T0133571

Contemporary High Performance Computing

From Petascale toward Exascale

Volume 3

Chapman & Hall/CRC
Computational Science Series

Series Editor: Sartaj Sahni

Data-Intensive Science
Terence Critchlow, Kerstin Kleese van Dam

Grid Computing
Techniques and Applications
Barry Wilkinson

Scientific Computing with Multicore and Accelerators
Jakub Kurzak, David A. Bader, Jack Dongarra

Introduction to the Simulation of Dynamics Using Simulink
Michael A. Gray

Introduction to Scheduling
Yves Robert, Frederic Vivien

Introduction to Modeling and Simulation with MATLAB° and Python
Steven I. Gordon, Brian Guilfoos

Fundamentals of Multicore Software Development
Victor Pankratius, Ali-Reza Adl-Tabatabai, Walter Tichy

Programming for Hybrid Multi/Manycore MPP Systems
John Levesque, Aaron Vose

Exascale Scientific Applications
Scalability and Performance Portability
Tjerk P. Straatsma, Katerina B. Antypas, Timothy J. Williams

GPU Parallel Program Development Using CUDA
Tolga Soyata

Parallel Programming with Co-Arrays
Robert W. Numrich

Contemporary High Performance Computing
From Petascale toward Exascale, Volume 3
Jeffrey S. Vetter

For more information about this series please visit:
https://www.crcpress.com/Chapman--HallCRC-Computational-Science/book-series/
CHCOMPUTSCI

Contemporary High Performance Computing

From Petascale toward Exascale

Volume 3

Edited by
Jeffrey S. Vetter

CRC Press
Taylor & Francis Group
Boca Raton London New York

CRC Press is an imprint of the
Taylor & Francis Group, an **informa** business

A CHAPMAN & HALL BOOK

CRC Press
Taylor & Francis Group
6000 Broken Sound Parkway NW, Suite 300
Boca Raton, FL 33487-2742

© 2019 by Taylor & Francis Group, LLC
CRC Press is an imprint of Taylor & Francis Group, an Informa business

No claim to original U.S. Government works

Printed on acid-free paper
Version Date: 20190124

International Standard Book Number-13: 978-1-1384-8707-9 (Hardback)

This book contains information obtained from authentic and highly regarded sources. Reasonable efforts have been made to publish reliable data and information, but the author and publisher cannot assume responsibility for the validity of all materials or the consequences of their use. The authors and publishers have attempted to trace the copyright holders of all material reproduced in this publication and apologize to copyright holders if permission to publish in this form has not been obtained. If any copyright material has not been acknowledged please write and let us know so we may rectify in any future reprint.

Except as permitted under U.S. Copyright Law, no part of this book may be reprinted, reproduced, transmitted, or utilized in any form by any electronic, mechanical, or other means, now known or hereafter invented, including photocopying, microfilming, and recording, or in any information storage or retrieval system, without written permission from the publishers.

For permission to photocopy or use material electronically from this work, please access www.copyright.com (http://www.copyright.com/) or contact the Copyright Clearance Center, Inc. (CCC), 222 Rosewood Drive, Danvers, MA 01923, 978-750-8400. CCC is a not-for-profit organization that provides licenses and registration for a variety of users. For organizations that have been granted a photocopy license by the CCC, a separate system of payment has been arranged.

Trademark Notice: Product or corporate names may be trademarks or registered trademarks, and are used only for identification and explanation without intent to infringe.

Visit the Taylor & Francis Web site at
http://www.taylorandfrancis.com

and the CRC Press Web site at
http://www.crcpress.com

Dedication

To my family, Jana and Alex.

Contents

2 Theta and Mira at Argonne National Laboratory   31

*Mark R. Fahey, Yuri Alexeev, Bill Allcock, Benjamin S. Allen, Ramesh
Balakrishnan, Anouar Benali, Liza Booker, Ashley Boyle, Laural
Briggs, Edouard Brooks, Phil Carns, Beth Cerny, Andrew Cherry, Lisa
Childers, Sudheer Chunduri, Richard Coffey, James Collins, Paul
Coffman, Susan Coghlan, Kathy DiBennardi, Ginny Doyle, Hal Finkel,
Graham Fletcher, Marta Garcia, Ira Goldberg, Cheetah Goletz, Susan
Gregurich, Kevin Harms, Carissa Holohan, Joseph A. Insley, Tommie
Jackson, Janet Jaseckas, Elise Jennings, Derek Jensen, Wei Jiang,
Margaret Kaczmarski, Chris Knight, Janet Knowles, Kalyan Kumaran,
Ti Leggett, Ben Lenard, Anping Liu, Ray Loy, Preeti Malakar, Avanthi
Mantrala, David E. Martin, Guillermo Mayorga, Gordon McPheeters,
Paul Messina, Ryan Milner, Vitali Morozov, Zachary Nault, Denise
Nelson, Jack O'Connell, James Osborn, Michael E. Papka, Scott
Parker, Pragnesh Patel, Saumil Patel, Eric Pershey, Renée Plzak,
Adrian Pope, Jared Punzel, Sreeranjani Ramprakash, John 'Skip'
Reddy, Paul Rich, Katherine Riley, Silvio Rizzi, George Rojas, Nichols
A. Romero, Robert Scott, Adam Scovel, William Scullin, Emily
Shemon, Haritha Siddabathuni Som, Joan Stover, Mirek Suliba, Brian
Toonen, Tom Uram, Alvaro Vazquez-Mayagoitia, Venkatram
Vishwanath, R. Douglas Waldron, Gabe West, Timothy J. Williams,
Darin Wills, Laura Wolf, Wanda Woods, and Michael Zhang*

3 Zuse Institute Berlin (ZIB)   63

Alexander Reinefeld, Thomas Steinke, Matthias Noack, and Florian Wende

4 The Mont-Blanc Prototype   93

Filippo Mantovani, Daniel Ruiz, Leonardo Bautista, Vishal Metha,
Fabio Banchelli, Nikola Rajovic, Eduard Ayguade, Jesus Labarta,
Mateo Valero, Alejandro Rico Carro, Alex Ramirez Bellido, Markus
Geimer, and Daniele Tafani

5 Chameleon   **123**

Kate Keahey, Pierre Riteau, Dan Stanzione, Tim Cockerill, Joe
Mambretti, Paul Rad, and Paul Ruth

8 Jetstream
189

Craig A. Stewart, David Y. Hancock, Therese Miller, Jeremy Fischer,
R. Lee Liming, George Turner, John Michael Lowe, Steven Gregory,
Edwin Skidmore, Matthew Vaughn, Dan Stanzione, Nirav Merchant,
Ian Foster, James Taylor, Paul Rad, Volker Brendel, Enis Afgan,
Michael Packard, Therese Miller, and Winona Snapp-Childs

14 Bridges: Converging HPC, AI, and Big Data for Enabling Discovery   355
Nicholas A. Nystrom, Paola A. Buitrago, and Philip D. Blood

17 CHPC in South Africa   423

Happy M Sithole, Werner Janse Van Rensburg, Dorah Thobye,
Krishna Govender, Charles Crosby, Kevin Colville, and Anita Loots

Preface

We are pleased to present you with this third volume of material that captures a snapshot of the rich history of practice in Contemporary High Performance Computing. As evidenced in the chapters of this book, High Performance Computing continues to flourish, both in industry and research, both domestically and internationally. While much of the focus of HPC is on the hardware architectures, a significant ecosystem is responsible for this success. This book helps capture this broad ecosystem.

High Performance Computing (HPC) is used to solve a number of complex questions in computational and data-intensive sciences. These questions include the simulation and modeling of physical phenomena, such as climate change, energy production, drug design, global security, and materials design; the analysis of large data sets, such as those in genome sequencing, astronomical observation, and cybersecurity; and, the intricate design of engineered products, such as airplanes and automobiles.

It is clear and well-documented that HPC is used to generate insight that would not otherwise be possible. Simulations can augment or replace expensive, hazardous, or impossible experiments. Furthermore, in the realm of simulation, HPC has the potential to suggest new experiments that escape the parameters of observability.

Although much of the excitement about HPC focuses on the largest architectures and on specific benchmarks, such as TOP500, there is a much deeper and broader commitment from the international scientific and engineering community than is first apparent. In fact, it is easy to lose track of history in terms the broad uses of HPC and the communities that design, deploy, and operate HPC systems and facilities. Many of these sponsors and organizations have spent decades developing scientific simulation methods and software, which serves as the foundation of HPC today. This community has worked closely with countless vendors to foster the sustained development and deployment of HPC systems internationally.

In this third volume of *Contemporary High Performance Computing* [1, 2], we continue to document international HPC ecosystems, which includes the sponsors and sites that host them. We have selected contributions from international HPC sites, which represent a combination of sites, systems, vendors, applications, and sponsors. Rather than focus on simply the architectures or applications, we focus on *HPC ecosystems* that have made this dramatic progress possible. Though the very word ecosystem can be a broad, all-encompassing term, it aptly describes high performance computing. That is, HPC is far more than one sponsor, one site, one application, one software system, or one architecture. Indeed, it is a community of interacting entities in this environment that sustains the community over time. In this regard, we asked contributors to include the following topics in their chapters:

1. Sponsor and site history

2. Highlights of applications, workloads, and benchmarks

3. Systems overview

4. Hardware architecture

5. System software

6. Programming systems

7. Storage, visualization, and analytics

8. Data center/facility

9. Site HPC statistics

Some of the authors followed this outline precisely while others found creative ways to include this content in a different structure. Once you read the book, I think that you will agree with me that most of the chapters have exceeded these expectations and have provided a detailed snapshot of their HPC ecosystem, science, and organization.

Why I Edited This Book

My goal with this series of books has been to highlight and document significant systems and facilities in high performance computing. With Volume 1, my main focus was proposed to be on the architectural design of important and successful HPC systems. However, as I started to interact with authors, I realized that HPC is about more than just hardware: it is an ecosystem that includes software, applications, facilities, educators, software developers, scientists, administrators, sponsors, and many others. Broadly speaking, HPC is growing internationally, so I invited contributions from a broad base of organizations including the USA, Japan, Germany, Australia, Spain, and others. The second volume is a snapshot of these contemporary HPC ecosystems. Each chapter is typically punctuated with a site's flagship system.

My excitement about volumes one and two of this book grew as I started inviting authors to contribute: everyone said 'yes!' In fact, due to the limitations on hardback publishing, we continued the series with this volume.

Helping Improve This Book

HPC and computing, in general, is a rapidly changing, large, diverse field. If you have comments, corrections, or questions, please send a note to me at `vetter@computer.org`.

Bibliography

[1] J. S. Vetter. Contemporary high performance computing: an introduction. In Jeffrey S. Vetter, editor, *Contemporary High Performance Computing: From Petascale Toward Exascale*, volume 1 of *CRC Computational Science Series*, page 730. Taylor and Francis, Boca Raton, 1 edition, 2013.

[2] J. S. Vetter, editor. *Contemporary High Performance Computing: From Petascale Toward Exascale*, volume 2 of *CRC Computational Science Series*. Taylor and Francis, Boca Raton, 1 edition, 2015.

Editor

Jeffrey S. Vetter, Ph.D., is a Distinguished R&D Staff Member, and the founding group leader of the Future Technologies Group in the Computer Science and Mathematics Division of Oak Ridge National Laboratory. Vetter also holds a joint appointment at the Electrical Engineering and Computer Science Department of the University of Tennessee-Knoxville. From 2005 through 2015, Vetter held a joint position at Georgia Institute of Technology, where, from 2009 to 2015, he was the Principal Investigator of the NSF Track 2D Experimental Computing XSEDE Facility, named Keeneland, for large scale heterogeneous computing using graphics processors, and the Director of the NVIDIA CUDA Center of Excellence.

Vetter earned his Ph.D. in Computer Science from the Georgia Institute of Technology. He joined ORNL in 2003, after stints as a computer scientist and project leader at Lawrence Livermore National Laboratory, and postdoctoral researcher at the University of Illinois at Urbana-Champaign. The coherent thread through his research is developing rich architectures and software systems that solve important, real-world high performance computing problems. He has been investigating the effectiveness of next-generation architectures, such as non-volatile memory systems, massively multithreaded processors, and heterogeneous processors such as graphics processors and field-programmable gate arrays (FPGAs), for key applications. His recent books, entitled "Contemporary High Performance Computing: From Petascale toward Exascale (Vols. 1 and 2)," survey the international landscape of HPC.

Vetter is a Fellow of the IEEE, and a Distinguished Scientist Member of the ACM. Vetter, as part of an interdisciplinary team from Georgia Tech, NYU, and ORNL, was awarded the Gordon Bell Prize in 2010. Also, his work has won awards at major venues: Best Paper Awards at the International Parallel and Distributed Processing Symposium (IPDPS), EuroPar and the 2018 AsHES Workshop, Best Student Paper Finalist at SC14, Best Presentation at EASC 2015, and Best Paper Finalist at the IEEE HPEC Conference. In 2015, Vetter served as the Technical Program Chair of SC15 (SC15 Breaks Exhibits and Attendance Records While in Austin). You can see more at https://ft.ornl.gov/~vetter.

Chapter 1

Resilient HPC for 24x7x365 Weather Forecast Operations at the Australian Government Bureau of Meteorology

Dr Lesley Seebeck

Former Group Executive of Data & Digital, CITO, Australian Bureau of Meteorology

Tim F Pugh

Director, Supercomputer Programme, Australian Bureau of Meteorology

Damian Aigus

Support Services, Data & Digital, Australian Bureau of Meteorology

Dr Joerg Henrichs

Computational Science Manager, Data & Digital, Australian Bureau of Meteorology

Andrew Khaw

Scientific Computing Service Manager, Data & Digital, Australian Bureau of Meteorology

Tennessee Leeuwenburg

Model Build Team Manager, Data & Digital, Australian Bureau of Meteorology

James Mandilas

Operations and Change Manager, Data & Digital, Australian Bureau of Meteorology

Richard Oxbrow

HPD Systems Manager, Data & Digital, Australian Bureau of Meteorology

Naren Rajasingam

HPD Analyst, Data & Digital, Australian Bureau of Meteorology

Wojtek Uliasz

Enterprise Architect, Data & Digital, Australian Bureau of Meteorology

John Vincent

Delivery Manager, Data & Digital, Australian Bureau of Meteorology

Craig West

HPC Systems Manager, Data & Digital, Australian Bureau of Meteorology

Dr Rob Bell

IMT Scientific Computing Services, National Partnerships, CSIRO

1.1 Foreword

Supercomputing lies at the heart of modern weather forecasting. It coevolves with the science, technology, means of the collection of observations, the needs of meteorologists, and the expectations of the users of our forecasts and warnings. It nestles in a web of other platforms and networks, applications and capabilities. It is driven by, consumes, and generates vast and increasing amounts of data. And it is part of the global effort by the world's meteorological agencies to collect data, understand the weather, and look ahead to generate forecasts and warnings on which human activity is based. Given the complexity of the overall task and the web of supporting capability, to talk about the supercomputing component alone seems reductionist. And yet it is a feat of human engineering and effort that we do well to recognise. These are capabilities that drive the data and information business that is the Bureau – the growing benefits available through more data, increasing granularity and frequency of forecasts, and better information to the Bureau's customers – no more and no less than to the scientists or the meteorologists.

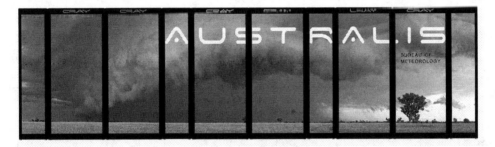

FIGURE 1.1: Australis compute racks as seen in the Data Centre

The Bureau's current supercomputer, Australis, was delivered on time and within budget, with the supercomputer itself, a Cray XC40, bought at a capital cost of \$A80 million[8]. The programme extends from 2014-15 through 2020-21. Within that period, the Bureau continues to keep pace with the relentless demands of the data, the models and user needs, and explore new, improving ways to extract value from both data and capability. It also has to contend with an increasingly challenging operating environment; their effective use placing growing demands on organisations in terms of skills, operating costs, and security.

On a personal note, arriving at the start of the programme to replace the existing supercomputer, I was fortunate to have a highly capable team led by Tim Pugh. To continue to be an effective contributor to the field, both the Bureau – and Australia – need to nurture and grow the technical skills, deep computational understanding, insights that build and shape the field of high performance computing and to exploit that capability. This chapter sets out the Australian Bureau of Meteorology's supercomputing capability, and in doing so helps contribute to that effort.

Dr Lesley Seebeck
Former Group Executive of Data & Digital, CITO,
Australian Bureau of Meteorology

1.2   Overview

The Australian Government's Bureau of Meteorology has had the responsibility of providing trusted, reliable, and responsive meteorological services for Australia - all day, every day – since 1908. Bringing together the ever-expanding world-wide observation networks, and improving computational analysis and numerical modelling to deliver the Bureau's exceptional predictive and analytical capability, we are able to undertake the grand challenge of weather and climate prediction.

Australia is a country with a landmass marginally less than the continental United States, but with a population 13 times smaller. Australia is not only vast, it is also harsh. With just 9% of the landmass suitable for farming, and the main population living along the cooler coastal regions, the climate of the continent plays a significant role in defining the life of the country.

Around the country there are climate pockets similar to those found on every other continent; Sydney shares a climate similar to South Africa, Canberra is most like Rome, Melbourne like the San Franciso Bay area, Perth like Los Angeles, Darwin like Mumbai, Hobart like Southern Chile and the UK. Across the centre are deserts, which, though sparsely populated, still contain major population centres like Alice Springs and the mining town of Kalgoorlie.

Against this backdrop the Bureau and its forecasting team strive to provide timely weather products to cover the entire continent and its climate variations, as well as managing its weather responsibilities for Australia's Antarctic Territory (a 5.9 million square kilometre area, 42% of the Antarctic continent), on a 24x7x365 basis. As if this wasn't a significant enough daily endeavour, the Bureau also manages a suite of on-demand emergency forecasts to cover the extreme weather events of the region; tsunami, cyclone, and bushfire (wildfire). They regularly run in the extreme weather season (December - April) and are also ready to go as and when they are required. Australia as an island continent also provides a full oceanographic suite of forecasting.

The Bureau of Meteorology has the unique numerical prediction capabilities required to routinely forecast the weather and climate conditions across the Australian continent, its territories, and the surrounding marine environment. When this capability is utilised with modern data and digital information services, we are able to issue timely forecasts and warnings to the Australian public, media, industries, and Government services well in advance of an event. These services are essential to ensure the nation is prepared to act when faced with an event, and to mitigate the loss of property and lives. As a prepared nation, we have been very successful in reducing the loss of lives and improving the warnings over the years, and will continue to improve with each advance in key areas of science, numerical prediction, observing networks, and computational systems.

Modern weather and climate prediction requires a significant science investment to achieve modelling advances that lead to enhanced forecast services. The science investment comes from the Bureau and its local partners in the Commonwealth Scientific and Industrial Research Organization (CSIRO) and Australian universities and international partners. The Bureau is a member of the Unified Model (UM) partnership [9], which is lead by the UK Met Office.

These partnerships bring together the required breadth of science, observations, and modelling expertise to develop the global data assimilation and forecast models to high resolution, convection permitting models, and the forthcoming multi-week and seasonal coupled climate models. Today the Bureau assimilates data from more than 30 different satellite data streams, surface observations, aircraft and balloon observations, and radar observations coming next. All these capabilities talk to the sophistication of numerical prediction modelling and why the Bureau needs such scientific partnerships, observation networks, and computing capability to continuously deliver better products.

The Bureau strategy is to focus on customer needs to deliver more accurate and trusted forecasts through its High Performance Computing (HPC) and numerical prediction capability. Australian businesses, agriculture, mining, aviation, shipping, defence, government agencies, and citizens are all beneficiaries of more timely and accurate weather forecasts, the multi-week climate outlooks, seasonal climate and water forecasting, and climate change projections. The Bureau's customers have an interest in decision-making across many time-scales, and value an ability to change decisions (and derive value) well beyond the one-week lead time typically associated with weather forecasts.[12]

The size of the HPC system is dependent on these factors; the number of modelling suites; the numerical weather prediction models cost and complexity, arising from finer grid resolutions; the need to consider a range of probable future atmospheric states (ensemble modelling); and the need to couple physical modelling domains (i.e. atmosphere, ocean, sea ice, land surfaces) to better capture physical interactions leading to improve simulations and forecast skill. Typically, the numerical prediction models are sized to the available computing capacity, thus constraining the modelling grid resolution.

1.2.1   Program Background

In-house computing came to the Bureau of Meteorology in 1967 with the commissioning of an IBM360/65. Previous to this, weather computations were compiled from 1956 using the Barotropic model running on CSIRAC, Australia's first digital computer. From 1964 the Bureau used the CSIRO CDC 3600 based in Canberra. A year later in 1968 a second IBM 360/65 was installed and run in parallel. Such was the public interest in the IBM systems that they were displayed on the ground floor of the World Met Centre building in central Melbourne with floor to ceiling windows for public viewing. The machines remained on display until the Bureau moved offices in 1974. The systems were replaced in 1982 by a Fujitsu M200 mainframe.

The Bureau's "supercomputer" era started in 1988 with the arrival of an ETA 10-P "Piper". A second ETA 10-P enroute to the Bureau was damaged by a forklift on the loading dock; it was unfortunately irreplaceable. Following ETA's reincorporation into the Control Data Corporation in 1990, CDC replaced the system with a Cray® X-MP and then in 1992, a Cray Y-MP was acquired. The Cray platform delivered the Bureau's Global Atmospheric Spectral Prediction (GASP) model at 250km and a 75km regional atmospheric model nested in the global model.

In 1997, the CSIRO and the Bureau collaborated again, forming the High Performance Computing and Communications Centre (HPCCC), which jointly operated a succession of NEC SX systems until 2010. The SX-5 further developing the global and regional models, and the SX6 finally delivered global and regional resolutions of 80km and 37km respectively.

The Bureau then replaced the NEC system with a Sun Constellation in 2009. This was acquired through a joint procurement with the National Computational Infrastructure (NCI) at the Australian National University – NCI is a collaborative research computing facility supported by the Australian Government. An Oracle HPC 6000 "Ngamai" then replaced the Bureau's Sun HPC system in 2013. The computational power of the Sun and Oracle machines facilitated continuous improvement of the real-time forecast/assimilation models to deliver a seasonal climate model at 250km resolution, global model at 25km, regional model at 12km, and city models at 4km.

In 2013, the Bureau entered the National Computational Infrastructure (NCI) partnership that forms part of the Bureau's ongoing commitment to the scientific community, working to advance weather and climate research and development within the region. It has facilitated the adoption of a software life cycle process for numerical prediction products; the Australian Community Climate Earth System Simulator (ACCESS) [4] and the Unified Model/Variational Assimilation (UM/VAR) weather modelling suites as well as ocean and marine modelling suites.

This continuing development of the Bureau's numerical modelling and prediction products have delivered an operational service for the routine and real-time demands of 24x7x365 weather, climate, ocean, and hydrological forecast services.

In July 2015 to meet the growing demand, the Bureau entered into a contract with Cray to acquire a Cray XC40 system called "Australis" to support its operational HPC requirements for improved numerical prediction and forecast services. The Cray computational systems married Intel processors, Lustre, the Network File System (NFS) filesystems, and PBS Pro job scheduler system to provide the backbone of the Bureau's HPC capability. The computational power of Australis facilitates improvements of the forecast/assimilation models to deliver a seasonal climate model at 60km resolution, global model at 12km, regional model at 4km, and city models at 1.5km. Australis also provides ensemble modelling capability to enable probabilistic forecasts to improve decision support systems.

The Bureau's current HPC platforms consist of several systems, an Exemplar used by system administrators to test system upgrades and patches; a small Development system for scientists and software developers called "Terra"; and the Australis operational system, a mission critical system for severe weather forecasting and environmental emergency response.

1.2.2   Sponsor Background

The Bureau is an Australian Government funded organisation. For the duration of its 109 years it has been mandated to provide the expertise and services needed to assist Australians in preparing for and responding to the harsh realities of the country's natural environment.

Through regular forecasts, warnings, monitoring, and advice spanning the Australian region and the Antarctic territory, the Bureau now provides one of the most widely used and fundamental services of government. In recent years the Bureau's position, both regionally and globally, as a provider of weather products in the Asia Pacific region has seen its profile rise in the governmental sphere. The importance of the HPC platform delivering time-sensitive weather predictions is widely recognised.

The HPC system needs to support the Bureau's mission with many aspects of the system being highly available and resilient to meet the critical forecast service requirements. It has resulted in a unique Supercomputer configuration, dedicated to delivering high quality, timely products on a 24x7x365 schedule.

The amount of observation data available to the Bureau has increased dramatically over recent years, predominately satellite imaging and its increasing resolution of 1km or less. Local and international observations are also universally collected using automatic weather stations and shared through global networks with the Bureau for our weather forecast models.

A consequence of this is the ability for the models to run at a higher grid resolution and produce greater accuracy. The previous Bureau HPC platforms were found to be consistently over-committed with operational and research computing half way through their life. In common with other Met centres, we have observed over many cycles where the system starts its life with 25% capacity dedicated to operations and 75% to research and development, ending with 80% for operations and 20% for research. This results in a constrained capacity for research and development projects that delay improvements until the next investment cycle.

In response to this, the Bureau changed its strategy to separate research and operational computing investments. Research computing moved to a collaborative national peak facility at NCI in 2013. New Government funding was obtained in 2014 for the replacement of the Bureau's existing Oracle HPC system with one delivering the computing capability to improve its numerical weather prediction applications and forecast services for severe weather events through improved accuracy, more up to date forecasts, increased ability to quantify the probability of forecast outcomes, and responding on-demand to extreme weather and hazard events as they develop.

Within the Bureau, the HPC platform sits in the Data & Digital Group of the organisation. The weather products are developed by the Research and Development branch in a collaborative relationship with the HPC technical team and National Forecast Services. This relationship of a scientific need meeting a technical service has been the internal driver for the system's upgrades.

1.2.3 Timeline

The timeline for the latest system design, development, procurement, installation, and use is shown in Table 1.1 below.

TABLE 1.1: Australis Implementation Timeline.

Date	Milestone Description	Reference Name
15 Jul 2015	Completion of Supercomputer and Procurement Issue of Official Order for Australis System Data Centre preparations for water-cooled Cray	Contract Signing with Cray Inc.
25 Nov 2015	Cray XC40 site preparations completed, system delivered, and installation commenced	Installation commencement.
15 Mar 2016	Supercomputer acceptance testing completed including 30 day availability test meeting 30 day service levels. Cray hand over of system to the Bureau. Cray to meet service levels and provide 24x7 support. Software porting from existing HPC system to new Cray XC40 began following acceptance.	Australis System Readiness Completed.
30 Jun 2016	Commissioning of replacement Supercomputer for routine 24x7 operational forecast services. Operational readiness acceptance testing and trials by the Bureau completed.	Australis Commissioning.

1.3 Applications and Workloads

The dominant applications on the system are focused on National Weather Prediction. Weather forecasts are produced using Numerical Weather Prediction model (NWP) outputs. These models deliver critical guidance within the core forecast process and in the direct generation of some products.

The Bureau runs an extensive suite of models, across multiple domains (atmosphere, ocean, land, water), and across multiple spatial scales and forecast lead times (from hours to days to weeks to months). Bureau HPC capability and infrastructure is built to ensure both a very high level of reliability of forecast generation and its timeliness of delivery - HPC attributes that distinguish it from workloads in other fields, such as research.

Improvements in the forecast quality of NWP over the decades have been driven by three key factors:

1. Improved understanding of atmospheric physics, and how that understanding can be encapsulated in a numerical model;

2. Use of more observation data and observation types, together with increasingly sophisticated mathematical methods in the "Data Assimilation" process that generates the initial atmospheric state from which a forecast simulation is produced;

3. Increasing HPC capacity, which has enabled models to run at higher-resolution to better resolve physical features and processes within a given production time-window.

Our daily runs include; Global NWP, Global Wave, Global Ocean, Australian Regional NWP, Regional Wave, and six regions of high-resolution NWP models for Victoria/Tasmania, New South Wales, Queensland, South Australia, Western Australia, and Northern Territory. A single high-resolution convection resolving NWP model of the Australian continent is desirable but computationally unattainable due to resource costs. Antarctic forecasting currently uses the Global NWP model for guidance. Our severe weather modelling consists of tropical cyclone prediction, fire weather prediction, flood forecasting, and environmental emergency response to chemical, volcanic, nuclear, and bio-hazard events. Additional modelling runs for global climate forecasting use the Predictive Ocean Atmosphere Model for Australia (POAMA) ensemble with a 250km grid resolution, and a new ACCESS coupled climate model with a 60km grid is being readied for multi-week and seasonal climate forecast services. Further predictive modelling includes ocean tides, storm surge, tsunami, coastal ocean circulation, space weather, hydrology, and stream flow.

1.3.1 Highlights of Main Applications

The Numerical Weather Prediction (NWP) models focus on predicting the future state of the atmosphere on timescales from hours to days, and are one of the key domains supported by Bureau HPC capability. Many of the models are refinements of the Australian Community Climate and Earth-System Simulator (ACCESS)[4].

In common with many other applications of Computational Fluid Dynamics, NWP models work by approximating the known (but largely unsolvable) partial-differential physics equations that govern fluid flow and energy, by a very large set of (solvable) algebraic and numeric equations, through a process of "discretisation" - breaking the atmosphere up into

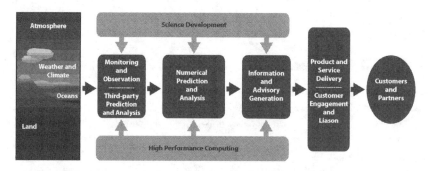

FIGURE 1.2: The Bureau's Numerical Prediction Value Chain

small volumes ("grid-cells") in a similar way a digital camera approximates an image in an array of pixels. The smaller the grid-cells, the higher the fidelity, the more accurate detail the model can produce, but higher resolution comes at a greater computational cost. A rule of thumb is a doubling of horizontal grid resolution results in 10 fold increase in compute costs. To best manage this detail/cost trade-off, the Bureau runs a number of NWP systems for spatial resolution and forecast lead time including:

"ACCESS-G" – the Bureau's global NWP system. This model covers the entire globe at a resolution of approximately 25km today, 12km in development, and produces forecasts out to ten days. It answers questions around large-scale meteorology, such as "where is that cold-front likely to be five days from now?" A new 18-member global ensemble system is in development at a resolution of 33km to derive probabilistic forecast information for feeding decision support systems.

"ACCESS-R" – the Bureau's regional NWP system covers mainland Australia and a significant expanse of surrounding ocean at a resolution of approximately 12km today, 4km in development. ACCESS-R produces forecasts out to three days. Whilst ACCESS-R does not simulate the atmosphere outside its region, it is influenced by it and references the "boundary data" provided by ACCESS-G. Thus, ACCESS-R is a nested, downscaled system of ACCESS-G, and its forecast quality is dependent on the quality of the ACCESS-G forecast. ACCESS-R is also focused on large-scale meteorology, but its higher resolution enables it to better address questions such as "Are the winds associated with the cold front likely to intensify over the next 24 hours?" or "How is the motion/structure of that cold front likely to change as it moves over a mountain range?"

"ACCESS-C" – the Bureau city-scale NWP system covers the country's major population centres at a resolution of approximately 1.5km. It produces forecasts out to 36 hours. It depends on ACCESS-R for its boundary data, as well as specification of the initial state of the atmosphere. At this high-resolution, the model begins to have an ability to mimic, though not perfectly simulate, aspects of weather at local scales. Whereas ACCESS-G and ACCESS-R provide a longer-range view as to the large-scale conditions that may favour thunderstorm formation in a particular region, ACCESS-C better simulates the thunderstorm itself, the weather near coastal regions and mountains and projected rainfall for streamflow and flood forecasts. A new 18-member city ensemble system is in development at a resolution of 2.2km to derive probabilistic forecast information for feeding decision support systems.

"ACCESS-TC" – the model optimised for forecasting the behaviour of tropical cyclones. A new deterministic model at 4km resolution will produce more accurate forecasts for tropical cyclone path, intensity, and structure including when and where it will cross the coast.

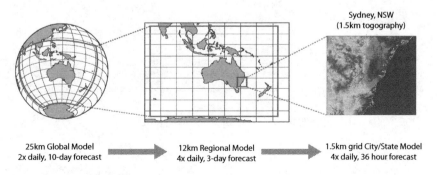

FIGURE 1.3: Numerical Weather Prediction Cascading Domains

Cascading or "coupling" of individual NWP models, and now ensemble modelling, has placed additional stress on HPC capacity in terms of forecast timeliness and peak demand for the compute and data storage resources. This characteristic typically sets the compute resource capacity limits or size of the system.

1.3.2   2017 Case Study: From Nodes to News, TC Debbie

On 22nd March 2017, a weak area of low pressure developed over the Coral Sea, in the Milne Bay Province of Papua New Guinea. Using a consensus of computer models from around the globe, including the ACCESS-G and ACCESS-R running on Australis, meteorologists in the Bureau of Meteorology's Tropical Cyclone Warning Centre in Brisbane were able to assess the potential for the tropical low to develop into a tropical cyclone and the possible directions that the system might move over the following days. The Bureau's embedded meteorologists at Queensland Fire and Emergency Services were also able to use the computer model outputs to provide briefings on the range of scenarios that could occur to assist state and local government planning.

Following an assessment of the computer model guidance available at the time, meteorologists in the Brisbane Tropical Cyclone Warning Centre decided to issue to the first Tropical Cyclone Watch for the developing tropical low on 24th March. Moving into the 25th March, the Bureau of Meteorology declared that the system had formed into a tropical cyclone and as a result gave it the designation of Debbie[2]. The declaration of the system as a Tropical Cyclone led to the initiation of the ACCESS-TC model, also running on Australis. The system was heading south.

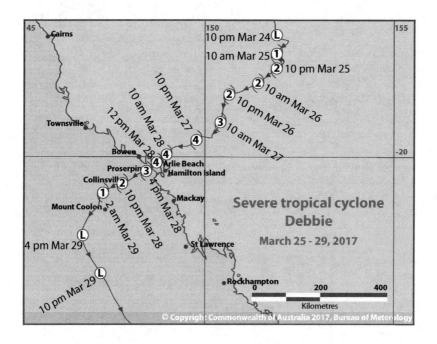

FIGURE 1.4: Path of Tropical Cyclone Debbie

Working with a combination of automatic weather station observations, satellite information, and data from the various weather models, meteorologists continued to make projections of the likely development and trajectory of the system. Further warnings were issued and possible evacuations were considered by emergency authorities. Passing over the

Coral Sea the system had developed into a Category 2 cyclone by 26th March. On 27th March Debbie strengthened quickly from a Category 2 to a Category 4 severe tropical cyclone as it continued heading toward the Queensland coastline.

The storm then continued developing until it crossed the coastline at Airlie Beach at midday on 28th March with sustained winds of 195 km/h. Bureau observing equipment on Hamilton Island Airport was damaged by the storm at around 11am. Prior to this, a peak wind gust of 263 km/h was recorded; this being the highest ever wind gust recorded in Queensland.

All the while Bureau staff were using the predictions from the ACCESS-G, ACCESS-R, ACCESS-C, and ACCESS-TC systems to update forecasts and warnings for communities in the expected path of the storm, and for those likely to experience damage to property and danger to life. Using the new Australis system, forecast models were produced every 6 hours, using guidance from the newest higher resolution ACCESS-C2 model covering the highly populated area of southeast Queensland. The model provided output to provide guidance on potential rainfall totals across southeast Queensland; this gave important input into decisions surrounding Severe Weather Warnings and Flood Warnings.

Ex-tropical cyclone Debbie tracked south then southeast over the Sunshine Coast and Brisbane during the afternoon and evening of Thursday, 30th March. The storm continued to move south across Queensland and into New South Wales; the forecasting responsibilities moved to the regional office in Sydney. Debbie finally left the Australian mainland on 31st March. As a severe weather system it continued across the Tasman Sea, where it caused further significant flooding in the Bay of Plenty region of New Zealand on 6th April[6].

1.3.3   Benchmark Usage

Benchmarks for the HPC platform are something that the Bureau uses for procurement, in system balance and design, application performance, system acceptance and diagnostics, routine sustained system performance reporting, contract measure of system performance, and assessment of new technology for future investments. From an operational viewpoint, with a system that has a focus on delivering a high quality product 24x7x365, routine benchmarks on sustained system performance are used to assess the overall performance of scheduler loads and system resourcing, computational performance, network and storage performance, power consumption, and operating system and application runtime system performance of our operational environment.

With such a continuous and complex workflow, we found placing the focus on measuring the ongoing performance of the system using SSP (Sustained System Performance) to be most operationally beneficial.

1.3.4   SSP - Monitoring System Performance

An ongoing concern for running an operational supercomputer is to detect any issues in this environment that might affect the performance of the system. While the Bureau runs a fairly predictable job mix, those jobs are not suited to detect issues in the system. Most jobs utilise iterative solvers or handle a varying amount of data, all of which makes the runtimes of most jobs variable. A hidden issue in the system causing a slowdown might not be picked up while monitoring the runtime of operational work load on Australis. For instance, a sensor and power supply issue is known to force the downclocking of a processor - and hence affecting the application performance.

A common approach to monitoring the system performance is to use standard benchmarks metrics like floating point performance, memory bandwidth, network performance and IO bandwidth. However none of these benchmarks give a holistic view of the overall HPC system, each one only picks certain aspects of the overall system.

The Bureau uses a different approach for monitoring the performance of the system by defining a set of five typical applications run as a standard set of benchmarks. This set represents the mix of applications running on the system routinely, but uses a fixed set of input data. The benchmarks in this set are three different UM (Unified Model) simulations at different resolutions (from a low-resolution climate model to a global model), a data assimilation, and an ocean simulation, as illustrated in Table 1.2.

TABLE 1.2: SSP Benchmarking.

Benchmark	Runtime (seconds)	Number of cores	Performance per core
1. UM N1024L85 (12 hour simulation)	828.754	2088	0.00208
2. UM N512L85 (3-day simulation)	578.409	1656	0.003758
3. UM N216L85 (5-day simulation)	296.314	1320	0.009204
4. 4DVAR N320L70	1253.057	1536	0.00187
5. OFAM3 (1-day simulation)	409.443	480	0.018318
Overall SSP value		25,614	123.45

The runtime of each of those five benchmarks is used to compute a performance per core value (column 4). These five performance values are then averaged using a geometric mean and multiplied with the number of cores in the system, resulting in one overall SSP (Sustained System Performance) number.

Because each simulation uses the same input data, the runtimes of each benchmark should report very little variation. Consequently the overall SSP figure should be within variance. Any significant change in the runtime behaviour, in any of those applications, would result in a significant change of the reported SSP figure, indicating that the system has an issue that would cause runtime degradation.

The full SSP suite is run once a week at a quiet time on the system. The individual runtimes, as well as the overall SSP figure, are reported monthly by Cray; these values are monitored by the Bureau to look for any degradation of the overall system performance.

A similar SSP setup was used on the Bureau's previous supercomputers. Some interesting issues discovered included:

1. A 7% performance loss was detected over a six-month period. While an OS update would have likely solved this issue, the associated risk of an OS update (loss of official support since newer kernels might not yet be certified to work with other components of the system, and the risk of introducing new problems) prevented an OS update from happening. Instead it was decided to reboot all nodes regularly, which solved the performance slowdown observed by the SSP.

2. A BIOS update contained an incorrect setting (hardware prefetch was disabled). The BIOS update was rolled out as nodes were rebooted. The SSP value early on indicated a system issue. Correlating the used nodes with lower SSP results soon indicated that recently rebooted nodes showed the slowdown, and closer analysis resulted in detecting the changed BIOS setting.

SSP tests are also used to evaluate new system software. The approach is somewhat different from the weekly SSP system tests; the tests will only be run on demand, i.e. when a new version of software is installed and needs to be evaluated (typically before it is made available on the system). In this scenario it is rare for the same binary to be used more than once (except to make sure we are getting statistically significant results). In contrast, the system-testing SSP suite will keep the same binaries for repeated cycles.

Due to the difficulties involved in verifying an application, running suites tend not to update to a newer compiler or system library until absolutely required. The SSP suite mirrors this and keeps on running with the previously compiled binary, in order to accurately reflect the mix running on the system. Once enough newly compiled software is running on the system, the system SSP suite is recompiled, and a new baseline is established.

1.4   System Overview

The Bureau of Meteorology relies on multiple supercomputing environments supporting its complete Software Development Lifecycle (SDLC); Research & Development, Performance Testing, Trial and Verification, Pre-Production, and Production stages. The hardware supporting these environments is located in either the Bureau's Data Centres or the National Computation Infrastructure (NCI). Its parts are defined as either physical or logical partitions of the system depending on the function.

The Research and Development teams in collaboration with our partners at the NCI facility conduct scientific studies to understand, develop, and validate weather and climate science using the national peak computing facility and their 1.7 Petaflop machine called Raijin.

The Pre-Production and Production computing is performed on our Cray XC40 supercomputer called Australis. Performance model testing and validation, and trial and verification during Pre-Production is performed on the Australis Staging partition. Production modelling is performed on the Australis Production partition with resilience provided by Australis Staging partition.

In the near future the Bureau will promote another machine into Production to deliver post-processing facilities for Australis called Aurora. The work currently underway is discussed in section 1.12.

1.4.1   System Design Decisions

The Cray XC40 system has been sized to support a maximum forecast load that includes enhanced 3-hour model runs, concurrent with model processing for exceptional weather events, comprising 3 tropical cyclones and 4 severe weather events.

The HPC design assumed a single Supercomputer system segmented into two parts. Each part is a Cray XC40 and is housed in its own room in the Bureau's data centre. These parts are designated one for operational use and the other for Pre-Production or Staging. Each part is designed to operate (power up or power down) independently of the other to allow maintenance to be performed without interrupting operational jobs running on the system.

The Bureau designates its HPC cluster members as Australis East/West with the system running an option for a Staging and Production function. The batch and suite schedulers run on servers external to the HPC enclosures. Using high availability configurations, the

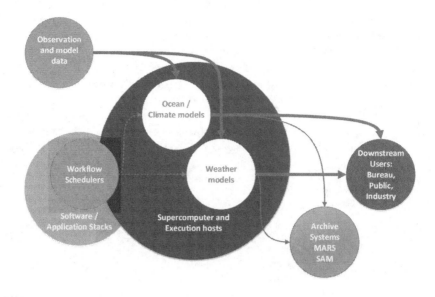

FIGURE 1.5: HPC Environment at the Bureau

schedulers are able to survive single points of failure independent from Australis and can maintain operational workflow into the HPC systems. This element of the configuration is seen as a key element in the HPC system meeting its uptime objective.

The operational benefit of this arrangement is that if an unplanned fault occurs on the part running the Bureau's operational services, the system administrators are able to move operations to the other part and restart the last computational jobs and thus minimise the effect of unplanned outages on the Bureau's operations. This design allows the Bureau's numerical forecast services to achieve a 99.86% uptime service level, a figure that equates to less than 1 hour of downtime per month.

1.5   Hardware Architecture

The Australis platform was envisaged as a two phase deployment. The first phase delivered in Q4 2015 was operational at the end of Q2 2016 and boosted the Bureau's compute capacity over 16 fold on the system it replaced. The second phase, scheduled for deployment in 2018, will double the capacity again. The final system, which follows a heterogeneous design, will deliver a fit for purpose platform for the Bureau's operations.

In addition to Australis, there are two further XC40 systems, a development platform currently with 7.5% the capacity of Australis, and an exemplar system designed specifically for testing settings and operating system updates before they are applied to Australis.

1.5.1   Australis Processors

All the nodes that run NWP jobs are using Intel® Xeon® Haswell 12-core E5-2960V3 2.66GHz processors. Applications are compiled with the Haswell specific feature set selected.

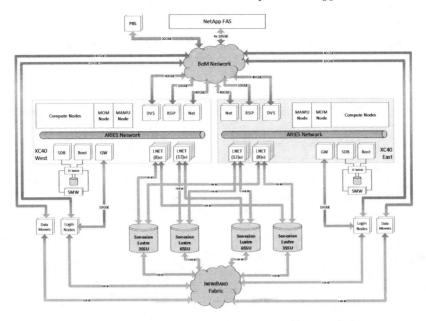

FIGURE 1.6: Australis Platform Logical Architecture

This processor was selected as the best processor performance when running the SSP benchmark. The use of hyperthreading is enabled on a per job basis; thus an application can utilise either 24 physical cores or 48 virtual cores per node.

The service blades for the XC40 system use Intel Xeon Sandy Bridge processors; therefore these are not used to run any NWP jobs.

1.5.2 Australis Node Design

There are three classes of nodes in Australis.

1.5.2.1 Australis Service Node

The first is the service blade, which is used to allow the machine to operate. Each service blade can hold two servers with IO slots. Service blades fulfill a number of different roles:

1. Boot and SDB nodes - these nodes provide a boot function and a System Database

2. Network Router nodes (Net) - these nodes provide the capability to route packets to and from a Cray Aries^{TM} network to the corporate network.

3. DVS – Data Virtualisation Service nodes provide a method to mount external NFS file systems (our Netapp FAS) into the Aries network.

4. RSIP – Realm Specific IP-Address nodes provide a service similar to Network Address Translation. They allows nodes on the Aries network to send packets to and get return packets from our HPC services. RSIP is typically used for lower level communications like DNS, LDAP, software license management, workflow status, etc.

5. LNET – these nodes route Lustre files system traffic from the Aries network through to the Sonexion® Lustre® appliances via InfiniBand^{TM} .

1.5.2.2   Australis Compute Node

The other type of blade is a compute blade. Each compute blade has 4 compute nodes. These Extreme Scalability nodes are used for the following:

1. Parallel compute jobs – the OS runs a minimal operating stack image.

2. MOM nodes - Machine Oriented Miniserver nodes. These are the nodes that launch the parallel compute jobs. They run PBS daemons to facilitate this and use ALPS to launch the jobs across the parallel nodes. They utilise an API to communicate with ALPS.

3. MAMU nodes - Multiple Application, Multiple User. These nodes provide the capability for small jobs from 1 to 24 cores. Jobs cannot span across multiple MAMU nodes. More than one job and more than one user can be utilising a MAMU node at a time.

TABLE 1.3: Australis Server Configuration.

Feature	Australis (2015)
Node Architecture	Cray XC40
CPU	Intel Xeon E5-2690 v3
CPU microarchitecture	Haswell
CPU Frequency (GHz)	2.60
CPU Count per Node	2
CPU cores per node	24
Node Memory Capacity (GB)	128
Node PCIe®	Gen 3
Interconnection Network	Aries
Compute Racks	12 (liquid cooled)
Number of compute nodes	2176
Number of MAMU nodes	136
Peak FLOP Rate (TF)	1660
Number of service nodes	64
Number of external nodes	16

1.5.3   External Nodes

A number of nodes are implemented outside the Cray XC40 chassis, with each performing a specific function.

1. Login nodes – these are the external facing servers for users to login to the system (via jump boxes). They also provide access to PBS queues for automatic builds of software in all but the Production environment.

2. DataMover nodes – these external facing servers have 40GbE connections to our corporate data Staging network. This is where large file transfers into and out of the supercomputer environments take place. It is also where the backup copy of data from the Production disks to the Staging disks is performed. This leaves the compute nodes free to do computation and for the DataMovers to do the storage based operations.

3. PBS nodes – These nodes are located externally to the Australis cabinets and are used to schedule the jobs in both the Production and Staging XC40 machines. More information is given in section 1.6.3 'Schedulers'. The design factors leading to the decision to locate the PBS nodes externally were discussed in Section 1.4.1

4. Suite Scheduler nodes – SMS and Cylc services provide routine operations workflow management, event triggers, and scheduling for Australis.

5. All the nodes located externally from the XC40 cabinets are managed by Bright Cluster Manager.

1.5.4 Australis Memory

The system memory architecture uses commodity 32GB DDR3, 2133MHz DIMM modules with chipkill advanced ECC[3]. Each processor uses 4 memory channels with one DIMM per channel with a measured 59GBps or 118GBps per node. The RAM is directly connected to the Intel Xeon processors. The jobs that use multiple nodes do so via Message Passing Interface (MPI) and there is no global RAM space defined.

1.5.5 Australis Interconnect

Australis uses a Cray custom interconnect, called Aries, inside the XC40 cabinets. It utilises a Dragonfly topology that incorporates three different layers of connectivity[5]. The first and lowest latency is the chassis interconnect and connects only within a chassis (each chassis houses 16 blades). The next level is an electrical group that uses copper interconnects, and for the XC40 liquid cooled system it connects 6 chassis together. The final level is based on optical fibres and connects each electrical group to all the other electrical groups. All ethernet traffic to and from each system is routed via physical firewall appliances. The Test and Development systems do not use Aries to communicate directly with the Staging and Production facilities.

1.5.6 Australis Storage and Filesystem

Australis utilises four Lustre file systems. Each Lustre file system is contained within a Cray Sonexion 2000 appliance, delivering Australis a total of 4PB. The Lustre storage network is currently implemented using FDR (Fourteen Data Rate) InfiniBand, while future upgrades will deploy EDR (Enhanced Data Rate) InfiniBand. This will double the Lustre storage capacity and bandwidth/throughput.

In the current Australis system, two of the Sonexion storage systems are large and twice the size of the two smaller systems. One large and one small Sonexion storage system are configured as a pair; one pair is used for the Production system and the other for the Staging system. The Staging storage pair also provides space for a limited copy of the Production data. The storage systems are accessed via symbolic links so that the Production data location can be redirected by simply reallocating the links. This design also allows for maintenance of the storage systems as well as recovery from unplanned outages.

Applications replicate data from the primary to the secondary Lustre file system at an appropriate point in each run cycle. Typically this occurs at application restart, next start, or when results are produced. The majority of the data on the Lustre file systems is considered to be transient and as such is not backed up, apart from the previously mentioned replicated data. The NWP Model Suite also archives data to one or more systems external to the Supercomputer. The Models are also aware of the status of each Sonexion file system and will either perform their data copy or abort that step when only one of the Production or Staging storage services is available.

The Cray Sonexion product is basically an appliance, and updates to it are performed mostly while the file system is offline. This means that storage failover methods are utilised during the updates.

Two NFS servers support the Cray XC40's by providing a small amount of persistent storage for critical software and data. The home directories on the XC40 computers are located on the NFS file systems; data protection is implemented using file based snapshots, file replication, and traditional backups. The home directories' file systems hold the persistent data required by the supercomputer to run the Production workload.

TABLE 1.4: Australis Storage Configuration.

Feature	Australis (2015)
Global Parallel Storage Architecture	Cray Sonexion 2000
Storage Filesystem	Lustre 2.5
Interconnection	FDR InfiniBand
Storage Racks	4
Total number of OSS	36
Storage Capacity	4320TB
Storage Bandwidth	135 GB/s
Storage Gateway to Aries method	LustreNet Routing
Total number of LNET routers	40
Shared NFS Storage Architecture	NetApp FAS 8040 Clustered Pair
Storage Filesystem (other)	NFS 4.0
Interconnection (NFS)	Ethernet (10/40Gbit)
Storage Gateway to Aries method	Cray DVS
Gateway nodes	4

1.6   System Software

1.6.1   Operating System

Australis currently uses a Cray customised version of SuSE Linux Enterprise Server 11 SP3 for extreme scalability applications and a full SuSE Linux for MOM and MAMU workflows. This environment, called 'CLE', is currently running Version 5.2 UP04. This is used on all the nodes including the management nodes. Future upgrades will include an update to SLES 12 and CLE 6.0.

1.6.2   Operating System Upgrade Procedure

As previously noted the Bureau HPC system must be highly available for its 24x7x365 mission. When needed, operating system updates are applied from Test, to Staging, and then promoted onto Australis. The Australis upgrade process is depicted in Figure 1.7. Staging is updated first; when that partition achieves stability, Staging is suspended and the Production environment is made active on the just updated partition. Provided this partition remains stable the remainder of the system is updated and the Staging workload resumes on the last upgraded partition. This method provides a fail-back option in the case of issues with Production. It is quicker and easier to do this than to attempt to roll-back all the updates that were applied, but sometimes that course of action may be the option chosen.

TABLE 1.5: Software Configuration.

Feature	‖ Australis (2015)
Login Node OS Compute Node OS Parallel Filesystem	SLES 11 SP3 / CLE 5.2 SLES 11 SP3 / CLE 5.2 Lustre 2.5.2
Compilers	Intel 2016 / 2017 GNU 5.2 Cray Development Toolkit
Message Passing Interface (MPI)	‖ Cray MPI
Notable Libraries	HDF5 netcdf Intel Math Kernel Library
Job Scheduler Resource Manager	PBS Pro 12.2 ALPS and PBS Pro
Debugging Tools Performance Tools	Allinea DDT / Forge TAU HPCToolkit NVIDIA® Visual Profiler

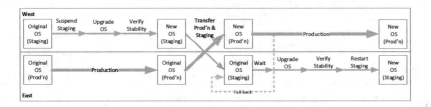

FIGURE 1.7: Australis Operating System Upgrade Process

1.6.3 Schedulers

A key tool in the ongoing delivery of the operational HPC's is our use of schedulers. Managing the complex daily schedule requires management of both jobs and the system resources on the HPC platform.

In operation, the job scheduler has three goals: first the priority scheduling goal, then the backfill scheduling goal, and finally the job pre-emption goal.

1. The priority scheduling goal is to run the most important time-critical jobs first; the environmental emergency response, the on-demand severe weather prediction, and finally the routine weather prediction jobs within the daily production time-window.

2. The backfill scheduling goal is to run the greatest aggregate sum of non-time critical jobs when computing resources are available, such as climate, ocean prediction, and reanalysis jobs. This results in the highest utilisation of the system.

3. The job pre-emption goal is to stop the minimum set of jobs required to allow priority jobs to run immediately. The suspend-resume pre-emption scheduling is a key feature of our system, which is used to effectively achieve both priority scheduling and backfill scheduling goals.

The pre-emption scheduling will target backfill jobs that can be suspended in memory when time-critical jobs are ready to run. When the priority job has completed, the backfill job is resumed. This means that the elapsed time of a backfill job does not need to fit within an available time slot in the operational schedule. The resource requirements for the backfill job do need to be met. The large memory compute nodes make the pre-emption scheduling achievable. Overall this allows us to achieve the highest utilisation of the system and achieve the production schedule of our business.

The HPC platform currently uses two schedulers (SMS and Cylc) and a workload manager (PBS Professional) to manage the daily work flow. The schedulers are used to feed the workload manager. Of the 20 plus weather modelling suites the Bureau runs regularly, the ACCESS suites are the most resource hungry. Running up to 8 times in any 24 hour period, they need to be managed alongside the Seasonal, Wave, Ocean, and Ocean forecast models, as well as a fleet of smaller NWP suites. Currently, the Bureau PBS scheduler runs up to 60,000 jobs per day across Australis production and staging.

1.6.3.1   SMS

Developed by European Centre for Medium-Range Weather Forecasts (ECMWF) the Supervisor Monitor Scheduler (SMS) has been the backbone of the HPC's delivery platforms for two decades. Written in C, it allows extensive customisations of task environments. SMS allows submission to multiple execution hosts using one or more batch schedulers, with suites scheduled according to time, cycle, suite, task family, and individual task triggering.

The key to the longevity of SMS is that it was always a product developed specifically to cycle numerical prediction workflows. The 20 years of continual development of SMS has contributed to HPC's high rates of uptime and timeliness of delivery. Such a long evolution and refinement has made it a very stable and reliable product. SMS, however, is now a decade outside of its operational lifetime and support from ECMWF has ended; the responsibility for support and development now falls in-house at the Bureau. The limitations of its interface and its alert and monitoring connectivity eventually drove a decision to seek a new workflow scheduler.

1.6.3.2   Cylc

The ACCESS suite of weather prediction jobs that deliver the main product from the Bureau are based on the Unified Model (UM) modelling software from the UK Met Office. Cylc as a workflow scheduler [10] is integrated in these models along with the suite configuration package Rose. Both these products use Python as the programming language.

Adopting Cylc as the new workflow scheduler will deliver significant time saving benefits with a simplified localisation process for every ACCESS model update. The Cylc service, like SMS, provides our IT Operators with status and alerts relating to running modelling suites and product generation. The deployment of Cylc continues and is expected to run into 2018 with an expected retirement of SMS towards 2020.

1.6.3.3   PBS Professional

PBS Pro 12.2 is a Cray specific release of the PBS Pro^{TM} software that facilitates Cray Application Level Placement Scheduling (ALPS) to manage the system's compute, memory, and storage resources.

Workflow jobs are passed from SMS or Cylc to PBS Pro for scheduling and execution when system resources are available. PBS Pro runs virtual Staging and Production queues to manage the upstream workloads distributing the jobs across the Staging and Production platform. PBS Pro also generates the data used to analyse the system utilisation, leading to improved job management, baseline capacity planning, and future upgrade planning.

1.7 Programming System

Software development for cloud or traditional server deployment has utilized a "dev/stage/prod" or "dev/test/prod" lifecycle for some time. It has delivered significant benefits to application resilience, at relatively low cost in those environments. HPC environments, however, are more complex and costly, and maintaining independent infrastructure is a challenge for many organisations.

The Australis environment has provided some separation between each stage in the development lifecycle, allowing the Bureau HPC engineering to benefit from many of the efficiencies that are inherent to cloud-based engineering models. This has enabled the team to pursue enhancements to automation and automated testing without risking operational stability, in particular using a partitioned area of the environment for testing and evaluation of systems.

Integrating with automated software validation tools such as Jenkins, Artifactory, Ansible®, and PyTest (among many others) has enabled a systematic record of provenance (knowing exactly what code produced the running binaries and scripts), easier rollback (easy availability of prior versions), and strong guarantees around the validation of the systems in operation.

Git was also adopted for version control for software development and configuration release. There has been clear value in moving to Git for version control, due to its improved ability for managing code and merging changes. Supporting multiple team structures is more easily done with a more powerful version control system.

Adopting these approaches has not been straightforward. There have been challenges in introducing new ways of working to long-standing teams, and architectural challenges integrating the automation tools.

Software engineering processes in other industries have achieved a far greater agility than in the world of NWP systems development. In an agile environment, the time from the development of a change to its operational implementation can be as little as a day, or even minutes in some cases. The challenges of managing complex numerical behavior mean this agility has not yet been achieved in the Bureau's HPC NWP domain. More work is required to provide the system modularity required for these approaches to apply fully.

1.7.1 Programming Models

A weather forecast suite consists of more than just the big models; typically there are several dozen scripts and programs related to pre- and post-processing. Porting a forecast suite involves two complementary tasks, porting the scripts and recompiling and tuning the actual executables. When the new HPC first became available, the Model Build Team had experience and expertise in current software engineering practice, but they lacked specialist skills and experience in the porting and tuning of operational software for Cray XC40 computers.

Thus the task of the initial porting of the numerical modelling software and workflows to Cray XC, and subsequent tuning, fell to the Scientific Computing Services and their Computational Science team to configure the user and application environment. Its staff then trained the Model Build team, Research & Development, and National Operations Centre staff on the specifics of the Cray XC40 environment and compilers so they could complete the application porting to Australis.

1.7.2   Compiler Selection

There are three different compiler environments available on Australis, The Intel Compiler Suite, the Cray Compiling Environment, and the GNU Compiler Collection. Based on past experiences, the Intel compiler had been found to deliver better performance than the GNU compilers. As all the Bureau applications on the previous supercomputer had been compiled with the Intel compilers, a comparison project between the Intel and Cray compilers was started. Early results indicated that the porting effort when using the Cray compiler was significantly higher. Several applications had problems when compiled with the Cray compiler. This was not typically caused by bugs in the Cray compiler, but had various other reasons:

1. Some algorithms are numerically sensitive to floating point optimisations, which are different between different compilers.

2. Several applications assumed that variables were initialised with zero. This had been working fine with the Intel compiler, but with the Cray compiler those applications aborted or caused incorrect results.

3. It can also be assumed that since all applications had been compiled for years with the Intel compiler, any compiler bugs that existed with the Intel compiler had been worked around (e.g., using special compiler flags to remove certain code transforms, or code restructuring).

Early measurements showed no clear performance advantage when using the Cray compiler so a decision was made to use the Intel compiler for all porting to the new Cray systems, which benefits from the implicit knowledge contained in the mature build scripts.

Porting using the newer Haswell optimised Intel compilers revealed some issues with older code. Whilst most instances were easy to remedy, some more complex examples required compiling with the Sandy Bridge options to avoid incorrect results.

In February 2016 the HPC platform began using the Intel V16 compilers, switching to V17 at the end of 2016. These compilers have so far proven themselves to be stable and suitable for compiling newer NWP models for Australis.

1.7.3   Optimisations

Since all the codes had previously been optimised with the Intel compilers, only a little effort was required to tune the existing applications. Working with the Cray hardware platform (processors, operating system, network & storage) the runtime environment of those jobs had to be adjusted. The Model Build team frequently used Cray's grid reorder tool to change the 'processes to nodes' mapping to minimise internode communication. Results from these changes delivered up to a 5% performance increase.

Further testing investigated the number of nodes required to allow each job to finish within the required time. In each case various domain decompositions were tested to find the one that gave the best performance. For the NWP Unified Model, used for the global, regional, and city forecasts, an additional IO server needed to be configured. The IO servers have their own topology and configuration, and free-up capacity in computation nodes. In some cases the Bureau utilised a simple in-house written "experiment manager" to search the multi-dimension search space for the best combination of parameters.

Running applications on partial nodes was also tested. On the previous HPC platform, it was found that some applications executed more quickly when using only part of the cores on a node – in some cases on a 16 core node, only 12 cores would be used. Partial node usage increases the memory bandwidth per processes and can give more third level cache per process, resulting in a shorter execution time[1]. Our measurements so far have not indicated any need to do this on the Cray XC40 platform.

Additional work was necessary for hybrid codes that utilised MPI and OpenMP® for parallel processing. Using the Intel compiler with its own thread-binding mechanism and environment variables was found in some cases to interfere with the thread-binding setup by the Cray application scheduler.

One unexpected problem encountered was a huge runtime variation in jobs that heavily utilise scripts (jobs starting more than 50,000 processes). The issue was traced to caching issues with the NFS file system. This drove the decision to move those centrally provided scripts from NFS and onto Lustre, and resulted in much improved application performance.

1.8 Archiving

Two archival systems are in place to handle data related to the input and output data from Australis, Oracle's Hierarchical Storage Manager (OHSM, formally known as SAM-QFS), and Meteorological Archival and Retrieval System (MARS) from the European Centre for Medium-Range Weather Forecasts (ECMWF).

1.8.1 Oracle Hierarchical Storage Manager (SAM-QFS)

Oracle Hierarchical Storage Manager (OHSM), previously known as SAM-QFS, archives unstructured data and is housed on an Oracle T5-2 clustered system. Details of the system are shown in Table 1.6

TABLE 1.6: OHSM (SAM-QFS) System Configuration.

Feature	Australis (2015)
Host	Oracle T5-2
Host Operating System	Solaris 11
CPU	Sparc
RAM	256GB
Archival Software	OHSM v6.1
Disk	DELL/EMC Unity 500 100TB
Tape	StorageTek T10000C 10 Drives
Network	10Gb Ethernet 4 Connections

Data is moved onto and off SAM-QFS using network copy programs (such as scp) from Data Mover nodes on the edge of the Crays.

1.8.2 MARS/TSM

MARS archives and retrieves structured data to and from tape, and is optimised for expected retrieval patterns. MARS is a bespoke archive solution designed and developed by the ECMWF.[7]

Meteorological Archival and Retrieval System (MARS) features:

1. Numerical Prediction (NP) specific archival system for gridded and observation datasets developed and maintained by the ECMWF

2. Metadata database and disk front-end for tape storage

3. 2.5PB of operational archive, growing 1+TB per day

4. Up to 60,000+ transactions per day

5. File formats: GRIBL, GRIBZ, & BUFR [11].

TABLE 1.7: MARS System Configuration.

Feature	‖ Australis (2015)
Host	DELL R730
Host Operating System	Linux 6
CPU	E5-2643
RAM	128
Network	10Gb Ethernet
	4 Connections
Tape	StorageTek T10000D
	10 Drives
TSM version	7.1

MARS provides a layer to archive/move the data to tape; in our case IBMs Spectrum Protection (previously Tivoli Storage Manager, TSM) is used to archive the data to tape. The system supporting the MARS service and TSM is described in Table 1.7.

1.9 Data Center/Facility

The Bureau's HPC platform is housed in a commercial data centre with a tier 3+ uptime rating, and is located in the state of Victoria, Australia. The facility has a PUE rating of 1.3. The space the Bureau utilises for its data centre has been divided into 3 separate rooms. The first two each house 50% of the Cray XC40 liquid cooled system. The rooms have sufficient cooling capacity, up to 980kW per room, for the anticipated mid-life upgrade. Each of those rooms has a separate power feed; a loss of a power feed will only affect one of the two rooms. The data centre provides redundant and separate liquid cooling loops to each Cray XC40.

The third room has redundant power feeds that incorporate dual feeds to all the racks; this enables all the Cray infrastructure services devices to have dual power supplies; these are fed from independent power sources. This room houses the Management, PBS Pro, Login, and Data Mover nodes for Australis; the Cray Sonexion and DDN GPFS (IBM Spectrum Scale™ General Parallel File System) storage systems. It also houses other infrastructure, filesystems, and data storage. This room is air-cooled only and built to use cold aisle containment.

The extra walls were required to isolate the rooms and include fire protection. This means the layout of our data centre is not the same that other customers have within the same facility. The Bureau needed to work with the data centre to alter their standard layouts and customise the airflows and other aspects of the facility to its needs.

1.10   System Statistics

1.10.1   Systems Usage Patterns

Australis has four principal Production run times each day (00:00 UTC, 06:00 UTC, 12:00 UTC & 18:00 UTC). The model runs include Global, Global Wave, Global Ocean, Australian Regional, Regional Wave, and six high-resolution state/city runs for Victoria/-Tasmania, New South Wales, Queensland, South Australia, Western Australia, and Northern Territory. Antarctic forecasting uses data from the Global model. Additional Model runs for climate forecasting use the Predictive Ocean Atmosphere Model for Australia (POAMA) ensemble with a 250km grid resolution.

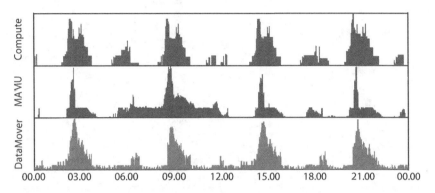

FIGURE 1.8: Australis NWP Time-critical Processing Load

A sample of system usage patterns on the Production platform can be seen in Figure 1.8. The Time-critical Processing Load graph shows the regularity of the load created by the 6-hourly Production jobs on the HPC system.

Notes: This load graph omits the impact of the many non time-critical jobs that run on Australis. These jobs include ocean and climate models, and they tend to use a lot of the HPC system capacity that otherwise might seem to be unused. In addition, noticeably more HPC system capacity will be consumed when the higher-resolution models currently being planned are moved to production.

Figure 1.9 shows the rise in the number of production jobs since the Australis HPC system inception. Staging jobs are not shown.

1.11   Reliability

In striving to achieve a robust 24x7x365 platform we identified four key areas to optimise the workflow and balance the competing loads.

1. Compute capacity to run jobs from PBS Pro

2. Datamover capacity to stage files

3. Storage disks for short term files on Lustre

4. SSH access to pull files

Identifying and focusing on these areas allowed us to establish processes to monitor and support each key area. In normal operation each node is allocated directly to particular PBS Pro queues; this is where a process allows specific groups of nodes to be allocated to either Production or Staging queues.

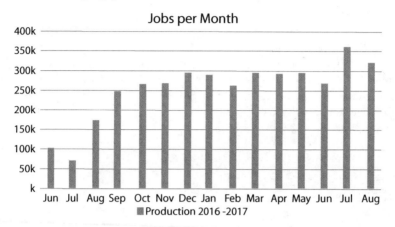

FIGURE 1.9: Australis Production Jobs per Month

1.11.1   Failover Scenarios

Maintaining operations 24x7x365 are important to the Bureau's forecasting services. The system has been designed to survive many different types of compute and storage failures.

1.11.2   Compute Failover

The changeover operation of compute nodes from Staging to Production can be performed without interruption to Production queues. However our preferred process is to first stop and drain all running jobs on the Staging systems. In the case of a system failure where the status of the jobs that were running on the (failing) Production nodes is unknown, the process is to ensure that all the Staging nodes have been drained (often forcibly) and then power off all the nodes previously allocated to Production. Production is then started on what was the Staging server. The failed nodes are rebooted; any issues are then fixed and the system is brought back on-line, returning to service as the Staging server. In this way the Bureau strives to minimise outages and ensure that the system is returned to full service as quickly and efficiently as possible.

A fault occurring on the Staging server can be resolved without disrupting Production.

1.11.3   Data Mover Failover

Data movers are allocated to Production or Staging in groups. At present there is a direct relationship of data movers to compute nodes, so they are usually swapped from Staging to Production at the same time.

1.11.4   Storage Failover

As previously mentioned there are two distinct groups of Lustre filesystems. The first is for Production data (Group P) and the second for Staging data (Group S). By design the Group S also holds a copy of important Production data. When needed for recovery, NWP applications can be reconfigured to collect their Production data from the Group S area relatively easily. Before doing so, this data may need to be rolled back to the last known good state.

The available modes of operation of the storage systems is shown in Figure 1.10. These range from Normal mode through Failover, Recovery, and Isolated modes, and are discussed further below.

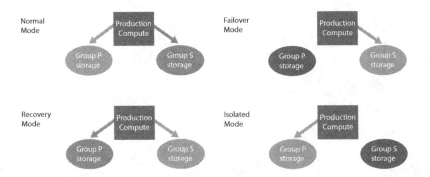

FIGURE 1.10: File Storage Operations Modes

1.11.4.1   Normal Mode

All filesystems are available. Production writes to Group P storage and stores a copy of the important data on Group S storage.

1.11.4.2   Failover Mode

The Group P storage is unavailable. All running jobs need to be restarted from last known state and now use Group S for input/output. In this state there is no copy of important data taken. The next mode will be Recovery, which can be switched to without requiring any jobs to be stopped.

1.11.4.3   Recovery Mode

All filesystems available, but Production still uses Group S. This mode is used so that the Group P file system can get a copy of the recovery data before we return to normal mode - which is what happens after being in recovery mode. Normally 24 hours are allotted for this to take place, however the process can be sped up or run manually for certain applications. It depends on how long the Group P file system was unavailable. Changing from Recovery to Normal mode requires stopping all running jobs.

1.11.4.4   Isolated Mode

The Group S storage is unavailable. Production continues to run without an interruption; however creating the copy of important backup data won't take place.Transitioning to this mode usually only takes place from the normal mode and can be achieved while jobs are still running in Production.

1.11.5   SSH File Transfer Failover

Some applications, such as the suite scheduler, require SSH access to retrieve files. To facilitate this, a F5 load balancer is used to poll the data movers to check their availability and to determine which PBS Pro queues they are allocated to. From this, a dynamic DNS entry is generated for those clients that need to run SCP (secure copy). If a target node becomes unresponsive, it will be removed from the list maintained by the F5, and when a queue is switched, the list updates within a few minutes.

1.12　Implementing a Product Generation Platform

During the time in which we have been preparing this chapter, the HPC team at the Bureau have been readying the environment to transition to a data-intensive product generation platform called "Aurora". The Bureau's aim is to decouple, or reduce, the modelling dependencies, improve forecast product longevity, reduce disruptions to business, and to improve:

1. Data processing performance; to provide a greater breadth of applications

2. Standard data processing levels; to improve data asset management

3. Standard methods; to improve software reuse and scientific integrity

4. Common data services; provides ease and consistency of product data access

5. API management; providing security and management of data requests

There are two major thrusts in the product generation platform: the splitting of pre-/post processing from model simulation and the decoupling of model data outputs from the forecast products and services that the Bureau's customers are interested in.

This split of compute and post-processing will allow the Bureau's HPC platform to adopt a more agile approach to managing its numerical modelling and weather products, so that modelling changes have fewer dependencies and thus lower development costs with shorter delivery times.

Separating the numerically intensive compute from the I/O intensive requirement offers many benefits to our operations. Currently the platform's resources are constantly managed to favour the intensive compute for the NWP modelling rather than the intensive data processing that delivers the forecasting products.

Separating these two functions will free the XC40 to focus on improving compute intensive functions. The CS400 post-processing platform will be allowed to specialise in delivering better I/O performance, optimised applications and products, with the ability to support innovations in areas like machine learning and visualisation.

Post-processing tasks are much more granular than NWP model suites. The existing scheduling tools – Cylc and PBS – are not fully fit to address such fine-grained requirements. Post-processing tasks change frequently in response to evolving customer requirements. To support such flexibility and agility of the development and operations, the future post-processing framework will be highly dynamic and configurable, with event-based declarative flow like the Dask.distributed package. This package is a distributed dispatcher, with a pool of workers that scales on demand through PBS.

There are other benefits that are considered important; in the present arrangement, system upgrades affect the whole environment in our 24x7x365 operational model, and is an ongoing risk. In the split platforms, the scope of adverse impact is halved. Resource management on the platform, currently a significant overhead for live operations, will also ease. This decoupling concept and platform approach is not unique to the Bureau. It has been

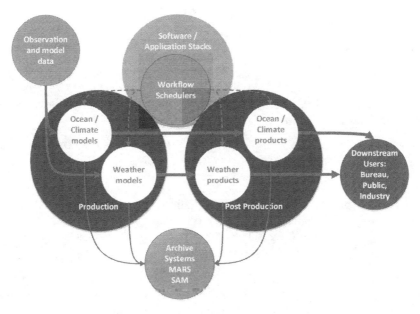

FIGURE 1.11: HPC Product Generation

used successfully at other National Meteorology centres; however our choice of hardware solution is different and worth a discussion.

The post processing platform is being built around two Cray CS400 systems. Each scalable CS400 platform comprises 16 compute nodes and 4 GPU nodes, each with 1.6TB NVMe flash storage, 3 service nodes, and 2 management nodes running Bright Cluster Manager. The platform will also mount the Cray XC40 Lustre filesystem, and its own GPFS filesystem, which is better equipped to manage the intensive I/O workloads. The configuration is based on a simplified design philosophy where each CS400 cluster is interconnected over InfiniBand and have their own dedicated storage based on DDN GRIDScaler® GS14KX hardware.

Currently the CS400 cluster represents a compute count of 40 nodes, 1440 Intel Broadwell cores, 8 NVIDIA® Tesla® K80 GPU's, 10.24TB of RAM, and 4PB of GPFS data storage with 300TB of SSD flash storage.

The post processing will use IBM's Spectrum Scale (GPFS) as its parallel file system. All CS400 clients run GPFS client software while the DDN storage run embedded GPFS Network Shared Disk(NSD) servers. In addition to this, each CS400 cluster has a dedicated LNET Node that provides access to the Australis global file systems. Each Compute, GPU and Service node also runs a version of lustre client to enable it to access the Australis global file systems.

We believe we are one of only a few HPC organisations utilising both Lustre and GPFS.

Our early testing using IOR (IO performance benchmark tool) measures 35GB/second across 16 nodes. Our calculations show that there is performance growth headroom within the DDN storage stack; however the more limiting performance bottleneck is the choice of FDR in our InfiniBand network (this is consistent with Lustre networking today). To improve storage performance, the Bureau will be moving to InfiniBand EDR in the mid-life upgrade.

Once the Aurora platform is in place, the Bureau will continue to work towards establishing a content delivery network with data supplied by the post processing platform.

Bibliography

[1] Ilia Bermous, Joerg Henrichs, and Michael Naughton. Application performance improvement by use of partial nodes to reduce memory contention. *CAWCR Research Letters*, pages 19–22, 2013. http://www.cawcr.gov.au/researchletters/CAWCR_Research_Letters_9.pdf#page=19, [accessed 31-August 2017].

[2] Bureau of Meteorology, Queensland Regional Office. Severe Tropical Cyclone Debbie. Press Release, 29 March 2017. http://www.bom.gov.au/announcements/sevwx/qld/qldtc20170325.shtml, [accessed 31-August-2017].

[3] TJ Dell. A white paper on the benefits of chipkill – correct ECC for PC server main memory. Technical report, IBM Microelectronics Division, November 1997. http://www.ece.umd.edu/courses/enee759h.S2003/references/ibm_chipkill.pdf, [accessed 31-August-2017].

[4] Tom Keenan, Kamal Puri, Tony Hirst, Tim Pugh, Ben Evans, Martin Dix, Andy Pitman, Peter Craig, Rachel Law, Oscar Alves, Gary Dietachmayer, Peter Steinle, and Helen Cleugh. *Next Generation Australian Community Climate and Earth-System Simulator (NG-ACCESS) - A Roadmap 2014-2019.* The Centre for Australian Weather and Climate Research, June 2014. http://www.cawcr.gov.au/technical-reports/CTR_075.pdf, [accessed 31-August-2017].

[5] J Kim, WJ Dally, and D Abts. Technology-Driven, Highly-Scalable Dragonfly Topology. In *ACM SIGARCH Computer Architecture News*, volume 36, pages 77–88. IEEE Computer Society, 2008.

[6] Anna Leask, Kurt Bayer, and Lynley Bilby. Tropical storm Debbie – a day of destruction, despair and drama. *New Zealand Herald*, 7 April 2017. http://www.nzherald.co.nz/nz/news/article.cfm?c_id=1&objectid=11833401, [accessed 10-October-2017].

[7] Carsten Maass. MARS User Documentation. October 2017. https://software.ecmwf.int/wiki/display/UDOC/MARS+user+documentation, [accessed 10-October-2017].

[8] Bureau of Meteorology. New supercomputer to supercharge weather warnings and forecasts. Press Release, July 2015. http://media.bom.gov.au/releases/188/new-supercomputer-to-supercharge-weather-warnings- and-forecasts/, [accessed 31-August-2017].

[9] UK Met Office. Unified Model Partnership, October 2016. https://www.metoffice.gov.uk/research/collaboration/um-partnership, [accessed 31-August-2017].

[10] Hilary J Oliver. Cylc (The Cylc Suite Engine), Version 7.5.0. Technical report, NIWA, 2016. http://cylc.github.io/cylc/html/single/cug-html.html, [accessed 31-August-2017].

[11] World Meteorological Organization. WMO International Codes, December 2012. http://www.wmo.int/pages/prog/www/WMOCodes.html, [accessed 31-August-2017].

[12] QJ Wang. Seasonal Water Forecasting and Prediction. Technical report, CSIRO, 2013. http://www.bom.gov.au/water/about/waterResearch/document/wirada/wirada-long-term-factsheet.pdf, [accessed 10-October-2017].

Chapter 2

Theta and Mira at Argonne National Laboratory

Mark R. Fahey, Yuri Alexeev, Bill Allcock, Benjamin S. Allen, Ramesh Balakrishnan, Anouar Benali, Liza Booker, Ashley Boyle, Laural Briggs, Edouard Brooks, Phil Carns, Beth Cerny, Andrew Cherry, Lisa Childers, Sudheer Chunduri, Richard Coffey, James Collins, Paul Coffman, Susan Coghlan, Kathy DiBennardi, Ginny Doyle, Hal Finkel, Graham Fletcher, Marta Garcia, Ira Goldberg, Cheetah Goletz, Susan Gregurich, Kevin Harms, Carissa Holohan, Joseph A. Insley, Tommie Jackson, Janet Jaseckas, Elise Jennings, Derek Jensen, Wei Jiang, Margaret Kaczmarski, Chris Knight, Janet Knowles, Kalyan Kumaran, Ti Leggett, Ben Lenard, Anping Liu, Ray Loy, Preeti Malakar, Avanthi Mantrala, David E. Martin, Guillermo Mayorga, Gordon McPheeters, Paul Messina, Ryan Milner, Vitali Morozov, Zachary Nault, Denise Nelson, Jack O'Connell, James Osborn, Michael E. Papka, Scott Parker, Pragnesh Patel, Saumil Patel, Eric Pershey, Renée Plzak, Adrian Pope, Jared Punzel, Sreeranjani Ramprakash, John 'Skip' Reddy, Paul Rich, Katherine Riley, Silvio Rizzi, George Rojas, Nichols A. Romero, Robert Scott, Adam Scovel, William Scullin, Emily Shemon, Haritha Siddabathuni Som, Joan Stover, Mirek Suliba, Brian Toonen, Tom Uram, Alvaro Vazquez-Mayagoitia, Venkatram Vishwanath, R. Douglas Waldron, Gabe West, Timothy J. Williams, Darin Wills, Laura Wolf, Wanda Woods, and Michael Zhang

Argonne National Laboratory

2.1 ALCF Overview

The U.S. Department of Energy (DOE) maintains a collection of open-access research facilities, called user facilities, that play a central role in the nation's leadership in science. Constructed and operated by various DOE Office of Science programs, these facilities house cutting-edge machines and instruments intended to deliver the greatest scientific impact.

In 2003, the DOE issued a bold plan, "Facilities for the Future of Science: A Twenty-Year Outlook," [24] outlining its goals and objectives for Office of Science large research facility projects for the coming two decades. Advanced scientific computing emerged as a top-ranked priority. And with that, the agency laid out a strategy to partner with U.S. computer vendors and support an integrated program of hardware and software investments designed to optimize computer performance for scientific problems, and then open those high-performance computing (HPC) resources at no cost to the scientific community, including industry, to accelerate discoveries on numerous fronts.

By prioritizing scientific computing and establishing the leadership computing program nearly 15 years ago, the Office of Science set a new course in how scientific inquiry is done. Today, computational science supports a significant portion of the nation's scientific output, and its impact is expected to increase with the advent of exascale computing capabilities.

2.1.1 Argonne Leadership Computing Facility

The Argonne Leadership Computing Facility (ALCF) at Argonne National Laboratory is one of two leadership computing facilities in the nation fully dedicated to open scientific research. Established in 2006, the ALCF builds and operates state-of-the-art computing resources and employs HPC experts and computational scientists to assist users at all stages of the process.

The ALCF currently operates two petascale machines – an IBM Blue Gene/Q and an Intel-Cray XC40 system – and a range of other resources used for testing and development, data analysis, visualization, and more.

Through substantial awards of computing time, largely awarded through two major DOE programs, researchers from the private sector, academia, and government laboratories conduct major simulation campaigns aimed at solving today's biggest science problems.

The diversity of projects underway on any given day of the year (ALCF's major resources run 24 hours a day, seven days a week) push the limits of knowledge in their respective fields. Perhaps their one commonality is that the work can't be done in traditional scientific settings, using traditional scientific methods, and certainly not at the traditional pace.

In addition to delivering breakthrough simulation science, leadership computing facilities are also keeping pace with the analysis needs of numerous disciplines that are generating increasingly massive amounts of data from large-scale experiments and observations. To facilitate the investigation of these vast data sets, the ALCF also maintains a high performance resource dedicated to visualization and analysis, with a priority policy favoring interactive data exploration. Significantly, the resource shares the same high-speed parallel filesystem as the compute resources, eliminating the need to transfer data to perform exploration.

The ALCF supports investigations that help advance our fundamental understanding of how things work, provide technological solutions to a wide range of problems, and keep the nation safe and competitive. To date, the ALCF has delivered billions of computing hours in support of achievements in physics, chemistry, materials science, biological sciences, and more – and expects to deliver billions more in the years to come.

2.1.2 Timeline

2004 Argonne forms the Blue Gene Consortium with IBM, made up of government labs, universities, and industrial organizations that were interested in the evaluation and use of the IBM Blue Gene family of high-performance computers. The Blue Gene/L supercomputer debuts in November 2004.

2005 Argonne installs a 5-teraflops Blue Gene/L for evaluation.

2006 The ALCF is established.

2009 The ALCF deploys a Blue Gene/P named Intrepid that debuts at #4 on the Top500 List [7].

2010 Intrepid ranks #1 on the Green500 List [6].

2011 Intrepid ranks #1 on the inaugural Graph500 List [5].

2012 The ALCF undergoes major facility upgrades in preparation for the Blue Gene/Q (BG/Q) named Mira. Mira goes online and debuts at #3 on the Top500 list.

2014 The DOE announces the Collaboration of Oak Ridge, Argonne, and Lawrence Livermore (CORAL) initiative, a $525 million project to upgrade existing leadership systems to help the nation accelerate to next-generation exascale computing.

2015 Through the CORAL initiative, the DOE announces a $200 million investment to deliver a next-generation supercomputer, Aurora, to the ALCF. The ALCF selects 10 Early Science projects for its intermediary system, a Cray XC40 named Theta.

2016 The ALCF installs Theta. The Theta Early Science Program begins.

2017 Theta opens to the full user community and begins to support ALCC awards in July.

2.1.3   Organization of This Chapter

Section 2.2 presents an overview of the Argonne Leadership Computing Facility, including details on recent and future upgrades. Section 2.3 describes the ALCF's newest supercomputer that officially entered production mode in July 2017. Section 2.4 presents the ALCF's IBM Blue Gene/Q Mira and some of the major scientific accomplishments it has enabled over the past four years. Sections 2.6 and 2.5 present an overview of the ALCF job failure analysis system and the Cobalt resource scheduler – two important system software features unique to the facility.

2.2   Facility

ALCF resources are housed in a 25,000 sq. ft. data center in Argonne's Theory and Computing Sciences (TCS) Building. This data center has a concrete base, a 4-foot raised floor, and mechanical rooms containing conventional facility support infrastructure (UPS, AHUs, etc.) located to the east and west sides of the center.

2.2.1   Mira Facility Improvements

Many of the details in this section were previously documented by Bailey et al. [10]. Data center preparations for Mira included power and cooling upgrades and floor reinforcement (see Section 2.4 for more on Mira).

Power: The power upgrades resulted in 20 MW of electrical capability in a redundant configuration, or 40 MW for a non-redundant configuration. The maximum electrical load for the BG/Q resources and supporting computing infrastructure (filesystems, visualization, networking, etc.) is approximately 6 MW of power, with an expected load of 4 MW. These improvements included the addition of three 3,000 kVA secondary unit substations in the TCS electrical room, ten 5,000 A distribution panels installed along the east wall of the data center, and six 200 kVA power distribution units in the data center.

Cooling: The BG/Q compute racks are approximately 91% liquid cooled, and 9% air cooled [23]. The rack cooling required installation of a closed liquid cooling process loop with two 1,300-ton chillers that runs underground from a chilled water plant (CWP) to the TCS and back. The design incorporated a water-side economizer, which maximizes free cooling capabilities whenever weather conditions are favorable. Oversized cooling towers were installed to increase the capacity of the chilled water that could be produced via free cooling operation. Multiple blended modes were also designed into the CWP sequences, which allows simultaneous operation of free cooling and centrifugal chiller cooling during high demand scenarios. The two high-efficiency chillers provide 0.571 kW/ton at maximum load conditions. During the winter, when temperatures are optimal for free cooling, the CWP potentially can avoid using 2,174,040 kW-hr by not operating the chillers. The loop from the CWP enters the building and goes to a heat exchanger, shared by an internal cooling loop. The external loop provides the cooling water, exchanges heat with the internal loop, and then returns it to the CWP. The chilled loop setpoint is 64°F, maintains water pressure at 25 lbs./sq. in., and a flow of 25 gal./min. The BG/Q can sustain temperature increases to 74 degrees Fahrenheit without issue. Flow changes are less tolerable.

Floorspace: The BG/Q compute and I/O node racks occupy about 2,000 sq. ft. of floor space in the south half of the data center. The Mira compute racks are laid out in three rows of 16 racks each, with two racks of I/O forwarding nodes (IONs) located at

FIGURE 2.1: TCS chillers and Mira water process loop.

the end of each row. (Previous BG/Q installations located the IONS on top of each rack.) The complementary infrastructure (storage, management, network, and visualization) along with six other BG/Q racks occupy an additional 500 sq. ft. of floor space.

Floor load: A structural load analysis determined that the existing floor pedestals and floor tiles were insufficient support for the BG/Q racks, each of which weigh about 4,300 pounds[1], hence, heavy duty pedestals and floor tiles were installed around and under the BG/Q racks.

FIGURE 2.2: Heavy duty floor pedestals for Mira.

2.2.2 Theta Facility Improvements

In June 2016, the ALCF installed a Cray XC40 named Theta (refer to Section 2.3 for more on Theta), requiring additional facility upgrades. Many of these details appear in Harms et al. [18].

Power: No additional electrical capacity was required, however, to avoid electrical interruptions, all work had to be planned to coincide with existing machine maintenance schedules. The first challenge was how to bridge the 120-foot span between Theta and the

---

[1]Slightly less than other BG/Q installations since the IONs are not located on top of each rack but in separate racks.

data center substations. A ceiling-mounted busway with six 1200 A bus ducts was installed, terminating at six new electrical panels, as shown in Figure 2.3. In addition, whips were installed from the panels to support up to 24 480 V racks and four power distribution units (PDUs) providing 208 V service.

Cooling: The engineering team redesigned the closed water loop to accommodate an additional system with different flow requirements; namely, the BG/Q requires a constant flow while the XC40 does not. Since Mira's cooling loop was designed with stubs and valves to accommodate additions, the piping and valves could be installed without affecting the existing loop until the final connection, charge, and commission. The impellers on the water loop were also upgraded to increase the water flow rate to compensate for Theta's additional heat load (see Figure 2.3). Since the pumps were originally installed in an N+1 configuration, the impeller changes could be done without impacting normal operations. The final system upgrade commission was done during a maintenance period.

FIGURE 2.3: Theta busway installation and cooling loop pumps.

Floorspace: The XC40 compute, management, and I/O racks occupy about 1,000 sq. ft. of floor space in the northeast portion of the data center. The Theta compute racks are laid out in two rows: 12 racks in one and eight in the other, with room to add four more. The management and I/O racks and two Liebert PDUs are inline with the first row of compute racks (to the south). Behind the first row of I/O and management racks (to the east) is a test and development air-cooled XC40 and its management rack.

Floor load: The raised floor was upgraded exactly as was done for Mira. The existing floor tiles were replaced with heavy duty tiles, increasing the maximum weight capacity from 925 pounds to 5,400 pounds. The floor pedestals were upgraded with 2 mm thick steel pedestals taking the support capacity to 9,000 pounds.

2.3   Theta

Theta, a Cray XC40 system based on the second-generation Intel Xeon Phi processor, will enable breakthrough computational science and engineering research, while providing a platform to help ALCF users transition their applications to the Intel Xeon Phi architecture.

FIGURE 2.4: Theta.

2.3.1 Architecture

Theta is part of the Cray line of supercomputers and continues the ALCF's architectural direction of highly scalable, homogeneous many-core systems. The primary components of this architecture are the second-generation Intel Xeon Phi Knights Landing (KNL) many-core processor and the Cray Aries interconnect. The Theta XC40 system has a peak performance of 11.69 petaflops (PF) with key architecture specifications shown in Table 2.1. The full system consists of 24 racks containing 4,392 compute nodes with an aggregate 281,088 cores, 69 terabytes (TB) of in-package, high-bandwidth, multi-channel memory (IPM), and 824 terabytes of DRAM. Compute nodes are connected into a three-tier Aries dragonfly network. A single Theta cabinet contains 192 compute nodes and 48 Aries chips. Each Aries chip can connect up to 4 nodes and incorporates a 48-port Aries router which can direct communication traffic over electrical or optical links [9]. Additionally, each node is equipped with 128 GB solid state drive (SSD) resulting in a total of 549 TB of solid state storage on the system.

TABLE 2.1: Theta Hardware Configuration

Node architecture	Cray XC40
CPU	Intel Xeon Phi 7230
CPU microarchitecture	Silvermont
CPU count per node	64
Node memory HBM/DDR (GB)	16/192
Interconnection network	Cray Aries
Compute racks	24
Total number of nodes	4,392
Peak FLOP rate (TF)	11.69
Lustre clients	4,392
Data servers	56
Metadata servers	4
LNET routers	30
Capacity (useable) (PB)	9
Peak B/W (GB/s)	240
GPFS/DVS nodes	60

2.3.1.1   Processor

Each Theta compute node consists of one KNL processor, 192 GB of DDR4 memory, 128 GB SSD, and a PCI-E connected Aries network interface controller (NIC). The KNL processor, shown in Figure 2.5 is architected to have up to 72 compute cores with multiple versions available containing either 64 or 68 cores. Theta contains the 64-core 7230 KNL variant. On the KNL chip, the 64 cores are organized into 32 tiles with two cores per tile, connected by an on-chip mesh network and with 16 GB of in-package, multi-channel DRAM memory. The core is based on the 64-bit Silvermont microarchitecture [26] with six independent out-of-order pipelines, two of which perform floating point operations. Each floating point unit can execute both scalar and vector floating point instructions, including earlier Intel vector extensions, in addition to the new AVX-512 instructions. The peak instruction throughput of the KNL architecture is two instructions per clock cycle, and these instructions may be taken from the same hardware thread. Each core has a private 32 KB L1 instruction cache and 32 KB L1 data cache. The key Theta node characteristics are summarized in Table 2.2.

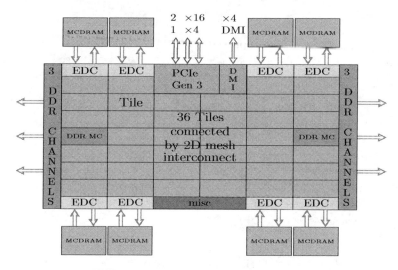

FIGURE 2.5: Intel Xeon Phi Processor

TABLE 2.2: Theta Node Architecture

Processor core	KNL (64-bit)
Speed	$1,100 - 1,500$ MHz
# of cores	64
# of HW threads	4
# of nodes/rack	192
Peak per node	2,662 GFlops
L1 cache	32 KB D + 32 KB I
L2 cache (shared)	1 MB
In-package memory	16 GB
Main memory	192 GB
NVRAM per node	128 GB SSD
Power efficiency	4,688 MF/watt [6]

Other key features of the node include:

1. Simultaneous multi-threading (SMT) via four hardware threads.

2. Two new independent 512-bit wide floating point units, one unit per floating point pipeline, that allow for eight double precision operations per cycle per unit.

3. A new vector instruction extension, AVX-512, that leverages 512-bit wide vector registers with arithmetic operations, conflict detection, gather/scatter, and special mathematical operations.

4. Dynamic frequency scaling independently per tile. The fixed clock "reference" frequency is 1.3 GHz on 7230 chips. Each tile may run at a lower "AVX frequency" of 1.1 GHz or a higher "Turbo frequency" of 1.4–1.5 GHz depending on the mix of instructions it executes.

2.3.1.2 Memory

With the KNL, Intel has introduced on-chip IPM comprised of 16 GB of DRAM (MC-DRAM) integrated into the same package with the KNL processor. In addition to on-chip memory, two DDR4 memory controllers and six DDR4 memory channels are available and allow for up to 384 GB of off-socket memory. Theta contains 192 GB of DDR4 memory per node. The two memories can be configured in multiple ways, as shown in Figure 2.6 [25].

- Cache mode. The IPM memory acts as a large, direct-mapped, last-level cache for the DDR4 memory

- Flat mode. Both IPM and DDR4 memories are directly addressable and appear as two distinct non-uniform memory access (NUMA) domains

- Hybrid mode. One half or one quarter of the IPM configured in cache or flat mode with the remaining fraction in the opposite mode

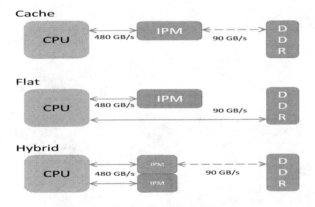

FIGURE 2.6: Intel Xeon Phi Memory Modes [25].

This configurable, multi-component memory system presents novel programming options for developers.

2.3.1.3 Network

The interconnect used in Theta is a three-level dragonfly topology network using the Cray Aries interconnect. Four Theta nodes are connected to a single Aries chip via a PCI-E

Gen3 interface, as show in Figure 2.7. The Aries chip contains four NICs for the attached nodes and 40 bi-directional network ports operating each way at 4.7 GB/s for the optical links and 5.25 GB/s for the electrical links. The first two levels, shown in Figure 2.8 (rank-1 and rank-2), are copper based with 10.5 GB/s bi-directional bandwidth per link and the rank-3 level is optical with 9.38 GB/s per link. The two-level network containing the high-speed, low-cost electrical links is referred to as an electric group, and a group contains up to 384 nodes within a pair of Cray XC cabinets. Optical cables are used for the long links interconnecting the groups. Each node has a peak injection bandwidth of 16 GB/s and the total system injection bandwidth is 39 TB/s. Theta's bisection bandwidth, which depends on the number of optical links interconnecting the groups, is around 10.12 TB/s.

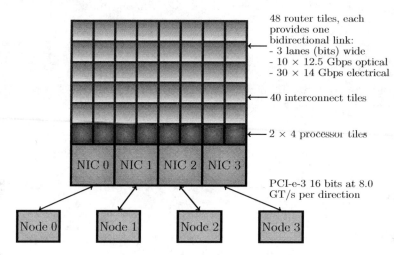

FIGURE 2.7: Cray Aries Router

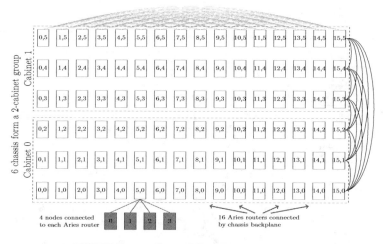

FIGURE 2.8: Cray XC40 Dragonfly Group

2.3.1.4   Storage System

The details in this section are taken from Harms et al. [18]. The primary storage system for Theta is the Cray Sonexion 3000 Lustre Storage System summarized in Table 2.1. The

Sonexion 3000 itself is managed by a Sonexion Management Unit (SMU). The SMU is a high availability (HA) pair of servers, each with an Intel Xeon E5-2609 v3 CPU with six cores at 1.9 GHz and 64 GB of RAM. The SMU manages the configuration for all the Sonexion components.

There are also two Metadata Management Units (MMUs). Each MMU is comprised of two servers, each with an Intel Xeon E5-2618L v3 with eight cores (HyperThreading enabled) at 2.30 GHz and 64 GB of RAM. One MMU contains the Lustre Metadata Server (MDS), Lustre Management Server (MGS), and the Lustre Metadata Target (MDT) drives. The other MMU is an Additional DNE Unit (ADU) which contains two distributed namespace (DNE) servers that provides the capability to spread metadata operations over multiple servers. Each MDS and DNE has a single MDT.

Lastly, there are 28 Scalable Storage Units (SSUs). Each SSU is comprised of two Lustre Object Storage Servers (OSS) in an active-active failover pair with the Object Storage Target (OST) drives. Each OSS is SAS attached to a 5U 84 drive disk enclosure. There are a total of 82 SAS drives and two SSD drives in this enclosure. The SAS drives are 6 GB/7200 RPM drives and are configured using a parity declustered RAID [19] code called GridRAID [41 (8+2+2)]. The GridRAID configuration will present a pair of 41 disk RAID arrays (OST), one to each of the two OSS servers in the SSU. The two SSD drives are used by Lustre as journals for ldiskfs functions and are not used to directly store Lustre file system data. Each of the 56 OSS servers is responsible for a single OST when not in a failover state. If one of the OSSs in a pair fails, the surviving OSS takes over the failed OSS's OST and serves both OSTs in the SSU. The 56 GridRAID OSTs contain a total of 2,296 6 TB SAS drives, yielding a 9 PB usable capacity.

The OSS, MDS, and MGS servers, as well as the Theta login servers and LNET routers, are connected to the ALCF InfiniBand Storage Area Network (SAN). All of the Sonexion servers are connected to an internal Ethernet management network as well. The Theta login servers and LNET routers are configured with Lustre version 2.7.1 and the Sonexion servers are configured with Lustre version 2.7.19.

2.3.2   System Software

Cray XC systems like Theta run the Cray Linux Environment (CLE). The CLE is a distributed system of service node and compute node components. CLE includes Cray's customized version of SUSE Linux Enterprise Server (SLES). This full-featured operating system (OS) runs on administrative service nodes, which use specialized daemons and applications to operate and manage the system, as well as login services that are the users' gateway to the machine.

The compute nodes by default run a special, optimized version of SLES. This optimized version has relatively few services running, thereby providing support for application execution without the overhead of a full-featured OS. Cray calls this "Extreme Scalability Mode" (ESM). Minimizing non-essential OS threads and processes is key to providing a highly scalable environment, thereby minimizing jitter.

Cray also supports what they call Cluster Compatibility Mode (CCM) which allows independent software vendor (ISV) and third party applications to run out of the box. These applications require some of the OS services and/or a more traditional Linux network stack that are not present in ESM.

Alternatively, ALCF is planning to support containers on Theta. Containers allow applications with complex requirements or OS functionality that may not be present under CCM. ALCF staff are currently in the process of testing several options including Singularity, Shifter, and Docker.

2.3.2.1   Systems Administration of the Cray Linux Environment

Cray's release of CLE 6.0/SMW 8.0 (code-named Rhine/Redwood) introduced a number of changes intended to increase the simplicity and maintainability of system configuration. Of these changes, the integration of the Ansible configuration management tool was the most significant [20]. At the core of the system is a wrapper called `cray-ansible` that creates a large number of Ansible variables based on a collection of files known as the "config set." All nodes are initially provisioned with a relatively generic filesystem image based on the class of node (compute, login, or service), then further customized with `cray-ansible` during boot. As with all Cray systems, configuration data is distributed from the System Management Workstation (SMW), which serves as a central point of control for the entire system.

As with all large system deployments, good configuration management is crucial to the long-term stability of Theta. Like other sites, ALCF has added additional organizational structure and processes to `cray-ansible` and image management in CLE 6.0 [20]. Of primary importance is the use of a Git repository to store copies of the main configuration directories on the SMW. Changes are first made on the administrator's local machine, then submitted as a merge request to a local Gitlab instance for others to review before the changes are made "live" on the SMW. This review phase increases the visibility of changes and reduces the likelihood of mistakes in configuration. Likewise, ALCF makes heavy use of its testing and development system, a single-cabinet XC40 named Iota, on which all major software and configuration updates are applied before reaching Theta.

2.3.2.2   Scheduler

The ALCF uses the Cobalt scheduler and resource manager (SRM) [1], which was originally developed at Argonne and is maintained by the ALCF. For an in-depth description of Cobalt, please refer to Section 2.5. Since Cobalt is the SRM on all ALCF production systems – including BG/Q systems, general Linux clusters, and resources in Argonne's Joint Laboratory for System Evaluation (JLSE) platforms – it was imperative to extend the management capabilities of Cobalt to the Cray XC40.

As reported in Harms et al. [18], the Cobalt component-based architecture was extended to include a component specifically intended to communicate with Cray's Application Level Placement Scheduler (ALPS) [11], as well as support job-to-resource-association mechanisms that would be specific to the Cray XC40. The ALPS interface was used for its reliability and clean abstraction layer. Of note, Cobalt's job pre- and post-scripts are used to provide a mechanism for on-the-fly memory mode control via CAPMC [21], allowing users to request different KNL memory/NUMA modes per job [17].

2.3.3   Programming System

2.3.3.1   Programming Models

Theta supports both distributed memory, shared memory, and partitioned global address space (PGAS) programming models like the various prior generation Cray XT, XE, XK, and XC models.

Cray provides an implementation of MPI based on MPICH and implements the MPI-3.0 standard. The Cray MPI (as well as other communication libraries) is layered on top of the Generic Network Interface (GNI) and Distributed Shared Memory Application (DMAPP) [14] communication services. The GNI API includes two sets of function calls: user-level high-performance applications (uGNI) and kernel-level driver functions (kGNI). uGNI and DMAPP provide low-level communication services to user-space software. uGNI directly ex-

TABLE 2.3: Software Configuration

Feature	Software
Login Node OS	SLES 12.0
Compute Node OS	CLE 5.2
Parallel Filesystem	Lustre 2.7.19
Compilers	Intel 17.0
	Cray Compiler 8.5
	GNU 6.3
	LLVM 4.0
MPI	(Cray) MPICH 2 (default)
	Intel MPI
Notable Libraries	HDF5
	netcdf/pNetCDF
	Cray Math Library
	Intel Math Kernel Library
	PETSc
	Trilinos
	FFTW
Scheduler & Resource Manager	Cobalt
Debugging Tools	Allinea DDT
	ATP/STAT (Cray)
Performance Tools	TAU
	Darshan
	HPCToolkit
	Perftools (Cray)

poses the communications capabilities of the Cray network application-specific integrated circuit (ASIC). DMAPP implements a logically shared, distributed memory (DM) programming model.

Cray supports the OpenMP shared-memory parallel-programming paradigm within a node on Theta. Multiple threads of execution perform tasks defined implicitly or explicitly by OpenMP directives. By default, threads are pinned to a processor core, but the application launcher `aprun` supports options to control thread placement. POSIX threads (`pthreads`) are also supported with a compute node and they are an API to a shared-memory threaded programming interface also obeying the same `aprun` runtime options.

Theta also supports partitioned global address space (PGAS) communication libraries and languages, including SHMEM [15], Co-Array Fortran [13], and Unified Parallel C [12]. These are layered on top of uGNI and DMAPP, just like MPI. SHMEM is a shared memory access library of logically shared and distributed memory access routines. Similar to MPI (MPI and SHMEM form Cray's Message Passing Toolkit), SHMEM calls pass data between cooperation processes in a one-sided fashion; that is, a process puts or gets data without acknowledgment from another process. Co-Array is a small extension to Fortran 95/2003 that provides an explicit notation for data decomposition in the Fortran language. UPC is a C language extension that provides a uniform programming model for both shared and distributed memory hardware.

2.3.3.2 Languages and Compilers

Theta supports the Intel compiler, Cray compiler, GNU compiler, and the LLVM compiler. The Intel, Cray, and GNU compilers are fully integrated into the Cray XC Programming Environment, which means Cray provides integrated support for their own libraries and tools with these compilers.

The Intel, Cray, and GNU compilers support the three primary languages C, C++, and Fortran; and also support the programming models MPI, SHMEM, OpenMP, and Pthreads described above. Co-Array Fortran and UPC support are only natively supported by the Cray compiler.

The LLVM compilers have been integrated into Theta's software environment. LLVM compilers include Clang, supporting C and C++, and Flang, supporting Fortran. Clang and Flang share almost all basic command-line flags with the GNU compilers, and, as a result, these compilers can be integrated with Cray's modules system using a set of wrapper scripts named after the corresponding GNU compilers.

The LLVM compilers support auto-vectorization using the AVX-512 instruction set and can generate calls to Intel's SVML vector math library. Clang also supports AVX-512 vector intrinsics like the Intel and GNU compilers. The LLVM OpenMP runtime library is ABI compatible with both Intel's and GNU's OpenMP libraries. Clang also includes support for link-time optimization (LTO), both traditional monolithic and the new scalable "thin" LTO. Moreover, Clang also supports a wide array of instrumentation-based debugging tools, such as Address Sanitizer and Thread Sanitizer, that can be used to debug programs with low overhead.

Cray provides a set of universal compiler wrappers: ftn (for Fortran), cc (for C), and CC (for C++). These wrappers invoke the compilers appropriate for the user's selected programming environment. Flags to enable compilation of MPI programs, to cross-compile for the KNL's architecture, and to make available software from the user's currently loaded modules, are added automatically. This latter capability is implemented on top of the pkg-config system.

Intel's ISPC compiler, which provides a domain-specific language for implementing vector kernels and built on LLVM, is installed.

2.3.4 Deployment and Acceptance

Theta was delivered, installed, configured, and accepted over a three-month period from June 2016 to September 2016 [18]. This period was divided into five phases: Site Configuration, Acceptance Test Preparation (ATP-P), Early Science Testing, Functional and Performance Acceptance (ATP-FP), and Stability Acceptance (ATP-S). Successfully completing the previous phase was a requirement for starting the next.

During the Site Configuration and ATP-P phases, the machine was installed, configured to integrate into the ALCF infrastructure, and acceptance tested and verified to function as expected. After all the AT applications were verified to run correctly, Theta was turned over to the Early Science Program (ESP) users (see Section 2.3.5) for two weeks, allowing ESP users early access to Theta for porting and scaling tests. Half of the ESP projects ran successfully at scale during this two week period.

2.3.4.1 Benchmarks

Theta's performance was evaluated using the Sustained System Performance [4] (SSP) method developed by the National Energy Research Scientific Computing Center (NERSC) for the NERSC8 acquisition. Six of the eight SSP reference applications were selected: AMG2013, GTC, MILC, MiniDFT, MiniFE, and MiniGhost. Table 2.4 presents the SSP results achieved.

The final SSP achieved was 172.28 TF. All of the SSP applications were run in the KNL cache quadrant mode [17].

In addition to the SSP benchmarks, the Sandia MPI Benchmark (SMB), STREAM Triad, and I/O benchmarks were evaluated. The SMB [3] measures message rates of a given

TABLE 2.4: Theta SSP Results

Benchmark	Nodes	Pi
AMG2013	768	0.012061731
GTC	1,200	0.049908531
MILC	384	0.056735604
MiniDFT	47	0.392259086
MiniFE	2,662	0.013050658
MiniGhost	768	0.124849456
Geomean	-	0.052865462
SSP		171.2840965

message size between endpoint pairs using eight nodes. The SMB benchmark was tested with 8-byte and 1024-byte message sizes obtaining message rates of 16.1 mmps and 7.3 mmps, respectively.

The STREAM [22] benchmark measures memory bandwidth for different workloads, but only the *Triad* results were evaluated. Table 2.5 shows the STREAM results. The KNL MCDRAM memory modes (Section 2.3.1.2) evaluated were flat, cache, and 50/50 hybrid. All were run under quadrant NUMA mode. A workload much larger than the available high-bandwidth memory (HBM) was also evaluated under 50/50 hybrid memory mode to evaluate the DDR memory. Results shown reflect a single node with 64 MPI processes with a single thread.

TABLE 2.5: Theta STREAM Results

Mode	Size (GiB)	BW (GiB/s)
Flat	7.8	447.9
Cache	7.8	308.2
Hybrid (50/50)	7.8	442.5
Hybrid (50/50)	97.6	57.9

Two different I/O benchmarks were used to evaluate the Lustre filesystem: IOR and mdtest. The IOR [2] benchmark was used to evaluate the Lustre filesystem's I/O bandwidth using an optimal workload. IOR was run with the following arguments: *-a POSIX -e -g -[wr] -t 64M -b 12g -F -k -E -o file*. The IOR write bandwidth was benchmarked at 247 GB/s and read bandwidth benchmarked at 235 GB/s.

The mdtest [8] benchmark was used to evaluate metadata rates of the Lustre filesystem. The mdtest application ran across the entire machine, using 3,240 nodes. The Lustre volume was configured with no DNE support, so this test measured the rate of a single MDS/MDT. Mdtest was run with the following arguments: *-i 1 -d /lus/theta-fs0/... -n 10*. Table 2.6 shows the mdtest results.

2.3.4.2   Applications

In addition to the performance benchmark applications, applications were selected that are representative of common ALCF workloads. These applications were used to verify the functionality of the KNL architecture and scalability of these workloads on that architecture. Table 2.7 shows the applications along with their scaling factor observed during ATP-FP and ATP-S.

TABLE 2.6: Theta mdtest Results

Operation	Rate (ops/s)
Directory creation	24,129.947
Directory stat	133,717.879
Directory removal	11,199.838
File creation	43,459.599
File stat	130,676.940
File read	93,707.416
File removal	29,923.935
Tree creation	194.406
Tree removal	42.541

TABLE 2.7: Theta Science Applications

Application	Description	Small (nodes)	Large (nodes)	Scaling factor
AMG2013	parallel algebraic multigrid solver	216	3072	14.2x
CAM-SE	high-order methods modeling environment for atmospheric climate modeling	256	1024	4x
HACC	N-body methods for formation of structure in collisionless fluids under the influence of gravity in an expanding universe	96	3240	33.75x
HSCD	turbulent combustion	4	128	32x
LAMMPS	molecular dynamics	128	2048	16x
NEKbone	computational fluid dynamics with spectral element method	216	3240	15x
MILC	quantum chromodynamics (su3_rhmd_hisq)	128	3072	24x
QBOX	first-principles molecular dynamics	216	3240	15x
QMCPACK	continuum quantum Monte Carlo	216	3240	15x

2.3.5 Early Science and Transition to Operations

In preparation for standing up next-generation systems, ALCF hosts the ESP [16], where participants prepare a set of applications for the architecture and scale of the future systems. The ALCF team sometimes refers to ESP as the *applications-readiness* program – a partnership among ALCF, system vendors, and the ESP project teams. ALCF gives training on the future hardware and its programming, including at least one hands-on workshop when sufficient early hardware is available. As soon as possible, ALCF provides access to simulators and previous-generation hardware, as well as preproduction silicon for the next-generation system. The benefits of the ESP are manifold:

- Ensure that future ALCF systems deliver science on day one. The ESP projects are excellent candidates for the first batch of production Innovative and Novel Computational Impact on Theory and Experiment (INCITE) and ASCR Leadership Computing Challenge (ALCC) projects once the system is in production.

- Vet and harden the new system hardware and software using real applications running at large scale.

- Develop and optimize libraries and tools for the new system. In addition to the Early Science projects, ALCF supports an omnibus project to develop scientific libraries and performance tools. Early Science projects depend on some of these libraries, and use the tools. Having this infrastructure in place and debugged before the new system goes into production is an important prerequisite for production users.

The program begins about two years prior to planned acceptance-testing of the system. Projects are chosen competitively based on a call for proposals. Authors propose an ambitious scientific run campaign to be executed on the future system. Proposals detail any required code development and a plan for porting and optimizing to the next-generation system. The ALCF evaluates proposals based on their potential scientific impact; potential for success and high performance on the future system; and ability of the proposed project team to deliver. Reviewers may include ALCF staff, as well as staff from Oak Ridge Leadership Computing Facility (OLCF) and NERSC, as part of coordination and collaboration among the three Office of Science compute facilities' applications-readiness programs. Beyond these merit reviews, ALCF staff optimize project selections to ensure:

- diversity of scientific areas, sampling the spectrum of science in the expected production workload

- diversity of algorithms and numerical methods

- strategic importance, for example filling gaps in science areas or methods from applications-readiness programs at other facilities

Each project has a designated point of contact in ALCF's computational science team, and a funded, two-year postdoctoral researcher. The Early Science postdocs work closely with the project principal investigator (PI) and team, but also have ALCF staff mentors. Funding ALCF postdocs also helps to develop the next generation of computational scientists in leadership-scale computing. Each project receives a significant award of computer time on the future system. ALCF dedicates the entire system for 3–6 months after acceptance but before a transition to production to the Early Science projects. The goal of ALCF is for each project to complete or make significant headway on their proposed run campaigns in the Early Science period; however, they may continue running for the remainder of that calendar year while sharing the system with other users.

The Theta Early Science program was under a compressed time frame; therefore, three projects were pre-selected, and then a call was issued in April 2015 where three more projects were selected in July 2015, see Table 2.8. An unexpectedly strong response to the call resulted in the selection of six additional Tier 2 projects, see Table 2.8. The Tier 2 projects were offered the same training and early hardware access as the six Tier 1 projects, but a funded postdoc and a large allocation for science runs were not provided. The Tier 2 projects were allowed to run in a low-priority mode, and several projects made good progress on science runs that way. The dedicated Early Science period ran from October 2016 through early April 2017.

The ALCF will collect a set of technical reports from the Theta ESP projects describing what they did to port and optimize their applications for the KNL/XC40 architecture.

TABLE 2.8: Theta ESP Tier 1 and 2 Projects.

Tier 1 Project Title	Principle Investigator	Application Code(s)	Research Domain
Scale-resolving simulations of wind turbines with SU2	Juan Alonso, Stanford University	SU2	engineering
Large-scale simulation of brain tissue: Blue Brain Project	Fabien Delondre, Ecole Federale Polytechnique de Lausanne	CoreNeuron	biological sciences
First-principles simulations of functional materials for energy conversion	Giulia Galli, University of Chicago	Qbox, WEST	materials science
Next-generation cosmology simulations with HACC: challenges from baryons	Katrin Heitmann, Argonne National Laboratory	HACC	physics
Direct numerical simulations of flame propagation in hydrogen-oxygen mixtures in closed vessels	Alexi Khokhlov, University of Chicago	HSCD	chemistry
Free energy landscapes of membrane transport proteins	Benoit Roux, University of Chicago	NAMD	biological sciences
Tier 2 Project Title	**Principle Investigator**	**Application Code(s)**	**Research Domain**
Electronic-structure-based discovery of hybrid photovoltaic materials on next-generation HPC platforms	Volker Blum, Duke University	FHI-aims, GAtor	materials science
Flow, mixing, and combustion of transient turbulent gaseous jets in confined cylindrical geometries	Christos Frouzakis, Swiss Federal Institute of Technology Zurich	Nek5000	engineering
Advanced electronic structure methods for heterogeneous catalysis and separation of heavy metals	Mark Gordon, Iowa State University	GAMESS	chemistry
Extreme-scale unstructured adaptive CFD: from multiphase flow to aerodynamic flow control	Kenneth Jansen, University of Colorado Boulder	PHASTA	engineering
The hadronic contribution to the anomalous magnetic moment of the muon	Paul Mackenzie, Fermilab	MILC, CPS, Chroma	physics
Quantum Monte Carlo calculations in nuclear theory	Steven Pieper, Argonne National Laboratory	GFMC	physics

These will be made available to the community in the second half of 2017, and ALCF will host community-accessible presentations from the projects on this technical work.

2.4 Mira

Mira, ALCF's 10-petaflops IBM Blue Gene/Q supercomputer, was deployed in 2012 and debuted at #3 on the Top500 list. Mira's 786,432 cores and 768 TB of memory make it one of the most powerful supercomputers in the world. It also ranks among the most energy-efficient, owing to its innovative chip designs and unique water-cooling system. Mira is still the primary production machine at ALCF, providing roughly 6 billion core hours yearly. With many years of service to leadership computing, this section provides an abbreviated look at the architecture, how the Mira ecosystem has evolved, notable science accomplishments, and system statistics.

FIGURE 2.9: Mira.

2.4.1 Architecture and Software Summary

The IBM BG/Q supercomputer system was developed in partnership with IBM and Lawrence Livermore National Laboratory (LLNL). It was funded by the National Nuclear Security Agency (NNSA) at LLNL and by the DOE Office of Science at Argonne. The BG/Q was the third generation of supercomputers developed by this partnership, after the BG/L and the BG/P.

Chapter 10 of the 2013 Contemporary High Performance Computing book (CHPC) [10] was dedicated to the BG/Q series of machines, and covered applications, benchmarks, system hardware, and software, along with some early system statistics about Mira. Storage, visualization, and analytics strategy were described as well. At the time of publication, Mira had been recently accepted and was being prepared for production use. The following paragraphs summarize major characteristics of the BG/Q architecture as presented in the 2013 CHPC book chapter.

The following summarize major characteristics of the BG/Q architecture. The BG/Q is the third generation in the IBM Blue Gene line of supercomputer systems. The BG/Q processor is an IBM PowerPC A2 at 1.6 GHz and 16 cores per node. The system combines processors, memory, and communication functions on a single chip. A single compute card contains a compute chip with 16 GB of DDR3 memory. Logically, this entity (chip plus memory) is known as an I/O node when located in an 8-way I/O drawer, or as a compute node when located in a 32-way node board assembly. Sixteen node boards are arranged into a midplane, which takes up half a rack and totals 512 compute nodes. Two midplanes are stacked vertically into a BG/Q rack. A rack therefore contains 1,024 compute nodes, with an aggregate peak performance of 209.7 TF.

Mira has a peak performance of 10 PF. It is configured as 48 racks of BG/Q with a total of 49,152 nodes, 786,432 cores, 768 TB RAM, and a 5D torus interconnect. The system also has a total of 384 I/O nodes.

The operating systems for the BG/Q inherit the dual-kernel architecture of previous Blue Gene machines. I/O nodes run a Linux-based operating system and serve as a proxy to and from the external network. The compute nodes run a Blue Gene customized OS called CNK (Compute Node Kernel). CNK connects to the I/O nodes for file I/O, sockets, and job and tool interaction. CNK leverages a 17th core for operating system functions to further isolate jitter. This core is used for control message processing, I/O messaging, special hardware event and error processing, debugger protocols, and application agent threads.

The BG/Q control system is designed to seamlessly scale from a half rack of hardware (512 nodes), to greater than 256 racks (over 260 thousand nodes). The BG/Q introduced several new capabilities to the control system that included the following: HA through automatic failover with job continuation to remove a single point of failure; subblock jobs for increased flexibility in job scheduling; a unified scheduling mechanism for simplified job control; and an enhanced event analyzer. The BG/Q control system uses a DB2 database for persistent storage of machine configuration, active and historical jobs, and operational status. The control system software runs on the BG/Q Service Node and manages the information stored in this database.

The BG/Q system supports the concept of subdividing the machine's resources into logical entities known as blocks. These blocks are electrically isolated from one another; and may be as small as 32 nodes and as large as the entire machine. The minimum block size may be larger on certain systems; as a block must have at least one connected I/O node. Larger blocks utilize optical cables to complete a multi-dimensional torus network, whereas smaller blocks are networked through their encompassing node boards and midplanes.

The BG/Q control system extends this capability by providing subblock jobs. These jobs can range in size from one to 512 nodes, and a decision is made at job-launch time instead of at block boot time. The size of the job must be rectangular; where each of the five dimensions can only be one, two, or four nodes. This allows greater use of the machine with less fragmentation for capacity workloads that do not occupy the entire system.

The BG/Q introduced the Toolkit for Event Analysis and Logging (TEAL), an event analysis framework based on the BG/P Event Log Analysis (ELA) and Federation ELA. It is designed as a pluggable processing pipeline that allows different components to use connectors to log events, analyze the events, create and log alerts, and deliver the alerts to interested parties. TEAL supports the processing of events as they occur, i.e., real-time analysis, and events that have occurred in the past, i.e., historic analysis. Analyzers specific to BG/Q look for events taking hardware offline, such as compute nodes, I/O nodes, bulk power modules, and cables. Events causing abnormal job termination are also analyzed. Listeners can be configured to send an email, write to a file, or invoke an external program.

Within the programming models and messaging, some of the novel capabilities introduced include scalable atomic primitives, shared addressing in CNK, lockless queues, collective network, and shared address collectives. In the languages and compilers sub-section, the authors cover four key areas of innovation: OpenMP support in XL's SMP runtime; the exploitation of Quad Processing extension (QPX) to the Power Instruction Set Architecture instructions using automatic vectorization; Transactional Memory (TM) support; and Speculative Execution (SE).

Many tools have been developed for the BG/Q system over the past five years. The ALCF user guide lists the most commonly used performance tools in the ALCF environment at: http://www.alcf.anl.gov/user-guides/performance-tools-apis. The most commonly used debuggers and profilers are here: http://www.alcf.anl.gov/user-guides/debugging-profiling.

2.4.2 Evolution of Ecosystem

Mira was deployed in 2013 as a 48-rack, 48K node, BG/Q system with a single-rack debugging system named Cetus; a second, single-rack testing and development system named Vesta; and an associated visualization and analysis resource named Tukey. All these systems shared the same IBM GPFS filesystems. Two 8-frame Spectra Login T950 tape libraries were also part of the initial Mira ecosystem (although originally installed in 2009). Over time, the ecosystem has evolved in a few key areas. Figure 2.10 shows the Mira ecosystem since 2015.

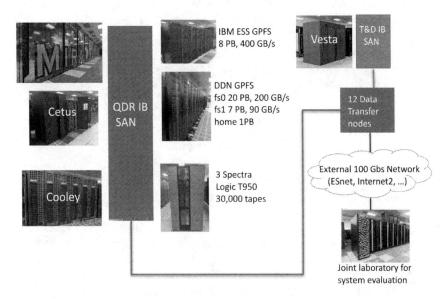

FIGURE 2.10: Mira ecosystem.

The evolutionary change started with a lesson learned from ALCF's previous IBM system, Intrepid, which contained a single GPFS filesystem. By putting all the resources in a single filesystem, users could see a higher realizable bandwidth. However, that single filesystem was also a single point of failure, with time-consuming `fsck` checks extending any filesystem outage. For Mira, a second smaller, less powerful GPFS filesystem was added to the design for disaster resilience reasons. These two filesystems are home to all the projects that run on Mira. If one filesystem becomes unavailable, production jobs can still run off the other.

Owing to acceptance considerations, a second rack of BG/Q was deployed to Vesta, Mira's testing and development system. The addition was a significant improvement from a scheduling perspective, as a 2-rack system requires additional links allowing for more thorough testing. Vesta, with its own independent GPFS filesystem, is truly a first-level testing and development system that can be used to test system and filesystem software without any impact on the production equipment. Vesta is also a place where potentially disruptive projects can run – for instance, projects testing OS development such as Plan9 and ZeptoOS.

With IBM discontinuing the Blue Gene line of supercomputers and hardware support, ALCF bought four more racks of BG/Q in 2014, which became the "new" Cetus. These racks were bought primarily as hardware replacement inventory, but quickly became an excellent place for second-level testing and development, user debugging and scaling studies, and small, long-running simulations. Off-loading these workloads further optimized scheduling of leadership computing jobs on Mira. As of January 1, 2015, all hardware replacements on Mira would come from ALCF inventory, the original Cetus rack, and then from Vesta or Cetus racks.

A third GPFS filesystem was obtained for two reasons: to address the difference in performance users experienced depending on which filesystem they used, and to gain experience in the operational challenges that come with a burst buffer. This third filesystem, designed to operate as a cache, would have no data permanently stored there, and therefore was not a capacity expansion. To date, this experiment is still in progress, and no decision has been made if the solution will work as a cache/burst buffer or be repurposed as a third filesystem. The addition provides a much higher bandwidth than the other two GPFS filesystems combined (realized performance of 400 GB/s vs 200 GB/s and 90 GB/s). Even though it is not in production yet, the design has informed ALCF about burst buffer operational difficulties.

Mira's data analysis resource, Tukey, was replaced in 2015 with a new resource named Cooley. Although the number of nodes and the number of processors remained similar (now 126 nodes with 12 cores each), the computing power tripled, and, more importantly, the new resource has significantly more memory per node at 384 GB (as compared to Tukey's 64 GB per node), for a total of 47 TB of memory. Similarly, with upgraded GPUs and NVIDIA Tesla K80s GPU accelerators, GPU memory per node doubled on Cooley to 24 GB, totaling 3 TB. The increase was a direct response to the needs of the users to have more memory per node for data analysis and visualization. Since Tukey and the newer Cooley share the same filesystem with Mira, users do not need to move their data to get to the analysis resource. Cooley has an FDR Infiniband (IB) based interconnect and utilizes QDR IB uplinks to the Mira storage area network (SAN).

In 2016, a third 8-frame Spectra Logic T950 tape library was installed. The tape libraries are the basic component of the ALCF archive solution, with the High Performance Storage System (HPSS) as the user-facing tool providing high speed data transfer to and from the data repository. HPSS was first deployed at the ALCF in 2009 and currently stores more than 38 PB of data. The HPSS infrastructure includes redundant core servers, a 1.2 PB disk cache residing on DDN SFA12K-40 storage, a NetApp resident DB2 metadata repository, and three 8-frame Spectra Logic T950 tape libraries. High speed parallel data transfer is accomplished through multiple data mover servers directly attached to both the disk cache and tape storage. There are approximately 23,500 LTO6 tapes residing in the three tape libraries; LTO6 being the currently configured tape technology. Technology refreshes are planned for every two generations.

Client access to HPSS is granted through HSI/HTAR and Globus GridFTP. HSI provides additional parallelism with multiple concurrent transfers for small files and dispatches multiple third party transfer agents for larger files. The transfer agent eliminates the requirement for data to traverse the network. GridFTP also includes a striped transfer feature for parallelism.

Archived data is initially written to the disk cache and is migrated to tape based on predefined policies. Small files are written to single tapes while larger files may be written to striped tape sets. Data remains in the disk cache until the predefined purge policy determines that the cache usage threshold has been reached. Data may be retrieved from the disk cache or from tape.

The hierarchical storage management (HSM) feature of HPSS, known as GPFS/HPSS Interface (GHI) was deployed on one of the project file systems in 2016. GHI provides space management and disaster recovery for the managed file system. Policy driven migrations, retrievals, and purges allow it to work quietly in the background. Deployment on the second project file system is scheduled for this year. The GHI namespace in HPSS currently contains more than 6 PB of project data from the managed file system. GHI has shown impressive aggregate transfer rates of 10 GB/s by utilizing multiple GHI manager nodes.

2.4.3 Notable Science Accomplishments

Miras mission is to provide orders of magnitude more computing time to science projects than is typically awarded elsewhere. The DOE's two primary allocation programs for awarding time at ALCF, INCITE and ALCC, were introduced in Section 2.3.5. The peer-reviewed award selection process also includes a readiness assessment of the proposed work. Readiness is defined as both the need for leadership computing and the ability of their workflow and applications to succeed at the needed scale. Need is defined as requiring any combination of compute, data, hardware, or software resources otherwise unavailable. INCITE projects are awarded for up to three-year terms. Since 2013, Mira has supported 168 INCITE projects (27 in 2013, 40 in 2014, 37 in 2015, 34 in 2016, and 30 in 2017), with an average award in 2017 of 117 million core-hours. Projects come from a broad range of science domains using simulation science, data analytics, and learning workloads.

Work on Mira has resulted in hundreds of peer-reviewed papers over the past decade. A few highlights are given here:

- In 2005, a semi-trailer truck hauling 35,000 pounds of explosives through Utah crashed and caught fire, which resulted in a massive explosion brought on by a process called deflagration-to-detonation transition (DDT). A University of Utah research team used Mira to virtually recreate the explosion to better understand the DDT process and potential mitigation strategies, including alternative packing arrangements and storage techniques. The effort will ultimately help improve the safety of transporting explosive devices on our roads and railways.

- In the standard model of cosmology, dark energy and dark matter together account for 95 percent of the mass energy of the universe, but their origins remain a mystery. An Argonne research team used Mira to carry out some of the largest and most detailed simulations of the universe ever performed. This project has resulted in the first simulations that are accurate enough to compare with state-of-the-art sky surveys. The insights gained from these simulations will suggest new theoretical approaches, as well as new methods for the design and cross-correlation of observational probes of structure formation.

- Advanced green energy and propulsion systems that deliver improved energy efficiency and yields from renewable sources have driven the development of accurate, high-fidelity simulation capabilities at GE Global Research. The inability of traditional computational fluid dynamics methods to accurately and consistently characterize turbulent mixing processes in shear flows and boundary layer flows had slowed the drive to higher efficiencies and lower emissions. A GE research team used ALCF computing resources to develop a simulation methodology that captured such phenomena accurately. Information derived from these simulations is key to designing and developing quieter, more efficient wind turbines and jet engines.

- Superlubricity, a state in which friction essentially disappears, is a highly desirable property for automobiles, wind turbines, and countless other mechanical assemblies that lose efficiency to friction. Argonne scientists used Mira to identify and improve a new mechanism for eliminating friction. The simulation results fed into the development of a hybrid material that exhibited superlubricity at the macroscale in laboratory experiments for the first time. The material could potentially be used for applications in dry environments, such as computer hard drives, wind turbine gears, and mechanical rotating seals for microelectromechanical and nanoelectromechanical systems. In addition, the knowledge gained from this study is expected to spur future efforts to develop materials capable of superlubricity for a wide range of mechanical applications.

2.4.4   System Statistics

The careful collection of data allows ALCF to produce statistics that accurately measure how well the facility is performing. ALCF takes action based upon these statistics to ensure that utilization, allocation percentages, and job size meet or exceed expectations.

Figure 2.11 shows the availability metrics from Mira. Availability of the machine has been over 90% for almost its entire service period.

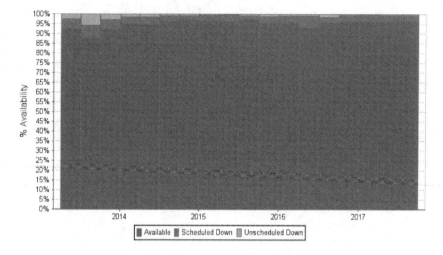

FIGURE 2.11: Mira availability and utilization.

Figure 2.12 shows the overall utilization and utilization by allocation program. Utilization started out at approximately 65% in 2013 and quickly rose to the 80%-90% range, and has been holding steady in the 90%-95% range ever since. Since 2014, the target allocation percentages for the INCITE, ALCC, and DD allocation programs have been 60%, 30%, and 10%, respectively.

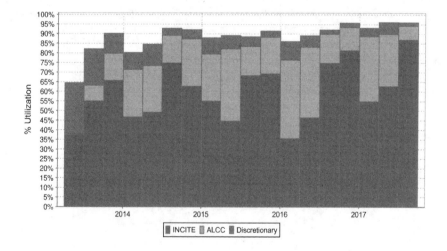

FIGURE 2.12: Mira utilization by program.

Table 2.9 shows the mean time to interrupt and mean time to failure numbers from 2013 through 2017. Mean Time to Interrupt (MTTI) is defined as time, on average, to any full outage on the system, whether unscheduled or scheduled. It is also known as Mean Time Between Interrupt. Mean Time to Failure (MTTF) is defined as the time, on average, to an unscheduled outage on the full system. ALCF's biweekly maintenance schedule caps MTTI at 14 days, but does not directly impact MTTF.

TABLE 2.9: Mira MTTI and MTTF by Year

Year	MTTI	MTTF
2013	4.2	10.5
2014	9	25.8
2015	9.5	24.2
2016	10	40.5
2017	10.2	35.3

Figure 2.13 shows job usage by size. On Mira, capability is defined as split into two parts: Capability (indicated by the color orange in the figure) is defined as using eight racks or more (16.7%), and High Capability (indicated by the color purple in the figure) is defined as running on 16 racks or more (33.3%). High Capability is a subset of Capability. The graph shows approximately 70% of all usage falls into the Capability category.

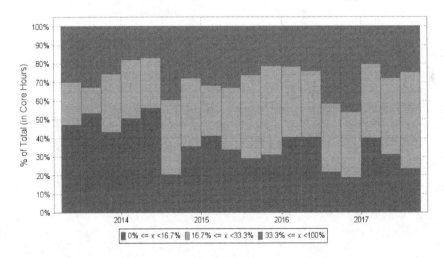

FIGURE 2.13: Mira job usage by size.

Figure 2.14 shows usage by science area. It clearly shows a wide range of science domains making use of the leadership computing resources.

2.5 Cobalt Job Scheduler

The ALCF uses an Argonne-developed and internally supported job scheduler called Cobalt. Its origins are in a DOE program called the "Scalable Systems Software Project" in the late 1990s, which later went on to become the SciDAC Scalable Systems Software ISIC. The decision to use Cobalt goes back to the origins of the ALCF and one of its priorities,

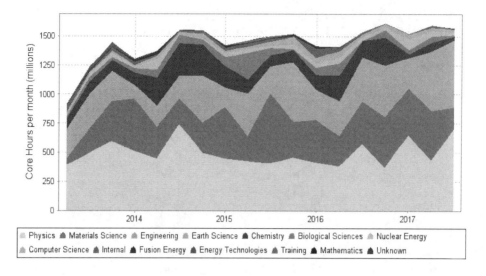

Physics   Materials Science   Engineering   Earth Science   Chemistry   Biological Sciences   Nuclear Energy   Computer Science   Internal   Fusion Energy   Energy Technologies   Training   Mathematics   Unknown

FIGURE 2.14: Mira usage by science area.

which was to support Operating Systems research at scale. The nature of this mandate required a scheduler that could boot alternative operating systems on the Blue Gene. At that time, the only scheduler that supported the Blue Gene was IBM's LoadLeveler, but it did not support alternate operating systems. The only remaining option was to modify an open source scheduler and add the required features. Other open source alternatives were available, but Cobalt was developed at Argonne and provided significant advantages in terms of rapid development cycles and testing coordination.

The ALCF's latest system, Theta (Section 2.3) is a Cray XC40, and the ALCF will continue to run the Cobalt scheduler because significant mission critical functionality has been built into it and allows the ALCF to rapidly respond to the changing needs of the facility, providing a competitive advantage.

The ALCF has developed scheduling algorithms that allow machine utilization greater than 90%, while also significantly favoring large-scale capability jobs up to and including single jobs that consume the entire machine. Hooks in Cobalt allow the ALCF deep and rapid visibility into the operational state of the scheduler. This allows us to drive reporting and enable troubleshooting of system problems far better than would a commercial scheduler.

Energy is one of many "first class" constraints that will need to be considered in the scheduling algorithms on future capability class systems. Energy-aware scheduling was added and evaluated around 2010. At the time, the decision was that the improvements did not outweigh the disadvantages, particularly user confusion with regard to why jobs were not being run. With the increase in power consumption of the latest and projected future ALCF machines, this area is once again receiving significant attention.

Burst buffers are another resource that are already appearing in DOE large-scale systems that are highly constrained and will need to be managed. Other resources, such as network bandwidth, storage space, and potentially even network accessible RAM may be constrained as well. Scheduling for multiple "first class" resources will have a significant impact on the success and utilization of future systems, and Cobalt will allow the ALCF to develop and tune those algorithms to precisely meet the science needs of its users.

Cobalt utilizes a component daemon architecture that allows rapid deployment to new supercomputing architectures without compromising support for existing architectures Mira (Section 2.4), the Cooley cluster, and Theta XC40 [18]. The code that handles most of the scheduling is identical, with the exception of a component that has architecture-specific allocation and resource tracking details (the "system" component) and, possibly, a system-specific user-script launch component. Where possible, vendor-provided resource monitoring and resource locking mechanisms are used, such as MMCS on the Blue Gene platform or ALPS on Cray systems. In most cases, this also allows Cobalt to avoid needing to run a daemon on the compute resources themselves. Where a resource manager is not available, such as Cooley, Cobalt can be set up to act as the primary one.

Scheduling policy at the ALCF is not primarily driven by traditional resource utilization. While robust utilization of the system is both important and achieved, the need for INCITE and ALCC workloads to run, even if they do not ideally utilize the machine, and the requirement that a certain amount of the core hours delivered, be run via what are considered "capability" jobs, which are typically 20% of the overall system size or larger, take precedence over pure utilization. Owing to these requirements, queueing and job scoring policy are set up in such a way that capability-sized workloads are incentivized. To enable maximum delivery of users' allocated time on these systems, users are given full priority so long as they have time left in their allocation, regardless of how much they have run recently on the system. To ensure that resources are free for a large capability class job, or a job from an INCITE or ALCC project, Cobalt will drain system resources until sufficient resources are available to run a job, given that there is sufficient hardware in working order to do so.

Utilization is a very important goal, nonetheless. Cobalt uses draining to ensure that resources are made available to the highest scored jobs at any time, but draining can incur a significant cost. To mitigate this cost, Cobalt uses a system-customized backfill algorithm to efficiently recover drained resources and run jobs opportunistically on draining resources without delaying the start time of the top-scored jobs. Even projects that have used their allocation and "gone negative" may submit jobs to a special low-priority backfill-only queue, though any job on the system is eligible for backfill and will be considered in score-order. This algorithm maintains a high (greater than 90%) utilization rate while ensuring delivery of key metrics.

2.6 Job Failure Analysis

Job Failure Analysis (JFA) is the process of identifying the root cause of the failure of a batch job that runs on the supercomputer. A batch job is a user created script or binary submitted to the scheduler (Section 2.5) run on the supercomputer in the order defined by the site's priority policy. The failure of that job is detected by a non-zero exit code or no exit code from the job or subcomponent of the job called a task.

The JFA process started with Intrepid, a BG/P. JFA helped the machine administrators improve reliability and availability by more clearly highlighting recurring failures. Before JFA, such investigations were a manual and labor intensive process that often took more than a day each week to complete.

Today, more directly accessible data is available for the administrators to determine root cause for each failure. Data exists in system logs, job outputs and errors, databases, and emails among many other places. All data is automatically pulled into a structured, central database to reduce the data complexity and normalize the data for analysis. This process, called an Extract Transform Load (ETL), allows application of System Logic, which is different for each machine. For example, even though Mira, Cetus, and Vesta are all BG/Qs, they have different network wiring, which effects how the system reacts to node failures, filesystem usage, and so forth. An example of the System Logic applied to jobs, tasks, or reservations to their hardware locations can be seen in Figure 2.15.

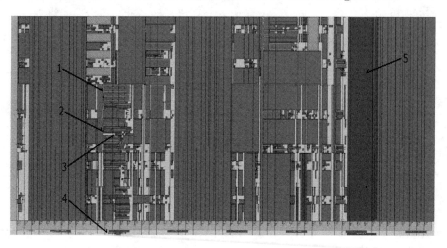

FIGURE 2.15: Mira machine time overlay.

In Figure 2.15, the x-axis is time and is binned weekly, and the y-axis contains nodes/midplanes from 0 to 95, top to bottom, respectively. Each box references a job, task, or reservation. The figure has five annotations: (1) is a failed job; (2) is a fatal RAS; (3) is a hardware reservation outage; (4) is the name of the reservation; (5) is a scheduled maintenance. This graphs allows visual inspection of the area of each event and the intersection in time and space of an event with other events. This information is invaluable for error detection and validation of the data.

Applying system logic before information goes into the database allows for simpler, less error prone analysis later. A central system manages the processing of ETLs and allows rerunning if a failure occurs. Each ETL is idempotent, greatly reducing the chance of generating bad or duplicate data.

JFA is an evolving process. New projects and applications, new systems, and previously unseen system faults drive refinement of existing and definition of new logic. Because the process started with very coarse grain collection and automation, it has allowed easier refinement and adaptation over time to suit the facility's needs. Events are prioritized, which allows easier root cause analysis. First temporal and spatial correlations are applied to account for system or external events. Next, institutional logic is applied to account for known application behavior – for example, some applications do not return a zero exit code on success. Institutional logic allows quick determination if a system fault – a network or filesystem outage, for example - affected multiple jobs, or a batch of jobs from a particular project all completed normally. As new errors are discovered or new application behavior is identified, the process is refined and re-prioritized.

There are many failures that JFA detects, and some examples are below. However, final root cause is determined by a site administrator. If the automatic recommendation and administrator decision differ, the logic is re-evaluated and refined if necessary and possible.

Node failures are a common cause. While it seems simple to detect, there is no direct link between a task and a failed node. A direct link would be information in the task about the node failure or the node failure providing information on the jobs it killed. To make it easier, the team applies temporal/spatial correlation, based on System Logic, to greatly simplify the linking of the tasks to node failures.

Jobs exceeding requested walltime is another common cause. This can be caused be a system fault – the filesystem became unresponsive – or because the user modified the application, resulting in decreased performance. Multiple and coherent data sources are critical to identify the root cause.

As previously noted, some applications simply return a non-zero exit code on success. Over time, common ones have been identified with other differentiating failure signatures defined based on job output and error messages.

There are multiple reasons for looking at each failure. The foremost reason is determining the mean time to job failure based on component. By understanding the system faults, effort can be directed to solve underlying systemic faults. It also provides trend data to identify possible emerging issues. A second reason is to expose newly introduced causes of failure. Firmware, software, and replacement hardware can all cause subtle issues. Seeing new failures after these events is a useful indicator that something unintended was introduced. The temporal and spatial correlation is an especially useful determination tool that highlights failures directly after particular software or hardware changes. Graphical representations of the failures are also extremely useful. A final reason is that such analysis simplifies and provides a more accurate account of the facility's availability and utilization metrics. These data help ensure the facility is providing stable and useful resources for the scientific community.

2.7 Acknowledgments

This material is based on work done by the Argonne Leadership Computing Facility, a U.S. Department of Energy Office of Science User Facility supported under contract DE-AC02-06CH11357.

We would like to acknowledge all ALCF staff, past and present, who have contributed to the deployment and operation of Mira and Theta.

Bibliography

[1] COBALT: Component-based lightweight toolkit. http://trac.mcs.anl.gov/projects/cobalt.

[2] Parallel filesystem I/O benchmark. https://github.com/LLNL/ior.

[3] Sandia MPI Micro-Benchmark Suite (SMB). http://www.cs.sandia.gov/smb/.

[4] Sustained System Performance (SSP). http://www.nersc.gov/users/computational-systems/cori/nersc-8-procurement/trinity-nersc-8-rfp/nersc-8-trinity-benchmarks/ssp/.

[5] The Graph 500 – June 2011. http://www.graph500.org.

[6] The Green 500 – June 2010. http://www.top500.org/green500.

[7] The Top 500 – June 2008. http://www.top500.org.

[8] mdtest, 2017. https://github.com/MDTEST-LANL/mdtest.

[9] Bob Alverson, Edwin Froese, Larry Kaplan, and Duncan Roweth. Cray XC Series Network. http://www.cray.com/sites/default/files/resources/CrayXCNetwork.pdf.

[10] Anna Maria Bailey, Adam Bertsch, Barna Bihari, Brian Carnes, Kimberly Cupps, Erik W. Draeger, Larry Fried, Mark Gary, James N. Glosli, John C. Gyllenhaal, Steven Langer, Rose McCallen, Arthur A. Mirin, Fady Najjar, Albert Nichols, Terri Quinn, David Richards, Tome Spelce, Becky Springmeyer, Fred Streitz, Bronis de Supinski, Pavlos Vranas, Dong Chen, George L.T. Chiu, Paul W. Coteus, Thomas W. Fox, Thomas Gooding, John A. Gunnels, Ruud A. Haring, Philip Heidelberger, Todd Inglett, Kyu Hyoun Kim, Amith R. Mamidala, Sam Miller, Mike Nelson, Martin Ohmacht, Fabrizio Petrini, Kyung Dong Ryu, Andrew A. Schram, Robert Shearer, Robert E. Walkup, Amy Wang, Robert W. Wisniewski, William E. Allcock, Charles Bacon, Raymond Bair, Ramesh Balakrishnan, Richard Coffey, Susan Coghlan, Jeff Hammond, Mark Hereld, Kalyan Kumaran, Paul Messina, Vitali Morozov, Michael E. Papka, Katherine M. Riley, Nichols A. Romero, and Timothy J. Williams. Blue Gene/Q: Sequoia and Mira. In Jeffrey S. Vetter, editor, *Contemporary High Performance Computing: From Petascale toward Exascale*, chapter 10, pages 225–281. Chapman & Hall/ CRC, 2013.

[11] Cray. *CLE User Application Placement Guide*, S-2496-5204 edition.

[12] Cray. *Cray C and C++ Reference Manual*, (8.5) S-2179 edition.

[13] Cray. *Cray Fortran Reference Manual*, (8.5) S-3901 edition.

[14] Cray. *XC Series GNI and DMAPP API User Guide*, (CLE6.0.UP03) S-2446 edition.

[15] Cray. *XC Series Programming Environment User Guide*, (17.05) S-2529 edition.

[16] Argonne Leadership Computing Facility. Early science program, 2010. http://esp.alcf.anl.gov.

[17] Sunny Gogar. Intel Xeon Phi x200 processor - memory modes and cluster modes: Configuration and use cases. *Intel Software Developer Zone*, 2015. http://software.intel.com/en-us/articles/intel-xeon-phi-x200-processor-memory-modes-and-cluster-modes-configuration-and-use-cases.

[18] Kevin Harms, Ti Leggett, Ben Allen, Susan Coghlan, Mark Fahey, Ed Holohan, Gordon McPheeters, and Paul Rich. Theta: Rapid installation and acceptance of an XC40 KNL system. In *Proceedings of the 2017 Cray User Group*, Redmond, WA, May 2017.

[19] Mark Holland and Garth A. Gibson. Parity declustering for continuous operation in redundant disk arrays. In Richard L. Wexelblat, editor, *Proceedings of the 5th International Conference on Architectural Support for Programming Languages and Operating Systems*, volume 27. ACM, New York, NY, 1992.

[20] Paul Peltz Jr., Adam DeConinck, and Daryl Grunau. How to automate and not manage under Rhine/Redwood. In *Proceedings of the 2016 Cray User Group*, London, UK, May 2016.

[21] Steven Martin, David Rush, and Matthew Kappel. Cray advanced platform monitoring and control (CAPMC). In *Proceedings of the 2015 Cray User Group*, Chicago, IL, April 2015.

[22] John D. McCalpin. Memory bandwidth and machine balance in current high performance computers. *IEEE Computer Society Technical Committee on Computer Architecture (TCCA) Newsletter*, pages 19–25, December 1995. http://tab.computer.org/tcca/NEWS/DEC95/dec95_mccalpin.ps.

[23] James Milano and Pamela Lembke. *IBM System Blue Gene Solution: Blue Gene/Q Hardware Overview and Installation Planning*. Number SG24-7872-01 in An IBM Redbooks publication. May 2013. ibm.com/redbooks.

[24] Department of Energy (DOE) Office of Science. Facilities for the Future of Science: A Twenty-Year Outlook, 2003. https://science.energy.gov/~/media/bes/pdf/archives/plans/ffs_10nov03.pdf.

[25] Scott Parker, Vitali Morozov, Sudheer Chunduri, Kevin Harms, Chris Knight, and Kalyan Kumaran. Early evaluation of the Cray XC40 Xeon Phi System Theta at argonne. In *Proceedings of the 2017 Cray User Group*, Redmond, WA, May 2017.

[26] Avinash Sodani. Knights Landing (KNL): 2nd Generation Intel Xeon Phi. In *Hot Chips 27 Symposium (HCS), 2015 IEEE*, Cupertino, CA, August 2015. http://ieeexplore.ieee.org/document/7477467/.

Chapter 3

Enabling HPC Applications on a Cray XC40 with Manycore CPUs at ZIB

Alexander Reinefeld, Thomas Steinke, Matthias Noack, and Florian Wende
Zuse Institute Berlin

3.1 Overview

Zuse Institute Berlin (ZIB) has been at the forefront of high-performance computing since its foundation in 1984. Apart from operating HPC systems for scientists and researchers in North Germany [1], ZIB conducts research in applied mathematics and computer science. A strong background in computer architecture, low-level system software, and a tight link to application developers allows ZIB to foster the early adoption of innovative system architectures for the HPC user community.

Since 2013, ZIB operates two systems: *Konrad*,[1] a Cray XC40/30 with a sustained performance of 1 PFLOPS, and a Cray XC40 *Test and Development System*[2] (TDS) with Intel Xeon Phi Knights Corner (KNC) coprocessors initially, and with Intel Xeon Phi Knights Landing (KNL) nodes at the time of the writing of this text. The TDS is furthermore

---

[1]Technical details can be found in a previous volume of this book [1] and on the web at https://www.hlrn.de/home/view/System3/CrayHardware.

[2]Funded jointly by the HLRN consortium.

equipped with a few Cray DataWarp nodes to explore the potential of burst buffers for certain workloads. The two systems are depicted in Fig. 3.1 and 3.2, respectively.

FIGURE 3.1: Cray XC40/30 *Konrad* at ZIB (picture: Jürgen Keiper).

3.1.1   Research Center for Many-Core HPC

The *Research Center for Many-core High-Performance Computing* at ZIB was founded in October 2013 with support by Intel Corporation. As one of the first Intel Parallel Computing Centers (IPCC) in Europe, its mission is to foster many- and multi-core technology in HPC and Big Data Analytics. For selected workloads from various science domains—materials science and nanotechnology, atmosphere and ocean flow dynamics, astrophysics, drug design, particle physics, and data analytics—the focus is on optimizing the respective codes for performance and scalability on many-core processors. For both the HLRN user community and external collaborators, ZIB provides the technical infrastructure and staff to port and "modernize" the codes jointly with their owners.

In this chapter we focus on our experiences with the Cray TDS running real-world HPC applications in realistic settings. For the first generation Intel Xeon Phi coprocessors (KNC), several obstacles had to be cleared to fit into the HPC context. Addressing multiple levels of parallelism—process, thread, and data level—and identifying code sections suited to be offloaded to the coprocessor (Sec. 3.4.2) posed the main challenges. The second generation Intel Xeon Phi processors (KNL) allow for a more convenient integration into HPC application development and usage by removing the necessity to program a heterogeneous system, as was the case for the KNC and its corresponding host system. With its on-chip high-bandwidth memory, however, KNL poses a further optimization challenge that adds to those for the KNC.

3.1.2   Timeline

The Cray TDS with the first generation of Intel Xeon Phi coprocessors (KNC) was installed in fall 2014. It comprised 16 compute nodes, each of which with a 10-core Intel

FIGURE 3.2: Cray XC40 Test and Development System with Intel Xeon Phi and Cray DataWarp nodes.

Ivybridge host-CPU and one Intel Xeon Phi 5120D coprocessor (60 CPU cores clocked at 1.05 GHz, 8 GiB GDDR5 main memory). For the code development, only Intel compilers and libraries could be used together with Cray MPI(CH).

In August 2016, the Cray TDS was upgraded to host Intel's second generation Xeon Phi processors (KNL). The system comprises 80 compute nodes with one Intel Xeon Phi 7250 processor (68 CPU cores clocked at 1.4 GHz, 16 GiB MCDRAM) and 96 GiB DDR4 main memory each. Opposed to the former installation, the Cray, Intel, and GNU software stack can be used for code development and program execution and profiling. This includes the access to optimized libraries and performance analysis tools. Additionally, 10 Cray DataWarp nodes provide a globally accessible filesystem with a total capacity of 32 TiB on SSDs.

Since September 2016, the Cray TDS is open for code developers to explore the capabilities of the KNL for their workloads. The TDS user community includes various national and international collaborators, e.g. from the Czech Republic, France, the UK, and the USA.

3.2 Applications and Workloads

The TDS serves as a prototype for next-generation many-core supercomputer installations at ZIB. With its 80 compute nodes, it allows mid-sized scalability experiments to run on the current Intel Xeon Phi (KNL) platform. Together with ZIB staff, HPC users can prepare their codes for upcoming novel architectures with increasingly more CPU cores, wider SIMD units, and deeper memory hierarchies.

Within ZIB's IPCC activities, relevant HPC applications were selected for code modernization. The science domains covered and the selected codes include: materials science

(VASP), biology (HEOM, GLAT), high energy physics (BQCD), photovoltaics (HEOM), and atmospheric and ocean fluid dynamics (PALM).[3]

VASP is the *Vienna Ab-initio Simulation Package* for atomic scale materials modeling, e.g. electronic structure calculations and quantum-mechanical molecular dynamics, from first principles [8, 9, 10].

HEOM is an implementation of the *Hierarchical Equations of Motions* for studying energy-transfer in light-harvesting molecular complexes on heterogeneous platforms.

GLAT is a program package for efficient thermodynamical simulation and analysis of molecules on heterogeneous high performance computer platforms using *Global Local Adaptive Thermodynamics.*

BQCD (*Berlin Quantum Chromodynamics*) is a Hybrid Monte Carlo program that simulates lattice QCD with dynamical Wilson fermions [13].

PALM (*PArallelized Large-Eddy Simulation Model*) enables large-eddy simulations of atmospheric and oceanic flows that are especially designed for performing on massively parallel computer architectures [12].

Three of the codes are described in more detail below: VASP serves as a case study for SIMD vectorization in the non-trivial case (Sec. 3.4.1), GLAT utilizes the offloading library HAM (Sec. 3.4.2), and HEOM serves as a demonstrator for runtime kernel compilation with KART (Sec. 3.4.3).

3.2.1 VASP

The *Vienna Ab-initio Simulation Package* is a widely used materials science application to do ab-initio electronic structure calculations and quantum-mechanical molecular dynamics simulations using pseudopotentials or the projector-augmented wave method and a plane wave basis set [8, 11]. VASP computes an approximate solution to the many-body Schrödinger equation either within Density Functional Theory (DFT) to solve the Kohn-Sham equation or through the Hartree-Fock (HF) approximation to solve the Roothaan equation—hybrid functionals that mix the HF approach with DFT, Green's functions methods, and many-body perturbation theory are also implemented.

The MPI-only VASP (current official release) is parallelized in two levels: at the high level, the bands are distributed over MPI tasks, and at the lower level, the coefficients of each band are distributed across multiple MPI tasks. In general, executing VASP is dominated by back and forth FFTs (from/to the real space to/from the Fourier space), and complex and real matrix multiplications. Most of the communication is spent in reduction operations. Details about a hybrid MPI/OpenMP implementation of VASP including **SIMD** optimizations are briefly described in Sec. 3.4.1 and detailed in [27].

3.2.2 GLAT

The *Global Local Adaptive Thermodynamics* performs Hybrid Monte Carlo simulations for molecules parameterized by the MMFF force field. Uncoupling of Markov chains on different simulation levels allows coarse to fine tuning of different parallelization strategies. Currently, the code approaches hybrid parallelization through MPI with OpenMP and CUDA, respectively. In case of running GLAT on a heterogeneous system with coprocessors (e.g. Intel Xeon Phi (KNC)) or accelerators (e.g. Nvidia GPGPUs), highly parallel code

---

[3]Some of these codes are included in the *HLRN Benchmark Suite* for the procurement of the next North German supercomputer HLRN IV.

sections, like the computation of non-bonding interactions involving solvent molecules, are offloaded to the coprocessor or accelerator, whereas sections that are dominated by control flow and housekeeping remain on the host CPU.

Techniques to scale out GLAT's computational demanding part comprise low-latency (remote) offloading from a multi-core CPU to many-core compute nodes via **Offload Over Fabric** (detailed in Sec. 3.4.2), as well as multi-threading and **SIMD** vectorization of (data) parallel loops (Sec. 3.4.1).

3.2.3 HEOM

The Hierarchical Equation of Motion (HEOM) method provides an exact solution to non-Markovian quantum dynamics in the presence of thermal fluctuations and dissipation. HEOM is the standard reference method for quantum dynamics simulations of excitation energy transfer in molecular complexes and for computing the resulting optical spectra. The quantum mechanical state is represented by a reduced density matrix for the subsystem of interest, while the state vector of the surrounding environment is encoded in a (in principle infinite) set of auxiliary density operators (ADOs). With decreasing temperature the number of physically relevant ADOs increases exponentially, leading to an increased memory demand to represent the quantum state of the system. The coherent dynamics of the system is described by the Liouville von Neumann equation, which requires computing in each time propagation step the commutator of the Hamiltonian matrix with all density matrices, including the ADOs. The overall time evolution of the quantum system is obtained by a standard Runge Kutta integration scheme, or if less memory consumption is warranted, by a Taylor integration scheme. After each propagation step neighbor exchanges between ADOs are performed for the non-commutator parts.

The accelerated HEOM variant developed at ZIB distributes the ADOs across compute nodes in addition to a parallelization on each compute device. In the productions version, OpenCL is used for the on-node parallelization of the commutator computation driven by the time integration schema implemented in OpenCL as well. With slight variations in work item granularity, the OpenCL part performs reasonably well on both GPUs (Nvidia, AMD) and many-core CPUs (Intel Xeon Phi).

Looking forward towards a broader OpenMP support including on GPUs, an OpenMP version of HEOM in which the OpenCL kernels are replaced by OpenMP 4 implementations is used [17] in combination with **Kernel Compilation At RunTime** as described in Section 3.4.3.

3.3   System Hardware Architecture

Beside conventional CPUs building up most (super) computers for some decades already, first Nvidia and AMD GPGPUs (around 2008) and later Intel's many-core Xeon Phis (around 2012) were added to reach the PetaFLOP mark and to go beyond. The Cray TDS at ZIB comprises 80 compute nodes with Intel Xeon Phi (KNL) processors. As outlined in Sec. 3.1.2, it is our second installation of Xeon Phi (co-)processors, and it serves as an evaluator of novel many-core architectures to conduct the decision making process regarding future computer installations at ZIB. In this section, we give a brief overview of the Intel Many Integrated Core (MIC) architecture and the products Xeon Phi KNC and

KNL—Table 3.1 compares both of the two against a standard (server) CPU installed in the field.

TABLE 3.1: Comparison of current multi- and many-core CPUs: Intel Xeon E7-8890v4, Intel Xeon Phi 7120 (KNC), and Intel Xeon Phi 7290 (KNL) as representatives.

	Standard CPU	Xeon Phi (KNC)	Xeon Phi (KNL)
CPU cores			
count	≤ 24	≤ 61	≤ 72
frequency [GHz]	≤ 3.4	≤ 1.3	≤ 1.7
threads per core	2	4	4
SIMD width (32-bit)	8	16	16
System memory	DDR4	GDDR5	DDR4 + MCDRAM
size [GiB]	≤ 3072	≤ 16	$\leq (384, 16)$
bandwidth [GiB/s]	≤ 85	≤ 350	$\leq (115, 500)$
TFLOPS (32-bit)	≤ 1.7	≤ 2.4	≤ 6.0
TDP	$\leq 165\,\mathrm{W}$	$\leq 225\,\mathrm{W}$	$\leq 260\,\mathrm{W}$

3.3.1 Cray TDS at ZIB with Intel Xeon Phi Processors

This section complements with Sec. 3.1.2 and points out the characteristics of the hardware configurations of the two-phase installation of ZIB's Cray TDS in 2014 and 2016 (Table 3.2).

TABLE 3.2: Cray TDS hardware configuration at ZIB.

Feature	Phase 1 (September 2014)	Phase 2 (August 2016)
Node architecture	Cray XC30	Cray XC40
CPU model	Intel E5-2670v2	Intel Xeon Phi 7250
CPU microarchitecture	Ivybridge	Knights Landing
CPU count per node	1	1
CPU core frequency (GHz)	2.5	1.4
CPU on-chip memory (GiB)	-	16 (MCDRAM)
Node main memory (GiB)	32	96
Node PCIe	Gen 3	Gen 3
coprocessor model	Intel Xeon Phi 5120D	-
coprocessor count per node	1	-
coprocessor main memory (GiB)	8	-
Network interconnect	Cray Aries	Cray Aries
Network ports per node	1	1
Number of compute nodes	16	80
Number of burst buffer nodes	8	10
Peak TFLOPS (32-bit)	6.4 + 32.2	418

Software Environment   The software environment of the Cray TDS includes the Cray Linux Environment CLE 6.0 (for KNL) and the system is connected to the global parallel file systems of the production system, i.e., two Lustre 2.5.4 file system and a HOME appliance accessible via NFS. The typical set of compilers (Intel, Cray CCE and GNU) are provided as listed in Table 3.3.

TABLE 3.3: Cray TDS software configuration at ZIB.

Feature	With KNC Nodes	With KNL Nodes
Login node OS	SLES SP 11.3	SLES SP 12.0
Compute node OS	CLE 5.2	CLE 6.0
Parallel filesystem	Lustre 2.5.4	
Compilers	Intel 15	Intel 17
	-	Cray CCE 8.6.0
	-	GNU 6.3.0
MPI	Cray MPICH	
Notable libraries	Cray libsci	
	Intel Math Kernel Library	
	FFTW	
	Boost	
Job scheduler	Moab	
Resource manager	Torque	
Debugging tools	Allinea DDT	
Performance tools	Cray Performance Analysis Tools (PAT)	
	Intel VTune, Advisor	

3.3.2 Intel Xeon Phi 71xx (Knights Corner—KNC)

The Xeon Phi (KNC) is an x86-based many-core coprocessor that implements Intel's MIC architecture [2, 5]. It offers up to 61 in-order 64-bit CPU cores, 512-bit SIMD vector processing, 4-way hardware multi-threading per core, and up to 16 GiB GDDR5 ECC main memory. The Xeon Phi device is connected to the host system via PCIe 2.0. Its cores, the memory controllers, and the PCIe client logic are connected by a bidirectional on-chip ring interconnect. On Xeon Phi 7-series devices, 61 cores provide up to 1.2 TFLOPS double precision (2.4 TFLOPS single precision) performance and 352 GiB/s memory bandwidth.

The Xeon Phi runs a fully user-accessible Linux OS, which together with other operational software and services is provided by the Intel Many-core Platform Software Stack (MPSS). Unlike GPGPUs, the Phi can thus act as an autonomous compute node with its own IP address.

3.3.3 Intel Xeon Phi 72xx (Knights Landing—KNL)

The Xeon Phi Knights Landing (KNL) is Intel's 2nd generation MIC architecture [26]. It complements the KNC by some features that bring it closer to a standard multi-socket CPU node. Its up to 72 out-of-order CPU cores are grouped into two, forming so-called tiles (see Fig. 3.3), which in turn are organized into sub-NUMA domains when booted into sub-NUMA cluster mode SNC2 or SNC4. The processor then appears as a two- or four-socket CPU system. Otherwise, when booted into any of the other modes, all cores reside within the same NUMA domain, making the KNL appear as one big many-core chip to the operating system and user. This allows developers to stick with standard programming models and patterns, e.g., MPI and OpenMP including SIMD support.

The KNL is the first Intel processor that introduces high-bandwidth on-chip memory (Multi-Channel DRAM - MCDRAM), which can be configured at boot time to either serve as a 16 GiB shared last level cache, a 16 GiB scratch pad memory, or as a mix of the two (see Fig. 3.4). With theoretical up to 500 GiB/s memory bandwidth, MCDRAM can bridge the bottleneck to the rather "slow" main memory (up to 384 GiB DDR4 memory with up to 115 GiB/s bandwidth), or it can directly feed the CPU cores when holding the

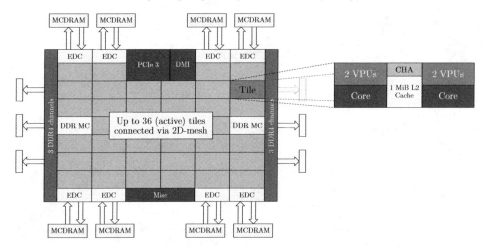

FIGURE 3.3: Intel Xeon Phi (KNL) processor [26] with up to 72 cores grouped into tiles of 2 cores each. There are two vector processing units (VPUs) per core. Two cores within the same tile share 1 MiB L2 data cache and the caching home agents (CHA), which connect the tile to the 2D mesh and hold a portion of the distributed tag directory.

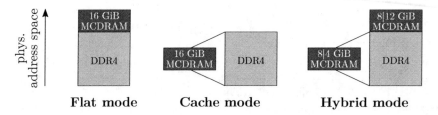

FIGURE 3.4: Three MCDRAM modes on KNL, which are configured at boot time: In the *flat mode* (left) both MCDRAM and DDR4 appear in the same physical address space and are managed individually. The *cache mode* (middle) uses the MCDRAM as a last level cache for DDR4 access. The *hybrid mode* (right) uses part of the MCDRAM as a cache for DDR4 access and the rest is mapped into the same physical address space as the DDR4 memory.

entire workload, thereby replacing a main memory access. Note that it is up to the user to effectively utilize the MCDRAM.

3.4   Many-Core in HPC: The Need for Code Modernization

It is widely believed that the core-count in future processors will rapidly grow. For this reason we decided to offer our HPC users a small-scale Cray TDS with many-core processors at a very early stage, so that they can gradually adapt ("modernize") their codes to meet the new hardware features even before large-scale many-core HPC systems with millions of cores are available. Challenges to be tackled by the users include the transition from multi-processing to multi-processing plus multi-threading as well as heterogeneous parallelism, fine grained data-level parallelism through SIMD vectorization, overlapping of computation and communication, and the extended memory hierarchy on the Intel Xeon Phi KNL. In the following sections, we motivate the necessity to modernize/adapt codes and we describe

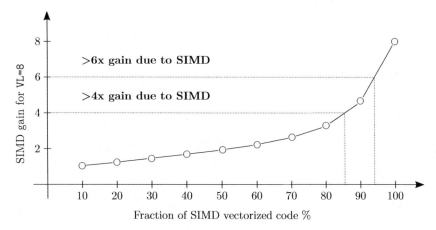

FIGURE 3.5: Amdahl's law for SIMD parallelism with vector length VL=8. About 85% of the code needs to be vectorized to gain the overall performance of the program by a factor 4, thereby achieving at most 50% of the theoretical peak performance. Peak performance can be reached only with 100% of the code be vectorized. SIMD vectorization thus is essential for an application to run efficiently on modern (many-core) CPUs.

some advanced techniques and software libraries that we provided in order to make the life for our HPC users a bit easier.

3.4.1 High-level SIMD Vectorization

While keeping core frequencies within the 2-3 GHz range, CPU vendors started to increase the core count on a die almost two decades ago along with multiplying the size of the per-core *Single-Instruction Multiple-Data* (SIMD) vector units starting from 64-bit (MMX) to 512-bit (AVX-512) on current Intel Xeon Phi products and Intel Skylake server CPUs. *Data-level parallelism* through the SIMD execution model and widely used process- and thread-level parallelism thus have to complement each other to leverage the hardware capabilities of modern CPUs (see Fig. 3.5).

From the programmers point of view, SIMD appears as an additional level of parallelism to be approached within the process or process + thread context. For that to happen, already existing tasks need to be split further into groups of VL sub-tasks that can be operated in *lock-step*, with each sub-task assigned to a so-called SIMD lane. The group size VL equals the number of SIMD lanes that are specific to the hardware platform and the type of data to be processed. For the Xeon Phi, for instance, VL=8 in case of operating 64-bit words, e.g., double-precision floating point numbers. The key difference to process- and thread-level parallelism is the circumstance that in the SIMD context all sub-tasks within a group share the same program counter (state). As a consequence, control flow divergences in the code can cause a serialization of the sub-tasks (Fig. 3.6), opposed to a concurrent execution with processes/threads. It is the lock-step execution scheme that makes SIMD optimization of parallel computer programs much more difficult than optimizing for multi-processing or -threading.

Compiler-Driven Vectorization Modern compilers are capable of vectorizing[4] loop structures automatically provided that in doing so the resulting program does not show

---

[4]The terms "vectorization" and "SIMD vectorization" are used interchangeably.

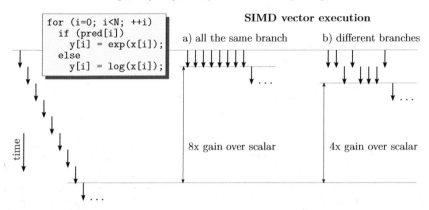

FIGURE 3.6: SIMD execution (with `VL=8`) of a simple loop structure with control flow divergence. We distinguish two cases: a) all sub-tasks in a group take the same branch, that is, either the `if` or the `else` branch; b) different branches are taken. Compared to executing the loop iterations one after the other (scalar), a) can achieve 8x and b) 4x performance gain, respectively.

erroneous behavior. However, in many cases, for instance, information about aliasing of the data to be processed is missing (or cannot be deduced from the program/function context), causing the compiler to be pessimistic about SIMD vectorization. Programmers then have two ways to approach this issue: first, hinting the compiler via compiler directives to enforce vectorization, and second, manual vectorization using assembly, SIMD intrinsics or C++ wrapper classes. Beside being applicable within the C/C++ programming language only, the latter additionally suffers the fact that it is specific to a particular hardware platform as manual vectorization in these cases basically means to instruct the compiler which SIMD instructions to use, potentially conflicting with compiler-internal optimization strategies. A more convenient way to SIMD vectorization is compiler directives—manual vectorization should be the last resort.

With OpenMP 4 [7], the programmer got means to enforce vectorization of loops and functions through a hand full of directives that can be used within the Fortran and C/C++ programming language, and more important, across different compilers. A comprehensive overview of OpenMP 4 SIMD constructs can be found in [20, 21].

The following pseudo-code demonstrates the use of these directives for both loops (via `#pragma omp simd` within `foo`) and functions (via `#pragma omp declare simd` for `bar`):

```
#pragma omp declare simd
void bar(double& x, double& y) { y = log(x); }

void foo(double* x, double* y, int n) {
  #pragma omp simd
  for (int i=0; i<n; ++i)
    bar(x[i], y[i]);
}
```

For function `foo` the compiler has to assume that `x` and `y` point to overlapping data (aliasing) and SIMD vectorization of the loop inside `foo` might be unsafe.[5] Real-world codes, however, exhibit much more complex loop structures than shown in the example above, e.g. those containing *nested branching, conditional and nested function calls*, mathematical function calls (which not every compiler can provide SIMD versions of), and some more.

---

[5]Modern compilers, will generate two versions of the loop that can be switched between at runtime depending on whether there is aliasing or not.

Enhancing Compiler-Driven Vectorization   When using compiler directives for complex loops and functions, everything related to *SIMD vectorization of the respective code section(s) happens behind the curtains*. The programmer then relies on the compiler's vectorization capabilities, which might be unfavorable if the program then shows erroneous behavior or if the performance gain due to SIMD is behind the expectations. In both cases there are only a few ways to approach these issues. Assuming the programmer did use the directives correctly—including the requirement that the code under debate is SIMD vectorizable at all—the erroneous behavior might have been introduced by the compiler itself during vectorization or it is subject to side effects that in the scalar case do not occur. Without diving deep into the program execution using a debugger, there is almost nothing that can be done to fix that issue. Even if the problem has been identified, what is the next step then? How to adapt the scalar code to eliminate a bug that does not occur in the scalar case? Similarly, finding performance bottlenecks can be challenging as the adjusting screws are confined to some clauses that can be used to extend the compiler directives. Identifying the reason for the performance not matching the expectations requires using profiling tools, and the findings then are for the SIMD vectorized program for which the code is not available as it has been generated by the compiler automatically.

To overcome these limitations, which are mainly rooted at the programmer who is required to stay within the scalar-world when writing down the code, we need to place ourselves somewhere in between compiler-driven vectorization and manual vectorization. This can be easily done by *coding with high-level vector data types together with compiler directives* [28]. The following pseudo-code illustrates that approach for the code shown before:

```
#define VL64 8

typedef struct {
  double x[VL64];
} vec_real64_t __attribute__((aligned(64)));
typedef struct {
  bool x[VL64];
} mask_real64_t;
...
void vbar(vec_real64_t& x, vec_real64_t& y, mask_real64_t& m) {
  #pragma omp simd
  for (int ii=0; ii<VL64; ++ii)
    if (m.x[ii]) y.x[ii] = log(x.x[ii]);
}
void vfoo(double* x, double* y, int n) {
  vec_real64_t vx, vy;
  mask_real64_t m;
  for (int i=0; i<n; i+=VL64) {
    #pragma omp simd
    for (int ii=0; ii<VL64; ++ii) {
      m.x[ii] = (i+ii)<n ? true : false;
      if (m.x[ii]) vx.x[ii] = x[i+ii];
    }
    vbar(vx, vy, m);
    #pragma omp simd
    for (int ii=0; ii<VL64; ++ii)
      if (m.x[ii]) y[i+ii] = vy.x[ii];
  }
}
```

The data types `vec_real64_t` and `mask_real64_t` are defined in a generic way through platform-dependent `VL64`.[6] The definition of `vbar` follows from that of `bar` by replacing

---

[6]When compiling with the GNU or the Intel C++ compiler and specifying `-maxv512f` and `-xcore-avx512`, respectively, the literal `__AVX512F__` will be defined.

scalar by vector arguments and by introducing an additional mask argument m. The mask then can be used within vbar to retain the original content of y on those SIMD lanes for which the mask signals false (the SIMD lane is then said to be inactive). It further can be of advantage to explicitly address the masking in the user-code to optimize for cases where all SIMD lanes are active or inactive. The former allows continuing working without masking as all SIMD lanes are active anyway, whereas the latter allows skipping entire code blocks, for instance. Within vbar and vfoo, vectors are processed element-wise with SIMD promoted via OpenMP 4 compiler directives. This way, both the definition of the vector data types as well as the means to enforce vectorization is generic and portable across compilers.

Among the advantages of coding with high-level vectors over leaving everything to the compiler, in case of staying with scalar code and SIMD compiler directives, is

- writing explicit vector code that is *portable across platforms and compilers*, and gives more flexibility for debugging and performance tuning.

- *mixing scalar and vector code in a natural way*—as far as we know, there is no means to switch between SIMD and scalar execution within a SIMD context when using directives.

- *defining SIMD vector functions manually*—not all compilers implement the declare simd feature.

Using these high-level vectors of course might require re-writing (large) portions of the scalar code. However, approaching SIMD explicitly is inevitable to run the corresponding program on today's and upcoming computer platforms efficiently as illustrated in Fig. 3.5. For many real-world codes with thousands of lines of code and non-trivial loop structures, it is much too simplistic to assume that introducing some compiler directives here and there will result in an effective SIMD version of the code.

Calling Tree Vectorization   Among the compute intensive code sections in the user-level part of VASP (see Sec. 3.2.1) is those using hybrid functionals. For certain classes of work-loads a non-negligible amount of time is spent in the ggaall_grid subroutine containing within its hotspot loop the subroutine/function[7] call hierarchy:

```
void ggaall_grid(..) {
  ..
  /* hotspot loop */
  for (int i=0; i<n; ++i) {
    ggaall(..)
       +-> calc_expchwpbe_sp(..)
       |     +-> ex(..)
       |     +-> ex_sr(..)
       |     +-> vx(..)
       |     +-> vx_sr(..)
       |     +-> wpbe_spline(..)         /* called 5 times */
       |           +-> wpbe_splin2(..)
       +-> corunsppbe(..)
             +-> gcor2(..)
  }
  ..
}
```

Any of the listed functions (calc_expchwpbe_sp, ex, etc.) contain a mix of scalar code

---

[7]We do not distinguish between "subroutine" and "function" hereafter. Instead we will use "function" in any case.

and simple loops with low trip counts, conditional code execution including function calls, and math function calls. SIMD vectorization within these functions would be less effective with respect to the overall program performance. We thus vectorize along the calling hierarchy using SIMD functions. The latter—mentioned early in this section already—can be thought of as vector expansions of scalar functions, either via the OpenMP 4 `declare simd` construct or high-level vectors as discussed before. With the former, we achieved moderate success with the Intel compiler only: the GNU Fortran compiler (we tested GNU 6.3 and 7.1) seems to support the `declare simd` construct only to some extent and failed to generate an executable. Using high-level vectors, we achieved with the Intel compiler a factor 1.5x gain over the pure OpenMP 4 SIMD version on both platforms considered: Intel Haswell CPU and Intel Xeon Phi (KNL). With the GNU compiler we got parts of the code vectorized, but the most relevant ones were missed.

Table 3.4 summarizes the execution times (in seconds) spent in the `ggaall_` grid subroutine for the two different SIMD versions on a Haswell CPU and a Xeon Phi (KNL). The numbers within braces refer to the gains over the reference (more details can be found in [27]).

TABLE 3.4: Execution time (in seconds) of the hotspot loop in `ggaall_grid` in VASP on an Intel Haswell CPU and an Intel Xeon Phi (KNL). The "reference" refers to the optimized scalar code, while the other two are for SIMD vectorized code via the OpenMP 4 `declare simd` construct, and with high-level vectors.

	gfortran-6.3		ifort-17 (update 2)	
	Haswell	Xeon Phi	Haswell	Xeon Phi
reference	93s	168s	80s	96s
declare simd	–	–	59s (1.35x)	22s (4.36x)
high-level vectors	74s (1.26x)	98s (1.71x)	42s (1.90x)	14s (6.86x)

Loop Splitting and Mixing of Scalar and Vector Code One kind of computation implemented in VASP (see Sec. 3.2.1) for which a significant amount of time is spent in the user code is the integration of the dynamically screened two electron integrals over frequency.

The loop structure for this computation is as follows:

```
int n = 1;
for (int i=0; i<n_omega; ++i) {
  if ((i*delta)>omega[n+1]) {
    while (true) {
      n = n+1;
      if (omega[n+1]>(i*delta)) break;
    }
  }
  tmp = f(screened_2e_int[n], screened_2e_int[n+1]);
  .. /* computation using 'tmp' */
}
```

SIMD vectorization of the i-loop suffers from the above mentioned loop dependences introduced by determining the n-values. All computations starting at line "`tmp = .. ,`" however, are independent of the computations in other iterations. We therefore split the i-loop into chunks of size `VL64`, and further decompose the resulting inner loop over `ii`, ranging from 0 to `min(VL64, n_omega - i) - 1`, into 3 parts l_k:

```
   int n = 1;
   for (int i=0; i<n_omega; i+=VL64) {
     int ii_max = min(VL64, n_omega-i);
     vec_int64_t vn;
11: for (int ii=0; ii<ii_max; ++ii) {
       if (((i+ii)*delta)>omega[n+1]) {
         while (true) {
           n = n+1;
           if (omega[n+1]>((i+ii)*delta)) break;
         }
       }
       vn.x[ii] = n;
     }
     vec_real64_t vtmp;
12: for (int ii=0; ii<ii_max; ++ii) {
       int nn = vn.x[ii];
       vtmp.x[ii] = f(screened_2e_int[nn], screened_2e_int[nn+1]);
     }
     #pragma omp simd
13: for (int ii=0; ii<ii_max; ++ii) {
       .. /* computation using 'vtmp' */
     }
   }
```

l_1, the pre-computation of the n-values, l_2, gathering all needed data into **vtmp** indexed through **n** (this results in gather loads), and l_3, the actual computation using **vtmp**. Both, the second and third inner most loops are candidates for SIMD vectorization. However, we annotate only the third one using OpenMP 4 directives, and let the compiler decide about vectorization of the second loop. Depending on whether the target platform supports vector gather operations, the latter will be vectorized or not. As the loop splitting into parts requires storing (or "backing up") those intermediate values computed in l_q and needed in at least one other $l_{q' \geq q}$ (e.g., **vn** and **vtmp**, our high-level vector approach is the natural way for an effective implementation as it allows mixing scalar and vector code. Vectorization of the original code is currently impossible with OpenMP 4 SIMD constructs, because with the i-loop defining the SIMD context, there is no means to enforce the serialization of l_1 and at the same time to keep the intermediate n-values needed to serve subsequent data access(es).

Table 3.5 summarizes the execution times (in seconds) spent in the integration procedure on a Haswell CPU and a Xeon Phi (KNL). Both the GNU and the Intel compiler achieved success in vectorizing the high-level vector code, although the Intel compiler generates the faster executable for the Xeon Phi (KNL); more details can be found in [27].

TABLE 3.5: Execution time (in seconds) of the integration of the dynamically screened two electron integrals over frequency in VASP on an Intel Haswell CPU and an Intel Xeon Phi (KNL).

	gfortran-6.3		ifort-17 (update 2)	
	Haswell	Xeon Phi	Haswell	Xeon Phi
reference	12.8s	44s	11.1s	29s
high-level vectors	6.9s (1.86x)	6.8s (6.47x)	6.6s (1.68x)	4.2s (6.90x)

3.4.2   Offloading over Fabric

Scaling offload applications across a Xeon Phi cluster or supercomputer requires hybrid programming approaches, usually MPI + X, where X is an offload programming model. We developed a framework based on heterogeneous active messages (HAM-Offload) that provides the means to offload work to local and remote (co)processors using a unified offload API [18]. Since HAM-Offload provides similar primitives as current local offload frameworks, existing applications can be easily ported to overcome the single-node limitation while keeping the convenient offload programming model. We demonstrate the effectiveness of the framework by using it to enable a real-world application, the GLAT code for thermodynamical simulations of molecules, to use multiple local and remote Xeon Phis. The evaluation shows a good scaling behavior. Compared with Intel LEO[8], there is no performance penalty but even up to 14% gain for local offloads.

Offload programming, or offloading, refers to writing programs that are executed on a distinguished *host* system, and during their execution place work on one or more offload *targets* for faster processing. Targets typically are local accelerators such as Xeon Phi co-processors (KNC) and GPGPUs, but can also be the same processor that is executing the host process or remote resources accessible via a fabric. An overall performance gain due to offloading can only be achieved if the reduced runtime for the offloaded computation super-compensates the overhead costs for the offload itself. These costs comprise communication (the transfer of code and data to and from the accelerator), synchronization, and additional software overheads of the used offload framework. It is the main optimization goal for every implementation of the offload programming model, which is minimizing these costs.

Scaling offload applications beyond the limited compute performance and device memory provided by the accelerators within a single node requires the use of remote devices over fabric. Usually, this requires a mix of offloading and another programming model that deals with distribution aspects, e.g., message passing via MPI. The Xeon Phi's flexibility, that comes with native program execution and the availability of low-level APIs provided by the the Intel Many-core Platform Software Stack (MPSS), allows pursuing new approaches that would not be possible with GPGPUs. With the second generation Xeon Phi (Knights Landing) as bootable CPU, heterogeneity moves from the inter-node level to the intra-node level. That is, on large supercomputers with Xeon and Xeon Phi partitions (e.g. NERSC's Cori), sometimes referred to as co-cluster as opposed to co-processor, offloading programs can use *offload over fabric* to combine the strength of both processor architectures.

HAM-Offload provides the means to offload computations to any number of local and remote compute devices that are able to run a process, e.g., Xeon hosts, and Xeon Phi processors and coprocessors. The framework draws on Heterogeneous Active Messages [16, 18][9] that allow remote code execution with little overhead beyond the bare communication cost. Instead of using a hybrid programming model, such as MPI + X, to overcome the single-node limitation of other offload models, HAM-Offload provides intra- and inter-node offloading within a unified API, which uses either Intel's *Symmetric Communication InterFace* (SCIF) or standard MPI as its back-end. This allows applications to be scaled from a single node to a Xeon Phi cluster without leaving the convenient offload programming model. Arbitrary offload patterns like Phi-to-Phi or reverse offloading, involving any number of hosts and coprocessors, can be realized. This expands the class of problems that can be handled within the offload programming model. HAM-Offload provides similar primitives as other offload solutions, such that porting pre-existing applications is easy. It is solely implemented

---

[8]Language Extension for Offload

[9]HAM and HAM-Offload were first published in 2014 providing offload over fabric years before the first vendor implementation.

by means of C++ without any language extensions, which avoids dependencies on specific development tools and compilers.

Heterogeneous Active Messages   The offload framework described here and referred to as *HAM-Offload* is built on top of *HAM*, which is a C++ template library that provides a highly efficient means to create type-safe Heterogeneous Active Messages.

Heterogeneous here means that communicating processes can execute different binaries of the same program source, which are compiled for different instruction set architectures (ISA) or optimized for different processors. This allows us to implement offloading using a symmetric execution model, where each runs differently compiled binaries of the same program. Heterogeneous active messages can be transferred via any reliable communication channel. HAM-Offload provides communication back-ends for SCIF and MPI. The overall architecture is depicted in Figure 3.7.

When implementing an offload mechanism, the first problem is how to get the code to the offload target. In HAM-Offload, this problem is solved by deploying the program binary compiled for the MIC architecture to the device prior to its execution. Since host and coprocessor each run a binary compiled from the same source, all code is available on both sites.

The second problem is to actually execute code on the coprocessor. This requires the transfer of execution onto the coprocessor device. HAM's active message approach extends the idea of directly transferring code addresses, which necessitates identical binaries on all communication partners, by adding a very efficient address translation that allows for heterogeneous binaries. The next paragraph details this mechanism. Insights into the implementation of LEO are provided in [14]. Additional information on HAM can be found in [16, 18].

Implementation Details   HAM is implemented as a C++ template library. This allows us to leverage the strengths of the C++ type system, template meta-programming, and runtime type information (RTTI) to implement the basis for a light-weight offload mechanism that works without language extensions. Although HAM is motivated by efficient offloading for the Xeon Phi, it is designed as an independent software layer and can be used in any context where heterogeneous active messages might be useful.

In conventional message passing systems like MPI, messages are passive pieces of data. In contrast, active messages are units of execution that contain or reference code to run upon receipt. A common and efficient way to implement this concept is to include the code address of a handler function into the message. When a message is received, the code at the embedded handler address is executed. The address of the message's payload is passed as

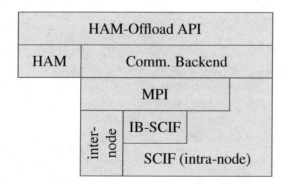

FIGURE 3.7: Layered architecture of the HAM-Offload framework.

an argument to its handler. In object-oriented active message systems, where messages are callable objects, the handler's job is to perform a type conversion from the typeless bytes of a network buffer back to an object of the actual message type, which can then be called like a function.

The problem here is to know the remote handler address when sending a message. The basic idea is to add a level of indirection by sending some reference to the handler inside each message that can be converted to the respective address by the receiver. HAM implements this by using the C++ type-system and RTTI to build look-up tables containing the local handler addresses of each process during initialization and linking the table indices with the active messages types. The sent messages contain globally valid handler indices which can be acquired from the message type and converted into the local handler address both ways in $O(1)$ for minimal overhead. This functionality is implemented in pure C++ (including an ABI [4] constraint for RTTI names) without the need for a language extension like Intel LEO or OpenMP 4.x.

HAM-Offload API   HAM-Offload complements the functionality of HAM with a unified intra- and inter-node offload API as a front-end. The API is designed to offer the same basic primitives as LEO with its `#pragma offload` directives. This makes it easy to port existing code, and allows for a direct performance comparison of intra-node offloading. Unlike LEO, all operations of HAM-Offload are available as library calls and not as a language extension based on directives. This makes the framework compiler independent. We describe here some of the HAM-Offload API functions.

Code that is to be offloaded with HAM-Offload has to be encapsulated in a function. This function together with its arguments can then be passed to the `f2f()` (short for function to functor) generator mechanism that creates a callable functor object. The offload of this functor is then performed by calling either `sync()` or `async()` with the offload target and the functor as arguments. In the case of an asynchronous offload, the result is a `future` object that resynchronizes to the offload when it is read and the return value is not already available.

All messages, and thus the contained functor objects, must be bit-wise copyable by the communication back-end. HAM-Offload provides a `Migratable` wrapper template that can be specialized for any type to provide serialization (conversion constructor) and de-serialization (conversion operator).

Remote memory is allocated via `allocate()`, returning a special `remote_ptr` object that ensures local and remote addresses cannot be mixed up without the compiler complaining about it. A corresponding `free()` operation deallocates the memory. Transfers between coprocessor and host memory are performed by means of a `read()` and `write()` function corresponding to LEO's `offload_transfer` directive. The `copy()` operation allows a direct copy between two target devices, which has no counterpart in LEO and OpenMP 4.x where all data goes through the host.

Additionally, the HAM-Offload API offers utility functions to query the available offload targets and their properties, e.g. the device type, or whether they are local or remote.

Communication Back-Ends   HAM-Offload uses an abstract communication back-end that is currently implemented for Intel SCIF and MPI. Each back-end provides the means to send messages, to transfer data, to address processes, and to allocate (remote) memory. The latter makes sure that memory fulfills alignment requirements or is pre-registered for RMA (Remote Memory Access). SCIF is the fastest and most low-level API for communication between the host and its local Phi coprocessors, but does not support inter-node communication (for more details on the SCIF back-end see [16]).

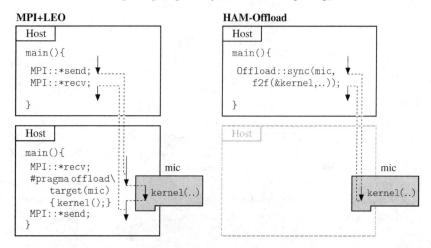

FIGURE 3.8: Synchronous "remote offload" execution of `kernel()` on Xeon Phi using MPI + Intel LEO (left), and HAM-Offload (right).

The MPI back-end allows the use of any number and combination of local and remote compute devices where an MPI process can be spawned. The arbitrary mapping of MPI processes to available Xeon and Xeon Phi KNL hosts, and Xeon Phi coprocessors allow patterns like conventional host-to-coprocessor offloading, remote offloading, coprocessor-to-coprocessor offloading, or reverse coprocessor-to-host offloading [23], illustrated in Figure 3.8.

Performance of Microbenchmarks   To quantify the overheads of HAM-Offload we carried out microbenchmarks and compared the cost for an empty offload with the round-trip time (RTT) of the different communication paths between host and target. Since any offload operation (with resynchronization) needs at least a single round trip, this reveals the overhead introduced by our framework on top of the unavoidable communication cost of the respective back-end. The round-trip times were measured with the Intel MPI PingPong benchmark, and with self-written SCIF code which uses remotely mapped memory that offers the lowest latency via SCIF.

The results for local offloads in comparison with LEO are shown in Figure 3.9. HAM-Offload adds only $1.4\,\mu s$ to the RTT of SCIF, and $3.4\,\mu s$ to MPI's RTT. Compared with LEO, which uses SCIF, the overall offload overhead measured for HAM-Offload is around 18.7 times smaller using SCIF and 1.8 times smaller using MPI. These values show that the active message mechanism behind HAM effectively minimizes the software overheads for remote code invocation and allows more fine-grained offloads.

Figure 3.10 depicts the results for all communication paths offered by the MPI back-end. The overhead ranges from 10.7 % to 43.2 % of the overall offload time, which is between $0.3\,\mu s$ and $7.5\,\mu s$ in absolute numbers. Besides the software overhead of HAM-Offload, the values also contain additional overhead of Intel's multi-threaded MPI library over the single threaded library used by the Intel MPI benchmark.

Molecular Simulations with GLAT Using HAM-Offload   When running GLAT, which is written in Fortran, many metastable states are sampled concurrently by spawning multiple OpenMP threads, where each thread performs the Hybrid Monte Carlo (HMC) sampling with the option to offload the expensive calculation of the solvation forces to a Phi

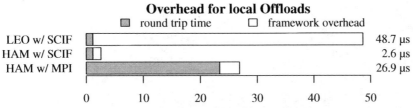

FIGURE 3.9: Costs for an empty local offload using LEO and HAM-Offload (with its SCIF and MPI back-ends). Printed times reflect overall transfer times. The SCIF and MPI RTT is $1.2\,\mu s$ respectively $23.4\,\mu s$.

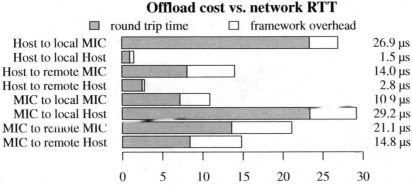

FIGURE 3.10: Execution times for an empty offload using HAM-Offload. The round-trip times (RTT) have been determined with the Intel MPI Benchmark for each communication path. Printed values represent the total offload times.

device. By enabling concurrent HMC samplings, the Phi is used as a shared (co)processor posing non-trivial challenges regarding the design of the offload patterns.

The integration of accelerator support into GLAT is through a C++ library that encapsulates all bookkeeping concerning the offload mechanism. The library contains wrapper functions to place work on the Xeon Phi and to get results of the calculations from it, and, in the case of HAM-Offload, to initialize and shut down the HAM-Offload runtime.

Code sections within the accelerator-enhanced GLAT library that have been modified for LEO could easily be adapted to HAM-Offload. Since HAM-Offload requires explicit memory allocation and transfer, like CUDA or OpenCL, it is more transparent to the programmer, and the memory management with HAM-Offload integrates better into our C++ code base.

Figure 3.11 demonstrates how to transform the offload pattern from LEO to HAM-Offload for an offload kernel _k(). With LEO (left-hand side), the offload in `glat::kernel()` is achieved by means of the `#pragma offload` compiler directive. Along with that, all necessary pointers are recovered and the kernel execution is made asynchronous via the `signal` clause. Within the offload region the kernel _k() is invoked, and its return value is stored to where _e points to. To actually obtain the return value, `glat::getEnergy()` synchronizes to the signal `sig` and then reads the value pointed to by _e.

With HAM-Offload (right-hand side), a functor `func` is created that encapsulates the function call together with its argument list. Via `Offload::async()` the functor is sent to the offload target for execution, and control is given back to the calling thread or process. The return value of `async()` in this case is a `future<double>` object, which later is used to synchronize to the offload and to eventually obtain the return value of the kernel _k(). Compared to LEO, HAM-Offload requires less code, because redeclaration and reintroduction of variables around and within the `#pragma offload` clauses is not necessary.

Intel LEO	**HAM-Offload**
	`#include <ham/offload.h>`
`__attribute__((target(mic)))` `double _k(double*);`	`double _k(remote_ptr<double>);`

`void glat::kernel(){`
  `//load member pointers onto`
  `//function stack`
  `double *_x=this->x;`
  `double *_e=this->e;`
	`void glat::kernel(){`

`#pragma offload target(mic)\`
  `in(_x:length(0) REUSE)\`
  `in(_e:length(0) REUSE)\`
  `signal(&this->sig)`
  `{`
    `*_e=_k(_x);`
  `}`
`}`
	`auto func=f2f(&_k,this->x);`
	
	  `//future<double> e;`
	  `this->e=Offload::async(`
	       `this->target,func);`
	
	`}`

`double glat::getEnergy(){`
  `double *_e=this->e;`
  `double retValue;`
	`double glat::getEnergy(){`

`#pragma offload target(mic)\`
  `in(_e:length(0) REUSE)\`
  `wait(&this->sig)`
  `{`
    `retValue=*_e;`
  `}`
  `return retValue;`
`}`
	`//future<double> e;`
	  `return e.get();`
	`}`

FIGURE 3.11: C++ methods for GLAT using kernel offloading via Intel LEO and HAM-Offload. For LEO, member pointers need to be placed onto the function stack to use them for the offload—on Xeon Phi the respective object does not exist and hence the pointers would not be valid. All LEO and HAM-Offload specifics are marked boldface. The function _k() is a dummy function here, representing an application kernel.

Application Benchmarks with GLAT   As a performance measure the number of billion particle-particle interactions per second (short: "GigaInteractions/s") is used (larger values are better).

GLAT performs multiple almost independent HMC samplings in a concurrent manner using OpenMP. Throughout the HMC sampling, each OpenMP host thread creates a Markov chain of conformations, and uses kernel offloading to the coprocessor to speed up force computations. We use 16 OpenMP threads per offload for single-coprocessor setups, and up to 30 OpenMP threads for scaling experiments with multiple coprocessors. Without offloading, each kernel uses 2 OpenMP threads on the CPU.

For benchmarking, we used a large simulation setup with a small peptide surrounded by 1750 water molecules, and a small setup where an octanol molecule is surrounded by a number of water molecules ranging from 100 to 1000. Figure 3.12 shows the results for a single Xeon Phi KNC offload target with concurrent kernel execution whereas all offloaded kernels use 16 OpenMP threads for a total of up to 224 concurrent threads. The upper plot compares the runtimes of the CPU reference, the LEO variant, and the HAM-Offload implementation with its different back-ends for the large setup. For all numbers of concurrent Markov chains, the HAM-Offload version of GLAT using the SCIF back-end is either equally fast or slightly faster than LEO. Due to the kernel runtimes being in the order of milliseconds, the offload overhead has no significant impact on the overall performance. The

MPI back-end, i.e., offload over fabric, is at most 6 % slower, possibly caused by contention on MPI resources. Whether an offload via MPI is local or remote does not impact the observed application runtime. Offloading to the Xeon Phi KNC in general accelerates the application as a whole by up to a factor of 2.5.

The bottom plot of Figure 3.12 depicts the result of an octanol simulation for a varying number of water molecules. The latter determines the workload on the Phi, and thus the kernel runtime. The results show the increasing impact of the offload overhead for smaller offloads. A decreased offload size leads to an increased relative speedup of the HAM-Offload implementation over its LEO counterpart, which demonstrates the benefit of HAM's low overhead. The relative speedup ranges from 1.1 for 1000 water molecules to 2.6 for 100 molecules. The degradation of the overall application performance with a decreasing problem size is a consequence of the increased ratio of overhead to actual computation. It is not only caused by offloading, but for the greater part by multi-threading inside the kernel.

To evaluate the weak and strong scaling behavior across multiple remote Xeon Phi coprocessors, we conducted experiments using up to 15 remote coprocessors. We use the same simulation scenario as for a single offload target: a small peptide consisting of 77 atoms surrounded by 1750 water molecules. To assess strong scaling, we always simulate 60 Markov chains, and scale the threads per offload with the number of coprocessors to achieve a constant number of 120 threads per Phi. Both weak and strong scaling lie within

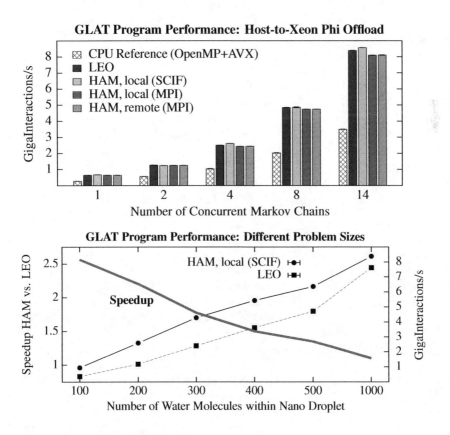

FIGURE 3.12: Performance of GLAT. *Top:* The number of concurrent Markov chains is varied over {1,2,4,8,14} for the small simulation setup (see text). Performance is measured in "GigaInteractions/s" including all overheads (higher values are better). *Bottom:* Speedups and performance results for large simulation setup (see text).

our expectation and show good scaling behavior with a parallel efficiency of 62% for using 15 remote KNC targets for offload.

3.4.3   Runtime Kernel Compilation with KART

Many HPC application codes implement generalized solutions for their respective domains. They typically provide a selection of algorithms that are used for different workloads or combinations of input sets. Whilst the applications grow with adding more methods and features, there is also a growing demand for applying a subset of methods to restricted workloads. Such use cases do not require the full complexity and flexibility of the original implementations. Hence users strive for optimizing their (limited) workloads by tuning the implementations. This starts with algorithmic optimizations, delivering different implementations of the original algorithm, such as reducing dimensions or replacing algorithms that work better for smaller problem sizes.

More than 40% performance gain on the Xeon Phi KNC were reported for the WSM6 proxy code [3] due to re-compiling the code for a specific input. For the DL_MESO code, an even larger 5-fold performance improvement was achieved by enabling better SIMD optimizations for the compiler's auto-vectorizer[25]. Clearly, knowledge on the runtime context of a unit of code would allow to optimize for specific memory access strides, eliminate conditional code, or apply workload-dependent loop transformations.

A typical approach to remedy this is to apply multi-versioning, that is, generating multiple specialized instantiations of the same function, loop, or code fragment. This can be achieved by using dedicated implementations, like C++ template specializations, or pre-processor macros, for example. Compilers can also emit versioned code to handle aligned versus unaligned data, to create different code paths for different instructions sets (e.g. SIMD, AVX), or to avoid SIMD vectorization for too small loop trip counts, to name just a few. Because multi-versioning can dramatically increase the code size, compilers usually only generate a few code versions and provide a general code path as fallback.

Programmers may add compilation hints with pragmas/directives or attributes, but these optimizations can only be applied for a small set of categories of workloads. Moreover, they increase the code size and make the code harder to maintain. While it is easy to provide different optimizations for different dimensionality of input data sets, it is much harder to do so for different memory access patterns, access strides, or loop trip counts.

As a more versatile solution we designed *Kernel-compilation At RunTime* (KART) [19], a light-weight, flexible runtime-compilation framework. It allows to optimize for values that manifest as constants during runtime but were not known at compile time. KART is particularly beneficial for many-core architectures like the Xeon Phi, whose microarchitecture is more sensitive to code-optimizations. For frequently used kernels, the improved optimization outweighs the runtime compilation overhead. We also regard this approach as a solution for OpenMP[*] [22] applications to benefit from the same dynamic recompilation advantages that OpenCL[*] [6] and CUDA[*] [15] provide.

Design Considerations   KART is designed as an abstract and flexible solution that provides an API to use any installed command-line compiler from within the application and then incorporate the resulting object code into the running program. It gives the highest flexibility, as any compiler, even for different languages, can be used. It can defer the compilation of performance critical-code sections until execution time and apply the best-optimizing compiler for a specific code fragment and target architecture, or to multi-version a kernel using different compilers and facilitate auto-tuning. Also different (hand-written) implementations of the same kernel can be used. Thereby the optimization is not only de-

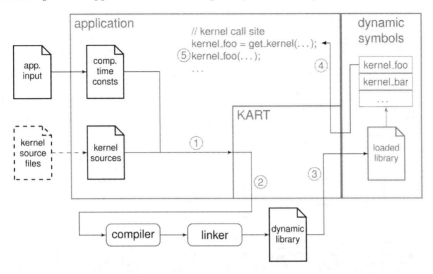

FIGURE 3.13: Schematic of KART: 1) Compile-time constants derived from the input and kernel source code are passed to KART. 2) KART starts a system compiler and linker to create a dynamically linked library. 3) The library is dynamically linked into the application. 4) The application queries KART using the kernel's function name to get a callable function pointer. 5) The kernel is invoked.

fined by compiler capabilities and varying compile-time constants, but also by the user at the algorithmic level. Kernels can be supplied in languages different from that of the host application, which increases the flexibility, e.g., by using C SIMD intrinsics within a Fortran application.

The KART Library   KART[10] provides application developers with the means to compile and use pieces of code at runtime with minimal overhead and maximal flexibility. KART resembles a simple build system with a library interface. It offers a slim API to compile a code fragment given either as a text string or a source file, and to call the result after compiling the code. KART is implemented in C++ using several Boost libraries [24] and provides APIs for C, C++, and Fortran, so far.

As illustrated in Fig. 3.13, any compiler can be used by invocation of command-line compilers and linkers in a separate process at runtime to create a shared library from a given source. The resulting library is then linked to the running program via `dlopen()` and the included functions can be accessed and executed using their (symbolic) name. Constants can be integrated into the runtime-compiled code by either generating the corresponding lines before passing the code to KART, or can be specified using compiler command line options (e.g. `-DNAME=VALUE`).

A *toolset* abstraction encapsulates the specification of a compiler and linker command, as well as different sets of options. Toolsets are defined in small configuration files. A default toolset file can be set via an environment variable.

The second main abstraction is the *program*, which is constructed from either a string or a file containing the source code. The program is then built using a toolset. Once built, callable function pointers can be acquired by specifying a name, and optionally a signature to ensure type-safety in C++. Previously built programs can be rebuilt with a different toolset. This allows to apply many configurations to the same code, e.g., for benchmarking

---

[10]KART is available on GitHub, https://github.com/noma/kart

```
#include "kart/kart.hpp"

// signature type
using my_kernel_t = double(*)(double, double);
const char my_kernel_src[] = R"kart_src(
extern "C" {

// original function
double my_kernel(double a, double b)
{ return a * b * CONST; }

})kart_src"; // close raw string literal

int main(int argc, char** argv)
{
    // create program
    kart::program my_prog(my_kernel_src);
    // create default toolset
    kart::toolset ts;
    // append a constant definiton (runtime value)
    ts.append_compiler_options(" -DCONST=5.0");
    // build program using toolset
    my_prog.build(ts)
    // get the kernel
    auto my_kernel =
        my_prog.get_kernel<my_kernel_t>("my_kernel");

    /* ... application code ... */

    // call the kernel as usual
    double res = my_kernel(3.0, 5.0);

    /* ... application code ...  */
}
```

FIGURE 3.14: This example shows how to embed a kernel as source code and compile it at runtime using KART. The highlighted lines show what is needed to introduce KART. Raw string literals, as provided by C++11, can be used to embed source code without having to escape some characters.

or auto-tuning codes, or in cases when compiled-in data changes, like loop trip counts or sizes of data structures after a load-balancing step.

In addition to C++ there is an API for C and Fortran. The C API is a wrapper around the C++ implementation that uses opaque handles and functions, instead of objects and methods. The Fortran interface is a set of bindings for the C API using the Fortran 2003 BIND attribute and iso_c_binding intrinsic module.

GNU-compiled C/C++ applications can use the most recent Intel C++ compiler to generate performance-critical code using its vectorization capabilities in addition to the input-specific compile-time constants. Fortran codes could use a C/C++ compiler to facilitate manual vectorization for kernels via C SIMD intrinsics. A benchmark or auto-tuning code could use KART to automatically evaluate different compilers and sets of options, e.g., for different optimization levels, pre-fetching settings, or numerical precision levels.

How to Use KART? Fig. 3.14 shows a simple example, where the function my_kernel is compiled at runtime. For a single function, wrapping the original code into a raw string literal, as shown in the example above, is sufficient. If the needed source code already is a separate compilation unit or gets larger, it is more convenient to use source files instead of embedded strings.

There are two ways to specify dependencies and other compile/link options: toolset configuration-files, intended for the compiler and the host-specific part (often non-portable), and methods called at runtime for the application-specific part. This way, the source code remains portable.

For existing code, the most convenient way of integrating runtime compilation would be a directive-based approach, where code is simply annotated as runtime compilation target. A mechanism like the one provided by KART could become part of a widely accepted and standardized programming model like OpenMP in a future version. However, this would mean giving up the flexibility to use any compiler and the library-only implementation.

Adapting Existing Code When adapting a code, the best method is identifying hotspots whose index computations, memory access patterns, loop counts, and branching predicates depend on input data. Once identified, it can be recompiled using compile-time constants for a few inputs to estimate the potential gain before restructuring the code. The runtime gain determines an upper bound for the acceptable compilation overhead. The process is very similar to adapting an application for offloading to an accelerator—without the need to rewrite kernels in another language and optimize them for the accelerator's architecture. The intrusiveness of incorporating runtime kernel compilation into an existing code base depends on the current code structure, as the build-time and run-time compiled source needs to be separated. For a well-structured code base, this means identifying the compilation units and adding the KART API calls into the application's initialization phase. For the HEOM Hexciton benchmark, 23 new lines of code were added and the interface of the benchmarking function was modified.

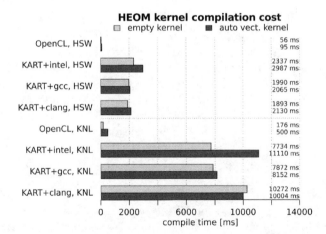

FIGURE 3.15: Runtime compilation overhead for the HEOM Hexciton and an empty kernel. There is a high constant cost for any compilation regardless of the code size. Only the Intel compiler adds significant cost to the empty kernel, but also generates the fastest auto vectorized code. OpenCL's compiler is two orders of magnitude faster, due to the library ABI and less indirectly included headers. The Xeon Phi (KNL) values suffer from the lower single thread performance. (The benchmark systems are an Intel Xeon Phi 7210 (KNL), and a dual socket Intel Xeon E5-2630 v3 (HSW) node. The software versions are: Intel OpenCL Runtime 16.1.1, Intel C++ Compiler 17.0.2, GCC 6.3.0, and Clang 4.0.0.)

The Runtime Compilation Overhead First we investigate the trade-off between the runtime compilation overhead and kernel speed-up. The overhead introduced by KART is

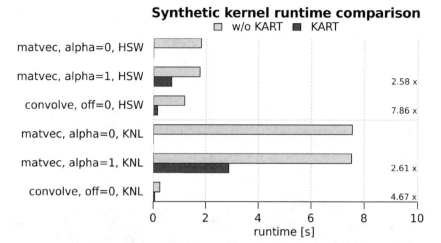

FIGURE 3.16: Speed-ups for two synthetic kernels *matvec* (single threaded) and *convolve* (OpenMP). The speed-ups do not include the compilation overhead, as this would require defining a somehow "realistic" number of kernel calls. A compile-time known *alpha=0* entirely removed the computation loops. The average compilation times for each kernel ranges from 0.87 to 0.93 s on the Xeon (HSW) and 3.43 to 3.54 s on the Xeon Phi processor (KNL).

largely determined by the invoked compiler and linker. Runtime compilation techniques pay off when the accumulated runtime savings of all kernel calls exceed the runtime compilation cost.

Fig. 3.15 shows the compilation cost using Intel OpenCL as a reference and KART with different compilers. The linking step took roughly two thirds of the time. The timings for the empty kernels show that there is a large constant cost coming with the command line compilers. This includes starting processes and lots of file operations when handling dependencies like a large set of header and library files, all not present in OpenCL. A library interface to existing compilers together with a set of small headers and libraries specifically optimized for compilation time could improve the situation. For commercial compilers, additional time is lost for fetching licenses from a file system or network. Caching the compilation results between application runs could mitigate these costs if the actual reuse is high.

Performance on Synthetic Kernels We have selected two kernels to highlight the principal usefulness of runtime compilation for HPC kernels: a) a one-dimensional linear convolution with an offset into the input vector (for different threads), and b) a matrix vector multiplication with scaling (*alpha*). To give the compiler's optimizer some optimization headroom, we assume the scaling to be 0.0 or 1.0, and matrix *a* to have just one column. This simulates cases where the compiler can remove invariant statements and/or loops. Both kernels have been compiled via KART and as ordinary C functions with all parameters as arguments (e.g. *alpha*, *rows*, and *cols* for kernel *matvec*).

Fig. 3.16 shows the results. For the *matvec* kernel, the compiler was able to entirely eliminate the loops for *alpha=0* and even showed a 2.6x kernel speed-up for *alpha=1* where the inner-most loop was removed since there is only one column of matrix *a*. For the *convolve* kernel, having *offset*, *input size*, and *kernel size* known by the compiler could improve kernel runtimes by 7.9x.

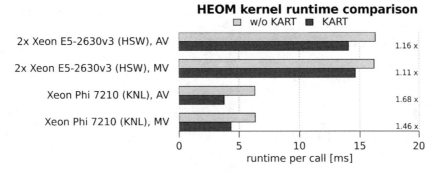

FIGURE 3.17: Runtimes and speed-ups achieved by using KART for the OpenMP version of the HEOM benchmark. Matrix size and number of matrices read from the input are used as compile-time constants during runtime compilation. AV is automatic and MV is manual vectorization. Amortization of compile time requires 1321 and 15117 calls on Xeon (HSW) and Xeon Phi (KNL), respectively. Typical application runs need 10^3 to 10^6 calls.

Performance Improvement on HEOM   We integrated KART into the OpenMP version of HEOM (Sec. 3.2.3) to build the different kernel variants at runtime and enable the use of input-specific constants at kernel compile time. Two constants, the matrix dimension and the number of matrices of the central HEOM data structure are most relevant for the memory access pattern and the loop counts.

Fig. 3.17 shows the results. The plotted values are from the best-performing kernel variants using the Intel C++ compiler. The highest speed-up of 2.6x was observed for Clang on the Xeon CPU with the manually vectorized kernel, but the absolute runtime was still slower than that of the code generated by the Intel C++ compiler. The Intel Xeon Phi benefits much more from the compiler optimizations because its light-weight cores and the missing L3 cache require better optimized code than the Haswell architecture.

3.5   Summary

The existence of many-core computer architectures results from the inevitable need to improve energy efficiency for floating point computations on the way to exascale machines within a feasible power budget. With its Xeon Phi products, Intel aims at providing to the user a familiar environment which in terms of both hardware and software shares many commonalities with standard (Intel) CPU platforms, but offers a better FLOP/Watt ratio and high bandwidth memory (HBM).

At ZIB, we operate an 80 node Cray XC40 Test and Development System (TDS) with Intel Xeon Phi (KNL) processors. As of its installation, users have the opportunity to run their codes on this next-generation many-core architecture, experience the differences to a standard CPU system, and eventually adapt their codes to make them benefit from the new platform. This "modernization"-process addresses all the different levels of parallelism needed to keep the many cores busy across a multi-node installation: process-level, thread-level and data-level parallelism. Techniques shown here, like compiler-directive based SIMD-vectorization through OpenMP 4.x, or input-dependent function specialization through runtime compilation with KART are only a few helpful examples to achieve this.

With the Xeon Phi—due to its large number of light-weight CPU cores and wide SIMD vector units—we experienced that the sum of all of these adaptations often requires funda-mental changes in the code, affecting data layouts, parallelization strategies, and algorithms used. The good news is that most of the work results in a double-benefit, meaning changes targeting the many-core platform improve performance on the current multi-core systems as well, rendering it a strong investment into the future.

Within the Research Center for Many-core High-Performance Computing, we work together with users and HPC vendors to coordinate and facilitate the whole-program-optimization process for applications frequently used on the current HLRN-III supercom-puter. We generalize our findings and develop novel programming approaches and tools, such as the presented HAM-Offload framework and KART runtime-compilation library. Such strategic collaborations between vendors, code owners, and HPC-centers are key to adapting the huge amount of existing code in a productive and effective process, in order to be ready for the next generation of supercomputers.

Acknowledgments   This work is carried out within the "Research Center for Many-Core High-Performance Computing" —the IPCC at ZIB with support from Intel Corporation. We thank the "The North-German Supercomputing Alliance" for providing access to the HLRN-III production system 'Konrad' and the Cray TDS system with Intel Xeon Phi KNC/KNL nodes. We thank the Vienna VASP team, in particular Martijn Marsman and Georg Kresse, Jeongnim Kim and their team at Intel, and Zhengij Zhao (NERSC) for the close collabo-ration on tuning VASP for the Xeon Phi. We thank Frank Cordes (GETLIG&TAR GbR) for contributing the GLAT code.

Bibliography

[1] Wolfgang Baumann, Guido Laubender, Matthias Luter, Alexander Reinefeld, Christian Schimmel, Thomas Steinke, Christian Tuma, and Stefan Wollny. *Contemporary High Performance Computing: From Petascale toward Exascale*, volume 2, chapter HLRN-III at Zuse Institute Berlin, pages 81–114. Chapman & Hall/CRC, 2015.

[2] Heinecke, A. and Klemm, M. and Bungartz, H. J. From GPGPU to Many-Core: Nvidia Fermi and Intel Many Integrated Core Architecture. *Computing in Science and Engineering*, 14:78–83, 2012.

[3] Tom Henderson, John Michalakes, Indraneil Gokhale, and Ashish Jha. Chapter 2 - Numerical Weather Prediction Optimization. In James Reinders and Jim Jeffers, editors, *High Performance Parallelism Pearls*, pages 7 – 23. Morgan Kaufmann, Boston, 2015.

[4] Intel Corporation. *Itanium ABI, v1.86*.

[5] Jeffers, James and Reinders, James. *Intel Xeon Phi Coprocessor High Performance Programming*. Morgan Kaufmann Publishers Inc., San Francisco, CA, USA, 1st edition, 2013.

[6] Khronos OpenCL Working Group. The OpenCL Specification, Version 2.2, March 2016. https://www.khronos.org/registry/cl/specs/opencl-2.2.pdf.

[7] Michael Klemm, Alejandro Duran, Xinmin Tian, Hideki Saito, Diego Caballero, and Xavier Martorell. Extending OpenMP* with Vector Constructs for Modern Multicore

SIMD Architectures. In *Proceedings of the 8th International Conference on OpenMP in a Heterogeneous World*, IWOMP'12, pages 59–72, Berlin, Heidelberg, 2012. Springer-Verlag.

[8] G. Kresse and J. Furthmüller. Efficiency of ab-initio total energy calculations for metals and semiconductors using a plane-wave basis set. *Comput. Mater. Sci.*, 6(1):15 – 50, 1996.

[9] G. Kresse and J. Hafner. *Phys. Rev. B*, 47:558, 1993.

[10] G. Kresse and D. Joubert. *Phys. Rev.*, 59:1758, 1999.

[11] G. Kresse, M. Marsman, and J. Furthmüller. VASP the Guide. http://cms.mpi.univie.ac.at/vasp/vasp/vasp.html, April 2016.

[12] B. Maronga, M. Gryschka, R. Heinze, F. Hoffmann, F. Kanani-Shring, M. Keck, K. Ketelsen, M. O. Letzel, M. Shring, and S. Raasch. The Parallelized Large-Eddy Simulation Model (PALM) version 4.0 for atmospheric and oceanic flows: model formulation, recent developments, and future perspectives. *Geosci. Model Dev.*, 8:1539–1637, 2015.

[13] Y. Nakamura and H. Stüben. BQCD - Berlin quantum chromodynamics program. In *PoS (Lattice 2010)*, page 40, 2010.

[14] Chris J. Newburn, Rajiv Deodhar, Serguei Dmitriev, Ravi Murty, Ravi Narayanaswamy, John Wiegert, Francisco Chinchilla, and Russell McGuire. Offload Compiler Runtime for the Intel Xeon Phi Coprocessor. In *Supercomputing*, pages 239–254. Springer Berlin Heidelberg, 2013.

[15] John Nickolls, Ian Buck, Michael Garland, and Kevin Skadron. Scalable Parallel Programming with CUDA. *Queue*, 6(2):40–53, March 2008.

[16] Matthias Noack. HAM - Heterogenous Active Messages for Efficient Offloading on the Intel Xeon Phi. Technical report, ZIB, Takustr.7, 14195 Berlin, 2014.

[17] Matthias Noack, Florian Wende, and Klaus-Dieter Oertel. Chapter 19 - OpenCL: There and Back Again. In James Reinders and Jim Jeffers, editors, *High Performance Parallelism Pearls*, pages 355 – 378. Morgan Kaufmann, Boston, 2015.

[18] Matthias Noack, Florian Wende, Thomas Steinke, and Frank Cordes. A Unified Programming Model for Intra- and Inter-Node Offloading on Xeon Phi Clusters. In *International Conference for High Performance Computing, Networking, Storage and Analysis, SC 2014, New Orleans, LA, USA, November 16-21, 2014*, pages 203–214, 2014.

[19] Matthias Noack, Florian Wende, Georg Zitzlsberger, Michael Klemm, and Thomas Steinke. KART – A Runtime Compilation Library for Improving HPC Application Performance. In *IXPUG Workshop "Experiences on Intel Knights Landing at the One Year Mark" at ISC High Performance 2017, Frankfurt, Germany*, June 2017.

[20] OpenMP Architecture Review Board. *OpenMP Application Program Interface, Version 4.0*, 2013. http://www.openmp.org.

[21] OpenMP Architecture Review Board. *OpenMP Application Program Interface, Version 4.5*, 2015. http://www.openmp.org.

[22] OpenMP Architecture Review Board. OpenMP Application Program Interface, Version 4.5, 2015. http://www.openmp.org/.

[23] Scott Pakin, M. Lang, and D.K. Kerbyson. The Reverse-Acceleration Model for Programming Petascale Hybrid Systems. *IBM Journal of Research and Development*, 53(5), 2009.

[24] Boris Schling. *The Boost C++ Libraries*. XML Press, 2011.

[25] Sergi Siso. DL_MESO Code Modernization. Intel Xeon Phi Users Group (IXPUG), March 2016. IXPUG Workshop, Ostrava.

[26] Avinash Sodani, Roger Gramunt, Jesús Corbal, Ho-Seop Kim, Krishna Vinod, Sundaram Chinthamani, Steven Hutsell, Rajat Agarwal, and Yen-Chen Liu. Knights Landing: Second-Generation Intel Xeon Phi Product. *IEEE Micro*, 36(2):34–46, 2016.

[27] Florian Wende, Martijn Marsman, Zhengji Zhao, and Jeongnim Kim. Porting VASP from MPI to MPI + OpenMP [SIMD]. In *Proceedings of the 13th International Workshop on OpenMP, Scaling OpenMP for Exascale Performance and Portability*, IWOMP'17, 2017. Accepted for publication.

[28] Florian Wende, Matthias Noack, Thomas Steinke, Michael Klemm, Chris J. Newburn, and Georg Zitzlsberger. Portable SIMD Performance with OpenMP* 4.X Compiler Directives. In *Proceedings of the 22nd International Conference on Euro-Par 2016: Parallel Processing - Volume 9833*, pages 264–277, New York, NY, USA, 2016. Springer-Verlag New York, Inc.

Chapter 4

The Mont-Blanc Prototype

Filippo Mantovani, Daniel Ruiz, Leonardo Bautista, Vishal Metha
Barcelona Supercomputing Center

Fabio Banchelli, Nikola Rajovic, Eduard Ayguade, Jesus Labarta, Mateo Valero
Barcelona Supercomputing Center and Universitat Politècnica de Catalunya

Alejandro Rico Carro
Arm Ltd.

Alex Ramirez Bellido
Google Inc.

Markus Geimer
Jülich Supercomputing Centre

Daniele Tafani
Leibniz Supercomputing Centre

4.1   Overview

The evolution of High-Performance Computing (HPC) systems was mainly driven for decades by the need to reduce time-to-solution and increase the resolution of models and problems being solved by a particular program. In this evolution towards better system performance, important milestones were achieved by using commodity technology. Examples are the ASCI Red and the Roadrunner supercomputers, which broke the 1 TFLOPS and 1 PFLOPS barriers, respectively, by using commodity technologies initially designed for other markets. Driven by a much larger market, these commodity components tend to evolve faster than their special-purpose counterparts, eventually achieving the same performance and eventually surpassing or replacing them. For this reason, RISC processors displaced vector processors, and x86 displaced RISC.

Nowadays commodity is in the embedded/mobile processor segment, for which cost and energy efficiency are key drivers. Mobile processors are developing very fast, and are still not at a point of diminishing performance improvements from new designs. Furthermore, they have been progressively incorporating the capabilities that make them capable to support the HPC software stack and applications. Similarly, the embedded market size and endless customer requirements allow for constant investments into innovative designs, and rapid testing and adoption of new technologies. For example, LPDDR memory technology was first introduced in the mobile domain and has recently been proposed as a memory solution for energy proportional servers [11]. The Mont-Blanc prototype [15] described in this chapter has been the first of a kind exploring the use of mobile processors in relatively large systems targeting real HPC applications.

4.1.1   Project Context and Challenges

As part of the initiatives towards Exascale funded by the European Commission, the Mont-Blanc project aimed at exploring the possibility of delivering HPC capabilities by using System-On-Chips (SoCs) initially developed for smartphones and tablets. The vision was that components developed for a huge market (embedded and mobile) for which cost and energy efficiency were key drivers could be leveraged to deliver cost effective solutions to the ever growing population of highly demanding applications. ARM was the chosen architecture because it was a standard in the mobile and embedded market with interest in researching the possibilities of going HPC, which later cemented in the design of ARM-based HPC systems.

The main motivation for evaluating the feasibility of mobile SoC was the fast growing market for which they are produced. Since 2011 this market has been evolving in different directions: on one hand the size and growth rate of the market is lowering the prices of the technology involved; on the other hand the computational requirements of the mobile market make the computational power of mobile SoCs grow fast. This growth speed, both in terms of volume and computational power, is higher than the one of server market, making therefore this technology extremely appealing for emerging computational challenges.

But the feasibility of adopting these mobile SoC for building future HPC systems should be done considering the challenges already identified in the race to Exascale computing systems. In the next paragraphs we outline how these challenges need to be further analyzed when the use of technologies from the mobile and embedded markets is considered:

Energy. Scaling the power consumption of current HPC systems to Exascale is not a viable option. General agreement in the community set the power budget for the first Exascale system to 20 MW. That was the first motivation when back in 2011 the Mont-Blanc project decided to explore the possibility of using technologies developed for a type of market that is extremely sensible for power consumption (mobile market). However, these systems were not initially conceived to be integrated into HPC-class systems, introducing other challenges like thermal instability, as explained in Section 4.5.1.

Concurrency and heterogeneity. Development of larger and more efficient computing system implies dealing with higher levels of concurrency: this trend is true for high-end HPC systems and, even more, in the case of systems based on mobile devices. These devices offer lower computational power than their counterparts in the server market, requiring the use of a higher (often one order of magnitude) number of computational elements in order to reach the same overall computational power. Moreover, mobile SoCs often offer heterogeneous architectures that need to be exploited in order to achieve maximum performance. Both aspects have a clear impact in programming, requiring the exploitation of much higher degrees of concurrency and dealing with different computational paradigms. The Mont Blanc project addressed these issues by developing and improving performance analysis tools (to understand the complexity) and programming models (to improve programming productivity).

Variability and resiliency. With the tremendous reduction in feature sizes and the huge amount of devices at the electronic level, larger and larger variability is to be expected in the characteristics and delivered performance of components within a large scale system. Other sources of variability may originate in system software components. The need to tolerate such variability and adapt to its possibly dynamic behavior is an additional challenge to be faced by a holistic system architecture.

Cost. As mentioned before, due to the high production volume of mobile technology, the price of mobile SoCs remains low while their computational power is growing quickly. As a consequence of this, it is a foreseeable continuing trend that it will be possible to buy a mobile SoC at a price $50\times$ cheaper than a server processor, with almost the same computational functionalities and between $10\times$ and $4\times$ less computational power. Meanwhile other ARM-based chips, targeting the server market, appeared on the market, carrying higher performances and higher prices. How this correlates to the Total Cost of Ownership (TCO) of a large datacenter was a question mark in 2011.

Although the proposals and ideas in the Mont-Blanc project were initially driven by the Exascale challenges mentioned in the previous paragraphs, partners in the project were keeping an eye on the emerging non-HPC workloads, like Big Data and Cloud, which were becoming more and more relevant, with huge impacts at the industrial and academic level. These emerging workloads could widen the spectrum of applicability that large highly parallel machines need to be able to efficiently handle. In this direction, Section 4.3.2 describes the effort made to deploy and evaluate the suitability of the Mont-Blanc prototype for the OpenStack Cloud environment.

Finally, the recent appearance of high-end ARM-based SoC targeting the server market, has motivated a change in the overall project focus towards high-end server technologies. Proof of this new tendency is the announcement in June 2017 of the commercialization by Bull/ATOS of a new ARM-based platform, based on Cavium ThunderX 2 high-end SoC, partially developed within the third phase of the Mont-Blanc project. To explore all the issues mentioned above and research on how to address them, the Mont-Blanc project targeted the three objectives listed in the following section.

4.1.2 Objectives and Timeline

The initial Mont-Blanc project was established having the following goals in mind:

1. to design and deploy a sufficiently large HPC prototype system based on the mobile commodity technology available at the time the project started;

2. to port and optimize the necessary software stack to give support to the development and execution of HPC applications;

3. to port and optimize a set of HPC applications to be run on the prototype developed and deployed.

Figure 4.1 shows the timeline with the major milestones for the Mont-Blanc prototype. The Tibidabo prototype [16], funded by PRACE, showed the viability of the Mont-Blanc idea, integrating 256 embedded boards housing one Tegra 2 SoC each. Shortly after, the Mont-Blanc project started evaluating the different SoCs available [18, 14, 5]. Once the SoC selection finalized, the board design and prototype production started, in parallel with a system software development phase. The project successfully ended on July 14th 2015, making the system openly available for evaluation to the scientific and technical community.

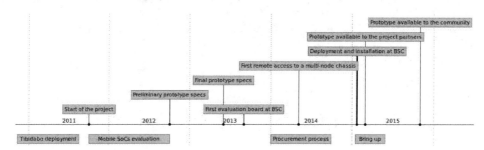

FIGURE 4.1: The Mont-Blanc prototype timeline

4.2 Hardware Architecture

This section presents the architecture of the Mont-Blanc prototype (shown in Figure 4.2). The peculiarities of each building block in the system are highlighted in the following subsections.

4.2.1 Compute Node

The Mont-Blanc compute node is a *Server-on-Module* architecture. Figure 4.3 depicts the Mont-Blanc node card (Samsung Daughter Board or SDB) and its components. Each SDB is built around a Samsung Exynos 5250 SoC integrating two ARM Cortex-A15[1] CPUs @ 1.7 GHz sharing 1 MB of on-die L2 cache, and a mobile 4-core ARM Mali-T604

---

[1]Implementation of the ARMv7-a architecture.

FIGURE 4.2: Physical view of the Mont-Blanc system (left) and blade (right).

GPU @ 533MHz. The SoC connects to the on-board 4 GB of LPDDR3-1600 RAM through two 32-bit memory channels shared among the CPUs and the GPU, providing a peak memory bandwidth of 12.8 GB/s.

The node interconnect is provided by the ASIX AS88179 USB 3.0 to 1 GbE bridge and an Ethernet PHY. An external 16 GB μSD card provides the boot-loader, OS system image, and local scratch storage.

The node connects to the blade through proprietary bus routing Ethernet signals using a PCI-e 4× form factor edge connector (EMB connector).

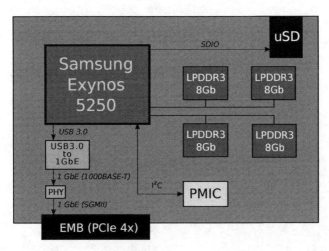

FIGURE 4.3: The Mont-Blanc node block scheme (not to scale).

4.2.2 Blade

Figure 4.4 describes the architecture of the Mont-Blanc blade (Ethernet Mother Board, or EMB, depicted in Figure 4.2). Each EMB blade hosts 15 SDB nodes that are interconnected through an on-board 1 GbE switch fabric. The switch provides two 10 GbE up-links. In addition, the EMB provides management services, power consumption monitoring of SDBs, and blade level temperature monitoring. The EMB enclosure is air-cooled through the fans installed on the front side.

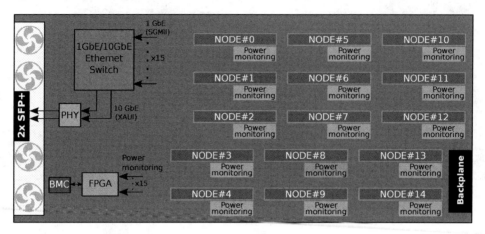

FIGURE 4.4: The Mont-Blanc blade block scheme.

4.2.3 The Overall System

The entire Mont-Blanc prototype system (shown in Figure 4.2) fits into two standard 42U-19″ racks. Each Mont-Blanc rack hosts up to four 7U Bullx chassis, which in turn integrate nine EMB blades each. In addition, racks are populated with two 2U 10 GbE Cisco Nexus 5596UP top-of-the-rack (TOR) switches, one 1U prototype management 1GbE switch[2], and two 2U Intel-based storage nodes.

System interconnect   The Mont-Blanc prototype implements two separate networks: the 1 GbE management network and the 10 GbE MPI network. The management network is out of the scope of this chapter, thus we depict the implementation of the MPI interconnect in Figure 4.5.

As mentioned before, the first level of switching is provided inside the EMB blades using a 1 GbE switch fabric providing two 10 GbE up-links. Switching between EMB blades occurs at the TOR switches with a switching capacity of 1.92 Tbps per switch. The TOR switches are directly interconnected with four 40 GbE links.

Storage   The Lustre parallel filesystem is built on a Supermicro Storage Bridge Bay based on x86-64 architecture, with a total capacity of 9.6 TB and providing 2-3.5 GB/s read/write bandwidth (depending on the disk zone). Each storage node is connected to the two TOR switches using two 10 GbE links.

Cooling   Compute nodes are passively cooled using a top-mounted heat sink, while blades provide active air-cooling through variable speed front-mounted fans in a temperature control loop.

---

[2]Not visible, mounted on the back.

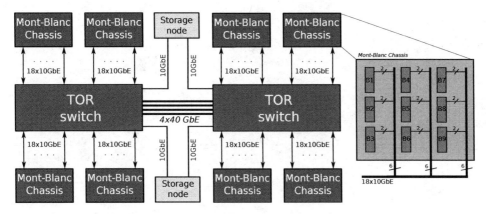

FIGURE 4.5: The Mont-Blanc system interconnect.

Power monitoring infrastructure The Mont-Blanc prototype provides a unique infrastructure for high-frequency measurements of power consumption at the granularity of a single compute node, scaling to the whole size of the prototype.

The Mont-Blanc system features a digital current and voltage meter in the power supply rail to each SDB. An FPGA on each EMB accesses the power sensors in each SDB via I2C and stores the averaged values every 1.120ms in a FIFO buffer. The Board Management Controller (BMC) on the EMB communicates with the FPGA to collect the power data samples from the FIFO buffer before storing them in its DDR2 memory along with a timestamp of the reading. User access to the data is then provided by the BMC over the management Ethernet through a set of custom Intelligent Platform Management Interface (IPMI) commands.

To provide application developers with power traces of their applications, the power measurement and acquisition process is conveniently encapsulated and automated in a custom-made system monitoring tool. The tool has been developed with a focus on simplicity and scalability by respectively employing Message Queue Telemetry Transport (MQTT) for lightweight transport messaging, and Apache Cassandra, a scalable, distributed database for storing the acquired power data along with other time-series based monitoring data. A set of command line tools and a special API provide users with the ability to access the raw monitoring data or to plot and correlate information from different data sources throughout the system.

4.2.4 Performance Summary

Figure 4.6 shows the peak performance at the SDB node, EMB blade, and chassis and entire system levels for CPU and GPU separately. The whole system has a peak performance of 107.7 TFLOPS SP and 30.3 TFLOPS DP.

The two Cortex-A15 cores provide a peak performance of 27.2 GFLOPS in single-precision (SP) and 6.8 GFLOPS in double-precision (DP). The performance disparity comes from the fact that the SIMD unit, code-named NEON, only supports SP floating-point (FP) operations, thus DP FP instructions execute in a scalar unit.

The on-chip 4-core Mali-T604 GPU provides 72.5 GFLOPS SP and 21.3 GFLOPS DP. The total node performance is 99.7 GFLOPS SP and 28.1 GFLOPS DP.

Due to the 32-bit nature of the SoC architecture, each node integrates only 4 GB of

Compute Node		
	CPU	**GPU**
Compute element	2×ARM Cortex-A15	1×ARM Mali-T604
Frequency	1.7 GHz	533 MHz
Peak performance (SP)	27.2 GFLOPS	72.5 GFLOPS
Peak performance (DP)	6.8 GFLOPS	21.3 GFLOPS
Memory (shared)	4 GB LPDDR3-800	
Blade = 15×Node		
Peak performance (SP)	408 GFLOPS	1.08 TFLOPS
Peak performance (DP)	102 GFLOPS	319.5 GFLOPS
Memory	60 GB	
Chassis = 9×Blade		
Peak performance (SP)	3.67 TFLOPS	9.79 TFLOPS
Peak performance (DP)	0.92 TFLOPS	2.88 TFLOPS
Memory	540 GB	
System = 8×Chassis		
Peak performance (SP)	29.38 TFLOPS	78.3 TFLOPS
Total (SP)	*107.7 TFLOPS*	
Peak performance (DP)	7.34 TFLOPS	23 TFLOPS
Total (DP)	*30.3 TFLOPS*	
Memory	4.32 TB	

FIGURE 4.6: Mont-Blanc compute performance summary.

memory. The high node integration density of 1080 nodes (2160 cores) in 56U (over 19 nodes per U) adds up to 4.32 TB of memory and an aggregate 13.8 TB/s memory bandwidth.

4.3   System Software

The work done in the Mont-Blanc project has been crucial to mature the HPC software stack on ARM architectures. Today, working with the Mont-Blanc prototype feels like working with any other HPC cluster.

Each SDB node runs Ubuntu 14.04.1 Linux on top of the customized Linaro Kernel version 3.11.0, which enables a user space driver for OpenCL programming of the ARM Mali-T604 GPU. The rest of the software stack components are shown in Figure 4.7.

Compilers		
GNU	JDK	Mercurium
Scientific libraries		
ATLAS LAPACK SCALAPACK FFTW		
BOOST clBLAS clFFT PETSc HDF5		
Performance analysis		**Debugger**
EXTRAE Paraver Scalasca		Allinea DDT
Runtime libraries		
Nanos++ OpenCL OpenMPI MPICH3		
Cluster management		
SLURM Nagios Ganglia		
Hardware support		**Storage**
Power monitor		LustreFS
Operating System		
Ubuntu		

FIGURE 4.7: The Mont-Blanc software stack.

A very relevant part of the Mont-Blanc software stack is the OmpSs programming model [7], provided by the Mercurium compiler and the Nanos++ runtime. OmpSs is a task-based programming model with explicit inter-task dataflow that allows the runtime system to orchestrate the out-of-order execution of the tasks, selectively off-loading of tasks to the GPU when possible, or running them on the CPU if the GPU is busy. Applications ported to OmpSs can make simultaneous use of the CPU and the GPU, dynamically adapting to load unbalanced situations.

4.3.1 Development Tools Ecosystem

The Mont-Blanc partners developed an integrated tool stack supporting both ARM-based platforms and the OmpSs task-based programming model. This stack includes both commercial and open-source tools for debugging, performance analysis, performance prediction, and automated kernel optimization.

Debugging. The Allinea Forge tools suite consisting of the MAP profiler and DDT debugger have been ported to the ARMv8 architecture. In addition, DDT has been tightly integrated with the Temanejo debugger [12] for task-parallel, data-dependency driven programming developed by HLRS. While Allinea DDT focuses on the traditional aspects of parallel debugging (i.e., call stack and variable inspection, execution stepping, breakpoints, process and thread control, etc.), Temanejo allows the inspection of the task-dependency graph maintained by a tasking runtime system such as the Nanos++ runtime for OmpSs, and to control the task execution order. As a result of this project, the two debuggers can be launched from each other, execution stepping control can be transferred between them, and program information can be exchanged via a newly developed inter-process communication protocol.

Application performance analysis. The tool suites developed by BSC [2] – consisting of the Extrae trace generation package and the Paraver trace analysis tool [13] – and by JSC [9] (among others) – consisting of the instrumentation and measurement infrastructure Score-P [10], the automatic trace analysis toolset Scalasca [8], and the Cube performance report visualizer [19] – have been ported to the ARM architecture and extended to seamlessly support applications using a combination of different programming models. Here, a particular focus was placed on asynchronous execution, for example, through the use of task-based programming (OmpSs, OpenMP), OpenCL, or CUDA. The two tool suites have been integrated via a newly developed plugin interface for the Cube performance report visualizer, which allows the display of results generated by the Paraver tools suite within the Cube graphical user interface as well as the steering of the Paraver visualization from Cube.

Application performance prediction. Along the same lines, the Dimemas developed at BSC [1] framework has been extended to support predictions of applications using acceleration devices.

Automated kernel optimization. The consortium has also focused on automatic optimization of compute kernels. In this context, CNRS developed the BOAST meta-programming framework [20] to produce portable and efficient kernels for HPC applications. With BOAST, kernels and their possible optimizations are described in a domain-specific language. Based on this input, many variants of the kernel are automatically generated and benchmarked, exploring the design space in an intelligent way to find a (near-)optimal solution for the given target platform. In this feedback loop, the MAQAO tool [6] – which has been ported to the ARM platform by INRIA – has been tightly integrated to provide detailed information in particular regarding memory accesses, and to provide additional hints to the user on how to improve the description of the kernel (e.g. to allow for a better automatic vectorization). Automatically tuned kernels using this approach can outperform hand-optimized kernels.

Contribution to standards.   Finally, BSC and JSC actively contributed to the OpenMP tools working group in an effort to standardize the OpenMP Tools Application Programming Interface for Performance Analysis (OMPT). In particular, the partners substantially contributed to the definition of an API to monitor task executions as well as their dependencies that block the execution of subsequent tasks. Besides, draft versions of the standard document have been reviewed and prototypically implemented in the Nanos++ OmpSs runtime, the measurement infrastructures Score-P and Extrae, as well as the Temanejo debugger, both to gain experiences and to identify possible shortcomings early on. As a result of these activities, the OMPT proposal passed the necessary second vote for acceptance into the "TR4: OpenMP Version 5.0 Preview 1" document in the OpenMP Architecture Review Board - the OpenMP standardization body - on November 1, 2016. The availability of a portable interface to the OpenMP runtimes of different vendors, including the Nanos++ OmpSs runtime, in the upcoming OpenMP 5.0 standard with major contributions from the partners is an outstanding achievement.

4.3.2 OpenStack

OpenStack is a cloud environment used for large amounts of compute, storage, and networking resources. The Mont-Blanc prototype has been deployed with the Juno edition of OpenStack and evaluated for performance and portability of Virtual Machines, and architectural design and suitability for OpenStack cloud environment.

VM installation and performance on Mont-Blanc node.   The Mont-Blanc SDB node includes the ARM hardware virtualization extensions (VE). The virtual machines run on top of KVM paired with QEMU with libvirt API layer that allows configuring and launching of Virtual Machines through XMLs. QEMU supports vexpress-a15 machine type with KVM. So as a first step we bootstrap the Linux image and install corresponding vexpress kernel and the device tree binary (dtb) file to create a raw image and fire up the VM and test for its performance using LM bench.

Installation on Mont-Blanc.   Figure 4.8 shows the architecture of OpenStack on the Mont-Blanc cluster. The picture shows a single compute node, which can then be replicated as required.

For the controller node, we create a virtual machine and run it using libvirt on a Mont-Blanc node. This allowed us to take snapshots of the working controller machine and restore the state and OpenStack environment in case of failures.

The controller VM.   This has a MySQL server binded with a static IP address to allow any other compute node's SQL client to communicate. The Rabbit-mq server is used as a message passing interface. The NOVA conductor is the heart of OpenStack, scheduling VM and managing compute nodes. GLANCE is an image storing device that manages images and allows storing snapshots in an image repository. KEYSTONE is an identity service, tightly integrated with SQL server for managing users and administrators of OpenStack. HORIZON, also called dashboard, provides a graphical interface using Apache Server. Dashboard integrates all the underlying OpenStack services.

The compute node.   OpenStack compute specific services are installed on bare metal. NOVA-compute is associated with launching VMs, using qemu and kvm. It also creates lib-

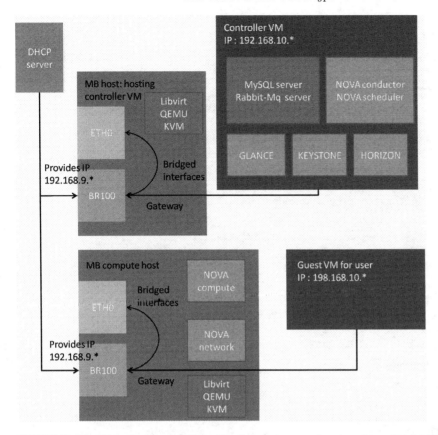

FIGURE 4.8: Distribution of OpenStack services and networking for building Mont-Blanc cloud.

virt VM description XML and loads images from the GLANCE repository. For the purpose of creating suitable libvirt XML, we modify the driver files of NOVA compute on each compute node, allowing us to pass kernel, dtb tree, initrd image, and command line arguments for selecting boot partition to qemu-kvm while booting a virtual machine. NOVA-network, networking configuration for booting VM, provides IP and Flat interface and gateway servers for VMs.

4.4 Applications and Workloads

This section presents a comparison between the Samsung dual-core Exynos 5250 SoC (first introduced in Q3 2012) running at 1.7 GHz used in the Mont-Blanc prototype and its contemporary 8-core Intel Xeon E5-2670 server processor (first introduced in Q1 2012) running at 2.6 GHz used in the MareNostrum 3 supercomputer [3]. Each MareNostrum 3 node is a dual-socket implementation using DDR3-1600 memory DIMMs. A side-by-side comparison is shown in Figure 4.9.

In terms of methodology, the following subsections present and discuss both core-to-core and node-to-node performance as well as energy figures when executing the Mont-Blanc

	CPU	GPU	CPU	GPU
Frequency [GHz]	1.7		2.6	
# sockets	1		2	
Peak FP-64 [GFLOPS]	6.8	21.3	332.8	-n/a-
Memory BW [GB/s]	12.8		51.2	
Network BW [Gb/s]	1		40	
Intersocket BW [GB/s]	-n/a-		32	

FIGURE 4.9: Mont-Blanc vs MareNostrum 3: node performance comparison.

benchmark suite [17] (see Figure 4.10). We report performance (execution time) and energy differences by normalizing to that of MareNostrum 3. We obtain node power using the power monitoring infrastructure of the Mont-Blanc prototype (see Section 4.2.3), and the node energy consumption in MareNostrum 3 provided through LSF job manager.

Tag	Full name
2dc	2D convolution
amcd	Markov Chain Monte Carlo method
dmm	Dense matrix-matrix multiplication
hist	Histogram calculation
ms	Generic merge sort
nbody	N-body calculation
3ds	3D volume stencil computation
fft	One-dimensional Fast Fourier Transform
red	Reduction operation
vecop	Vector operation

FIGURE 4.10: List of Mont-Blanc benchmarks.

4.4.1 Core Evaluation

Figure 4.11 presents the performance comparison on a core-to-core basis between the Mont-Blanc prototype and MareNostrum 3 supercomputer. This comparison using single-threaded runs gives the baseline performance difference between both cores without the interference of scheduling and synchronization effects of parallel runs.

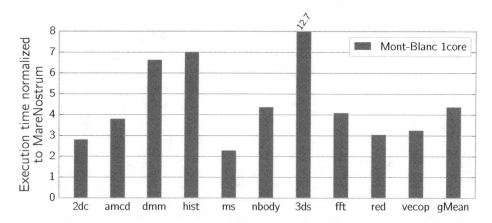

FIGURE 4.11: Mont-Blanc benchmarks: core-to-core performance comparison.

Across the benchmark suite, Mont-Blanc is between 2.2× and 12.7× slower on a per core basis. On average, across the entire suite, a Mont-Blanc processor core is 4.3× slower than that of MareNostrum 3.

4.4.2 Node Evaluation

Figure 4.12 compares performance and energy consumption on a node-to-node basis between the Mont-Blanc prototype and the MareNostrum 3 supercomputer.

Given the characteristics of the Mont-Blanc SoC and its software stack, we evaluate three different computing scenarios: homogeneous CPU computing with OpenMP, heterogeneous CPU + GPU with OpenCL, and heterogeneous with OmpSs.

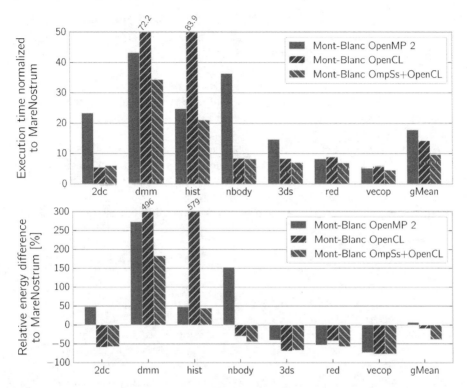

FIGURE 4.12: Performance (top) and Energy (bottom) comparison between Mont-Blanc and MareNostrum 3.

Comparing CPU-only computing, a dual-core Mont-Blanc node is on average 18× slower than a 16-core MareNostrum 3 node. When using OpenCL to off-load all compute tasks to the GPU, Mont-Blanc is 14× slower than MareNostrum 3. Finally, using OmpSs to efficiently offload computation to both the GPU and the CPU, we significantly reduce the gap to only 9× across the benchmark suite.

Energy-wise, when using only the CPUs, a Mont-Blanc node consumes 7% more energy compared to a MareNostrum 3 node. As we close the performance gap, Mont-Blanc nodes become more energy efficient on average: from consuming 10% less energy when using only GPU, to consuming 40% less energy when using both GPU and CPU cores.

Our results show that, when using the embedded GPU, Mont-Blanc can be significantly more energy-efficient than a homogeneous cluster like MareNostrum 3. However, Mont-Blanc needs applications to scale up between 10× to 15× more nodes in order to match performance, and interconnection network performance is critical for that.

4.4.3   System Evaluation

Figure 4.13 shows the scalability of a set of MPI applications in terms of strong and weak scaling on the Mont-Blanc prototype. Each graph is accompanied with the corresponding parallel efficiency graph to provide more details about the applications scalability. Note that 16 Mont-Blanc nodes already span 2 EMB blades, and 32 nodes span 3 EMB blades. Also, most applications had their baseline run with > 1 node due to the 4GB/node DRAM limitation.

5 out of 8 applications show linearly scalability up to hundreds of nodes, with 4 of them still running at $> 50\%$ efficiency at the full scale of the system. BQCD and QE exhibit quick strong scaling degradation, but still run at $< 50\%$ efficiency on 64 nodes. The worst case is for SMMP, which quickly degrades starting at 32 nodes. Parallel efficiency drops to 50%, and performance flattens and even degrades at 512 nodes. Our results show that it is reasonable to scale applications to 16 nodes to compensate for the difference with a MareNostrum 3 node. However, not all applications will scale further to compensate for multiple MareNostrum 3 nodes.

Weak scaling results are much better. Most of the applications still run at $> 70\%$ efficiency at the maximum problem size. Notably, CoMD and SMMP run at $> 90\%$ efficiency, but QE and MP2C degrade to 60% efficiency. Detailed performance analysis reveals the causes for lack of scalability: besides the low bandwidth/high latency GbE network, the system suffers from lost packets in the interconnect, each incurring at least one Retransmission Time Out (RTO) and load imbalance introduced by scheduler preemptions. This is explained in detail in Section 4.6.2.

4.4.4   Node Power Profiling

Energy has two dimensions: power and time. Execution time depends on how the application performs on the underlying architecture. Power depends on how much the application stresses compute resources, processor physical implementation, and SoC power management. The power monitoring infrastructure in the Mont-Blanc prototype (Section 4.2.3) helps the user to reason about both factors. Comparing the power of different mappings[3] (CPU, GPU, or CPU+GPU), the user can estimate the speed-up required to compensate the power differences and run the system at the best energy efficiency point.

Figure 4.14 shows a high sampling rate power profile of one Mont-Blanc node for different mappings of the execution of the 3D-stencil benchmark. The different mappings include one CPU core (sequential), dual core (OpenMP), GPU (OpenCL), and GPU + 1 CPU (OmpSs).

Node idle power is 5.3W. This includes the static power of all components given that frequency scaling is disabled for benchmarking purposes. The average power consumption when running on one and two CPU cores is 7.8W and 9.5W respectively. This includes the power consumption of the SoC, memory subsystem, and network interface.

Node power when using the GPU and the GPU + 1 CPU is 8.8 and 11W, respectively. When running on the GPU alone, one of the cores is still active as a helper thread that synchronously launches kernels to the GPU and therefore blocks until they complete. When running OmpSs on the GPU + 1 CPU, one of the cores is the GPU helper and the other one runs a worker thread and contributes to computation, thus adding that extra power.

Results show that the extra power required by OmpSs because of adding one CPU core to GPU computation could outweigh the performance improvement, in turn leading to a higher energy-to-solution in the 3D stencil (3ds) benchmark (as we show in Figure 4.12).

From the results with other benchmarks, node power varies across different workloads although it remains in the same range seen in Figure 4.14. The maximum power seen for

---

[3]Counting only elements contributing to the computing.

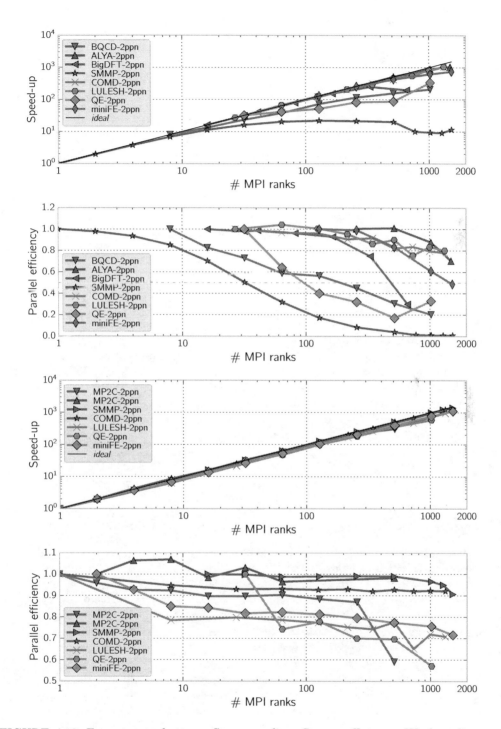

FIGURE 4.13: From top to bottom: Strong scaling, Strong efficiency, Weak scaling, and Weak efficiency.

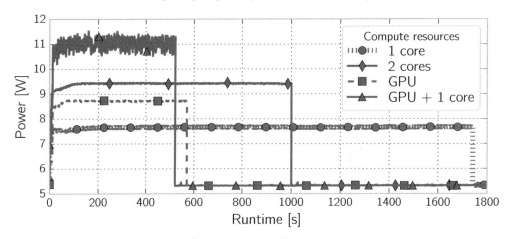

FIGURE 4.14: Power profile of different compute to hardware mappings for 3D-stencil computation. Note: markers are only to distinguish lines, not actual sampling points.

executions with two CPU cores is 14W, and 13.7W for executions with GPU plus one CPU core.

This shows the relevance of the power measurement infrastructure in the Mont-Blanc prototype. It explains where and how the power is being spent, even at high frequencies. The ability to visualize power over time is even more valuable for applications showing different phases that may benefit from different CPU-GPU mappings. This way, the user can identify the best mapping for each application phase.

In systems without a power profile (which just provide the total job energy consumption), such analysis requires a less accurate and time-consuming trial-and-error approach looking at power deltas over multiple runs of different configurations.

4.5   Deployment and Operational Information

The Mont-Blanc prototype has been deployed next to MareNostrum 3, the largest supercomputer in Spain, TIER-0 machine of the PRACE infrastructure and one of the top supercomputers in the world. The datacenter contains 160 square meters from which only 120 can be used for IT equipment. Outside the chapel resides the infrastructure equipment that provides a maximum of 5 MW with 3 transformers. The infrastructure also has 7 chillers which provide cold water that is distributed between 2 heat exchangers for those racks that are cooled with read door exchangers, and 6 computer room air handler units for those racks that are air cooled.

A total of 351 users have had access to the Mont-Blanc prototype in order to run their simulations and scientific applications, more than 35000 different jobs have been executed on the Mont-Blanc prototype since its deployment, in May 2015. Figure 4.15 shows the occupation statistics as reported by the SLURM job scheduler for the period between May 2nd 2015 and March 1st 2016. Even though it is based on mobile technology, the platform showed a good reliability during the duration of the project. During operational time the prototype had in fact only ~27% downtime, mostly due to prototype reconfiguration and some hardware issues. The following section analyzes one of the most impacting issues that

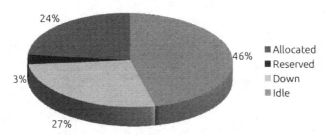

FIGURE 4.15: SLURM job statistics from May 2nd 2015 to March 1st 2016.

affected the Mont-Blanc prototype deployment: instability and variability due to thermal issues.

4.5.1 Thermal Experiments

Once the Mont-Blanc prototype was deployed and made available to execute applications and benchmarks to test the stability of the cluster, a high variability across the executions was observed, The variability was randomly caused by just some nodes, but were more frequent when executing large MPI executions using a large number of nodes. The misbehavior was studied both at node and blade level.

For this analysis the High Performance Linpack benchmark (HPL) was separately executed on all the nodes of one blade, systematically monitoring the following metrics: SoC temperature, CPU frequency and power consumption on each node, motherboard temperature, switch temperature, power consumption, and speed of the fans for each blade.

Figure 4.16 shows for a time frame of ~1.5 hours the fan speed of the blade (top) and the temperature of the nodes (bottom). When the temperature of the motherboard passes a threshold, the fans are activated at a higher RPM. After some time of stronger air flow, the overall temperature becomes lower, resulting in the fans also lowering their frequency. Even if with some time shift due to measurement buffering, a clear correlation is visible.

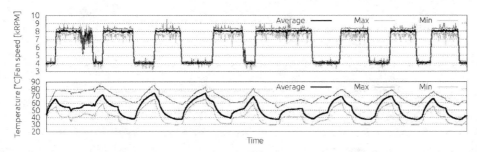

FIGURE 4.16: Thermal study of the original blade firmware: blade fan speed and (top), average temperature of the nodes (bottom).

This is the expected behavior; however, looking more carefully at the bottom part of Figure 4.16, one can observe a pretty large variation of the temperature of the compute node, and especially the maximum temperature ranging between 80 and 90 °C, close to throttling threshold.

Analyzing the operational frequency of the compute nodes, we spotted several nodes dropping their frequency to half the maximum in correspondence to high values of temperature. Those nodes were in fact suffering the automatic thermal throttling, a behavior of the hardware that is automatically limiting the frequency in case of reaching a temperature threshold (85°C) in order to avoid damage to the hardware. It is important to note that the frequency is not restored to its maximum once the temperature issue is solved, creating an obvious performance imbalance. This behavior is also confirmed by the power consumption of those nodes: whenever nodes throttle, power consumption also drops.

In order to fix the thermal throttling problem, we considered *i)* to increase the speed of the fans with a firmware update at blade level; *ii)* to power off nodes more affected by thermal throttling; *iii)* to modify the Linux kernel handling the throttling mechanism to ensure that frequency is restored once the thermal issue is solved.

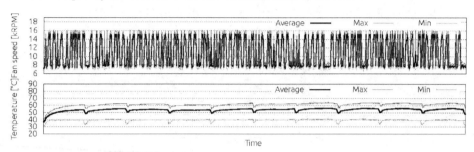

FIGURE 4.17: Thermal study of the improved blade firmware: blade fan speed and (top), average temperature of the nodes (bottom).

As a kernel update would have required a long outage time, we discarded the third option. The other two options were implemented and deployed. After the deployment of the fixes, we executed the same sanity checks on all the blades. Results corresponding to one execution of HPL on a critical blade are shown in Figure 4.17. We can observe that the higher fan speed corresponds to an obvious benefit in terms of temperature of the nodes, but also implies a higher power consumption of the blades (between 7 and 20% depending on the load). However, since some throttling problem still occurred on some nodes, we also powered down the most critical position, corresponding to node id 12, of each blade. The problem has been attributed to the physical design of the blade, which did not provide the appropriate air flow to these nodes.

4.6   Highlights of Mont-Blanc

As authors of this chapter, we decided to highlight in the following section the three main features that in our opinion make the Mont-Blanc prototype a perfect playground for detecting, measuring, studying, and alleviating effects of behaviors that will appear in future HPC systems.

The first study, presented in Section 4.6.1 and derived from [4], shows the results of a reliability study of the low power DDR3 memory system installed in the Mont-Blanc prototype. As the memory technology is inherited from a mobile market, it does not include error protection hardware support. Is it feasible to think about cost-efficient next generation HPC platforms with reduced hardware techniques for memory error protection?

Following the same line of questions, the second contribution in Section 4.6.2 analyzes the network retransmission issues and the noise introduced by the operating system. The limitations observed studying real HPC workloads on the Mont-Blanc prototype are similar to the ones we can expect in a large future HPC system where millions of threads will concur for a limited set of heterogeneous resources orchestrated by several instances of complex operating systems. Can we tune our systems and adapt the runtime in order to help HPC applications to survive in this "noisy" environment?

Our last highlight goes for the power monitoring system deployed at system level on the Mont-Blanc prototype. Being able to easily monitor the fine grained power consumption of large jobs is the first step for developing energy efficient improvements of next-generation HPC systems. This is the kind of in depth analysis offered in Section 4.6.3.

4.6.1 Reliability Study of an Unprotected RAM System

The Mont-Blanc prototype has allowed us to characterize DRAM memory errors on a large system operating without hardware ECC (i.e., the machine does not detect errors at the hardware level) and Low Power DDR technology (i.e., the supply voltage of LPDDR is lower, 1.2V, than standard DDR3, 1.5V). We note that a lower supply voltage makes the chip more susceptible to soft errors or silent data corruption since the critical charge to flip a bit is lower with lower voltage.

Memory error scanning tool. For the analysis it was necessary to develop a software level memory corruption detection mechanism that could run for long periods of time to gather enough data to guarantee statistical significance.

For each node, the memory scanning tool creates log entries when it starts/ stops scanning and when it detects a memory error. We orchestrate the execution of the memory scanner tool only when the node is idle by using the job scheduler and its *prologue* and *epilogue* scripts. The epilogue script contains a command that triggers the start of the memory scanning tool when a job completes. The memory scanner is basically an infinite loop; inside the loop every memory word is written with a specific value. At every iteration, the values are checked and updated with the bitwise negated value. If the expected and actual values do not match, an error is recorder in a log. The memory scanner continues executing on the node until a new job is scheduled. At this moment, the memory scanner receives a SIGTERM signal from the prologue and exits the infinite loop. After that, the new scheduled job starts execution.

Error extraction methodology. As explained above, the scanning tool logs every error observed in the system. However, not every error log is an independent error. In many cases, a fault in a memory cell manifests as many consecutive error logs over time, but they are all related to the same original root cause: a fault in one memory cell. Even if such a fault produced many incorrect values for thousands of consecutive iterations, **we count this as one single memory error** [4].

Memory scanned. A total of 923 compute nodes were continuously scanned for memory errors from February 2015 to February 2016 inclusive, accumulating over 4.2 million node-hours of error monitoring and logging over 25 million error logs. The study covered a total of $12,135$ Terabyte-hours of memory analysis.

Figure 4.18 shows the total number of hours that each node was scanned during the entire period of the study. In the figure, we map the system in 63 blades with 15 SoC per blade, each SoC being an independent node. We see that the first blades do not perform any error monitoring in the first SoC; this is because they are dedicated as login nodes.

Observe that the SoC number 12 of most blades did not get much monitoring time. As explained in Section 4.5.1, this node suffered from overheating due to its location in

---

[4]Given that we filter multiple error logs originating on the same root cause and count them as one single fault, we use the terms memory fault and memory error interchangeably in the remainder of this chapter.

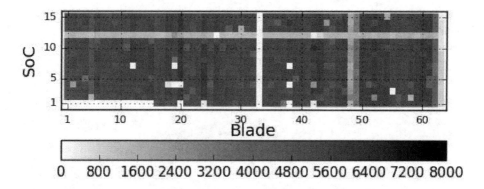

FIGURE 4.18: Hours each node was scanned for memory errors.

the blade. The system administrators decided to turn them off for long periods of time. There are also a few SoC that never got scanned as they were shut down due to hardware issues. Most nodes got about 5000 hours of error monitoring, which is more than half of the total period of the study. This large number of monitoring hours gives us a fair degree of statistical confidence on the results.

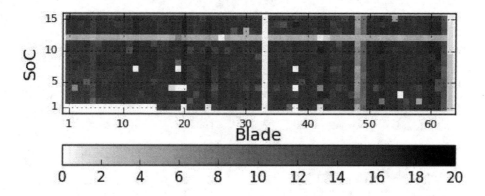

FIGURE 4.19: Amount of memory analyzed per node (Terabyte-Hours).

Figure 4.19 shows the total terabyte-hours that each node was scanned during the period of the study. We observe a strong correlation between this figure and the previous one, showing that a node with more hours of monitoring also scanned more memory, but we also see the presence of a few more marked differences between SoCs, compared to the previous figure. Overall, the vast majority of nodes scanned about 15 terabytes-hours, showing a rather homogeneous distribution.

Failure rate. At the end of the study, the error monitoring tool had logged over 25 million errors. Such a large number of errors is completely out of the expected failure rate for the studied prototype in normal conditions. As previously mentioned, not every error log is an independent memory error. Moreover, a simple analysis showed that over 98% of the observed failures came from the same node. This node was a faulty node that was removed from the job scheduler pool and is a classic case of a node that gets replaced in production systems. Thus, this node was also removed from the error characterization study. After these filters, the system logged over 55,000 independent memory errors, which corresponds to a node experiencing a memory error every 41 hours, or the cluster experiencing an error every 10 minutes. This raw failure rate is somewhat larger than expected, but it can be explained as we will see in the rest of this study.

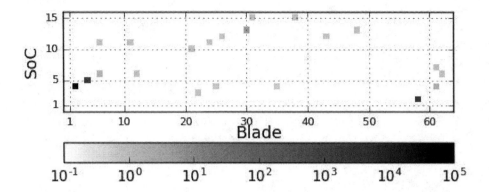

FIGURE 4.20: Number of independent memory errors for each node.

To analyze how the memory errors were distributed in the system, the heat map in Figure 4.20 was plotted. The map shows the raw number of memory errors observed for each node during the study. A first observation is that most of the nodes did not show any failure during the study (white color in the figure). Also, most nodes with failures had only one failure (dark blue spots). A few other nodes had thousands of failures (yellow, orange, and red spots). Note that these represent the raw number of errors and does not take into account the amount of time each node was scanned for errors. However, the most faulty nodes show orders of magnitude higher error rates than most other nodes, much higher than the difference of time scanned between nodes.

Multiple simultaneous corruptions. During this study we observed a total of 85 failures that corrupted multiple bits of a memory word. From those 85 cases, 76 were double-bit errors, which would be detected in a SECDED-protected system, potentially resulting in a process or system crash depending on the location and severity of the error in system memory space. The other 9 memory errors corrupted more than 2 bits, which could pass undetected by the ECC protection, leading to silent data corruption.

It is worth highlighting that about 90% of corrupted bits switched from 1 to 0 and only 10% the other way around. This is an indication that in the large majority of corruptions, the affected memory cell loses some charge. Another observation is that the majority of the multiple bit corruptions occur in the least significant bits of the word.

We observed that most double-bit errors were accompanied by other errors occurring simultaneously in other regions of the memory. We suspect that the affected memory cells are in physical proximity or alignment (row, column, bank); however, the memory controller maps them to different address words. These observations suggest that the root cause of such simultaneous errors could be linked to local hardware defects due to manufacturing variability, but they could also be related to external factors that affect multiple regions of the devices at the same time.

Relation between detectable and undetectable errors. The previous analysis gives us some correlations between correctable and uncorrectable (detectable) errors. Now we try to analyze the relation between detectable and undetectable errors. In particular, we focus on errors with more than 3 bit-flips. Not only did we not find any errors occurring at the same time, but in addition, those nodes did not show any other error during the entire study. Those 7 undetectable errors occurred in 5 different nodes that did not show **any** other error in the whole period. In fact, 4 of those undetectable errors occurred in a node that had only the one error. Moreover, other nodes did not log any strange activity at the time of those undetectable errors. That is to say, *those cases of undetectable errors are extremely silent* in that they are both undetectable by hardware mechanisms and completely uncorrelated to detectable errors.

We noticed that 6 of these errors occurred before we turned off the overheating nodes and 4 of the concerned nodes are located near them. Overheating could have partially damaged part of the memory, making them more prone to SDC. Unfortunately, these errors occurred before we started to login the temperature of the system, so we do not know the temperature of the concerned nodes at the moment of the corruption. However, temperature seems to be an unlikely direct cause given that no other errors were logged. Independent of the root cause, it is surprising that no other corruption was detected in those nodes or in other nodes at the same time.

Conclusion.   The study presented in this first author's choice study revealed the presence of multiple single-bit errors occurring simultaneously in different regions of the memory. Moreover, a large fraction of double-bit errors happened simultaneously with single-bit errors in other parts of the memory, showing a correlation between correctable and uncorrectable errors. Furthermore, we present disturbing evidence of SDC occurring in an isolated and independent fashion, making it extremely hard to detect and/or predict.

4.6.2   Network Retransmission and OS Noise Study

The use of commodity technologies was also considered when choosing the interconnection network for the Mont-Blanc prototype and software infrastructure. In this second author's section, we analyze the effect of choosing an Ethernet based network, as well as operate a standard instance of the Linux operating system of each of the Mont-Blanc compute nodes. Two particular issues are discussed in this section: retransmissions due to lost packets in the network and system noise due to pre-emptions.

Lost packets.   First we evaluate the impact of network retransmission that happen in the system. For the study, we used one of the applications analyzed in Section 4.4.3: CoMD. Figure 4.21 shows an execution profile for a real execution and a simulated one, using Dimemas, in which all network retransmissions were eliminated. Both traces have the same time scale. The x axis represents time, the y axis represents the process number.

The simulated profile shows that the native execution suffered from a lot of lost packets (most application's communication phases suffer from at least 1 retransmission), reducing performance by $1.47\times$. This is of course application dependent, and depends on the communication patterns, message sizes, volume of communication, etc.

Further analysis of the duration of MPI send operations shows that CoMD experiences multiple retransmissions per packet, with an average MPI send duration of 158ms (compared to 50ms optimum), and often reaching 400ms.

The top part of Figure 4.22 shows the performance degradation as a function of how many nodes experience a retransmission penalty on every message they send. The results show that the penalty is linear with respect to the retransmission delay. But more important, the results show that as soon as one node has to retransmit, the whole application pays almost the full penalty.

The bottom part of Figure 4.22 shows the performance degradation as a function of how many messages need to be retransmitted (by any node). The results show that the

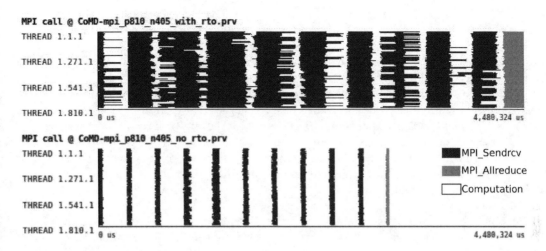

FIGURE 4.21: Illustration of the packet loss effect on MPI parallel applications. Packet loss in place (top) and No packet loss (bottom).

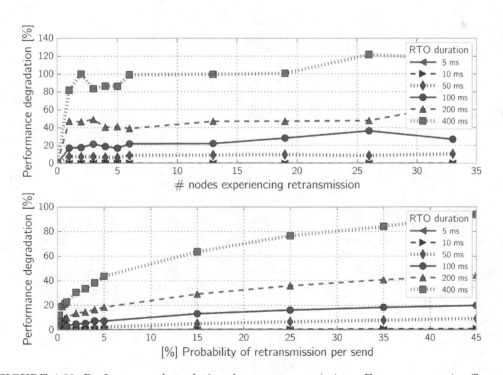

FIGURE 4.22: Performance degradation due to retransmissions: Every message is affected for selected nodes (top) and Random messages are affected (bottom).

penalty is linear with the retransmission delay and the retransmission probability. Both results combined indicate that it is important to avoid retransmissions in the whole system, or to cluster retransmissions in time, because as soon as one node has to retransmit, it does not matter if others also have to retransmit. For example, a glitch in a switch that causes all nodes connected to it to retransmit would have a similar penalty to a glitch in the NIC of one of the nodes, forcing it alone to retransmit.

To minimize the penalty of retransmissions, we reduced the RTOmin parameter in the TCP/IP stack from the default 200ms to 5ms (the lowest possible in our system). While the lowering of RTOmin parameter reduces retransmission penalties, it would be desirable implementing Retransmission Early Detection (RED) to reduce the effects of retransmissions. However, packet loss does not exclusively happen at switch buffers, but we also observed that nodes can drop packets. In addition, our blade switches, which forward most of the network traffic, do not support Explicit Congestion Notification (ECN) markings, thus not being able to control transmission rates.

Pre-emptions. The second issue commented in this section is system noise produced by pre-emptions, again for the same application also used before: CoMD. Figure 4.23 shows a histogram of the duration of computational phases in the real application execution. The gradient color shows the total time spent in computation phase of a given duration (green/light is low, blue/dark is high).

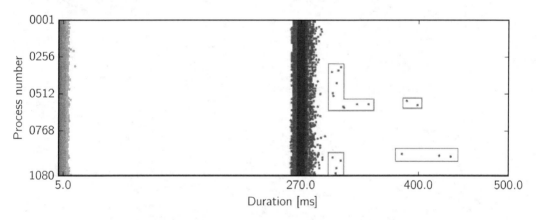

FIGURE 4.23: 2D Histogram of computational phases duration.

The figure shows two main regions of 5ms and 270ms durations. The x axis represents bins of durations, the y axis represents process number. Gradient coloring: green-blue. Coloring function: logarithmic. We matched the 5ms regions to the TCP/IP retransmissions (matching the 5ms RTO setting, and confirming that many processes suffer retransmissions). Then, the remaining time was spent in 270ms regions, matching the duration of one inner iteration of the application. Beyond the 270ms boundary, we identified a set of outliers taking significantly more time (marked with red polygons). Checking the IPC of these computation phases, we confirmed that the divergence in execution time is not related to load imbalance in the application. There were external factors introducing this variation. We attributed them to scheduler preemptions, which produced OS noise.

Based on these observations, further simulations of different noise injection frequencies and noise duration were performed, whose main results indicate that the performance impact of OS noise is linear with the probability of noise being injected, and the ratio for the noise duration to the computational burst. That is, applications with short computational bursts are more prone to suffer OS noise performance degradation than applications with long computational bursts.

4.6.3   The Power Monitoring Tool of the Mont-Blanc System

As extensively reported in this chapter, the primary objective of the Mont-Blanc project has been to design and realize an energy-efficient HPC prototype based on commercially available, off-the-shelf embedded technologies. One of the key requirements for achieving this result relies in the capability of retrieving and storing detailed information on the power consumption of the system. In this regard, a holistic power monitoring tool has been developed for keeping track of the power and energy consumed by the platform at node level and for making this information available to the resource and job management system. Aside from standard health monitoring features such as hardware failure detection, this further enables the opportunity of defining novel energy-aware scheduling strategies and/or energy-based user accounting policies for a more energy-efficient operation of the prototype.

Power acquisition process and software architecture of the power monitoring tool. The tool has been designed to fit the custom nature of the architecture of the Mont-Blanc prototype and the specific "out-of-band" process for acquiring power consumption data at node level. More in detail, each compute node has a dedicated power sensor installed on its hosting blade. This last also comprises a Board Management Controller (BMC), which, among other tasks, is responsible for managing data communication between system management software and platform hardware. The blade further hosts an FPGA responsible for handling the parallel collection and pre-processing of power consumption readings. The acquisition of power samples is realized as follows: every 1120ms, the FPGA accesses all the power sensors of the 15 SDBs hosted in the blade via I^2C at the same time; each of the obtained 15 power values corresponds to an average of 16 power samples (at node level) performed in an interval of time of approximately 70ms. Once acquired by the FPGA, the 15 power values are stored in an internal FIFO buffer. The BMC polls the FPGA buffer every 500 ms retrieving all the available power samples, subsequently associating a time stamp to the readings and storing them in its DDR2 memory. The data can finally be retrieved via customized Intelligent Platform Management Interface (IPMI) raw commands.

The envisioned Mont-Blanc power monitoring tool conveniently encapsulates the power sample acquisition process described so far with the software architecture illustrated in Figure 4.24. Specifically, the tool consists of three major software components:

- a key-value store, responsible for storing the monitored power data,

- one or more "pushers", for polling out-of-band power consumption data from the BMC of the monitored device according to a specific protocol (in the Mont-Blanc system case, via IPMI),

- one or more "collect agents", which gather all the power data acquired by the pushers and transmit it to the key-value store.

Application example of the power monitoring tool in the Mont-Blanc prototype. Despite its simplicity, the tool proves to be very effective in finding common sources of errors in the power measurement setup, such as synchronization gaps between the database and the BMCs, unusual power consumption values due to potential hardware failures, as well as other irregularities. As an exercise, the power monitoring tool was extensively tested in order to verify that sensor data would be properly collected. Specifically, a small test script was

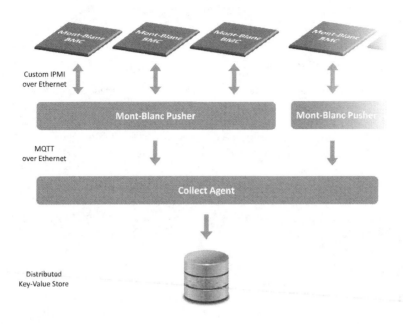

FIGURE 4.24: Software architecture of the power monitoring tool.

written that performs 5 cycles of CPU-intense calculations for 30 seconds, followed by 30 seconds of idle. If both the power data acquisition and storage processes work as expected, the 5 application cycles should be clearly visible in the application's power trace obtained from the database (as correctly depicted in Figure 4.25 Left). It should be noted that the CPU-intense phases run fully out of the CPUs L1 cache, meaning there is no stress on the memory or the GPU resulting in lower power consumption than other benchmarks. To assess the Mont-Blanc prototype's power measurement correctness, the test benchmark was executed on all compute nodes and the resulting graphs have undergone visual inspection.

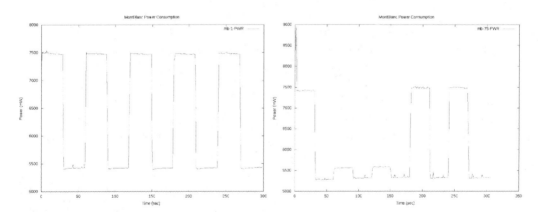

FIGURE 4.25: Power trace of the power cycle test application. Node behaves as expected (left) and with power and performance issues (right).

This analysis revealed a couple of blades in which for some of the nodes, the power and performance was not stable across iterations (as shown in Figure 4.25 Right). Further experiments showed that the drop in power consumption always came along with a drop in compute performance at which it became clear that this rather exhibits a performance problem instead of a problem in the power measurement setup. Since other users of the machine also experienced issues related to performance variations, the problem was subsequently narrowed down to a cooling issue that could be mitigated by moving towards a more aggressive fan speed policy and disabling of peculiar nodes. After these changes, subsequent runs of the test application no longer exhibited this power and performance variation.

To ensure that the prototype was in good shape, histograms of the temperature and power distribution were generated from the data obtained before and after stabilizing the system. Figure 4.26 shows that the new fan speed policy was successful in lowering SoC temperatures (with the aim to avoid any temperature related throttling).

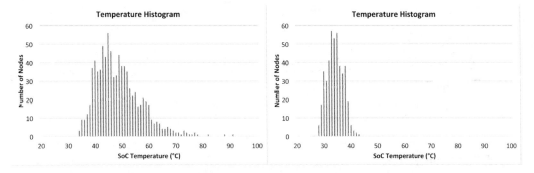

FIGURE 4.26: Temperature histogram of the prototype's SoC temperatures. Initial system (left) and Reworked system (right).

4.7 Acknowledgments

The research leading to results reported in this chapter has received funding from the European Commission's Seventh Framework Programme [FP7/2007-2013] and Horizon 2020 under the Mont-Blanc projects, grant agreements number 288777, 610402, and 671697. The project also received support from national funding agencies, including the Spanish Government through Programa Severo Ochoa (SEV-2015-0493), by the Spanish Ministry of Science and Technology (project TIN2015-65316-P), and by the Generalitat de Catalunya (grants 2017-SGR-1328 and 2017-SGR-1414). Authors also acknowledge Oriol Vilarrubi Barri and the Operations Department at the Barcelona Supercomputing Center for their support in the deployment of the prototype.

Bibliography

[1] Rosa M. Badia, Jesus Labarta, Judit Gimenez, and Francesc Escale. DIMEMAS: Predicting MPI applications behavior in Grid environments. In *Workshop on Grid Applications and Programming Tools (GGF8)*, volume 86, pages 52–62, 2003.

[2] Barcelona Supercomputing Center. BSC Performance Analysis Tools. https://tools. bsc.es/.

[3] Barcelona Supercomputing Center. MareNostrum III (2013) System Architecture. https://www.bsc.es/marenostrum/marenostrum/mn3.

[4] Leonardo Bautista-Gomez, Ferad Zyulkyarov, Osman Unsal, and Simon McIntosh-Smith. Unprotected Computing: A Large-scale Study of DRAM Raw Error Rate on a Supercomputer. In *Proceedings of the International Conference for High Performance Computing, Networking, Storage and Analysis*, SC '16, pages 55:1–55:11, Piscataway, NJ, USA, 2016. IEEE Press.

[5] Kallia Chronaki, Alejandro Rico, Rosa M Badia, Eduard Ayguadé, Jesús Labarta, and Mateo Valero. Criticality-aware dynamic task scheduling for heterogeneous architectures. In *Proceedings of the 29th ACM on International Conference on Supercomputing*, pages 329–338. ACM, 2015.

[6] Lamia Djoudi, Denis Barthou, Patrick Carribault, Christophe Lemuet, Jean-Thomas Acquaviva, William Jalby, et al. Maqao: Modular assembler quality analyzer and optimizer for Itanium 2. In *The 4th Workshop on EPIC architectures and compiler technology, San Jose*, volume 200, 2005.

[7] Alejandro Duran, Eduard Ayguadé, Rosa M Badia, Jesús Labarta, Luis Martinell, Xavier Martorell, and Judit Planas. OmpSs: a proposal for programming heterogeneous multi-core architectures. *Parallel Processing Letters*, 21(02):173–193, 2011.

[8] Markus Geimer, Felix Wolf, Brian JN Wylie, Erika Ábrahám, Daniel Becker, and Bernd Mohr. The Scalasca performance toolset architecture. *Concurrency and Computation: Practice and Experience*, 22(6):702–719, 2010.

[9] Jülich Supercomputing Centre. Jülich Supercomputing Centre – HPC technology. http://www.fz-juelich.de/ias/jsc/EN/Research/HPCTechnology/PerformanceAnalyse/ performanceAnalysis_node.html.

[10] Andreas Knüpfer, Christian Rössel, Dieter an Mey, Scott Biersdorff, Kai Diethelm, Dominic Eschweiler, Markus Geimer, Michael Gerndt, Daniel Lorenz, Allen Malony, et al. Score-P: A joint performance measurement run-time infrastructure for Periscope, Scalasca, TAU, and Vampir. In *Tools for High Performance Computing 2011*, pages 79–91. Springer, 2012.

[11] Krishna T. Malladi, Benjamin C. Lee, Frank A. Nothaft, Christos Kozyrakis, Karthika Periyathambi, and Mark Horowitz. Towards Energy-proportional Datacenter Memory with Mobile DRAM. In *Proceedings of the 39th Annual International Symposium on Computer Architecture*, ISCA '12, pages 37–48, 2012.

[12] Mathias Nachtmann and José Gracia. Enabling model-centric debugging for task-based programming models–a tasking control interface. In *Tools for High Performance Computing 2015*, pages 147–160. Springer, 2016.

[13] Vincent Pillet, Jesús Labarta, Toni Cortes, and Sergi Girona. Paraver: A tool to visualize and analyze parallel code. In *Proceedings of WoTUG-18: transputer and occam developments*, volume 44, pages 17–31. IOS Press, 1995.

[14] Nikola Rajovic, Paul M. Carpenter, Isaac Gelado, Nikola Puzovic, Alex Ramirez, and Mateo Valero. Supercomputing with commodity CPUs: Are mobile SoCs ready for HPC? In *Proceedings of the International Conference on High Performance Computing, Networking, Storage and Analysis*, SC '13, pages 40:1–40:12, New York, NY, USA, 2013. ACM.

[15] Nikola Rajovic, Alejandro Rico, Filippo Mantovani, Daniel Ruiz, Josep Oriol Vilarrubi, Constantino Gomez, Luna Backes, Diego Nieto, Harald Servat, Xavier Martorell, Jesus Labarta, Eduard Ayguade, Chris Adeniyi-Jones, Said Derradji, Hervé Gloaguen, Piero Lanucara, Nico Sanna, Jean-Francois Mehaut, Kevin Pouget, Brice Videau, Eric Boyer, Momme Allalen, Axel Auweter, David Brayford, Daniele Tafani, Volker Weinberg, Dirk Brömmel, René Halver, Jan H. Meinke, Ramon Beivide, Mariano Benito, Enrique Vallejo, Mateo Valero, and Alex Ramirez. The Mont-blanc Prototype: An Alternative Approach for HPC Systems. In *Proceedings of the International Conference for High Performance Computing, Networking, Storage and Analysis*, SC '16, pages 38:1–38:12, Piscataway, NJ, USA, 2016. IEEE Press.

[16] Nikola Rajovic, Alejandro Rico, Nikola Puzovic, Chris Adeniyi Jones, and Alex Ramirez Tibidabo: Making the case for an ARM-based HPC system. *Future Generation Computer Systems*, 36:322–334, July 2014.

[17] Nikola Rajovic, Alejandro Rico, James Vipond, Isaac Gelado, Nikola Puzovic, and Alex Ramirez. Experiences with Mobile Processors for Energy Efficient HPC. In *Proceedings of the Conference on Design, Automation and Test in Europe*, DATE '13, pages 464–468, San Jose, CA, USA, 2013. EDA Consortium.

[18] Nikola Rajovic, Lluis Vilanova, Carlos Villavieja, Nikola Puzovic, and Alex Ramirez. The low power architecture approach towards exascale computing. *Journal of Computational Science*, 4(6):439–443, 2013.

[19] Pavel Saviankou, Michael Knobloch, Anke Visser, and Bernd Mohr. Cube v4: From performance report explorer to performance analysis tool. *Procedia Computer Science*, 51:1343–1352, 2015.

[20] Brice Videau, Kevin Pouget, Luigi Genovese, Thierry Deutsch, Dimitri Komatitsch, Frédéric Desprez, and Jean-François Méhaut. BOAST: A metaprogramming framework to produce portable and efficient computing kernels for hpc applications. *The International Journal of High Performance Computing Applications*, page 1094342017718068, 2017.

Chapter 5

Chameleon: A Scalable Production Testbed for Computer Science Research

Kate Keahey, Pierre Riteau

Computation Institute, University of Chicago

Dan Stanzione, Tim Cockerill

Texas Advanced Computing Center

Joe Mambretti

Northwestern University

Paul Rad

University of Texas at San Antonio

Paul Ruth

Renaissance Computing Institute

5.1   Overview

5.1.1   A Case for a Production Testbed

Computer Science experiments, whether they comprise the development of new system tools and algorithms or performance evaluation of new hardware, typically require direct access to resources that support deep reconfigurability, the ability to work in an isolated environment, as well as experimenting at scale and on up-to-date hardware. Direct access and *deep reconfigurability*, including e.g., the ability to make modifications to the firmware, reboot from a custom kernel, or change a range of other options in the configuration stack, is essential for the experimenter to fully explore a range of interesting phenomena. Strong isolation between different experiments is fundamental to the observation process: it ensures that the results of the experiments are not impacted by the activities of other users or the system and is typically provided by giving a user a *lease*: a temporary, exclusive ownership of a resource between well-defined points in time. And finally, the ability to experiment at scale and on state-of-the-art hardware ensures the research on the platform can be impactful as new hardware features, such as e.g., the introduction of hardware virtualization [65], often revolutionize the technological needs and open up new opportunities for research.

These requirements conflict with configuration provided by traditional resources targeting domain applications that provide only a very narrow interface to the user (usually via job submission) as well as most private and commercial clouds that support a shared environment, typically limit reconfigurability options, or offer their capabilities at small scales only. Configuration trade-offs with these systems range from complexity (i.e., users who simply want to run jobs on supported environments versus users who want to experiment with building such environments) to utilization and cost (i.e., the need for isolated experimental environments conflicts with the desire to amortize costs possible in multi-tenant environments). In recognition of this fact, operating institutions typically set up dedicated testbed resources for the specific purpose of experimenting with a new architecture or serving as a testing and integration environment for tools and systems prior to their deployment on production scale resources.

The word "testbed" is thus typically associated with such special access resources. Such systems typically serve small groups of users with special access privileges, at scales that correspond to the amount of amortization this usage can give, and operate under the policy that "things may break", possible to arbitrate in a small group. In contrast to this type of an experimental testbed, Chameleon's goal is to provide a *production testbed*, i.e., to define a set of production services that will enable its users to allocate, for a limited period of time, a private testbed that will support all the kind of exploration possible in a small dedicated testbed—or more. This mode of usage makes it possible for many users to have exclusive usage of part of the testbed at different times and thus arbitrate access across a larger user community. This in turn allows for better leverage of investment in testbed resources, both as to scale and state-of-the-art, and thereby ultimately makes Computer Science experimentation and exploration cheaper and more accessible.

As a production testbed, Chameleon allows users to create private testbeds composed of potentially hundreds of nodes of different architectures, thousands of cores, and PBs of storage out of a total of 600+ nodes and 5 PB of storage deployed by the system. The private testbeds created by users may choose from a wide array of innovative hardware comprising fast interconnects, a variety of accelerators and memory devices, or innovative architectures such as ARMs, Atoms, or FPGAs. Those resources are available on a national scale and are currently used by 1,800+ users working on 250+ research and education projects.

Our goal of building a production testbed received substantial assistance from the fact that today's cloud technologies have matured to the point where it is possible for us to build a system largely based on a commodity, widely supported open source cloud computing software, specifically OpenStack [51]. While we had to adapt and extend OpenStack to make it a suitable tool for our goals, the benefits of working with a widely supported system allow us to leverage a considerable community investment into its maintenance and further development, as well as allow us to leverage the familiarity with the system already existing in the community of both operators and users. Since our extensions and modifications are contributed back to the project, we are also enabling a new application for cloud technology: a production testbed. Ultimately, our intent is to leverage the confluence of developments in cloud computing infrastructure and better understanding of experimental requirements for Computer Science to make production testbeds more sustainable and thus enable more experimentation of all kinds.

The idea of a production testbed is not new. Grid'5000 [10, 6] in France has developed a testbed providing deeply reconfigurable leases to its users over the last decade, though its capabilities do not focus exclusively on support for Computer Science experiments and include support for domain science work as well. In the United States, the Emulab [66] project, the PRObE project [24], which deployed Emulab on retired clusters donated by DOE facilities, and the CloudLab project [58], which represents most recent deployment of Emulab, have all worked within roughly the same model. The most significant difference in our approach is that while all these systems develop custom software to implement this model, Chameleon builds on a widely-used commodity software project and works with the community to extend it to fit our use case.

Other significant production testbeds included the OpenCirrus [4] and FutureGrid [64, 23] projects, which also operated on the idea of providing a reconfigurable resource lease to a user though in the case of both, this lease was implemented by virtual machine deployment rather than bare metal reconfiguration. While this type of lease is capable of supporting some of Computer Science research projects, it does not support many projects in e.g., virtualization, operating systems, and power management that require direct access to the hardware (i.e., without the additional layer of a hypervisor). More recently, a similar mode of providing resources has been provided by resources such as Jetstream [61], Bridges [53], Comet [62]—as well as commercial clouds [2, 28, 45].

Another type of production testbed focuses primarily on providing capabilities for networking experiments and extends the concept of a lease (implemented either via virtualization or bare metal reconfiguration) into the networking area by creating the concept of a slice, an isolated virtual circuit suitable for conducting experiments. The PlanetLab testbed [15] was a pioneer in this area and the GENI [7] project developed its concepts and continues to provide a platform for this type of research. As we seek to provide corresponding capabilities in the networking area (see Section 5.9.1), the differences here focus primarily on hardware configuration of the testbed: Chameleon hardware strategy focuses on achieving scale within sites at the cost of having relatively few sites, while the networking testbeds emphasize wide distribution at the cost of allocating very few resources per site.

5.1.2 Program Background

The Chameleon project was developed under a three-year mid-scale infrastructure grant awarded in the fall of 2014 by the National Science Foundation (NSF) under solicitation NSF 13-602 [46] for the development and deployment of a research infrastructure supporting exploration on topics ranging from cloud computing architectures and virtualization, to software-defined networking technologies, cyber-physical systems, high-performance computing, and innovative applications. The ultimate intent of the platform was to enable researchers to go beyond the use of existing commercial cloud offerings and allow them to influence such offerings in the future.

The Chameleon project is led by the University of Chicago in collaboration with partners in Northwestern University, Ohio State University (OSU), Texas Advanced Computing Center (TACC), and University of San Antonio (UTSA).

The original NSF Cloud solicitation anticipated two phases of the NSFCloud program. During the first 3-year phase to be completed in the fall of 2017 a supplement investment in the networking capabilities of the testbed added the Renaissance Computing Institute (RENCI) to the list of partners. The project was reviewed in the Spring of 2017 and subsequently awarded phase 2 funding for another 3 years, starting in October 2017.

5.1.3   Timeline

The Chameleon project started in October 2014. The first months were devoted to establishing basic user services for Chameleon users on hardware repurposed from an earlier FutureGrid project [23, 64] of which both the University of Chicago and TACC were partners. In parallel with these activities, we evaluated technology suitable for the implementation of a production testbed as described above and meeting our criteria of sustainability. OpenStack with the Ironic component (implementing bare metal reconfiguration) was selected as a result. Accordingly, in January 2015 we began construction of a technology preview of CHameleon Infrastructure (CHI) based on OpenStack, which implemented core capabilities of the testbed. The technology preview was released in early April 2015, still on FutureGrid hardware. In June 2015, we accepted the majority of the new Chameleon system hardware, consisting of 12 racks of homogenous nodes (42 Intel Haswell compute nodes + 4 storage nodes per rack) distributed between the University of Chicago and TACC and configured it with the technology preview; it was made available to early users in June of 2015. By the end of July 2015 this initial system was publically released. In September of 2015 we made available a KVM cloud on a modest partition complementing the bare metal reconfiguration capabilities of the testbed and serving primarily educational projects.

The following years saw the incremental deployment of new CHI capabilities and new hardware. Roughly every quarter we added new capabilities including console access, appliance catalog and appliance management tools, support for complex appliances, and a variety of ease of use improvements. We also added new hardware capabilities ranging from global store to heterogeneous elements including memory hierarchy nodes, a variety of GPUs, FPGAs, ARM, and Atom processors, as well as low-power Xeons. As of this writing, Chameleon is entering phase 2, which will deploy new hardware, broaden the experimental capabilities to support a significantly larger set of networking experiments, and add another dimension to the testbed by providing repeatability mechanisms.

5.2   Hardware Architecture

The original Chameleon system was designed to cover a wide range of community needs. The guiding principles of our hardware design were a trade-off of two concerns: on one hand we wanted the users to have the flexibility to explore tradeoffs and alternatives in every hardware aspect, including processor, storage, and network, and on the other we wanted to provide them sufficient size to test research ideas at scale. We solved this trade-off by first allocating most of our investment into large-scale homogenous hardware, that was then concentrated in one institution (TACC), then adding heterogenous elements onto this homogenous base, and finally supplementing it with a smaller investment in stand alone heterogeneous clusters representing different architectures.

5.2.1 Projected Use Cases

The design of the hardware required reflection about the types of research that the "cloud research community", broadly defined, might undertake, in order to configure a system that would properly support them. The testbed is intended to support a wide variety of architecture tradeoffs, for instance, what is the potential benefits of thick cores vs thin cores in cloud applications? What alternative processor architectures should be considered in the cloud? What impacts are there to alternative network architectures? How might storage—both local and remote—be optimally configured, and what is the benefit of alternative storage technologies? At an application level, user might wish to consider alternative strategies for fault tolerance and load balancing. An important use case was to consider impacts of distributed data centers in cloud applications, from the perspective of latency, reliability, or quality of service. The team considered what might a researcher want to measure and observe for each of these use cases, and at what scale these might be most relevant.

The team tailored the Chameleon design in phase 1 (below) to enable all of these research cases. Observations of how the user community took advantage of this design follows the hardware description, and led to some alterations in our approach in the second phase of the project. Following our principles, Chameleon is designed to be multi-site, to address the distributed cases above, to have heterogeneity to support various architectural tradeoffs, yet to have suitably large homogenous partitions to support scaling studies. At the same time, the design of both hardware and software were focused on allowing a greater degree of configurability than would be permitted in the commercial cloud, to support all of the use cases above.

5.2.2 Phase 1 Chameleon Deployment

The Phase 1 architecture consists of a set of *standard cloud units (SCUs)*, each of which contains 42 capable compute nodes, 4 storage nodes attached to 128TB of local storage in configurable arrays, and an OpenFlow [43] compliant network switch. The SCUs are supplemented by a set of *heterogeneous cloud units (HCUs)* that were deployed over the life of phase 1 of the project and incorporate a wide variety of alternate processor and network technologies within the testbed.

The testbed also includes a *shared infrastructure* that includes a persistent storage system accessible across the testbed, a top level network gateway to allow access to public networks, and a set of management and provisioning servers to support user access, control, monitoring and configuration of the testbed. The testbed is physically distributed between the two operating sites (UC and TACC) connected by 100Gbps Internet2 links, to allow users to examine the effects of a distributed cloud. The conceptual architecture of the phase 1 testbed is shown in Figure 5.1.

Standard Cloud Units The standard cloud unit is a self-contained rack with all the components necessary to run a complete cloud infrastructure, and the capability to combine with other units to form a larger experiment. The original racks consisted of 42 Dell R630 and R730 servers; each with 24 cores delivered in dual socket Intel Haswell processors, each with 128GB of RAM. In addition to the compute servers, each unit contained storage provided by four Dell FX2 servers, each of which have attached 16 2TB hard drives, for a total of 128TB of raw disk storage per unit (and more than a PB throughout the testbed of user-configurable storage). Each node in the SCU is connected to a Force 10 switch at 10Gbps, with 160Gbps of bandwidth to the core network from each SCU. The total system contains 12 SCUs (2 at UC and 10 at TACC) for a total of more than 13,000 cores, 50TB of RAM, and 1.5PB of configurable storage in the initial phase 1 SCU subsystem.

Heterogeneous Cloud Units   There are several hardware related scenarios that can not be explored through a homogeneous testbed. The debate between "thick core and thin core" continues to be active in the community for a variety of algorithms and power consumption scenarios, as well as a strong interest in cloud applications that utilize accelerators or reconfigurable hardware. Increasingly, there is renewed interest not only in coprocessors, such as GPUs, but also reconfigurable hardware such as FPGAs, and specialized processors such as Tensor Processing Units (TPUs). The HCUs provide alternate hardware to allow a fuller exploration of the space. The testbed evolved over time, based on both user demand and hardware availability, throughout phase 1 of the project. One rack was equipped with an EDR InfiniBand rack to explore alternate networks (additional networking technologies are being deployed in phase 2). Different processor types were also deployed in HCUs, including 24 ARM64-based microservers, 8 Intel Atom-based microservers, and 8 low-power Xeon microservers. A number of nodes were equipped with GPUs; initially with NVIDIA K80 and M40 GPU cards, and later with P100 cards. A final upgrade to the phase 1 system

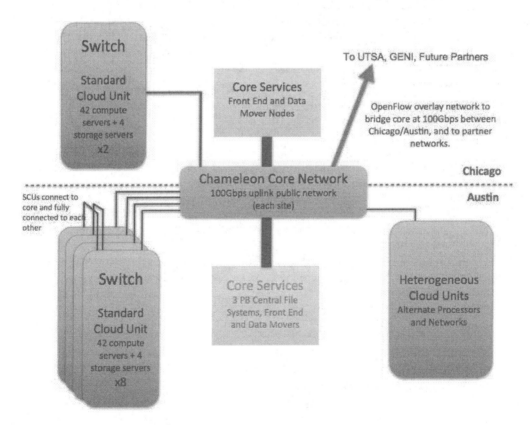

FIGURE 5.1: Chameleon Architecture.

consists of additional P100 GPUs deployed in servers with NVLINK connectivity between the GPUs in each server. Four additional servers were equipped with Altera FPGAs.

Testbed Networking   Networks continue to evolve, and the network fabric is as much a part of the research focus of Chameleon as the compute or storage. Each Chameleon node connects to this network at 10Gbps, and from each unit four 40Gbps uplinks provide 160Gbps per rack to the Chameleon core network. The core switch aggregates to 100Gbps Ethernet links, which connect to the backbone 100Gbps services at both UC and TACC. A separate 1 Gbps Ethernet management network extends to every node, to maintain monitoring and connectivity when the research network is either isolated from the public networks or otherwise in an experimental mode. An Enhanced Data Rate (EDR) InfiniBand network (104Gbps) was also deployed on one SCU rack.

Shared Infrastructure   While different types of storage are made available to researchers as part of node allocations, Chameleon also provides a shared storage system to store appliances, experimental data, and other artifacts. The shared storage consists of more than 3.6PB of raw disk in the initial configuration, which is partitioned between an appliance/image store and an object store that provides persistent storage for experiments. A dozen management nodes provide for login access to the resource, data staging, system monitoring, and hosting a variety of other resources described in the following sections.

5.2.3   Experience with Phase 1 Hardware and Future Plans

Experience with the first phase of Chameleon have yielded lessons learned for the future expansion of our system, as well as production testbeds in general. First, we believe that Chameleon represents adequate scale to address most experimental scenarios that have been brought to the system thus far: researchers are more commonly seeking a diversity of capabilities or a particular capability than the full scale of the testbed. Second, our experience has been that newly released technologies are in constant demand. Each enhancement we have made to the system has brought a few new projects; both new users, and new kinds of research, from the addition of FPGAs, low power processors, or new generations of GPUs. Third, we have observed that some of those capabilities have emerged since the initial proposal was submitted four years ago—our ability to be flexible and adapt the testbed was an asset, and will likely continue to be over the next several years.

Three particular very specific sub-groups were identified as needing specialized capabilities, and in areas that have changed substantively since the phase one submission. First, we see disproportionate growth in demand for experiments related to machine and deep learning; and particularly demand for GPUs to support this work. Second, a subset of the community wishes to exploit more flexible software defined networking (SDN) capabilities— and this market has matured in many ways since the initial proposal, when most vendors had a "toe in the water" with SDN, but there was no coherent adoption of even proper subsets of standards. Finally, there is demand for a wider range of storage options—faster local scratch storage, and more types of persistent storage at each site.

Given these considerations, our phase 2 investments will focus on adding specific capabilities and refresh at smaller scales, rather than attempting a large expansion or costly forklift upgrade of the full system. Accordingly, we plan a modest refresh of the SCUs via an acquisition of four additional Dell EMC PowerEdge SCUs: three containing the latest generation of Intel Xeon processors (Skylake) (two at Chicago and one at TACC), and a fourth containing the following generation of Intel processor Ice Lake (TACC). The nodes will be expanded to 2U chassis, to provide the maximum flexibility in allowing for additional expansion cards. We will further add an additional 16 nodes with 32 top of the line

NVIDIA GPUs—perhaps the most oversubscribed component in Chameleon today—with eight nodes at each site. To address the need for SDN experimentation we plan to acquire DP2000 series switches from Corsa; the two DP2400 switches with 100 Gb uplinks to be deployed at Chicago and a single DP2200 switch at TACC. This will allow 100Gb end-to-end testing over the WAN with full SDN capability at each end. Finally, we will add additional storage servers to increase persistent object storage at Chicago and 150TB of NVMe storage at TACC across a subset of compute nodes to create high speed local scratch storage pools. As in phase 1, some of our investment will be reserved to respond to user demand or new technologies in a flexible manner.

5.3   System Overview

The existing Chameleon system is distributed over two sites; University of Chicago and Texas Advanced Computing Center (TACC) connected with a 100Gps ESNET network link. The majority of SCUs (10) were deployed at TACC in order to create a large homogeneous partition for Big Compute experiments with 2 deployed at University of Chicago; users can use the same appliances along with the same hardware type on either site providing redundancy in case of site failures. TACC also hosts 3.6 PB of dual replicated global store used for experimental data storage as well as the heterogeneous systems.

Currently, all of the hardware at University of Chicago, 7.5 of the homogeneous racks at TACC (including nodes with heterogeneous add-ons), and all of the stand-alone heterogeneous hardware (comprising ARM, Atom, and low power Xeons) are configured with CHI (see Section 5.4) to support deep reconfigurability for systems experiments. A partition of 2 homogeneous racks at TACC is currently configured as an easy to use OpenStack/KVM cloud to support educational and "paradigm testing" projects that explore the usefulness of cloud computing for innovative applications.

The division into bare metal (CHI) and KVM cloud partitions allows us to balance control versus complexity as reflected by the needs of different types of users: on the one hand, users who require deep control but also have the level of skill required to program it, and on the other hand users who require a relatively simple and standard environment. The balance between the rack allocations can be adjusted to provide more resources to one group or the other as needed. One half rack at TACC is under long-term reservation due to ongoing need to provide an integration environment for the system itself.

5.4   System Software

We have developed CHameleon Infrastructure (CHI) using primarily OpenStack, a widely used and supported open source infrastructure, complemented by other open source components partially developed by ourselves. Below we first define the services we consider critical to the operation of a Computer Science testbed and then we describe how those services were implemented in Chameleon.

5.4.1   Core Services

We define a *Computer Science experimental workflow* as consisting of the following key components: (1) experiment design, where a user designs an experiment to support his or her hypothesis, (2) definition and identification of resources required to carry out the experiment, (3) allocation or leasing, i.e., claiming temporary ownership of those resources, (4) resource configuration, where the user configures the experimental environment, (5) the experiment itself, where the user conducts the experiment and observes, measures, and records relevant qualities, and (6) analysis. While the first and the last stage of this workflow will differ significantly depending on the nature of the experiment, the four middle stages have requirements that are relatively consistent across different systems experiments and thus require specific services to support them. Below, we focus on these four stages and define a minimal set of core services and their properties that a CS testbed has to implement.

Resource Discovery. When selecting resources for their experiments, users need resource representation that is both *fine-grained* and *up-to-date*: systems experimenters need to know at a glance what specific cache hierarchies or I/O device specifications might be, a BIOS update might change performance characteristics of a system, while e.g., replacing a faulty disk for the exact same model might result in a different power signature of the component leading to a potentially inconsistent experimental configuration. It follows that a testbed resource description must reflect all those fine-grained qualities, potentially down to the level of serial numbers of individual components (so that a change may be detected), and reflect any updates as soon as they are made—automatically if possible to eliminate human error factor. To make it easier to identify changes, as well as provide a record of testbed state at any particular time for reproducibility purposes, a testbed should be *versioned*; in this way differences in results from experiments run on different testbed versions can be compared and reasoned about. Finally, it is important that users have the ability to *verify dynamic changes* (e.g., different memory allocation relating to memory errors) directly before the experiment.

Resource Allocation. Systems experiments typically require *exclusive ownership* of resources (isolation) to ensure that the results are not impacted by factors outside of the experimenter's control. Especially in exploratory phases, they also frequently require interactive access. Allocating resources thus requires creating a *lease*: a temporary ownership of resources limited by well-defined points in time. While on-demand leases are the most convenient for the user, it is unlikely that a large number of resources—extending to potentially the whole testbed—will be available on demand. For this reason, to provide for experiments at scale we also need to support *advance reservations* (of which on-demand leases are a special case) that allow users to allocate large amounts of resources if reserved sufficiently far in advance. In addition, since many Computer Science experiments exhibit a pattern where the same set of actions may be enacted over different environments, it is important to separate resource allocation and configuration (unlike e.g., in Amazon-style clouds where a specific VM image is tied to a lease).

Configuration. Once a user obtains an allocation/lease of nodes, the next task is to reconfigure those nodes. The core requirement of Computer Science experiments is the ability to accomplish such configuration at a very low level—change the operating system and potentially firmware, explore different operating system kernels, or interact with the system via the serial console—this is sometimes referred to as "bare metal access". At a most basic level, a user should be able to deploy an *appliance* [59] (a generic name that can describe a virtual machine image, a bare metal image, or a container) representing the desired environment, and thus create an *instance* (an interactive environment based on such appliance), modify it in various ways such as e.g., changing the kernel, and ultimately *snapshot* it (i.e., save changes to the appliance/image) so that it can be used for future experiments or shared with others. To enable such sharing, the testbed should provide facilities for publishing appliances; referencing these appliances along with testbed version and specific resources used provides a basis for repeatability, i.e., recreating the experimental environment accurately and cost effectively. This facility will also allow testbed operators to publish the most popular appliances (such as e.g., frequently used Linux distributions, software essential to programming specialized hardware, or popular software stacks) to facilitate experimentation. Last but not least, testbed services should provide support for orchestration of *complex appliance* deployments—such as virtual clusters or cloud configurations—so that the contextualization [36] step of those deployments, and thus recreation of environments underlying complex experiments, can be handled automatically.

Monitoring. Once resources are discovered, allocated, and configured, the experimenters can use them interactively or explore a variety of experiment management tools [12] to automate and structure their experiments. The testbed can assist in recording, aggregating, and making accessible monitoring information consisting of system metrics, metrics from specialized hardware, or user-provided ones.

5.4.2   Implementation

We started the implementation of CHI with a detailed definition of the APIs and properties of the key testbed services described above shortly after the project has started. This was followed by an in-depth evaluation of the available technologies. The purpose of the evaluation was to determine what technologies most closely matched our requirements for specific services, whether and how they could be extended to match them, whether and how those technologies could be combined, and what combination of technologies presented the most promising solution. In addition to evaluating functionality, we also considered non-functional factors such as sustainability, scalability, and robustness of the proposed solutions.

As a result of the evaluation we chose to base the bulk of our system on OpenStack-/Ironic [35] (Juno release [50]), use resource modeling and discovery tools developed by the Grid'5000 project [6], and implement the remainder of the system using our own development and tools. While the decision to base the system on OpenStack represented a short-term risk—OpenStack was not targeting our use case and Ironic, which implements bare metal configuration, was not yet a standard component in the Juno release—it also represented potential advantages. They include access to past and future upgrades, more significant broader impact for our project as we share our development effort with a broader community, reduction of our maintenance footprint, and leverage of increasing familiarity with OpenStack of both potential users and operators at academic institutions.

This section describes the implementation of the system. A diagram of this implementation, in particular the mapping of critical services onto specific technology components as well as integration points between those components, is shown in Figure 5.2. We discuss below the implementation details of our approach.

The *Chameleon Resource Discovery* was implemented using an adaptation of the Grid'5000 Resources Description and Verification software [42]. It defines a fine-grained resource model, represented as JSON documents [11], and provides a suite of tools that generate semi-automated fine-grained inspection of the hardware using tools such as e.g., Ohai [14], hwloc [27], or lshw [41]. The ability to generate this information automatically is important as it relieves the system administrator from reviewing and updating resource information manually, which is error-prone and effort-intensive (and thus subject to postponement). The Grid'5000 resource description suite also provides the ability to generate

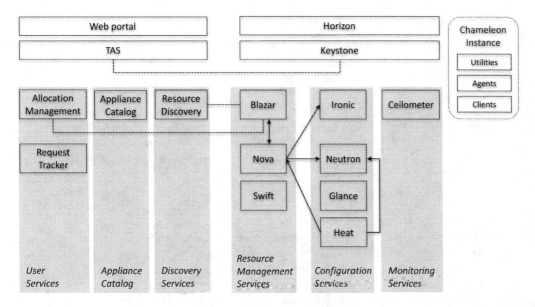

FIGURE 5.2: Chameleon Components. The shaded grey colums show the sorftware used to implement the core services. The dashed lines show points where integration/synchronization of different components is taking place.

versions of this testbed description, a critical reproducibility factor. As an example, as of the time of this writing, Chameleon resource description has gone through 53 versions.

The resource model is made available in two formats: a JSON format for command line access, scripting, and generation of resource model used by the resource allocation services, as well as human readable format implemented in the Chameleon portal [63] by our team. Another Grid'5000 tool, g5k-checks, a Ruby utility that can be run after the user logs into their experimental environment, compares the JSON description with the resource information available at runtime; it has been adapted (and renamed cc-checks) to provide the dynamic verification capability that allows users to run a "sanity check" to verify that the resources are indeed as advertised.

The *Resource Allocation Services* allow users to allocate nodes, racks, VLANs, and storage objects in the global store. Allocating a node implies access to all the hardware on the node, including storage disks and devices such as accelerators. Using this approach, users can for example allocate all storage nodes across different racks to create a private storage cluster. Finer-grained allocation was not considered useful as allocating a component available on a node used by another user would lead to contention for resources such as I/O bandwidth and make isolation between experiments hard to implement—however, users are of course able to experiment with approaches implementing such isolation within their allocations. Allocating a full rack is accomplished by allocating all the nodes in the rack and has the advantage of providing isolated access to network internal to the rack.

We implemented our node resource allocation service based on OpenStack Nova [49]. However, since Nova does not provide advance reservations, staff at University of Chicago revived the Blazar project [8], initially proposed for energy management [18], and improved it to provide a production-quality reservation service. This involved developing such features as cleanup of resources between leases, keeping historical lease data, and allowing operators to analyze utilization over time. We also made adaptations in both Nova and Ironic OpenStack components to allow advance reservations of bare-metal nodes. Since on-demand requests are a special case of advance reservations, the resulting system covers both (on-demand requests are made possible by currying the advance reservation function with current time and date). To make it easier to determine resource availability at a glance, we developed a visualization tool showing active leases and pending reservations for each node in the system. As in the case of resource discovery, this information is available via the service interfaces and command line tools as well as through a web portal implemented by OpenStack Horizon extended to support Blazar. Storage object allocation in our global store has been implemented by using an unmodified OpenStack Swift service deployment.

The core *Configuration Service*—deploying appliances (described in detail in Section 5.5) to create instances—is implemented via a combination of OpenStack Ironic [35] that implements bare metal reconfiguration (as opposed to deploying KVM virtual machines used in the most popular configuration of OpenStack), Glance [25] for image/appliance management and storage, meta-data services for instance configuration (e.g., setting up SSH keys on deployed instances so that users can log in), Neutron [47] for network management, and Heat [29] for complex appliance deployment and orchestration. Ironic relies on IPMI and PXE booting to restart a node using a dedicated in-RAM deployment environment, which sets up the disk as an iSCSI target on which the Ironic service writes the appliance image onto disk, before rebooting using the appliance environment. Whole disk image boot is supported making it possible to efficiently reboot from custom kernel or experiment with a range of kernel parameters. Console access can also be configured with shellinabox [32].

Since OpenStack does not provide a snapshotting facility for bare-metal nodes, we implemented it by including in our appliances a small utility that creates a QCOW2 image [56] of the root file system (using tools from libguestfs) and transferring it to Glance. This gives users a quick way to create a new appliance: they can use one of the Chameleon provided appliances, modify it, and save the modified appliance by using snapshotting.

Some experimental environments, such as virtual clusters or datacenter deployments, are complex in that they consist of multiple nodes, configured to take on various roles, and share information that is generated or assigned only at deployment time, such as hostnames, IP addresses, or security keys. Deploying such environments requires orchestrating role assignment and information exchange during the deployment process; if executed manually it is both error prone and time expensive. Chameleon uses Heat [29] to automate this process. Heat takes as input, appliances that consist not only of images but also of a template describing how to orchestrate their deployment (what we call complex appliances). Heat takes as input, an appliance that consists of images as well as a template that describes how to orchestrate the deployment of those images and what information to exchange between them. In addition, a user can parameterize the deployment of templates by e.g., the number of compute nodes in an OpenStack deployment.

The only network configuration available in Ironic until the OpenStack Newton release [31] was a single flat network shared between tenants and the control plane, which means that all nodes within a site were using a single L2 and L3 network during bare metal deployment and cleanup as well as during experiments. This was a severe limitation: users running DHCP servers needed to carefully configure them to avoid impacting other experiments; allocation of IP addresses for bridged virtual machines running on bare metal nodes needed to be done via a specific Chameleon API to avoid conflicts, etc. Moreover, stitching Chameleon nodes with a remote VLAN (e.g., with a GENI slice) could not be done without stitching the entire Chameleon site, which is insecure and impractical.

To provide a solution in this space, we developed an implementation for tenant network isolation on bare metal, based on dynamic VLANs. Our implementation relies on minor code modifications to Neutron and Nova, the addition of switch tag and port number information for each Ironic node, and an OpenDaylight (ODL) VM capable of configuring VLAN tagging on individual ports of our Dell S6000 network switches.

While the shared flat network remains the default configuration, any user who requests the creation of a tenant network in Neutron gets assigned a VLAN tag from a range defined by the administrators. This can be requested via any of the Chameleon interfaces: the Horizon web interface, the Neutron command line, the Neutron API, or indirectly via an orchestration service such as OpenStack Heat. Users are also instructed to create a Neutron router for this network to ensure that traffic can reach it.

When users launch bare metal instances attached to a tenant network, Nova schedules them on specific nodes and, for each of them, retrieves switch tag and corresponding port number from Ironic. This information is communicated to Neutron, which via its ODL ML2 driver requests the ODL controller to tag the node's port with the VLAN allocated for the tenant network (support for interfacing ODL with our Dell S6000 switches was implemented by Dell Inc.). The opposite action happens during termination of instances, with nodes being moved back to the VLAN corresponding to the single shared network. To summarize, each node can dynamically added to specific VLANs while in use (hence the name *dynamic VLANs*).

This mechanism ensures that all L2 traffic is isolated within its own VLAN. It also provides the building blocks for stitching to slices of other testbeds, by connecting multiple VLANs together via AL2S as explained in more detail in Section 5.9.1. While the existing system works well, since our implementation was developed, the OpenStack community has released support for multi-tenancy in Ironic [33], which we plan to compare to ours and consider for adoption in the future.

The *Monitoring Service* is currently implemented by Ceilometer [13], collects information from agents present on Chameleon appliances. The agents currently provide information from standard metrics (CPU, memory, network, disk usage, etc.). Due to Ceilometer scalability challenges (most operations are $O(n)$ where n is the number of samples recorded), we reduce the number of samples by sending metrics only once per minute by default and emptying the Ceilometer database approximately every month (as defined by our policies). In addition, we provide a library to a RAPL interface to provide power and energy usage metrics contributed by one of our users (due to fine-grained character of the information, it is currently not exported to Ceilometer though users can input averaged qualities). Given its scalability shortcomings we are planning to replace Ceilometer with Gnocchi [26] in the future.

The *Chameleon user services* allow users to create and manage accounts, user profiles, and projects. This functionality is not significantly different from what is typical for other resources and is implemented by TAS, a proprietary account management system implemented and operated by TACC. Our web portal provides a user-friendly interface to TAS in the form of a dashboard that displays information about user allocations. Another such interface, an administrator dashboard backed up by a variety of scripts developed as part of the resource management components, allows the testbed operators to assess the state of the testbed. Users communicate with the support team via Request Tracker (RT), a ticket-tracking system, also made available via the user dashboard.

5.5 Appliances

Appliances, i.e., bare metal images, are the main equivalent of "programming tools" in Chameleon. An appliance [59] represents a record of an experimental environment and can be implemented as a virtual machine (VM) image, a container (e.g., Docker) image, or a bare metal image. The key core Chameleon services allow users to create, deploy, save, and share appliances representing their experimental environments.

Chameleon appliances are built to a common format: QCOW2 whole disk images that are configured to boot successfully on either site (useful when moving from site to site quickly), with site-specific data being passed dynamically via Nova vendor data [48]. Each appliance contains utilities and services common to all Chameleon appliances. These include common utilities such as snapshotting, cc-checks, and instrumentation packages, the Ceilometer and Heat agents (both can be disabled), command-line clients for key Chameleon services, and standard development and configuration management tools such as Puppet [55] and Ansible [3].

Our appliances are generated using diskimage-builder [20], a tool developed by the OpenStack community for automatically building customized operating-system images. We start from existing cloud images, e.g., those created by the Ubuntu and CentOS projects, and apply customization elements: installation of packages, modification of configuration files, etc. These elements are packaged together with a script invoking diskimage-builder and published on GitHub, where users can track changes, propose improvements, and most importantly use our recopies as basis for developing their own. This is important from reproducibility as well as maintainability perspective: while Chameleon appliances provide a direct route to repeat the deployment of the exact same environment, a recipe provides a vehicle for inspection of how that environment was created, as well as opportunity to update or extend this workflow with minimum effort.

To make it easy to browse, identify, and publish appliances we developed a Chameleon appliance catalog. While many images are made public by their authors when uploading to Glance, the appliance catalog allows users to publish appliance meta-data (including documentation and information about support) that are easy to search and thus make discovery and indexing possible. The catalog consists of a web portal display backed by an SQL database in which the information is stored. The Chameleon team developed and supports multiple appliances including base images, such as CentOS 7 and Ubuntu (multiple versions), heterogeneous hardware support such as CUDA images for our GPU nodes, or popular applications such as NFS, OpenStack, or MPI. Below, we discuss highlights of specific Chameleon appliances.

5.5.1   System Appliances

The Chameleon team has developed and supports system appliances to provide access to the variety of hardware on Chameleon and to match the demands of our user community. System appliances are base images typically used by our users to start their experiments: they deploy a base image, modify its configuration and snapshot—or use appliance configuration tools described above to create an appliance based on base image recipes for long-term maintenance. Our system appliances are based on two of the most popular Linux distributions: CentOS and Ubuntu.CentOS, a free derivative distribution of Red Hat Enterprise Linux (RHEL), is often used in scientific environments and in the industry. Ubuntu, part of the Debian family, is often popular among developers.

In addition to basic appliances customized for Chameleon, we also maintain hardware-specific appliances providing drivers and frameworks to support the variety of hardware available on Chameleon: CUDA appliances for our NVIDIA GPUs (using both CentOS 7 and Ubuntu 16.04), an appliance including the Altera OpenCL Runtime Environment to support our FPGA accelerators, and an appliance compatible with our ARM64 hardware. The purpose of those appliances is to help users get started with new architectures quickly, instantly equipped with all the required tools. Finally, individual appliances also include popular applications such as e.g., Docker [44].

5.5.2 Complex Appliances

Complex appliances allow users to deploy whole clusters of interconnected resources such as HPC clusters or cloud configurations. The Chameleon team provides complex appliances for popular applications that allow users to deploy NFS clusters, MPI clusters (based on the MPICH3 implementation), as well as an OpenStack cloud based on the DevStack configuration. Other appliances specialize on providing KVM virtual machines with efficient access to InfiniBand interconnects, e.g., MPI over SR-IOV with MVAPICH2-Virt [39] or RDMA for Apache Hadoop [38].

5.6 Data Center/Facility

Chameleon is distributed over two sites connected by highly sophisticated networking facilities allowing users to build experiments both on a data center level and distributed.

5.6.1 University of Chicago Facility

The Chicago portion of the system is housed in space leased from the Supercomputing Support Facility, a state of the art data center located in the Theory and Computer Science Building on the Argonne National Laboratory campus just outside Chicago. This facility provides 25,000ft2 of 48" raised floor space, 18MW of power (including 2.25 MW of UPS), redundant 2 ton centrifugal water chillers providing air cooling for the room, plus off-site redundant chilled water supply for water-cooled machines and to back up internal chillers. Highly reliable electrical power is supplied by ComEd.

5.6.2 TACC Facility

The Texas portion of the system is housed in the TACC machine room located in the Research Office Complex Building on the J. J. Pickle Research Campus of the University of Texas at Austin. This facility provides 14,000ft2 of raised floor space, nearly 10MW of IT power, and 4,000 tons of chilled-water cooling capacity. Highly reliable electrical power is supplied by the City of Austin.

5.6.3 Wide-Area Connectivity

The two primary Chameleon sites are interconnected to two national 100 Gbps R&E WAN network backbones. The local sites have devices connected at 10 Gbps each, to switches with 100 Gbps uplinks to these national WAN networks. Consequently, Chameleon can support 100 Gbps end-to-end testing over the WAN with complete SDN capabilities on both sides. One major driver of Big Data applications today is machine learning for analysis of large scale real time data. In large part, the requirements of such applications require transporting extremely large volumes of data E2E across thousands of miles with high reliability. The WAN networks used by Chameleon are designed and engineered for such large scale transfers, unlike the general commodity Internet, which is designed to support millions of small flows, not high capacity E2E data flows. The capability provided by Chameleon also includes high performance direct integration of the WAN paths with edge devices. Currently Chameleon is also exploring options for connecting to emerging large scale GPU based machine learning testbeds, to enable these testbeds to be used for Big Data analytics.

5.7   System Management and Policies

Chameleon is organized as a set of research or education projects, each providing resources for a number of users. Projects are headed by PIs, generally required to be a faculty member or research scientist as they carry responsibility for the users they add to their projects. The project application process is simple and based on a brief description of proposed research or education activities that typically get processed within one business day.

Each project is awarded an allocation of 20,000 Service Units (SUs), which equates to one hour of wall clock time on a single compute server (for virtual machines, an SU is 24 cores with up to 128 GiB of RAM). This allocation value has been calculated to balance the needs of the PI (i.e., cover an amount of experimentation needed to obtain a significant result) and fairness to other testbed users (it represents roughly 1% of six months' capacity of the testbed as calculated on the date of public release). Different components of the system may be charged differently (e.g., storage nodes are charged at double the rate of a compute node). PIs can both renew (extend the duration) and recharge (add service units) their allocations as needed. The renewal process gives us insight into what our users are doing and any publications that may have resulted from their work on Chameleon.

The project allocations are meant to limit frivolous usage of the system. However, shortly after the public release it became clear that more restrictive measures were needed as many users would allocate resources even if they were not in constant use, which prevented others with immediate experimental needs—in particular large-scale experimental needs—from using the testbed. To address this issue, we introduced a lease limit of one week that can be easily extended by the user 48 hours before lease expiration if there is no advance reservation for their resource. While this provided a solution in that the usage levels dropped significantly and large-scale leases again became possible—it requires users to plan better and structure their experiment such that they can potentially redeploy them. To some extent, this is simply good experimental discipline—and we will continue to develop tools that foster it.

5.8   Statistics and Lessons Learned

As of the end of September 2017, more than 2 years from the announcement of public availability at the end of July 2015, Chameleon has served over 1,800 users (including 210 project PIs) and over 250 research and education projects at 116 different institutions in 33 states. Our user community consists primarily of researchers, with only around 15% of our users coming from educational projects. Our users have reported over 100 research publications and presentations resulting from their use of Chameleon.

On average, every 4 days a new Chameleon project comes online with relatively linear addition of projects to date. The research projects range in scope from operating systems research, virtualization, security, networking, to resource management and distributed computing. These projects account for over 3,000,000 SUs delivered, which makes for an average utilization of 35%. Most of those SUs were spent on the bare metal partition; more than 2,500 leases have been successfully executed there, accounting for 2,400,000 SUs. 450 users from 128 research projects have launched 70,000 VMs on the OpenStack KVM partition accounting for 20% of the total SUs delivered.

Deep reconfigurability is the most fundamental difference between a CS testbed and traditional method of providing resources targeting domain sciences and has implications ranging from interfaces, artifacts, sharing, and security models, to ease/cost of use and operation that make those models conflicting. Providing the right level of reconfigurability (i.e., the right interfaces) can be a balancing act that requires ongoing community feedback. For example, early after the public release we were forced to recalibrate the provided capabilities as it rapidly became apparent that rebooting from custom kernel—or rebooting kernels with different parameters—were highly desired features and thus important to optimize for; we thus prioritized support for whole disk image boot and released it soon after to fulfill this demand. On the other hand, the requests for BIOS reconfiguration were few and since so far they concerned only the BIOS settings we were able to handle them via help desk. At the same time, we became aware of interest in more structured management of firmware in general so that our eventual solution in this space will address this broader problem. An interesting case was providing the broadest possible access to FPGAs: since Quartus Prime in the FPGA SDK is protected by export controls, while all users can access the nodes, only users from countries not excluded by export controls can compile OpenCL kernels. We solved this problem by setting up a separate server to compile OpenCL kernels that only verified users from allowed countries can access.

With a homogeneous partition of 294 nodes/7,056 cores, expandable to 420 nodes/10,080 cores, Chameleon supports the largest homogeneous partition of all the Computer Science experimental cloud infrastructures to date in terms of cores [6, 7, 24, 21]. Our experiences to date indicate that it is adequate in terms of size for the current needs of our community: our usage data on the CHI partition indicate that requests with node count 16 or more accounted for 36% of the SUs delivered and requests with node count 32 or more for 18%. Our most popular resources are unquestionably the GPUs: NVIDIA K80 and M40 offerings (available since 07/2016) have seen 50% utilization to date (this includes the rampup period of several months when the resource was new and the utilization low).

At the same time, an important lesson learned has been that providing resources for large-scale experiments requires more than hardware and the inherent scalability of all infrastructure components. We already described the need for advance reservations to provision large numbers of nodes. However, the ability to orchestrate the deployment of a complex appliance also plays a significant role as most of the large-scale deployments represent a configured entity such as a virtual cluster. We were only able to provide this capability 15 months after the public release, and there is a correlation between large scale requests and requests for extending lease limits. Those limits were introduced in the first place to enable such requests; all of this indicates that support for automation of experiment preparation—in other words, repeatability—is a critical requirement. Incidentally, similar mechanisms are needed for popular heterogeneous hardware, in particular GPUs: their popularity resulted in multiple back to back advance reservations and no availability for significant periods of time. In response we both invested more heavily into this highly contested resource and are now fine-tuning our policies to balance the interests of individual users and fairness to all users more efficiently.

Our project demonstrated that core capabilities of an experimental testbed for Computer Science, that used to require custom developed software for the entirety of the software stack as in [6, 7], can now be built from open source commodity components, specifically an Infrastructure-as-a-Service implementation with support for bare metal reconfiguration. We used the OpenStack implementation, but any other implementation providing a scalable and robust services and features similar to those described in Section 5.4.1 would work well. These capabilities were supplemented by resource discovery services adapted from the Grid'5000 project [42] to reflect the community-specific need for a fine-grained and versioned testbed resource model.

We currently estimate that only about 25% of the entire system was based on our own development, most of it contributed back to the OpenStack project, and all of it made available as open source. The most important capabilities developed by the Chameleon team are the revival and extension of the OpenStack Blazar project (advance reservations), the implementation of appliance management, appliance snapshotting, and catalog (in addition to configuring multiple appliances), lease monitoring displays, monitoring and instrumentation agents, and the user portal.

Developing CHI based on OpenStack required a significant amount of expertise primarily because many components were not designed for our specific use case, and thus needed to be adapted or extended. Many were also in early development cycle; in particular, Ironic in the Juno release, underlying our public release was not yet an official OpenStack component. And finally, Infrastructure-as-a-Service systems are inherently complex simply because the functionality they implement is complex. However, once developed, our approach can be packaged to make the cost of subsequent installations and operation very low; now that the core functionality has been implemented, this has become one of our main future objectives.

Building on top of an open source project brings many advantages. First, it brings a significant return on investment in terms of a steady stream of features in past and future upgrades. In our case, upgrading from Juno to the Liberty release brought support for whole disk image boot critical to supporting custom kernel experiments. The upcoming short term upgrades will bring support for multi-tenant networks and security groups for Ironic, better support for non-x86 architecture that will e.g., allow us to support whole disk image boot on our ARM nodes and easier to use console access. Longer-term we expect support for configuring multiple network interfaces on bare metal nodes [34] that will allow users to experiment with complex network topologies, read support for storage volumes from multiple hosts [16] (and write support from single hosts [17]) that will allow users to manage access to experimental data more easily and efficiently. While installing and, in some cases, integrating/customizing these upgrades to the testbed as required will still require a certain amount of effort, this effort will be fractional compared to implementing these features ourselves.

Second, it allows us to share our development effort with a broader community. The most significant example of contributions by Chameleon staff is the revival of the OpenStack Blazar project, extending Nova to provide advance reservations. As a result, University of Chicago is now recognized as a key contributor to Blazar, working with a team including members from NTT and NEC, interested in using it for the Open Platform for Network Functions Virtualization (OPNFV). Since Blazar was recently recognized as a core component of OpenStack, these contributions also extend our impact from the thousands of users of Chameleon to potentially millions of OpenStack users.

Last but not least, building on open source is a core element of our sustainability strategy as it drastically reduces our maintenance footprint—as well as future development investment, given the upcoming features described above. Finally, it leverages increasing familiarity with OpenStack—of both potential users and operators—at academic institutions by significantly cutting the costs of adoption or creating a desirable set of skills.

5.9 Research Projects Highlights

5.9.1 Chameleon Slices for Wide-Area Networking Research

The NSF CC*Data SciDAS project [57] has the goal of bridging the gap between science and cyberinfrastructure. One of the research challenges being addressed by SciDAS is management of data, controlled by geographically distributed institutions, and used by applications running on a variety of mid- and large-scale distributed computational systems that cannot be located near the data source. Toward this goal, SciDAS aims to dynamically create high-performance isolated networks between mid-scale computational clusters and remote data repositories.

Chameleon's deeply programmable mid-scale testbed is ideal for emulating the diverse and large-scale computational infrastructure configurations available today but is limited to only two sites and supported dynamic VLANs only local to the site (see Section 5.4.2) at the time our experiments started. Therefore, to create conditions where we can experiment with isolated networks on a highly distributed set of sites, we first needed to extend Chameleon's ability to create dynamic isolated networks into the wide area, and secondly do it in such a way that it could connect to and leverage a large body of distributed resources such as the one provided by the GENI testbed [7]. ExoGENI's [5] wide footprint and deeply programmable network stack (that can be used to provide wide-area isolated circuits called slices in GENI parlance) was ideal for this purpose as it is able to provide both advanced network functionality and can also connect to any cooperating data repository. Integrating these capabilities into the Chameleon stack would thus enable emulation of arbitrary compute facilities connected across dedicated wide-area circuits to real data repositories.

Building on the existing dynamic VLANS, we augmented Chameleon to include support for GENI-style WAN stitching of Chameleon slices to external cyberinfrastructure and testbeds (including GENI). Stitching is the action of creating wide-area isolated circuits (i.e., slices) via appropriate (local and wide-area) networking mechanisms. Extending the testbed with this new capability gave us support for experiments that require both compute and network at-scale. In general, such experiments may range from large-scale Computer Science research in networking and distributed systems to innovative high-performance and high-throughput domain science experiments requiring advanced wide-area network capabilities.

More specifically, with slice stitching in Chameleon, users can create dynamic VLANs from special pools that extend to named stitching points outside of Chameleon (typically an Internet2 AL2S URN [30]). From the perspective of the Chameleon user, the first step to stitching is identical to allocating a regular dynamic VLAN except that he/she must specify that the VLAN be allocated from the appropriate stitching pool. After the VLAN is allocated, the user controls a dynamic VLAN that ends on a specific I2 AL2S URN. Completion of the stitch depends on the external cyberinfrastructure which the user wishes to connect to the Chameleon slice. If the Chameleon slice is being stitched to GENI, the user must make a request to ExoGENI to create a slice that includes a stitchport specifying the named stitching point of the Chameleon dynamic VLAN (i.e. the I2 AL2S URN). The instantiated ExoGENI slice will include a network circuit that connects to Chameleon slice enabling L2 network traffic to move between the slices. Although, this example depicts stitching to an ExoGENI slice, it should be noted that any external cyberinfrastructure that can create I2 AL2S circuits can be stitched to a Chameleon slice.

Stitching Chameleon resources to external cyberinfrastructure enables wide-area networking research that is not possible on either the Chameleon or GENI testbeds alone. It allows SciDAS to leverage the Chameleon platform features, such as the availability of Infini-Band, GPUs, and large-scale resources to emulate systems such as clouds, high throughput computing (HTC), and high performance computing (HPC) systems and connect them using isolated circuits, through ExoGENI, to real and emulated data repositories distributed across many institutions. In this environment we could now experiment with hardware and software configurations as well as new algorithms that lead to increased performance and ease of use.

More specifically, the experiment designed by the SciDAS team is working toward using Chameleon to optimize performance of applications across different computational and data management models. The SciDAS team works with several applications that utilize large amounts of data from the NIH National Center for Biotechnology Information (NCBI). As part of this experiment, they have automated the deployment of Chameleon resources directly connected to the NCBI. For example, in a recent experiment, 20 Chameleon hosts at UC were configured to emulate the Open Science Grid (OSG) [54] by supporting the Pegasus Workflow Management System [19] and HTCondor [22]. A Chameleon stitchable dynamic VLAN was connected, through ExoGENI, to a L2 connection into the NCBI data repository. A Genomics workflow that requires, potentially, terabytes of data from NCBI was executed on Chameleon nodes and the data transferred over the isolated high-performance network providing a valuable proof of concept of how such systems can be built. In the near future we will explore the scaling properties of this system, scaling it to experiment on hundreds of compute nodes, and explore the performance characteristics of the compute, storage, and end-to-end visibility and control of every aspect of the cyberinfrastructure will enable SciDAS researchers to identify and optimize their system for performance, security, and efficiency, as well as perform controlled experiments that will prove their optimization was responsible for any observed effects. The deeply configurable nature of Chameleon will allow the SciDAS team to emulate many common compute facilities utilized by their applications.

5.9.2   Machine Learning Experiments on Chameleon

Machine learning and deep learning [60] has been increasingly in the forefront of Computer Science exploration. With the availability of large data sets and high performance compute nodes, training a complex deep neural network model is both feasible and cost-effective. However, due to the computational complexity of learning algorithms while using large data sets, the computation capacity of the compute nodes becomes the critical factor in learning systems. To meet the computational complexity of learning algorithms, much attention has focused on leveraging high performance compute nodes with specialized Graphical Processing Units (GPU).

Deep Learning is a new branch of Machine Learning research, which allows artificial neural networks (ANNs) with large numbers of hidden layers to learn and abstract representations of data automatically. On a high level, working with a deep learning model is a two phase process after designing an ANN model, (i) training phase: the model is trained in a supervised fashion using labeled data samples of inputs and desired output to train its parameters using some sort of stochastic gradient descent algorithms to minimize the error function; (ii) inference phase: the trained model is deployed to run inference to recognize and process unknown inputs. Training and evaluating a deep neural network often requires huge amounts of data sets and capable compute nodes according to the problem at hand.

Understanding human emotion and behavior at a personal level is important in many aspects of cyber security and human-machine teaming and cooperation. Mapping human emotions from a variety of sources such as facial images and audio and video streams are quintessential for numerous security and affective computing research. In our research, we designed deep learning convolution neural network (CNN) models to conduct face detection, face re-identification, and emotion from live multi-cameras streaming to Chameleon. CNN models are widely used for image recognition, pattern recognition, speech recognition, natural language problems, etc. [9, 52, 40]. A CNN model [37] usually consists of one or more convolution layers, pooling layers, and fully connected layers. We have designed and trained the models with over two million labeled images including a variety of faces with different poses and emotions. Chameleon Swift object storage enables us to store our large disparate data sets for this research. The multi-tenant Chameleon Swift storage provides sufficient access control policies for sensitive data access. As the amount of data and complexity of the network increases, so does the computational complexity. Hence, training a deep neural network can take days or even months depending on the model and data complexities. GPU compute nodes available in Chameleon significantly speed up the training procedure, up to 100 times faster than their CPU counterparts, by parallelizing the convolution operations in the many cores of the GPU. Once the neural network model is trained and saved, the trained model, which typically consists of 240 million parameters, can be used for inference by passing one or many inputs at a time. Since the size of the trained parameters or embedding models are fractions of training data sets, deploying them for inference phase does not require heavy compute intensive nodes with large storage. The choice of the right hardware for inference depends upon requirements such as latency to get results from trained model, model size, local storage type and size, etc.

Chameleons GPU-enabled compute and storage resource heterogeneity is essential for building large deep learning models today but is limited to only a small number of GPU-enabled servers. Chameleon is well suited for data and compute intensive research as it presents us with a variety of compute and storage options for training and inference phases of our research. As an example, our neural network is capable of predicting basic human emotions such as anger, sadness, disgust, and fear on Chameleon, which provide impressive results after fine-tuning the model. The CNN used in our system consists of 7 layers: 3 convolutional layers, 2 max-pooling layers, and 2 fully connected layers. Figure 5.3 shows the architecture of our CNN model and the associated configuration parameters. The network is trained on 35,000 frontal face images with different emotions and poses.

Our experimental configuration on Chameleon consists of the following elements: (1) data stored on the Chameleon Swift, a highly available, distributed object/blob store, (2) Chameleon bare metal nodes with GPUs and (3) appliance with Google TensorFlow Graph Computation Library and Django Framework for API data access. We use a range of different types of GPUs available on Chameleon including NVIDIA Tesla K80 GPU with 24 GB of memory, NVIDIA Tesla M40 GPU with 12 GB of memory, and NVIDIA Tesla P100 GPU with 32 GB of memory for the training phase. Each of the compute nodes has access to the Chameleon Swift object storage over an internal high-speed network with an average of 446

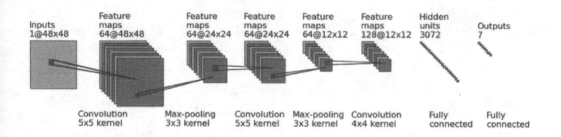

FIGURE 5.3: The trained CNN architecture used for emotion detection.

MB/s read speed and 52.4 MB/s write speed for a variety of object sizes. This allows for big data-centric computing models for streaming applications and other real-time applications.

To facilitate an easy replication of our experiments or enable others to work on similar experiments, we have configured a TensorFlow appliance which includes the Google Tensor-Flow library [1] that can be used to perform graph computation. The TensorFlow appliance is an OpenStack Heat-based complex appliance and can be deployed on multiple GPUs. The appliance is available via the Chameleon appliance catalog. Once deployed, users have access to the deep learning platform and the Chameleon Swift storage for carrying out compute intense deep learning.

Bibliography

[1] Martín Abadi, Ashish Agarwal, Paul Barham, Eugene Brevdo, Zhifeng Chen, Craig Citro, Greg S. Corrado, Andy Davis, Jeffrey Dean, Matthieu Devin, et al. Tensorflow: Large-scale machine learning on heterogeneous distributed systems. *arXiv preprint arXiv:1603.04467*, 2016.

[2] Amazon Web Services. Elastic Compute Cloud (EC2). https://aws.amazon.com/ec2/, 2017. [Online; accessed 28-July-2017].

[3] Ansible HQ. Ansible. https://www.ansible.com, 2017. [Online; accessed 28-July-2017].

[4] Arutyun I. Avetisyan, Roy Campbell, Indranil Gupta, Michael T. Heath, Steven Y. Ko, Gregory R. Ganger, Michael A. Kozuch, David O'Hallaron, Marcel Kunze, Thomas T. Kwan, et al. Open Cirrus: A Global Cloud Computing Testbed. *Computer*, 43(4):35–43, 2010.

[5] Ilia Baldine, Yufeng Xin, Anirban Mandal, Paul Ruth, Chris Heerman, and Jeff Chase. ExoGENI: A Multi-Domain Infrastructure-as-a-Service Testbed. *Testbeds and Research Infrastructure. Development of Networks and Communities*, pages 97–113, 2012.

[6] Daniel Balouek, Alexandra Carpen-Amarie, Ghislain Charrier, Frédéric Desprez, Emmanuel Jeannot, Emmanuel Jeanvoine, Adrien Lèbre, David Margery, Nicolas Niclausse, Lucas Nussbaum, Olivier Richard, Christian Pérez, Flavien Quesnel, Cyril Rohr, and Luc Sarzyniec. Adding Virtualization Capabilities to the Grid'5000 Testbed. In Ivan I. Ivanov, Marten van Sinderen, Frank Leymann, and Tony Shan, editors, *Cloud Computing and Services Science*, volume 367 of *Communications in Computer and Information Science*, pages 3–20. Springer International Publishing, 2013.

[7] Mark Berman, Jeffrey S. Chase, Lawrence Landweber, Akihiro Nakao, Max Ott, Dipankar Raychaudhuri, Robert Ricci, and Ivan Seskar. GENI: A federated testbed for innovative network experiments. *Computer Networks*, 61:5–23, 2014. Special issue on Future Internet Testbeds – Part I.

[8] Blazar contributors. Welcome to Blazar! — Blazar. http://blazar.readthedocs.io/en/latest/, 2017. [Online; accessed 28-July-2017].

[9] A. Boles and P. Rad. Voice biometrics: Deep learning-based voiceprint authentication system. In *2017 12th System of Systems Engineering Conference (SoSE)*, pages 1–6, June 2017.

[10] Bolze, Raphaël and Cappello, Franck and Caron, Eddy and Dayde, Michel and De-sprez, Frédéric and Jeannot, Emmanuel and Jégou, Yvon and Lanteri, Stephane and Leduc, Julien and Melab, Nouredine and Mornet, Guillaume and Namyst, Raymond and Primet, Pascale and Quétier, Benjamin and Richard, Olivier and El-Ghazali, Talbi and Touche, Iréa. Grid'5000: A Large Scale And Highly Reconfigurable Experimental Grid Testbed. *International Journal of High Performance Computing Applications*, 20(4):481–494, 2006.

[11] T. Bray. The JavaScript Object Notation (JSON) Data Interchange Format. RFC 7159, RFC Editor, March 2014.

[12] Tomasz Buchert, Cristian Ruiz, Lucas Nussbaum, and Olivier Richard. A survey of general-purpose experiment management tools for distributed systems. *Future Generation Computer Systems*, 45:1–12, 2015.

[13] Ceilometer contributors. Welcome to the Ceilometer developer documentation! — ceilometer documentation. https://docs.openstack.org/developer/ceilometer/, 2017. [Online; accessed 28-July-2017].

[14] Chef contributors. About Ohai — Chef Docs. https://docs.chef.io/ohai.html, 2017. [Online; accessed 28-July-2017].

[15] Brent Chun, David Culler, Timothy Roscoe, Andy Bavier, Larry Peterson, Mike Wawr-zoniak, and Mic Bowman. PlanetLab: An Overlay Testbed for Broad-Coverage Services. *ACM SIGCOMM Computer Communication Review*, 33(3):3–12, 2003.

[16] Cinder contributors. Attach a Single Volume to Multiple Hosts — Cinder Specs. https://specs.openstack.org/openstack/cinder-specs/specs/kilo/multi-attach-volume.html, 2015. [Online; accessed 28-July-2017].

[17] Cinder contributors. Add Volume Connection Information for Ironic Nodes — Ironic Specs. https://specs.openstack.org/openstack/ironic-specs/specs/approved/volume-connection-information.html, 2016. [Online; accessed 28-July-2017].

[18] Marcos Dias de Assuncão, Laurent Lefèvre, and Francois Rossigneux. On the impact of advance reservations for energy-aware provisioning of bare-metal cloud resources. In *2016 12th International Conference on Network and Service Management (CNSM)*, pages 238–242, Oct 2016.

[19] Ewa Deelman, James Blythe, Yolanda Gil, Carl Kesselman, Gaurang Mehta, Sonal Patil, Mei-Hui Su, Karan Vahi, and Miron Livny. Pegasus: Mapping Scientific Work-flows onto the Grid. In *Grid Computing*, pages 131–140. Springer, 2004.

[20] Diskimage-builder contributors. Diskimage-builder Documentation. https://docs.openstack.org/developer/diskimage-builder/, 2017. [Online; accessed 28-July-2017].

[21] D. Duplyakin and R. Ricci. Introducing configuration management capabilities into CloudLab experiments. In *2016 IEEE Conference on Computer Communications Workshops (INFOCOM WKSHPS)*, pages 39–44, April 2016.

[22] EM Fajardo, JM Dost, B Holzman, T Tannenbaum, J Letts, A Tiradani, B Bockelman, J Frey, and D Mason. How much higher can HTCondor fly? In *J. Phys. Conf. Ser.*, volume 664. Fermi National Accelerator Laboratory (FNAL), Batavia, IL (United States), 2015.

[23] Geoffrey C. Fox, Gregor von Laszewski, Javier Diaz, Kate Keahey, José Fortes, Renato Figueiredo, Shava Smallen, Warren Smith, and Andrew Grimshaw. FutureGrid: A Reconfigurable Testbed for Cloud, HPC, and Grid Computing. In *Contemporary High Performance Computing: From Petascale toward Exascale*, Chapman & Hall/CRC Computational Science, pages 603–636. Chapman & Hall/CRC, April 2013.

[24] Garth Gibson, Gary Grider, Andree Jacobson, and Wyatt Lloyd. PRObE: A Thousand-Node Experimental Cluster for Computer Systems Research. *USENIX; login*, 38(3), 2013.

[25] Glance contributors. Welcome to Glance's documentation! — glance documentation. https://docs.openstack.org/developer/glance/, 2017. [Online; accessed 28-July-2017].

[26] Gnocchi contributors. Gnocchi – Metric as a Service. http://gnocchi.xyz, 2017. [Online; accessed 28-July-2017].

[27] Brice Goglin. Exposing the Locality of Heterogeneous Memory Architectures to HPC Applications. In *Proceedings of the Second International Symposium on Memory Systems*, MEMSYS '16, pages 30–39. ACM, 2016.

[28] Google Compute Platform. Compute Engine - IaaS. https://cloud.google.com/compute/, 2017. [Online; accessed 28-July-2017].

[29] Heat contributors. Welcome to the Heat documentation! — heat documentation. https://docs.openstack.org/developer/heat/, 2017. [Online; accessed 28-July-2017].

[30] Internet2. Advanced Layer 2 Service. https://www.internet2.edu/products-services/advanced-networking/layer-2-services/, 2017. [Online; accessed 28-July-2017].

[31] Ironic contributors. Ironic Release Notes: Newton Series (6.0.0 - 6.2.x). https://docs.openstack.org/releasenotes/ironic/newton.html, 2016. [Online; accessed 28-July-2017].

[32] Ironic contributors. Configuring Web or Serial Console — ironic documentation. https://docs.openstack.org/developer/ironic/deploy/console.html, 2017. [Online; accessed 28-July-2017].

[33] Ironic contributors. OpenStack Docs: Multi-tenancy in the Bare Metal service. https://docs.openstack.org/ironic/latest/admin/multitenancy.html, 2017. [Online; accessed 28-July-2017].

[34] Ironic contributors. Physical Network Awareness — Ironic Specs. https://specs.openstack.org/openstack/ironic-specs/specs/not-implemented/physical-network-awareness.html, 2017. [Online; accessed 28-July-2017].

[35] Ironic contributors. Welcome to Ironic's developer documentation! — ironic documentation. https://docs.openstack.org/developer/ironic/, 2017. [Online; accessed 28-July-2017].

[36] K. Keahey and T. Freeman. Contextualization: Providing One-Click Virtual Clusters. In *2008 IEEE Fourth International Conference on eScience*, pages 301–308, Dec 2008.

[37] Yann LeCun, Yoshua Bengio, et al. Convolutional networks for images, speech, and time series. *The handbook of brain theory and neural networks*, 3361(10):1995, 1995.

[38] Xiaoyi Lu, Md. Wasi-ur Rahman, Nusrat Islam, Dipti Shankar, and Dhabaleswar K. (DK) Panda. *Accelerating Big Data Processing on Modern HPC Clusters*, pages 81–107. Springer International Publishing, 2016.

[39] Xiaoyi Lu, Jie Zhang, and Dhabaleswar K. (DK) Panda. *Building Efficient HPC Cloud with SR-IOV Enabled InfiniBand: The MVAPICH2 Approach.* Springer International Publishing, 2017.

[40] J. Lwowski, P. Kolar, P. Benavidez, P. Rad, J. J. Prevost, and M. Jamshidi. Pedestrian detection system for smart communities using deep convolutional neural networks. In *2017 12th System of Systems Engineering Conference (SoSE)*, pages 1–6, June 2017.

[41] Lyonel Vincent. Hardware Lister (lshw). http://www.ezix.org/project/wiki/HardwareLiSter, 2017. [Online; accessed 28-July-2017].

[42] David Margery, Emile Morel, Lucas Nussbaum, Olivier Richard, and Cyril Rohr. Resources Description, Selection, Reservation and Verification on a Large-Scale Testbed. In Victor C.M. Leung, Min Chen, Jiafu Wan, and Yin Zhang, editors, *Testbeds and Research Infrastructure: Development of Networks and Communities: 9th International ICST Conference, TridentCom 2014, Guangzhou, China, May 5-7, 2014, Revised Selected Papers*, pages 239–247. Springer International Publishing, 2014. DOI: 10.1007/978-3-319-13326-3_23.

[43] Nick McKeown, Tom Anderson, Hari Balakrishnan, Guru Parulkar, Larry Peterson, Jennifer Rexford, Scott Shenker, and Jonathan Turner. OpenFlow: Enabling Innovation in Campus Networks. *ACM SIGCOMM Computer Communication Review*, 38(2):69–74, 2008.

[44] Dirk Merkel. Docker: Lightweight Linux Containers for Consistent Development and Deployment. *Linux Journal*, 2014(239):2, 2014.

[45] Microsoft Azure. Virtual machines – Linux and Azure virtual machines. https://azure.microsoft.com/services/virtual-machines/, 2017. [Online; accessed 28-July-2017].

[46] National Science Foundation. CISE Research Infrastructure: Mid-Scale Infrastructure - NSFCloud (CRI: NSFCloud). https://www.nsf.gov/pubs/2013/nsf13602/nsf13602.htm, 2013. [Online; accessed 28-July-2017].

[47] Neutron contributors. Welcome to Neutron's developer documentation! — neutron documentation. https://docs.openstack.org/developer/neutron/, 2017. [Online; accessed 28-July-2017].

[48] Nova contributors. Vendordata — nova documentation. https://docs.openstack.org/developer/nova/vendordata.html, 2017. [Online; accessed 28-July-2017].

[49] Nova contributors. Welcome to Nova's developer documentation! — nova documentation. https://docs.openstack.org/developer/nova/, 2017. [Online; accessed 28-July-2017].

[50] OpenStack contributors. Openstack Juno — OpenStack Open Source Cloud Computing Software. https://www.openstack.org/software/juno/, 2014. [Online; accessed 28-July-2017].

[51] OpenStack contributors. OpenStack Open Source Cloud Computing Software. https://www.openstack.org, 2017. [Online; accessed 28-July-2017].

[52] S. Panwar, A. Das, M. Roopaei, and P. Rad. A deep learning approach for mapping music genres. In *2017 12th System of Systems Engineering Conference (SoSE)*, pages 1–5, June 2017.

[53] Pittsburgh Supercomputing Center. Bridges. https://www.psc.edu/bridges, 2017. [Online; accessed 28-July-2017].

[54] Ruth Pordes, Don Petravick, Bill Kramer, Doug Olson, Miron Livny, Alain Roy, Paul Avery, Kent Blackburn, Torre Wenaus, Frank Würthwein, et al. The Open Science Grid. In *Journal of Physics: Conference Series*, volume 78. IOP Publishing, 2007.

[55] Puppet. Puppet. https://puppet.com, 2017. [Online; accessed 28-July-2017].

[56] QEMU contributors. QCOW2. http://bit.ly/qcow2, 2017. [Online; accessed 28-July-2017].

[57] Renaissance Computing Institute. Scientific Data Analysis at Scale (SciDAS). http://renci.org/research/scientific-data-analysis-at-scale-scidas/, 2017. [Online; accessed 28-July-2017].

[58] Robert Ricci, Eric Eide, and The CloudLab Team. Introducing CloudLab: Scientific Infrastructure for Advancing Cloud Architectures and Applications. *USENIX ;login:*, 39(6), December 2014.

[59] Constantine Sapuntzakis, David Brumley, Ramesh Chandra, Nickolai Zeldovich, Jim Chow, Monica S. Lam, and Mendel Rosenblum. Virtual Appliances for Deploying and Maintaining Software. In *Proceedings of the 17th USENIX Conference on System Administration*, LISA '03, pages 181–194, 2003.

[60] Jürgen Schmidhuber. Deep learning in neural networks: An overview. *Neural networks*, 61:85–117, 2015.

[61] Craig A. Stewart, Timothy M. Cockerill, Ian Foster, David Hancock, Nirav Merchant, Edwin Skidmore, Daniel Stanzione, James Taylor, Steven Tuecke, George Turner, et al. Jetstream: A self-provisioned, scalable science and engineering cloud environment. In *Proceedings of the 2015 XSEDE Conference: Scientific Advancements Enabled by Enhanced Cyberinfrastructure*, page 29. ACM, 2015.

[62] Shawn M. Strande, Haisong Cai, Trevor Cooper, Karen Flammer, Christopher Irving, Gregor von Laszewski, Amit Majumdar, Dmistry Mishin, Philip Papadopoulos, Wayne Pfeiffer, Robert S. Sinkovits, Mahidhar Tatineni, Rick Wagner, Fugang Wang, Nancy Wilkins-Diehr, Nicole Wolter, and Michael L. Norman. Comet: Tales from the long tail: Two years in and 10,000 users later. In *Proceedings of the Practice and Experience in Advanced Research Computing 2017 on Sustainability, Success and Impact*, PEARC17, pages 38:1–38:7. ACM, 2017.

[63] The Chameleon project. Chameleon Cloud Homepage. https://www.chameleoncloud.org, 2017. [Online; accessed 28-July-2017].

[64] The FutureGrid project. FutureGrid. http://www.futuregrid.org, 2015. [Online; accessed 28-July-2017].

[65] Leendert van Doorn. Hardware Virtualization Trends. In *Proceedings of the 2nd International Conference on Virtual Execution Environments*, pages 45–45, 2006.

[66] Brian White, Jay Lepreau, Leigh Stoller, Robert Ricci, Shashi Guruprasad, Mac Newbold, Mike Hibler, Chad Barb, and Abhijeet Joglekar. An integrated experimental environment for distributed systems and networks. In *Proceedings of the Fifth Symposium on Operating Systems Design and Implementation*, pages 255–270. USENIX Association, December 2002.

Chapter 6

CSCS and the Piz Daint System

Sadaf R. Alam, Ladina Gilly, Colin J. McMurtrie, and Thomas C. Schulthess

Swiss National Computing Centre-CSCS

6.1 Introduction

"Piz Daint" is the flagship supercomputer of the Swiss National Supercomputing Center (CSCS) and the workhorse of the "User Lab", a high-performance computing research infrastructure that serves science in Switzerland and Europe. The initial 12-cabinet prototype, installed in autumn 2012, was the first large Cray XC installation, larger than the 4-cabinets demonstrator of DARPA High Performance High Productivity (HPCS) program[1]. This was extended to 28 cabinets with hybrid, GPU accelerated nodes in autumn of 2013. After the most recent upgrade in late 2016, the system was equipped with new hybrid nodes composing Intel Xeon E5-2690 v3 (aka Haswell) host processors that are paired with NVIDIA P100 (aka Pascal) GPU accelerators. Furthermore, the system was "merged" with eight Cray XC40 cabinets equipped with dual socket multi-core Intel Xeon E5-2695 v4 (aka Broadwell) nodes.

After the latest extension that is currently underway, the system will consist of 28 Cray XC50 cabinets with 5,320 hybrid GPU accelerated nodes, 10 Cray XC40 cabinets with 1,815 dual-socket multi-core nodes, all integrated within one common Cray Aries network fabric that has a three-level dragon fly topology. The system has 14 DataWarp[2] nodes and two Lustre-based Sonexion scratch filesystems. Overall the system has over 12 Petabytes of scratch storage and over 80 Terabytes of DataWarp (burst buffer) intended to be used as fast storage for interactive and data analytics workloads. Detailed systems specifications of Piz Daint can be found at http://www.cscs.ch/computers/piz_daint/.

6.1.1 Program and Sponsor

CSCS is a unit of ETH Zurichi (Swiss Federal Institute of Technology in Zurich), one of Europe's leading universities. ETH Zurich is an institution of the ETH Domain and is federally funded. The Swiss High-Performance Computing and Networking (HPCN) initiative is one of several strategic investments into research infrastructures made by the ETH Board, the governing body of the ETH Domain. The HPCN initiative was approved by the Swiss Parliament in December 2009 and consisted of three investment areas:

1. A new data center for CSCS in Lugano;

2. A network of application software and numerical libraries development projects at Swiss universities, and;

3. The development and procurements of a petascale supercomputing system.

ETH Zurich matches these investments by funding the operational costs of the centre. These encompass operational and maintenance costs for the data centre and systems including power for the centre and payroll for the CSCS staff. The CSCS staff has tripled since the beginning of the HPCN initiative. At time of writing, about 10% of the center's staff is funded by third parties.

The CSCS User Lab is therefore funded through ETH Board's investment in the HPCN initiative and ETH Zurich's matching contribution of operational costs. Within the ETH Domain, User Labs are openly accessible research infrastructures, the resources of which are allocated through competitive peer review processes. User Lab projects are open to all scientists and no quotas exist for Swiss researchers. CSCS has been running a transparent,

---

[1]https://www.darpa.mil/about-us/timeline/highhroductivity-computing-systems
[2]https://www.cray.com/datawarp

excellence driven review process for the Swiss Tier-1 program since 2008. This process served as a template for improving the review process of PRACE Tier-0 projects. PRACE stands for the Partnership of Advanced Computing in Europe. CSCS is one of five PRACE hosting members. Both processes allocate resources based on excellence in sciences, are open to scientists irrespective of their origins, and are reviewed by a panel whos members are not competing for resources within the same program. While some of the other PRACE Tier-0 systems have to honour national quotas, the Swiss system is solely committed to funding the best science.

The HPCN User Lab resources, i.e. the majority of the hybrid nodes of Piz Daint, are allocated for Tier-0 (40%) and Tier-1 (60%) projects, respectively. Tier-0 projects require in excess of one million node hours that are allocated through PRACE. According to PRACE guidelines, projects that require less than one million node hours on Piz Daint are considered Tier-1. Tier-1 projects are managed by a national review process. Hence, for Piz Daint, review processes for Tier-0 and Tier-1 project allocations are similar.

6.1.2 Timeline

The first 12 cabinets of Piz Daint were installed at CSCS in October 2012. Cray's product name for the architecture that evolved from the DARPA HPCS Cascade program at the time was XC30 [5]. These first 12 cabinets were populated entirely with multi-core nodes with two Intel Xeon E5-2670 v1 (aka SandyBridge) processors (Table 6.1). For the first six month until March 2013, this system served to harden the Cray Aries network technology at scale, as the previous DARPA demonstrator only consisted of four cabinets (two electrical groups). This hardening and early science phase was completed on schedule and, from April 2013 onward, Piz Daint has been operational as the flagship system of the HPCN User Lab.

The co-design project that is briefly outlined in the next section was successfully completed in the autumn of 2013 and resulted in the upgrade and extension of Piz Daint to 28 Cray XC30 cabinets with 5,272 hybrid, GPU accelerated nodes that consisted of a Sandy-Bridge host processor and a NVIDIA Tesla K20X (aka Kepler) accelerator (see Table 6.1). This completed the initial buildup of Piz Daint.

In 2014, CSCS replaced its previous flagship Supercomputer "Monte Rosa", a 16-cabinet Cray XE6 system with dual-socket nodes containing 16-core AMD Interlagos processors, with seven cabinets of Cray XC40 that had two Intel Xeon E5-2690 v3 (Haswell) processors per node. This system serves as a supplement to the User Lab and hosts HPC cluster services for several Swiss Universities and other institutions of the ETH Domain. This system also included DataWarp nodes to support a burst buffer of over 80 TB, in order to gain experience with data science workloads that had to access millions of unstructured files. In spring 2016 these Cray XC40 cabinets were upgraded to Intel E5-2695 v4 (Broadwell) processors and, in the autumn of the same year, it was extended by an additional Cray XC40 cabinet and integrated into a single system with the 28 hybrid cabinets.

Concurrently to the integration of the hybrid and the multi-core partitions, the 28 hybrid cabinets were upgraded to Cray XC50 with nodes that consist of an Intel Haswell host processor and a NVIDIA Pascal GPU. With this setup, the design of the hybrid partition of Piz Daint was complete. Apart from a significant upgrade in compute and memory performance due to the Pascal GPUs with the on-die HBM-2 memory, the nodes were now balanced from a network perspective. With the upgraded processors, the host would now communicate over PCIe 3.0 16x with the GPU accelerator and the Aries NIC (previously the SandyBridge host and K20X GPUs could only communicate over PCIe 2.0), which represents an increase of more than a factor of two bandwidth between the host and the GPU. With the new node configuration, the injection bandwidth into the network is about 10-20% lower than the effective bandwidth between the memory subsystems on the node.

TABLE 6.1: Performance characteristics during different phases of Piz Daint deployment since 2012. Piz Daint is currently a hybrid and heterogeneous system with multiple node configurations.

| | Phase I Multi-core XC30 | Phase II Hybrid XC30 | Phase III Hybrid and Heterogeneous | |
			Multi-core XC40	Hybrid XC50
Number of compute nodes	2,256	5,272	1,815	5,320
Peak Double-precision performance of system	0.75 PFlops	7.8 PFlops	2.195 PFlops	25.326 PFlops
CPU cores/sockets per node (Intel Xeon)	16/2 (E5-2670 v1)	8/1 (E5-2670 v1)	18x2/2 (E5-2695 v4)	12/1 (E5-2690 v3)
CPU memory per node	32 GBytes	32 GBytes	64 GBytes and 128 GBytes	64 GBytes
GPU SM devices per node (NVIDIA Tesla)	–	14/1 (K20X)	–	56/1 (P100)
GPU memory per node	–	6 GBytes GDDR5	–	16 GBytes HBM2
Double-precision GFlops per node	332.8 GFlops (CPU)	166.4 GFlops (CPU), 1311 GFlops (GPU)	1200 GFlops	500 GFlops (CPU), 4261 GFlops (GPU)
CPU memory bandwidth per node	102.4 GBytes/s	51.2 GBytes/s	136.5 and 153.6 GBytes/s	68.2 GBytes/s
GPU memory bandwidth per node	–	250 GBytes/s (ECC off)		732 GBytes/s
Host to GPU interface	–	16x PCIe 2.0	–	16x PCIe 3.0
Network and I/O interface	16x PCIe 3.0			
Network injection bandwidth per node	Approx. 10.2 GBytes/sec			

At the time of writing, two additional Cray XC40 cabinets are being added to the multi-core partition and DataWarp is being extended by adding nodes to the Cray XC50 partition. From spring 2018, the DataWarp nodes will be used for persistent storage in a fast, high-performance filesystem that is integrated with the fabric of the compute nodes. Experience with data science projects showed that this way of using DataWarp nodes has the potential to cover data analytics and interactive supercomputing workload requirements, especially for access patterns where performance is constrained by the Lustre file system.

Upgrading two systems with minimal interruption to the users required careful planning and some out of the box thinking (see Figure 6.1). This timeline shows the upgrade of Piz Daint hybrid nodes, the integration of Piz Dora multi-core nodes to the same high speed network fabric, as well as processes involved in ensuing the readiness of a petascale platform for the CSCS user communities.

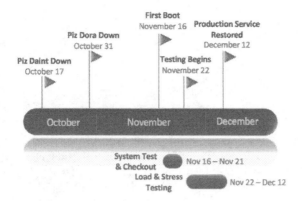

FIGURE 6.1: Timeline for the Piz Daint upgrade (Phase III) and the return to service for users. Key milestones highlighted in the timeline demonstrate efficient transition from installation to the operation phase in 2016. This timeline does not show installation and operation of Piz Daint test and development (TDS) platform and a single-cabinet system, which was deployed as a contingency plan for key customers during Piz Daint upgrade.

6.2 Co-designing Piz Daint

When planning what was later to become the Piz Daint supercomputer started in 2010, the goals defined by the HPCN initiative and co-financing of ETH Zurich were clear. Switzerland was aiming to develop one of the most modern petascale systems that had to be productive on a range of applications, as well as being energy efficient. ETH Zurich has a century-old tradition for investing in knowhow and minimizing overhead.

Within the context of the HPCN initiative and the structuring projects of what was later to become swissuniversities[3], ETH Zurich launched the platform for High-Performance and High-Productivity Computing (HP2C)[4] that funded 12 application development projects. These projects invested in the HPC development skills of existing application development teams at Swiss universities to motivate high-risk, high-reward development at scale. A now prominent example was the collaboration between ETHs Center for Climate Systems Modeling (C2SM), MeteoSwiss, and CSCS that totally refactored the dynamical core of the regional climate model COSMO [4], and would later become the first operational model to run on GPU accelerated systems in 2015[5]. In 2016, MeteoSwiss and CSCS won the Swiss Information and Communication Technology (ICT) award for this co-design initiative[6]. Recently, a team of scientists of ETH Zurich and MeteoSwiss performed near-global simulations on 4,888 GPU accelerated nodes of Piz Daint [6]. These runs outperformed the 2016 Gordon Bell Prize winner [17] running on the Taihu Light system by a factor 2 to 3. These simulations set a baseline for extreme-scale climate simulations, against which performance enhancements of future exascale computing systems can be measured.

The design tradeoffs for application performance are very different from those needed to create a supercomputer that ranks first on the top500 list. The dominant motif to iteratively solve the dense linear problem posed by the high-performance Linpack (HPL)

---

[3]https://www.swissuniversities.ch/en/
[4]http://www.hp2c.ch
[5]https://insidehpc.com/2015/09/swiss-cscs-to-power-weather-forecasts-with-gpus-on-cray-cs-storm/
[6]http://www.c2sm.ethz.ch/news/news/2016/11/meteoswiss-and-cscs-win-swiss-ict-award-2016.html

benchmark are matrix-matrix multiplication with an arithmetic density (the ratio between floating point operations and memory movements measured in terms of load/store operations) that increases linearly with problem size. The computation is dominated by floating point operations and data locality is straightforward to achieve with blocking techniques. Numerous problems in materials science, chemistry and condensed matter physics build on dense linear algebra as well, and are thus rather well represented by the HPL benchmark. However, this is not the case for many applications that solve partial differential equations on a grid.

Climate models, for instance, use low-order approximations for many physical processes. Consequently, the underlying atmospheric dynamics is solved most efficiently with low-order finite difference or finite volume methods. These methods, however, have very low arithmetic density and the computation is dominated by data movement. HPL is not a good metric for these applications and co-design of a computing system will require different tradeoffs.

Developing a machine from scratch, as was done for the Japanese K-Computer project [11], was not economically viable for CSCS. A Swiss system had to be built from commodity components, for which, at the beginning of this decade there were three architectural options:

1. **Multi-core:** The most widely used option prior to the installation of Piz Daint were distributed multi-core systems. The IBM BlueGene line of systems was the best at delivering high bytes per flop ratio on simple applications, such as lattice QCD, but they proved less successful for climate and other types of earth system models [9]. Thus, many distributed multi-core systems at the time were based on x86 processors from Intel or AMD. The drawback of this architecture was low memory performance.

2. **Hybrid Multi-core (GPU accelerated):** Memory performance could be improved with hybrid GPU accelerated nodes. With NVIDIAs introduction of error correcting memory and 64-bit floating point units into its Tesla line of GPU products, GPU-based systems could be built at scale. The first system was TSUBAME [10] of the Tokyo Institute of Technology that successfully supported numerous successful applications.

3. **Manycore (Intel Xeon Phi):** In 2011, Intel announced the new Xeon Phi product line that promised to combine the advantages of Xeon-based multi-core processors with the high concurrency and memory performance of GPU-based hybrid systems [3] [15]. While first large-scale supercomputers based on this technology were announced at the time, the performance advantages of Xeon Phi processors architecture on real applications had yet to be established.

CSCS would attempt to leverage technology development of the DARPA HPCS program in terms of programming environments, packaging technologies and networks. After IBM's demise in the Blue Waters project[7] and Crays focus on a collaboration with Intel[8], options for co-designing an energy efficient petascale systems were limited. Nevertheless, in fall of 2011, Cray and CSCS agreed to embark on a systematic application-based study to evaluate options for a high-end node design for what was later to become the Cray XC product line. The study was based on 9 of the application projects of the HP2C platform.

By spring 2012 the study showed that all three architectural options outlined above were viable. The specific node architectures Cray was considering were: dual multi-core nodes with Intel SandyBridge processors, as well as two hybrid options with an Intel SandyBridge host combined with an Intel Xeon Phi (aka Knights Corner or KNC) or an NVIDIA Kepler GPU, respectively. In fact, thanks to this collaboration, Cray added the GPU accelerated

---

[7]https://www.hpcwire.com/2011/08/08/ibm_bails_on_blue_waters_supercomputer/
[8]https://www.hpcwire.com/2012/04/25/intel_makes_a_deal_for_cray_s_interconnect_technology/

option to its product roadmap, and the detailed evaluation of the three node-architectures would continue over the summer. In 2012, Ramos and Hoefler performed a seminal study [12] of KNCs memory system that would explain why this generation of Xeon Phi processors would prove difficult to use in applications. Based on this, the KNC accelerated node option could be dismissed and the co-design effort focused entirely on comparing the GPU accelerated option with the multi-core-only baseline.

In October 2012, CSCS installed the first Cray XC system (see timeline of Piz Daint in Figure 6.1) and upgraded a Cray XE6 testbed system to a Cray XK6 with GPU accelerated nodes [1]. The latter was the first operational Cray XK7 system and would also serve as a test system for OLCF prior to the deployment of Titan[9]. Furthermore, in November 2012 CSCS selected two applications, the refactored version of COSMO [7] and CP2K [13], a well-known materials science code developed at the University of Zurich, for the final phase of the application-based co-designs of the system.

During the final year before the upgrade and extension to a 28 cabinet Cray XC30 with hybrid GPU accelerated nodes, the co-design process focused on developing the application and system software stack for both remaining node architectures and consideration. The target for the GPU accelerated nodes was to perform 1.5x over the adjusted baseline. The novelty of this co-design project was that the baseline performance was allowed to improve as the application and system software stack developed. This is important, since the refactoring of application would improve the sustained performance on both architectures.

6.3 Hardware Architecture

6.3.1 Overview of the Cray XC50 Architecture

The Piz Daint system, in its current incarnation, is a heterogeneous system composed of two distinct Cray XC series components merged together to form one system. The Cray XC50 portion of the system features XC-series compute blades that are a little longer than the earlier Cray XC30 and XC40 blades. As a result, the entire cabinet and service blade design has been altered in order to accommodate the longer compute blades. The system interconnect design is, however, unaltered and still features the Aries High Speed Network (HSN) so that it was possible to connect separate rows of both the Cray XC40 and XC50 cabinets together. Details of the hybrid and heterogeneous compute, storage and service blade configuration are provided in the following subsections.

6.3.2 Cray XC50 Hybrid Compute Node and Blade

The Cray XC50 represents Cray's latest evolution in system cabinet packaging. The new larger cabinets provide the necessary space to handle NVIDIA's Tesla® P100 GPU accelerator. While the cabinet width has not changed relative to the Cray XC30 or XC40, the cabinet's depth has increased in order to accommodate longer modules. The new Cray XC50 supports the same module layout as its predecessor, the Cray XC40. The cabinet contains 3 chassis, each with 16 modules, and each compute module provides 4 compute nodes for a total of 192 nodes per cabinet. The added depth provides the necessary space for full-sized PCI-e daughter cards that are used in the compute nodes. The use of a standard PCI-e interface provides additional choice and allows the systems to evolve over time.

---

[9]https://www.olcf.ornl.gov/computing-resources/titan-cray-xk7/

The XC50 compute nodes of Piz Daint have a host processor of an Intel® Xeon® CPU E5-2690 v3 @ 2.60GHz (aka 12-core Haswell). Each node has 64GB of DDR4 configured at 2133MHz. Along with the host processor, the Piz Daint XC50 compute nodes include an NVIDIA's Tesla P100 GPU accelerator with 16 GB of High Bandwidth Memory (HBM).

As can be seen in Figure 6.2, the new GPU accelerators require the full width of the XC50 compute module. The added length of the modules provides all the space needed to accommodate 4 nodes per compute module. In this layout, the Aries connection can be seen to the far left, followed by two compute nodes with their two GPUs and then another two compute nodes with their two GPUs. With this configuration there are two GPUs in series within a single airstream. This design differs from the previous hybrid XC30 design where there were 4 SXM form-factor GPUs in a single airstream, which was challenging from a cooling perspective. With the new design, the layout of the PCI form-factor GPUs in the cooling airstream was very similar to CS-Storm systems containing NVIDIA K80 GPUs that were already in production at CSCS. Hence, despite the fact that the Tesla P100 GPUs were new, the expectation was that there would not be problems with the cooling of the GPUs in the system. This was indeed found to be the case, and no GPU throttling was observed, even when running compute-intensive workloads such as HPL.

FIGURE 6.2: A hybrid Cray XC50 compute module containing four compute nodes and the Cray Aries network and routing card. Each node is composed of an Intel Xeon Haswell processor and an NVIDIA Tesla P100 GPU. Each Piz Daint cabinet can contain a maximum of 48 such modules.

6.3.3   Interconnect

The nodes in the Cray XC50 (see Figure 6.3) are connected via the Cray Aries High Speed Network (HSN) in a Dragonfly topology. The design utilizes 3 network ranks for communications in order to build full interconnectivity. Network Rank 1 is achieved through the chassis backplane for 16 modules. Network Rank 2 is built using electrical cables that connect six chassis from two adjacent cabinets forming a cabinet group. Each cabinet group is then connected via the Rank 3 optical network. While both Rank 1 and Rank 2 are fully connected for maximum bandwidth, Rank 3 is configurable. Rank 3 bandwidth is determined by the number of connected optical cables between cabinet groups and can be customised to meet the system requirements.

The basic building block of a Cray XC30 system from an interconnect point of view is a blade with a single Aries chip. There are 16 such chips connected within a chassis forming a fully connected, all-to-all electrical network. The second electrical group is composed of siz chassis. Within this second group, each Aries chip is connected to every other Aries chip within the same slot position. For example, Aries 0 is connected to five other Aries 0, Aries 1 to all other Aries 1 within a group, and so on. Details on the Cray XC30 Aries and the

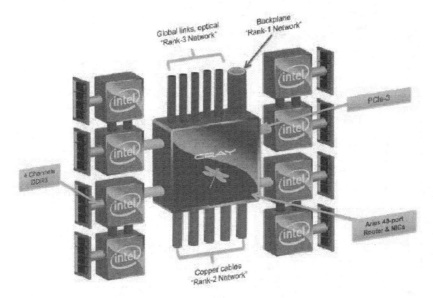

FIGURE 6.3: Inside of a Cray XC compute module with multi-core only nodees (image courtesy of Cray Inc.). Central part, the Aries network and routing chip is shown with links to all ranks, two electrical and one optical that comprise the dragonfly topology. A hybrid module has one Intel Xeon and one accelerator device (Tesla P100 for Cray XC50).

dragonfly topolgy can be found in [5]. Each electrical group (six chassis) is connected to another electrical group (six chassis) using optical links. The number of optical links can be customized for a given site. There are a total of 240 open optical ports per group. The performance characteristics of electrical and optical groups are slightly different.

Table 6.2 contains the configuration details of the Piz Daint HSN, in its latest incarnation.

6.3.4   Scratch File System Configuration

A high-bandwidth Lustre-based scratch file system is deployed on Piz Daint, which also went through an upgrade in two deployment phases. During the second phase of deployment, as the system increased from 12 cabinets to 28 cabinets, the capacity and bandwidth of the file system was increased. During the final deployment phase in 2016, a new generation of the Sonexion Lustre file system called Sonexion 3000 optimized for capacity was added. The current system contains two file systems: bandwidth optimized Sonexion 1600 from Phase II is still mounted; and capacity optimized Sonexion 3000 is added as a general purpose scratch file system. Table 6.3 highlights key features of the scratch storage during the deployement phases of Piz Daint.

The current Lustre parallel file system and storage environment has been reengineered to reflect user needs in terms of performance, capacity, stability and availability. The up-to-date layout is shown in Figure 6.4.

A review of the incidents related to the pre-upgrade Lustre scatch file system (/scratch/daint), which was based on Cray's Sonexion 1600 storage, showed a clear weakness in the handling of metadata operations. The file system was based on the Lustre 2.1 technology and was not able to efficiently manage heavy metadata workloads and, because of the shared-resource nature of the file system, other concurrent workloads on the system

TABLE 6.2: Performance characteristics of the high speed network during different deployment phases of Piz Daint. There is a single dragonfly network for the current installation of the hybrid Cray XC50 and multi-core Cray XC40 cabinets.

	Phase I Multi-core XC30	Phase II Hybrid XC30	Phase III Hybrid and Heterogeneous	
			Multi-core XC40	Hybrid XC50
Number of cabinets	12	28	10	28
Number of electrical groups	6	14	5	14
Number of Aries network and router chips	576	1344	480	1344
Number of optical ports (max)	1,440	3,360	1200	3360
Number of optical ports (connected)	360	3,276	1080	3024
Bisection bandwidth	4,050 GBytes/s	33,075 GBytes/s	40,612 GBytes/s	
Point to point bandwidth	8.5-10 GBytes/s			
Aggregate optical bandwidth	6,750 GBytes/s	61,425 GBytes/s	76,950 GBytes/s	
Global bandwidth per compute node	Approx 3 GBytes/s	Approx 11.6 GBytes/s	Approx 10.7 GBytes/s	

suffered because of this issue. The ability to mitigate these problems, without simply preventing heavy metadata workloads to run, was a key requirement in the new I/O backend design.

Another key factor for the new system design, together with the file system choices, was to improve the overall availability of Piz Daint. Due to the fact that /scratch/daint was the one and only file system available on the compute nodes, any incident or planned activity on the file system affected the entire system availability. The upgraded design for Piz Daint removed this single point of failure by introducing a second file system for compute nodes that could be used as the primary scratch parallel file system.

Hence the new file system, named /scratch/snx3000, is a Lustre scratch file system based on a Cray Sonexion 3000 appliance. The Sonexion 3000 is composed of 2 MDS (MetaData Server) nodes, with one of them also acting as MGS (Management Server) and 14 OSS (Object Storage Server) nodes configured in High-Availability (HA) pairs where each couplet has direct access to 82 8TB disk drives in the same SSU (Scalable Storage Unit) enclosure and a further 82 disk drives in the attached ESU (Expansion Storage Unit) enclosure. The system is thus composed of 10 SSUs and 10 ESUs for a total raw capacity of 13.12 PB and about 10 PB of usable capacity in the /scratch/snx3000 file system.

The Sonexion 3000 provides InfiniBand EDR connectivity but, because there was no EDR option available for XC50 service nodes during the deployment phase, /scratch/snx3000 is linked to Piz Daint LNET routers with FDR (4x links). This is not a strong bottleneck for peak I/O bandwidth performance however, because the I/O bandwidth provided by a single Sonexion 3000 OSS is referenced at 5 GB/s[10], which is less than the available bandwidth provided by FDR (4x links).

---

[10]http://docs.cray.com/PDF/XC_Series_Lustre_Administration_Guide_CLE_6.0_UP03_S-2648.pdf

TABLE 6.3: Setup and configuration of Lustre parallel file system (scratch) for the different deployment phases of Piz Daint. Currently, Piz Daint is configured with two Lustre file systems.

	Phase I Multi-core XC30	Phase II Hybrid XC30	Phase III Hybrid and Heterogenous	
			Multi-core XC40	Hybrid XC50
Storage capacity (scratch)	1.1 PBytes	2.6 PBytes	10 PBytes + 2.6 PBytes	
Storage units (Sonexion SSU)	10	24	(10 SSU + 10 ESU) + 24 SSU	
Storage servers (OSS)	20	48	20 + 48	
Storage targets (OST)	80	192	160 + 192	
File system bandwidth (theoretical max)	60 GB/s	144 GB/s	160 GB/s + 120 GB/s	
Metadata unit (MDS)	1	1	1 + 1	
Internel LNET routing nodes	12	34	22 + 26	
DVS servers (external file systems access)	4	8		
Total number of service nodes	24	52	68	
Resource management and login servers	4	5	5	

In addition to /scratch/snx3000, Piz Daint compute nodes also mount /scratch/snx1600, another Sonexion hosted Lustre file system designed and deployed together with the original Piz Daint as shown in Figure 6.4.

Combining the capacity of the two available scratch file systems, the upgraded Piz Daint has quadrupled the capacity available for computational output. Moreover the decision to put another Sonexion side by side, rather than upgrade or replace the original one, protects the machine from the original single point of failure, thereby enabling Piz Daint to be operational even without one of these two file systems.

6.4 Innovative Features of Piz Daint

Piz Daint is the first Cray XC50 system deployed. It features a number of unique and innovative aspects ranging from hardware configuration to resource management to policy configuration. This section compares and contrasts the node level aspects of its predeces-

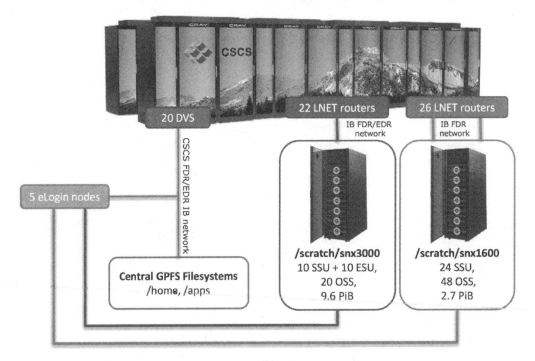

FIGURE 6.4: Schematic of the Piz Daint ecosystem highlighting the file system configuration. The key difference in the recent upgrade is the availability of both capacity and bandwidth optimized Lustre file systems.

sor Cray XC30 and Cray XC40 systems, discusses the versatility and complexity of CLE 6.0UP02, describes the new accessibility models for the compute nodes and details extensions to the system, specifically GPU monitoring, analysis, troubleshooting and diagnosis.

6.4.1 New Cray Linux Environment (CLE 6.0)

Along with the hardware upgrade, the new XC50 cabinets with the Tesla P100s required a move to CLE 6.0UP02 (Rhine) and SMW 8.0 (Redwood). Additionally, the external login (eLogin) servers are no longer managed by Bright Cluster Manager, but controlled by a new OpenStack-based Cray Management Controller.

The transition to this new operating environment required a completely fresh installation of the system. Many procedures have completely changed with regards to the administration of the system. The differences between the previous CLE5.2 and SMW 7.0 and the new system are themselves worthy of a paper and many have already been published [8]. There are some highlighted benefits that CSCS has taken advantage of in the initial months of deployment:

1. Node-Independent images: Prior to CLE6.0, all images booted a shared image and mounted a shared remote root. Node and class specific changes were handled using `xtopview` and `xtspec`, which were both quite limited in scope and also created a very non-standard `/etc` directory. CLE6.0 adds a new Cray Image Management and Provisioning Service (IMPS). This new system allows for individual nodes to run a much more standard SLES 12 image. A recipe system is used to define a list of packages that can be grouped into subrecipes and collections. These can be extended

and mixed to create a specialized image for a given node or class. The same image building is done for internal and external nodes, which allows for keeping site-specific changes in sync easily. Further configuration modifications can be automated at boot time using Ansible or SimpleSync;

2. The new standard SLES12 image provides a much more current software level and has also allowed for application such as Xorg (one of the most commonly used display servers among Linux users) to run without having to maintain a custom build. On the previous system, patches were required for Xorg in order to provide visualization capabilities to our users. With the new more standard SLES install, the only thing that needed to be done was add the Cray driver search path to the Xorg configuration file. Adding additional software is as easy as finding an RPM and adding it to the recipes. VirtualGL and TurboVNC were additional visualization software packages that became much simpler to support with this new image model;

3. Live Updates and Rolling Upgrades: Due to the fact that each image is self-contained, the nodes can now be modified live at a per-node granularity. These changes need to live in a ramdisk, however, so they come at the cost of reducing the available system memory. For this reason, only small changes are generally pushed out live. This has also allowed for security updates to be done without a reboot. Given that each node is running a standard SLES install, zypper can be run directly on booted nodes. Larger changes can be 'baked' into a new image and staged so the nodes pick up the changes as they are rebooted following job completion. There are utilities available to help automate this with the job scheduler;

4. Independent Programming Environment (PE) Image. This change has rendered the PE independent of the node images. This helps to keep the PE software and libraries in sync no matter which image is booted. This also extends to the eLogin nodes. The same software is seen system-wide through the use of bind mounts, and changes can be pushed out live.

While the process of learning the new system management workflow has taken some time, the above improvements have gone a long way towards increasing system availability and reducing downtime for maintenance activities.

6.4.2 Public IP Routing

Since compute nodes on a Cray XC are located on their own High Speed Network (HSN) with private IPs, the method used to provide external connectivity outside of the HSN is usually RSIP (Realm Specific Internet Protocol). The intended purpose of RSIP is to allow internal nodes to reach license or authentication servers external to the Cray system and has certain inherent limitations, in particular when it comes to reaching external entities that require multiple port connectivity (such as GridFTP) or when external entities require direct connectivity to nodes that are behind one or more RSIP servers.

As an alternative to using RSIP and by leveraging CSCS' network infrastructure and environment, nodes in the HSN of Piz Daint are configured with public IPs and use standard static routing through a set of service nodes with 40GbE connectivity to reach the outside world. Automatic load-balancing and resiliency in this scenario is not possible as the feature of the kernel IP_ROUTE_MULTIPATH that allows multiple default gateways is not enabled on compute nodes running Cray CLE 6.0 UP02. Cray is working on this front, but it is not yet clear when, and if, this feature will be enabled and supported. Hence, with this configuration, a portion of Piz Daint would be rendered unable to reach the external networks should one or more gateway service nodes fail and go down.

To partially overcome the above limitation, the external routing infrastructure has been configured to utilise a set of virtual IPs that float across the gateway service nodes to reach Piz Daint's internal nodes. These virtual IPs can be moved to different service nodes as needed and are automatically assigned by a tool named `keepalived`. Note that floating virtual-IPs can only exist on the external ethernet devices of the service nodes, as the current implementation of the HSN does not easily move IPs across nodes. However, since `keepalived` can identify and react when a member of the virtual IP pool goes down, it is possible to instruct the system to issue a massive `pdsh` command and alter static routes as needed.

With this configuration, compute nodes in Piz Daint are capable of reaching external services with no overhead due to address translation. This, in turn, not only enhances user experience in certain pre-existing workflows (remote visualization), but also allows the system to take on new and complex workflows.

6.4.3　GPU Monitoring

CSCS is no stranger to accelerated computing with GPUs. The experience gained from running Piz Daint with K20x GPUs was used to enhance diagnostic capabilities and catch suspect GPUs quickly. The years of experience have shown that existing automated diagnostics are very limited and often failed to remove suspect nodes from service.

Building upon the knowledge gained, CSCS was able to introduce an automated diagnostic that would remove suspect nodes from service. At the start and end of each batch job, a series of quick diagnostic checks are performed to establish the overall health of the GPU and the node. Any failure would result in the node being automatically placed in a special maintenance reservation for further investigation. The problem of continuing to use a suspect node on follow-on batch jobs has now been solved.

There are 9 automated checks that are performed as part of the Slurm prolog and epilog for every batch job on every node of that batch job. The accumulated checks take approximately 4 seconds to complete. Embedded in all the checks is one test to verify that a GPU actually exists and is reachable. When a compute node, which is supposed to have a working GPU installed, can no longer communicate with the GPU, the error "GPU is lost" is reported. Each of the custom diagnostic checks validates that a functioning GPU exists and as a result will catch a GPU that has truly failed.

A custom written test harness is used to perform these diagnostic checks. The harness allows for different modes of operation, including one for use in prologs and epilogs as well as running interactively. When a node is detected to be suspect and is removed from service, system administrators can rerun the tests with additional messaging options to confirm the error condition and determine a corrective course of action. Automatic detection and handling of errors means that it is possible to prevent other applications from being allocated a suspect GPU. The end result is fewer application failures due to known GPU errors.

6.4.4　System Management and Monitoring

Despite being the first Cray XC50 architecture upgrade incorporating pre-existing compute, storage, service and other peripheral components, the system installation, deployment and operational readiness was extremely efficient. As with any new system, it was anticipated to have some instability for the first 3 to 6 months as the hardware burns in. In addition to the general system hardware stability, software updates were also expected as fixes would be released. However, since opening the system to the CSCS user community, Piz Daint has been very stable. System management and monitoring tools have been developed specifically for Piz Daint as well as its ecosystem such as the shared storage to ensure high availability and reliability of services.

CSCS has many facilities in place to assist with the management and monitoring of Piz Daint. The main health of the system is monitored by Nagios, which implements checks from multiple different data sources. A large number of custom checks have been written that query various system services at regular intervals and are set to alert when certain thresholds have been crossed. Additionally, Ganglia has been setup to monitor loads, filesystems and memory metrics of the various internal and external service nodes on the system. These monitors are also used to feed Nagios alerts.

Another source of alerts is based on log messages. CSCS has set up graylog to consolidate all system logs to give a quick place to search for messages and correlate events. Additionally, GrayLog is configured to alert when certain triggers are seen. As mentioned in the previous section, GPU errors and draining nodes over threshold send an alert for further investigation, thus minimizing an impact on the productivity of users.

In addition to system health, various performance and environmental monitors are in place. The Cray Power Management Database (PMDB) is configured to gather frequent (1Hz) power consumption data across every node in the system. Due to the large amounts of data involved, only 8 hours of live data is currently configured to remain in database at any given time. This means that old data is constantly being retired and pushed off-system to archives. To help give a general idea of usage over time and keep the data manageable, every minute an average of the per-chassis power usage is sent to an external ElasticDB to allow for an overview of energy usage over time (see Figure 6.5). Slurm energy counters have also been enabled in the accounting database to give a rough estimate of energy usage per job. If additional analysis is necessary, the archived `pmdb` can be restored for access to more precise measurement data.

Additional Slurm data sent to this ElasticDB allows for dashboards to be created using Grafana. A high level system overview has been created allowing for quick visual appraisal of the health of the job scheduling system. Metrics such as system utilization by node type, as well as pending job breakdowns by both job type and project allocation, are shown. Additional dashboards have been created purely to analyze the performance of slurm, tracking metrics such as thread counts, cycle times and backfill statistics. This data has been very helpful in monitoring performance as scheduling parameters are modified to accommodate the new hybrid system workloads (see Figure 6.6).

6.5 Data Center/Facility

CSCS relocated to its new facility in Lugano, southern Switzerland, in 2012. The new site is composed of two separate buildings; a four-story glass-clad office building and a much more architecturally discrete data centre. The two buildings are connected via a footbridge on the first floor and via a tunnel underground.

6.5.1 Design Criteria for the Facility

From the outset of the construction project it was decided that the new facility should be designed for energy efficiency, flexibility and modularity. An ambitious target PUE of 1.25 was defined for the project in 2009. Thanks to continued optimisation efforts, the current average annual PUE stands at 1.2, despite the fact that the data centre is currently nowhere

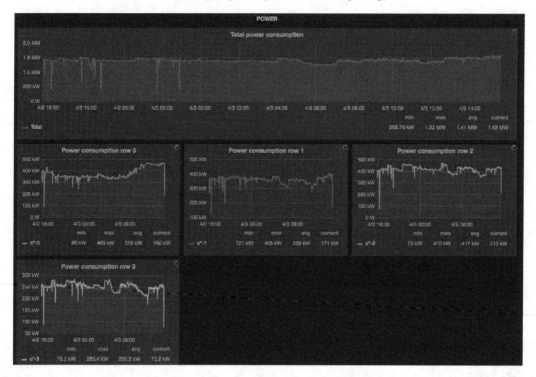

FIGURE 6.5: One of the power monitoring interfaces of Piz Daint. The Grafana dashboard shows overall power usage of the system over time as well as power usage for each of the four rows of Piz Daint.

near full design load. One of the key success factors in achieving this level of efficiency was the use of water from Lake Lugano for the cooling of the computers and buildings. A further important design decision was to reduce UPS power to critical services only, whilst running most of the large loads, including the User Lab production systems, on network power. The design of the building allows both the addition of chillers should the lake temperature increase and the addition of flywheel UPS systems should the quality of the power grid drop significantly. The pursuit of energy-efficiency also led to the decision that all systems sited at CSCS must be direct or hybrid cooled, in order to avoid having to plenum cool the entire data centre.

In terms of building design the three main design decisions were;

- The construction of a generous building envelope that would allow us to adapt to technology changes within the existing construction;

- A fully contiguous data centre space with no pillars;

- The innovative design of the raised floor as a 5.5m deep separate story in order to allow PDUs to be relocated from the data centre to the so-called "installation deck", as well as allowing cooling distribution loops for the separate systems to be built in this area.

This last design decision has proved particularly invaluable when siting new systems, as it allows significantly faster turn-around of infrastructure preparations for new machines thanks to preparation work being executed by large teams in the installation deck whilst operation continues unhindered in the machine room.

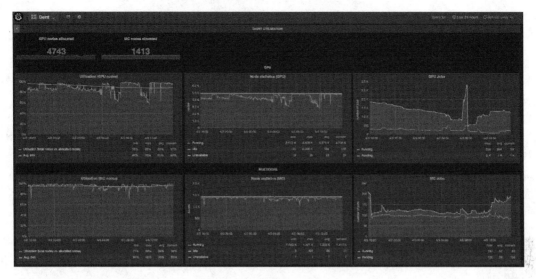

FIGURE 6.6: One of the Slurm statistics interfaces of Piz Daint. It shows total number of jobs, number of nodes in usage and additional statitics for hybrid and multicore partitions. Statistics for each slurm queue and for different time frames can also be viewed and analyzed through this interface.

6.5.2 Lake Water Cooling

In order to provide cooling for the entire CSCS infrastructure, water is extracted at a depth of 45m from Lake Lugano, where it has a constant year-round temperature of 6°C. It is then pumped the 2.8km to CSCS along an 800mm diameter pipeline. This allows CSCS to operate with cooling water of 9°C and upward, once losses along the pipeline and in the heat exchangers are accounted for. The lake water cooling system is designed for a capacity of 760l/s, of which 420l/s are exclusively reserved for CSCS cooling purposes whilst the remainder is made available to the local industrial works that also has the ability to draw heat from the return pipe to provide energy to urban heating networks in the future.

6.5.3 Cooling Distribution

The cooling distribution at CSCS is separated into the following loops:

- Lake water cooling loop, which connects the lake to the CSCS facility;

- Primary cooling loop, which provides water at two different temperatures throughout the centre;

- Secondary cooling loops, which provide cooling to the various systems sited within the CSCS facility.

All these loops are separated by heat exchangers in order to ensure better control of water quality and lower risk in the event of a leak. They are all powered by redundant pumps.

The primary cooling loop that is cooled by the lake water provides cooling in two different loops. The first, known as the low temperature loop, operates at 9°C with a return of 18°C; the second, known as the medium temperature loop, uses the return of the first loop and operates at 20°C with a return of 28°C. The first loop is used to cool highly energy-dense systems, whilst the latter is used to cool the less energy-dense systems that are housed in in-row cooling pods. The design of the cooling distribution allows for the addition of a high-temperature cooling loop that would use the return of the medium temperature loop.

The secondary cooling loops are designed and built to accommodate the specific needs of a given supercomputer and remain in place for the life-cycle of the computer.

6.5.4   Electrical Distribution

CSCS has a non-redundant 16kV power feed with a capacity of up to 25MW from the local sub-station that is located 25m behind the data centre. The electrical distribution was designed to allow the main medium voltage distribution to be built up front whilst the distribution from the transformers to the machine room is extended as and when needed. Currently 11MW of the total electrical capacity has been built out. The UPS distribution is designed to power up to 4MW of the total available power capacity. Power is provided to the installation deck at 400V and, where possible, this voltage is run all the way to the supercomputer.

6.5.5   Siting the Current Piz Daint System

6.5.5.1   Cooling

The current User Lab production system, Piz Daint, is connected to the low temperature cooling loop. The secondary cooling distribution was purposely built for the Piz Daint system. It has a separate cooling loop for each of the four rows, with a total of 4.8MW of cooling capacity. As with all systems, CSCS requires the vendor to ensure a minimum ΔT of 8°C between the inlet and the return water temperature, as well as no more than 5% heat loss to the ambient air in the data centre.

6.5.5.2   Power

Each rack is powered by two power lines and 125A breakers that are run from a total of 6 PDUs connected to network power. The blower cabinets are powered from the UPS-supplied building-automation PDUs. The connections are specified for a maximum load of 115kW per cabinet.

6.5.5.3   Challenges

The current system has seen a number of different upgrade steps on the way to its current dimension. Each of these upgrade steps has seen first-of-a-kind hardware sited at CSCS. This means that some of the infrastructure specifications only become available shortly before the installation, thus requiring that planning be kept flexible. The fact that CSCS has framework contracts in place with its planning team and contractors allows it to accommodate fast turnaround times for infrastructure projects and ensures great flexibility.

The design of the CSCS infrastructure has allowed the machine to be switched from the medium temperature to the low temperature loop in the space of 2 days, the installation to be extended as the machine grew and, especially during the last upgrade, the installation deck allowed the contractors to prepare significant parts of the new infrastructure ahead of the delivery and during full operation. Thanks to this, the entire upgrade project was turned around in just 8 weeks of downtime to the users.

FIGURE 6.7: A view of the upgraded Piz Daint (after the 2016 upgrade) and a view down to the rear of the CSCS machine room. Difference in the depth of cabinets for multi-core and hybrid rows can be observed in this view.

6.6 Consolidation of Services

CSCS's mission is to enable world-class scientific research by pioneering, operating and supporting leading-edge supercomputing technologies. Scientists today require an integrated support for not only massive computing resources but also complex workflows involving data analysis. Piz Daint offers a list of services for a diverse set of research communities. This includes computing, storage, data analysis and visualization, as well as middleware services for research communities that tend to have dedicated resources. Details and examples of how these services are enabled and supported are presented in the next subsections.

6.6.1 High Performance Computing Service

The programming and execution environment for high performance computing applications (HPC) before and after the upgrade remain the same. Major differences include CUDA 8 programming interface for Tesla P100 devices. The main programming environment, Cray, GNU, Intel and PGI are available together with the standard numerical libraries, including the libraries from the CUDA toolkit. Using appropriate SLURM seetings, Users can request a GPU device with different operating modes to share a GPU with multiple processes, as well as to control clock frequencies. Dynamic RDMA credentials (DRC) enable shared network access between different user applications and allow users to manage workloads and workflows on a Cray XC system.

The most notable feature of the upgraded Piz Daint system is the Tesla P100 GPU. Table 6.4 compares and contrasts key features of two generations of GPU devices highlighting performance, as well as funtionality improvements for HPC workloads.

Tesla P100 not only comes with increased compute and data processing power but also with a new computing model called sm_60. The new features include support for HPC and data analysis (deep learning) applications such as:

- Page migration engine;

- Unified memory;

- Support for FP16 for Deep Learning applications;

- Better atomics for parallel programming;

TABLE 6.4: Performance characteristics of two generations of NVIDIA Tesla GPU devices. Tesla K20X accelerator devices were added during the first hybrid upgrade of Piz Daint. Tesla P100 accelerator devices were added during the latest upgrade of Piz Daint.

Feature	Tesla K20X	Tesla P100
SMs	13	56
Base Clock	732 MHz	1328 MHz
GPU Boost Clock		1480 MHz
Double Precision Performance	1.31 TeraFLOPS	4.7 TeraFLOPS (not DGEMM)
Single Precision Performance	3.95 TeraFLOPS	9.3 TeraFLOPS
Half Precision Performance		18.7 TeraFLOPS
PCIe x16 Interconnect Bandwidth	16 GB/s bidirectional (PCIe Gen 2.0)	32 GB/s bidirectional (PCIe Gen 3.0)
Memory Interface	384-bit GDDR5	4096-bit (CoWoS HBM2 Stacked Memory)
Memory capacity	6 GB	16 GB
Memory Bandwidth	250 GB/s	732 GB/s
Compute capability	3.5	6.0

- Modified cache architecture to support data sharing;

- Shared memory block size has increased to 64 KB per SM.

6.6.2 Visualization and Data Analysis Service

Tesla P100 allowed CSCS to consolidate and offer visualization and data science services. The key features include:

- EGL enabled driver: EGL is an interface between Khronos rendering APIs (such as OpenGL, OpenGL ES or OpenVG) and the underlying native platform windowing system. EGL handles graphics context management, surface/buffer binding, rendering synchronization, and enables "high-performance, accelerated, mixed-mode 2D and 3D rendering using other Khronos APIs." From a user point of view, this means enabling graphics without running an X server[11];

- Deep Learning applications including cuDNN: The NVIDIA CUDA Deep Neural Network library (cuDNN) is a GPU-accelerated library of primitives for deep neural networks. cuDNN provides highly tuned implementations for standard routines such as forward and backward convolution, pooling, normalization and activation layers. cuDNN is part of the NVIDIA Deep Learning SDK. A number of GPU accelerated

---

[11]https://devblogs.nvidia.com/parallelforall/egl-eye-opengl-visualization-without-x-server/

frameworks, for instance, Caffe, CNTK, TensorFlow, etc. have been accelerated using this library[12] [16].

6.6.3   Data Mover Service

For some time now CSCS has had a data mover service that takes care of file transfer from within CSCS to the outside world and vice versa. During the planning phase of the upgrade, consideration was given to how this concept could be used to optimize and simplify internal data transfer in a standard job submission; the goal was to enable efficient workflow management on Piz Daint.

Prior to the upgrade, users at CSCS had 3 ways to move data between filesystems:

1. Interactively move data via the external login node (esLogin);

2. Move the data on the internal login node before or after the call of the `aprun` job;

3. Use a job on an external CSCS cluster for data movement.

Today with Native Slurm on Daint[13] that does not offer `aprun`, Option 2 above is slightly changed and the users have to `scp` data from a login node to the scratch filesystem. Moreover the decommissioning of the external cluster at CSCS removes Option 3.

Considering Option 1 as the sole data transfer alternative makes it impossible to have completely automated workflows where CSCS users can move files from and to the scratch filesystems in pre- and post-processing phases.

This clearly identified that CSCS needed a batch data transfer solution integrated with the Piz Daint environment. After doing the overall evaluation, it was decided to deploy four Data Mover nodes and include them as part of the Piz Daint Slurm configuration (see Figure 6.8). In the long-term however, once the new "Cross-cluster Job dependencies" feature of Slurm is available, the plan is to make the data mover nodes a separate Slurm cluster.

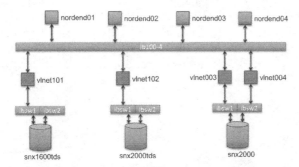

FIGURE 6.8: Schematic of CSCS Data Mover service for Piz Daint that allows for decoupled and efficient staging of data to and from Piz Daint. This service has a potential to be extended for emerging workflows and for hierarchical storage solutions such as DataWarp.

These four nodes have access to all the CSCS filesystems and they provide GridFTP[14], Copy and Move services. As a first step, in order to evaluate how the users would react to

---

[12]https://developer.nvidia.com/cudnn
[13]https://slurm.schedmd.com/SC13_BOFSC13_BOF_Cray.pdf
[14]http://toolkit.globus.org/toolkit/docs/latest-stable/gridftp/

handling their data transfer as pre- and post-process automating their job workflow, this service was introduced to a limited set of early users. This service since has proved useful and is currently in production on Piz Daint. As a step to further improve productivity of users, CSCS is looking into how to provide a Web interface to the Data Mover nodes. One of the options include the SLURM-WEB project[15].

6.6.4 Container Service

The concept of containerized applications is becoming increasingly popular because it allows users to develop, test and package applications onto *container images* that can then be shipped to a facility and executed at a larger scale. CSCS supports the utilization of containerized applications on Piz Daint by means of Shifter, a tool created by researchers at the National Energy Research Scientific Computing Center (NERSC), that allows users to run containerized applications on Cray XC systems.

As an early adopter, contributor and supporter of Shifter, CSCS builds, maintains and provides its own GPU-enabled version of Shifter that is regularly ported back to the mainstream GitHub repository[16]. In addition to benefiting certain traditional HPC applications and workloads, the container service allows Piz Daint to extend beyond traditional HPC and accommodate other types of workflows. For instance, the Swiss Institute of Particle Physics (CHIPP) is capable of running RedHat-based Large Hadron Collider (LHC) production jobs on Piz Daint, which runs SLES 12, without any change to their workflows.

6.6.5 Cray Urika-XC Analytics Software Suite Services

The combinition of new and unique features, performance gains, and addition and consolition of new services greatly benefit simulation science workloads and workflows on Piz Daint. At the same time, the services offerings and the presence of a GPU device that has been considered highly efficient for artificial intellegince applications[17] has opened up opportunties to accelerate data science workloads and workflows. A concrete example is Cray Urika-XC analytics software suite, which brings graph analytics, deep learning and big data analytics tools to the Cray XC supercomputers[18]. Open source analytics tools such as Apache Spark, R and other distributions are distributed as container images (using Shifter container). Not only does this allow users of Piz Daint access to the most commonly available tools on a scalable system, it also improves performance and efficiency of applications such as Apache Spark and Python by reducing overheads for the metadata accesses to the Lustre file system [2].

6.6.6 Worldwide Large Hadron Collider (LHC) Computing Grid (WLCG) Services

The Worldwide LHC Computing Grid (WLCG) project is a global collaboration of more than 170 computing centres in 42 countries, linking national and international grid infrastructures [19]. The mission of the WLCG project is to provide global computing resources to store, distribute and analyse the 50 Petabytes of data expected in 2017, generated by the Large Hadron Collider (LHC) at CERN on the Franco-Swiss border. WLCG is made

---

[15]http://edf-hpc.github.io/slurm-web/
[16]https://github.com/nersc/shifter
[17]http://www.nvidia.com/object/tesla-p100.html
[18]http://www.cray.com/products/analytics/urika-xc
[19]http://wlcg.web.cern.ch/

up of four layers, or "tiers"; 0, 1, 2 and 3. Each tier provides a specific set of services [20]. CSCS has operated a Tier-2 infrastructure for the Swiss Institute for High Energy Physicists (CHIPP) on a dedicated platform since 2008. This service is now offered on Piz Daint shared infrastructure. Certain abstractions were needed in order to ensure that this transition from a dedicated environment to shared environment is fully transparent to the end users and existing workflows for experiments including ATLAS, CMS and LHCb. The technologies and solutions that have been exploited in creating abstractions include containerisation, file system virtualisation, usage of public IP for compute nodes and utilisation of non-Lustre storage targets such as the Cray DataWarp technology. WLCG workload and its federated middleware for compute and data was constrained by the diskless compute nodes, Lustre file system and light-weight operating system. WLCG Tier-2 services have been operational since April 2017. Piz Daint is the first Cray XC platform that offers these services to three LHC experiments [14].

6.7 Acknowledgements

As is evident from the content of this chapter, the Piz Daint system has been through several incarnations and has grown in size and complexity at each successive step. At each point along this journey, significant efforts were made by CSCS staff, the Cray engineering team and the NVIDIA engineering team. Each upgrade presented its own set of challenges and pushed the envelope in some way. As a result the collective installation teams had to work together in a 3-way partnership, often exercising every part of CSCS from the facilities team and many external contractors through to the systems and storage teams, user engagement and support, human resources, business services, procurements department, communications and reception. Without the tireless work of these people and their counterparts on the side of Cray and NVIDIA, we would not have been able to achieve our objectives. Hence, it is with the utmost sincerity that we acknowledge and thank the many people involved for their professionalism, commitment, skill and adaptability in helping us navigate a difficult path, beset with many challenges, to reach this point. Furthermore, we would like to acknowledge the continued support from the Canton of Ticino, the City of Lugano, as well as the University della Svizzera Italiana. Last, but not least, we thank ETH Zurich and the ETH Board for their considerable foresight and commitment to providing the necessary longterm funding for these important activities that help to keep Swiss researchers at the forefront of scientific endeavour.

Bibliography

[1] S. Alam, J. Poznanovic, U. Varetto, N Bianchi, A. Pena, and N. Suvanphim. Early experiences with the Cray XK6 hybrid CPU and GPU MPP platform. *In Proceedings of the Cray User Group Conference*, 2012.

[2] N. Chaimov, A. Malony, C. Iancu, and K. Ibrahim. Scaling Spark on Lustre. *ISC High Performance 2016. Lecture Notes in Computer Science*, 9945, 2016.

---

[20]http://wlcg-public.web.cern.ch/tier-centres

[3] G. Chrysos and S. P. Engineer. Intel xeon phi coprocessor (codename knights corner). *In Proceedings of the 24th Hot Chips Symposium*, 2012.

[4] G. Doms and U Schattler. The non-hydrostatic limited-area model LM (lokalmodell) of DWD Part I: scientific documentation. *German Weather Service, Offenbach/M.*, 1999.

[5] G. Faanes, A. Bataineh, D. Roweth, T. Court, E. Froese, B. Alverson, T. Johnson, J. Kopnick, M. Higgins, and J. Reinhard. Cray cascade: a scalable hpc system based on a dragonfly network. *Proceedings of the International Conference on High Performance Computing, Networking, Storage and Analysis (SC 12)*, 2012.

[6] O. Fuhrer, T. Chadha, T. Hoefler, G. Kwasniewski, X. Lapillonne, D. Leutwyler, D. Lüthi, C. Osuna, C. Schär, T. C. Schulthess, and H. Vogt. Near-global climate simulation at 1 km resolution: establishing a performance baseline on 4888 gpus with cosmo 5.0. *Geoscientific Model Development Discussions (under review)*, 2017.

[7] O. Fuhrer, C. Osuna, X. Lapillonne, T. Gysi, B. Cumming, M. Biaco, A. Arteaga, and T. C. Schulthess. Towards a performance portable, architecture agnostic implementation strategy for weather and climate models. *Supercomputing frontiers and innovations*, 2014.

[8] G. Johansen. Configuring and customizing the cray programming environment on cle 6.0 systems. *In Proceedings of the Cray User Group Conference*, 2016.

[9] D. J. Kerbyson, K. J. Barker, A. Vishnu, and A. Hoisie. A performance comparison of current HPC systems: Blue Gene/Q, Cray XE6 and InfiniBand systems. *Future Gener. Comput. Syst.*, 30:291–304, January 2014.

[10] S. Matsuoka. Power and energy aware computing with tsubame 2.0 and beyond. In *Proceedings of the 2011 Workshop on Energy Efficiency: HPC System and Datacenters*, EE-HPC-WG '11, pages 1–76, New York, NY, USA, 2011. ACM.

[11] Y. Oyanagi. Lessons learned from the K computer project - from the K computer to Exascale. *Journal of Physics: Conference Series*, 523:012001, 06 2014.

[12] S. Ramos and T. Hoefler. Modeling communication in cache-coherent SMP systems: A case-study with Xeon Phi. In *Proceedings of the 22nd International Symposium on High-performance Parallel and Distributed Computing*, HPDC '13, pages 97–108, New York, NY, USA, 2013. ACM.

[13] O. Schütt, P. Messmer, J. Hutter, and J. VandeVondele. Gpu-accelerated sparse matrix-matrix multiplication for linear scaling density functional theory. *Electronic Structure Calculations on Graphics Processing Units: From Quantum Chemistry to Condensed Matter Physics*, 2016.

[14] G. Sciacca. ATLAS and LHC computing on Cray. *22nd International Conference on Computing in High Energy and Nuclear Physics*, 2016.

[15] A. Sodani, R. Gramunt, J. Corbal, H. Kim, K. Vinod, S. Chinthamani, S. Hutsell, R. Agarwal, and Y Liu. Knights landing: Second-generation intel xeon phi product. *IEEE Micro*, 36(2):34–46, 2016.

[16] M. Staveley. Adapting Microsoft's CNTK and ResNet-18 to Enable Strong-Scaling on Cray Systems. In *Neural Information Processing Systems (NIPS)*, 2016.

[17] Chao Yang, Wei Xue, Haohuan Fu, Hongtao You, Xinliang Wang, Yulong Ao, Fangfang Liu, Lin Gan, Ping Xu, Lanning Wang, Guangwen Yang, and Weimin Zheng. 10m-core scalable fully-implicit solver for nonhydrostatic atmospheric dynamics. In *Proceedings of the International Conference for High Performance Computing, Networking, Storage and Analysis*, SC '16, pages 6:1–6:12, Piscataway, NJ, USA, 2016. IEEE Press.

Chapter 7

Design Best Practices for Public Research High Performance Computing Centres

Ladina Gilly

Swiss National Computing Centre-CSCS

7.1 Introduction

Public research high performance computing (HPC) centres form a key part of the infrastructure backbone enabling scientific discovery, driving innovation and ensuring the competitive advantage and security of nations. A cost effective, flexible and energy efficient data centre design will safeguard the longevity of capital expenditure and contain operational costs, thereby securing the majority of public funds allocated to these national endeavours for the purpose of research.

By virtue of their mission, HPC centres find themselves at the forefront of computing development, and as such, are the first to experience the disruptive changes in technology and requirements brought about by the pursuit of ever-greater compute performance, which impact the requirements these systems make on the infrastructure and the building that host them. Past changes have included, but are not limited to, the transition from vacuum tube based systems in the 1940s to solid state transistor in the 1960s, as well as the move from liquid to air-cooling in the 80s and the subsequent return of liquid-cooling in the first decade of this century. Future challenges lie in the pursuit of exascale performance and the impending dusk of Complementary Metal-Oxide Semiconductor (CMOS) technology.

Funding agencies expect public research HPC data centres to achieve the usual lifetime of a building or infrastructure. This goal contrasts starkly with the expected three to five year lifecycle of supercomputers that is driven by the need to provide ever-greater compute performance.

Due to its mission, the use case of a public research data centre differs markedly from that of enterprise data centres that existing standards cater to. Defining design criteria for a data centre with a life expectancy of several decades, which must be able to accommodate multiple generations of HPC systems is, therefore, a complex task that requires a combination of engineering expertise, great curiosity and educated guesses about future IT technology developments.

It was the quest to understand key design criteria for HPC data centres that drove the author to survey HPC sites around the world during the summer of 2016 for her master thesis [10]. The result of the interviews with 18 public research HPC sites - all hosting systems that figure in the top 100 positions of the Top500 list of November 2015 - was a collection of current design best practices and decision processes that are presented in the section "Compilation of Best Practices".

The intent of the research was to provide future managers of construction projects with a compilation of best practices utilised by HPC data centres today. The interested reader can access the full master thesis on the CSCS website[1].

7.2 Forums That Discuss Best Practices in HPC

Whilst the enterprise data centre industry has had dedicated discussion forums since the advent of standards, exchanges between public research HPC centres on data centre design and infrastructure issues have only really caught on in recent years. Various workshops such as the "Department Of Energy (DOE) HPC Best Practice" workshop (2007 to 2011)[2] and its continuation from 2013 in the format of "The HPC Operations Review"[3], the "European HPC Centre Infrastructure Workshop"[4] series that has been running since 2008 and the annual Energy Efficiency HPC Working Group (EE HPC WG) workshops that have taken place since 2010 bear testimony to this[5]. These forums provide a great opportunity for sites to learn from the experiences of their peers.

7.3 Relevant Standards for Data Centres

A number of professional bodies and organisations provide standards specific to subsystems found in data centres such as power, cooling and ventilation. Each of these standards has their individual focus and will provide varying levels of detail.

---

[1] https://www.cscs.ch/publications/technical-reports/2016/data-centre-design-standards-and-best-practices-for-public-research-high-performance-computing-centres/

[2] http://www.nersc.gov/events/hpc-workshops/

[3] http://science.energy.gov/ascr/community-resources/workshops-and-conferences/hpc-operations-review-and-best-practices-workshops/

[4] http://www.cscs.ch/8th_european_hpc_infrastructure_workshop/index.htm

[5] https://eehpcwg.llnl.gov see "Conferences"

For this work the following data centre standards were studied:

- Uptime Institute Data Center Tier Classification and Performance Standard [25][11][12];

- ANSI/TIA-942 Telecommunications Infrastructure Standard for Data Centers [2];

- ANSI/BICSI 002-2014, Data Center Design & Implementation Best Practices [9];

- EN 50600/BSI Series [1][3][4][5][6][7][8];

- The American Society for Heating, Refrigeration and Air-Conditioning Engineers (ASHRAE) Datacom Series [13][14][15][16][17][18][19][20][21] [22][23][24].

As far as the fundamentals of design process, site selection, space planning and maintenance are concerned, the interested reader would be well served with the BICSI/ANSI 002-2014 standard. Networking and telecommunications people will find the TIA-942-A helpful, whilst the ASHRAE Datacom series provides in-depth and complementary information on a number of key topics for data centre operators.

The ASHRAE Datacom Series is the only standard to specifically address the requirements of high-density environments and HPC, as well as having a strong focus on metrics and energy efficiency. Liquid cooling is covered extensively and this is the only standard that covers particulate and gaseous contamination.

Interested readers from the HPC domain will find the ASHREA publication *Thermal Guidelines for Data Processing Environments* specifically addresses the high-density environment of high performance computing. It is important to note that although the publication *High Density Data Centres Case Studies and Best Practices* also specifically addresses the HPC environment, this book was published prior to the return of liquid cooling and therefore does not cover this topic.

7.4   Most Frequently Encountered Infrastructure Challenges

The infrastructure challenges most frequently encountered by the interviewed sites were:

- The choice of cooling technology and capacity, as well as the balance between different cooling technologies;

- The definition of power density and capacity;

- The difficulty in foreseeing future requirements and accommodating the disparate lifecycles of HPC systems and buildings;

- Environmental factors, increasing regulations and societal focus on these topics;

- The definition of raised floor ratings;

- How to commission liquid cooling;

- The definition of interfaces between the infrastructure and IT equipment.

Based on the discussion of these challenges with the interviewed sites and the strategies they have applied in tackling them, a set of successful strategies and approaches was deduced and compiled as a first set of best practices that is presented hereafter.

7.5   Compilation of Best Practices

The following section provides an overview of these successful approaches and strategies currently used by HPC sites that can be considered best practices. For ease of reference, they have been grouped and structured into topical areas.

7.5.1   Management Topics

Having adequate management tools and processes in place to accompany a data centre construction project is paramount to ensuring its success. The key points mentioned by the sites regarding management topics were:

- Have a clearly formulated and agreed business plan and, if applicable, also have a portfolio plan before you start. This will ensure that you know your assets and their limits and can plan for costs throughout the lifecycle. For new projects, this will allow you to clearly identify and defend your requirements for the design. Update these plans frequently;

- Build support for your project at each level so the funding request can be defended and supported by each in turn;

- Get full backing from all stakeholders to ensure everyone is on the same page and focused on the same goal;

- Know and understand government or other policy makers' requirements that will affect your project. This may include energy efficiency requirements, funding thresholds, carbon emissions, etc;

- Beyond the expertise in IT systems, invest in hiring (or at least contracting) the necessary skills in terms of electrical and mechanical engineering as well as building automation. This will be invaluable during the design and construction phase, but will also allow you to fine tune and optimise the facility when in operation, as well as ensuring that you have key knowledge about your facility in house;

- Ensure facility and IT system managers are both involved throughout the entire design and construction process to ensure optimal fit with requirements, shared responsibility for decisions and a smoother and faster handover to operations on completion of the project;

- Ask a lot of questions, exchange on best practices with peers and get regular updates from vendors about their technology roadmaps;

- Take the long view: understanding how technology changed in the past is valuable as a background when making guesses about the future. It will allow you to recognise repeat patterns and pre-empt them;

- Be aware of ASHRAE Datacom Series. ANSI/BISCI can provide a helpful basis if starting from scratch;

- Prior to talking to an A&E firm, put together a catalogue of your design and performance requirements, as well as any standards you want the design to adhere to;

- Define no more than five design features considered make or break to the success of the project. This will ensure that you do not make trade-offs in the wrong places and that you know where you can compromise;

- Review the different possible tendering processes and choose the one that best suits your needs. (See next section for further details)

7.5.2   Tendering Processes

The tendering process for the construction of a new data centre but also for extension projects throughout the lifetime of a data centre are key in ensuring you get the best value for your money and are able to turn projects around fast enough to match the IT procurement process. Below is the list of considerations by the interviewed sites regarding tendering:

- Previous data centre planning experience is imperative for your A&E partner. Experience of HPC is desirable;

- Possible tendering options:

  - Each trade is tendered singularly. High administrative overhead, potentially longer process, coordination onerous, responsibility and warranty grey zones;

  - A&E partner and general contractor: Separate tenders are put out for an A&E partner and a general contractor. Only two contractual partners. Potentially shorter process, responsibilities and warranty clearer. (Also referred to as design-bid-build in the U.S.);

  - Design-build (also referred to as Integrated Design): Single tender results in a contract with a combined team of A&E and contractors that go through the design and construction process together. Collaborative and iterative process. Allows for on-going optimisation and shorter turn-around of the project. The DOE High Performance and Sustainability Guidance[6] requires DOE sites to apply integrated design principles. This form of tendering is fairly recent and in Europe it is not yet widely applied because tendering processes and standard contracts have not yet been adapted to allow for them. Progress is being made on this front though, so it is worth looking into in detail.

- Consider buying the rights to bids that do not win so as to be able to integrate their best ideas in your final design;

- Consider tendering for framework contracts (also referred to as master contract) with A&E and key trades once you are in operation. This allows you to work with the same partners over a number of years, thereby accumulating knowledge and experience. It also enables you to turn around infrastructure upgrade projects faster because you do not need to tender for each one of these separately but can go directly to your framework partners.

---

[6]http://www.wbdg.org/pdfs/hpsb_guidance.pdf

7.5.3 Building Envelope

Two trains of thought emerged regarding this topic. The first and most frequently represented one amongst the interviewed sites advocates for building as large a building envelope as can be justified in order to be able to react to changes within this. In this case, the advice of one site to make sure you get your steel and concrete right is important, as is the advice of keeping some flexibility.

The second approach mentioned is to build a modular envelope and optimise it based on the known requirements whilst keeping it generic enough to modify if or when requirements change. In order to determine which approach best fits your requirements consider the following:

- Does your facility have a Public Relations role that will require it to be architecturally pleasing and designed to accommodate frequent visitors?

- Do your funding agencies prefer large and infrequent or smaller and incremental funding requests for infrastructure measures?

- How straightforward is it to get planning permission for a new building or building extension at your site?

Once you have your answers to the above, you should be able to choose which of the following two approaches best fits your situation:

- Big envelope: this approach entails building the biggest building envelope you can justify in order to be able to accommodate for changes within this framework. In this approach, the envelope is set but the infrastructure can still be designed and executed in a modular fashion. With this approach, it is important to invest in good quality for long lifecycle items (e.g. the raised floor) and include options for future developments in the design stage. Check that your site will be able to accommodate your future requirements in terms of electricity and water and check options for waste-heat re-use or free cooling;

- Modular envelope: this approach aims to provide the optimal structure for the known requirements that is sufficiently generic to be able to adapt to changes. Think of this as a box to which you attach the requisite services. Both the envelope and the infrastructure are modular.

7.5.4 Power Density and Capacity

Deciding the power density and capacity for a new data centre is a challenging task. The increasing power density of IT systems is pushing facilities to their limit. Fortunately, the move from 208V to 480V distributions for most HPC systems has eased the pressure at least in terms of space required for the electrical infrastructure. All interviewed sites still run their electrical distribution in Alternate Current (AC). One site is looking at testing Direct Current (DC) that is known to transmit power more efficiently.

Numerous sites used power capacity as a starting point in defining design for new data centres. The decision process applied was fairly similar and can be summed up as follows:

- Decide what compute capacity the site should be able to host as far out as imaginable;

- Extrapolate power and footprint for such a system based on today's technology, vendor R&D roadmaps and research;

- Assume the need to be able to host two of these systems in parallel for a limited amount of time when a new system comes online before the old one is retired. Add space, power and cooling capacity for miscellaneous systems and service area. This will allow you to extrapolate the amount of power and cooling capacity as well as the footprint you will need to design for;

- Design the envelope so it can accommodate the final capacity;

- Break infrastructure down into modules that can be added when needed;

- Pre-build connection points for addition of infrastructure modules.

Alternatively, build the optimal facility for the known requirements and keep it as generic as possible so as to be able to modify it to adapt to future changes in requirements.

7.5.5 Raised Floor

There are currently two lines of thought regarding raised floors. These are: to have a raised floor or to build slab on grade (i.e. not have a raised floor). The choice depends on the situation and preferences of a given site. The advice regarding raised floors the interviewees gave was to invest in the best raised floor attainable and make sure that the entire raised floor surface is uninterrupted in order to have full freedom when siting systems. The sites mention that although this increases the upfront cost, it is well worth the investment in order to ensure performance and avoid expensive and disruptive subsequent upgrades. Ratings for raised floor, support structure and cement slab need to be coherent in order to ensure the requisite performance of the structure.

- Raised floor: Allows you to run connections to IT equipment under the floor and if desirable to separate certain types of connections (e.g. water and electricity). The crux lies in the choice of the depth of the raised floor and the load ratings for it. If you elect to have a raised floor, consider the following:

  - Specify both a static and a point load rating;
  - Make sure the ratings are coherent and aligned with those for the raised floor structure and supporting building structure.
  - Invest in the highest rating you can afford, as this is more cost effective and less obstructive than a later upgrade.
  - Raised floor depth:
    * Check for limitations regarding this in building codes and other regulations as they may impact your operational processes;
    * Within these limitations maximise the depth of your raised floor in order to be able to accommodate all the connections as well as airflow if needed;
    * Consider making the raised floor a full storey below the machine room. This will allow you to locate electrical and mechanical distribution infrastructure directly below the systems, thus shortening the connections, improving efficiency and reducing the surface needed for these installations in other parts of the building. It also improves the ability to deploy infrastructure in a modular way more comfortably and without impacting operations in the machine room. Be sure to check fire codes if you pursue this as this will result in a fire zone of considerable volume;
    * Ensure the raised floor structure can support the weight of cable trays and piping.

- Slab on grade: Once you specify the load ratings for your cement slab, you do not need to worry about them again. All connections are run overhead together with lighting, fire detection and possibly extinguishing systems. The crux lies in the coordination of these. Given that at the time of writing, only one of the interviewed sites was in the planning process to apply this approach, the discussions did not provide a sufficient basis to formulate best practices.

7.5.6   Electrical Infrastructure

The interviewed sites noted the difficulty of specifying the power distribution and connections for future systems with yet unknown requirements as well as in planning for extra headroom and connection points, so as to be able to accommodate further growth and make the investment more durable. They also note the need to be careful to not end up with stranded[7] or trapped[8] capacity. Below are some of the approaches identified in mitigating this challenge.

- Define a standard electrical distribution and connection type for non-HPC hardware that will be hosted in your machine room. You can then make this a requirement in your procurements and it makes installation faster and allows you to move hardware around in the room more easily;

- HPC systems will mostly require 480V distribution;

- For HPC systems, build the main distribution up front. For the final distribution to the system you can either:

  - Reserve the build-out until you have the full requirements for the system and do this as part of the site preparation. Having framework contracts in place makes this considerably easier to turn around in the limited time available;

  - Build out the full distribution, in which case you will need to specify this in future systems procurements and require vendors to connect to them. This approach is unlikely to work for sites procuring first-of-a-kind systems.

- Keep distribution paths as short as possible;

- Integrate the ability to meter and monitor as much as possible. (See Measuring and Monitoring for more detail);

- AC or DC: currently none of the interviewed sites use DC distribution, but one site is preparing to test it. DC has efficiency advantages but does also come with an increased arc flash capability, and you will require specially trained facility staff to work in this environment. Because DC distribution is not mainstream, at this point the technology is more expensive than AC;

- Look at possibilities for using alternative/renewable energy sources;

- UPS: Evaluate the quality of your utility power supply in order to ascertain the frequency at which you may experience brownouts or blackouts. This evaluation, combined with your business case, should inform your decision to put in place a power protection strategy or integrate a future option for this in your design;

---

[7]Due to overprovisioning.
[8]Due to underuse.

- Make sure the utility company has sufficient power available for your planned capacity and be aware that load swings may adversely impact the utility;

- Earthing and electromagnetic compatibility (EMC) are of paramount importance in any data centre.

7.5.7 Cooling

The selection and capacity specification of cooling technologies is another area that many of the interviewed sites had found challenging. For new buildings, the challenge lies in deciding what cooling technologies to design for and how to define and balance their capacities. Older sites face the challenge of retrofitting for liquid cooling and having to define the temperature range and capacity for this.

Although sites agree that liquid cooling is a requirement for high-density environments and has the added benefit of being more energy efficient than air cooling, they are frustrated by the lack of uniformity in temperature ranges amongst different vendor solutions. Six sites also report increasing difficulty in fitting additional capacity into the same building envelope.

Below are some of the considerations based on the interviews that may help in defining the cooling capacity and balance between technologies:

- What are the environmental conditions you want to provide in the machine room that will allow you to accommodate a wide range of vendor technology?

- Can you re-use your waste heat or make it available to a third party for use now or in the future? Is waste-heat re-use a design driver and does it require you to use specific temperature ranges for your cooling? Note that this will impact your design choices as well as your future hardware choices.

- Evaluate and be aware of the trade-off between the savings of higher coolant temperatures vs. the impact this may have on the compute performance of your systems.

No matter which cooling technology(ies) are chosen, some basics will apply:

- Separate hot and cold;

- Use pumps with Variable Frequency Drives (VFDs) so you can accommodate different levels of operation efficiently;

- Size pumps to match operational range in order to avoid issues with cavitation;

- Define a standard cooling distribution for your nonHPC equipment (e.g. hot and cold aisles, in-row cooling, rear door heat exchangers). This makes installation faster and allows you to move hardware around in the room more easily;

- Keep distribution paths as short as possible.

- For HPC systems, build the main distribution up front. For the final distribution to the system, you can either:

  - Reserve the build-out until the full requirements for the system are received and do this as part of site preparation. Having framework contracts in place makes this considerably easier to turn around in the limited time;

  - Build out the full distribution, in which case you will need to define this in future systems procurements and require vendors to connect to them. This approach is unlikely to work for sites procuring first of a kind systems.

- Commissioning for a large capacity cooling plant in the absence of the heat load from the IT is non-trivial and should be considered from the outset. Two possible approaches are:

  – Point commissioning of flow rates and temperatures with final testing and acceptance delayed to when the load is installed;

  – Use of district hot water distribution to simulate heat load during commissioning phase;

  – Use of water-cooled load banks to simulate the load.

- For liquid and hybrid cooling you will also want to consider the following:

  – Define a temperature differential (ΔT) and a pressure differential (Δp) that you expect to see across your distribution as they will impact your overall cooling capacity;

  – Consider having cooling loops at different temperature ranges to be able to accommodate a wider range of hardware. Run these in cascade formation for improved energy efficiency;

  – Monitor and control water chemistry even when not required by a system vendor;

  – Divide different cooling loops (external, internal, IT) with heat exchangers so as to be able to separate different water chemistry requirements as well as avoid undesirable reactions between different materials used. This also reduces the amount of water in case of leakage or need for chemical treatment. This setup will facilitate running different temperature loops in a cascade formation;

  – Be aware of the weight that liquid cooling will add to your raised floor when you are defining the criteria for the same;

  – Due to the higher densities of liquid-cooled systems, there is less temperature buffer. For this reason, where systems are on protected power, the cooling distribution should have N+1 pumps and be on protected power so as to ensure continued circulation and avoid hardware damage.

7.5.8   Fire Protection

Fire protection is an important topic that will be subject to extensive regulations due to the amount of power present in these facilities.

- Invest in a Very Early Smoke Detection Apparatus (VESDA) system;

- Fire suppression: there are different directions of thought on this topic. The best choice for your site will depend on your preferences, budget and priorities.

  – In the U.S., the predominant choice is for either pre-action dry piping or wet-pipe systems.

  – In Europe, numerous sites use gas or water mist.

7.5.9   Measuring and Monitoring

- Invest in the ability to monitor and measure as much as possible. It will not only help with preventative maintenance (see next section for more detail) but also allow you to do such things as accurately measure TCO and energy efficiency. You cannot improve things that you cannot measure;

- Consider investing in a Data Centre Information Management (DCIM) system.

7.5.10   Once in Operation

- Measure and monitor as much as possible as this will facilitate understanding what the normal situation of your infrastructure is, thereby enabling you to detect failures before they arise and execute preventative maintenance;

- Following commissioning, spend time and effort optimising the infrastructure for maximum efficiency. This can noticeably reduce operating costs;

- Ensure that the requisite operational procedures are in place in order to avoid outages due to human error;

- When tendering for an HPC system, integrate the requirements of applications, systems and facilities to ensure procurement of a system best fitted to all requirements or that at least fits within the boundary conditions.

7.6   Limitations and Implications

The best practices collected herein are by no means complete and exhaustive, but should be seen as a basis upon which the community can build. They represent the opinions of the interviewed sites, based on their experiences. At times approaches between sites differ fundamentally, and in such cases both directions of thought are represented in the compilation. Any errors are the responsibility of the author alone, and it should be noted that the next disruptive change in technology might well require a substantial review of any of the best practices in the compilation.

7.7   Conclusion

Defining design criteria for a data centre with a life expectancy of several decades, that must be able to accommodate multiple generations of HPC systems, is a complex task.

It requires a combination of engineering expertise, great curiosity and educated guesses about future IT technology developments to allow the derivation of clear design requirement for the A&E partner whilst maintaining a maximum amount of flexibility to adapt to future changes.

The aim of this chapter was to provide managers of future HPC data centre construction projects with a collection of best practices as they are currently applied by the community.

Best practices for HPC data centres must continue to evolve with the technology they host. The current compilation can therefore only be a starting point for the community to build on. Further work in this context would be desirable and most useful to the community.

Bibliography

[1] British Standards Institution (2012). *EN 50600-1 Information Technology - Data centre facilities and infrastructures - Part 1: General concepts.* London, 2012.

[2] Telecommunications Infrastructure Association (2014). *Telecommunications Infrastructure Standard for Data Centers.* 2014. Available from: http://www.tia.org.

[3] British Standards Institution (2014a). *Information Technology. Data centre facilities and infrastructures. Building construction.* London, 2014.

[4] British Standards Institution (2014b). *Information Technology. Data centre facilities and infrastructures. Power distribution.* London, 2014.

[5] British Standards Institution (2014c). *Information Technology. Data centre facilities and infrastructures. Environmental control.* London, 2014.

[6] British Standards Institution (2014d). *Information Technology. Data centre facilities and infrastructures. Management and operational information.* London, 2014.

[7] British Standards Institution (2015). *Information Technology. Data centre facilities and infrastructures. Telecommunications cabling infrastructure.* London, 2015.

[8] British Standards Institution (2016). *Information Technology. Data centre facilities and infrastructures. Security Systems.* London, 2016.

[9] BISCI. *ANSI/BICS 002-2014, Data Center Design and Implementation Best Practices.* Tampa, FL, 3rd edition, 2014.

[10] Ladina Gilly. Data centre design standards and best practices for public research high performance computing centres. Master's thesis, CUREM - Center for Urban & Real Estate Management, University of Zurich, CH - 8002 Zurich, 8 2016. Available at: http://www.cscs.ch/fileadmin/publications/Tech_Reports/Data_centre_design_Thesis_e.pdf.

[11] The Uptime Institute. *Data Centre Site Infrastructure Tier Standard: Topology.* 2012. Available from: http://www.uptimeinstitute.com.

[12] The Uptime Institute. *Data Center Site Infrastructure Tier Standard: Operational Sustainability.* 2013. Available from: http://www.uptimeinstitute.com.

[13] American Society of Heating Refrigerating and Air-Conditioning Engineers (2007). *Structural and vibration guidelines for datacom equipment centers.* Atlanta, GA, 2007.

[14] American Society of Heating Refrigerating and Air-Conditioning Engineers (2008a). *Best practices for datacom facility energy efficiency.* Atlanta, GA, 2008.

[15] American Society of Heating Refrigerating and Air-Conditioning Engineers (2008a). *TC 9.9 Mission Critical Facilities Technology Spaces and Electronic Equipment (2008b): High Density Data Centers.* Atlanta, GA, 2008.

[16] American Society of Heating Refrigerating and Air-Conditioning Engineers (2009a). *Design considerations for datacom equipment centers.* Atlanta, GA, 2009.

[17] American Society of Heating Refrigerating and Air-Conditioning Engineers (2009b). *Real-time energy consumption measurements in data centers*. Atlanta, GA, 2009.

[18] American Society of Heating Refrigerating and Air-Conditioning Engineers (2011). *Green tips for data centers*. Atlanta, GA, 2011.

[19] American Society of Heating Refrigerating and Air-Conditioning Engineers (2012). *Datacom equipment power trends and cooling applications*. Atlanta, GA, 2012.

[20] American Society of Heating Refrigerating and Air-Conditioning Engineers (2013). *PUE: a comprehensive examination of the metric*. Atlanta, GA, 2013.

[21] American Society of Heating Refrigerating and Air-Conditioning Engineers (2014a). *Liquid cooling guidelines for datacom equipment centers*. Atlanta, GA, 2014.

[22] American Society of Heating Refrigerating and Air-Conditioning Engineers (2014b). *Particulate and gaseous contamination in datacom environments*. Atlanta, GA, 2014.

[23] American Society of Heating Refrigerating and Air-Conditioning Engineers (2015a). *Thermal guidelines for data processing environments*. Atlanta, GA, 2015.

[24] American Society of Heating Refrigerating and Air-Conditioning Engineers (2015b). *Server Efficiency - Metrics for Computer Servers and Storage*. Atlanta, GA, 2015.

[25] W. P. Turner, J. H. Seader, V. Renaud, and K. G. Brill. *Tier Classifications Define Site Infrastructure Performance*. 2008. White-paper available from: http://www.uptimeinstitute.org.

Chapter 8

Jetstream: A Novel Cloud System for Science

Craig A. Stewart
Indiana University Pervasive Technology Institute (IUPTI)

David Y. Hancock, Therese Miller, Jeremy Fischer
IUPTI

R. Lee Liming
University of Chicago

George Turner, John Michael Lowe
IUPTI

Steven Gregory, Edwin Skidmore
University of Arizona

Matthew Vaughn
Texas Advanced Computing Center, University of Texas at Austin

Dan Stanzione
Texas Advanced Computing Center, University of Texas at Austin

Nirav Merchant
University of Arizona

Ian Foster
University of Chicago and Argonne National Laboratory

James Taylor
Johns Hopkins University

Paul Rad
University of Texas San Antonio

Volker Brendel
Indiana University

Enis Afgan
Johns Hopkins University

Michael Packard
Texas Advanced Computing Center, University of Texas at Austin

Therese Miller

IUPTI

Winona Snapp-Childs

IUPTI

8.1   Overview

Jetstream[1] [45] is a first-of-a-kind cloud system funded by the National Science Foundation and by contributions from the several participants that created and now operate this system. It is a first-of-a-kind system in the sense that it is the first cloud system funded by the NSF accessible to and designed to be a resource for the national research community. Jetstream is also in a real sense a pilot project because the NSF has never before funded the creation of a cloud system. Proposing and implementing Jetstream was at times very much a process of putting a square peg into a round hole. Jetstream was funded through an NSF high performance computing (HPC) system acquisition solicitation, but the actual acquisition of the hardware from the vendor (Dell) was a small minority of the effort needed to put a cloud system into production.

The majority of the effort to implement Jetstream was the system integration and software installation done by the team of academic institutions that proposed the creation of Jetstream. The system software for Jetstream is mostly open source - it runs the widely used OpenStack cloud software system [51], as well as many other open software components. As we will explain in this chapter, the implementation of Jetstream was a useful learning experience for the NSF and other NSF-funded cyberinfrastructure implementers forming a model for OpenStack-based clouds that others may follow. Most importantly, it is now demonstrably useful to many researchers and students. Thus far Jetstream has been a significant success. It has been in production operation since June 2016. A total of 2,013 individuals currently have accounts on the system, and more than 8,500 users have run jobs on Jetstream via Science Gateways and workflow systems that operate on the system.

Jetstream is the first US-based cloud system designed specifically for production use by a national community of researchers from many disciplines and is thus a harbinger of things to come. It is a managed science cloud - a cloud managed for science. In our early experiences with Jetstream, we have already discovered an interesting and important difference between Jetstream and other major cyberinfrastructure resources: Jetstream is "programmable cyberinfrastructure." That is, the function and behavior of Jetstream can be configured and modified by users with no intervention of the systems administrators. Users have sudo privileges within their own virtual machines (VMs). Thus, users may independently and autonomously configure virtual clusters within Jetstream and implement and use tools that coordinate and orchestrate the use of many VMs or containers within Jetstream.

At over half a PetaFLOPS of peak theoretical processing capacity, Jetstream may well be the lowest of any high performance computing (HPC) system described in this book. However, "high performance computing" can be viewed as relative to what a given researcher or scholar is accustomed to using. In that sense a cloud system based on current-generation processors is indeed high performance computing and an important part of the national and international approach to advanced cyberinfrastructure and eScience.

In this chapter we describe the implementation of Jetstream focusing on: architectures; implementation approaches; lessons learned; uses and applications that constitute interesting departures from the traditional NSF-funded HPC systems and their users. In particular we will focus on the user communities that have made extensive use of Jetstream already, and what we have learned in roughly a year and a half of production operation of Jetstream.

---

[1]Craig A. Stewart and David Y. Hancock contributed equally to the creation of this report.

8.1.1 Jetstream Motivation and Sponsor Background

The National Science Foundation began providing what we now call cyberinfrastructure for the US research community in the 1980s with its supercomputer center program [28, 49]. The supercomputers created as national resources were available to researchers via a proposal process and were described as serving a "time machine" function - taking a small number of researchers from the (then) present into the future of supercomputer capabilities to solve the most computationally challenging problems in science.

Over time, in keeping with the NSF's general evolution of goals and concerns, the NSF put progressively more focus on broadening access to and utility of the cyberinfrastructure that it funds for use by the US national research community [49]. The most recent reset of NSF approaches to provisioning of cyberinfrastructure came with the creation of the XD (eXtreme Data) program that began with a series of solicitations in 2008 [30]. The NSF subsequently organized the delivery of cyberinfrastructure services into a central supporting organization called XSEDE (the eXtreme Science and Engineering Discovery Environment) [52], which coordinates access and support for cyberinfrastructure resources, and a group of Service Providers (SPs) that operate particular cyberinfrastructure resources accessible to the national research community via XSEDE and with support from XSEDE. The largest resources accessible via XSEDE are called "Level 1" SPs and are funded through a series of solicitations entitled "High Performance System Acquisition." The systems funded under this series of solicitations, prior to Jetstream, are listed in Table 8.1.

TABLE 8.1: High Performance System Acquisition Systems.

System	SP	Years in use	TFLOPS	Special Characteristics
Ranger	TACC	7	579.4	First system in the NSF "Path to Petascale" program
Kraken	NICS	5	607/1000	First PetaFLOPS system in the NSF "Path to Petascale" program
Keeneland	GA Tech	5	615	Early platform for GPU heterogeneous computing
Gordon	SDSC	5	340	Early use of flash memory for supercomputing
FutureGrid	IU led	5	54.8	Cloud testbed system
Stampede	TACC	4	5168	Heterogeneous computing with Xeon Phi
Wrangler	TACC led	4	Not applicable	NAND Flash storage utilized
Comet	SDSC	4	2000	HPC plus cloudmesh virtual cluster capabilities

Of the above, only FutureGrid and Wrangler were something other than a traditional supercomputer or HPC cluster (although several had interesting feature such as large-memory or accelerator-equipped nodes). FutureGrid [56] was an experimental grid / cloud system that was intended for computer science research and basically exempted from integration with XSEDE. The NSF has more recently funded two other experimental cloud systems independent of XSEDE, through other programs, called Chameleon and Cloudlab [28, 26, 29]. Wrangler is a data analytics and data storage system. All of the traditional supercomputers and HPC clusters funded by the NSF HPC acquisition solicitations were heavily used by a large group of researchers across the US who need batch-oriented supercomputers. But none of these resources were well suited to delivering modest amounts of computing power available interactively and on demand. And the best way to do that is via a cloud.

As of 2014, the NSF had never funded the creation of a general purpose cloud for production use, even though cloud computing was well established in the commercial space at that time. FutureGrid was and Chameleon and Cloudlab are meant to support experiments in cloud computing itself, and are focused on computer science research, not on producing production scientific results in other fields. So if the needs of a researcher working in any discipline other than computer science were best met by cloud computing resources, the only option was to turn to the commercial sector. The NSF had no cloud resources to offer.

Recognizing this lack of cloud resources in the NSF portfolio of advanced computing systems in particular as well as the general need to broaden the utility of the resources available through XSEDE, the NSF in its 2014 solicitation entitled "High Performance Computing System Acquisition: Continuing the Building of a More Inclusive Computing Environment for Science and Engineering" [18] put special focus on "non-traditional" high performance computing. It specifically stated that "The current solicitation is intended to complement previous NSF investments in advanced computational infrastructure by exploring new and creative approaches to delivering computational resources to the scientific community."

With existing NSF resources including several traditional HPC systems and with a new data-oriented resource already funded (Wrangler), we saw an opportunity and a need to create a cyberinfrastructure resource that addressed a very large group of researchers who needed modest amounts of computing power interactively and dynamically on demand - exactly what cloud computing does best.

We knew that a successful proposal to the NSF to fund a cloud resource would have to include clear evidence of specific needs for such a system and a clear and convincing plan for facilitating the adoption of a cloud system. The Texas Advanced Computing Center [50] agreed to partner with the Indiana University Pervasive Technology Institute [44] with IUPTI as the lead institution in a proposal to the NSF because of IUPTI's track record in needs analysis, strategies for adoption of computing resources, and past history of success with novel HPC systems. We used a well-established format and approach to use case analysis based on approaches of the Systems Engineering Institute at Carnegie Mellon University [25] and previously used by IUPTI and its collaborators within XSEDE [48, 47].

Based on the need to deliver cloud computing in a user-friendly way, the need to integrate a proposed cloud system with the XSEDE infrastructure and processes (as specified in the NSF solicitation), and an eye to attracting and supporting researchers in the biological community (which we believed to be the largest potential community of users who did not see batch-oriented supercomputing as helpful), IUPTI and TACC invited the following other organizations to participate in the Jetstream project with funding from the NSF for their part in this project:

- The University of Arizona, because of the user-friendliness of their Atmosphere interface for OpenStack clouds, as well as their leadership in the CyVerse project highlight (one of the two largest projects creating frameworks for biologically oriented computing) and experience with on-boarding first generation of domain scientists using cloud infrastructure [21, 27].

- The University of Chicago, for integration with XSEDE authentication (via Globus [53, 9]), as well as their expertise in data science and the "long tail" of science.

- Johns Hopkins University, because of their leadership of the Galaxy bioinformatics workflow system (the other of the two largest projects creating frameworks for biologically oriented computing) [3].

- Cornell University (because of their expertise in creating high quality online tutorials).

- University of Texas San Antonio (because of their expertise in cloud technology and their excellent outreach and educational activities).

During the planning for Jetstream, the largest amount of work done was the work reaching out to well established communities of researchers who we thought might find a cloud computing resource to be useful. From these conversations, we distilled a set of generalized use cases:

- A researcher wants straightforward access to specific, usually interactive, tools to analyze data delivered in a manner congruent with their normal operations and often driven by availability of new data.

- A related and also common use case we heard, generally from scientists who are developing new software, was: a tool producer develops new analysis routines and methods to address research bottlenecks, and needs to make said tool available to experimentalists without having them contend with technical complexities of operating system and software dependencies.

Among the use cases distinguished by mode of access or mode of use of CI resources, the following affect the largest number of users:

- Enhance ease of science gateway deployment. Science Gateways provide web-accessible implementations of particular analyses and scientific workflows.

- Facilitate reproducible data analyses. Enable reproducibility of data analyses and published research.

- Enable analysis of public data sets at small schools with limited CI budgets (including MSIs).

The disciplines and sub-disciplines from which representatives seemed most interested in the capabilities of cloud computing included biology, earth science and polar science, field station research, network science, observational astronomy, and the social sciences. We recognized early on a conundrum with our plans: there was no way that we could support the large diversity of access modalities and disciplines that had needs for cloud computing within the budget guidelines from the NSF for its HPC system acquisition. Also, we knew from our work with XSEDE that XSEDE did not have the resources to do so either. (Several of the Jetstream partners also are funded participants in or leaders of XSEDE, so we have good understanding of the constraints facing that project.) We adopted a strategy of identifying pre-existing disciplinary groups or academic leaders which had existing programs that we could leverage so that we could support leaders and organizations in the areas listed above, and then they could facilitate communities supporting their own use of Jetstream. We thus added several partners to the Jetstream project to complement the disciplinary expertise of the core proposing team, including:

- Johns Hopkins University (James Taylor and the Galaxy Project)

- The National Snow and Ice Data Center Network (earth and polar science)

- The Odum Institute at the University of North Carolina (social sciences)

- University of Hawai'i (oceanography, biology, outreach - also home to Stakeholder Advisory Board Chair Dr. Gwen Jacobs)

- University of Arkansas Pine Bluff

- National Center for Genome Analysis Support (bioinformatics)

With this set of funded and unfunded collaborators, we set out to create a cloud system that would attract many thousands of users. Our approaches to adoption strategy are rooted in sociological research on technology adoption [55] which finds that individuals choose whether or not to adopt a particular piece of new technology based on: performance expectancy (perceived value), effort expectancy (perceived ease of use), social influence, and facilitating conditions (including knowledge of a technology and the belief that end users will find it accessible). A cloud computing system, particularly with the Atmosphere user interface, provided a tool that we thought would be perceived to be useful and straightforward to use. The engagement of many disciplinary experts and communities provided social influences and facilitating conditions that we expected to encourage use of the system. All we needed then was a catchy name. The Jetstream name was motivated by the NSF solicitation and our plans to significantly broaden use of the resources funded by the NSF. In the upper atmosphere, the Jetstream constitutes the border between two very large air masses. As a cyberinfrastructure system, our intent was that Jetstream would function at the border of existing NSF-funded cyberinfrastructure and its users, and a new group of users who had not previously made use of the resources funded by the NSF.

8.1.2 Timeline

The Jetstream acquisition proposal was submitted to the National Science Foundation on May 15, 2014. Award notice was confirmed on November 20, 2014, in time to announce the project on the last day of the ACM/IEEE Supercomputing 2014 Conference in New Orleans, LA. The project start date on the cooperative agreement was December 1, 2014, which called for an initial Project Execution Plan (PEP) within 90 days of award execution. The technical team met in Arizona in mid-December to begin technical planning for the system, including scheduling and authentication. An all-hands meeting was held in January 2015 to fully discuss not only the hardware acquisition, but technical implementation of the software stack that would drive the cloud system.

Through this process, we formally established with the NSF the following planned functions for Jetstream:

- Offers "self-serve" academic cloud services, enabling researchers or students to select a pre-existing VM image or to create a new virtual environment for personalized research computing.

- Hosts persistent Science Gateways.

- Enables data movement, storage, and dissemination.
    - Jetstream supports data transfer with Globus Connect.
    - Users are able to store VMs in the Indiana University digital repository, IUScholarWorks, identified and discoverable with a Digital Object Identifier (DOI)

- Provides virtual desktop services delivered to tablet devices which increases access to CI for users at resource-limited institutions (e.g. small schools, schools in EPSCoR jurisdictions, and Minority Serving Institutions).

We wanted to mimic the functionality of commercial cloud systems with near 100 percent uptime. To do this, we installed the Jetstream production hardware in two different geographical regions - Indiana University, operated by the Pervasive Technology Institute (IUPTI) and the University of Texas Austin, operated by the Texas Advanced Computing Center (TACC). We also needed a test system, which was located at the University of Arizona, where we could test new software components for compatibility and reliability. A purchase agreement to acquire the proposed test system from Dell was executed on March 16, 2015, although the project execution plan (PEP) had not been reviewed and fully approved. This was necessary, in order to keep the project on schedule, with IU assuming financial responsibility. The delivery of the test system was made in April 27, 2015, in time to do performance tests and installation of the initial Jetstream software stack. We set up a Github instance, as well a Jira and Confluence, for project management and for tracking issues with the system deployment.

On May 1, 2015 the NSF program officer assigned to the Jetstream project confirmed that the NSF intended to expedite a peer review of the PEP, since this was a new and novel high performance computing system, with the goal of having it approved by late July, 2015. The peer review of the PEP began on May 18, 2015, and was submitted to the NSF DGA on July 18, 2015 and was added as an amendment to the cooperative agreement. Also, in progress at that time was a draft of the acceptance criteria and process, with Indiana University identified as the "system integrator" in the statement of work presented to Dell and the PEP referred to as the authoritative source of acceptance terms. The hardware purchase order was placed with Dell on July 29, 2015. The final Dell SOW was signed on July 31, 2015, after the PEP had been executed by the NSF. Production systems arrived at IU and TACC in mid-October, 2015.

TABLE 8.2: Acceptance timeline for Jetstream.

Acceptance Task	Jetstream-IU	Jetstream-TACC
Purchase order	07/29/2015	07/29/2015
System arrival	10/19/2015, 10/23/2015	10/16/2015
System boot	11/11/2015	11/03/2015
Functionality pass	01/14/2015	02/24/2016
14-day stability pass	04/21/2016	04/21/2016
NSF review	05/03/2016 - 05/04/2016	
Amended agreement	05/27/2016	

The production system acceptance timeline is outlined in Table 8.2. The NSF required an "early operations phase" that began on February 10, 2016. The "early operations phase" meant the system was available for use "as-is" and usage by friendly users and use was not charged against an allocation. A site review of the project was held May 3 & 4, 2016 at Indiana University to review project implementation, the early operations phase, the set of performance criteria set by the NSF. Table 8.3 shows the acceptance criteria and actual results of hardware and software performance tests.

8.1.3   Hardware Acceptance

The acceptance criteria included basic tests of hardware functionality. These were based - with modifications - on the benchmark tests traditionally used for NSF HPC system acquisitions. Rather than traditional HPC workloads, we had proposed a particular suite of services to be offered by Jetstream and proposed two production locations for one integrated cloud system. We therefore had to invent a set of tests to verify Jetstream's functionality as an integrated cloud system and for each of the four key functions we had agreed upon in the development of the Program Execution Plan that were described in Section 8.1.2.

As a first and most basic part of the system's acceptance, a number of tests were proposed to ensure that the performance of the cluster hardware was within the advertised specifications. Results for these acceptance tests are summarized in Table 8.3.

TABLE 8.3: Jetstream hardware performance functionality test results.

Test	Success criteria	Achieved values	Outcome
Single-Node Performance Tests			
High-Performance Linpack (HPL): Single node Linpack performance (for a problem size using at least half of the memory in a node)	VM performance 80% or more of that achieved in Linux OS	Achieved in Linux OS: Jetstream-IU 697 GFLOPS; Jetstream-TACC 701 GFLOPS Achieved inside VM: 678 GFLOPS Performance in VM: 97% of that in OS	G
STREAM: Single node OpenMP threaded performance (aggregate across the node)	65 GB/s	Jetstream-IU: 100 GB/s Jetstream-TACC: 113 GB/s	G
10 Gigabit Ethernet Bandwidth link performance: At least 1 GB/s for large-message point-to-point	1 GB/s	Jetstream-IU: 1.1 GB/s Jetstream-TACC: 1.2 GB/s	G
File System and Storage Benchmarks			
200 MB/s data transfer rate for data reads, 100 MB/s writes from within a virtual machine to the block storage (system totals). Initial tests done with dd. Subsequent tests done with IOR.	200 MB/s read, 100 MB/s write	Jetstream-IU: 273 MB/s read, 170 MB/s write Jetstream-TACC: 247 MB/s read, 251 MB/s write	G
Use nuttcp to analyze network bandwidth and packet loss[2]	N/A	Jetstream (both clouds): 1.2 GB/s, 0 packet loss	N/A
Use IOR to analyze network bandwidth and I/O to the storage systems[2]	N/A	Jetstream-IU: 263 MB/s read, 155 MB/s write Jetstream-TACC: 229 MB/s read, 235 MB/s write	N/A
System Reliability & Capacity			
Uptime for a period of 14 days	95%	100%	G
VMs simultaneously operating	320 per location	Jetstream-IU: 998 Jetstream-TACC: 832	G

[2]This test was not part of the initial acceptance test set; it was suggested by the review panel appointed by the NSF to review Jetstream.

[3]This test was not part of the initial acceptance test set; it was suggested by the review panel appointed by the NSF to review Jetstream.

8.1.4 Benchmark Results

When evaluating the performance of virtual machines it is necessary to understand the overhead induced by the underlying hypervisor. This insight can be gained by comparing performance results from benchmarks that are run within the VMs versus benchmarks run on the host server. The latter are often being referred to as the "bare metal" results.

The High Performance Computing Challenge (HPCC) benchmark suite is composed of seven benchmarks which measure various aspects of interest in a research computing system [14]. While Jetstream is not a typical distributed memory HPC system, characterizing those aspects measured by the HPCC at the single node level does provide important insights into the expected performance parameters a user might expect when porting their codes into the virtual environment. Results from various benchmarking tests are summarized in 8.4.

TABLE 8.4: Comparison of HPCC performance benchmarks running inside an instance vs. on bare hardware.

Benchmark	Units	Bare hardware	VM	% of bare hardware
HPL	GFLOPS	0.696	0.678	97.4%
DGEMM	GFLOPS	30.66	30.20	98.5%
FFTE	GFLOPS	13.75	9.215	67.0%
Random	Gup/s	0.364	0.288	79.2%
STREAM	GB/s	88	68	77.1%
PTRANS	GB/s	224	143	63.9%
Bandwidth	GB/s	26	23	88.5%
Latency	μs	0.482	0.471	97.6%

In general what we observed is that for benchmarks that are CPU bound, e.g. HPL and DGEMM, VM performance is nearly that of the bare metal results. On the other hand, bandwidth benchmarks requiring the movement of a significant amount of data through memory channels shows the influence of the hypervisor resulting in a 20-36% decrease in performance. One interesting result that we saw with the STREAM benchmark that we did not see with the other bandwidth bound benchmarks was that by reducing the number of cores by one, we were able to recoup much of the memory performance lost to the hypervisor.

8.1.5 Cloud Functionality Tests

In our proposal to the NSF we asserted that the production hardware located at IUPTI and TACC would function as an integrated cloud system. In consultation with the NSF, we developed a set of tests that by consensus we believed would demonstrate such integrated functionality. In particular, we committed to provide "self-serve" academic cloud services, enabling researchers or students to select a VM image from a published library, or alternatively to create or customize their own virtual environment for discipline- or task-specific personalized research computing. Authentication to this self-serve environment will be via Globus. Proof of functionality was agreed by NSF and the Jetstream team to consist of success in accomplishing the following tasks on Jetstream:

1. An authorized and knowledgeable user will be able to authenticate to the Jetstream user interface (which uses Globus as the mechanism for verification of credentials).

2. After so doing, an authorized and knowledgeable user will be able to launch a virtual machine from a menu of pre-packaged VMs on the production hardware located in Indiana or Texas.

3. After so doing, an authorized and knowledgeable user will be able to quiesce a VM image running on production hardware in Indiana or Texas, move it from one production system to another, and reactivate said VM.

4. An authorized and knowledgeable user can create and access persistent cloud storage on the Indiana or Texas production hardware.

5. An authorized and knowledgeable user can modify a preexisting VM image and manually store that VM image to one of the production locations within Jetstream.

Jetstream does all of these things, and does so now reliably. During the NSF review of Jetstream, we exhibited the ability to pass these tests in live demonstrations. The final version of the acceptance report submitted to the NSF [46] includes screen shots of the critical steps.

8.1.6 Gateway Functionality Tests

The Jetstream PEP also included functionality tests for supporting Science Gateways, developed by agreement between the NSF and the Jetstream team.The success criteria and demonstrated results of support for Science Gateways are shown in 8.5.

TABLE 8.5: Jetstream gateway functionality and performance tests.

Test	Success criteria	Key test metric result achieved	Outcome
Galaxy gateway availability and correct function	Gateway executes a known workflow in ≤125% of the time required to run on another XSEDE system	Normalized for clock speed, a known workflow completes in 80% of the time to run on Stampede	G
One other gateway functioning in XSEDE-environments will function on Jetstream	Gateway will operate correctly and be available within 2% of overall system availability in 14-day test period	SEAGrid operated continuously for 14 days	G

8.1.7 Data Movement, Storage, and Dissemination

The Jetstream PEP also included functionality tests for supporting data movement, storage, and dissemination. The proofs of functionality agreed to by consensus between NSF and the Jetstream leadership, and codified in the PEP, were as follows:

- An authorized and knowledgeable user can select a file to which they have rights on a system outside Jetstream, and move that file and save it on storage on Jetstream (with the condition that the file size is within the storage quota set for their use on Jetstream).

- An authorized and knowledgeable user can select a file to which they have rights on Jetstream, and move that file and save it on storage to a system on which that user has rights and which is accessible from open public networks (with the condition that the file size is within the storage quota set for their use on Jetstream).

- An authorized and knowledgeable user can successfully save a VM previously stored to disk storage on Jetstream into a format supported by DSpace, upload that file to IUScholarWorks *scholarworks.iu.edu*, and submit that document for publication via IUScholarWorks via online forms. Subsequent to that, the VM will appear in IUScholarWorks and the user will receive a DOI identifier for that object.

These tests were passed successfully in live demonstrations for the NSF review panel and documented via screen shots contained in [46].

8.1.8   Acceptance by NSF

On May 27, 2016 the NSF granted IU authority to pay Dell for the production hardware. The NSF declared the system in full production on June 1, 2016. The operations and maintenance phase began on that date. This means that: the Jetstream team was expected to keep the system up and running in compliance with the operational standards agreed to by the NSF and the Jetstream team; researchers using Jetstream were doing so on the basis of allocations applied and approved by XSEDE; and XSEDE was to begin providing support for users of Jetstream.

8.2   Applications and Workloads

We made it a primary goal to attract user communities that have been under-served by the national cyberinfrastructure. As shown in Table 8.6, Jetstream has excelled especially in three areas: biological sciences, computer science, and education. The nature of the cloud resource on demand, long runtime ability and lack of wall clock limitations, and ability to customize workflows is important for the first two. The growth of Jetstream for educational use has been a concerted effort by the Jetstream staff to demonstrate to educators and researchers the flexibility of Jetstream for courses and workshops. This not only gives the ability to have custom images tailored to the syllabus, it engages researchers and students, expanding their knowledge while also showing the value of Jetstream to their present and future work.

TABLE 8.6: Distribution of allocations by discipline for Jetstream PY1 and for all other systems supported and allocated via XSEDE.

Discipline or area of interest	# of Jetstream allocations	SUs allocated on Jetstream	% of SUs allocated on Jetstream	% of SUs allocated on other XSEDE-supported systems
Astronomy	2	1,108,096	3.04%	8.61%
Atmospheric sciences	4	2,752,400	7.55%	3.73%
Biological sciences	57	5,199,000	14.27%	4.95%
Campus/Domain champions	123	6,105,500	16.76%	0.09%
Computational science	11	1,150,000	3.16%	0.92%
Computer science	15	4,944,302	13.57%	1.8%
Education	24	2,847,600	7.82%	0.01%
Engineering	1	100,000	0.27%	3.81%
Geosciences	10	1,978,400	5.43%	2.87%
Humanities/Social sciences	10	560,000	1.54%	0.45%
Molecular biosciences	8	4,647,520	12.75%	17.65%
Network science	3	200,000	0.55%	0.06%
Ocean science	3	230,000	0.63%	1.30%
Physics	4	2,252,400	6.18%	16.43%
Training, development	11	2,362,000	6.48%	0.16%

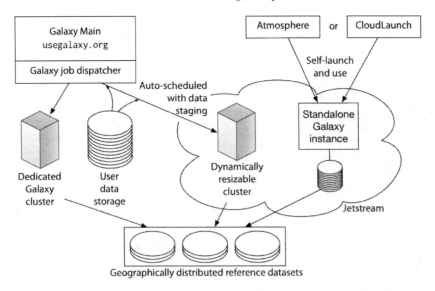

FIGURE 8.1: Integration of Galaxy with Jetstream.

8.2.1 Highlights of Main Applications

Applications on Jetstream are not viewed in the same way they would be for a traditional HPC environment. Instead of focusing on single applications, Jetstream looks at workflows and use cases. Based on actual usage today as well as interest from users who have contacted the Jetstream team, some of the most widely used applications on Jetstream are described below.

Galaxy is an "open, web-based platform for accessible, reproducible, and transparent computational biomedical research" [3]. It is one of the most popular bioinformatics workflow tools in existence. In the first 15 months of integration with Jetstream, more than 105,000 Galaxy jobs were successfully run on Jetstream on behalf of more than 8,500 users. Their jobs were submitted via the Galaxy Main gateway available at *usegalaxy.org* without any end-user intervention. This constitutes more than 15% of the total CPU use on Jetstream — Galaxy is the single most widely used application on Jetstream. In addition, it is possible to launch personal, dedicated Galaxy instances on Jetstream that have been pre-configured for immediate use. Self-launched instances have no usage quotas and come with over 150 tools installed with access to 4TB of reference genomic data, which is available as a shared, read-only, geographically distributed file system multiple Galaxy instances can connect to. Once instantiated, it is also possible for the user to install additional tools as needed on the standalone instance. Figure 8.1 captures the two modes of how Galaxy integrates with Jetstream.

The CyVerse project has also been a source of tools from the biology and bioinformatics communities ported to Jetstream from Cyverse, such as BWASP [6] and WQ-MAKER, a cloud native implementation of popular genome annotation package MAKER-P [8]. A general bioinformatics suite, Biolinux containing dozens of bioinformatics applications is also available and widely used on Jetstream.

R and RStudio are also applications that have been used frequently for courses and workshops. The interactive nature of Jetstream allows for more complex R calculations faster than they could on local workstations while letting researchers continue using the application interface that they are comfortable with. Jetstream provides R with support for the Intel compilers as well as GCC.

As noted before, education is a prime use case for Jetstream. To more fully examine education as a practical application of Jetstream, the Jetstream staff conducted a survey of Principle Investigators (PIs) with education allocations on Jetstream. The results of this survey were reviewed and published in a paper for SIGUCCS17 [16]. This survey explored some of the primary uses (applications) of Jetstream, one of them being Jetstream as an educational platform. Beyond that initial use of Jetstream as a base for education, there have been several highly used applications and workflows. Several courses and workshops in the survey used Galaxy as part of their workflows and Galaxy Main (*usegalaxy.org*) also utilizes Jetstream as an elastic computing resource for processing jobs that meet a certain profile [15].

The Volker Brendel lab at IU has based its training of graduate students on use of Jetstream. New students start their computational training in bioinformatics on Jetstream. The group maintains a handbook with short How-Tos that explain basic procedures in the group [5]. Implemented as a github repository, the handbook encourages contributions by all group members and works nicely to impart some of the basic group knowledge and protocols. The Brendel group has developed its own virtual machine image, called bgRAMOSE, based on Ubuntu 16.04, publicly available on Jetstream and described as follows: "This image provides a platform for Brendel Group RAMOSE workflows for computational genomics. ... we take every effort to design our workflows such that a user can generate reproducible, accurate, and meaningful results; our software is open (source), scalable, and easy to use (so that a typical genome laboratory team should be able to run it)... ." The image contains all common bioinformatics software used in the Brendel Lab. There are multiple benefits to this approach. New group members only need a little bit of training on how to use Jetstream. After that theyll have immediate access to a clean workspace with all our favorite tools accessible. The students own their own bgRAMOSE instances on Jetstream and can happily explore the consequences of sudo privileges without any possibility of causing harm outside their own VMs. And, students developing code or workflows for their own projects have the tools they need to communicate clearly what they have done and how someone else could reproduce their work. All in all, Jetstream has become the cornerstone of this lab's computational work.

Of course, the best indicators of the quality of a pudding comes from the dinner guests, not the cooks. The following are three examples of Jetstream used in novel and successful ways in education, by people who are users of Jetstream - not part of the Jetstream team:

- The Berkeley Institute for Data Science, University Of California, Berkeley has successfully used Jetstream as the basis for a day-long bootcamp in data science hosted at the University of California in San Francisco (UCSF). The use of Jetstream, rather than software installed on student laptops, was highly successful. Holdgraf et al. [22] described their experiences and offered insights for pedagogical approaches to computational education using Jetstream or other cloud resources.

- PoreCamp USA 2017 [19] a workshop for teaching processing of data for Nanopore based sequencing technology using Wrangler and Jetstream. Data from lab devices were streamed direct to Jetstream for real-time analysis.

- The ANGUS workshop on Next-Gen Sequence Analysis Workshop (2017) at UC Davis depended upon use of Jetstream for a two-week long workshop held in July of 2017 [7].

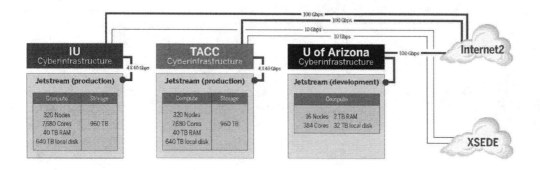

FIGURE 8.2: Jetstream system overview diagram.

8.3 System Overview

Jetstream consists of three components: Jetstream-IU, Jetstream-TACC, and Jetstream-AZ as illustrated in Figure 8.2. We designed Jetstream to deliver availability and reliability in a way that would mimic commercial cloud experiences and be manageable on an acquisition and implementation budget of less than $8M. The facilities in which the production systems are located are described in Section 8.7. Jetstream-AZ is housed at the University of Arizona and serves as a test and development environment.

The two production environments, evenly split between IU and TACC, are referred to as Jetstream-IU and Jetstream-TACC respectively. These are identical and each consists of compute nodes (320 Dell M630 blades), storage nodes (20 Dell R730 servers), and management nodes (7 Dell R630 servers). The system is based on Dell PowerEdge servers with a 10/40 Gbps Fat-Tree Ethernet network, oversubscribed 2:1 ratio [45]. Jetstream's most important innovations are in its reconfigurability and reliance on cutting edge open source software. For this reason the team elected to deploy a homogeneous, unaccelerated environment with reliance on a standard Ethernet fabric to help ensure reliability and stability. Each production environment has a peak capacity theoretical capacity of 258 TeraFLOPS for an aggregate of 516 TeraFLOPS between Jetstream-IU and Jetstream-TACC.

8.4 Hardware Architecture

8.4.1 Node Design and Processor Elements

Jetstream was implemented using three different Dell PowerEdge Servers; M630 blades that primarily host VMs and lightweight services, R630 servers for management, database, and load-balancing functions, and R730 servers for storage services. Each Dell PowerEdge server contains two Intel "Haswell" E5-2680v3 (12-core) processors operating at 2.5 GHz, 2133 MHz bus with 30 MB L3 cache, 12 x 256 KB L2 cache. The compute blades, storage servers, and management systems use the same processor.

The Dell PowerEdge systems use Intel's C610 chipset. The M630 nodes have a peak theoretical performance of 806.4 GigaFLOPS with the aforementioned processors. Each

M630 has a PERC H330 RAID controller and dual 1 TB 7.2K RPM NL-SAS 6 Gbps 2.5in Hot- plug system devices. Each R630 has a PERC H330 integrated RAID controller and dual 400 GB Solid State Drive (SSD) SATA Mix Use MLC 6 Gbps 2.5in Hot-plug system devices. Each R730 has a PERC H730P integrated RAID controller with 2 GB cache, dual 200 GB Solid State Drive SATA Mix Use MLC 6 Gbps 2.5in Flex Bay system devices, and twelve 4 TB 7.2K RPM NL-SAS 6 Gbps 3.5in Hot-plug Hard storage devices.

Each Dell M630, R630, and R730 has 24 DDR4 DIMM slots running at 2133MT/s. The M630's have 128 GB RAM whereas the R630 and R730's have 64 GB of RAM.

8.4.2 Interconnect

Dual Dell Networking MXL 10/40 Gbps Ethernet blade switches are used as leaf switches. Dell Force10 S6000 10/40 Gbps Ethernet switches are used for top-of-rack (ToR) switches and spine infrastructure. For Jetstream-IU and Jetstream-TACC, every sixteen M630 blades connect via bonded 2 x 10 Gbps links, using Intel X710 dual-port adapters, to the two Dell MXL switches in each blade chassis (with virtual link trunking enabled), which each uplink to the ToR Dell Force10 (F10) S6000 switches via two bonded 40 Gbps links resulting in 2:1 over-subscription to the blades. Each ToR S6000 then connects via 2 x 40 Gbps links into each of the two spine S6000 switches. The two spine F10 S6000 are cross linked at 3 x 40 Gbps for 120 Gbps aggregate. Each F10 S6000 spine switch is then uplinked to the data centers Science DMZ via 2 x 40 Gbps uplinks for a total of 4 x 40 Gbps. The R630 management and R730 storage nodes link into the F10 S6000 spine switch via dual bonded 10 Gbps links or 40 Gbps links using Intel X710 or XL710 adapters depending on their purpose. Three nodes utilize the XL710 adapters, two of which act as load-balancers for the entire cluster. Dell N3048 1 Gbps management Ethernet switch provide out-of-band management control of the overall system.

8.4.3 Storage Subsystem

Twenty Dell R730 servers form the storage environment for Jetstream. Jetstream does not leverage a traditional parallel filesystem as most HPC systems would. Jetstream uses Ceph for the storage environment, described in more detail in Section 8.5.5. Each R730 system has local SSD storage for caching and twelve 4 TB near-line SAS drives. As Jetstream was funded primarily as a computational resource, the storage capacity within the system is limited. The storage system is utilized for all block and object storage within each site. Individual instances have the options to use local ephemeral storage within their instance or leverage volumes (persistent block devices) that can be attached to individual instances. In either case, the block devices are formatted with EXT4 by default and served by Ceph. (Telemetry data from Ceilometer no longer uses the storage environment as its object storage due to the high IOPS required; instead PCI-based flash devices are used for collecting those data.)

8.5   System Software

8.5.1   Operating System

OpenStack is the "cloud operating system" that powers Jetstream. It is a collection of projects that provide services to orchestrate the delivery of computational, networking, and

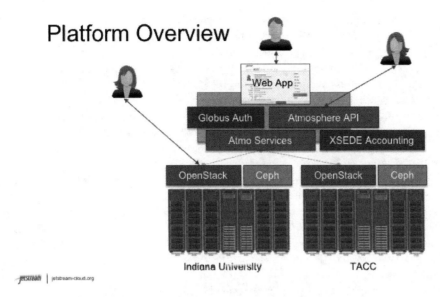

FIGURE 8.3: Jetstream Platform Overview.

storage resources. Each individual project is designed to work with the other projects but functions and is developed independently. Jetstream users interact with these projects and higher-level services as illustrated in Figure 8.3. The cloud infrastructure is based upon OpenStack with its ability to deliver virtualized compute capacity. The Atmosphere orchestration layer and interface provides the software interface directly experienced by the user as discussed in Section 8.6. Globus authentication services manage authentication of users, further discussed in Section 8.5.6, and enable rapid data movement into and out of, and data sharing on Jetstream. Users can also interact directly with Application Programming Interfaces (APIs) at the OpenStack layer for tighter integration with other systems or services such as web-based Science Gateways or on-demand scaling of workloads for computational or workshop needs.

Jetstream was originally deployed using services from the OpenStack fall 2015 Liberty release. The system has since been upgraded multiple times and as of summer 2017 is using OpenStack Ocata. The OpenStack community operates around a six-month, time-based release cycle with frequent development milestones [36]. Hosts that operate OpenStack and Atmosphere services currently use different operating systems: Ubuntu 14.04 for Atmosphere, Ubuntu 16.04 for databases and messaging, and Centos 7.3 for compute and OpenStack services. All projects follow similar design patterns, a stateless API server, agents that execute the requests from the API server, schedulers that direct the requests from the API server to the best execution agent, a database where all state is contained, and a message bus to transmit all RPC (remote procedure call) requests between components. The use of stateless agents and a message bus allow for horizontal scaling within a project, as well as high availability features. Jetstream takes full advantage of both horizontal scaling and high availability in its design as discussed in Section 8.5.2.

8.5.2   System Administration

OpenStack services on the Indiana University portion of the cloud use 882 host specific configuration files distributed among 290 hosts. OpenStack introduces deprecations and removals of configuration options with every release. Strong configuration management tools are essential for a large OpenStack deployment. Each partner selected the configuration management tool that they were most familiar with: SaltStack for IU and Puppet for TACC. One strength of SaltStack is the tight integration with git, allowing the production deployment directly from a public git repository [24]. Using salt and adapting the configuration from the Jetstream test cluster, OpenStack on the IU cloud was deployed between November 9, 2015 when the node operating systems were installed and December 15, 2015 when the first instance was started. Holiday and conference schedules left 17 business days during this period for deployment; a typical deployment for a cluster of this size is 60 business days. TACC has used Puppet for previous projects and opted to continue using it for deploying Jetstream. The publicly available IU salt configurations were reimplemented in Puppet and then applied at TACC.

Configuration management is also an important consideration with respect to system maintenance. A traditional HPC system is expected to take downtime for maintenance, which is possible because jobs have a fixed maximum duration. For every batch system, there is a time in the future where every running job will have terminated and a barrier can be placed beyond that time where no job will be started that will run past the barrier. This window of idle time can be used for maintenance on any subsystem that would cause failures in either the batch system itself or the jobs. A cloud system does not have instances with a fixed maximum duration nor does it queue requests to be serviced later, presenting two challenges not faced with a traditional HPC environment. Maintenance must be performed while the system is in use. As a result, we looked to enterprise and commercial cloud systems as examples for designing management plans. Load balancers servicing all cloud API requests are vital to rolling updates to cloud services. OpenStack services have large overlapping dependency trees, making service by service update on a single node likely to fail. Instead, a cloud service node is taken out of rotation and all services updated. Once fully updated, services are stopped on out-of-date nodes and the requests are directed to the updated node by the load balancers. With all services running on an updated node the remaining nodes are updated and put back into rotation. Similarly, rolling updates of compute nodes have instances migrated to idle updated hosts, updates performed, and updated compute nodes returned to service.

The most direct effect of configuration management for the end user is the use of Ansible by Atmosphere to add users to VMs just after instance boot. Instances boot without users save the root user. Other minor conveniences are deployed at immediately after boot like setting host names to match DNS names given to the public IP address and web desktop components. Also injected by Ansible is a Jupyter bootstrap script which performs the optional deployment of Jupyter in a single step and is launched through the "ezj" command within an Atmosphere-launched instance as discussed in Section 8.9.1.

8.5.3   Schedulers and Virtualization

Along with a lack of scheduled preventative maintenance, one of the significant challenges to operating a cloud-based environment is the absence of a traditional HPC scheduler or resource manager. A scheduler in the OpenStack Nova realm is no more than an algorithm for placement of resource requests on host systems. If no resources are available, one can retry the request, but there is not an option to queue that request as one would do with a traditional batch job. Jetstream first started with a placement strategy to optimize performance of individual virtual machine (VM) instances, and those instances were spread out among compute hosts. As resource utilization increased, this placement algorithm lead to the inability to launch larger VM instance sizes that occupy an entire physical host without action by administrators to migrate smaller instances to pack them on hosts where possible. Jetstream now operates with a placement policy that looks more like a best-fit strategy for instance placement. The absence of traditional HPC queuing and scheduling makes resource utilization planning and the allocation process more critical than in most environments, particularly when considering a deployment of limited size.

Jetstream uses KVM as the hypervisor for compute hosts with a configuration that allows live migration of VMs, removing the need for scheduled maintenance on most services in the software stack. The exception is the Atmosphere user portal which does not currently operate in a high-availability configuration. When Atmosphere is under maintenance, running instances are still accessible, and any services that leverage the OpenStack APIs are still available (E.g. users can still directly access their VMs and manage resources with OpenStack Horizon or command line interface tools). As seen in Section 8.1.2 the measured overhead for single-node HPL was less than 3% during acceptance testing, and large instances still have the ability to saturate a 10 Gbps link leaving little reason to operate in a bare-metal configuration that would not allow for live migration of instances. Single Root IO Virtualization (SRIOV) presents virtual machines with virtual PCI express interfaces multiplexed into a single real PCI Express device on the hypervisor. SRIOV is typically used to maximize performance of network interfaces and by virtue of presenting real hardware to the virtual machine excludes the possibility of live migration. Jetstream was able to achieve near line rate with acceptable latency without the use of SRIOV. Since Jetstream was awarded the use of containers and orchestration systems have increased rapidly, such services are available on Jetstream and discussed in Section 8.6.

Jetstream compute nodes have Intel Hyper-Threading enabled and a vCPU consists of a single Hyper-Threaded core. The currently available instance sizes for Jetstream are shown in Table 8.7. Jetstream limits over-subscription of physical cores and does not throttle IOPs per instance in order to be responsive to scientific, engineering, and educational workloads. This design decision is in direct contrast to most commercial and private cloud environments where resources such as CPUs, memory, and storage are often over-subscribed or constrained in order to pack the maximum number of instances per physical host, a strategy that's optimized for background or low-intensity web services.

TABLE 8.7: Jetstream instance "flavors"

Flavor	vCPUs	RAM (GB)	Storage	Max Per Node
tiny	1	2	8	46
small	2	4	20	23
medium	6	16	60	7
large	10	30	120/60*	4
xlarge	24	60	240/60*	2
xxlarge	44	120	480/60*	1

* Flavors updated March 2017; storage-rich flavors are no longer imaged.

8.5.4 Security

Jetstream's security concerns are drastically different from HPC systems as users are given root. Thus a multi-layered approach is paramount and perhaps even more critical. Automated external network-based scans are performed regularly for known vulnerabilities. Network intrusion detection systems monitor every network packet transmitted to and from the system. Real-time analysis is performed by a Bro cluster attempting to detect and notify of possible malicious activity. Alerts are treated as an opportunity to extend the teaching of best practices to users. The most common issues the Jetstream team encounters are user instances with unsecured MongoDB or Elasticsearch services. When simple mitigation is possible, like closing a port with a firewall rule or closing anonymous access, it is the preferred route. Atmosphere limits open ports <1024 but opens unrestricted ports, making it easier for most users to install and use common software packages. Atmosphere abstracts the details of security groups and network creation for ease of use reasons. Through the API side of Jetstream, one must specifically open each port or range of ports through manipulation of an instance's security policy which restricts network traffic through the hypervisor external to the instance and not through a local host-based firewall.

The nature of clouds in general, and certainly Jetstream, make it conducive to minimal investment in recovery, if one is following deployment best practices; a seriously compromised instance is destroyed rather than cleaned up and rescued. Currently IU is piloting updating all software packages in an instance on first boot. The trade-offs are a much lower likelihood of running vulnerable software in exchange for longer, possibly very long, boot times, as well as possibly breaking a user's software environment due to a package upgrade. Featured images are refreshed frequently ensuring that older vulnerable software is not supplied to users by Jetstream, but users must do this themselves for private images or images they maintain for a community of users.

8.5.5   Storage Software

Ceph [41] storage backs all aspects of Jetstream. It is a software defined object storage system that can assemble the objects for higher order semantics. Objects can be ordered with the use of read and write offsets to emulate block devices. This emulation of block devices with objects is the basis for all block devices on Jetstream including images, volumes, and instance root disks. Ceph has strong snapshot and copy on write capabilities used to do low cost thinly provisioned clones of images into root disks for instances. This capability greatly reduces the cost of instance startup. Centralized storage facilitates live migration of instances between hypervisors; only the processor state and memory contents need to be transfered. Ceph, by default uses host level replication to ensure high availability; the other option is erasure coding the objects and sharding between hosts. Data from images and ephemeral root disks are replaceable to a higher degree than data on volumes, hence they only have two replicas as opposed to three replicas for volumes. Ceph RADOS gateway implements the OpenStack Swift and Amazon Web Services S3 protocols for object storage. Object storage semantics do not have strong consistency properties, and expectations for latency are such that the trade-off of using erasure coding for object storage is acceptable. Consequently the object storage via Swift or S3 on Jetstream is erasure coded with 4 data blocks and 2 recovery blocks for a 50% overhead vs 300% for block storage with volumes.

Wrangler is similar to Jetstream in that it is a joint IU and TACC system with hardware housed at both sites. Wrangler's data oriented design and co-location with Jetstream allows XSEDE projects with big data and cloud needs to use both systems. By special arrangement, projects can have their portion of Wrangler's 10PB Lustre filesystem exported over NFS to their Jetstream virtual machines.

8.5.6   User Authentication

Jetstream aims to support researchers and teams who may be new to the national cyber-infrastructure. Consequently, the user experience for gaining access to the system must be as straightforward as possible. A web browser interface is essential. Jetstream's applications in campus bridging and science gateways [48] require a flexible identity system, notably allowing researchers and students to identify themselves via their campus authentication systems. As a resource allocated via the NSF's national allocation process [58], Jetstream must also be integrated with XSEDE's resource allocation system and allow use of XSEDE credentials.

From the start of this project we planned to use Globus Auth [53, 20] as Jetstream's user authentication mechanism. Globus Auth is part of the Globus platform-as-a-service (PaaS) operated for the research community by the University of Chicago. XSEDE already uses Globus Auth, and–via the CILogon service operated by NCSA [4] – Globus Auth allows user authentication via hundreds of college and university campuses and research organizations. Globus has since added support for Google and ORCID [37]. Because Globus Auth is based on the popular OAuth 2.0 [1] and OpenID Connect 1.0 [42] standards, the Jetstream team was able to use an open source Python client from Google to add Globus Auth's login function to its web interface. Globus Auth's application configuration allows Jetstream to require users to be registered with XSEDE. After a successful login, Jetstream receives the user's XSEDE identity regardless of how the user authenticated. This makes it easier to coordinate with XSEDE's allocation system. The details of Globus auth integration for the Atmosphere portal are described in Section 8.6.3.

8.5.7 Allocation Software and Processes

Jetstream is allocated entirely via the XSEDE Resource Allocation System (XRAS), including tracking of PI discretionary time. This process allows for various kinds of allocation awards, from Campus/Domain Champion awards for XSEDE advocates and programmers to startup allocations for beginning research and testing workflows. Education allocations are for those using an XSEDE resource for courses, tutorials, and workshops. Lastly, research allocations are the larger awards for continuing research into specific areas. These allocations are all valid for one year and all but startups are routinely eligible for renewal.

XSEDE allocations have no monetary cost, though they are assigned a monetary value. The "cost" of an XSEDE allocation comes in the form of writing a proposal to do a specific course of research or educational pursuit. The complexity ranges from the simple requirements of a startup allocation [59] to the slightly more involved education allocation [57] to the ten to fifteen page research allocation requirements [58]. These awards are given as resource time in service units (SUs). An SU on Jetstream is 1 virtual CPU (vCPU) for 1 hour. You can receive awards from a typical 50,000 SU startup up to millions of SUs on research allocations.

In addition, Jetstream has an allocation type that is not common in XSEDE: the Jetstream Trial Allocation (JTA). The JTA allows researchers and educators to try Jetstream on a limited basis to see if their needs might be met with a cloud service. JTA gives a streamlined process of getting an XSEDE Portal account and then simply clicking a button to request access [23]. This is intended to let potential users try Jetstream with little commitment or effort until they know if it might work for their needs. The intent is to lower the bar for bringing users to Jetstream.

The TACC Administration System (TAS) provides an integration layer between Jetstream and the XSEDE project. TAS was already in existence to support other TACC supercomputers and provided a complete interface to the XSEDE allocation systems. Within Jetstream, TAS performs five core functions: communication with XSEDE databases, interactions with both OpenStack and Atmosphere to provide user authorization and allocation information, maintaining LDAP information for Jetstream to consume, aggregating the two Jetstream site's usage data into a single resource for XSEDE, and providing reporting information. TAS receives allocation and user information from XSEDE and makes it available to Jetstream via an application program interface (API). Jetstream uses that information to control access to Jetstream itself as well as to determine the amount of SUs the user has available via their allocation and the dates that that allocation is valid. Conversely, Jetstream reports back the usage in SUs per user to TAS to be applied against the allocation. That in turn is reported back to the XSEDE central database where it can be reviewed by the PIs and resource managers in the XSEDE User Portal.

8.6   Programming System

Jetstream has multiple methods of access and working with virtual machines. The one envisioned in the original proposal was the Atmosphere user-friendly, web-based interface based on the original CyVerse (iPlant) interface. This interface was intended to make it easy for the novice researcher, educator, or student to use a VM environment without needing knowledge of networking or OpenStack functionality to achieve their goals. Lowering the bar to research computing has been a common theme when discussing users' needs.

Jetstream also intended to make the OpenStack Application Program Interface (API) available to science gateway developers and other power users. This was not intended to happen during early operations, being considered a "nice to have" service but not crucial to meeting our requirements as set forth in the award. There was enough demand for API services from almost the date Jetstream became public that it was accelerated into service considerably sooner.

Having the API service available makes a number of services possible. The key service it enables is hosting science gateways, as it allows for persistence of IP addresses. It also allows Jetstream users to take advantage of the nature of cloud computing and have truly programmable cyberinfrastructure available to them - a means of dynamically creating customized resources to meet their research or educational needs on demand.

8.6.1   Atmosphere

Atmosphere is an integrative, private, self-service, multi-cloud management platform designed to abstract and simplify the provisioning of cloud resources by orchestrating steps within OpenStack. Atmosphere provides a web-based interface for allowing users to manage the life cycle for their VMs, from searching, sharing, and launching VMs from its curated catalog. Users can easily monitor their consumption of cloud resources and readily de-provision their resources with a few clicks. The value to users is that Atmosphere empowers them to focus on their science rather than the minutiae of cloud-specific processes, allowing them to readily configure and customize VMs that can be shared with groups of collaborators or made publicly discoverable through its catalog.

Jetstream was the first computing system outside of the CyVerse organization to make use of CyVerse's Atmosphere platform. Atmosphere's core capabilities were extended to support pluggable integration with resource providers, making it easier for projects like Jetstream to adopt Atmosphere. Additionally, features necessary for support staff and site operators were enhanced to allow ancillary functions and tasks associated with managing cloud assets for Jetstream.

Atmosphere consists of three core components: Atmosphere middleware [11], Troposphere [13], and atmosphere-ansible [12]. The Atmosphere middleware generally refers to the set of services that monitor and communicates with OpenStack. The Atmosphere middleware also provides facilities to cache information about the cloud, execute operations in OpenStack asynchronously, and allow users to organize and add metadata to cloud assets.

Troposphere is the front-end user interface, allowing users to use their web browser to interact with Jetstream resources. Built on top of Django and javascript React, Troposphere communicates to the Atmosphere backend APIs for authentication, checking the state of their resources, and to take action on those resources. Atmosphere-ansible is the facility that installs and configures instances after being provisioned, and can work in conjunction with cloud-init. Because Atmosphere-ansible operates outside of the instance and can also perform operations within OpenStack, Atmosphere-ansible provides an additional mechanism to perform repeatable, critical configurations on an instance, such as ensuring security mechanisms are enforced before a user gains access to the instance.

8.6.2 Jetstream Plugins for the Atmosphere Platform

8.6.2.1 Authorization

As discussed in Section 8.5.6 Globus Auth had to be integrated into Atmosphere. A custom authentication and authorization plugin was added to Atmosphere for Jetstream called django-cyverse-auth [10]. When a user accesses the Atmosphere web interface without previously being authenticated, the user will be redirected to Globus Auth. Upon successful authentication and being redirected to Atmosphere, the TACC Administration System (TAS) validates the user to ensure he or she has at least one valid Jetstream allocation. Users authorized through TAS gain access to Jetstream and their cloud resources. Troposphere handles authorization failures by redirecting those users to a Jetstream-specific help page explaining how the user can enroll in Jetstream and gain access to a project allocation via XSEDE.

8.6.2.2 Allocation Sources and Special Allocations

In addition to the requirement that Jetstream users can only have access if they have at least one project allocation available, users can only interact with an instance while they have compute time remaining on their allocation. In order to facilitate this requirement, Atmosphere included a new, pluggable approach to creating, managing, and reporting on allocation sources. An allocation source is defined by its name, the compute allowed for the allocation source, and a start date and end date. An overview of allocation types and processes is described in Section 8.5.7.

A plugin was created for Jetstream to grant users access to an allocation source based on their XSEDE allocations available via the TAS APIs. Any instances created by that user must be assigned to an allocation source, although the user is allowed to change the allocation source, at runtime, if he or she has more than one available on his or her account.

To manage a user's compute usage for a given allocation source, Atmosphere opted for a solution that uses both a rules engine and event sourcing. By creating new events for allocation source renewed, allocation source created, allocation source compute allowed changed, user assigned allocation source and instance allocation source changed, we were able to calculate the compute usage for any given user, based on the current rules as laid out in the rules engine.

A new task was created specifically for Jetstream to handle the creation of reports on a user's compute usage. Those reports are then sent to the TAS API to be stored and included in the total compute used for the XSEDE project's allocation. When 100 percent of the allocation source has been consumed and the site operator has configured Atmosphere to enforce allocations, all of the instances that are associated with that allocation source will be shut down. Users who wish to start their existing instances and/or create a new instance will be required to have a new allocation source and/or request an extension of the existing allocation before they can continue using Jetstream.

In addition to creating a button in the XSEDE portal to request access to a Jetstream Trial Allocation (JTA) discussed in Section 8.5.7, the Atmosphere process had to be modified. Atmosphere supports the special JTA by including a plugin during the login step that is responsible for verifying with TAS API which projects a user can access. If the user is found to have access to one of the special allocations, as defined by the site operator, a custom (very limited) allocation and quota will be assigned until the user has been granted access to a formal project with a Jetstream allocation (E.g. startup, educational, or research allocation). Users who are not part of a special allocation will receive the normal, default quota and access to 100 percent of their allocation.

8.6.3 Globus Authentication and Data Access

In order to integrate Atmosphere with Globus, we wrote a new plugin for **django-cyverse-auth**. The **OAuthLoginBackend** was created to handle requests containing Globus OAuth tokens and allow the user to login with the Django builtin tools. On success, user data was retrieved from Globus and the associated Django user is updated to match the profile information. The **GlobusOAuthTokenAuthentication** was created to integrate Globus with the django-rest-framework library by reading API requests with the header: **Authorization GlobusToken** and ensuring the token's validity.

8.6.4 The Jetstream OpenStack API

The OpenStack APIs within Jetstream offer users the ability to leverage Jetstream in conjunction with other resources, applications, or science gateways via programmatic methods that are not available with most other NSF systems. Jetstream has two main methods for accessing the OpenStack API: the Horizon Dashboard [34] and the command line interface (CLI). Horizon is a web-based dashboard for controlling all aspects of OpenStack end user components like launching and maintaining VMs, building networks, working with automation such as Heat, etc. It gives a graphical representation to all of these components. Its similarity to Atmosphere is only in that they are both web-based interfaces for working with VMs. Horizon is focused on a fully-featured interface and not a user-friendly interface. It provides significantly more control and with that control, more complexity.

The CLI provides the same in-depth control of OpenStack VMs and services as Horizon. It does require that the user install the Python-based CLI clients [35] on the machine they plan to use to control OpenStack VMs and services. With the CLI, you can have interactive control over your OpenStack services or you can use shell scripts or other scripting to control them.

The last means of programmatically working with Jetstream via OpenStack is using the OpenStack Python SDK [32]. Using the Python SDK allows someone to truly have a programmable cyberinfrastructure on Jetstream. Aside from the OpenStack developed SDK there are many third party clients available to use against the publicly available RESTful OpenStack APIs. At this point, we are not aware of any end users making use of the SDK, though that could easily change.

8.6.5 VM libraries

Part of Jetstream's design is the ability to share virtual machine images that users can share and customize. From the start, Jetstream committed to providing academic self-serve cloud services that allow researchers or students to select from a library of curated images as well as community contributed VM images. The curated or featured images range from the base development images provided as a stable foundation to build customized workflows on to more specialized images such as those with Matlab, BioLinux, and R/RStudio. The community contributed images range from single scientific application images created by domain researchers to more complex images with many tools necessary for a number of different workflows. There really are few limits for what researchers or educators can build on Jetstream for their projects save for disk size limits available. And we have seen several researchers build VM images and then share them with the entire Jetstream community.

The Jetstream team is working with XSEDE to create a means for sharing VM images more generally, in ways that will make them easily usable on multiple cloud systems. Some of the options being explored are OpenStack specific such as using Heat templates [33] combined with cloud-init [54] to create a shareable, customizable, and more easily maintained set of images that can be shared with any OpenStack cloud. This would allow for consistency for users between academic clouds as well as making it easy for cloud operators to share those images easily, making any cloud-specific customizations in a text file and not in the image itself. Researchers and educators in turn could contribute their images back to the repository for portable domain science or education images that would benefit their communities.

8.7   Data Center Facilities

As previously described, Jetstream is a multi-site deployment in different regions of the country, a common practice for distributed cloud infrastructure. The production cloud components are sited within the IU Data Center on the Bloomington campus of Indiana University and within the TACC data center on the J.J. Pickle Research Campus of the University of Texas at Austin. The test and development environment is located on the campus of the University of Arizona in Tucson.

The production components are housed in similar environments at IU and TACC, both within machine rooms with at least 11,000 square feet of raised floor with under floor power, 208V in this case, and forced air cooling supplied by CRAC (Computer Room Air Conditioner) units. The IU facility uses under floor networking in standard cable trays for the system while TACC uses a combination of above-rack and below floor networking. Racks within the research machine room at IU rely on water cooling for primary heat extraction, in this particular case custom active rear-door heat exchangers from Motivair, model M8, were designed to fit standard APC 48U racks and provide for up to 29kW of heat extraction (approximately 8 tons of cooling) with an exhaust temperature of 75° F. Racks within the TACC data center rely on in-row cooling units from APC, model ACRC100, which are placed between the computer racks, and receive cold water from below floor pipes to cool rear-ingested hot air and exhaust cold air to the front.

There were no particular challenges in the installation and hosting of the system components. The Jetstream nodes are unaccelerated and consume less power and cooling per rack than many other high performance computing systems housed at IU and TACC. The water-cooled doors at IU connect to a separate rear-door cooling loop via hoses with 1 inch quick connect fittings.

Figure 8.4 shows a rear view of the Jetstream components at Indiana University and the Motivair M8 chilled doors in particular. If the doors are not functioning properly due to a fan or water temperature issue, the LED lights will change from blue to red, which is

FIGURE 8.4: Rear view of Jetstream-IU. Courtesy of David Y. Hancock.

particularly easy for IU Data Center Operations staff to spot on regular walk-throughs and notify the appropriate administrative or facility team.

8.8   System Statistics

Jetstream compiles monthly statistics on system usage, availability, and other related metrics for the National Science Foundation. These metrics give a good measure of the overall health of Jetstream as a project. Table 8.8 shows some of the prime metrics we record every month. As the table shows, Jetstream is generally meeting the goals initially set forth in the Project Execution Plan (PEP). The lone persistent exception is the metric for average utilization of CPU capacity. This was set at 6 percent overall (averaged over time and over the entire system, not just during the execution of one job on one set of nodes. On the one hand, average percent CPU utilization measures something that is not generally going to be the limiting factor for users of cloud resources. On the other hand, having this as a metric we report and track, and having what turns out to be a very high goal relative to past research cloud deployments, has helped us put greater focus on facilitating workflows that make heavy use of CPUs and generally doing everything we can to maximize the effectiveness with which the NSF investment in Jetstream is utilized.

Table 8.9 shows the breakdown of SUs made available to researchers on Jetstream. One key metric that will be added to this for subsequent reporting years is the number of allocation renewals. This will be important in highlighting the projects that continue to use Jetstream as a novel resource. While that in itself is not necessarily a measure of success, it does demonstrate that the PIs are willing to continue to use Jetstream for their research and not seek alternatives. As of September 1, 2017, there were 322 active XSEDE projects covering 59 fields of science and 2000+ active users representing 189 institutions. There are presently 9 active science gateways utilizing Jetstream. Of those users, over 600 undergraduate and graduate students were represented on education/teaching allocations.

TABLE 8.8: Operational metrics for Jetstream PY1 (through June 2017).

Metric	Goal	Achieved
System availability (uptime of the production hardware, as % of wall clock time)	95%	100%
Capacity availability (% of total capacity of Jetstream available for use over time)	95%	99.4%
Job completion success - featured VM launches that reported status to Atmosphere as active	96%	97.7%
Total number of distinct users	1000	1921
Use - mean number of VMs active 24 hour average	320	mean:512 peak:790
CPU % utilization	6%	mean:4.2% peak:21.6%
VM images published with a DOI via IUScholarWorks	10	11

8.9 Interesting Features

There are two features of Jetstream that are of overarching interest as regards deployment of cloud systems to support research. One was planned and intentional; the other became evident as a result of the activities of Jetstream users. Our plan from the beginning was for Jetstream to be a managed science cloud - a cloud managed for science. Certainly one can do scientific research on commercial cloud services, but research activities are at best a minor component of the commercial cloud industry's activities and business. For us, researchers were paramount and we manage and operate Jetstream from the interface down to the storage system for research, and the management and operation of Jetstream are done by people who are in contact with and embedded in the research communities making use of Jetstream. Supporting research and research education are our first priority, and that shows in practice. Jetstream also provides a communication and collaboration platform for software creators. A producer of research software can make that software available to the entire user population of Jetstream in a way that is not replicable (at the time this chapter was written) on any commercial cloud system.

The other feature that has emerged from observing users of Jetstream is the understanding that it is programmable cyberinfrastructure. (Co-PI Matthew Vaughn deserves credit for this felicitous construction). Anyone with an allocation on Jetstream can be rooted in his or her own little world, and that world can be expanded within the Jetstream system bounded only by other uses of the system and the amount of resource allocated to a particular user. Thus we see individual users autonomously implementing and using cloud orchestration and container tools such as Docker, Jupyter, and Mesos, controlling system resource usage and job flow independent of systems administrators and in keeping with researcher needs. It is this sort of capability that has caused us to refer to Jetstream as "programmable cyberinfrastructure." The new book *Cloud Computing for Science and Engineering* by Foster and Gannon [17] discusses cloud computing in general and focuses on three commercial public clouds (Amazon, Google, and Microsoft) and Jetstream. This book contains extensive dis-

TABLE 8.9: Total Allocations for Jetstream, including Q3PY2.

	Q3PY2 Total (Jun-Aug 2017)	Total (through Aug 2017)
Startup		
Total requests	40	148
SUs requested	1,250,000	3,367,840
SUs awarded	1,250,000	3,367,840
Educational		
Total requests	11	33
SUs requested	2,728,000	9,428,000
SUs awarded	2,728,000	9,428,000
Campus Champion/Staff		
Total requests	46	180
SUs requested	2,050,000	6,401,000
SUs awarded	2,050,000	6,401,000
Supplemental/Discretionary		
Total requests	2	17
SUs requested	2,885,120	11,734,182
SUs awarded	2,885,120	11,734,182
Research		
Total requests	5	27
SUs requested	2,458,720	21,332,544
SUs awarded	2,458,720	28,832,544
Total requests and allocations		
Total requests	104	405
SUs requested	11,371,840	52,263,566
SUs awarded	11,371,840	59,763,566

cussions of many of the ideas regarding cloud computing for science and engineering that we have touched on in this book chapter. One other feature of interest regarding Jetstream as a federal investment is the development of new testing and reporting requirements. The development of acceptance tests for Jetstream, done through collaboration of the Jetstream team and the NSF, has set useful precedents for how cloud resources acquired by the NSF are developed and put into production. We also think that the precedent of having the CPU utilization is one that should be continued and extended to other systems funded by the NSF. This is only one of many metrics one might track on any computational system, and consideration of CPU utilization in isolation of other usage metrics would be unhealthy. However, having to track and report CPU utilization has resulted in the Jetstream team putting more emphasis on cultivating uses and user communities that have needs for CPU-intensive tasks than we would have in the absence of this as a reportable metric. As a result, the average levels of CPU utilization of Jetstream have been increasing over time, and more computational work is being done on Jetstream than before. We think the reporting of CPU utilization for all NSF-funded systems (or all federally-funded systems) could lead to more emphasis generally on computational efficiency and effectiveness of workloads run on US national cyberinfrastructure.

8.9.1   Jupyter and Kubernetes

JupyterHub, developed by University of California Berkeley [2], allows one user of a cloud resource to let other users interact with a resource in an organized, regimented manner via remote (web) interface. For workshops or courses, it lets an instructor standardize an environment and have a consistent workflow [39]. Jupyter notebooks have become more common in instructional settings and a number of Jetstream PIs are utilizing it for their academic use. Jetstream, through the Atmosphere-ansible, makes Jupyter available for simple installation via the 'ezj' command. This allows for a standalone Jupyter installation on any Atmosphere-launched instance quickly and easily.

Taking this concept one step further involves creating a means to auto-scale Jupyter's resource. Zero to JupyterHub started this process using commercial clouds. They have begun working with it on Jetstream with Kubeadm Bootstrapper - part of the Kubernetes project [38]. While still in the alpha stage, it is under active development and is expected to be working fully on Jetstream by late 2017. This initial effort to combine education tools along with a container orchestration engine will help enhance Jetstream as a teaching and learning environment. And, these uses of Jupyter and Kubernetes are perfect exemplars of the concept of programmable cyberinfrastructure

8.10   Artificial Intelligence Technology Education

The University of San Antonio (UTSA) OpenCloud Institute (*opencloud.utsa.edu*) has developed an educational AI-Thinking platform on Jetstream [40] to help address the current high demand for skilled AI talent. The UTSA AI-Thinking platform provides an easy-to-use environment for students and offers instructors access to valuable knowledge-based extracted by AI about the students' activities. UTSA's AI Thinking platform was implemented in classes at UTSA, within the Electrical and Computer Engineering department, in the 2016 academic year and within the department of Information Systems and Cyber Security in 2017. All the interface libraries were pre-installed on the Jetstream cloud environment and other learning modules requested by the students were added to the platform. Overall, students and instructors rated the class experience with Jetstream as a big success, and the use of this AI platform is being expanded at UTSA.

8.11   Jetstream VM Image Use for Scientific Reproducibility - Bioinformatics as an Example

A problem prominent in the field of bioinformatics (but certainly not unique to it) is the lack of actual reproducibility of published work. The current standard is to make all primary data accessible via download from public repositories, provide key derived data as supplementary files on a journal website, and describe the steps taken from raw data to derived data in the papers method section and supplementary information. In practice, this allows an educated guess as to what was done. Rarely are all relevant steps fully documented, and the same holds for program versions and parameters. Moreover, the code that was used in the original work may not run on the reader's workstation.

From a scientific standpoint, the above scenario is challenging because it means that the analysis of experiments is not replicable [43]. For computational analysis of experimental data, everything being done should be bitwise reproducible (with caveat that some workflows might include an intentional stochastic component). Galaxy, discussed earlier, focuses on reproducibility of workflows. With current technologies, a Jetstream VM image provides an elegant solution. The Volker Brendel Lab at IU publishes all of the tools, data, and analysis used in each of its publications in a way that allows a reader to exactly reproduce

- and if desired extend - the analysis of the data in any of the lab's peer-reviewed publications. A combination of bash scripts and Makefiles for GNU make capture every bit of the data generation, guaranteed to work on an appropriately sized VM on Jetstream. As images can be archived on Jetstream (with DOI; see *https://jetstream-cloud.org/support/doi-requests.php*), the use described here may well become part of the future standard for scientific computational reproducibility.

8.12   Running a Virtual Cluster on Jetstream

XSEDE has created something called the "community software repository" which includes a set of RPMs that enables anyone to straightforwardly create a fully functional cluster (including open source job management tools). These tools are available from a YUM repository [31]. With these tools, a user can create a cluster running within Jetstream as part of educational activities or as another way to orchestrate and manage resources within Jetstream. We expect this capability to be particularly useful in educational and training settings in which students are learning to create and administer high performance computing clusters.

Acknowledgments

This material is based upon work supported in part by the National Science Foundation under Award 1445604. We thank all the staff of the Jetstream partner organizations for making Jetstream such a success so far. The Indiana University Pervasive Technology Institute and our partners have also supported Jetstream implementation. Other federal funding has supported many other efforts that have contributed to the success of the Jetstream project and have supported science and engineering research done on Jetstream, including:

- The Galaxy Project is supported in part by NSF, NHGRI, The Huck Institutes of the Life Sciences, The Institute for CyberScience at Penn State, and Johns Hopkins University.

- CyVerse is supported by the National Science Foundation under Award Numbers DBI-0735191 and DBI-1265383. URL: www.cyverse.org

- Globus is developed and operated by the University of Chicago and Argonne National Laboratory, and is supported by funding from the Department of Energy, the National Science Foundation, and the National Institutes of Health.

- XSEDE (the Extreme Science and Engineering Discovery Environment), which is supported by National Science Foundation grant number ACI-1548562.

- Wrangler is supported in part by the NSF via award ACI-1447307.

- The work done by the University of Texas at San Antonio was supported by the UTSA Cloud and BigData Laboratory and Rackspace, Inc.

- The work of the Volker Brendel group at Indiana University has been supported in part by a number of grants from the NSF, including NSF IOS-1221984 and NSF IOS-1238189.

- The National Center for Genome Analysis Support (NCGAS) has been deeply involved in support of bioinformatics software on Jetstream. NCGAS is supported by NSF award 1458641.

Any opinions expressed here are those of the authors and do not necessarily represent the opinions of any funding agencies.

We thank reviewers of earlier versions of this report. We also wish to thank the staff who have worked with us during all phases of this project. We most particularly thank our primary vendor partner Dell and our primary vendor representative Jamie Stevens for their partnership in this adventure. We also thank our collaborators at the University of Hawaii, University of Arkansas, University of Colorado/CIRES, Penn State University, University Of North Carolina Chapel Hill, Jackson State University, Mathworks, Inc., and the National Center for Genome Analysis Support.

Bibliography

[1] The OAuth 2.0 Authorization Framework. Technical report, 10 2012.

[2] JupyterHub, 2017.

[3] Enis Afgan, Dannon Baker, Marius vandenBeek, Daniel Blankenberg, Dave Bouvier, Martin Čech, John Chilton, Dave Clements, Nate Coraor, Carl Eberhard, Bjrn Grüning, Aysam Guerler, Jennifer Hillman-Jackson, Greg VonKuster, Eric Rasche, Nicola Soranzo, Nitesh Turaga, James Taylor, Anton Nekrutenko, and Jeremy Goecks. The Galaxy platform for accessible, reproducible and collaborative biomedical analyses: 2016 update. *Nucleic Acids Research*, 44(W1):W3–W10, 7 2016.

[4] Jim Basney, Terry Fleury, and Jeff Gaynor. CILogon: A federated X.509 certification authority for cyberinfrastructure logon. *Concurrency and Computation: Practice and Experience*, 26(13):2225–2239, 9 2014.

[5] Volker Brendel. Brendel Group Handbook, 2015.

[6] Volker P Brendel. BWASP, 2017.

[7] C. Titus Brown. Next-Gen Sequence Analysis Workshop (2017) angus 6.0 documentation, 2017.

[8] M. S. Campbell, M. Law, C. Holt, J. C. Stein, G. D. Moghe, D. E. Hufnagel, J. Lei, R. Achawanantakun, D. Jiao, C. J. Lawrence, D. Ware, S.-H. Shiu, K. L. Childs, Y. Sun, N. Jiang, and M. Yandell. MAKER-P: A Tool Kit for the Rapid Creation, Management, and Quality Control of Plant Genome Annotations. *PLANT PHYSIOLOGY*, 164(2):513–524, 2 2014.

[9] Kyle Chard, Ian Foster, and Steven Tuecke. Globus: Research Data Management as Service and Platform, 2017.

[10] CyVerse. Django.

[11] CyVerse. Atmosphere, 2017.

[12] CyVerse. Atmosphere-Ansible, 2017.

[13] CyVerse. Troposphere, 2017.

[14] Jack Dongarra and Piotr Luszczek. HPC Challenge: Design, History, and Implementation Highlights. In Jeffrey Vetter, editor, *Contemporary High Performance Computing: From Petascale toward Exascale*, chapter 2, pages 13–30. Taylor and Francis, CRC Computational Science Series, Boca Raton, FL, 2013.

[15] Jeremy Fischer, Enis Afgan, Thomas Doak, Carrie Ganote, David Y. Hancock, and Matthew Vaughn. Using Galaxy with Jetstream. In *Galaxy Community Conference*, Bloomington, IN, 2016.

[16] Jeremy Fischer, David Y Hancock, John Michael Lowe, George Turner, Winona Snapp-Childs, and Craig A Stewart. Jetstream: A Cloud System Enabling Learning in Higher Education Communities. In *Proceedings of the 2017 ACM Annual Conference on SIGUCCS*, SIGUCCS '17, pages 67–72, New York, NY, USA, 2017. ACM.

[17] Ian Foster and Dennis B. Gannon. *Cloud computing for science and engineering*. Massachusetts Institute of Technology Press, 2017.

[18] National Science Foundation. High Performance Computing System Acquisition: Continuing the Building of a More Inclusive Computing Environment for Science and Engineering, 2014.

[19] Genomics and Bioinformatics Service at Texas A&M. PoreCamp USA.

[20] Globus. Globus.

[21] Stephen A. Goff, Matthew Vaughn, Sheldon McKay, Eric Lyons, Ann E. Stapleton, Damian Gessler, Naim Matasci, Liya Wang, Matthew Hanlon, Andrew Lenards, Andy Muir, Nirav Merchant, Sonya Lowry, Stephen Mock, Matthew Helmke, Adam Kubach, Martha Narro, Nicole Hopkins, David Micklos, Uwe Hilgert, Michael Gonzales, Chris Jordan, Edwin Skidmore, Rion Dooley, John Cazes, Robert McLay, Zhenyuan Lu, Shiran Pasternak, Lars Koesterke, William H. Piel, Ruth Grene, Christos Noutsos, Karla Gendler, Xin Feng, Chunlao Tang, Monica Lent, Seung-Jin Kim, Kristian Kvilekval, B. S. Manjunath, Val Tannen, Alexandros Stamatakis, Michael Sanderson, Stephen M. Welch, Karen A. Cranston, Pamela Soltis, Doug Soltis, Brian O'Meara, Cecile Ane, Tom Brutnell, Daniel J. Kleibenstein, Jeffery W. White, James Leebens-Mack, Michael J. Donoghue, Edgar P. Spalding, Todd J. Vision, Christopher R. Myers, David Lowenthal, Brian J. Enquist, Brad Boyle, Ali Akoglu, Greg Andrews, Sudha Ram, Doreen Ware, Lincoln Stein, and Dan Stanzione. The iPlant Collaborative: Cyberinfrastructure for Plant Biology. *Frontiers in Plant Science*, 2:34, 7 2011.

[22] Chris Holdgraf, Aaron Culich, Ariel Rokem, Fatma Deniz, Maryana Alegro, and Dani Ushizima. Portable Learning Environments for Hands-On Computational Instruction. *Proceedings of the Practice and Experience in Advanced Research Computing 2017 on Sustainability, Success and Impact - PEARC17*, pages 1–9, 2017.

[23] Jetstream. Trial Access Allocation, 2017.

[24] John Michael Lowe, Michael Packard, and C. Bret Hammond. Jetstream Salt States.

[25] Ruth Malan and Dana Bredemeyer. Functional Requirements and Use Cases. Technical report, 2001.

[26] Joe Mambretti, Jim Chen, and Fei Yeh. Next Generation Clouds, the Chameleon Cloud Testbed, and Software Defined Networking (SDN). In *Proceedings of the 2015 International Conference on Cloud Computing Research and Innovation (ICCCRI)*, ICCCRI '15, pages 73–79, Washington, DC, USA, 2015. IEEE Computer Society.

[27] Nirav Merchant, Eric Lyons, Stephen Goff, Matthew Vaughn, Doreen Ware, David Micklos, and Parker Antin. The iPlant Collaborative: Cyberinfrastructure for Enabling Data to Discovery for the Life Sciences. *PLOS Biology*, 14(1):e1002342, 1 2016.

[28] National Science Foundation. Cyberinfrastructure: From Supercomputing to the TeraGrid, 2006.

[29] National Science Foundation. CISE Research Infrastructure: Mid-Scale Infrastructure - NSFCloud (CRI: NSFCloud), 2013.

[30] National Science Foundation. TeraGrid Phase III: eXtreme Digital Resources for Science and Engineering (XD), 2008.

[31] Jp Navarro, Craig A Stewart, Richard Knepper, Lee Liming, David Lifka, and Maytal Dahan. The Community Software Repository from XSEDE: A Resource for the National Research Community.

[32] OpenStack Foundation. Getting started with the OpenStack SDK, 2017.

[33] OpenStack Foundation. Heat, 2017.

[34] OpenStack Foundation. Horizon Dashboard, 2017.

[35] OpenStack Foundation. OpenStack Clients, 2017.

[36] OpenStack Foundation. OpenStack Roadmap, 2017.

[37] ORCID Inc. ORCID — Connecting Research and Researchers.

[38] Yuvi Panda and Andrea Zonca. kubeadm-bootstrap, 2017.

[39] Project Jupyter team. Zero to JupyterHub with Kubernetes, 2017.

[40] Paul Rad, Mehdi Roopaei, Nicole Beebe, Mehdi Shadaram, and Yoris A. Au. AI Thinking for Cloud Education Platform with Personalized Learning. In *51st Hawaii International Conference on System Sciences*, Waikoloa Village, HI, 2018.

[41] Inc. Red Hat. Ceph Homepage - Ceph, 2017.

[42] FN Sakimura, J Bradley, M Jones, B de Medeiros, and C Mortimore. OpenID Connect Core 1.0 incorporating errata set 1, 2014.

[43] C.A Stewart. Preserving Scientific Software . . . in a Usable Form? *EDUCAUSE Review*, 2016.

[44] C.A. Stewart, V. Welch, B. Plale, G. Fox, M. Pierce, and T. Sterling. Indiana University Pervasive Technology Institute, 2017.

[45] Craig A Stewart, David Y. Hancock, Matthew Vaughn, Jeremy Fischer, Lee Liming, Nirav Merchant, Therese Miller, John Michael Lowe, Daniel Stanzione, Jaymes Taylor, and Edwin Skidmore. Jetstream - Performance, Early Experiences, and Early Results. In *Proceedings of the XSEDE16 Conference*, St. Louis, MO, 2016.

[46] Craig A. Stewart, David Y. Hancock, Matthew Vaughn, Nirav C. Merchant, John Michael Lowe, Jeremy Fischer, Lee Liming, James Taylor, Enis Afgan, George Turner, C. Bret Hammond, Edwin Skidmore, Michael Packard, and Ian Foster. System Acceptance Report for NSF award 1445604 High Performance Computing System Acquisition: Jetstream - A Self-Provisioned, Scalable Science and Engineering Cloud Environment. Technical report, Indiana University, Bloomington, IN, 2016.

[47] Craig A Stewart, R Knepper, Andrew Grimshaw, Ian Foster, Felix Bachmann, D Lifka, Morris Riedel, and Steven Tuecke. Campus Bridging Use Case Quality Attribute Scenarios. Technical report, 2012.

[48] Craig A. Stewart, Richard Knepper, Andrew Grimshaw, Ian Foster, Felix Bachmann, David Lifka, Morris Riedel, and Steven Tueke. XSEDE Campus Bridging Use Cases. Technical report, 2012.

[49] Craig A. Stewart, Richard Knepper, Matthew R Link, Marlon Pierce, Eric Wernert, and Nancy Wilkins-Diehr. Cyberinfrastructure, Cloud Computing, Science Gateways, Visualization, and Cyberinfrastructure Ease of Use. In Mehdi Khosrow-Pour, editor, *Encyclopedia of Information Science and Technology*. IGI Global, Hershey, PA, fourth edition, 2018.

[50] University of Texas at Austin, Texas Advanced Computing Center, 2017.

[51] The OpenStack Foundation. OpenStack, 2017.

[52] John Towns, Timothy Cockerill, Maytal Dahan, Ian Foster, Kelly Gaither, Andrew Grimshaw, Victor Hazlewood, Scott Lathrop, Dave Lifka, Gregory D. Peterson, Ralph Roskies, J. Ray Scott, and Nancy Wilkens-Diehr. XSEDE: Accelerating Scientific Discovery. *Computing in Science & Engineering*, 16(5):62–74, 9 2014.

[53] Steven Tuecke, Rachana Ananthakrishnan, Kyle Chard, Mattias Lidman, Brendan Mc-collam, Stephen Rosen, and Ian Foster. Globus Auth : A Research Identity and Access Management Platform. In *IEEE 12th International Conference on eScience*, Baltimore, Maryland, 2016.

[54] Ubuntu. Cloud-Init, 2017.

[55] Venkatesh Viswanath, Michael G Morris, Gordon B Davis, and Fred D Davis. User Acceptance of Information Technology: Toward a Unified View. *MIS Quarterly*, 27(3):425–478, 2003.

[56] Gregor von Laszewski, Geoffrey C. Fox, Fugang Wang, Andrew J. Younge, Archit Kulshrestha, Gregory G. Pike, Warren Smithy, Jens Vöcklerz, Renato J. Figueiredox, Jose Fortesx, and Kate Keahey. Design of the Futuregrid experiment management framework. In *2010 Gateway Computing Environments Workshop, GCE 2010*, 2010.

[57] XSEDE. XSEDE Education Allocations, 2017.

[58] XSEDE. XSEDE Research Allocations, 2017.

[59] XSEDE. XSEDE Startup Allocations, 2017.

Chapter 9

Modular Supercomputing Architecture: From Idea to Production

Estela Suarez, Norbert Eicker, and Thomas Lippert

Jülich Supercomputing Centre - Forschungszentrum Jülich GmbH, Leo Brandt Strasse, 52428 Jülich (Germany)

This chapter describes a new heterogeneous architecture created at the Jülich Supercomputing Centre (JSC), its motivation and the development path that led to its final realization. Because it covers a broader scope involving several hardware platforms, the chapter is structured in the following way: first an overview of the Jülich Supercomputing Centre is given, to explain its context and background. In section 9.2 a historical view of the architectures and main systems co-developed at JSC is given, which led to the actual Modular Supercomputing Architecture. Section 9.3 describes the JSC application portfolio and how the newly developed architecture aims to match it. An overview of the systems built following the Modular Supercomputing approach is given in section 9.4, elaborating on their detailed hardware implementation in section 9.5. The software and programming environments implemented to support the new architecture are described in sections 9.6 and 9.7, respectively. Section 9.8 treats the cooling and facility infrastructures. Finally, section 9.9 concludes the chapter with a look into the future of the Modular Supercomputing Architecture.

9.1   The Jülich Supercomputing Centre (JSC)

The *Forschungszentrum Jülich* (FZJ) [9], with a staff of over 5,000 employees, is one of Europe's largest research centers. It pursues cutting-edge interdisciplinary research to address the grand challenges facing society in the fields of health, energy and environment, and information technologies. As a member of the German research *Helmholtz Association* [12] (HGF), FZJ hosts world-class instruments used by internal and external researchers to conduct their work: supercomputers for simulations, unique analytical and characterization equipment, imaging techniques for medicine, nanotechnology tools, etc.

The *Jülich Supercomputing Centre* [16] (JSC) within FZJ plays a key role in the above-mentioned activities. Founded in 1987, JSC has extensive expertise in providing supercomputer services and support to national and international user communities. With over 200 employees, JSC is the largest of the three national supercomputing centres in Germany. In 2009 JSC became the first European supercomputing center with Petaflop capability in PRACE (*Partnership for Advanced Computing in Europe [21]*), which bundles European computing centres to collectively offer computing resources to users.

The operation of large scale HPC-systems is only one of the aspects that JSC covers to provide supercomputing services to the wider scientific community. Additionally, JSC strives to guarantee optimal user support, continuously developing the simulation methodology, parallel algorithms and new programming and visualisation techniques, as well as carrying out intensive research in core areas of the computational sciences. Researchers who apply for computing time at the JSC's systems are supported by a continuously growing number of domain-specific Simulation Laboratories (*SimLabs* [15]). At present, JSC runs nine SimLabs covering diverse fields such as Biology, Plasma Physics, Climate Sciences, and Neuroscience. The SimLabs offer support to specific scientific communities, and contribute through co-design to the research and development of HPC technologies.

Furthermore, JSC actively participates in designing and building its next generation supercomputers. Key in this context are the in-house development of open source software and tools, and the development of innovative HPC architectures. For this purpose tight, long-term collaborations (the so-called *Exascale Laboratories*) have been established with the world-leading technology providers IBM, Intel, and NVIDIA. The Exascale Labs, in combination with German- and European-funded R&D initiatives, enable JSC to apply co-design strategies and explore new concepts and technologies.

9.2   Supercomputing Architectures at JSC

Through very close collaboration with the providers, JSC is able to address its users' requirements when procuring production systems. To achieve the best possible price-performance ratio the focus is put in the selection and optimal integration of the best suited off-the-shelf components. In particular, JSC has since long designed the architecture of its systems employing its expertise in cluster configuration, network topologies, and cluster management software [54].

New concepts and technologies are first tested in prototypes and, once validated, employed in the next generation large scale production systems. For this purpose a number of small to medium size computing systems are being operated at JSC. Current examples are an Intel Xeon Phi (KNL) system for the lattice-QCD community (*QPACE3* [22]), the two pilot systems for the Human Brain Project [14] (*JURON* and *JULIA*), and the DEEP prototypes [6]. The latter will be explained in more detail in section 9.5.

Based on the experience gathered with prototypes, the design of the JSC production systems was chosen. The following three subsections describe how this work has led to an architectural evolution at the computing centre: from a dual supercomputing approach to a Modular Supercomputing architecture.

9.2.1   The Dual Supercomputer Strategy

Back in 2004, JSC constructed a modern computer room to host its new *JUMP* system: an IBM p690 Cluster with a total of 1,312 processors and 5 Terabytes internal memory (128 gigabytes per node). JUMP initially achieved a maximum performance of 5.6 TFlop/s (it became number 21 in the TOP 500 list [26] at the time of its inauguration), to be later scaled-up to a total of 9 TFlop/s. However, already quite early in the operation cycle of JUMP, the JSC-team realized that for the given number of users and allocation of computing time, a further growth of capability computing on JUMP would have actually decreased the overall efficiency. The reason was that many applications were not scaling well to very large number of processes. These users, who were working at their sweet spot, would not have profited from policies preferring jobs with very large processor numbers.

As a solution, the *dual supercomputer strategy* [50] was conceived. It consisted on running two large-scale HPC-systems simultaneously: a highly flexible, general purpose cluster (for low/medium scalable applications), and a massively-parallel system (for highly scalable applications).

The realisation of the dual concept started in 2005/2006 with the installation of *JUBL*, a 46 Teraflop/s BlueGene/L system with 16,384 processors. Before being admitted to the machine, the scalability of a code had to be proven (up to a minimum of 1,024 processors). At the same time, JSC made a strong investment in terms of personnel resources to provide training and support for users in order to scale-up applications and increase the JUBL portfolio. This lead to a substantial improvement on scalability for several applications, a number of them up to the full machine.

However, in many cases the scientific problem was intrinsically in conflict with a massively parallel execution of the code and ran much more efficiently on the JUMP cluster. This finding confirmed the importance of continuing the dual hardware strategy, regularly upgrading and modernising its two branches in a staged manner, with each system reaching a life-time of about five years (see Figure 9.1).

General purpose cluster branch   The JUMP system was replaced in 2009 by *JUROPA*, a large compute cluster increasing the power of its predecessor by more than a factor of 25. This cluster was designed and built by JSC together with partners from industry. The operating system software running on the machine was *ParaStation*, developed jointly by ParTec (a Munich based software company) and JSC. With a peak performance of about 300 TFlop/s and 79 Terabyte main memory, *JUROPA* was the 10th fastest computer in the world at the time of deployment.

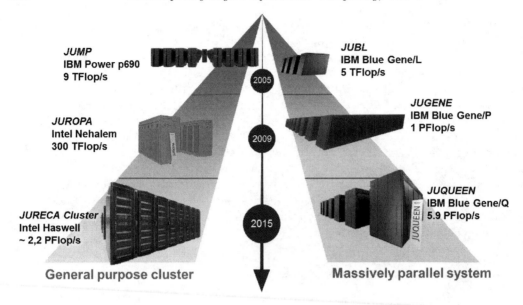

FIGURE 9.1: Dual architecture strategy driven at JSC for the past years.

JUROPA was substituted in July 2015 by the 2.2 PFlop/s *JURECA Cluster* [45], which continues in operation today. Its configuration is described in detail in section 9.5.3.

Massively parallel branch   Given the success of JUBL and to keep-up with the large user demand, JSC deployed already by end of 2007 the IBM BlueGene/P system *JUGENE*, which was the second fastest computer in the world at the time of installation (222.8 TFlop/s peak performance). After a later scale-up [31], JUGENE reached 1 PFlop peak performance and was kept in operation until 2012.

At that time, the IBM BlueGene/Q system *JUQUEEN* [53] was installed. With almost 6 PFlop/s performance, nearly half a million processors (28,672 nodes with 16 cores each) and 448 Terabytes main memory (16 GB/node), JUQUEEN became the fastest system in Europe at the time of installation. This water-cooled system was also among the most energy efficient supercomputers in the world, with a performance/power ratio of approximately 2 Gigaflop/s per Watt. To help users migrating their codes and leverage performance, porting and tuning workshops were organised. In this context, the *High-Q Club* [13, 32] was established: a showcase for production codes able to scale up to the entire JUQUEEN, i.e., capable of using all its 458,752 cores.

JUQUEEN continues in operation today and its decommissioning is planned for Q1/2018.

Storage system   Data movements between the JSC machines are minimised by running a common *GPFS* file system on all of them. This storage system is mounted from the central Jülich Storage Cluster (*JUST*) [17], which is in fact the only physical connection between the two branches of the dual supercomputing approach. To keep pace with the performance increase of the compute systems, JUST is also regularly upgraded. The last JUST upgrade was done in 2013, soon after JUQUEEN's installation [32]. As a result, the storage bandwidth increased from about 60 GByte/s to 200 GByte/s (by increasing the number of disks), and a much better protection against failures was achieved (thanks to the installation of the GNR (GPFS Native Raid) software). The next generation of JUST is planned for early 2018.

9.2.2   The Cluster-Booster Concept

Even if a user can have access to both JUQUEEN and JURECA, distributing a code over both platforms is cumbersome due to their different software environments and the lack of an inter-system high-speed network connection. To fill the gap between the two branches of the dual supercomputing strategy, the ***Cluster-Booster architecture*** [37] was created. Primary goals were to enable a larger amount of codes exploiting the advantages of highly scalable systems, and improving the energy-efficiency and scalability of cluster computers.

For the latter, the standard approach is building clusters using heterogeneous nodes, in which multi-core CPUs are hosting one or more accelerators (many-core CPUs or graphic processing units (GPU)). This *host-device(s)* approach is efficient and scalable, but presents some caveats: latency penalties and bandwidth limitations on the GPU-to-GPU communication due to the node's PCIe bus, GPU-specific programming environments requiring high code re-factoring efforts, static assignment of GPU to CPU resources, etc.

The Cluster-Booster architecture proposed to integrate heterogeneous computing resources at the system level, instead of doing so at the node level (see Figure 9.2). This translates into extracting the accelerators from the host nodes and moving them into a stand-alone cluster of accelerators, which received the name of ***Booster***. The Booster was attached to a standard HPC-Cluster via a high-speed network. This connection, together with a uniform software stack running over both parts of the machine, enables them to act together and be used by applications as one single system.

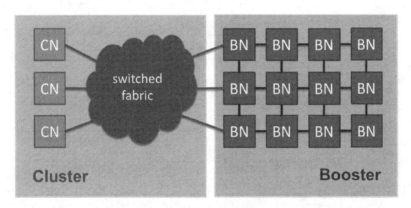

FIGURE 9.2:   Sketch of the Cluster-Booster architecture. *CN*: Cluster node (general purpose processor), *BN*: Booster node (autonomous many-core processor).

The ratio of the amount of work to be executed by the commodity CPUs in the Cluster and the accelerators in the Booster is different in each application. Accordingly, in the Cluster-Booster architecture no constraints are put on the combination of nodes that an application may select, and resources are reserved and allocated dynamically. This has two important effects: Firstly each application can run on a near-optimal combination of resources and achieve excellent performance. Secondly all the resources can be put to good use by a system-wide resource manager allowing combining the set of applications in a complementary way, increasing throughput and efficiency of use for the overall system.

Until recently the type of kernels to be offloaded onto accelerators was very limited due to their inefficient data-exchange capabilities with other accelerators. In the Booster, however, accelerators communicate directly with each other through the high-speed network, allowing for full codes with intensive internal communication to run on the system. In this way, the Booster can be regarded as a massively parallel system on its own, so that highly scalable codes running well on BlueGene should also fit very well with the Booster. Applications with low/medium scalable parts (as the ones described in section 9.3) can run the highly scalable parts on the Booster and leave those less scalable to profit from the high single-thread performance of the Cluster.

The Cluster-Booster architecture enables for the first time mapping the intrinsic scalability patterns of applications onto the system hardware. In this way, the limitation posed by the less-scalable parts of codes is alleviated, and the overall scalability of the full code should improve.

The first two prototypes of the Cluster-Booster architecture were developed and built within the European-funded research projects[1] *DEEP* [5] (*Dynamical Exascale Entry Platform*) and *DEEP-ER* [4] (*DEEP-Extended Reach*). The DEEP prototype and its software stack were designed to support mainly HPC applications. In DEEP-ER, additional non-volatile memory (NVM) layers were integrated and network-attached memory technologies were prototyped. Both extensions enabled advanced scalable high-performance I/O and resiliency strategies. The precise hardware and software configurations of the DEEP and DEEP-ER prototypes are described in sections 9.5.1 and 9.5.2, respectively.

The Cluster-Booster approach is now going into production, with the recent installation of a Booster attached to the JURECA Cluster. The JURECA Booster, a 5 PFlop Intel Xeon Phi (KNL) system, was deployed at the end of 2017. Its precise hardware configuration is described in section 9.5.3.

9.2.3   The Modular Supercomputing Architecture

While the Cluster-Booster architecture is being implemented in production, the JSC-team is already working on the development of its next generation systems. The underlying concept in a Cluster-Booster system is to break with the tradition of replicating many identical (potentially heterogeneous) compute nodes, and integrate instead the heterogeneous computing resources at the system level. This concept is being extended and generalised in the *Modular Supercomputing Architecture*.

The Modular Supercomputer Architecture (Figure 9.3) connects compute modules with different hardware and performance characteristics with each other to create a single heterogeneous system. Each module is a parallel, clustered system of potentially large size. A federated network connects the module-specific interconnects. This approach brings substantial benefits for heterogeneous applications and work-flows since each part can be run on an exactly matching system, improving time to solution and energy use. It is therefore ideal for supercomputer centres running heterogeneous application mixes (higher throughput and energy efficiency). The Modular Supercomputing Architecture also offers valuable flexibility to system operators, allowing the set of modules and their respective size to be tailored to the centre's actual portfolio and usage. Modules with disruptive technologies, such as neuromorphic or quantum devices, can also be included in a Modular Supercomputer to satisfy the needs of specific user communities.

The Cluster-Booster machines deployed until now (see section 9.5) are in principle Modular Supercomputers with two modules. However, their designs and software stacks were not foreseen for further extensions. The real generalisation of the concept will be first re-

---

[1]In this chapter the term *DEEP projects* will be used when referring globally to the research projects DEEP, DEEP-ER, and DEEP-EST. These three European funded projects are strongly connected with each other, but do focus on different research topics. The DEEP project (2011-2015) introduced the Cluster-Booster concept, building the first hardware prototype and developing its full software and programming stack. The DEEP-ER project (2013-2017) focused on I/O and resiliency: it built a small-size, memory-enhanced Cluster-Booster prototype and implemented advanced I/O and resiliency software. The DEEP-EST project (2017-2020) will realise a Modular Supercomputing prototype addressing the requirements of HPC and HPDA users.

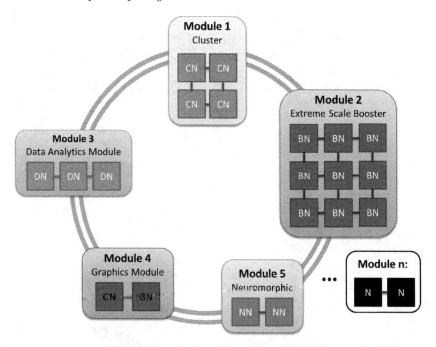

FIGURE 9.3: Sketch of the Modular Supercomputing Architecture (*CN*: Cluster node, *BN*: Booster node, *DN*: Data Analytics node, *GN*: Graphics node, *NN*: Neuromorphic node).

alised in the ***DEEP-EST*** (*DEEP - Extreme Scale Technologies*) research project, which started in July 2017 and will run for three years. One of the most important contributions expected from DEEP-EST is the development of resource management software and scheduling strategies to deal with any given number of compute modules. To demonstrate its capabilities, a three-module prototype will be built, which shall cover the needs of both HPC and high performance data analytics (HPDA) workloads.

The implementation of the Modular Supercomputing architecture in a large-scale production system will start already in parallel to DEEP-EST. The installation of the ***JUWELS*** Cluster is planned already in Q2/2018, with further modules coming around the 2020 time-frame.

9.3 Applications and Workloads

The provision of supercomputer resources at JSC is executed by the *John von Neumann Institute for Computing* (NIC). This independent institution organises and coordinates a half-yearly peer-review process with international expert-referees that evaluate the project-applications and allocate the computing time according to their scientific excellence. This process, which has meanwhile been adopted by other German and European HPC centers, ensures an effective usage of the HPC infrastructure. Users come mostly from German and European universities and research institutes, with a smaller proportion of industrial provenance. The relative quantity of regional, national, European, and international users is determined by the funding sources that contribute to cover the costs of the computers procurement and operation. This leads to JUQUEEN (which is funded by national sources), being used mostly by German and European users, while JURECA (funded by the Helmholtz Association) serves mainly regional and national users.

The main role of JSC is enabling outstanding research in fields encompassing astrophysics, computational biology and biophysics, chemistry, earth and environment, plasma physics, computational soft matter, fluid dynamics, elementary particle physics, computer science and numerical mathematics, condensed matter, and materials science. Accordingly, the application portfolio running on the JSC systems is highly multidisciplinary, as outlined in Figure 9.4. These applications are very diverse not only with regards to the research fields that they address, but also to the algorithms, numerical methods, and parallelisation strategies that they employ. Therefore, all computer architectures developed at JSC aim at fulfilling a very wide set of user requirements.

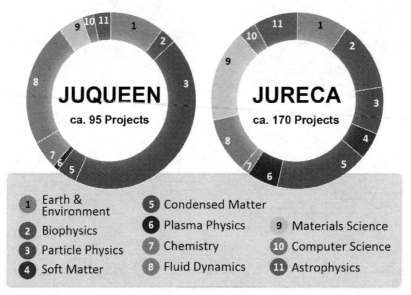

FIGURE 9.4: Computing time assigned to different research fields on the JUQUEEN and JURECA systems (as of May 2017).

The dual supercomputing strategy described in section 9.2.1 has been very successful in fulfilling the needs of both highly scalable HPC applications (with the massively parallel platform), and low/medium scalable codes requiring high single-thread performance (with the general purpose cluster). Analysing the respective applications, one can observe that the highly scalable codes often present very regular communication patterns and manage relatively reduced amounts of data, while the less scalable ones manage more data and access it using more complex communication patterns.

However, a more detailed analysis revealed that many of the latter codes include highly scalable code-parts, too. In particular, applications simulating multi-scale or multi-physics problems, or coupling different models to describe highly complex phenomena, do show a mix of concurrency patterns: parts of these applications are highly scalable, while others are intrinsically limited in scalability. Due to Amdahl's law, these codes are not able to scale-up properly in a BlueGene/Q machine like JUQUEEN. However, ignoring their high-scalable parts and running them on the general purpose cluster would waste both resources and power. The Cluster-Booster concept described in section 9.2.2 was designed to address this issue.

New user communities with new requirements are joining the JSC portfolio. Examples are High-Performance Data Analytics (HPDA), machine learning, and interactive supercomputing. One of the main challenges raised by the convergence between HPC and HPDA is finding an architecture that can match well the requirements of both application fields.

Traditional HPC applications are usually iterative and rely heavily on a small number of numerical algorithmic classes (like the original Berkeley *seven dwarfs* [30]) that operate on relatively small data sets and accrue very high numbers of floating point operations across iterations. HPC systems have been optimised according to these requirements, and it felt justified to rank these machines purely on their Flop/s performance for DGEMM [26]. With the years this has led to rather monolithic systems where the amount of memory per core is steadily decreasing.

However, the complexity and memory requirements of HPC codes are increasing, leading to a dissonance with these traditional systems. In addition, the desire to support the HPDA workloads rapidly emerging from the *Big Data* community clearly requires a change in systems architecture, since these will exhibit less *arithmetic intensity* and require additional classes of algorithms to work well (see e.g. advance deep learning neural network algorithms). Moreover some scientific fields like brain research are expected to make use of both technologies – HPC and HPDA – to the same degree in the future. The Modular Supercomputing Architecture (see section 9.2.3) has been designed precisely to provide a platform best fitting diverse, increasingly complex, and new-coming applications.

To make sure that the implementations of first the Cluster-Booster and now the Modular Supercomputing Architecture really became usable and beneficial for a large and multidisciplinary portfolio of applications as the one shown in Figure 9.4, a number of *co-design* applications were included in the DEEP projects.

9.3.1   Co-design Applications in the DEEP Projects

A total of 15 application teams bringing full-fledged HPC and HPDA applications are or have been actively involved in the DEEP projects. Their requirements strongly influence the choice of hardware components for the prototypes, which functionality the software and programming environment provide, and how the architecture itself is evolving in time. At the same time, code-modernisation has brought significant improvements to the applications themselves, in terms of better performance, new capabilities, and higher resilience to failures. In this context, it is important to mention that the changes included in the codes are not exclusive to run on a Modular Supercomputer, but are more general and in the end beneficial on any modern HPC system.

The DEEP co-design applications are listed below, including their field of research, the name of the application, and the institution driving the particular application effort within the DEEP projects. More details on the codes are available at the given bibliographic references.

- **Neuroscience simulations**: NEURON [48] by EPFL (École Polytechnique Fédérale de Lausanne) and NEST [18] by NMBU (Norges Miljø- og Biovitenskapelige Universitet).

- **Space weather simulation**: iPiC3D [55] and xPic [47] by KU Leuven (Katholieke Universiteit Leuven).

- **Climate simulation**: EMAC [34] by CYI (The Cyprus Institute).

- **Computational fluid engineering**: AVBP [1] by CERFACS (Centre Européen de Recherche et de Formation Avancée en Calcul Scientifique).

- **High temperature superconductivity**: TurboRVB [39] by CINECA (Consorzio Interuniversitario del Nord-Est per il Calcolo Automatico).

- **Seismic imaging**: RTM [23] by CGG (Compagnie Générale de Géophysique) and FWI [10] by BSC (Barcelona Supercomputing Center).

- **Human exposure to electromagnetic fields**: GERShWIN [49] by INRIA (Institut National de Recherche en Informatique et en Automatique).

- **Computational earthquake source dynamics**: SeisSol [24] by LRZ (Leibniz-Rechenzentrum der Bayerischen Akademie der Wissenschaften).

- **Radio astronomy**: the SKA data analysis pipeline [25] by ASTRON (Netherlands Institute for Radio Astronomy).

- **Lattice QCD**: CHROMA [2] by the University of Regensburg.

- **Molecular dynamics**: GROMACS [11] by NCSA (Bulgarian National Center for Supercomputing Applications).

- **Data analytics in Earth Science**: piSVM and HPDBSCAN [44] by the University of Island (Haskoli Islands).

- **High Energy Physics**: CMSSW [3] by CERN (Conseil Européen pour la Recherche Nucléaire).

The above codes have demonstrated the high flexibility of the concept, which enables very different use models on the system. Developers of monolithic, high scalable applications (e.g. CHROMA) typically run their codes fully on the Booster. Applications combining different physical models, such as EMAC – which couples and is atmospheric with a chemistry model – were distributed between various modules according to their concurrency levels (Cluster and Booster in the EMAC case). Results obtained with xPic demonstrate the benefit of mapping this way the specific characteristics of an application onto the hardware modules [47]. Codes aiming at interactive supercomputing such as CoreNeuron ran the simulation on the Booster, steering and visualising it on the Cluster side. Also users running application pipelines employ different modules for each component of their work flow. This is the case of the space weather application from KU Leuven, which analyses satellite data on the Data Analytics Module, uses the Cluster to calculate the propagation of the ejected solar particles from Sun to Earth, and distributes their interaction with the Earth's magnetosphere between Cluster and Booster.

The large variety of fields covered by the DEEP co-design applications is well visible in the list above. Their co-design input, based on their diverse requirements and code characteristics, has led to the system design described in the following sections.

9.4   Systems Overview

The **Modular Supercomputing Architecture** proposes a new way of integrating heterogeneous hardware at system level. To demonstrate the potential of this new philosophy and progressively refine and improve different aspects of the concept, various prototype systems have been built before its final realisation in a production machine.

1. The DEEP prototype: the first Modular Supercomputer ever built, with one Cluster and two Booster modules. The second of these Boosters, a small-size prototype called GreenICE Booster, was built to test a newer generation network fabric and an innovative immersion cooling technology (see section 9.5.1).

2. The DEEP-ER prototype: this second generation Cluster-Booster system is of much smaller size than the previous one, but is enhanced with a multi-level memory hierarchy that enables new I/O and resiliency strategies.

3. The JURECA production system: the existing JURECA Cluster has recently (end 2017) been complemented with the 5 PFlop JURECA Booster, becoming the first Modular Supercomputer in production.

Their hardware components (details in section 9.5) have been chosen taking the newest technology available at each point in time. The software stacks (see sections 9.6 and 9.7) are very similar in all platforms and aim always at exposing the standard functionality and programming environments commonly available in HPC systems.

9.4.1 Sponsors

European, national (German), and regional (North Rhine-Westphalia) funding sources have contributed to the development, construction and procurement of the above mentioned Modular Supercomputers.

The DEEP projects (DEEP, DEEP-ER, and DEEP-EST) received funding from the European Commission's programs for research, technological development, and demonstration, at funding rates that vary depending on the framework program and the partner provenance (academia vs. industry). The matching co-finance comes from the internal budget of the partners involved in the projects. JSC co-financed its own personnel costs and the hardware components. Additionally, JSC paid fully the operational costs for the prototypes. JSC's internal budget comes from national sources, channelled through the Helmholtz Association (HGF). Ultimately, the amount of funding received from the HGF comes to 90% from the German Federal Ministry of Education and Research, and to 10% from the North Rhine-Westphalia Ministry for Culture and Science.

Funding for the procurement and operation of the JURECA system, on the other hand, is of pure national (German) origin and was granted by the Helmholtz Association through the program *Supercomputing & Big Data*.

9.4.2 Timeline

Figure 9.5 shows the time frames in which the DEEP and JURECA systems have been designed, developed, and deployed.

The DEEP prototypes[2], and especially the first generation (DEEP), are the result of ambitious research and development projects. The first (DEEP) Booster, in particular, was constructed using custom hardware components, designed and built exclusively for the project. This approach requires higher development effort and implies also higher risks, which translate into long design, construction, and bring-up phases for this system. There was however no alternative, since at the time no off-the-shelf cluster of autonomous accelerators was available on the market.

The situation changed with DEEP-ER, thanks to new self-booting many core processors appearing in the market. Therefore, this time the prototype is based on standard components, which accelerated the whole process. Custom hardware was built only for the network attached memory (see section 9.5.2), which is included in Figure 9.5 as part of the Booster.

---

[2]When using the term in plural (*DEEP prototypes*), the authors refer globally and indistinctly to the hardware platforms deployed in the DEEP and DEEP-ER projects. *DEEP prototype* refers to the first generation (built in the DEEP project), and *DEEP-ER prototype* to the second.(built in the DEEP-ER project).

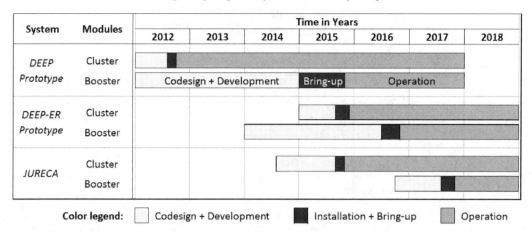

FIGURE 9.5: Timeline for the development of the DEEP, DEEP-ER, and JURECA systems.

The JURECA system has been developed in co-design with the provider companies. To satisfy production quality and stability of the system, a much more conservative philosophy was applied, based on the selection of off-the-shelf components. This approach largely reduces the design and development phases and simplifies the bring-up and installation processes.

9.5 Hardware Implementation

The Cluster parts of the DEEP prototypes and JURECA are relatively standard general-purpose systems, employing the newest Intel Xeon generation at the time of their deployment. Their Boosters are based on Intel Xeon Phi many-core processors. The first generation (Knights Corner, KNC) was used in DEEP to create a unique custom-hardware Booster, while the second generation (Knights Landing, KNL) was integrated in DEEP-ER and JURECA using off-the-shelf components.

Table 9.1 gives an overview of the hardware configuration for all the systems built at JSC following the Modular Supercomputing architecture. For the sake of brevity, only the main compute parts of the systems are included in the table. In the first generation DEEP prototype only the large scale Cluster and Booster are described, leaving the small GreenICE Booster for section 9.5.1. In the case of the JURECA Cluster only the compute nodes are described. For the sake of presentation the GPU accelerated partition of JURECA – which amounts to only 4% of the system – is skipped. For more details on the JURECA Cluster configuration, including a description of its 12 visualization nodes and 12 login nodes, see [45].

The remainder of this section describes the hardware implementation of the three systems in more detail. System software and programming environments are explained in sections 9.6 and 9.7, respectively. Information on the room infrastructure is given in section 9.8.

TABLE 9.1: Hardware Configurations

	Feature	DEEP (1st generation prototype)	DEEP-ER (2nd generation prototype)	JURECA
Cluster	Deployment date	2012	2015	2014
	Integrator	Eurotech	SAR	T-Platforms
	Chassis architecture	Aurora		V5050
	Node architecture	Aurora Blade	SuperMicro	V-Class V210S/F
	PCIe	Gen 2	Gen 3	Gen 3
	CPU	Intel Xeon	Intel Xeon	Intel Xeon
	processor number	E5-2680	E5-2680v3	E5-2680v3
	microarchitecture	Sandy Bridge	Haswell	Haswell
	cores(threads)	2×8(32)	2×12(48)	2×12(48)
	frequency (GHz)	2.7	2.5	2.5
	CPUs per node	2	2	2
	memory per node (GB)	32 RAM	128 RAM 400 NVM	128/256/512 RAM
	Network technology	InfiniBand	EXTOLL	InfiniBand
	generation	QDR	Tourmalet A3	EDR
	topology	fat-tree	3D torus	full fat-tree
	Compute Racks	1/2 (double sided)	1/3	29
	Cluster node count	128	16	1,872
	Cluster peak performance (TFlop/s)	45	16	1800(CPU) + 440(GPU)
Booster	Deployment date	2012	2015	2014
	Integrator	Eurotech	none (JSC)	DELL
	Chassis architecture	Aurora		
	Node architecture	Aurora Blade	Intel Adams Pass	C6320P
	PCIe	Gen 1	Gen 3	Gen 3
	CPU	Intel Xeon Phi	Intel Xeon Phi	Intel Xeon Phi
	processor number	7120X	7210	7250F
	microarchitecture	KNC	KNL	KNL
	cores(threads)	61(244)	64(256)	68(272)
	frequency (GHz)	1.2	1.3	1.4
	CPUs per node	1	1	1
	memory per node (GB)	16 RAM	16 MCDRAM 96 DDR4 400 NVM	16 MCDRAM 96 DDR4
	Network technology	EXTOLL	EXTOLL	Omni-Path
	implementation	FGPA (Altera Stratix V)	ASIC Tourmalet A3	
	topology	3D torus	torus	full fat-tree
	Compute Racks	1 (double sided)	1/4	23
	Booster node count	384	8	1640
	Booster peak performance (TFlop/s)	500	20	5000
Total	Racks	2 (double sided)	1	52
	Total peak performance (TFlop/s)	545	36	7200

9.5.1 First Generation (DEEP) Prototype

The DEEP prototype consists of two modules (Cluster and Booster), served by a common set of login nodes and external storage servers. All together the DEEP prototype reaches a total peak performance of about 550 TFlops. Part *a)* of Figure 9.6 shows a picture of the first generation DEEP prototype installed at JSC. The front rack (with blue cables) is the Booster. The one in the back (with screens) is the Cluster. Between them a rack of air-cooled power supplies is located.

DEEP Cluster The DEEP Cluster, installed in 2012, is an off-the-shelf Aurora Cluster manufactured by the company Eurotech. The Aurora line comes with double-sided racks (H 2260 mm × W 1095 mm × D 1500 mm), hosting up to 16 chassis. These contain a number of direct liquid-cooled node-blades. In the case of the DEEP Cluster, only 8 chassis were

a) DEEP Prototype

b) DEEP-ER Prototype

FIGURE 9.6:   Pictures of the DEEP prototypes. *a)* First generation(DEEP); *b)* Second generation (DEEP-ER).

installed, each containing 16 Intel Xeon (Sandy Bridge) direct-liquid cooled node-blades. The 128 blades, equipped with two Intel Xeon E5 2680 processors each, are interconnected by a Mellanox InfiniBand ConnectX fabric using QDR-generation technology.

DEEP Booster   The DEEP Booster is based on custom hardware, designed and built entirely within the DEEP research project. The first step for building a Booster, i.e. a cluster of accelerators, is to select a *stand-alone accelerator* processor. At the end of 2011, when the DEEP project started, there was no such device on the market. All existent devices at that time (GPUs and many-core processors) required a host processor both for booting and for managing communication through a standard high-speed network, making them *slaves* of a host CPU.

The DEEP team found a solution in using the Intel Xeon Phi (KNC) coprocessor in combination with the EXTOLL [7] interconnect. The EXTOLL network is a switchless solution in which host interface, network interface controller, and router are completely integrated in one-chip. Each chip gives 7 interconnect links, which naturally allows bulding a 3-D torus using six of them. The 7th link provides further connection possibilities (e.g. short-cuts in the 3-D torus) and has been employed in the DEEP Booster to attach the interface nodes. Further details of the EXTOLL design and capabilities are given in [38]. Each compute node in the DEEP Booster contains one KNC attached via PCIe to an Altera Stratix V FPGA running the EXTOLL network protocol. The FPGA implements EXTOLL's NIC and acts as the PCIe root port.

The physical connection between the Cluster and Booster sides of the system is done via interface nodes. Each of them contains a general purpose (Intel Xeon i7) server CPU, with an InfiniBand HCA and an EXTOLL NIC plugged into a PLX PCIe switch. The CPUs of the interface modules run the inter-module bridging protocol (see section 9.6.3) and play an initiator role in the remote-booting process of the Booster nodes. Without a host CPU, booting the KNC is achieved exploiting EXTOLL's ability to transparently forward PCIe packets [38].

The DEEP Booster rack is, as the Cluster, a double-sided, direct water-cooled Eurotech's Aurora rack. It holds 12 chassis, each containing 16 double-node blades (i.e. 32 individual nodes) and two interface nodes. Compute and interface blades are plugged into a passive backplane, through which the chassis-internal network links are routed. The inter-chassis links are implemented with copper cables. The Booster network topology is a (8×6×8) 3D torus. EXTOLL 7th links connect inside each chassis the Booster compute nodes with the interface nodes, and through them with the Cluster part of the Modular Supercomputer.

GreenICE Booster   The ASIC version of EXTOLL (code-named Tourmalet) was available too late for its integration in the large DEEP Booster, so that FGPAs had to be employed to implement the EXTOLL network protocol. The main difference between the FGPA and the ASIC versions is that the latter achieves about 7× higher link bandwidth and 8× lower latency. To evaluate the use of this high-speed network in a Booster-like system, a small prototype – called *GreenICE Booster* – was built in the last months of the DEEP project [33]. It differs from the large DEEP Booster previously described not only in its network implementation, but also in its overall physical integration and cooling.

Each GreenICE Booster node consists of a KNC (Intel Xeon Phi 7120D) and an EXTOLL network interface card (NIC) (a Tourmalet PCIe card [8] in which the EXTOLL ASIC is embedded). The EXTOLL NICs are interconnected to each other via copper cables that realize a 3-D torus topology. Groups of 8 KNC and 8 Tourmalet cards share the same backplane, which is mainly responsible for conducting the PCIe signals between KNC and NIC and for providing the necessary electrical power to both of them. A GreenICE chassis includes 4 such dense backplanes, i.e. a total of 32 Booster nodes.

FIGURE 9.7: Picture of the GreenICE Booster chassis (outside its rack).

The GreenICE chassis is built as an hermetically closed container, filled with the Novec [27] cooling liquid produced by 3M. All KNC and Tourmalet cards together with the backplanes and cables are immersed in this fluid, which dissipates the heat produced during operation. The Novec liquid boils at 49° C. In direct contact with the hot electronic components, Novec evaporates. Its gas bubbles – less dense than the liquid form of Novec – transport the absorbed heat to the upper part of the chassis basin, where they get in contact with a water cooling serpentine. There Novec condensates and the liquid droplets fall down to the lower part of the basin, closing the cooling cycle. Figure 9.7 shows a picture of the GreenICE Booster chassis deployed in the DEEP project.

Interface nodes connect the GreenICE Booster with the DEEP Cluster[3], and are implemented as standard air-cooled Xeon servers (equipped with a Tourmalet card and a Mellanox FDR InfiniBand adapter) sitting in the upper part of the rack. Their role is the same as in the large Booster: remote-booting the KNCs and driving the communication between the DEEP Cluster and the GreenICE Booster.

9.5.2   Second Generation (DEEP-ER) Prototype

The DEEP-ER prototype consists of one Cluster and one Booster module integrated in a single, standard 19" rack (see Part *b)* of Figure 9.6), which also holds the storage system (one meta-data, two storage servers, and 57 TB storage in spinning disks). A uniform high-speed EXTOLL interconnect runs across Cluster and Booster, connecting them internally, between each other, and with the storage. The Tourmalet A3 product generation has been selected. It relies on an ASIC-based NIC that provides six[4] links of 100 Gbit/s bandwidth each, and contains logic for highly efficient message transmission and DMA.

The DEEP-ER system is smaller than its predecessor (all together 24 nodes with a total 36 TFlop/s peak performance) but is enhanced with advanced memory technologies, in particular non-volatile and network attached memories (NAM). With them, a multi-level memory hierarchy has been built, which provides scalable I/O performance and enables the implementation of innovative I/O and resiliency techniques (see 9.7.3). The total memory capacity of the system is 8 TByte.

Given the size of the system and the strong focus of the DEEP-ER project on software development, the construction of the prototype was kept as simple as possible, employing off-the-shelf, air-cooled hardware components. A climate machine in the computer room provides the needed cooling capacity for the prototype.

DEEP-ER Cluster   The DEEP-ER Cluster is composed of 16 SuperMicro servers (1U high ×19" wide). Each server hosts an Intel Xeon (Haswell) processor, one EXTOLL Tourmalet card, and and a non-volatile memory device (see 9.5.2). The latter are connected to the processor board via PCIe gen3. Copper cables running between the Tourmalet cards build-up a 4×2×4 torus, with links going towards the storage servers, the Booster part, and the NAMs.

DEEP-ER Booster   The DEEP-ER prototype profited from the evolution of the Intel Xeon Phi processor line. The second generation of this product, code-named *Knights Landing* (KNL), is a self-booting many-core processor, which greatly eases the construction of a Booster. A further important feature for DEEP-ER is KNL's larger memory capacity, with high bandwidth 16 GB MCDRAM, and the possibility to additionally plug 6 memory DIMMs. In the prototype these were populated with a total of 96 GB DDR4 memory, fitting the requirements established by the co-design applications.

The 8 servers that constitute the Booster part of the system are of the model code-

---

[3]There is no direct connection between the large Booster and the GreenICE Booster, as none of the co-design applications intended to distribute code over the two Boosters.

[4]The 7th link, though available also in the Tourmalet ASIC, is not easily accessible in the current PCIe board and has therefore not been used in the DEEP-ER Booster.

named *(Adams Pass)*, from which four of them fit into a 2U server. However, in our case only the two lower servers could populate each chassis. The reason is that the NVMe cards had to be located on the upper slot (connected via a flat PCIe cable), since there was not enough space within the server enclosure to fix both the NVMe device and the EXTOLL Tourmalet. The network topology chosen for the Booster is a (2×2×2) torus.

Memory technologies All nodes in the DEEP-ER prototype (in both Cluster and Booster) feature a **non-volatile memory (NVM)** device for efficiently buffering I/O and storing checkpoints. The chosen technology is Intel's DC P3700, an SSD replacement device with 400 GByte capacity that provides high speed, non-volatile local memory, attached to the node with 4 lanes of PCIe. Extensive experiments and a wide range of measurements with I/O benchmarks and application mock-ups have been performed, which show substantial performance increases over conventional best-of-breed SSDs, in particular for scenarios with many parallel I/O requests, and over state-of-the art I/O servers.

DEEP-ER has also introduced an innovative memory concept: the **network attached memory (NAM)**. It exploits the remote DMA capabilities of the EXTOLL fabric, which enable remotely accessing memory resources without the intervention of an active component (such a CPU). Packed into a PCIe add-on card, the NAM combines Hybrid Memory Cube (HMC) devices with a state-of-the-art Xilinx Virtex 7 FPGA to create a high-speed memory device that is directly attached to the EXTOLL fabric, and is therefore globally accessible by all nodes in the system. The FPGA implements three functions: the HMC controller, the EXTOLL network interface with two full-speed Tourmalet links, and the NAM logic. The HMC controller has been developed by UHEI and its design has been released as Open Source [19].

A *libNAM* library has been implemented to give system and application software running on the DEEP-ER prototype access to the NAM memory pool, and to enable the execution of any pre-defined functions in the NAM logic. As a first NAM use-case, a checkpointing/restart function has been implemented. It uses the NAM FPGA to pull the required data from the compute nodes and locally calculate the parity information.

The DEEP-ER prototype holds two NAM devices, each with 2 GByte capacity. Their small size is due to limitations of current HMC technology. Future implementations can, however, increase capacities and may trigger a rethinking of memory architectures for HPC and data analytics. In fact, the NAM-concept is going to be further developed within the successor project DEEP-EST.

9.5.3 JURECA

The JURECA Cluster, running since 2015 as JSC's general purpose production cluster, has received a Booster module that is attached to it since the end of 2017.

JURECA Cluster The JURECA Cluster [45] (see Part a) in Figure 9.8) consists of 1872 compute nodes, accompanied by additional 24 nodes used for login, visualization, etc. Each node is equipped with two 12-core Intel Xeon E5-2680 v3 processors clocked at 2.5 GHz. The compute nodes present various memory sizes and a maximum memory bandwidth of 136 GB/s. Most of the nodes (1,680) have 128 GB of DDR4 memory. From the remaining nodes, 128 contain 256 GB and 64 have even 512 GB. Furthermore, 75 nodes are accelerated with two nVIDIA K80 graphic processing units (GPGPU) each.

The interconnect is Mellanox EDR (extended data rate) InfiniBand (100 Gb/s link bandwidth and $1\mu s$ MPI latency). Each node hosts a ConnectX-4 HCA, attached to a first layer of 36-port switches. The spine of the fabric is build out of three 648-port Omni-Path director switches, leading to a full fat-tree topology without any pruning. With it,

a) JURECA Cluster

b) JURECA Booster

FIGURE 9.8: JURECA system, composed of interconnected Cluster and Booster.

full bisection bandwidth and non-blocking communication for appropriate communication patterns is achieved.

In order to provide I/O capabilities to JURECA's users, it is connected to JSC's central GPFS storage cluster JUST via a set of Mellanox gateway routers bridging between the internal EDR InfiniBand fabric and the facility's Ethernet backbone using 40 G technology.

JURECA Cluster system usage   Figure 9.9 shows how the JURECA Cluster reaches nearly 90% productive usage. The first four months of operation (July to October 2015) correspond to the first phase of the installation, in which only 4 of the Cluster racks were available to users. The Cluster started full operation in November 2015. The down-time in December 2016 was due to problems with the GPFS file-system, caused by a software bug.

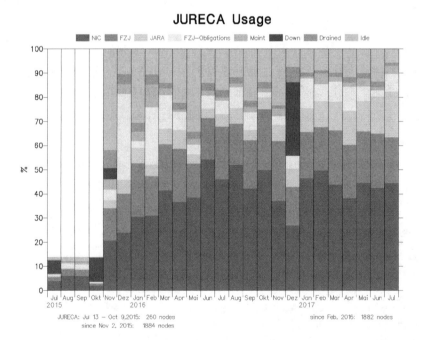

FIGURE 9.9: Usage of the JURECA Cluster.

The different colors in Figure 9.9 show the distribution of the compute time over the various pools of users. Regional users are grouped under *FZJ* and *JARA*; German-wide users belong to *NIC*; national and international users working closely together with JSC through specific research collaborations are accounted under *FZJ-obligations*.

JURECA Booster Recently JSC has extended the JURECA system by a Booster based on Intel's Xeon Phi processors of the KNL generation (see Part b) in Figure 9.8). For this, a total of 1,640 Booster nodes, each one hosting a 68-core Intel XeonPhi 7250-F many-core CPU, are utilized. Each processor contains 16 GB of high-bandwidth MCDRAM and is accompanied by 96 GB of DDR4 memory. The -F version of KNL has Intel's Omni-Path fabric on board. The Booster nodes form their own full fat-tree fabric, which allows high flexibility in the communication patterns of the highly scalable parts of the applications to run on the Booster. The fat-tree topology is set-up with a first layer of 48-port switches, accompanied by a spine-layer build out of Omni-Path director switches.

In order to embed the JURECA Booster in the existing environment, two types of gateway nodes are included in the system. On the one hand 198 MPI Router nodes attach the Booster to the JURECA Cluster bridging between their respective Omni-Path and Infini-Band fabrics. Each of the MPI Router nodes hosts a Mellanox ConnectX-4 Host Channel Adapter and a Intel Omni-Path Host Fabric Adapter. The nodes are powered by a single 14-core Intel Xeon E5-2690 v4 processor, which translates between the two fabric protocols and hosts 64 GB of DDR4 memory. On the other hand, 26 GPFS router nodes bridge to the facility Ethernet backbone using 40 G Ethernet. These nodes are populated with two 14-core Intel Xeon E5-2690 v4 processors each. Besides 32 GB of DDR4 memory, each of the GPFS router nodes host an Intel Omni-Path Host Fabric Adapter and an Intel XL710 Dual Port 40 G NIC.

9.6 System Software

The software environment used in the DEEP prototypes and the one installed in JU-RECA have many points in common. The few differences between them come mostly from the more conservative philosophy inherent to a production system as JURECA, compared to the more experimental character of the DEEP research prototypes (newer, higher-risk approaches can be tried out when full-time operation is not a requirement). The most important software components are summarised in Table 9.2.

9.6.1 System Administration

The cluster management software running on the general-purpose clusters at JSC is ParaStation V5 [20], an Open Source middleware developed and maintained by the ParaStation consortium, in which JSC is one of the key members. ParaStation contains multiple components covering the most important functionalities for management of large-scale, high-performance computers. These range from low level (e.g. process management for parallel and serial jobs, support for various high-speed network, hardware monitoring, resource management), to the higher layers of the programming environment (e.g. MPI, high-performance parallel file copy).

Its MPI programming environment (ParaStation MPI) is based on MPIch and relies on its own communication library, named *pscom*. It is highly scalable and extendible through

TABLE 9.2: Software configuration

Feature	DEEP prototypes	JURECA
Login Node OS Compute Node OS Cluster Management Parallel Filesystem	Linux CentOS 6.9 Linux CentOS 7 ParaStation ClusterSuite GPFS 4.2 (/home) BeeGFS 2015.03 (/work)	Linux CentOS 7 Linux CentOS 7 ParaStation ClusterSuite GPFS 4.2
Compilers	Intel 2017.2.17 Fortran, C/C++ Compiler GNU 5.3 PGI 13.4	GNU 5.4.0 PGI 17.3
Parallel Programming	ParaStation MPI 5.1.9 OpenMP Intel MPI 5.1 OmpSs	ParaStation MPI 5.1.9 OpenMP Intel MPI 2017.2.174 MVAPICH2 (2.2-GDR) NVIDIA CUDA 8 OpenCL OpenAcc
Notable Libraries	Intel Math Kernel Library 2017.2.174 SIONlib 1.7.1 HDF5 1.8.18 netcdf 4.2 PETSc 3.7.4 SCR 1.1.8 Exascale10	SIONlib 1.7.1 HDF5 1.8.18 netcdf 4.4.1.1 PETSc 3.7.6 (and 3.7.5)
Job Scheduler Resource Manager	Moab / SLURM Torque/SLURM + ParaStation psmgmt	SLURM SLURM + ParaStation psmgmt
Debugging Tools	Intel Inspector TotalView	
Performance Tools	Scalasca 2.0b3 Intel Advisor 17.1 Intel Inspector 17.1 Intel VTune 17.1 Vampirtrace 5.14.3 Extrae/Paraver 2.5.1	Scalasca 2.3.1 Intel Advisor 17.2 Intel Inspector 17.3 Intel VTune 17.4 TotalView 2017.0.12 Allinea Performance Reports

a plugin system and supports many different interconnects without application re-linking. The best communication path between each two nodes is chosen automatically at application start-up. Within the DEEP projects, *pscom* has been extended with new plugins for EXTOLL and the EXTOLL-InfiniBand network-bridging protocol (see section 9.6.3. This way, ParaStation MPI covers all possible communication paths within the DEEP prototypes. For JURECA, new *pscom* plugins for the Booster's Omni-Path network and the Omni-Path to InfiniBand bridging protocol have been recently implemented.

9.6.2 Schedulers and Resource Management

One of the main differences between DEEP's and JURECA's software environments is the utilization of different packages for resource management and scheduling. JURECA employs SLURM [52], while the Torque [29] and Maui [28] combination is used in the DEEP and DEEP-ER prototypes. This is the result of a strategic decision taken at JSC shortly before the deployment of the JURECA Cluster. At that time, and to profit from SLURM's much wider use and active development in the HPC community, JSC decided to move from

Torque-Maui/Torque-Moab into SLURM for all its production cluster systems. Sticking to the new policy, the DEEP prototypes originally installed with the old management software have been migrated to SLURM. The modifications to the resource management required to support a Modular Supercomputer, which had been implemented in Torque/Maui within the DEEP project, are currently being ported to SLURM.

Independently of the underlying software, in order to properly support a Modular Supercomputer the resource management system must be able to handle its heterogeneity. In particular it must be able, for any particular job, to simultaneously allocate nodes within several compute modules, while being aware of their different node configurations.

Figure 9.10 shows schematically three fictive application-workloads with different profiles running on a Modular Supercomputer composed of 5 compute modules.

- Workload 1: a *classic* HPC application with a large highly scalable code part running on the Booster and a smaller low scalable part running on the Cluster.

- Workload 2: a typical HPDA application, which runs mostly on the data-analytics module, using the Cluster module for pre-processing and the Graphics module for visualisation of the results.

- Workload 3: a neuroscience application starting on the Cluster module, running simulations on the Neuromorphic module and using GPGPUs on the Graphics module to run arithmetic-intensive kernels.

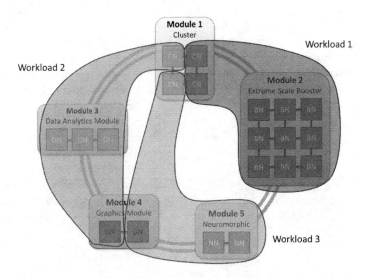

FIGURE 9.10: Three application workloads running on a Modular Supercomputer.

The management and scheduling systems employ heuristics to determine the optimal distribution of user-codes on the system, and to order them in the queue. Goals of the optimisation algorithms are to give all applications their required resources and globally achieve maximal system utilisation. From the system perspective the latter is more important, as it leads to a higher scientific throughput. Full system utilisation is possible with a good mix of diverse applications or, looking it from the opposite perspective, with a system design tailored to the specific application portfolio.

To explain how the users interact with the scheduler in a Modular Supercomputer, let's consider as an example Workload 1 in Figure 9.10: an application that starts its execution on the Cluster part of a Modular Supercomputer and runs part of its code on the Booster module. In that case, the user places a request to the job scheduler via a modified version of the qsub command:

```
qsub -l nodes=cn:cluster+bn:booster "mpiexec -np n <exec>"
```

where *cn* and *bn* denote the number of Cluster and Booster nodes, respectively. Within the application, MPI_Comm_spawn calls are used to run their highly scalable code parts on the Booster, as described in section 9.7.1. The scheduler then passes lists of all the allocated resources to ParaStation's process management system.

Resource allocation may be *static* (with all needed nodes allocated before the job starts and remaining reserved until if is terminated), or *dynamic*. In the latter case, an application calling MPI_Comm_spawn may request more Booster nodes than initially allocated. When this happens, the MPI runtime forwards the request to the resource manager. Depending on the current load of the machine, it may block the application until enough nodes are available, or until an optionally specified timeout expires, in which case the call fails. When the resources are available, these are associated to the application, which starts running on the reserved nodes. If the allocation is *dynamic*, nodes are freed and allocated to other users as soon as the spawned tasks are done. In the *static* case all resources are freed once the full application run is completed.

9.6.3   Network-bridging Protocol

In a Modular Supercomputer, the interconnect does not necessarily need to be the same in all modules. In fact, the first DEEP prototype and JURECA do present different network technologies in their Cluster and Booster parts (see section 9.5).

For applications to run distributed on modules with different interconnects, a very efficient network bridge is needed. In DEEP, a so-called *Cluster-Booster protocol* was written to bridge between InfiniBand (FDR) and EXTOLL. Invisible to the user, this bridging protocol is called by the MPI library when data has to be transfered between application parts running on separate modules. DEEP's Cluster-Booster protocol provided significant performance benefits compared to a standard store-and-forward implementation. A detailed discussion of the design and implementation of this protocol, and benchmarks of the results obtained can be found in [36].

For the JURECA system, an own bridge-protocol is being developed at JSC, together with its partners ParTec and Intel. It will run on JURECA's interface nodes and seamlessly connect the InfiniBand EDR network of the JURECA Cluster, with the Omni-Path fabric of its Booster.

9.6.4   I/O Software and File System

Some of the first DEEP users found the memory and storage capacity of the first generation DEEP prototype was too small, especially on the Booster side of the machine. Therefore, the second generation prototype (DEEP-ER) introduced a memory hierarchy (see 9.5.2) as basis to a scalable I/O infrastructure. The resulting I/O software platform combines the parallel I/O library SIONlib with the BeeGFS parallel file system. Together, they enable the efficient and transparent use of the underlying hardware and provide the functionality and performance required by data-intensive applications and multi-level checkpointing-restart techniques.

The I/O library SIONlib [42, 43] acts as a concentration-layer for applications to most efficiently use the underlying file system. SIONlib compacts all the data that applications performing task-local I/O need to store into one or very few large files, easily manageable by the file system. SIONlib runs on JURECA and the DEEP prototypes. In particular, it plays a key role on the second generation (DEEP-ER) system, where it builds a bridge between the I/O and resiliency components of the software stack. SIONlib is used to copy local checkpoints into the NVM of a companion (*buddy*) node for redundancy, and to efficiently store checkpoint-data in the global file system. Both functions work in combination with the scalable checkpointing library SCR (see section 9.7.3).

The file system on JURECA is GPFS. Though the DEEP prototypes are also connected to this central JSC infrastructure (used for the `/home` directories), their effective (`/work`) global parallel file system is BeeGFS [40]. BeeGFS provides a solid, common basis for high-performance, parallel I/O operations. Advanced functionalities, such as a local cache layer in the file system, have been added within the DEEP-ER project. The cache domain – based on BeeGFS on demand (BeeOND) [41] – stores data in fast node-local non-volatile memory devices and can be used in a synchronous or asynchronous mode. This speeds up the applications' I/O operations and reduces the frequency of accesses to the global storage, increasing the overall scalability of the file system.

9.7   Programming Model

An important amount of the work performed in the DEEP projects was related to the development of a programming environment that maximally reduces the effort of porting applications to the new platform. The components of the programming model were consciously selected to be the de-facto standard in HPC: MPI+OpenMP. Adjustments and extensions have been implemented on their lower layers to properly support the Modular Supercomputing architecture.

This approach aims at hiding the hardware complexity from the end-user. Runtime environments supporting the hardware features of each module have been implemented. For example, the MPI library running on each module is specifically optimized for the network fabric installed on it, and it automatically calls the low-level network bridging protocol whenever an application communicates between two modules with different fabrics. Admittedly, in such a case the interface nodes increase the communication latency. The impact of this restriction is however minimal for the performance of the overall application, since the programming model for a Modular Supercomputer foresees partitioning applications at boundaries involving low-frequency communication and limited data volume. This is a consequence of the fact that large portions of the application – comprising internal inter-node communication – run on each compute module, so that collective operations happen mostly within the modules, and not between them. Therefore, in this scenario the term *kernel*, which is commonly used to describe parts of codes running on accelerators, is not appropriate. On a Modular Supercomputer the term *part* has been chosen to describe the portion of an application offloaded from one compute module to another.

9.7.1   Inter-module MPI Offloading

The actual offloading process between modules is kept as close to existing standards as possible. The dynamic process model of MPI-2, namely `MPI_Comm_spawn`, has been chosen to perform the offloading mechanism (see Figure 9.11). It allows spawning processes from one module to another and provides an efficient way of exchanging data between them using MPI semantics.

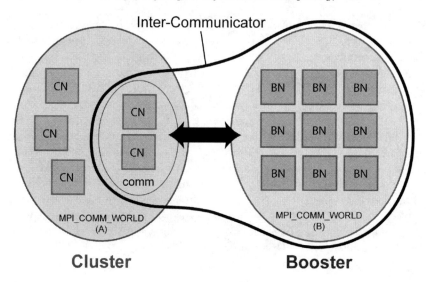

FIGURE 9.11: `MPI_Comm_spawn` schematics, describing the example of an application starting on the Cluster and offloading a part of its code to the Booster. (*CN*: MPI process on Cluster node; *BN*: MPI process on Booster node).

`MPI_Comm_spawn` is a collective operation performed by a subset of the processes of an application starting on a specific module. Its call requires as input the binary-name and the number of new processes to be started. A new inter-communicator is returned, providing a connection handle to the children. Each child calls then `MPI_Init`, as usual, and gets access to the inter-communicator via `MPI_Get_parent`. Both parts of the applications – the part containing the `main()` function, and the offloaded part – have their own `MPI_COMM_WORLD`s providing full MPI functionality on either side, and are connected to each other via inter-communicators.

The intra-module MPIs, together with the offloading mechanism and the network-bridging protocol, constitute a *global MPI*, i.e. an MPI implementation that is usable on all node types and allows for communication between nodes sitting on different modules. Its implementation uses ParTec's ParaStation MPI (see section 9.6.1), which runs on all Modular Supercomputers at JSC.

The code changes needed to map an application (xPic) onto the two parts of the DEEP-ER prototype using ParaStation global MPI, and results demonstrating the gained performance gain are discussed in [47].

9.7.2   OmpSs Abstraction Layer

For a programmer, actively employing the `MPI_Comm_spawn` primitive means coordinating and managing two or more sets of parallel MPI processes, explicitly sending the required data from one side to the other. This approach may become cumbersome for large and complex applications. To reduce this porting effort, an abstraction layer sitting on top of the global MPI has been implemented within the DEEP project. It enables application developers offloading large complex tasks by simply annotating with *pragmas* the parts of their codes that shall run in a different compute module to where the `main()` function is located.

The abstraction layer is based on the OmpSs data-flow programming model [35, 51]. This OpenMP 4.0-like environment exploits task-level parallelism and supports asynchronicity,

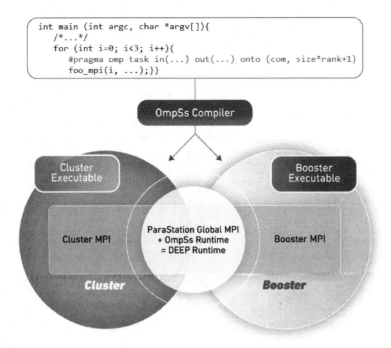

```
int main (int argc, char *argv[]){
    /*...*/
    for (int i=0; i<3; i++){
        #pragma omp task in(...) out(...) onto (com, size*rank+1)
        foo_mpi(i, ...);}}
```

FIGURE 9.12: Workflow of an application running across the Cluster and Booster modules with the OmpSs abstraction layer.

heterogeneity, and data movement. Using OmpSs, an application's code is annotated with OpenMP-like pragmas that indicate data dependencies between the different tasks of the program. Taking these dependencies into account, the OmpSs runtime decides on the order of the tasks and whether concurrent execution is allowed, creating a task dependency graph at run-time. All this information is used to schedule the tasks on the available devices.

Figure 9.12 shows the workflow of an application that starts on the Cluster module and sends a part of its code (an OmpSs task) to the Booster. For this purpose, a single OmpSs pragma is included in the source code. It indicates the data that the task needs as input, the data that it generates as output, and the destination to where it shall be sent, with a given communicator and size. The OmpSs source-to-source compiler interprets this pragma and generates two executables: one for the part of the code to run on the Cluster, and one for the part that shall run on the Booster. The OmpSs runtime cooperates then with the global MPI layer to transparently manage all data transfers between the MPI processes running on the two modules.

9.7.3 Resiliency Software

Within the DEEP-ER project OmpSs has been further extended to improve application's resiliency against transient hardware failures. Failed OmpSs tasks can now be restarted at their last checkpoint, without losing the work that had been performed in parallel by other OmpSs tasks of the same code. To support this task-based resiliency functionality, the ParaStation management daemon has been extended with an interface for querying resiliency-related status information from the MPI layer and thus also from the OmpSs runtime environment. ParaStation MPI itself is now able to detect, isolate, and clean up

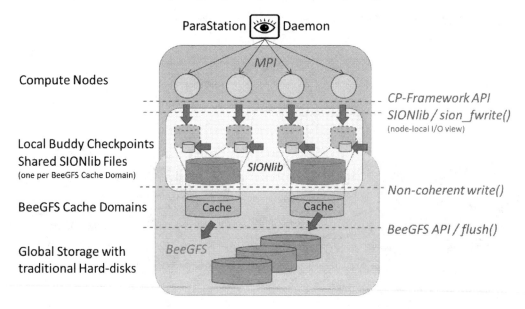

FIGURE 9.13: Buddy-checkpointing software stack in the DEEP-ER prototype.

failures of MPI-offloaded tasks, which can be then independently restarted without requiring a full application recovery.

Complementing the task-based resiliency mechanism, traditional user-level application checkpoint-restart is applied. The Scalable Checkpoint-Restart library (SCR) offers a flexible interface for applications to perform checkpoints and restart from them in case of failure. The user only needs to call the library and indicate the data required by the application to restart execution. SCR decides based on a failure model (specifically developed for the DEEP-ER prototype) where and how often checkpoints are performed, and keeps a database of checkpoints and their locations in preparation for eventual restarts.

Results obtained by applications showing the benefit of applying the I/O and resiliency features developed in DEEP-ER are discussed in [46].

A *buddy-checkpointing* functionality has been implemented in the DEEP projects – combining SCR, ParaStation MPI, SIONlib, and BeeGFS – to save data on the node-local storage and keep a copy on a companion node (see Figure 9.13). In case of hardware failure, the data lost on the damaged node can be recovered from its *buddy* and the application can continue with minimum time-loss. SCR keeps track of the association between host nodes and buddies; SIONlib takes care that all MPI processes running on a single node jointly write their checkpoint-date into a single file in the buddy-node; and BeeOND saves the data itself on the cache-file system on the local NVM, transferring it asynchronously to the permanent global storage.

Last, but not least, SCR and SIONlib have been extended to enable the use of the DEEP-ER network attached memory (NAM) pool. Together, they call libNAM to trigger parity computation on the NAM. This enables application developers to transparently perform checkpointing/restart to/from the NAM without modifying their codes.

9.8 Cooling and Facility Infrastructure

The DEEP prototypes and the JURECA system are manufactured by different hardware providers with diverse integration approaches, which translates into the use of different cooling technologies.

- DEEP prototype (first generation): Eurotech's Cluster and Booster modules use direct water cooling for all nodes. The small GreenICE Booster uses two-phase immersion cooling to extract heat from electronics, plus a water cooling loop to condensate the immersion-coolant. Power supplies, login nodes, and external storage are air cooled.

- DEEP-ER prototype (second generation): completely air-cooled.

- JURECA Cluster and Booster: air cooling with water-cooled rack doors.

Physically, the DEEP and JURECA systems are located in two different computer rooms at JSC, which present also quite different infrastructures. JURECA sits in the same large hall with JUQUEEN and JUST, while the DEEP prototypes are hosted in a smaller room specially reserved for experimental systems. Since the cooling technology and room infrastructure in the production hall is rather standard, only the free cooling infrastructure of the DEEP room is described here.

Free cooling in the DEEP computer room   One of the objectives of the DEEP projects is to investigate means to keep the power consumption of HPC systems at bay. In this context, the first generation DEEP prototype was designed to employ free cooling.

The use of dry coolers instead of chillers to keep the cooling liquid of a system at an acceptable temperature (up to 40° C) saves a significant amount of power. However, the use of warm-coolant also poses some challenges in system integration and maintenance. To efficiently cool a high performance computer at these temperatures, the chosen coolant has to be very effective in removing and transporting the heat away from the electronics. Direct water cooling was the solution chosen for the first DEEP prototype. Aluminium cold-plates were designed with a *Manhattan* profile exactly matching the node boards. These cold plates are plugged via quick-disconnects into chassis-level water distribution bars, which are connected via tubes to the room infrastructure pipes.

Figure 9.14 depicts a simplified scheme of the water cooling infrastructure implemented for the DEEP prototypes. The Cluster and Booster modules of the first DEEP generation are both water-cooled systems. The internal (primary) cooling loop of each part of the system runs from the DEEP computer room down to the cellar of the building, where pumps and heat exchangers are located. One of the heat exchangers puts the primary cooling loop in contact with the secondary loop. This runs from the cellar to the outer part of the building, where a dry cooler is located. The dry cooler is ultimately responsible for keeping the temperature of the secondary loop below 35° C, which guarantees an inlet temperature in the primary loops below 40° C. A second heat exchanger brings the primary loop in contact with the central cool water distribution of Forschungszentrum Jülich. This connection is foreseen only as backup, for the very rare occasions (the few hottest days in the summer) in which the outside air temperature becomes too high to operate the system using only free cooling.

The primary cooling loop of the DEEP Booster is split into two branches: one for the large Booster, and one for the small GreenICE Booster. Valves and control sensors at various parts of the infrastructure guarantee that the coolant is kept at the desired temperature

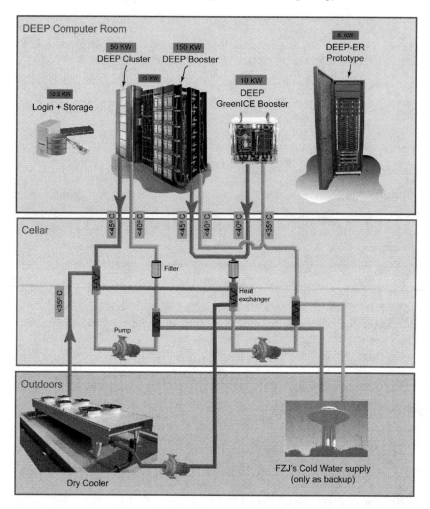

FIGURE 9.14: Schematics of cooling infrastructure for the DEEP prototypes. The DEEP prototype (Cluster and Booster) use direct water cooling, as well as the DEEP GreenICE Booster. Login nodes and the second generation prototype (DEEP-ER) employ air-cooling.

and pressure at each point of the loop. Additionally, probes of the primary loop coolants are taken regularly to analyse their chemical composition. Conductivity and pH are particularly carefully controlled.

9.9   Conclusions and Next steps

The Modular Supercomputing Architecture is the result of more than a decade experience gathered at the Jülich Supercomputing Centre (JSC) in the co-development, operation, and maintenance of high performance computers. The motivation behind this new approach to heterogeneous computing is to enable a most efficient use of the computing resources, while providing application developers with all necessary tools to take the step from Petascale to Exascale computing.

JSC recognized very early that no single technology could ever satisfactorily fulfill the requirements of all its diverse user communities, especially, if the resulting HPC system should become both user-friendly and energy efficient. Therefore, JSC initiated a dual supercomputing approach by simultaneously operating two production machines: a general purpose cluster and a massively parallel computer. Users were channelled to the system that best suited their needs: low/medium-scalable with high data-management to the cluster, and high-scalable to the massively parallel. However, an intermediate type of application was identified, which could profit from some characteristics of both architecture branches. This led JSC to create the Cluster-Booster architecture, which basically brings the dual supercomputing approach into one single platform. This concept has been implemented already in two prototype systems (DEEP and DEEP-ER), and is currently going into production with JURECA.

The Modular Supercomputing architecture generalizes the idea of segregating heterogeneous resources into individual, interconnected compute modules. Advantages are expected – as demonstrated with the Cluster-Booster approach – from the high flexibility that the concept offers to users, its perfect match for very diverse application requirements [47], and the possibility to naturally integrate exotic technologies not yet widely available in the HPC environment.

The DEEP-EST research project will create a first incarnation of the Modular Supercomputer Architecture and demonstrate its benefits. The exact configuration of the DEEP-EST prototype, which shall be installed in 2019, will be determined in close co-design between applications, system software, and system component architects. It will include three modules: a general purpose Cluster module and an extreme scale Booster (together supporting the full range of HPCs applications), and a Data Analytics module (specifically designed for high-performance data analytics (HPDA) workloads). The goal is to cover the needs of both HPC and HPDA user communities, contributing to the convergence of both worlds. It shall also allow methodologies applied on HPC and HPDA to be combined for solving increasingly complex simulation and data analysis scenarios. Proven programming models and APIs from HPC (MPI and OpenMP/OmpSs) and from HPDA will be extended. Added to a significantly enhanced resource management and scheduling system, the resulting software stack shall enable straightforward use of the new architecture and achieve highest system utilisation and performance. Six ambitious, full-fledged applications from HPC and HPDA domains will drive the co-design, serving to evaluate the DEEP-EST prototype and demonstrate the benefits of its innovative Modular Supercomputer Architecture.

Already now JSC is preparing the first step towards the implementation of the concept at large scale. In fact, the JUWELS system will be a Modular Supercomputer. Its first module, a general purpose Cluster, will be installed in Q2/2018. In the next few years, it will be complemented with further modules, with hardware and software designs tailored to JSC's user's needs.

9.10   Acknowledgments

The authors would like to thank the JSC staff and all people and partners involved in the DEEP projects, for their engagement and strong commitment, which led to the results described in this chapter. Also, the authors thank Dr. D. Krause for discussing and proof-reading the JURECA sections, Dr. W. Frings, U. Frings, and Dr. F. Janetzko for the information on JURECA and JUQUEEN user profiles included in Figures 9.4 and 9.9, and A. Kreuzer and J. Kreutz for proof-reading the DEEP prototype's data in Tables 9.1 and 9.2.

The research leading to these results has received funding from the European Community's Seventh Framework Programme (FP7/2007-2013) under Grant Agreement n° 287530 (DEEP) and 610476 (DEEP-ER), and from the Horizon 2020 Programme (H2020-FETHPC) under Grant Agreement n° 754304 (DEEP-EST). The present publication reflects only the authors' views. The European Commission is not liable for any use that might be made of the information contained therein.

Bibliography

[1] AVBP website at CERFACS. http://www.cerfacs.fr/avbp7x/. Accessed: 2017-07-28.

[2] Chroma github repository. https://jeffersonlab.github.io/chroma/. Accessed: 2017-07-28.

[3] CMS software github repository. https://github.com/cms-sw/cmssw. Accessed: 2017-07-28.

[4] DEEP-ER project website. http://www.deep-er.eu. Accessed: 2017-07-16.

[5] DEEP project website. http://www.deep-project.eu. Accessed: 2017-07-16.

[6] DEEP prototype website. http://www.fz-juelich.de/ias/jsc/EN/Expertise/Supercomputers/DEEP/DEEP_node.html. Accessed: 2017-07-16.

[7] EXTOLL GmbH website. http://www.extoll.de. Accessed: 2017-07-23.

[8] EXTOLL Tourmalet. http://www.http://extoll.de/products/tourmalet. Accessed: 2017-07-23.

[9] Forschungszentrum Jülich website. http://www.fz-juelich.de/en. Accessed: 2017-07-09.

[10] Full Wave Inversion (FWI) code in DEEP-ER. http://www.deep-projects.eu/applications/project-applications/enhancing-oil-exploration.html. Accessed: 2017-07-28.

[11] GROMACS application website. http://www.gromacs.org/. Accessed: 2017-07-28.

[12] Helmoltz association website. https://www.helmholtz.de/en/. Accessed: 2017-07-09.

[13] High-Q club website. http://www.fz-juelich.de/ias/jsc/EN/Expertise/High-Q-Club/_node.html. Accessed: 2017-08-10.

[14] Human Brain Project pilot systems website. http://www.fz-juelich.de/ias/jsc/EN/Expertise/Supercomputers/HBPPilots/_node.html. Accessed: 2017-07-16.

[15] JSC Simlabs website. http://www.fz-juelich.de/ias/jsc/EN/Expertise/SimLab/simlab_node.html. Accessed: 2017-08-07.

[16] Jülich Supercomputing Centre website. http://www.fz-juelich.de/ias/jsc/EN. Accessed: 2017-07-09.

[17] JUST: Jülich Storage Cluster website. http://www.fz-juelich.de/ias/jsc/EN/Expertise/ Datamanagement/OnlineStorage/JUST/JUST_node.html. Accessed: 2017-07-16.

[18] NEST code website. www.nest-simulator.org. Accessed: 2017-07-28.

[19] OpenHMC. http://www.uni-heidelberg.de/openhmc. Accessed: 2017-07-26.

[20] ParaStation V5 website. http://www.par-tec.com/products/parastationv5.html. Accessed: 2017-07-26.

[21] Prace website. http://www.prace-ri.eu. Accessed: 2017-08-07.

[22] QPACE3 website. http://www.fz-juelich.de/ias/jsc/EN/Expertise/Supercomputers/ QPACE3/_node.html. Accessed: 2017-07-16.

[23] Reverse time migration (rtm) code website. http://www.cgg.com/en/What-We-Do/ Subsurface-Imaging/Migration/Reverse-Time-Migration. Accessed: 2017-07-28.

[24] SeisSol application website. http://www.seissol.org/. Accessed: 2017-07-28.

[25] SKA data analysis pipeline in DEEP-ER. http://www.deep-projects.eu/applications/ project-applications/radio-astronomy.html. Accessed: 2017-07-28.

[26] Top 500 list. https://www.top500.org/lists/. Accessed: 2017-06-26.

[27] 3M. Novec. http://multimedia.3m.com/mws/media/569865O/3mtm-novectm-649-engineered-fluid.pdf?&fn=Novec649_6003926.pdf.

[28] Adaptive Computing. Maui. http://www.adaptivecomputing.com/products/ open-source/maui/.

[29] Adaptive Computing. TORQUE Resource Manager. http://www.adaptivecomputing. com/products/open-source/torque/.

[30] Krste Asanovic, Ras Bodik, Bryan Christopher Catanzaro, Joseph James Gebis, Parry Husbands, Kurt Keutzer, David A. Patterson, William Lester Plishker, John Shalf, Samuel Webb Williams, and Katherine A. Yelick. The landscape of parallel computing research: A view from Berkeley. Technical Report UCB/EECS-2006-183, EECS Department, University of California, Berkeley, Dec 2006.

[31] Norbert Attig, Florian Berberich, Ulrich Detert, Norbert Eicker, Thomas Eickermann, Paul Gibbon, Wolfgang Gürich, Wilhelm Homberg, Antonia Illich, Sebastian Rinke, Michael Stephan, Klaus Wolkersdorfer, and Thomas Lippert. Entering the Petaflop-Era - New Developments in Supercomputing. In *NIC Symposium 2010 / ed.: G. Münster, D. Wolf, M. Kremer, Jülich, Forschungszentrum Jülich, IAS Series Vol. 3. - 978-3-89336-606-4. - S. 1 - 12*, 2010. Record converted from VDB: 12.11.2012.

[32] Dirk Brömmel, Ulrich Detert, Stephan Graf, Thomas Lippert, Boris Orth, Dirk Pleiter, Michael Stephan, and Estela Suarez. Paving the Road towards Pre-Exascale Supercomputing. In *NIC Symposium 2014 - Proceedings*, volume 47 of *NIC Series*, pages 1–14, Jülich, Feb 2014. NIC Symposium 2014, Jülich (Germany), 12 Feb 2014 - 13 Feb 2014, John von Neumann Institute for Computing.

[33] Ulrich Bruening, Mondrian Nuessle, Dirk Frey, and Hans-Christian Hoppe. *An Immersive Cooled Implementation of a DEEP Booster*, pages 30–36. Intel Corporation, Munich, 2015.

[34] Michalis Christou, Theodoros Christoudias, Julian Morillo, Damian Alvarez, and Hendrik Merx. Earth system modelling on system-level heterogeneous architectures: EMAC (version 2.42) on the Dynamical Exascale Entry Platform (DEEP). *Geoscientific model development*, 9(9):3483 – 3491, 2016.

[35] Alejandro Duran, Eduard Ayguadé, Rosa M. Badia, Jesús Labarta, Luis Martinell, Xavier Martorell, and Judit Planas. OmpSs: A proposal for programming heterogeneous multi-core architectures. *Parallel Processing Letters*, 21(02):173–193, 2011.

[36] Norbert Eicker, Andreas Galonska, Jens Hauke, and Mondrian Nüssle. *Bridging the DEEP Gap - Implementation of an Efficient Forwarding Protocol*, pages 34–41. Intel Corporation, Munich, 2014.

[37] Norbert Eicker and Thomas Lippert. An accelerated Cluster-Architecture for the Exascale. In *PARS '11, PARS-Mitteilungen, Mitteilungen - Gesellschaft für Informatik e.V., Parallel-Algorithmen und Rechnerstrukturen, ISSN 0177-0454, Nr. 28, Oktober 2011 (Workshop 2011), 110 - 119*, 2011. Record converted from VDB: 12.11.2012.

[38] Norbert Eicker, Thomas Lippert, Thomas Moschny, and Estela Suarez. The DEEP Project - An alternative approach to heterogeneous cluster-computing in the many-core era. *Concurrency and computation*, 28(8):23942411, 2016.

[39] Andrew Emerson and Fabio Affinito. Enabling a Quantum Monte Carlo application for the DEEP architecture. In *2015 International Conference on High Performance Computing Simulation (HPCS)*, pages 453–457, July 2015.

[40] Fraunhofer Gesselschaft. BeeGFS website.

[41] Fraunhofer Gesselschaft. BeeOND: BeeGFS On Demand website.

[42] Jens Freche, Wolfgang Frings, and Godehard Sutmann. High Throughput Parallel-I/O using SIONlib for Mesoscopic Particle Dynamics Simulations on Massively Parallel Computers. In *Parallel Computing: From Multicores and GPU's to Petascale, / ed.: B. Chapman, F. Desprez, G.R. Joubert, A. Lichnewsky, F. Peters and T. Priol, Amsterdam, IOS Press, 2010. Advances in Parallel Computing Volume 19. - 978-1-60750-529-7. - S. 371 - 378*, 2010. Record converted from VDB: 12.11.2012.

[43] Wolfgang Frings, Felix Wolf, and Ventsislav Petkov. Scalable Massively Parallel I/O to Task-Local Files. In *Proceedings of the Conference on High Performance Computing Networking, Storage and Analysis, Portland, Oregon, November 14 - 20, 2009, SC'09, SESSION: Technical papers, Article No. 17, New York, ACM, 2009.ISBN 978-1-60558-744-8. - S. 1 - 11*, 2009. Record converted from VDB: 12.11.2012.

[44] Markus Götz, Christian Bodenstein, and Morris Riedel. HPDBSCAN - Highly parallel DBSCAN. In *Proceedings of the Workshop on Machine Learning in High-Performance Computing Environments - MLHPC '15*, page 2. Workshop Workshop on Machine Learning in High-Performance Computing Environments, subworkshop to Supercomputing 2015, Austin (Texas), 15 Nov 2015 - 15 Nov 2015, ACM Press New York, New York, USA, Nov 2015.

[45] Dorian Krause and Philipp Thörnig. JURECA: General-purpose supercomputer at Jülich Supercomputing Centre. *Journal of large-scale research facilities*, 2:A62, 2016.

[46] Anke Kreuzer, Jorge Amaya, Norbert Eicker, Raphaël Léger, and Estela Suarez. The DEEP-ER project: I/O and resiliency extensions for the Cluster-Booster architecture. In *Proceedings of the 20th International Conference on High Performance Computing and Communications (HPCC)*, Exeter, UK, 2018. IEEE Computer Society Press. (accepted for publication).

[47] Anke Kreuzer, Jorge Amaya, Norbert Eicker, and Estela Suarez. Application performance on a Cluster-Booster system. In *Proceedings of the 2018 IEEE International Parallel and Distributed Processing Symposium (IPDPS) Workshops Proceedings (HCW)*, *IPDPS Conference*, Vancouver, Canada, 2018. (accepted for publication).

[48] Pramod Kumbhar, Michael Hines, Aleksandr Ovcharenko, Damian Alvarez, James King, Florentino Sainz, Felix Schürmann, and Fabien Delalondre. Leveraging a Cluster-Booster Architecture for Brain-Scale Simulations. In *Proceedings of the 31st International Conference High Performance Computing*, volume 9697 of *Lecture Notes in Computer Science*, pages 363 – 380, Cham, Jun 2016. 31st International Conference High Performance Computing, Frankfurt (Germany), 19 Jun 2016 - 23 Jun 2016, Springer International Publishing.

[49] Raphäel Léger, Damian Alvarez Mallon, Alejandro Duran, and Stephane Lanteri. Adapting a Finite-Element Type Solver for Bioelectromagnetics to the DEEP-ER Platform. In *Parallel Computing: On the Road to Exascale*, volume 27 of *Advances in Parallel Computing*, pages 349 – 359. International Conference on Parallel Computing 2015, Edinburgh (UK), 1 Sep 2015 - 4 Sep 2015, IOS Press Ebooks, Sep 2016.

[50] Thomas Lippert. *Recent Developments in Supercomputing*, volume 39 of *NIC series*, pages 1–8. John von Neumann Institute for Computing, Jülich, 2008. Record converted from VDB: 12.11.2012.

[51] Programming Models @ BSC. The OmpSs Programming Model, 2013.

[52] SchedMD. SLURM website. https://slurm.schedmd.com/.

[53] Michael Stephan and Jutta Docter. JUQUEEN: IBM Blue Gene/Q Supercomputer System at the Jülich Supercomputing Centre. *Journal of large-scale research facilities*, 1:A1, 2015.

[54] Estela Suarez, Norbert Eicker, and Thomas Lippert. Supercomputing Evolution at JSC. volume 49 of *Publication Series of the John von Neumann Institute for Computing (NIC) NIC Series*, pages 1 – 12, Jlich, Feb 2018. NIC Symposium 2018, Jülich (Germany), 22 Feb 2018 - 23 Feb 2018, John von Neumann Institute for Computing.

[55] Anna Wolf, Anke Zitz, Norbert Eicker, and Giovanni Lapenta. Particle-in-Cell algorithms on DEEP:The iPiC3D case study. volume 32, pages 38–48, Erlangen, May 2015. PARS 15, Potsdam (Germany), 7 May 2015 - 8 May 2015, PARS.

Chapter 10

SuperMUC - the First High-Temperature Direct Liquid Cooled Petascale Supercomputer Operated by LRZ

Hayk Shoukourian

Leibniz Supercomputing Centre (LRZ) of the Bavarian Academy of Sciences and Humanities
Boltzmannstraße 1, 85748 Garching bei München, Germany

Arndt Bode

Leibniz Supercomputing Centre (LRZ) of the Bavarian Academy of Sciences and Humanities
Boltzmannstraße 1, 85748 Garching bei München, Germany
Technische Universität München (TUM), Fakultät für Informatik I10
Boltzmannstraße 3, 85748 Garching bei München, Germany

Herbert Huber

Leibniz Supercomputing Centre (LRZ) of the Bavarian Academy of Sciences and Humanities
Boltzmannstraße 1, 85748 Garching bei München, Germany

Michael Ott

Leibniz Supercomputing Centre (LRZ) of the Bavarian Academy of Sciences and Humanities
Boltzmannstraße 1, 85748 Garching bei München, Germany

Dieter Kranzlmüller

Leibniz Supercomputing Centre (LRZ) of the Bavarian Academy of Sciences and Humanities
Boltzmannstraße 1, 85748 Garching bei München, Germany
Ludwig-Maximilians-Universität München (LMU), MNM-Team
Oettingenstraße 67 D-80538 München, Germany

10.1 Overview

The Leibniz Supercomputing Centre (Leibniz-Rechenzentrum, LRZ) [20] of the Bavarian Academy of Sciences and Humanities (Bayerische Akademie der Wissenschaften, BAdW)

[6] is the IT service provider for Munich's universities and to a number of scientific institutions in the greater Munich area as well as in the state of Bavaria. LRZ is a member of the Gauss Centre for Supercomputing (GCS) [9] alliance, which aims to provide the most powerful supercomputing infrastructure in Europe for tackling various research and industrial challenges present in a wide range of disciplines. GCS is the alliance of the three German supercomputing centres, namely: High Performance Computing Center Stuttgart (HLRS) [15], Jülich Supercomputing Centre (JSC) [19], and LRZ. Besides offering state of the art High Performance Computing (HPC) infrastructure in Europe, GCS also provides training for national as well as for European HPC communities. The high-end systems deployed at the three GCS centers are complementary to ensure the support for a broad spectrum of large-scale applications. Additionally, all three centers provide a wide range of tools and support in order to further help users in their application development, porting, and tuning procedures.

The pyramid shown in Figure 10.1 summarizes the concept of how the scientific community is provided with access to supercomputing systems on the national and European level. SuperMUC, LRZ's flagship system, consisting of two installation phases with an aggregated peak performance of 6.8 PetaFLOPS, is a GCS Tier-1 system and one of the PRACE (Partnership for Advanced Computing in Europe) Tier-0 systems.

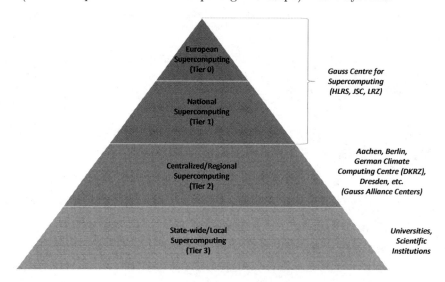

FIGURE 10.1: HPC provision pyramid

SuperMUC and its supporting building facility (described in Section 10.5) have been equally funded by the federal government of Germany and the Free State of Bavaria. The employee costs are covered mainly by the Free State of Bavaria and by accompanying funds from the European Union, the German Federal Ministry of Education and Research, and other third-party research funds.

10.1.1   Timeline

The procurement process for SuperMUC Phase1 started in Feburary 2010. Eight participation requests were obtained - with five of which, in March 2010, the first dialogue process was initiated with planned three phases of negotiations. The first phase assumed submission of offers by July 2010. Two bidders were selected for the second dialogue phase, which started in August. During this phase, the system performance with respect to various benchmarks representing LRZ's user load as well as with respect to system configurations (e.g. number of processors, cache sizes, memory bandwidth, structure of internal network, etc.) were examined. The final selection for the IBM [16] system was met in November 2010. This was followed by contractual negotiations and an eventual contractual agreement in December 2010. SuperMUC Phase1 (described in Section 10.2) was delivered in the beginning of 2012 and was ready for operations by the end of May. The migration system, referred to as SuperMIG, with peak performance of 78 TFLOPS (slightly higher than the predecessor HLRB2 system) was already installed in May 2011. In order to support users in the transition from the SGI ALTIX system with a virtual shared memory architecture, SuperMIG was configured with large per node memories (256 GByte per node). Starting from the middle of September 2011 SuperMIG was fully operational, which implied the complete shutdown of the HLRB2 system. SuperMUC Phase1 provided a peak performance 3.2 PetaFLOPS. Figure 10.2 summarizes the development of HPC at LRZ during the past 26 years.

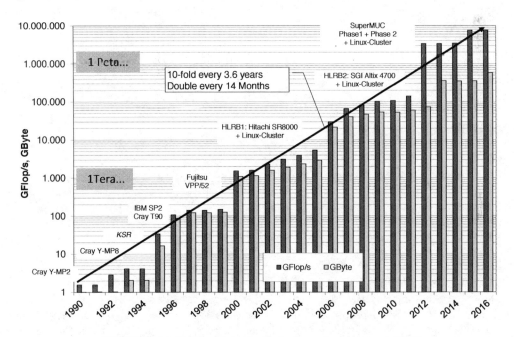

FIGURE 10.2: The history of peak performance at LRZ

In June 2015, the extension of SuperMUC, referred to as Phase2, was officially put into operation. It provided an additional boost of 3.6 PetaFLOPS in the system peak performance. This was achieved by an addition of 86,016 processing cores that lifted the maximum theoretical computing power of SuperMUC to 6.8 PetaFLOPS. Phase2 did not contain any accelerator components allowing users to run their applications on the extension part without major modifications and porting efforts.

Although Phase2 provided similar system performance as Phase1, it only occupied a quarter of its floor space. This is a perfect showcase for Moore's Law, which, by implication, postulates that the system performance would quadruple in the 3 years between the installation of the two phases at an identical footprint. It was also more energy-efficient than Phase1 with 1.9 GFLOPS/W vs the provided 0.85 GFLOPS/W by Phase1.

10.2 System Overview

SuperMUC is the first High-Temperature (ASHRAE W4 chiller-less [2]) Direct Liquid Cooled (HT-DLC) Petascale supercomputer installed worldwide. Its active components (e.g. processors, memory, etc.) are directly liquid cooled with an inlet water temperature of up to 45 °C.

FIGURE 10.3: The SuperMUC system[1]

The bulk of the first installation phase of SuperMUC consists of 18 direct liquid-cooled thin node islands representing the IBM [16] iDataPlex DX360M4 Intel Sandy Bridge system, 1 air-cooled fat node island representing a BladeCenter HX5 Westmere-EX Xeon E7-4870 10C based system, and 1 air-cooled many cores nodes island representing the iDataPlex DX360M4 Ivy-Bridge (IvyB) and Xeon Phi 5110P system (Table 10.1). All compute nodes within an individual island are connected via a fully non-blocking Infiniband network (QDR fat nodes, FDR10 thin nodes). The 18 thin node islands contain 147,456 processor cores in 9216 compute nodes that deliver 3.18 PetaFLOPS theoretical peak performance. The system was the fourth fastest supercomputer in the world and the fastest in Europe at its installation (TOP500 list [32] July 2012). The fat node island (Westmere based nodes) as well as the many cores island (Xeon Phi and Ivy-Bridge nodes) are not included in the TOP500 performance value. It is based solely on the performance of the Sandy Bridge nodes. Each node of the thin node islands is equipped with two 8 core Intel Sandy Bridge-EP Xeon E5-2680 8C processors [18], with a maximum operating frequency of 2.7 GHz (maximum Turbo frequency varies from 3.1 GHz to 3.5 GHz depending on the used number of cores), and a Thermal Design Power (TDP) [14] of 130 W. The size of shared memory per node is 32 GByte. The energy-efficiency of SuperMUC Phase1 is 0.85 GFLOPS/W (Green500 list [10]).

---

[1]Blade pictures from Torsten Bloth

The second installation phase of SuperMUC, referred to as SuperMUC Phase2, is an IBM/Lenovo [21] NeXtScale nx360M5 WCT Intel Haswell system with 3.57 PetaFLOPS of theoretical peak performance and was the 21 fastest supercomputer in the world at its installation time in June 2015 [32]. Phase2 shows a 1.9 GFLOPS/W efficiency (Green500 list [10]). It consists of 6 islands, where each island comprises 512 compute nodes. All compute nodes within an individual island are connected via a fully non-blocking Infiniband FDR14 network. Each compute node features two 14 core Intel Haswell Xeon E5-2697 v3 processors, with a maximum operating frequency of 2.6 GHz (maximum Turbo frequency varies from 3.1 GHz to 3.6 GHz [17]), and a TDP of 145 W. The size of memory per node is 64 GByte.

Both phases have a high speed interconnect between the islands, which enables a bi-directional bi-section bandwidth ratio of 4:1 (intra-island/inter-island). There is no direct Infiniband connection between two phases; data sharing takes place only via shared file system. That is the reason why both phases have separate TOP500 entries.

Figure 10.3 shows the Phase1 and Phase2 installations and the pictures of the direct liquid cooled node designs. Apart from differences in node design, it can be seen that one blade of Phase2 encompasses two compute nodes. For Phase1, the power supply sits on the side of the node with a separate air channel in order to not draw cold air over the liquid cooled node. For Phase2 a standard rack design was used (which is deeper than Phase1 racks) and, therefore, the power supplies are behind the node.

SuperMUC uses IBM's General Parallel File System (GPFS) with 15 Pbyte of capacity and with an aggregated throughput of 350 GB/s. Both phases of SuperMUC use the IBM LoadLeveler [1] as a resource management and scheduling system. Additionally, SuperMUC is connected to powerful visualization systems: LRZ maintains a large 4K stereoscopic powerwall and a 5-sided CAVE artificial virtual reality environment that allow for impressive visualization of scientific data.

Tables 10.1 and 10.2 draw the summary of the system hardware and software configurations, while Table 10.3 describes the programming environment and outlines the currently available main development tools. More information regarding currently available software applications at LRZ can be found in [3].

10.3 Applications and Workloads

Tables 10.4 and 10.5 show the Phase1 and Phase2 usage data with respect to the: *(i)* provided CPU hours; *(ii)* number of distinct users, and *(iii)* number of distinct projects. As can be inferred, the aggregated core hour usage of SuperMUC has been growing since its installation in 2012, reaching to 1628 million CPU hours in 2016 and accumulating to overall 5096 million CPU hours for its four years operational time frame.

SuperMUC distinguishes itself by its versatile usability due to its homogeneity and standard instruction set architecture. Figure 10.4 shows the compute time percentage utilization share of individual scientific disciplines. As was observed for previous years, the usage of SuperMUC is again dominated by computational fluid dynamics and astrophysics domains. A trend of increasing usage is seen for the disciplines of bio and life sciences. LRZ has recognized more than expected improvements in average parallel code scalability, achieved through both system software improvements and by the efforts of application support groups from LRZ and IBM, as well as strong support from the users including algorithm and refactoring groups especially at Technical University of Munich.

Table 10.6 recaps the usage share of SuperMUC by individual institutions for 2016. The

TABLE 10.1: Technical data summary for hardware configuration of SuperMUC

Installation Phase		Phase1			Phase2
Installation Date	2011	2012	2013		2015
Island Type	Fat Nodes	Thin Nodes	Many Cores Nodes		Haswell Nodes
System	BladeCenter HX5	IBM System x iDataPlex dx360M4	IBM System x iDataPlex dx360M4		Lenovo NeXtScale nx360M5 WCT
Total Number of Islands	1	18	1		6
Node Count per Island	205	512	32		512
Processors per Node	4	2	2 (IvyB) 2.6 GHz + 2 Phi 5110P		2
Cores per Processor	10	8	8 (IvyB) + 60 (Phi)		14
Logical CPUs per Node	80	32	32 (host) + 480 (Phi)		56
Processor Type	Westmere-EX Xeon E7-4870 10C	Sandy Bridge-EP Xeon E5-2680 8C	Ivy-Bridge (IvyB) and Xeon Phi 5110P		Haswell Xeon Processor E5-2697 v3
Nominal Frequency (GHz)	2.4	2.7	1.05		2.6
Thermal Design Power (W)	130	130	225		145
Total Size of Memory (TByte)	52	288	2.56		194
Memory per Core (GByte)	6.4	2	4 (host) + 2 x 0.13 (Phi)		2.3
Size of Shared Memory per Node (GByte)	256	32	64 (host) + 2 x 8 (Phi)		64
Bandwidth to Memory per Node (Gbyte/s)	136.4	102.4	Phi: 384		137
Interconnect Technology	Infiniband QDR	Infiniband FDR10	Infiniband FDR10		Infiniband FDR14
Intra-Island Topology	Pruned Tree 4:1	Non-Blocking Tree	N.A.		Non-Blocking Tree
Inter-Island Topology					Pruned Tree 4:1
Bisection Bandwidth of Interconnect (TByte/s)	12.5				5.1
Login Servers for Users	2	7	1		5
Size of parallel storage (SCRATCH/WORK) (Pbyte)			3.5 (+ 3.5 for replication)		
Size of NAS storage (HOME) (PByte)			15		
Aggregated bandwidth to/from parallel storage (GByte/s)			350		
Aggregated bandwidth to/from NAS storage (GByte/s)			12		
Capacity of Archive and Backup Storage (PByte)			>30		
Total Peak Performance (PFLOPS)	0.078	3.2	0.064 (Phi)		3.58
Total HPL Performance (PFLOPS)	0.065	2.897	N.A.		2.814
Typical Power Consumption (MW)		< 2.3			~ 1.1
Power Consumption at HPL (MW)		3.4			1.48
Energy Efficiency (GFLOPS/W)		0.85			1.9

TABLE 10.2: Technical data summary for system software configuration of SuperMUC

Installation Phase	Phase1	Phase2
Operating System		Suse Linux Enterprise Server (SLES)
Resource Management and Scheduling System		IBM LoadLeveler
Parallel Filesystem for SCRATCH and WORK		IBM GPFS
File System for HOME		NetApp NAS
Archive and Backup Software		IBM TSM
System Management		xCat from IBM

TABLE 10.3: Summary of the programming environment and the available main application software

Product Name	Short Description
Programming Paradigms	
MPI	Message Passing Interface
OpenMP	Open Multi-Processing
PGAS	Partitioned Global Address Space
Tools	
Intel Inspector	Allows to perform correctness checking on multi-threaded applications
Intel Amplifier	Allows to perform performance analysis on multi-threaded applications
Intel Advisor	Allows to identify optimization possibilities in the applications
Intel Tracing Tools VAMPIR/NG	MPI profiling tools
Marmot	MPI error detection tool
MPIP	Tool for profiling the communication of MPI applications
Periscope Scalasca	tools for performance analysis
Valgrind	Tool for correctness checking of programs (memory management, threading, etc.) that uses a virtual execution environment
PAPI	Performance Application Programming Interface: allows to valuate hardware performance counters
Forcheck	Tool for static analysis of Fortran code
Eclipse CDT	Integrated Development Environment for C/C++/Fortran/Java
Languages	C C++ Fortran Java
Debuggers	
gdb	GNU debugger
(x)pgdgb	PGI debugger
ddt	Allinea DDT

usage share of PRACE has been drastically reduced, since LRZ has mainly fulfilled the contractual obligations for the first period of PRACE in previous years.

The list below presents the main scientific highlights accomplished with the help of SuperMUC.

- **Seismic Science Project SeisSol**
  SeisSol, a software to simulate earth quakes, achieved performance of 1.42 PetaFLOPS

TABLE 10.4: SuperMUC Phase1 usage data

Year	System usage in Mill CPU hours	Number of Distinct Users	Number of Distinct Projects
2012	136.15	574	205
2013	993.42	864	244
2014	1100	897	294
2015	1031	803	278
2016	1001	676	269

TABLE 10.5: SuperMUC Phase2 usage data

Year	System usage in Mill CPU hours	Number of Distinct Users	Number of Distinct Projects
2015	206.5	298	136
2016	626.5	563	224

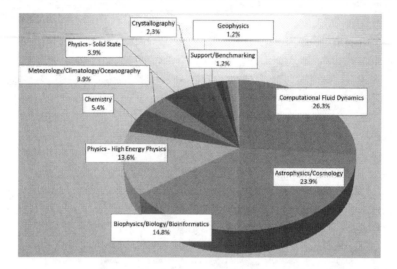

FIGURE 10.4: Core hour usage of different HPC applications at LRZ

Institution	Share of used CPU hours
Universities	61.2%
Max Plank	27.3%
Helmholtz	6.7%
LRZ	3.2%
PRACE	1.5%
Others	0.1%

TABLE 10.6: SuperMUC's usage share by individual institutions

for a weak scaling test that corresponds to 44.5% of SuperMUC's peak processing performance - first sustained PetaFLOP (1.09 PetaFLOPS) performance was achieved [7].

- **Extreme Scale-Out campaign in 2015 on SuperMUC Phase2** with following highlights:

(a) Largest cosmological hydrodynamics simulation to date (10% of the visible universe simulated using the Gadget code), Box0 of the Magneticum-Project [22];

(b) Largest pseudo-spectral simulation of interstellar turbulence [35];

(c) Improvement of the molecular spectra simulation by a factor of 100 with the help of the simulation software IPHIGENIE/CPMD [24, 13].

- **Massively-parallel free-energy prediction for drug design**
  Simulations ran on SuperMUC for 37 hours, using nearly all of SuperMUC's 250,000 compute cores combined. The simulation helped in creating a roadmap for advancing the medicines from trials to market in a shorter time, for anticipating effectiveness of a given drug for individual patients, or for anticipating the possible side-effects [8].

SuperMUC specifically addresses the needs for very large applications capable to use a large portion of the configuration or even the full system. To support the development and tuning of such grand scale applications even better, LRZ in conjunction with the hardware and software vendors regularly offers "Extreme Scale" events with on-site support of additional personnel for scaling and tuning of the applications. In order to allow extreme scale applications to run, the system or major parts of it must be empty from other smaller applications. This tends to slightly reduce the overall average usage of the system in case not enough small short running applications are available to bridge the time to make the system empty. However, it is the explicit and successful strategy of LRZ to specifically support extreme scale applications (see [23]).

10.4 System Stability

Figures 10.5 and 10.6 show some of SuperMUC's Phase1 and Phase2 components that saw the highest failure rates in 2016. As can be seen, the Dual In-line Memory Modules (DIMMs) show the highest failure rates for both installation phases. CPU failure rates remained low for both phases during 2016. On the other hand, the failure rates of Infiniband Cables (IB Cables) and Cards (IB Cards) were substantially higher for Phase1.

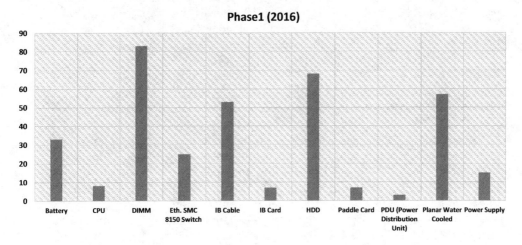

FIGURE 10.5: Components of Phase1 with highest failure rates in 2016

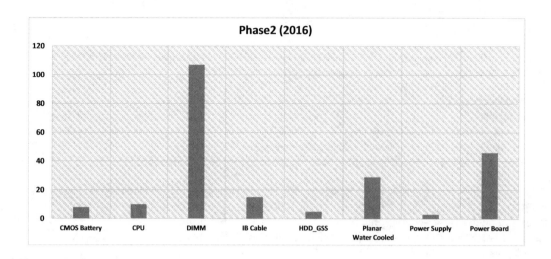

FIGURE 10.6: Components of Phase2 with highest failure rates in 2016

These and other production material faults were among the main challenges during the four years of SuperMUC's operation, since they led to degradation of system stability until they were identified and resolved. However, in general, the SuperMUC system proved to be stable.

10.5   Data Center/Facility

Figure 10.7 shows the outer view of the Leibniz Supercomputing Centre. The HPC systems are deployed in the twin cube illustrated in the lower left side. LRZ's hot water cooling infrastructure was installed in 2011 as part of the data center extension in preparation for SuperMUC Phase1. The twin cube has an IT equipment floor space of $3160 m^2$ ($34019 ft^2$ encompassing 6 rooms on 3 floors) and an infrastructure floor space of $6393 m^2$ ($68819 ft^2$).

The bulk of SuperMUC's heat is removed via the hot-water cooling loops that operate typically at 35 °C. At LRZ's southern German location, this water temperature can be sustained year-round by means of free (chiller-less) cooling. The term "hot water" refers to ASHRAE's W4 specification (i.e., facility supply water temperature ranging from 2 °C to 45 °C) [2].

Figure 10.8 illustrates the schematic overview of LRZ's chiller-less (also called hot water) cooling infrastructure, consisting of four identical cooling circuits. Each cooling circuit has a 2 MW wet cooling tower (*KLT11, KLT12, KLT13,* and *KLT14,* see "boxes" in the left upper corner of the twin win cubes in Figure 10.7). On average, at least two cooling circuits are active, the third and the fourth are added depending on the load.

Each of these four circuits consists of two distinct subcircuits. In **subcircuit I** redundant pumps circulate an ethylene glycol water mix (to prevent the water from freezing) via the corresponding cooling tower KLT_i that rejects the heat. The cooled water is sent back to the heat exchanger. In **subscircuit II** the water enters the cooling circuit from the distribution

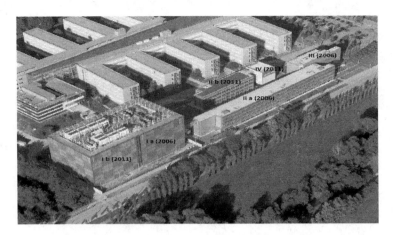

FIGURE 10.7: Leibniz Supercomputing Centre

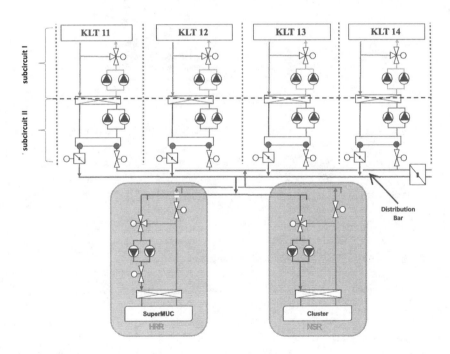

FIGURE 10.8: Schematic overview of LRZ's chiller less cooling infrastructure

bar via a hydraulic gate. The water then flows with the help of a redundant pump pair to the heat exchanger and back again via a hydraulic gate to the distribution bar. From this distribution bar, two floors (HRR and NSR used by SuperMUC and other direct liquid cooled systems run by LRZ) are supplied with chiller-less liquid cooling connections. Each IT system's cooling infrastructure is further separated from the LRZ's internal cooling loop via heat exchangers.

10.6   R&D on Energy-Efficiency at LRZ

Figure 10.9 shows the trend of energy costs for LRZ from 2000 till 2016 (with an estimate for 2017). As can be seen the energy costs have notably increased since 2000 from around 0.5 Mill EUR to 6.8 Mill EUR in 2016. This increase is mainly due to ever larger system sizes that, despite significant improvements in energy efficiency, cause higher power consumption (Figure 10.10). Additionally, electricity prices rose from 0.07 EUR in 2000 to 0.157 EUR in 2016 (partially caused by the German policy to raise consumption taxes to support renewable energy).

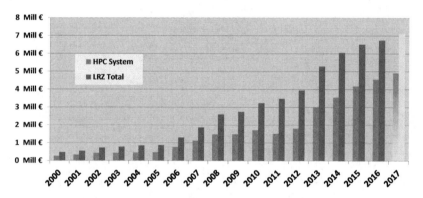

FIGURE 10.9: Trend of Energy Costs for LRZ from 2000 till 2016, and prediction for 2017

The mentioned increased power consumption of HPC systems does not only translate to high operational costs but also, as discussed by Bates et al. [5], to high carbon footprints, affecting the environment, and limiting the further expansion of HPC data centers. Thus, the reduction of power/energy consumption is a critical challenge for LRZ and HPC data centers in general and consequently, energy efficiency is a focal point of research at LRZ.

A general basis for building frameworks aimed towards energy efficiency management of HPC systems was suggested in [34]: the 4 Pillar Framework. Figure 10.11 illustrates the main set of influencing parameters on overall energy efficiency of a typical HPC data center: building and cooling infrastructure (*Pillar I*); supercomputer hardware (*Pillar II*); systems software and tools (*Pillar III*); and application and algorithms (*Pillar IV*).

To improve data center energy efficiency one needs to take a holistic approach that includes all the 4 pillars, as well as data center requirements and mission goals, combined with outside influences and constraints. For that reason LRZ is conducting research in various energy-efficiency related topics: *from* performance, energy, and power monitoring [26], [11]; *over* application tuning [12] and performance/power/energy consumption prediction [27], [28]; *to* energy-aware resource management and scheduling [4], [25]; and cooling infrastructure analysis [29], [30], [31].

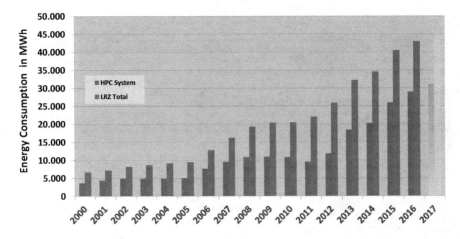

FIGURE 10.10: Trend of Energy Consumption for LRZ from 2000 till 2016, and prediction for 2017

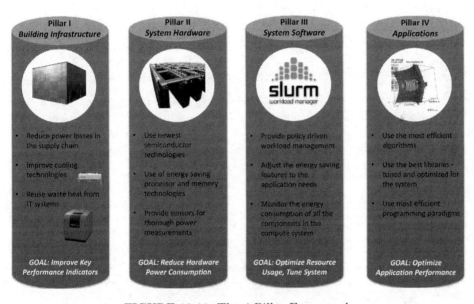

FIGURE 10.11: The 4 Pillar Framework

Some of these aspects are covered by PowerDAM, the Power Data Aggregation Monitor developed at LRZ [26, 25]. PowerDAM is a unified energy measuring and evaluating toolset for HPC data centers. It is aimed towards collecting and correlating energy/power consumption-relevant data of a data center (e.g., environmental information, site infrastructure, information technology systems, resource management systems, and applications), thus covering a wide range of power and energy consumption analysis capabilities. Figure 10.12 gives a high-level overview of PowerDAM.

PowerDAM uses agent-based data communication models for actual sensor data retrieval from the monitored systems/entities. These agents reside on the monitored entity and push the requested sensor data over the network. PowerDAM collects and analyzes these data and finally stores them in a database for further evaluation. One of the available evaluation metrics is the Coefficient Of Performance (COP) of hot water cooling circuits that can be

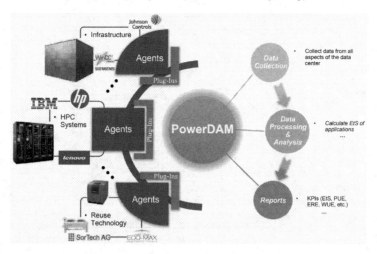

FIGURE 10.12: PowerDAM overview

calculated by PowerDAM for any given time frame. The COP of a cooling loop is defined as the fraction of the produced cold Q and the consumed amount of electrical power P:

$$COP = \frac{Q}{P} \qquad (10.1)$$

Figure 10.13 illustrates the COPs of LRZ's hot water and cold water (mechanical chiller supported, ASHRAE W1/W2, inlet temperature of 14 °C) cooling loops for the year of 2016 [29].

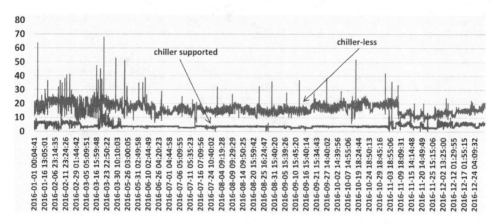

FIGURE 10.13: COP's of LRZ's warm and cold water cooling loops for 2016

As can be seen, the COP of the chiller-less (warm water) cooling was on average 3 times better than the COP of chiller supported (cold water) cooling. Additionally, the COP of warm water cooling was on average higher in winter than in summer. This is due to the fact the COP is largely influenced by the power consumption of the cooling tower fans that need to run less during cold weather. The drop in the COP of warm water cooling, observed in November, was caused by the decrease in the IT system inlet temperature by 9 °C (from 39 °C to 30 °C), which caused activation of an additional cooling tower (and its fans), increasing the power consumption and thus causing a drop in COP. For that reason, the inlet temperature was thereafter increased (in December) by 3 °C, bringing the COP of warm water cooling circuit back to 20.

To eliminate such drops in the efficiency of the cooling infrastructure in the future, LRZ is actively investigating the interoperability between the target HPC systems and the building infrastructure of the supercomputing site. A recent research presented in [30] suggested a machine learning approach, referred to as Infrastructure Data Analyser (IDA) framework, to model the COP of HPC data center's hot water cooling loops. The suggested model was validated using LRZ's operational data: Figure 10.14 shows the 2016 COP prediction results for the LRZ's warm-water cooling infrastructure, when the network was trained using the 2015 operational data. The tuple on the top of the figure indicates the Root Mean Squared Error (RMSE) and Mean Absolute Error (MSE) of the prediction. During the period of [2016-Apr-01 till 2016-June-01] the graph has less variability since some of the operational data, due to building automation system maintenance, was not completely available.

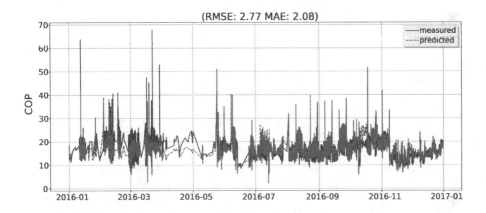

FIGURE 10.14: Complete COP model prediction results for 2016 when trained using the 2015 data

The initial goal set for the network was to check if it is possible to construct a network with a relative small amount of operational (unsanitized/not pre-processed) data that will be capable of predicting accurately the fluctuations of the cooling efficiency with respect to different infrastructural configurations. As can be seen, the network was also capable of predicting the irregular drop in the COP caused in the beginning of November 2016. The above presented COP prediction accuracy should increase with additional input data pre-processing, as well as with a larger training data set.

Future work will include the training of the suggested IDA framework for specific operational scenarios so that it encompasses the irregular annual environmental variations and has a sufficient spectrum on the data center's operational conditions, as well as development of an interface to the resource management and scheduling system(s) that will use the information provided by IDA for further enhancement of currently available power/energy-aware resource management and scheduling techniques.

Finally, as the vision of LRZ is to reduce the overall power consumption of the data center, a large number of additional measures were implemented and are in production use of the center:

- reuse of waste heat for heating/cooling of the buildings;

- reuse of waste heat to produce chilled water using adsorption machines [33];

- automatic frequency control as part of the energy/power-aware resource management and scheduling system; and

- continuous enhancement of the building infrastructure based on production experience as well as results from modeling/simulation.

Bibliography

[1] IBM: Tivoli workload scheduler LoadLeveler, 2015.

[2] American Society of Heating, Refrigerating and Air-Conditioning Engineers, 2016.

[3] Applications Software at LRZ, 2017.

[4] Axel Auweter, Arndt Bode, Matthias Brehm, Luigi Brochard, Nicolay Hammer, Herbert Huber, Raj Panda, Francois Thomas, and Torsten Wilde. A Case Study of Energy Aware Scheduling on SuperMUC. In *Proceedings of the 29th International Conference on Supercomputing - Volume 8488*, ISC 2014, pages 394–409, New York, NY, USA, 2014. Springer-Verlag New York, Inc.

[5] Natalie Bates, Girish Ghatikar, Ghaleb Abdulla, Gregory A Koenig, Sridutt Bhalachandra, Mehdi Sheikhalishahi, Tapasya Patki, Barry Rountree, and Stephen Poole. Electrical grid and supercomputing centers: An investigative analysis of emerging opportunities and challenges. *Informatik-Spektrum*, 38(2):111–127, 2015.

[6] Bavarian Academy of Sciences and Humanities, 2017.

[7] Alexander Breuer, Alexander Heinecke, Sebastian Rettenberger, Michael Bader, Alice-Agnes Gabriel, and Christian Pelties. Sustained petascale performance of seismic simulations with seissol on supermuc. In *International Supercomputing Conference*, pages 1–18. Springer, 2014.

[8] GCS: Delivering 10 Years of Integrated HPC Excellence for Germany, Spring 2017.

[9] Gauss Centre for Supercomputing, 2016.

[10] Green500, 2016.

[11] Carla Guillen, Wolfram Hesse, and Matthias Brehm. The persyst monitoring tool. In *European Conference on Parallel Processing*, pages 363–374. Springer, 2014.

[12] Carla Guillen, Carmen Navarrete, David Brayford, Wolfram Hesse, and Matthias Brehm. Dvfs automatic tuning plugin for energy related tuning objectives. In *Green High Performance Computing (ICGHPC), 2016 2nd International Conference*, pages 1–8. IEEE, 2016.

[13] Nicolay Hammer, Ferdinand Jamitzky, Helmut Satzger, Momme Allalen, Alexander Block, Anupam Karmakar, Matthias Brehm, Reinhold Bader, Luigi Iapichino, Antonio Ragagnin, et al. Extreme scale-out supermuc phase 2-lessons learned. *arXiv preprint arXiv:1609.01507*, 2016.

[14] John L Hennessy and David A Patterson. *Computer architecture: a quantitative approach*. Elsevier, 2012.

[15] HLRS High Performance Computing Center Stuttgart, 2017.

[16] IBM, 2016.

[17] Intel. Intel Xeon Processor E5 v3 Product Family. Processor Specification Update, August 2015.

[18] Intel, 2016.

[19] Jülich Supercomputing Centre (JSC), 2017.

[20] Leibniz Supercomputing Centre (LRZ) of the Bavarian Academy of Sciences and Humanities, 2017.

[21] Lenovo, 2016.

[22] Magneticum: Simulating Large Scale Structure Formation In the Universe, 2014.

[23] Wagner S., Bode A., Brüchle H., and Brehm M. *Extreme Scale-out on SuperMUC Phase 2*. 2016. ISBN: 978-3-9816675-1-6.

[24] Magnus Schwörer, Konstantin Lorenzen, Gerald Mathias, and Paul Tavan. Utilizing fast multipole expansions for efficient and accurate quantum-classical molecular dynamics simulations. *The Journal of chemical physics*, 142(10):03B608_1, 2015.

[25] Hayk Shoukourian. *Adviser for Energy Consumption Management: Green Energy Conservation*. PhD thesis, München, Technische Universität München (TUM), 2015.

[26] Hayk Shoukourian, Torsten Wilde, Axel Auweter, and Arndt Bode. *Monitoring Power Data: A first step towards a unified energy efficiency evaluation toolset for HPC data centers*. Elsevier, 2013.

[27] Hayk Shoukourian, Torsten Wilde, Axel Auweter, and Arndt Bode. Predicting the Energy and Power Consumption of Strong and Weak Scaling HPC Applications. *Supercomputing Frontiers and Innovations*, 1(2):20–41, 2014.

[28] Hayk Shoukourian, Torsten Wilde, Axel Auweter, Arndt Bode, and Daniele Tafani. *Predicting Energy Consumption Relevant Indicators of Strong Scaling HPC Applications for Different Compute Resource Configurations*. To appear in the proceedings of the 23rd High Performance Computing Symposium, Society for Modeling and Simulation International (SCS), 2015.

[29] Hayk Shoukourian, Torsten Wilde, Herbert Huber, and Arndt Bode. Analysis of the efficiency characteristics of the first high-temperature direct liquid cooled petascale supercomputer and its cooling infrastructure. *Journal of Parallel and Distributed Computing*, 107:87 – 100, 2017.

[30] Hayk Shoukourian, Torsten Wilde, Detlef Labrenz, and Arndt Bode. Using machine learning for data center cooling infrastructure efficiency prediction. In *Parallel and Distributed Processing Symposium Workshops (IPDPSW), 2017 IEEE International*, pages 954–963. IEEE, 2017.

[31] The SIMOPEK Project. http://simopek.de/, 2016.

[32] Top500, 2017.

[33] T. Wilde, M. Ott, A. Auweter, I. Meijer, P. Ruch, M. Hilger, S. Khnert, and H. Huber. Coolmuc-2: A supercomputing cluster with heat recovery for adsorption cooling. In *2017 33rd Thermal Measurement, Modeling Management Symposium (SEMI-THERM)*, pages 115–121, March 2017.

[34] Torsten Wilde, Axel Auweter, and Hayk Shoukourian. The 4 pillar framework for energy efficient hpc data centers. *Computer Science - Research and Development*, pages 1–11, 2013.

[35] Compressible Turbulence World's Largest Simulation of Supersonic, 2013.

Chapter 11

The NERSC Cori HPC System

Katie Antypas Brian Austin, Deborah Bard, Wahid Bhimji, Brandon Cook, Tina Declerck, Jack Deslippe, Richard Gerber, Rebecca Hartman–Baker, Yun (Helen) He, Douglas Jacobsen, Thorsten Kurth, Jay Srinivasan, and Nicholas J. Wright

NERSC, Lawrence Berkeley National Laboratory

11.1 Overview

11.1.1 Sponsor and Program Background

The National Energy Research Scientific Computing Center (NERSC) is the mission high performance computing facility for the Department of Energy's Office of Science (DOE SC). NERSCs primary goal is to accelerate scientific discovery for the DOE SC workload through high performance computing, related technology development and data management and analysis. Toward this end, NERSC provides large-scale, state-of-the-art computing, storage and networking for the DOE SCs unclassified research programs.

With thousands of users from universities, national laboratories and industry, NERSC supports a large and diverse research community. The NERSC workload represents the wide variety of research performed by its users, including simulations that run at the largest scales. In addition, the analysis of massive datasets is becoming increasingly important at NERSC in support of DOE SC experimental facilities. Over the years, NERSC's resources have contributed to ground breaking science. Five of NERSC's users have won the Nobel Prize and each year over 2000 publications are attributed to using NERSC's systems.

The NERSC Center was founded in 1974 at Lawrence Livermore National Laboratory and became the first unclassified computing center. At the time, the Center was focused on fusion energy research. In 1983 the Center's focus expanded to support high performance computing to all the programs in what is now the Department of Energy Office of Science. In 1996 NERSC moved to Berkeley Lab and became part of the Computing Sciences program. In 2000, NERSC outgrew its location on the main Berkeley Lab campus and temporarily moved to the Oakland Scientific Facility while a new facility was built to house the supercomputers and staff. More than a decade later, in 2016, NERSC moved back to the main Berkeley Lab campus into a state-of-the-art energy efficient building.

The Cori system, a 30PF Cray XC system, described in detail in this chapter, was designed to support data intensive workloads and be a platform that would begin to transition the user community to more energy efficient architectures. Preparing for and deploying the Cori system [7] in a brand new facility was a top priority for NERSC in 2016.

11.1.2 Timeline

The Cori system was procured as part of the Alliance for Application Performance at Extreme Scales (APEX), a partnership between Berkeley Lab, Los Alamos National Lab and Sandia Lab. The intention of the collaboration was to procure two systems in the 2016 time frame that would begin to serve to transition the user community to more advanced architectures on the path to exascale. One system would be installed at LANL, in partnership with Sandia and the other would be installed into the new Wang Hall facility at Berkeley Lab for NERSC. The systems were procured through a competitive process and Cray was selected as the vendor for the Cori system. The Cori system was delivered in two phases. The first phase, known as the Cori Data Partition, or Cori Haswell, was delivered in the fall of 2015 and was the first system installed into the new Wang Hall facility. The second phase of Cori, the KNL partition, was delivered in the summer of 2016 and installed and integrated into NERSC later that year. The system was accepted in 2016. Early users from the NERSC Exascale Science Application Program (NESAP) were the first enabled on the system and given priority access to the system until it transitioned into production on July 1st, 2017.

11.2 Applications and Workloads

As the mission high performance scientific computing facility for the Office of Science in the United States Department of Energy, NERSC supports research in a wide variety of disciplines, including climate modeling, research into new materials, simulations of the early universe, analysis of data from high-energy physics experiments, investigations of protein structure, and many others.

NERSC has a diverse user base of over 6,000 users in more than 700 projects running more than 600 different codes. However, the top ten codes make up 50% of the workload, and the top 25 codes make up more than 2/3 of the workload. But even these 25 codes are quite diverse in both application area as well as execution characterization. Codes run at NERSC utilize all seven original motifs (Dense Linear Algebra, Sparse Linear Algebra, Computations on Structured Grids, Computations on Unstructured Grids, Spectral Methods, Particle Methods and Monte Carlo) and more.

11.2.1 Benchmarks

Benchmarking is essential for ensuring that HPC systems provide correct results and satisfactory performance, both upon installation and throughout the lifetime of the machine. [29] Benchmarks may be designed to test specific aspects of system performance (i.e., the STREAM micro-benchmark measures memory bandwidth) or the performance of a complete scientific application. While NERSC routinely performs and monitors the performance of several micro-benchmarks, we emphasize the importance of application benchmarks (over micro-benchmarks and kernels) because application performance is a direct indication of the experiences of our users and requires balanced integration of the entire stack of system hardware and software stack. By focusing on applications rather than micro-benchmarks, the risk of tuning the system for niche uses that do not benefit real simulation codes is avoided.

The APEX benchmark suite [6] used to evaluate Cori consists of eight applications:

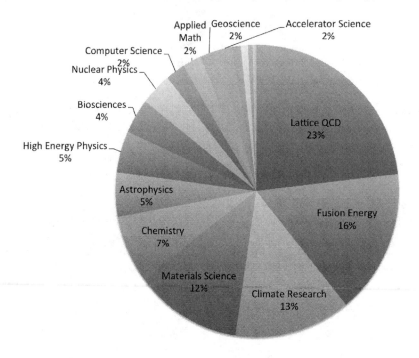

FIGURE 11.1: NERSC 2016 usage by science category.

- *GTC:* 3D gyrokinetic particle-in-cell simulation of Tokomak fusion devices

- *MILC:* Lattice Quantum Chromodynamics

- *MiniDFT:* Plane-wave density functional theory

- *MiniFE:* Finite element generation, assembly and solution of an unstructured grid problems

- *MiniGhost:* 3D finite difference stencil

- *AMG:* Algebraic multigrid solver for linear systems

- *UMT:* 3D, deterministic multigroup photon transport simulation on unstructured meshes

- *SNAP:* discrete ordinates neutral particle transport

The first three of these codes (GTC, MILC and MiniDFT) were carefully selected to represent a cross-section of the NERSC workload in terms of node-hours used, algorithmic diversity and coverage of scientific domains. The remaining applications were selected by other members of the APEX partnership and are similarly important to their workloads, but also relevant to NERSC. (For example, the stencil algorithms and communication patterns exercised by MiniGhost appear in many NERSC codes as well.)

The Sustained System Performance (SSP) is the primary metric used to evaluate Cori's performance. SSP is simply the average (geometric mean) of the FLOP rate achieved by each application in the benchmark suite, scaled to the full size of the size of the system.[29] Cori's SSP, using the benchmarks, is 562 GF/s, a 10.8× improvement over Hopper, the Cray XE6 system that preceded it.

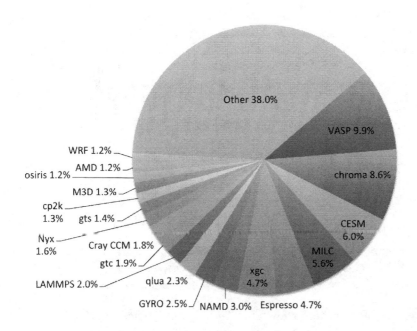

FIGURE 11.2: Top 20 codes used at NERSC in 2016.

11.3 System Overview

NERSCs newest supercomputer, named Cori after Nobel prize winning biologist Gerty Cori, introduces the NERSC user community to the advanced energy efficient architectures necessary to reach exascale levels of performance. Cori is a Cray XC40 system made up of three primary components. The main system, a Cray XC40, is the compute pool, the external login nodes allows users to access the system, and the scratch storage, a Cray Sonexion 2000.

The XC40 has two compute pools consisting of 9,688 single socket nodes with Intel Xeon Phi Knights Landing (KNL) manycore processors. Cori also has 2,388 dual-socket Intel Xeon Haswell nodes on the same Cray Aries high-speed interconnect network. This mix of node types makes Cori a novel system at this scale in HPC. In addition, the system has a Burst Buffer, a schedulable, fast, flash-based, intermediary storage pool between the compute pool and the Lustre file system, The burst buffer has a capacity of 1.6 PB and a bandwidth of over 1.5 TB/sec. The storage system is a 28 PB Lustre file system contained in 18 cabinets of Cray Sonexion 2000 racks providing over 700 GB/second of IO performance.

11.4   Hardware Architecture

The system design of the XC40 is similar to previous Cray architectures. Compute nodes are placed 4 to a compute blade, 16 blades make up a chassis and there are three chassis per cabinet, leading to a maximum of 192 nodes per cabinet. The cabinets are cooled transversely with air that passes through a water-cooled radiator. Cori can use inlet water up to 75 degrees.

11.4.1   Node Types and Design

There are two basic blade types, compute and service. Each compute blade has 2 processor daughter cards each of which contains 2 nodes. The compute nodes contain either an Intel Haswell or Intel Knights Landing processor.

11.4.1.1   Xeon Phi "Knights Landing" Compute Nodes

These single socket nodes contain an Intel Xeon Phi "Knights Landing" (KNL) Many Integrated Cores (MIC) processor. This features 68 cores per node with 4 hardware threads each, 512 bit vector units, 16 GB on-package MCDRAM (Multi-Channel DRAM) high bandwidth memory and 96 GB of DDR4 memory (6 channels).

The peak performance of each node is approximately 3 Tflops, and measured DGEMM performance is 2.1 TF/s. The MCDRAM memory can sustain 415 GB/s on STREAM triad and the DDR memory can sustain 90 GB/s. The two different memory types on the KNL processor allow different configurations of the memory (which can be changed with a reboot). The node can either be configured with the MCDRAM as a cache for the DDR4 memory, or with a flat memory space covering both memory types. If the MCDRAM is configured as a cache, a performance penalty is incurred and the STREAM triad bandwidth drops to 315 GB/s.

In order to obtain good performance from the KNL nodes, it is essential to use many of the 68 cores to make full use of the vector units and to use the MCDRAM as much as possible.

11.4.1.2   Xeon "Haswell" Compute Nodes

These dual socket nodes contain two 16 core Intel Xeon E5-2698 v3 "Haswell" processors running at 2.3 GHz and 128 GB of DDR4 memory running at 2133 MHz. Each core supports two hyperthreads and has two 256-bit wide vector units. Each core has a peak performance of 36.8 Gflops, making the peak performance of the node 1.2 TFlops. Each socket supports 4 memory channels giving a peak memory bandwidth of 137 GB/s and a STREAM triad bandwidth of 115 GB/s.

11.4.1.3   Service Nodes

The service blades have 2 nodes per blade. Each contains an Intel Xeon "Sandy Bridge" processor and has 2 PCIe gen3 slots available. Cori has several different types of service nodes: network, bridge (used for the Software Defined Networking (SDN) connections), Data Virtualization Services (DVS), DataWarp (burst buffer), Lustre Router (LNET), and Slurm controller nodes. What the node will be used for determines what type of HBAs are installed. The network, Slurm controller nodes and bridge nodes have 2 dual Mellanox (QDR-IB) cards installed that are connected using bonded vlans to the NERSC local internal and external networks. The internal network is used primarily for access to storage and external is used for LDAP, and general connections from outside the NERSC environment. The DVS nodes have one IB and one Ethernet card installed. The InfiniBand provides fast access to the NERSC global file systems and the Ethernet is used for the management connections to the NERSC global file systems. The LNET nodes have two Mellanox InfiniBand HCAs for access to Coris scratch file system.

11.4.2 Interconnect

The System uses a Cray proprietary network interconnect, referred to as Aries, in a Dragonfly topology. The Aries network interconnect is comprised of Aries chips and cabling. The Aries chip is comprised of four Network Interface Controllers (NICs) and a 48-port tiled high radix router. The NICs and router are all on a single die. The entire Cray XC interconnect consists of a direct network of Aries chips using copper and optical cabling. The Aries network interconnect connects all nodes (Compute, Service, and the Cray Burst Buffer if the option is exercised) in the Cray XC system. Each compute node connects to the Aries network via PCI express, at a peak bandwidth of 16 GB/s.

The dragonfly network has 3 levels. The lowest level connects each node in a chassis to each other, the second level connects each chassis in a pair of cabinets together, finally each cabinet pair is connected with optical cables to form the third level of the dragonfly. This leads to a maximum of 5 hops between any pair of nodes in the system. The peak bisection bandwidth of the machine is 45 TB/s. The Aries interconnect has numerous adaptive routing features designed to avoid congestion and hot spots.

11.4.3 Storage - Burst Buffer and Lustre Filesystem

The Burst Buffer (Cray DataWarp) is made up of service nodes that are peers on the Aries network with the compute nodes. Each contains 2 Intel P3608 SSD cards that provide 3.2 TB of available storage per card. The Burst Buffer is configured to use the Cray Data Virtualization Service (DVS) software to handle I/O transactions. In addition, numerous features to manage allocations of space on a per-job or persistent basis are provided by the Cray burst buffer service, which are accessible via the job scheduler.

The system also has a 30 PB Lustre file system based on the Cray Sonexion 2000 with 124 scalable storage units (SSUs) and 2 additional Distributed Namespace (DNE) units to provide both fast data paths and large storage capacity. Four additional metadata servers to help spread the metadata load increasing performance.

11.5 System Software

11.5.1 System Software Overview

The system software stack on Cori consists of several closely inter-related pieces: an independent operating system for each of the nodes in the system, management software for the collection of nodes that make up the system, and software for operating and managing system components, including the storage and compute resources as well as other services (login nodes external to the Cray Aries network, network gateway nodes, workload dispatch nodes, etc.). This section presents an overview of all this software as well as details on specific functionality and customizations that NERSC has enabled in order to support the workload that runs on Cori.

The Operating System on Cori is a variant of Linux. The compute nodes of the system run a modified version of the Linux kernel called Compute Node Linux. The operating system itself is based off the SuSE distribution and is, on external (user facing) and service nodes, the SLES software stack. Since the compute nodes on Cori are heterogenous, with both Knights Landing (KNL) nodes as well as Haswell (HSW) nodes, each of these variants of the compute nodes have different node images loaded on them. The service nodes, which include the (external) login nodes, compute gateway nodes, storage service nodes (including LNET nodes to talk to the Lustre filesystem servers), DVS nodes (for projection of the GPFS filesystems on to the compute nodes), and other management nodes for the system have a different full-featured SLES-based image loaded on them.

11.5.2 System Management Stack

The Cray system management software consists of two parts, the System Management Workstation (SMW) software and the Cray Linux Environment (CLE) software. The system software stack is pictured in Figure 11.3 below. The function of the system management

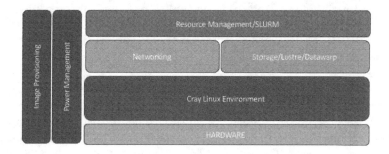

FIGURE 11.3: The system management software stack on Cori.

software on a Cray system is to generate system images for each of the different types of nodes on the system, deploy (boot) the nodes, configure them appropriately for the services they will provide and then, collect overall information about the system, including health information, performance information, etc. In addition, the system management software allows for managing nodes on an ongoing basis, including setting of various power states and rebooting of nodes.

NERSC's vision of the system management stack hews closely to this description, but expands on it by applying it in a uniform fashion to multiple systems. NERSC operates four very similar Cray systems, two large scale systems (Cori and a previous generation Cray system Edison) and two testbeds, one for each large scale system. Though there are some differences in hardware and scale, the intention is to manage them in as similar a way as possible. The system management methodology followed [27] allows NERSC to utilize the same system configuration method (Ansible) to operate all the Cray systems, with the software determining the appropriate configuration to apply to each system.

11.5.3 Resource Management

Within Cori, Intel's Knights Landing processors with High-Bandwidth memory (MC-DRAM) allows each node to be configured in twenty different configurations or "modes" [26].

While the vast majority of our workload can be run using one or two of these configurations, being able to provide users with the ability to select configurations and to quickly provide access to the appropriately configured resource is critical to the efficient operation of the system. NERSC utilizes the SLURM workload manager to provide users access to compute resources, and, in combination with Cray's DataWarp software, to associated Burst Buffer resources. We have worked extensively with SchedMD [28] to design and develop SLURM functionality that allows us to:

- Efficiently schedule and run a highly diverse workload on Cori, with job sizes spanning a single core to the entire 10,000+ nodes on the system

- Run jobs on an existing configuration of KNL nodes of varying modes and HSW nodes.

- Run single jobs across KNL and HSW nodes

- Quickly allocate and configure KNL nodes into a new mode (which requires a node reboot)

- Provide access to all the different storage resources (described below) for user jobs, if necessary, on demand

11.5.4 Storage Resources and Software

The Cori system supports both traditional HPC simulations as well as data analysis workloads. This spectrum of user needs requires an equally broad range of storage resources. Being able to provide the right kind of storage for jobs is a necessity if the system is to be utilized effectively. The Cori system provides users four different kinds of storage resources:

- The system-local, high-performance Lustre "scratch" filesystem.

- Center-wide, GPFS filesystems, providing home directories shared amongst all our systems, "Project"-specific storage space as well as "common" space for frequently and widely used libraries and programs.

- The I/O acceleration storage layer or "Burst Buffer" provided by Cray as the DataWarp system backed by the Lustre scratch filesystem.

- "Node-local" storage, created on demand on the scratch filesystem for jobs using Shifter.

All of these different storage resources can be seamlessly accessed by all jobs on the system. In addition, the Lustre filesystem is "external" and can be available to users even if the compute nodes are not. This is accomplished by use of Lustres LNET protocol and the use of dedicated LNET servers, allowing compartmentalized access to the storage system from the compute nodes of Cori, the external login nodes of Cori, the Cray XC-30 "Edison" system as well as dedicated Data Transfer Nodes (DTNs) optimized and used for wide-area network traffic and grid-based data transfer.

NERSC staff have also worked closely with Cray and SchedMD to develop the DataWarp software to support the needs of our Data-Intensive users. In addition to being able to request DataWarp storage on-demand per job, users are able to pre-stage data and store data on the resource both for the job lifetime alone as well as across multiple jobs. Future functionality being developed includes the ability to use the DataWarp layer as a transparent cache to the Lustre backing store.

11.5.5 Networking Resources and Software

Cori provides a high-performance network (Aries) between the compute nodes and between the compute and service nodes, resulting in a well-integrated system that allows for efficient communication within processes and for I/O traffic. For effective support of data-intensive workloads, however, external network connectivity at reasonably high-bandwidth and low latency is required. Crays standard solution for traffic out of the Aries network has been to use a combination of Realm-Specific Internet Protocol (RSIP) servers and traditional network gateways. For performance and reliability reasons this solution is not optimal for the NERSC workload. To allow for greater flexibility in shaping external traffic both in to and from the compute nodes of the system, we have replaced the RSIP nodes with bridge nodes that send and receive the traffic to and from software-based routers (Figure 11.4). The bridge nodes (each configured to handle a subset of the compute nodes) allow for communication between the Aries network and external Ethernet networks. In addition, to improve resilience, the bridge nodes can easily be configured to serve a different set of compute nodes in case of failure.

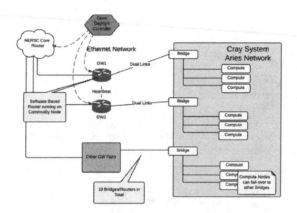

FIGURE 11.4: RSIP replacement configuration. (From [22].)

NERSCs vision of networking to Cori (and to Cray systems in general) is to provide our users with a fully software-defined network that can handle the needs of our most demanding data ingest requirements (such as the Light Sources) to configure and shape the network seamlessly between resources external and internal to the system.

11.5.6 Containers and User-Defined Images

The use of container technology has rapidly developed over the last few years to enable greater control of the system environment by users. Users, especially those who develop or use specialized software for simulation or analysis that is closely tied to a specific operating system environment, have found this to be an indispensable way to migrate their workload to different systems without explicitly porting the software over. To meet the needs of these users, we have investigated the use of Docker-like containers on Cori. Containers have, however, not been widely used in HPC environments for various reasons including security concerns with allowing user-defined environments in tightly integrated systems and a lack of easy to use tools to deploy them in such environments.

NERSC, in collaboration with Cray, developed a tool called Shifter [27], that allows the creation and distribution of Docker-like images on to the Cray platforms, including changes to support the use of the global filesystem, addressing security concerns of deployment of the user-defined images in a production environment, and most importantly, integration with the workload manager. These features allow users to generate images and simply submit a job that requests the image, which allows them to quickly use existing codebases to run jobs at very large scale on Cori. Users from light sources such as LCLS at SLAC and from high energy physics facilities such as the LHC have successfully utilized Cori this way [27].

In summary, a well-integrated, easy to deploy, manage and use system software stack is critical to the efficient operation and use of a large complex system such as Cori. NERSC's philosophy of not just taking what is provided with the system, but carefully picking the most useful parts of the stack, modifying it if needed, and adding functionality of interest to staff and users allows us to deploy a stable state-of-the-art system, both useful to users and one that allows for continuous improvement over its lifetime.

11.6 Programming Environment

11.6.1 Programming Models

The majority of existing HPC applications deployed on NERSC resources use MPI as their primary means of expressing parallelism after the transition from vector to distributed memory architectures. With 68-cores per Cori KNL node with four hardware threads each, pure MPI will still work for most applications at some level, though it will unlikely achieve optimal performance. The 512-bit wide vector processing units offer additional parallelism. Application developers will need to explore more on-node parallelism through threading and vectorization. Hybrid MPI/OpenMP is the most common programming model on Cori as it allows for existing MPI applications to be more gradually modified by adding OpenMP for thread scaling.

The key reason why a hybrid MPI/OpenMP programming model is needed on KNL is that a pure MPI approach may no longer fit in memory since each MPI task runs a copy of the program. The number of MPI tasks vs OpenMP threads will depend on the application and the specific MPI and OpenMP implementation for a given code. On Cori, applications often use a range of between 4 and 16 MPI tasks per node and 2 to 8 OpenMP threads per task. OpenMP introduces a compiler-directive agnostic way of expressing SIMD parallelism at the loop or function level; and it also allows a degree of application portability to a variety of supercomputing architectures.

While MPI+OpenMP is the most common programming mode, the Cori system supports other programming models and languages such as UPC, UPC++, PGAS, Pthreads, C++11, TBB, Kokkos and others. Applications can also use non-MPI solutions such as thread-aware task-based runtime system and abstractions (e.g., CHARM++, Legion and HPX).

11.6.2 Languages and Compilers

On the Cori system, three compilers are supported: Intel, Cray and GNU. Cray's PrgEnv modules initialize the programming environment for a specific compiler and simplify users experiences of building applications. The provided Cray compiler wrappers (ftn for Fortran, cc for C and CC for C++ codes) automatically link in necessary MPI and other Cray libraries that are loaded.

Each of these compilers support Fortran and C/C++11 language standards, and support OpenMP, SHMEM, Global Arrays, Pthreads. The Cray and Intel compilers support Fortran

CoArrays, UPC and the KNL MCDRAM memory placement extensions. Only the Cray compiler supports C/C++ CoArrays and OpenACC.

Java and Python libraries are available under the GNU programming environment. Python modules are available for scalable service via Data Virtualization Service (DVS) on the compute nodes.

11.6.3   Libraries and Tools

The default MPI library on Cori is Cray's MPICH, derived from Argonne National Laboratory MPICH [5]and implements the MPI-3.1 standard. Cray's MPICH has custom optimizations for the Aries interconnect and Intel Xeon Phi KNL architectures, which can be utilized via runtime tuning options for memory allocation in DDR or MCDRAM, IO hints, hugepages, adaptive routings, default message communication protocols, etc. User-level Generic Network Interface (uGNI) is available to directly program the Aries network. The Distributed Memory Applications (DMAPP) interface can be targeted at one-sided languages such as PGAS and SHMEM. Intel MPI and OpenMPI based on OpenFabrics [4] are also available.

Cray's Scientific and Math Libraries (CSML, more familiar to users as LibSci) include BLAS, CBLAS, LAPACK, ScaLAPACK, BLACS, PBLACS, Iterative Refinement Toolkit, and CrayBLAS. The Cray MPICH libraries and Cray's scientific libraries are loaded by default on Cori.

Other available common libraries are FFTW, PETSc, Trilinos, and Cray's Third Party Scientific Libraries and Solvers collections, which include MUMPS, ParMetis, SuperLU, SuperLU_DIST, Hypre, Scotch and Sundials. The available IO libraries are: NetCDF, Parallel NetCDF, HDF5, and Parallel HDF5, ADIOS.

Performance monitoring and profiling tools available on Cori include Cray's Performance Monitoring and Analysis Toolkit (CPMAT, more familiar to users as Perftools); Intels VTune and Advisor tools; Allineas MAP tool; Scalasca; TAU; and Barcelona Supercomputing Centers Paraver and Extrae. Debugging tools include Cray's CCDB, LGDB, Intels Inspector tool, Allinea DDT, and Totalview.

11.6.4   Building Software for a Heterogeneous System

The heterogeneous Haswell/KNL system is considerably more complex than a homogeneous cluster. Cori has both Haswell and KNL compute nodes, and all login nodes are Haswell. Compute nodes on Cori KNL are configured without the full build environment, thus applications targeting either Haswell or KNL must be built on the Haswell login nodes.

Executables that run on KNL need to be cross-compiled on Haswell to target KNL. The Cray provided target architecture modules craype-haswell and craype-mic-knl can easily be switched back and forth for building applications to run on the desired target compute nodes. Although a Haswell binary will run on KNL (but not vice-versa), that binary and the libraries it calls will use compiler optimizations targeting Haswell rather than KNL, so NERSC recommends that the appropriate target module be loaded when building applications. The Intel compiler has an optional flag of "-axMIC-AVX512,CORE-AVX2 to build a merged binary that contains instructions appropriate to both Haswell and KNL. This flag is handy when building applications to target both, especially those that will benefit from key numerical libraries that can take advantage of the KNL architecture.

A frequently-encountered difficulty when building software targeting the KNL nodes is that in some build systems (such as autoconf or cmake), a small test program needs to run in order to generate a Makefile. This will not work when building on Haswell for KNL since the binary targeted for KNL cannot run on Haswell. A workaround for this autoconf issue is to perform the configure step in the Haswell environment, then switch to the KNL environment before compile. The suite of CMake tools were created by Kitware in response to the need for a powerful, cross-platform build environment for open-source projects Cray has worked with Kitware to increase the compatibility of CMake with the programming environment on the Cray systems to enable cross-compiling [16].

NERSC is actively working on streamlining the software build process by using the Spack software package manager for building supported packages on all the Cray systems at NERSC, including Edison Ivy Bridge, Cori Haswell, and Cori KNL[31].

11.6.5 Default Mode Selection Considerations

KNL nodes have the option of being configured at boot-time in a variety of sub-NUMA clustering (SNC) modes and memory modes. Depending on the mode, a single KNL node can appear to the OS as having 1 (quad mode), 2 (snc2 mode) or 4 (snc4 mode) NUMA domains. It is also possible to configure the MCDRAM as a direct-map cache (cache mode) or to expose it as a directly accessible memory domain separate from the DDR (flat mode).

NERSC tested these different configurations with a variety of benchmark applications [6, 1] including MILC, GTC P, AMG, MiniDFT, SNAP and PENNANT and some user applications. In our testing it was found that the SNC modes introduce significant complexity into user job scripts, especially the snc4 mode due to additional NUMA issues caused by the uneven number of cores in each quadrant. We saw the differences from quad+cache from other modes are at most 5-10% differences.

The MCDRAM configured in flat mode outperforms cache mode by a few percent in memory bandwidth bound benchmarks such as STREAM when the working set size is less than 16 GB. In real applications, the performance difference is often minimal, with cache mode sometimes outperforming flat mode. Effectively utilizing a node configured in flat mode with data sizes larger than 16 GB requires memory to be directly allocated into the MCDRAM and requires additional programming effort. Utilizing the flat mode also introduces more settings into the standard batch script.

For these reasons we chose a default of quad,cache mode for our KNL nodes. However, for those users who are able to take advantage of other modes, we allow a fraction of the Cori KNL nodes to be rebooted by the job scheduler. We introduced this limit to avoid overhead related to rebooting nodes, which could last 30 min or longer for each reboot.

11.6.6 Running Jobs

On Cori, the scheduling software SLURM is used in 'native' mode, meaning SLURM directly manages the computing resources without going through another layer of the Cray Application Level Placement Scheduler (ALPS). Having 68 cores per KNL compute node, with 34 dual-core tiles and different cluster and memory modes, complicates the task placement for hybrid MPI/OpenMP applications. The general recommendations are: Use 64 cores per node in most cases and use 1 or 2 cores per node for core specialization, which is a feature designed to isolate system overhead (system interrupts, etc.) to designated cores on a compute node. The srun flags -c and –cpu_bind=cores are critical for getting the optimal process affinity. Without these, multiple MPI ranks will run on the same physical cores. The portable OpenMP process binding options (OMP_PROC_BIND and OMP_PLACES) are then used to fine tune thread affinity. Either numactl or the srun –mem_bind option can be used to specify how MCDRAM memory is used.

For running large jobs, we suggest users to sbcast (the SLURM command to broadcast) the executable to each compute node first before running the job to minimize the job startup delay, which can be up to several minutes sometimes. Using hugepages is generally recommended.

We provide an online Job Script Generator tool so users can input some simple run parameters and get a ready-to-use batch script. Pre-built binaries to report process and thread affinity information compiled with different compilers are prepared for users to check their desired run time settings for their applications.

11.7   NESAP

11.7.1   Introduction

The NERSC Exascale Science Applications Program (NESAP [11]) was established concurrently with the procurement of Cori in order to help users transition to advanced architectures like Intel's Xeon Phi, Knights Landing processor. The NESAP program provides support for preparing science applications for Cori not only by providing staff and postdoc resources, but also by connecting science code teams with vendor experts at Intel and Cray.

Since NERSC has more than 6,000 users running 700 different applications, it is not feasible to devote staff to each application running at the center. Instead, twenty application teams [9] were selected to participate in the NESAP program, from which an optimization strategy and set of best practices to share with the greater community would be created. The 20 selected applications cover all six programs within the Department of Energy Office of Science and represent about 60% of the overall NERSC CPU hours, either directly or as proxy codes. The selected codes are displayed in Table 11.1.

The domain scientists and application developers received intensive advanced training in the form of on-site visits from Intel and Cray staff, hackathons at Intel campuses as well as on-going collaborations with NERSC and Cray staff as part of a Center of Excellence. Furthermore, these teams had access to pre-production Xeon Phi hardware prior to the delivery of the Cori system, which significantly increased optimization productivity. Eight application teams were additionally paired up with postdoctoral researchers at NERSC who devoted a large fraction of their time to the profiling and optimization efforts.

The lessons learned from these efforts are extensively documented in general Xeon Phi documentation guidelines [12] as well as specialized case studies [10] on the NERSC website. This facilitates the dissemination of the knowledge gained to the rest of the NERSC user base.

11.7.2   Optimization Strategy and Tools

The Cori system uses the same Aries interconnect and dragonfly topology as its predecessor Edison [8]. The most disruptive changes in the system come from the novel architecture of the Intel Xeon Phi processor. Therefore, NESAP code optimization effort is mainly focused on node-level performance.

Compared to e.g. Xeon multi-core processors, the Intel Xeon Phi many-core chip features more (slower) cores, more hyper-threads, wider vector units supporting more complex instructions as well as high-bandwidth on-package MCDRAM. In order to obtain good code performance on Xeon Phi, it is mandatory to utilize at least some of these features. Navigating this complex optimization space is difficult and therefore NERSC developed an optimization strategy based on the roofline performance model [25, 38, 37, 14]. The approach includes the identification of hot kernels, i.e., code regions that consume a large

TABLE 11.1: Overview of NESAP applications.

Name	Scientific Field
ACME	Climate Modeling
BerkeleyGW	Materials Science
BoxLib	Multiple
CESM	Climate Modeling
Chombo-Crunch	Multiple
Chroma	Nuclear Physics
DWF	High Energy Physics
EMGeo	Geophysics
GROMACS	Materials Science
HACC	high Energy Physics
HISQ	High Energy Physics
HMMER	Bioinformatics
Meraculous	Bioinformatics
M3D	Fusion Research
MFDN	Nuclear Physics
MILC	High Energy Physics
MPAS-O	Climate Modeling
NWchem	Basic Energy Sciences
Parsec	Materials Science
Qbox	Materials Science
Quantum ESPRESSO	Materials Science
VASP	Materials Science
WARP	Accelerator Physics
XGC1	Fusion Research

fraction of the wall-time, and the determination of their arithmetic intensity and performance in terms of FLOPS/s. The data points are plotted on a 2D roofline plane and may be visually compared against the Xeon Phi roofline ceilings (determined by limits on memory bandwidth and cpu speed). The position of each of these kernels on the roofline relative to the ceilings indicate the most promising optimization targets. For example, it informs the user if a kernel is memory bound, compute bound or potentially latency bound. The model additionally allows a developer to visually track the effect of optimizations as they are implemented in an application.

In order to obtain the relevant performance metrics, NERSC developed a methodology in cooperation with Cray and Intel staff. This approach employs Intels VTune [2], SDE [15] and Vector Advisor [3] products. The latter recently incorporated a variant of the roofline mode, the so-called cache-aware roofline, into it's basic functionality.

Figure 11.5 depicts the performance of a specific kernel in the BerkeleyGW [24] application after a series of optimization steps (2 - addition of OpenMP, 3 - loop reordering for vector code generation, 4 - cache blocking, 5,6 - hyperthreading and refined vectorization).

Example Roofline Optimization Steps

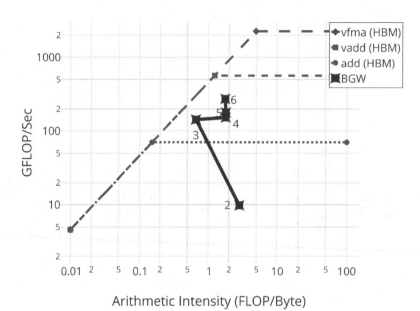

FIGURE 11.5: BerkeleyGW kernel trajectory after a series of optimization steps.

11.7.3 Most Effective Optimizations

As discussed before, the most promising optimizations for a given kernel depend on the position on the roofline plot. For memory-bound kernels, cache blocking and utilizing MCDRAM have proven to be most efficient. The former is especially important as Xeon Phi is not equipped with a comparably big L3 cache that can efficiently mitigate L2 misses. For compute-bound kernels on the other hand, efficient vectorization and instruction-level parallelism such as utilization of FMA instructions are the most promising optimization targets. However, this simple picture becomes complicated when considering more subtle effects such as hardware prefetching: if code is not sufficiently vectorized, single-word loads and stores can overwhelm the prefetcher while vectorized loads and stores reduce the number of in-flight memory operations by a factor of up to 32.

The following optimizations were identified as the most effective across a series of applications:

- *identifying and exploiting parallelism / creating more work for individual threads*: This may be the most important thing to consider when switching from multi-core to many-core architectures. Small OpenMP sections that do not contain enough work for multiple threads will hurt performance significantly due to implicit barriers at the end of these sessions. Where possible, loop nests should be collapsed to maximize parallelism.

- *loop tiling*: Cache blocking to achieve cache locality of heavily used arrays can be realized by reordering and tiling inner loops. This is especially important on Xeon Phi as there is no L3 cache to mitigate the impact of L2 misses on application performance. Unfortunately, as this is a manual code transformation rather than a directive, code can become less readable and more brittle. Nevertheless, it was found that blocking to shared L2, i.e., 512 KiB per core, performs best for most applications.

- *short loop unrolling*: short loops should be unrolled as they do not provide enough work either for threading or for vectorization.

- *ensuring efficient vectorization*: This can be a major challenge as it may entail loop restructuring as well as data layout transformations. Where the compiler fails to detect vectorization opportunities automatically, loops can be annotated with the OpenMP 4 `simd` pragmas to enforce the compiler to vectorize these loops.

- *using optimized mathematical functions*: AVX512 supports intrinsics for reduced precision divisions and certain expensive mathematical functions such as transcendentals. Those can be enabled by instructing the compiler to use a relaxed floating-point model.

11.7.4   NESAP Result Overview

Figure 11.6 shows the summary of the node-to-node code performance on Edison and Cori before and after applying optimizations. The numbers are collected from multi-node benchmarks representing larger scale science runs being performed by the teams.

The speedups are normalized with respect to the performance of the original (baseline) codes on Edison. The number of nodes for each application is displayed in parentheses.

One observes an approximate 3x speedup on average on Xeon Phi between original and optimized codes. Furthermore, one finds an approximate 1.5x average architecture advantage in favor of Cori (Xeon Phi) vs. Edison.

NERSC further studied impacts of various Xeon Phi-specific hardware features on application performance. Figure 11.7 shows the relative speedups when utilizing MCDRAM (in either cache or flat mode depending on the application preference) vs. ignoring the MCDRAM (running in flat mode utilizing only the traditional DRAM). In addition, one can compare performance when compiling with full-optimization (-xMIC-AVX512) vs. disabling vectorization (-no-vec -no-simd). It should be noted that the latter test does not include libraries or AVX intrinsic codes where such compiler flags are ignored. The NESAP optimization efforts overview and results are documented in more detail in [17, 30].

11.7.5   Application Highlights

This section presents some selected applications and the major optimizations used to improve their performance on Xeon Phi.

11.7.5.1   Quantum ESPRESSO

Quantum ESPRESSO is an open source density functional theory (DFT) code and widely used in Materials Science and Quantum Chemistry to compute properties of material systems, such as atomic-structures, total-energies, vibrational properties etc. Accurate calculations of important electronic properties, like band-gaps and excitations energies, are achievable for many systems through so called Hybrid Functional calculations employing a certain contribution for the exact exchange (exx) potential - which represents the contribution of the Pauli-Exclusion principle.

The most expensive part of an exact exchange (exx) calculation is the calculation of the exact exchange functional. This function represents essentially a sequence of element-wise products of large complex arrays interleaved with Fast Fourier Transforms (FFT) of

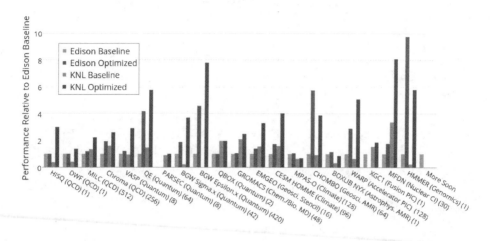

FIGURE 11.6: Applications performance relative to Edison baseline on multiple nodes. The number in parentheses represents the number of nodes used to measure performance.

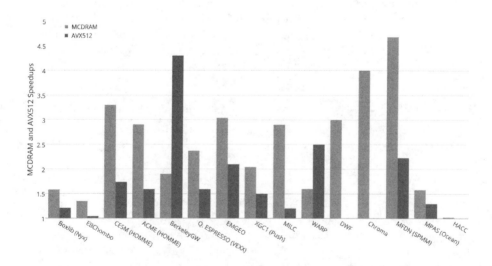

FIGURE 11.7: Applications performance speedup using MCDRAM vs. using DRAM (light bars) as well as using AVX512 vs. using AVX2 (dark bars).

these arrays. In the original code, the OpenMP parallelization was applied to the innermost loop, but the code performance did not scale beyond ~16 threads (cf. Figure 11.8). VTune profiling revealed that the run time of these sections was extremely short and thus overhead from forking and merging sections dominated. This problem was fixed by moving to a coarse grained parallelization, i.e., moving the OpenMP pragmas on the element-wise products from the inner to the outer loops. Since these sections are interleaved with FFTs, those loops had to be chunked into blocks and the sizes of the involved arrays had to be increased so that they can store results for a full chunk. This further enabled pooling of multiple FFTs within a chunk, which resulted in a ~20% performance improvement. On the element-wise products, the now doubly nested loops were additionally cache blocked into chunks of 2048 double-complex vectors. The two innermost loops were further decorated with `omp parallel for simd collapse(2)` directives in order to exploit full parallelization. In addition to this, MPI scaling was improved by re-arranging the data structure layout so that more parallelism relevant to this part of the calculation could be exploited. This change also enabled independent, node-local, FFTs, which significantly improved performance over the original distributed ones. In order to ensure compatibility between the exact exchange and the other parts of the calculation, a data structure transformation was performed. The overhead of this procedure is mitigated by the huge performance improvement gained in the expensive exact exchange calculation. Figure 11.9 displays the strong scaling for the full calculation (left panel) and the exact exchange part (right panel) for the original code (annotated QE 5.2.0) and our improved version.

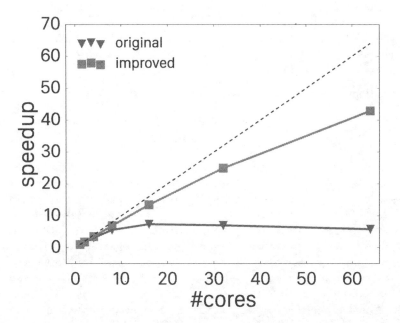

FIGURE 11.8: Strong thread scaling for Quantum ESPRESSO exact exchange calculations improved vs. original code for a system comprised of 64 water molecules.

More detailed discussions are available at [18, 13].

11.7.5.2 MFDn

Many-Fermion Dynamics—nuclear, or MFDn, is a configuration interaction (CI) code for nuclear structure calculations currently in use at multiple machines at NERSC, ALCF and OLCF for *ab initio* calculations of atomic nucei [21, 32, 33, 34]. To provide high accuracy

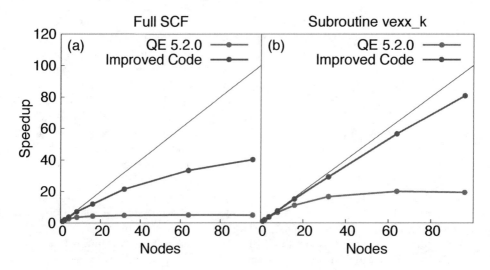

FIGURE 11.9: Multi-node scaling of full hybrid-DFT calculation (left) and of the exx-subroutine (right).

with realistic two and three-body forces with a CI code, a very large and sparse Hamiltonian is required, and therefore a highly scalable code is needed to effectively utilize the aggregate memory of a cluster. For problems of physical interest the matrix dimensions can exceed $10^{10} \times 10^{10}$ with over 10^{13} non-zero elements. The code is written in portable Fortran 90 with a hybrid MPI/OpenMP programming model.

A typical run of MFDn involves three phases:

- Matrix construction

- Obtain lowest eigenvalue/eigenvector pairs

- Compute observable properties

The matrix construction and computation of observables are compute intensive, but contain very few flops. The dominant operations are integer comparisons, bit operations and random access to lookup tables. In order to obtain good performance in these phases on Xeon Phi, improvements to data locality and efficient use of the vector units were essential. Promotion of occupied state bit masks from 32-bit to 64-bit integers, manual loop tiling and OpenMP 4.0 simd pragmas were used to improve vector and cache efficiency. The tile size is now a compile time option and a low multiple of the vector width is chosen in practice. Manual tiling and use of OpenMP pragmas instead of compiler options preserves the portability of the code.

The sparse matrix-matrix multiple kernel (SPMM) is the most expensive operation in the iterative eigensolver. Changing from the Lanczos to LOBPCG eigensolver enabled the use of SPMM, which has a higher arithmetic intensity than SPMV operations. Choosing the best number of MPI ranks per node and OpenMP threads per rank is also important on Xeon Phi.

The high OpenMP scalability of MFDn allows it to run with as few as 1 MPI rank per node (See Figure 11.10), which would be the preferred mode for best memory utilization. However, the best performance on Cori is obtained with multiple ranks as a single Xeon Phi core is not able to fully utilize the high speed network. Optimizations for MFDn resulted in better performance on all platforms and Xeon Phi saw more improvement than Xeon, highlighting that the Xeon Phi platform is more sensitive to code issues than Xeon.

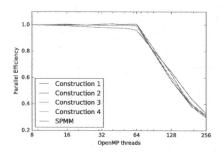

FIGURE 11.10: Strong thread scaling for MFDn for matrix construction and SPMM kernels.

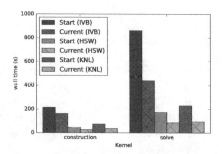

FIGURE 11.11: Comparison of effect of optimizations on 32 nodes of Edison, Cori-Haswell and Cori-KNL.

More detailed discussions are available at [23, 36].

11.8 Data Science

The Cori Haswell partition has been configured to specifically support large-scale data analysis. With increasing dataset sizes coming from experimental and observational facilities, including telescopes, sensors, detectors, microscopes, sequencers and, supercomputers, scientific users from the Department of Energy, Office of Science are increasingly relying on NERSC for extreme scale data analytics. To support these requirements, the Cori system includes hardware, software and policy changes to support this new and growing workload.

11.8.1 IO Improvement: Burst Buffer

One of the top improvements NERSC users consistently request in requirement reviews and feedback is better IO performance. To address this, Cori contains a Burst Buffer, based on the Cray DataWarp technology. This is an intermediate layer of non-volatile storage that sits between the fast on-node DRAM and the slower (but higher capacity) parallel file system (PFS). This Burst Buffer provides users with a configurable layer of fast IO that can improve application IO in several ways:

TABLE 11.2: Burst Buffer IOR performance, using 11120 compute nodes (HSW+KNL), 4 ranks per node.

	Posix FPP (GB/s)	MPIIO shared file (GB/s)	IOPs
Best measured read	1745	1320	28.2M
Best measured write	1566	1364	13.1M

- Improved IO bandwidth for reads/writes, for example, for checkpoint-restart applications.

- Improved performance for complex IO patterns, for example, high IOPS (IO operations per second).

- Improved capability for complex workflows, for example, combining simulation, analysis and visualization codes.

The DataWarp SSDs sit on specialized nodes that bridge the internal Aries interconnect of the compute system and the SAN fabric of the PFS, through the IO nodes. The flash memory is attached to Burst Buffer nodes that are packaged two nodes to a blade. Each Burst Buffer node contains an Intel Xeon processor with 64 GB of DDR3 memory and two 3.2 TB NAND flash SSD modules attached over two PCIe gen3 x8 interfaces. The Burst Buffer nodes are attached to the Cori Cray Aries network interconnect over a PCIe gen3 x16 interface. Each Burst Buffer node provides approximately 6.4 TB of usable capacity and a peak of approximately 5.7 GB/sec of sequential read and write bandwidth, with an aggregate bandwidth for the full Burst Buffer reaching over 1.7TB/sec and 28M IOPs (see Table 11.2 for details).

Access to the Burst Buffer resource is integrated with the SLURM scheduler. When a user submits a job requesting a Burst Buffer allocation, an XFS filesystem is mounted for that allocation so that the user sees a single namespace, even though data might be striped over several DataWarp nodes.

After considerable effort from NERSC staff and Cray engineers to refine the DataWarp performance, users generally see excellent performance from the Burst Buffer [20]. For example, the ATLAS collaboration has used the Burst Buffer to analyze data from the Large Hadron Collider [19], which typically involves several stages of filtering data to identify useful events for further analysis. This "derivation" process involves large I/O reads and is up to 7 times faster using the Burst Buffer compared to Cori Scratch (see Figure 11.12). Subsequent analysis stages of the filtered data exhibit a very different I/O pattern, requiring large amounts of small random reads and writes from the filtered data files. Obtaining an optimal performance in the analysis stage required tweaking the application caching from 2MB to to 100MB, which allowed the application to take better advantage of the available bandwidth to the Burst Buffer. This improved the application performance by a factor of 17, with the Burst Buffer out-performing Cori Scratch by a factor of 5 consistently at all job scales, as shown in Figure 11.13.

Another example application is the coupling of ChomboCrunch and Visit that demonstrates both high bandwidth and a complex workflow using the Burst Buffer [35]. Figure 11.14 illustrates that the simulation, visualization and analysis can be run simultaneously using the Burst Buffer, enabling higher spatial and temporal resolution, and Figure 11.15 shows that the bandwidth out-performs Lustre at all scales.

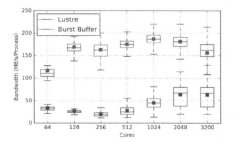

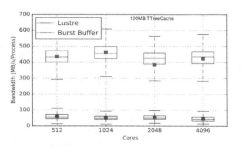

FIGURE 11.12: Comparison of application bandwidth to Cori Scratch file system (Lustre) and the Burst Buffer, for ATLAS data filtering.

FIGURE 11.13: Comparison of application bandwidth to Cori Scratch file system (Lustre) and the Burst Buffer, for ATLAS data analysis.

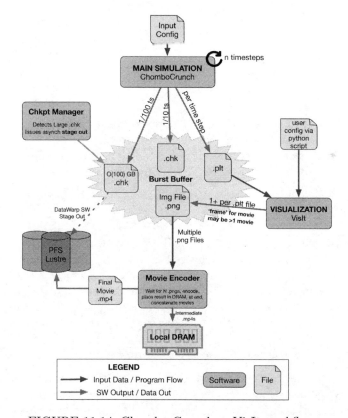

FIGURE 11.14: Chombo-Crunch + VisIt workflow.

11.8.2 Workflows

NERSCs mission has been expanding into closer interactions with experimental and observational facilities, whose users often have different requirements than traditional HPC modeling and simulation users. Users analyzing large data sets from an experimental facility have more complex workflows including filtering data, moving data and running multiple pipelined analysis codes on the data. The Cori system has been designed with data-intensive workflows in mind.

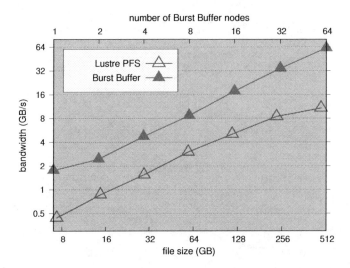

FIGURE 11.15: Chombo-Crunch I/O bandwidth scaling. The compute node to Burst Buffer node ratio is fixed at 16:1.

11.8.2.1   Network Connectivity to External Nodes

Many workflow systems are managed by a control node or database that manages the different tasks and stages in a workflow - this may be a persistent service that lives outside the Cori network. Individual workflow tasks may also need to pull down units of work or data, or publish results to/from a data service. Cori compute nodes therefore are able to talk to external services directly.

11.8.2.2   Burst Buffer Filesystem for In-situ Workflows

Multi-Stage Workflows will generate data between each step in the workflow - for example, a simulation generates data files, which need to be analyzed by an independent application, which then needs to be visualized by a third application (such as the Chombo-Crunch and Visit workflow mentioned in section 11.8.1 and [35]). As the size of the data grows, it becomes increasingly impractical to move the data in and out of the file system. The burst buffer provides a very convenient intermediate staging area for this data.

11.8.2.3   Real-time and Interactive Queues for Time Sensitive Analyses

Cori supports a real-time queue for time sensitive analyses. Users can request a small number of on-demand nodes if their jobs have special needs that cannot be accommodated through the regular batch system. The real-time queue enables immediate access to a set of nodes, for jobs that are under the real-time wallclock limit. Typically this is used for real time processing linked to an experiment (e.g., LCLS) or event (supernova). In addition to this, in mid-2017 NERSC began providing 192 nodes (Haswell and KNL) for high-turnaround 'interactive' usage. This allows all users to have instant turnaround for single analytics jobs (that can use multiple nodes for several hours).

11.8.2.4 Scheduler and Queue Improvements to Support Data-intensive Computing

In addition, the scheduler and scheduling policies we had traditionally used to support our modeling and simulation workloads proved inflexible for dealing with the more dynamic needs of data users. One of the key changes made to support this new workload was a change to Native SLURM. The schedulers closer ties to the compute nodes provide easier diagnostics, cleaner access to the data and faster startup. Users from experimental facilities also often come with expectations of a specific operating system or require a complex set of installed libraries. For these users, NERSC is allowing users to bring their own images to Cori, by way of a new capability called Shifter [8], which enables users to import and use their Docker containers.

11.9 System Statistics

As mentioned in Section 11.7.1, NERSC has over 700 projects and more than 6,000 users. To facilitate moving codes to the Intel Knight's Landing processors, the NESAP codes chosen covered a large spectrum of science fields within the DOE Office of Science mission. Since these teams had been working on their codes to prepare for the system, they were given exclusive and priority access to KNL nodes starting from November 2016. In January 2017, access to a subset of the KNL nodes was granted to all users for code development, debugging and optimization. Non-NESAP users started to gain full access to the KNL nodes once they had demonstrated some degree of application-readiness. The system entered full production mode in July 2017.

11.9.1 System Utilizations

Figure 11.16 shows the 30-day rolling medium utilization in node days on Cori KNL. NESAP users ramped up the system usage very quickly from the end of November 2016 to early January 2017. As shown in Figure 11.18, the system utilization has been mostly in the 90% range once users were provided access.

Figure 11.17 shows the breakdown of hours used on Cori KNL nodes from December 22, 2016 after Cori was accepted, through June 15, 2017. Lattice QCD codes were ready to use KNL before many others. VASP and Quantum Espresso are material science applications that NERSC installs on systems and users execute. The VASP and Quantum Espresso users were enabled mid-January, explaining the large usage in materials science.

The workload is highly parallel as indicated in the Job Size breakdowns in Figure 11.18. About half of the hours from January to June 2017 were used by jobs using more than 512 nodes and more than 25% of the total hours were used by jobs running on more than 1,024 nodes. The system utilization chart also indicated a couple of Cori system maintenance periods: February 28 to March 3, and April 18-21 for new cabinets integration, and March 22-24, 2017 for an OS upgrade.

11.9.2 Job Completion Statistics

Job completion statistics help to indicate how successfully user applications are running on the system and to discover potential system problems. On Cori, the SLURM accounting database is used to analyze success rate, failure categories and causes.

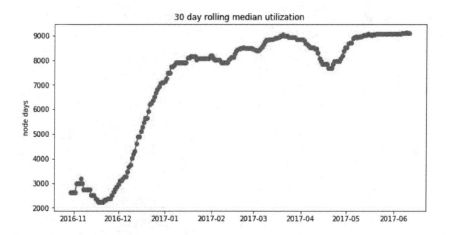

FIGURE 11.16: KNL system utilization from November 2016 to June 2017.

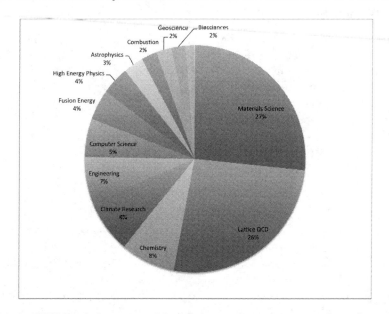

FIGURE 11.17: KNL node hours used by various science category from January to June 2017.

Figure 11.19 shows the percentage of KNL node-hours spent by jobs completed with each category. A small number of jobs in the categories of Node Fail, Boot Fail and Cancelled System are considered as job failures related to system issues. Jobs in the "Completed" category are completed successfully. Jobs in the Timeout categories are unknown of whether from system or user issues. Many NERSC workflows choose to intentionally timeout and restart from regular checkpointing data. Cancelled or Failed jobs can be from either user or system cause, which mostly represent user activities debugging their workloads.

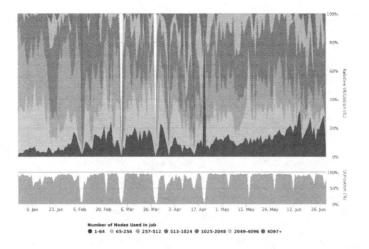

FIGURE 11.18: KNL Job size and system utilization from January to June 2017.

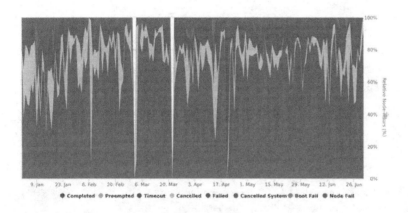

FIGURE 11.19: Job Completion Breakdown from January to June 2017.

11.10 Summary

In summary, the Cori system has been configured to support both large-scale simulation as well as extreme data analysis for the broad Department of Energy, Office of Science workload. With a number of new architectural features such as the Burst Buffer and the Knights Landing processor with many light weight cores and high bandwidth memory, users are getting exposed to new system features that are expected in next generation systems on the path to exascale. Through the NESAP program, users have optimized applications through improved parallelism and vectorization and the use of on-package memory. On average, NESAP applications have seen a 3x speedup on the Cori Knights Landing compute nodes.

Innovations such as Shifter and SDN as well as new queue policies to support data workloads have enabled the Cori system to support users from analyzing data from experimental facilities.

Since the system was installed, users have rapidly ported codes and system utilization has been high. NERSC is continuing to add new capabilities to the system, which will be in service for approximately 5 more years.

11.11   Acknowledgments

The authors would like to thank Woo-Sun Yang and Austin Leung for helping in collecting some system statistics. This research used resources of the National Energy Research Scientific Computing Center, a DOE Office of Science User Facility supported by the Office of Science of the U.S. Department of Energy under Contract No. DE-AC02-05CH11231.

Bibliography

[1] APEX Benchmarks. https://www.nersc.gov/research-and-development/apex/apex-benchmarks/.

[2] Intel VTune Amplifier. https://software.intel.com/en-us/intel-vtune-amplifier-xe.

[3] Intel®Advisor. https://software.intel.com/en-us/intel-advisor-xe.

[4] Libfabric OpenFabrics. https://ofiwg.github.io/libfabric.

[5] MPICH. http://www.mpich.org.

[6] NERSC-8 Benchmarks. https://www.nersc.gov/users/computational-systems/cori/nersc-8-procurement/trinity-nersc-8-rfp/nersc-8-trinity-benchmarks/.

[7] NERSC Cori System. https://www.nersc.gov/users/computational-systems/cori.

[8] NERSC Edison System. https://www.nersc.gov/users/computational-systems/edison.

[9] NESAP. http://www.nersc.gov/users/computational-systems/cori/nesap/nesap-projects.

[10] NESAP Application Case Studies. http://www.nersc.gov/users/computational-systems/cori/application-porting-and-performance/application-case-studies/.

[11] NESAP Projects. http://www.nersc.gov/users/computational-systems/cori/nesap.

[12] NESAP Xeon Phi Application Performance. http://www.nersc.gov/users/application-performance/preparing-for-cori/.

[13] Quantum ESPRESSO Case Study. http://www.nersc.gov/users/computational-systems/cori/application-porting-and-performance/application-case-studies/quantum-espresso-exact-exchange-case-study/.

[14] Roofline Performance Model. http://crd.lbl.gov/departments/computerscience/PAR/research/roofline.

[15] SDE: Intel Software Development Emulator. https://software.intel.com/en-us/articles/intel-software-development-emulator.

[16] Tips for Using CMake and GNU Autotools on Cray Heterogeneous Systems. http://docs.cray.com/books/S-2801-1608//S-2801-1608.pdf.

[17] Taylor Barnes, Brandon Cook, Douglas Doerfler, Brian Friesen, Yun He, Thorsten Kurth, Tuomas Koskela, Mathieu Lobet, Tareq Malas, Leonid Oliker, and et al. *Evaluating and Optimizing the NERSC Workload on Knights Landing.* Jan 2016.

[18] Taylor A. Barnes, Thorsten Kurth, Pierre Carrier, Nathan Wichmann, David Prendergast, Paul R.C. Kent, and Jack Deslippe. Improved treatment of exact exchange in quantum {ESPRESSO}. *Computer Physics Communications*, 214:52 – 58, 2017.

[19] W. Bhimji, D. Bard, K. Burleigh, C. Daley, S. Farrell, M. Fasel, B. Friesen, L. Gerhardt, J. Liu, P. Nugent, D. Paul, J. Porter, and V. Tsulaia. Extreme i/o on hpc for hep using the burst buffer at nersc. Computing in High-Energy Physics, 2016.

[20] W. Bhimji, D. Bard, M. Romanus, D. Paul, A. Ovsyannikov, B. Friesen, M. Bryson, J. Correa, G.K. Lockwood, V. Tsulaia, Byna S., S Farrell, D. Gursoy, C. Daley, V Beckner, B. Van Straalen, D. Trebotich, Tull C., G.H. Weber, N.J. Wright, K. Antypas, and Prabhat. Accelerating science with the nersc burst buffer. Cray User Group, 2016.

[21] S. Binder, A. Calci, E. Epelbaum, R. J. Furnstahl, J. Golak, K. Hebeler, H. Kamada, H. Krebs, J. Langhammer, S. Liebig, P. Maris, U.-G. Meißner, D. Minossi, A. Nogga, H. Potter, R. Roth, R. Skinński, K. Topolnicki, J. P. Vary, and H. Witała. Few-nucleon systems with state-of-the-art chiral nucleon-nucleon forces. *Phys. Rev. C*, 93(4):044002, 2016.

[22] R.S. Canon, T. Declerck, B. Draney, J. Lee, D. Paul, and D. Skinner. Enabling a superfacility with software defined networking. Cray User Group, 2017.

[23] Brandon Cook, Pieter Maris, Meiyue Shao, Nathan Wichmann, Marcus Wagner, John ONeill, Thanh Phung, and Gaurav Bansal. High performance optimizations for nuclear physics code mfdn on knl. In *International Conference on High Performance Computing*, pages 366–377. Springer, 2016.

[24] Jack Deslippe, Georgy Samsonidze, David A. Strubbe, Manish Jain, Marvin L. Cohen, and Steven G. Louie. Berkeleygw: A massively parallel computer package for the calculation of the quasiparticle and optical properties of materials and nanostructures. *Computer Physics Communications*, 183(6):1269 – 1289, 2012.

[25] Douglas Doerfler, Jack Deslippe, Samuel Williams, Leonid Oliker, Brandon Cook, Thorsten Kurth, Mathieu Lobet, Tareq Malas, Jean-Luc Vay, and Henri Vincenti. *Applying the Roofline Performance Model to the Intel Xeon Phi Knights Landing Processor*, pages 339–353. Springer International Publishing, Cham, 2016.

[26] P. Hill, C. Synder, and J. Sygulla. Knl system software. Cray User Group, 2017.

[27] D.M. Jacobsen. Extending cle6 to a multicomputer os. Cray User Group, 2017.

[28] M. Jette, D.M. Jacobsen, and D. Paul. Scheduler optimization for current generation cray systems. Cray User Group, 2017.

[29] William TC Kramer, John M Shalf, and Erich Strohmaier. The sustained system performance (ssp) benchmark.

[30] Thorsten Kurth, William Arndt, Taylor Barnes, Brandon Cook, Jack Deslippe, Doug Doerfler, Brian Friesen, Yu He, Tuomas Koskela, Mathieu Lobet, Tareq Malas, Leonid Oliker, Andrey Ovsyannikov, Samuel Williams, Woo-Sun Yang, and Zhengji Zhao. *Analyzing Performance of Selected Applications on the Cori HPC System.* Jun 2017. Accepted for IXPUG Workshop Experiences on Intel Knights Landing at the One Year Mark, ISC 2017, Frankfurt, Germany.

[31] Melara M, Gamblin T, Becker G, French R, Belhorn M, Thompson K, Scheibel P, and HartmanBaker R. Using spack to manage software on cray supercomputers. In *Proceedings of Cray User Group*, 2017.

[32] P. Maris, M. A. Caprio, and J. P. Vary. Emergence of rotational bands in ab initio no-core configuration interaction calculations of the Be isotopes. *Phys. Rev. C*, 91(1):014310, 2015.

[33] P. Maris, J. P. Vary, P. Navratil, W. E. Ormand, H. Nam, and D. J. Dean. Origin of the anomalous long lifetime of ^{14}C. *Phys. Rev. Lett.*, 106(20):202502, 2011.

[34] Pieter Maris, James P. Vary, S. Gandolfi, J. Carlson, and Steven C. Pieper. Properties of trapped neutrons interacting with realistic nuclear Hamiltonians. *Phys. Rev. C*, 87(5):054318, 2013.

[35] A. Ovsyannikov, M. Romanus, B. Van Straalwn, G. Weber, and D. Trebotich. Scientific workflows at datawarp-speed: Accelerated data-intensive science using nersc's burst buffer. IEEE, 2016.

[36] Meiyue Shao, Hasan Metin Aktulga, Chao Yang, Esmond G Ng, Pieter Maris, and James P Vary. Accelerating nuclear configuration interaction calculations through a preconditioned block iterative eigensolver. *arXiv preprint arXiv:1609.01689*, 2016.

[37] Samuel Williams, Andrew Waterman, and David Patterson. Roofline: An insightful visual performance model for multicore architectures. *Commun. ACM*, 52(4):65–76, April 2009.

[38] Samuel Webb Williams. *Auto-tuning Performance on Multicore Computers.* PhD thesis, Berkeley, CA, USA, 2008. AAI3353349.

Chapter 12

Lomonosov-2: Petascale Supercomputing at Lomonosov Moscow State University

Vladimir Voevodin, Alexander Antonov, Dmitry Nikitenko, Pavel Shvets, Sergey Sobolev, Konstantin Stefanov, Vadim Voevodin, and Sergey Zhumatiy

Research Computing Center of Lomonosov Moscow State University

Andrey Brechalov, and Alexander Naumov

T-Platforms Company

12.1 Overview

12.1.1 HPC History of MSU

The history of High Performance Computing at Lomonosov Moscow State University began with the creation of the Research Computing Center (RCC) in 1955. Since its inception, the MSU Computing Center was equipped with up-to-the-minute equipment. As early as December 1956, the Strela computer was commissioned. It performed complex calculations associated with the launch of the first Earth satellites, the first Soviet rockets to the Moon, as well as the first manned flight into space of Yuri Gagarin. In May 1961, the M-20 computer was installed; in 1966, BESM-4 arrived, and in 1968 Strela was changed to BESM-6, Russia's highest-performance computer at the time.

MSU developed its own computers too. Since 1959, an experimental model of a small computer Setun (Figure 12.1) had been operating — the country's first machine made of tubeless elements, and the first one in the world in the ternary numeral system. Setun was designed and manufactured at MSU RCC; in 1961, serial production of Setun computers began. Fifty computers were produced from 1961 to 1965.

FIGURE 12.1: Setun computer developed at MSU in 1959.

From 1955 until the beginning of the 1990s, more than 25 high-performance systems of different architectures had been installed and were actively used at Lomonosov Moscow State University. At the same time, a deep study of methods for solving applied problems using computers had been carried out, and these methods were introduced into the educational process at Lomonosov Moscow State University.

In 1999, the MSU Research Computing Center had chosen the cluster architecture as the basis for projected new computer systems. The first self-made cluster consisted of 18 nodes connected with the SCI network. Each node contained two Intel Pentium III 500 MHz processors, and its peak performance was 18 Gflops. Research groups formed around the first cluster started using a new type of technology — parallel computers with distributed memory in order to boost their research.

Then, in 2002, a cluster with a standard Fast Ethernet technology for communication followed with peak performance of 82 Gflops (Figure 12.2). In 2004, a cluster from Hewlett-Packard was installed with 160 AMD Opteron 2.2 GHz processors and InfiniBand network with a peak performance of 700 Gflops. In 2008, supercomputer Chebyshev entered into operation with a peak performance of 60 Tflops. It consists of 625 nodes and includes 1,250 quad-core Intel Xeon 5472 3.0 GHz processors. Almost immediately after its launch, the supercomputer was fully workloaded.

FIGURE 12.2: Computing cluster at RCC MSU, 2002.

Lomonosov supercomputer [14] (Figure 12.3) was initially installed at Lomonosov Moscow State University in 2009. This supercomputer was created by the Russian company T-Platforms. The official launch ceremony was attended by D.A. Medvedev, President of the Russian Federation, who proposed to name the supercomputer after the great Russian scientist of the 18th century M.V. Lomonosov. At launch time, a peak performance of Lomonosov was 420 Tflops, which allowed the supercomputer to lead the list of the most powerful computers in CIS and Eastern Europe, and rank 12th in the global Top500 list in November 2009.

By that time, the number of users of MSU supercomputing center had reached 250, and its resources were used by more than 50 organizations — MSU faculties, institutions of the Russian Academy of Sciences, and others. Only a year later, available resources of Lomonosov, which became the flagship of MSU supercomputing center, were not sufficient to deal with all the necessary workloads.

In 2012, after four stages of the supercomputer expansion process, Lomonosov was equipped with new 260 dual-processor compute nodes with quad-core Intel Xeon X5570 processors, 680 compute nodes with 6-core Intel Xeon X5670 processors, 777 compute nodes with two Intel Xeon E5630 CPUs and two NVIDIA X2070 computing accelerators, and 288 compute nodes with Intel Xeon X5570/X5670 processors and GPU accelerators. As a result of all modernizations, a peak performance of the computing system has been increased to 1.7 Pflops, and Linpack performance reached 901.9 Tflops, which resulted in efficiency of

FIGURE 12.3: 1.7 Pflops Lomonosov supercomputer.

53%. Its total amount of memory has increased to 92 TB, and the computer's peak power consumption was 2.6 MW.

The first stage of the Lomonosov-2 supercomputer (Figure 12.4) was installed at Lomonosov Moscow State University in 2014. This system was also created by the T-Platforms company. After some upgrades Lomonosov-2 became a new leader of Russian supercomputing. With 2.58 Pflops of peak performance, it was ranked 22nd in the global Top500 list in November, 2014. In 2017, Lomonosov-2 contains 1,472 compute nodes with Intel Xeon E5-2697 v3 processor and NVIDIA Tesla K40s GPU. Its peak performance is 2.96 Pflops, Linpack performance — 2.1 Pflops. Lomonosov-2 is ranked 59th in the Top500 list in June, 2017.

Taking the supercomputing road more than ten years ago, Lomonosov Moscow State University Supercomputing Center is planning to move forward to exaflops and further in the future. To learn more about the MSU Supercomputing Center, its facilities, projects, applications, and other activities, see [2].

12.1.2 Lomonosov-2 Supercomputer: Timeline

Supercomputer Lomonosov-2 was deployed in three stages:

1. Year 2014, May: Intel Xeon E5-2680v2 10C 2.8GHz, InfiniBand FDR, NVIDIA K40s, 6400 cores, peak performance 423 Tflops.

2. Year 2014, October: Intel Xeon E5-2697v3 14C 2.6GHz, InfiniBand FDR, NVIDIA K40s, 37120 cores, peak performance 2.575 Pflops.

3. Year 2016, May: Intel Xeon E5-2697v3 14C 2.6GHz, InfiniBand FDR, NVIDIA K40s, 42688 cores, peak performance 2.962 Pflops.

It is expected that the supercomputer will be upgraded up to 5 Pflops by the end of 2017 using NVIDIA P100 accelerators.

FIGURE 12.4: 2.9 Pflops Lomonosov-2 supercomputer.

12.2   Applications and Workloads

12.2.1   Main Applications Highlights

In the beginning of 2017, MSU's supercomputing center based on Lomonosov-2 provided computational resources for over 600 research projects. Scientific groups from MSU, Russian Academy of Sciences (RAS), other institutions from all over Russia and abroad collaborated in almost all areas of science. The most popular are Chemistry, Physics, and Mechanics, almost equally sharing 74% of the total number of projects, followed by Biology, Medical, and Geosciences (Figure 12.5).

Most of these projects are conducted in accordance with the priority directions of science and technology development of the Russian Federation with a special focus on nanosystems industry, life sciences, information and telecommunication systems, energy efficiency and nuclear energy, transport and aerospace systems, environmental science and management and informational security (Figure 12.6).

12.2.2   Benchmark Results and Rating Positions

Linpack and Top500

Since its inception in 2014, Lomonosov-2 has been included in a global Top500 ranking. In the June 2014 Top500 list edition, it ranked 129th with a peak performance of 423.4 Tflops, Linpack performance of 319.8 Tflops, and efficiency of 75.5%.

After the first expansion round, Lomonosov-2 was ranked 22nd in the November 2014 edition of Top500 list with the sustained performance of 1.85 Pflops.

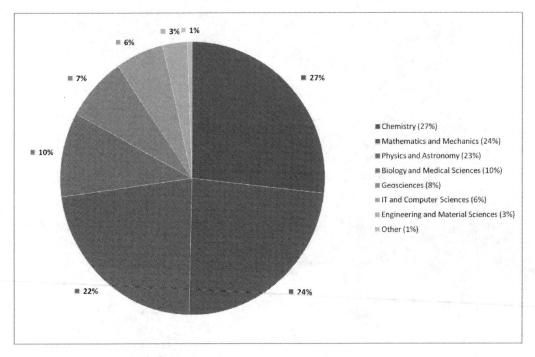

FIGURE 12.5: MSU supercomputing center's user research areas.

At the time of this writing (summer 2017) Lomonosov-2 is ranked 59th in the June 2017 Top500 list with a peak performance of 2.96 Pflops, Linpack performance of 2.1 Pflops, and efficiency of 71%.

Green500

With a power consumption of 1.079 MW and power efficiency of 1.948 Gflops/W, Lomonosov-2 was ranked 94th in the June 2016 Green500 list. And now it is ranked 135th in the June 2017 edition.

Top50

Since 2004, the Research Computing Center of Lomonosov Moscow State University and the Joint Supercomputer Center of the Russian Academy of Sciences have been keeping a list of the Top50 most powerful supercomputers in Russia and CIS [1]. It is issued twice a year, in March/April and September. In its compilation principle, this project is similar to the Top500 list — computers are ranked by their Linpack performance. Since the spring of 2015, Lomonosov-2 steadily has been ranking first, thus confirming its leading position in the Russian supercomputer industry.

12.2.3　Users and Workloads

The total number of MSU's supercomputing center users in 2017 exceeded 3000 including both research project members and students. The geography of collaboration inside Russia is shown on figure 12.7.

Scientific groups representing more than 350 organizations and institutions from over 50 cities of Russia use the HPC resources of MSU's supercomputer center. As many as 150 groups conduct collaborative research projects with international scientific groups from over 90 locations worldwide.

Usage of the computational resources of the center resulted in more than 1000 research

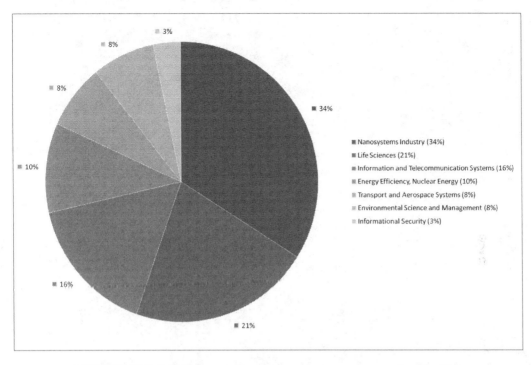

- Nanosystems Industry (34%)
- Life Sciences (21%)
- Information and Telecommunication Systems (16%)
- Energy Efficiency, Nuclear Energy (10%)
- Transport and Aerospace Systems (8%)
- Environmental Science and Management (8%)
- Informational Security (3%)

FIGURE 12.6: MSU supercomputing center's user research priorities.

papers published during 2016, with a noticeable number of publications in high-impact journals.

The average rate of job submission for Lomonosov-2 system is about 1000 jobs per day. The average wait time of a submitted job is 42 minutes.

Figure 12.8 illustrates the distribution of total consumed CPU hours by various classes of job sizes. Nearly 40% of resources are consumed by the jobs provided with a range of from 128 to 512 CPU cores.

12.3   System Overview

Today Lomonosov-2 (Table 12.1) contains 1472 compute nodes in 6 racks, 12 management nodes, 6 service nodes, and 2 storage system appliances.

Each compute node is an A-Class by the T-Platforms company. There are 6 T-Platforms A-Class racks; 5 of them are fully equipped with 256 compute nodes and the 6th rack is partially equipped with 192 compute nodes. InfiniBand and Ethernet switch systems, as well as compute nodes, are installed in A-Class system rack. All equipment in the A-Class system rack excluding PSUs are liquid-cooled by hot water (up to 45 degrees Celsius inlet temperature) to provide better energy efficiency.

All compute nodes (Figure 12.9) have the same configuration; each node has 64 GB memory, one Intel Xeon E5-2697 v3 processor with 14 physical cores, and one Nvidia Tesla K40 GPU in SXM form-factor. One rack contains up to 256 compute nodes (grouped by four on the one assembly with a single coldplate) organized into 8 pools, 2 assemblies of management nodes, ethernet switch, and auxiliary network InfiniBand switch. Each pool

FIGURE 12.7: MSU supercomputing center's user locations in Russia.

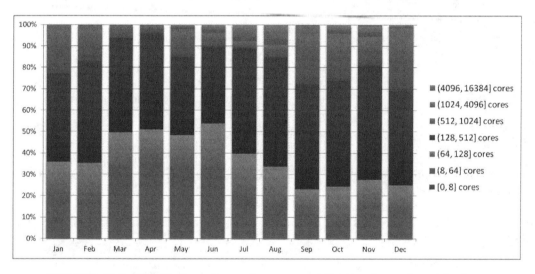

FIGURE 12.8: Distribution of overall resource utilization by various job sizes.

contains up to 32 compute nodes (in 8 assemblies), four 36-ports FDR InfiniBand switches for communication network connectivity, up to 2 Ethernet switches, and one FDR InfiniBand switch system to provide auxiliary network connectivity. Compute nodes are connected to the switches via backplane without extra cables.

Service nodes are based on T-Platforms V-Class blade systems and are used for various purposes. Two access nodes secure users access from Internet, users can compile their programs, upload and download files, submit batch jobs and control them from these nodes. Two nodes called monitors are dedicated to collecting and analyzing health, performance and other data from computing nodes, infrastructure and job control. Some data-collecting services are encapsulated into virtual machines based on Linux KVM technology. Virtualization allows to easily move these services between monitors in case of any troubles with physical server. Last two service nodes are "managers", they run subnet managers for InfiniBand networks, batch jobs manager, LDAP servers and core xCAT daemons for system management and OS provisioning.

TABLE 12.1: Lomonosov-2 supercomputer highlights.

Feature	Value
Nodes	1472
x86 cores	20608
GPUs	1472
Memory per node	64 GB
GPU memory	11.56 GB
HDD per node	n/a
GPU model	Tesla K40s
CPU model	Intel Xeon E5-2697 v3 2.6GHz
home filesystem	64 TB
scratch filesystem	433 TB
opt filesystem	30 TB

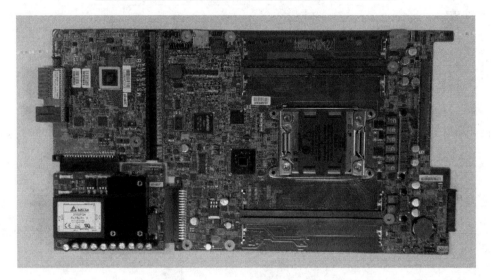

FIGURE 12.9: Compute node motherboard with power and interfaces boards.

12.4   System Software and Programming Systems

The operating system of Lomonosov-2 is Centos-7. The only additions are Mellanox InfiniBand drivers, Panasas drivers, and Lustre drivers.

Lomonosov-2 uses XCAT [7] to control all boot images for all nodes and power control via IPMI.

Several OpenMPI versions are available: 1.8.4, 1.10.7, and 2.1.1. Only OpenMPI supports the flattened butterfly topology of the InfiniBand network. Compiling can be done with GNU GCC/GFortran 4.8.5 or Intel Compiler. Intel MPI is not officially supported because of lack of support for the flattened butterfly topology.

For GPU utilization, CUDA versions 5.5, 6.5, and 8.0 are installed. Intel MKL is available for users to improve the performance of their applications.

Jobs control on Lomonosov-2 is secured by SLURM 15.08.1 [6] and the GLURMO custom job scheduler. System statistics are collected by collectd and nmond monitoring systems and then processed by OctoScreen [13] (visualizations) and OctoTron [8] (anomaly detection). Data about actually compiled and used programs and computational packages are collected by XALT software.

Several preinstalled packages are available for users: abinit, espresso, lammps, namd, nwchem, vasp, cp2k, gromacs, and magma. Most packages are compiled with CUDA support, and all of them support MPI.

Lmod compatible with Environment modules was used to control environments for different versions of software.

User access to the supercomputer via ssh and sftp is possible using key-based authentication only. For user management and troubleshooting, the Octoshell [12] system is actively used.

Table 12.2 shows the software configuration of the Lomonosov-2 supercomputer.

TABLE 12.2: Lomonosov-2 Software Configuration.

Feature	Software
Access Node OS	CentOS 7.1
Compute Node OS	CentOS 7.1
Home Filesystem	Panasas
Scratch Filesystem	Lustre 2.11
Compilers	Intel Compilers (C,C++,Fortran) 15.0 GCC Compilers (C,C++,Fortran) 4.8.5 CUDA 5.5 CUDA 6.5 CUDA 8.0
MPI	OpenMPI 1.8.4 OpenMPI 1.10.7 OpenMPI 2.1.1
Libraries	Intel MKL 15.0 Boost
Resource Manager	Slurm 15.08.1
Job Scheduler	GLURMO
Cluster Manager	Octoshell 2
Monitoring and Analysis Tools	collectd nmond Tentaviz OctoTron XALT
Applications	abinit 7.10.5 cp2k 3.0 gromacs 5.1.1 espresso 5.3.0 lammps magma 1.7.0 namd 2.11 nwchem 6.6 vasp 5.4.4

12.5   Networks

Mellanox dual-ports ConnectIB-based network module is installed in each compute node as well as the Gigabit ethernet controller. There are two independent FDR InfiniBand networks: communication network for MPI-like exchanges and auxiliary network for I/O operations for Lustre filesystem.

12.5.1   Communication Network

FIGURE 12.10: FDR Infiniband switches mounted on the coldplate.

The Communication network is used for MPI communications. Only compute nodes are connected to the communication network. The network is implemented using 36 ports FDR InfiniBand switches (Figure 12.10) which are installed in the A-Class racks. These switches are connected to the flattened butterfly topology 3x8x8, which allow to extend up to 4D flattened butterfly $4 \times 8 \times 8 \times 8$. This topology was chosen for the system after different topologies simulation based on the requirement for extending the cluster up to 16K compute nodes. Each switch has 8 internal ports connected to the backplane for compute nodes connections and 28 external FDR InfiniBand ports for switch-to-switch connectivity.

Figure 12.11 shows the flattened butterfly topology scheme.

T-Platforms modified version of the subnet manager has to be used to support such topology. There are some MPI libraries installed in the cluster but openmpi is the only recommended.

12.5.2   Auxiliary InfiniBand Network

The auxiliary network is implemented using FDR InfiniBand. The networks topology inside A-Class rack is fat tree with oversubscription factor 8 : 1. Each leaf switch combines

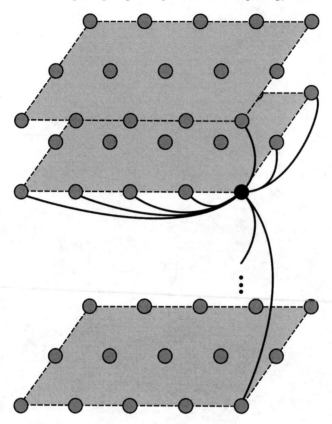

FIGURE 12.11: Flattened butterfly topology scheme.

32 compute nodes and has 4 uplinks going to 2 top-of-the-rack switches (2 links to each switch). The usage of two top-of-the-rack switches provides fabric redundancy. Each top-of-the-rack InfiniBand switches has 18 uplink ports; now each switch is connected by 3 FDR links to the Mellanox SX6536 core switch and connections are made to provide redundancy.

There are two pairs of 36 ports Mellanox MSX6025 switches providing connectivity for service nodes and Lustre servers. The major part of service nodes and Lustre servers is divided to failover pairs, so the servers in the same pair are connected to the different MSX6025 switches providing redundancy in case of switch system failure.

12.5.3   Management and Service Network

Management and Service network is used for compute nodes boot, job scheduling, monitoring, and remote control. Additionally, the Panasas storage system is accessible via the management network.

Management and Service network is based on the 10G/1G Ethernet protocols. Management and service traffics are isolated to different VLANs and subnets. There are two core 48-ports 10G Ethernet switches; some service nodes are connected by 10G Ethernet links directly to the core switches as well as the Panasas system, and other service nodes are connected by Gigabit Ethernet links to the Gigabit ethernet switches that are connected to the core switches.

Each compute node is connected via backplane to the Ethernet switch that is installed in the pool. This switch is connected to the level 2 Ethernet switches in the rack by cable connections and each level 2 switch is connected to the core switch by 10G ethernet uplink. Compute node remote management is provided by IPMI protocol including iKVM features.

12.6   Storage

Lomonosov-2 storage subsystem consists of two independent parallel filesystem appliances.

The first system is the PAS16 storage system, which includes 3 PAS16 DirectorBlades that are working in the failover cluster configuration and 8 PAS16 StorageBlades. The Panasas storage system is connected to the core Ethernet switches by 10G Ethernet and provides 1.5 GB/sec read and write bandwidth on the sequential I/O load, as well as 94 TB storage space capacity.

There are two data volumes on the Panasas system: /opt and /home.

/opt volume is accessible on the compute and access nodes and is used for storing common libraries, tools, and applications, and compilers, MPI libraries, CUDA libraries, etc. Some applications that are used for computations by the different users and groups are located on the /opt data volume as well.

/home volume is accessible only on access nodes and is used as the users home directories volume. /home volume is used by users for storing data and doing data processing on the access nodes (preprocessing, postprocessing, some reports generating, etc).

The second part is Lustre appliance which is based on the T-Platforms V200 servers for metadata and object data processing and EMC VNX5600 and VNX7600 block storage systems for the data storage. Lustre filesystem is accessible to the compute nodes as well as to the access nodes via auxillary InfiniBand fabric, and is used as the users home directories for the compute nodes (users have to copy applications and data to the Lustre filesystem before running code on the compute nodes). Open-source Lustre edition is used on the server and client sides.

The metadata processing part consists of two servers working in the failover mode that are directly connected by FibreChannel to the EMC VNX5600 block storage system equipped with SSD drives to provide better latency and random I/O performance.

There are four physical object storage servers, which are directly connected by 4 Fibre Channel 8Gb links to the EMC VNX7600 block storage. All Fibre Channel links are working in the link aggregation mode to provide maximum bandwidth as well as failover. There are 240 2TB HDDs divided to 24 RAID6 (8 + 2) LUNs on the block storage system side; each LUNs is used as the OST, so each server presents 6 OSTs. The object storage servers are divided to the failover pairs, so in case of server failure the second server is processing 12 OSTs.

MDS and OSS servers are connected to the two 36-ports Mellanox FDR InfiniBand switches, and these switches are connected to the core switch by 3 FDR InfiniBand links each.

Overall storage performance is 10 GB/sec on the read and write operations and about 380 TB raw capacity at the filesystem layer.

12.7   Engineering Infrastructure

12.7.1   Infrastructure Support

The power and cooling systems for Lomonosov-2 supercomputer follow the general segmentation guidelines. That means that the IT equipment in a HPC data center using the cluster-based architecture can be generally divided into two types (computing IT hardware and auxiliary IT hardware), each having its own requirements for engineering infrastructure fault tolerance and component redundancy [10].

In addition, they must meet the demands of the facility's IT equipment and engineering systems at full load, which includes up to 64 A-class systems and up to 80 auxiliary equipment U racks in 42U, 48U, and custom cabinets. At full capacity these systems including engineering infrastructure require 12,000-kW peak electric power capacity.

Utility power is designed to be provided by eight 20/0.4-kV substations, each having two redundant power transformers making a total of 16 low-voltage power lines with a power limit of 875 kW/line in normal operation.

Although no backup engine-generator sets have been provisioned, 28% of the computing equipment and 100% of auxiliary IT equipment is protected by UPS, providing at least 10 minutes of battery life for all connected equipment.

The engineering infrastructure also includes two independent cooling systems: a warm-water, dry-cooler type for the computational equipment and a cold-water, chiller system for auxiliary equipment. These systems are designed for normal operation in ambient temperatures ranging from -35 to $+35°C$ (-31 to $+95°F$) with year-round free cooling for the computing hardware. The facility also contains an emergency cooling system for auxiliary IT equipment.

The facility's first floor includes four 480-square-meter (m^2) rooms for computing equipment (17.3 kW/m^2) and four 280-m^2 rooms for auxiliary equipment (3 kW/m^2) with 2,700 m^2 for site engineering rooms on an underground level.

12.7.2   Power Distribution

The power distribution system is built on standard switchboard equipment and is based on the typical topology for general data centers. In this facility, however, the main function of the UPS is to ride through brief blackouts of the utility power supply for select computing equipment, all auxiliary IT equipment, and select engineering equipment systems. In the case of a longer blackout, the system supplies power for proper shutdown of connected IT equipment.

The UPS system is divided into three independent subsystems. The first is for computing equipment, the second is for auxiliary IT equipment, and the third is for engineering systems. In fact, the UPS system is deeply segmented because of the large number of input power lines. This minimizes the impact of failures of engineering equipment on supercomputer performance in general.

The segmentation principle is also applied to the physical location of the power supply equipment. Batteries are placed in three separate rooms. In addition, there are three UPS rooms and one switchboard room for the computing equipment that is unprotected by UPS. Figure 12.12 shows one UPS-battery rooms pair.

Three independent parallel UPS, each featuring $N + 1$ redundancy (see Figure 12.13), feed the protected computing equipment. This redundancy, along with bypass availability and segmentation, simplifies UPS maintenance and the task of localizing a failure. Con-

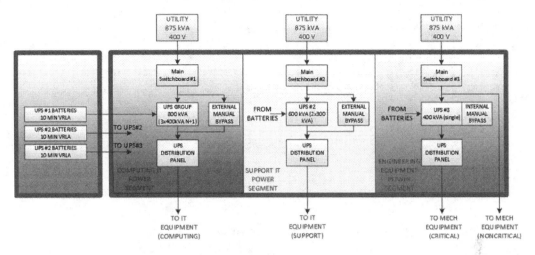

FIGURE 12.12: A typical pair of UPS-battery rooms.

sidering that each UPS can receive power from two mutually redundant transformers, the overall reliability of the system meets the owner's requirements.

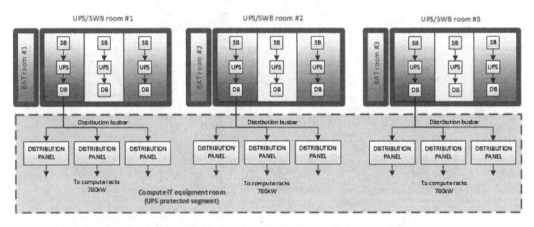

FIGURE 12.13: Power supply plan for computing equipment.

Three independent parallel UPS systems are also used for the auxiliary IT equipment because it requires greater failover capabilities. The topology incorporates a distributed redundancy scheme that was developed in the late 1990s. The topology is based on use of three or more UPS modules with independent input and output feeders (see Figure 12.14).

This system is more economical than a $2N$-redundant configuration while providing the same reliability and availability levels. Cable lines connect each parallel UPS to the auxiliary equipment computer rooms. Thus, the computer room has three UPS-protected switchboards. The IT equipment in these rooms, being mostly dual fed, is divided into three groups, each of which is powered by two switchboards. Single-fed and $N + 1$ devices are connected through a local rack-level ATS.

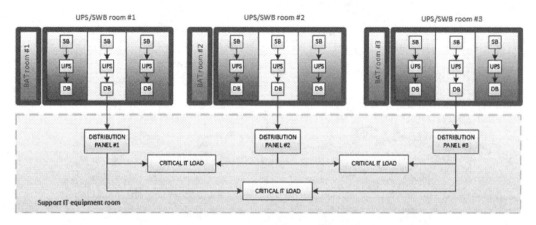

FIGURE 12.14: Power supply plan for auxiliary equipment.

12.7.3 Engineering Equipment

Some of the engineering infrastructure also requires uninterrupted power in order to provide the required fault tolerance. The third UPS system meets this requirement. It consists of five completely independent single UPS. Technological redundancy is fundamental. Redundancy is applied not to the power lines and switchboard equipment but directly to the engineering infrastructure devices.

The number of the UPS in the group (Figure 12.15 shows 3 of 5) determines the maximum redundancy to be $4 + 1$. This system can also provide $3 + 2$ and $2N$ configurations). Most of the protected equipment is at $N + 1$ (see Figure 12.15).

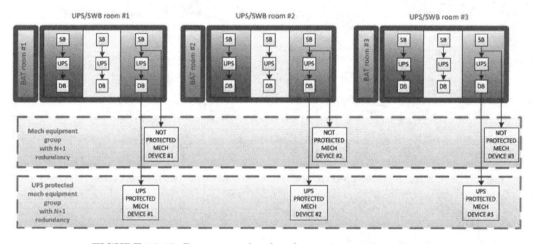

FIGURE 12.15: Power supply plan for engineering equipment.

In general, this architecture allows decommissioning of any power supply or cooling unit, power line, switchboard, UPS, etc., without affecting the serviced IT equipment. Simultaneous duplication of power supply and cooling system components is not necessary.

12.7.4 Overall Cooling System

The Lomonosov-2 supercomputer makes use of a cooling system that consists of two independent segments, each of which is designed for its own type of IT equipment (see

TABLE 12.3: Lomonosov-2 makes use of cooling system consisting of two independent segments.

Excess heat removal system segment	Equipment serviced by segment	Features	Key figures
"Hot" water segment	Computing equipment with direct liquid cooling	• Dry coolers (8 × 1080 with extension up to 10) • No DX cycle • 2-loop system with plate heat exchangers between loops • Coolant supplied directly to IT equipment	Inner loop coolant temperatures: Inbound — +44° Return — +50° Total removed power — up to 8300 kW.
"Cold" water segment	Auxiliary equipment and engineering equipment with air cooling	• External single-block chillers with "free cooling" mode are used (2 × 870 kW with extension up to 3). • 2-loop system with plate heat exchangers between loops (not accounting for internal loops of chillers). • Computer room air is cooled with conditioners	Inner loop coolant temperatures: Inbound — +12° Return — +17° Total removed power — up to 1700 kW.

Table 12.3). Both segments make use of a two-loop scheme with plate heat exchangers between loops. The outer loops have a 40% ethylene-glycol mixture that is used for coolant. Water is used in the inner loops. Both segments have $N + 1$ components ($N + 2$ for dry coolers in the supercomputing segment).

This system, designed to serve the 64 A-class enclosures, has been designated the hot-water segment. It almost completely eliminates the heat from extremely energy-intensive equipment without chillers (see Figure 12.16).

Dry coolers dissipate all the heat that is generated by the supercomputing equipment up to ambient temperatures of +35°C (95°F). Power is required only for the circulation pumps of both loops, dry cooler fans, and automation systems.

Under full load and in the most adverse conditions, the instant PUE would be expected to be about 1.16 for the fully deployed system of 64 A-class racks.

The water in the inner loop has been purified and contains corrosion inhibitors. It is supplied to computer rooms that will contain only liquid-cooled computer enclosures. Since the enclosures do not use computer room air for cooling, the temperature in these rooms is set at 30°C (86°F) and can be raised to 40°C (104°F) without any influence on the equipment performance. The inner loop piping is made of PVC/CPVC (polyvinyl chloride/chlorinated polyvinyl chloride) thus avoiding electrochemical corrosion.

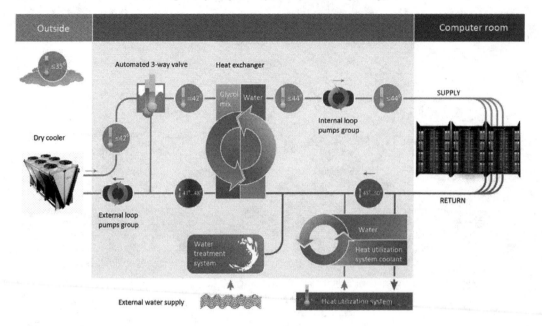

FIGURE 12.16: The "hot" water segment. Cooling system diagram.

12.7.5   Cooling Auxiliary IT Equipment

It is difficult to avoid using air-cooled IT equipment, even in a HPC project, so a separate cold-water [12−17°C (54−63°F)] cooling system was also deployed. The cooling topology in these four spaces is almost identical to the hot-water segment deployed in the A-class rooms, except that chillers are used to dissipate the excess heat from the auxiliary IT spaces to the atmosphere. In the white spaces, temperatures are maintained using isolated hot aisles and in-row cooling units. Instant PUE for this isolated system is about 1.80, which is not a particularly efficient system (see Figure 12.17).

If necessary, some of the capacity of this segment can be used to cool the air in the A-class computing rooms. The capacity of the cooling system in these spaces can meet up to 10% of the total heat inflow in each of the A-class enclosures. Although sealed, they still heat the computer room air through convection. But in fact, passive heat radiation from A-class enclosures is less than 5% of the total power consumed by them.

12.7.6   Emergency Cooling

An emergency-cooling mode exists to deal with utility power input blackouts when both cooling segments are operating on power from the UPS. In emergency mode, each cooling segment has its own requirements. As all units in the first segment (both pump groups, dry coolers, and automation) are connected to the UPS, the system continues to function until the batteries discharge completely.

In the second segment, the UPS services only the inner cooling loop pumps, air conditioners in computer rooms, and automation equipment. The chillers and outer loop pumps are switched off during the blackout.

Since the spaces allocated for cooling equipment are limited, it was impossible to use a more traditional method of stocking cold water at the outlet of the heat exchangers.

Instead, the second segment of the emergency system features accumulator tanks with water stored at a lower temperature than in the loop [about 5°C (41°F) with 12°C (54°F) in

FIGURE 12.17: Lomonosow-2 dry coolers and chillers site.

the loop] to keep system parameters within a predetermined range. Thus, the required tank volume was reduced to 24 m^3 (cubic meters) instead of 75 m^3, which allowed the equipment to fit in the allocated area. A special three-way valve allows mixing of chilled water from the tanks into the loop if necessary (see Figure 12.18). Separate small low-capacity chillers (two 55-kW chillers) are responsible for charging the tanks with cold water. The system charges the cold-water tanks in about the time it takes to charge the UPS batteries.

12.7.7   Efficiency

Usage of the segmented cooling system with high-temperature direct water cooling segment allows reducing its total cost of ownership by approximately 30% compared to data center cooling architectures based on direct expansion (DX) technologies.

12.8   Efficiency of the Supercomputer Center

The Research Computing Center of Lomonosov Moscow State University is developing a set of system tools for performing holistic analysis of supercomputer behavior that is being used on the Lomonosov-2 supercomputer. The main accent is on the efficiency of supercomputer usage in general and different supercomputer applications in particular. The set consists of 6 main software tools each being devoted to study its own particular aspect of supercomputer behavior like supercomputer job flow efficiency, supercomputer resources usage, etc. These tools are shown on Fig. 12.19 (circles), also mentioning supercomputer

FIGURE 12.18: Cold accumulators are used to keep system parameters within predetermined range.

entities that are being studied by them. Currently this set is being used only on MSU supercomputers, but it is portable and freely available to the supercomputer community. All main tools from this set are described below.

Any supercomputer behavior analysis is impossible without collecting enough data about a supercomputer state. There are a number of good existing monitoring systems that are currently being used for this purpose on modern supercomputers, but many of them lack a set of features that will be required in the future. For example, such systems should be scalable to millions of nodes, dynamically reconfigurable, easily expandable, able to deal with BigData problems concerning the amount of collected data. RCC MSU is developing the DiMMon monitoring system [15], having all these requirements in mind. One of the main features of the DiMMon system is dynamic reconfiguration — its operating modes, data path routes, and configuration parameters can be changed dynamically without needing to be restarted. Another useful capability is "on-the-fly analysis", which means that useful information is obtained from the raw monitoring data before being stored to the database. This, for example, enables one to calculate online performance metrics for individual jobs.

The DiMMon monitoring system is mostly aimed at performance monitoring but can be easily used for fitness monitoring as well.

Performance monitoring provides a lot of useful information about dynamics of supercomputer application execution, such as CPU user load, network usage intensity, efficiency of interaction with memory subsystem (e.g., number of cache misses or read/store operations per second), system load average, etc. This information forms the basis for another tool called JobDigest [11].

JobDigest processes monitoring data on a particular supercomputer job and generates a report containing a lot of useful information about this job dynamic behavior. Its main goal is to help users detect any efficiency problem in the particular job run and locate its root cause. For this purpose, JobDigest provides different types of information. The first part of the JobDigest report contains integral dynamic characteristics for a general description of job behavior. These characteristics describe average/minimum/maximum for all characteristics like CPU user load, load average, or memory usage intensity during the

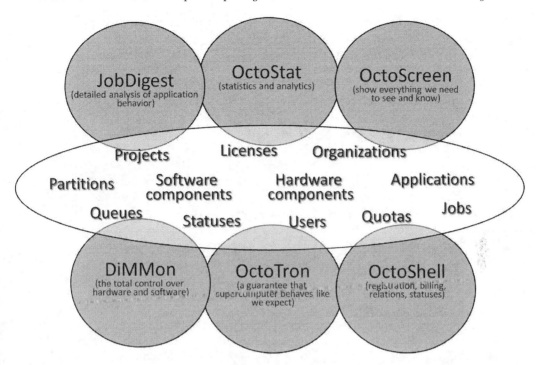

FIGURE 12.19: A set of tools being developed in RCC MSU for supercomputer behavior analysis.

job run. It helps to detect basic issues concerning overall resource usage — was GPU or InfiniBand used in this program, how fully CPU was used during job run, etc.

The second part of JobDigest provides timeline graphs showing the behavior of different characteristics in detail during the job run. Such graphs show, for example, how the value of CPU user load changed over time. This information helps to specify different execution stages in the program run (e.g., initialization, data read/store, main computational part, data exchange between processes, etc) and helps to locate potential performance bottlenecks.

Since performance monitoring data for the whole supercomputer job flow is being constantly collected and stored, JobDigest can provide an analysis report for any job executed on the supercomputer. It should be noted that this tool does not require any code instrumentation or any other actions from the user in order to provide reports.

In order to achieve efficient supercomputer management, it is necessary to analyze not only individual supercomputer applications but the whole supercomputer job flow as well. RCC MSU is developing a number of independent software utilities aimed at studying different aspects of supercomputer job flow behavior.

Each user can himself analyze reports generated by JobDigest for all his executed jobs, but it is a very hard and ineffective way to find possible efficiency issues. So a tool is being developed that is intended to scan through the whole supercomputer job flow and detect abnormally inefficient jobs, comparing to common values for jobs running on this supercomputer [16]. This tool uses performance monitoring data that is provided as an input to machine learning methods that classify each job run as definitely abnormal, normal, or suspicious. Last class means that the job is not surely very inefficient, but it definitely has some performance issues so it should be analyzed in detail. Currently this tool is capable of post-mortem analysis and provides a daily report with found jobs that should be further analyzed. It is planned to implement prompt user notification about found cases of low efficiency in order to operatively cancel jobs if needed.

Another utility is used to understand the efficiency of computational resource usage. It collects data from the resource manager (Slurm [6] is used both on Lomonosov and Lomonosov-2 supercomputers) and provides a variety of different graphs and charts describing resource usage statistics. These statistics show distribution of the amount of CPU*hours consumed by different users, efficiency of used policies and quotas, supercomputer load during different time periods, number of running/waiting jobs, etc. This information helps to evaluate overall efficiency and balance of resource usage.

The main goal of the last utility focused on supercomputer job flow analysis is similar to the previous one. But in this case performance monitoring data is again used, so it is possible to analyze resource usage not only from resource manager point of view, but studying different efficiency characteristics of executed jobs. For example, one can see the list of jobs with least load average value, top "communicative" jobs (most intensive usage of communication network), comparison of partition usage based on CPU user load or memory usage intensity, etc.

An important step to understanding the results obtained by any analysis tool is proper result representation. RCC MSU is developing OctoScreen — a tool suite for handy visualization for every need [13]. It provides a universal framework that is aimed to represent in a browser almost any kind of data about the supercomputer state. It can be used to provide a mobile version of a short digest with the most important information about the current supercomputer state, a timeline graph for system administrators about hardware failures and time spent on their fixing, a distribution of a temperature in the computer room, a geographical map with locations of current supercomputer users, etc.

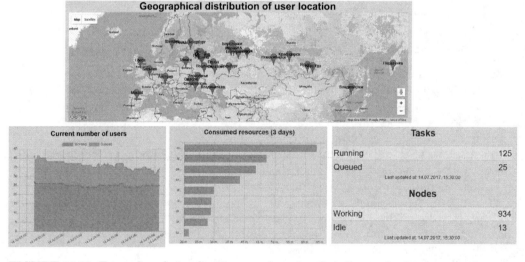

FIGURE 12.20: Examples of visualization graphs using OctoScreen for Lomonosov-2 supercomputer.

Several examples of graphs available for Lomonosov-2 are shown on Figure 12.20. These graphs are part of the "excursion screen" intended to illustrate current supercomputer state during lectures or excursions to the supercomputer center. The top picture shows geographical distribution of users' location. Pictures at the bottom show (from left to right): current number of users with jobs that are currently running/queued on Lomonosov-2 supercomputer; top users by the amount of consumed resources; current statistics on active nodes and tasks.

Efficiency of supercomputer usage also depends on the reliability of supercomputer hardware and software components. In order to achieve efficient management it is important to control everything and to react promptly to any emergency situation. That is the reason RCC MSU is developing Octotron system [8] (available on Github [4]). Octotron is based on a formal model of the supercomputer, which describes in detail all supercomputer components and their interconnection. This model can be referred as "theory", describing the way the supercomputer is expected to behave. The "practice" can be described in a usual way by the means of monitoring systems. The main goal of the Octotron system is to constantly compare "theory" and "practice" and react accordingly in case anything does not match. Such an approach allows the detection not only of simple emergency situations (like hardware component failure or overheating, or software service not working) but also more complex cases that require analysis of a set of conditions. For example, Octotron can detect component operating modes mismatch, which may occur in the case of different modes on two ports of one Ethernet cable, or control ratio between number of failed and working sensors for checking temperature in the hot aisle.

The model is represented as a graph with different SW/HW components as vertices and their dependencies as edges. Edges can be of different types: "contain", "power", "infiniband", etc. Each vertex or edge can include a number of attributes each describing one element that should be controlled. Detected mismatches are described as a set of rules that check specific correlation between values described in "theory" (formal model) and "practice" (monitoring data). If a rule is violated, a specified reaction is triggered. There are different types of automatic reactions available in Octotron: logging, SMS/email notification of system administrators, equipment shutdown, restarting software services, or executing custom administrator scripts.

Control of supercomputer usage efficiency and reliability is an essential part of efficient supercomputer management. Another important part is convenient work management. System administrators are often required to install and maintain a whole set of different independent software tools intended to solve particular issues — user management, support (ticket management, forums, wiki,...), resource management, service monitoring, etc. This is a complex task that usually leads to a lot of manual operations, consistency errors, and bad portability.

The OctoShell system [12] developed in RCC MSU is intended to help solve this task. It works as a single entry point for every type of user (common users, administrators, management) working on mentioned services. This helps to automate different standard routines and easily maintain consistency. OctoShell is used as a primary work management tool in the MSU Supercomputer center for project management, providing and managing access, equipment service, user support, etc. Currently OctoShell is used by more than 600 active projects and helps to resolve ~1000 user requests per year. The OctoShell system is open source and can be found on Github [3].

The fundamental problem of high-performance computing is the necessity for accurate coordination of algorithm and program structure with hardware features leading to high efficiency. Capabilities of modern computers are great, but if there is no coordination between the algorithmic implementation on the given hardware platform, the resulting efficiency of the implementation can be very low. But main features of algorithms are independent from any computational system. From this point of view a detailed description of an algorithm's features is essential. The AlgoWiki project [5, 9] started with deployment of the Lomonosov-2 supercomputer is an open encyclopedia of algorithms' properties and features of their implementations on different hardware and software platforms from mobile to extreme scale, which allows for collaboration with the worldwide computing community on algorithm descriptions.

Bibliography

[1] A list of Top50 most powerful supercomputers in Russia and CIS. http://top50.supercomputers.ru.

[2] Moscow University Supercomputing Center. http://hpc.msu.ru.

[3] Octoshell source code. https://github.com/octoshell/octoshell-v2.

[4] Octotron framework source code. https://github.com/srcc-msu/octotron.

[5] Open Encyclopedia of Parallel Algorithmic Features. http://algowiki-project.org.

[6] Slurm — cluster management and job scheduling system. https://slurm.schedmd.com.

[7] xCAT. http://xcat.org/.

[8] A. Antonov, D. Nikitenko, P. Shvets, S. Sobolev, K. Stefanov, Vad. Voevodin, Vl. Voevodin, and S. Zhumatiy. An approach for ensuring reliable functioning of a supercomputer based on a formal model. In *Parallel Processing and Applied Mathematics. 11th International Conference, PPAM 2015, Krakow, Poland, September 6-9, 2015. Revised Selected Papers, Part I*, volume 9573 of *Lecture Notes in Computer Science*, pages 12–22. Springer International Publishing, 2016.

[9] A. Antonov, V. Voevodin, and J. Dongarra. Algowiki: an Open encyclopedia of parallel algorithmic features. *Supercomputing Frontiers and Innovations*, 2(1):4–18, 2015.

[10] A. Brechalov. Moscow State University Meets Provides a Facility That Meets HPC Demands. *Uptime Institute Journal*, 6:50, 2016.

[11] B. Mohr, E. Hagersten, J. Gimenez, A. Knupfer, D. Nikitenko, M. Nilsson, H. Servat, A. Shah, Vl. Voevodin, F. Winkler, F. Wolf, and I. Zhukov. The HOPSA Workflow and Tools. In *Proceedings of the 6th International Parallel Tools Workshop, Stuttgart, 2012*, volume 11, pages 127–146. Springer, 2012.

[12] D.A. Nikitenko, Vad.V. Voevodin, and S.A. Zhumatiy. Octoshell: Large supercomputer complex administration system. In *Proceedings of the 1st Russian Conference on Supercomputing — Supercomputing Days 2015*, volume 1482 of *CEUR Workshop Proceedings*, pages 69–83, 2015.

[13] D.A. Nikitenko, S.A. Zhumatiy, and P.A. Shvets. Making Large-Scale Systems Observable — Another Inescapable Step Towards Exascale. *Supercomputing Frontiers and Innovations*, 3(2):72–79, 2016.

[14] V. Sadovnichy, A. Tikhonravov, Vl Voevodin, and V. Opanasenko. Lomonosov: Supercomputing at Moscow State University. In *Contemporary High Performance Computing: From Petascale toward Exascale*, Chapman & Hall/CRC Computational Science, pages 283–307, Boca Raton, United States, 2013.

[15] K.S. Stefanov, Vl.V. Voevodin, S.A. Zhumatiy, and Vad.V. Voevodin. Dynamically Reconfigurable Distributed Modular Monitoring System for Supercomputers (DiMMon). volume 66 of *Procedia Computer Science*, pages 625–634. Elsevier B.V., 2015.

[16] Vl.V. Voevodin, Vad.V. Voevodin, D.I. Shaikhislamov, and D.A. Nikitenko. Data mining method for anomaly detection in the supercomputer task flow. In *Numerical Computations: Theory and Algorithms, The 2nd International Conference and Summer School, Pizzo calabro, Italy, June 20-24, 2016*, volume 1776 of *AIP Conference Proceedings*, 2016.

Chapter 13

Electra: A Modular-Based Expansion of NASA's Supercomputing Capability

Rupak Biswas

NASA Ames Research Center

Jeff Becker, Davin Chan, David Ellsworth, and Robert Hood

CSRA LLC—NASA Ames Research Center

Piyush Mehrotra

NASA Ames Research Center

Michelle Moyer, Chris Tanner

CSRA LLC—NASA Ames Research Center

William Thigpen

NASA Ames Research Center

13.1   Introduction

NASA has increasingly relied on high-performance computing (HPC) resources for computational modeling, simulation, and data analysis to meet the science and engineering goals of its missions in space exploration, aeronautics, and Earth and space science. The NASA Advanced Supercomputing (NAS) Division at Ames Research Center in Silicon Valley, Calif., hosts NASA's premier supercomputing resources, integral to achieving and enhancing the success of the agency's missions. NAS provides a balanced environment, funded under the High-End Computing Capability (HECC) project, comprised of world-class supercomputers, including its flagship distributed-memory cluster, Pleiades; high-speed networking; and massive data storage facilities, along with multi-disciplinary support teams for user support, code porting and optimization, and large-scale data analysis and scientific visualization.

However, as scientists have increased the fidelity of their simulations and engineers are conducting larger parameter-space studies, the requirements for supercomputing resources have been growing by leaps and bounds. With the facility housing the HECC systems reaching its power and cooling capacity, NAS undertook a prototype project to investigate an alternative approach for housing supercomputers. Modular supercomputing, or container-based computing, is an innovative concept for expanding NASA's HPC capabilities. With modular supercomputing, additional containers—similar to portable storage pods—can be connected together as needed to accommodate the agency's ever-increasing demand for computing resources. In addition, taking advantage of the local weather permits the use of cooling technologies that would additionally save energy and reduce annual water usage.

The first stage of NASA's Modular Supercomputing Facility (MSF) prototype, which resulted in a 1,000 square-foot module on a concrete pad with room for 16 compute racks, was completed in Fall 2016 and an SGI (now HPE) computer system, named Electra, was deployed there in early 2017. Cooling is performed via an evaporative system built into the module, and preliminary experience shows a Power Usage Effectiveness (PUE) measurement of 1.03. Electra achieved over a petaflop on the LINPACK benchmark, sufficient to rank number 96 on the November 2016 TOP500 list [14]. The system consists of 1,152 InfiniBand-connected Intel Xeon Broadwell-based nodes. Its users access their files on a facility-wide filesystem shared by all HECC compute assets via Mellanox MetroX InfiniBand extenders, which connect the Electra fabric to Lustre routers in the primary facility over fiber-optic links about 900 feet long. The MSF prototype has exceeded expectations and is serving as a blueprint for future expansions.

In the remainder of this chapter, we detail how modular data center technology can be used to expand an existing compute resource. We begin by describing NASA's requirements for supercomputing and how resources were provided prior to the integration of the Electra module-based system.

13.2   NASA Requirements for Supercomputing

NASA's research-oriented science and aeronautics projects rely on very large-scale, high-fidelity simulations to advance the understanding of a broad spectrum of topics, such as Earth's weather and climate, galaxy formation, solar magnetic fields, and complex aircraft aerodynamics. Some of these intensive simulations require system capabilities that can handle long-running computations using upwards of 70,000 cores each, utilizing a sizable portion (25% or more) of the system at one time. The system must also support more than 1,500 users and be able to run hundreds of jobs simultaneously; individual jobs must not adversely affect the performance of other jobs that are also being executed. In addition, NASA's engineering-oriented efforts, such as launch and crew exploration vehicle development, often require high-throughput system capacities to rapidly process large sets of moderate-scale computations—typically, 500–4,000 cores each—in order to analyze a wide range of flight conditions and vehicle design variations.

The high demand for compute resources and the need to meet mission critical deadlines mean that any downtime related to maintenance activities must be minimized. High availability is also required for time-sensitive, mission-critical analyses that can be performed on demand—for example, immediate analyses of anomalous events during space missions, such as debris strikes, or timely weather prediction analyses that can aid preparations for dangerous storms.

NASA's HECC users run more than 1000 applications covering various programming paradigms and languages, and numerous classes of algorithms, data structures, and communication/memory access patterns. Of these, 12 applications are responsible for approximately 50% of the resource usage. The performance of these key applications—used heavily in aerospace vehicle design and Earth and space sciences research—must be taken into careful consideration when selecting system and processor types, hardware architectures, storage and filesystems configurations, and so on. In addition, to handle an increasing and evolving workload over time, the system must be expandable while still providing a consistent user interface over its lifetime.

Collectively, these diverse NASA project needs, analysis applications, and access requirements drive many of the key decisions to procure, configure, and regularly upgrade the agency's supercomputing systems. In the next section, we describe the capability into which the new MSF and Electra system were integrated.

13.3   Supercomputing Capabilities: Conventional Facilities

13.3.1   Computer Systems

Prior to deploying the MSF, the NAS supercomputing resources comprised four platforms, all manufactured by SGI (now HPE):

- Pleiades: NASA's flagship supercomputer, a distributed-memory cluster containing four generations of Intel processors (described in more detail below).

- Endeavour: A shared-memory, single system image (SSI) computer that replaced the Columbia SSI cluster, which was the predecessor to Pleiades.

- Merope: A system containing older processor nodes removed from Pleiades to accommodate its expansion, located about a mile from the main NAS facility.

- hyperwall: A 128-node visualization cluster with a wall of 128 screens arranged in an 8x16 configuration.

The initial deployment of Pleiades, in 2008, comprised 100 racks with 12,800 quad-core Intel Xeon E5472 (Harpertown) processors. At 487 teraflops (TF) (LINPACK), it was the third-most powerful supercomputer in the world at that time. Subsequent expansions added Intel X5570 (Nehalem), X5670 (Westmere), E5-2760 (Sandy Bridge), E5-2680v2 (Ivy Bridge), E5-2680v3 (Haswell), and E5-2680v4 (Broadwell) multi-core processors. Currently, Pleiades comprises 160 racks (11,440 nodes) containing Sandy Bridge, Ivy Bridge, Haswell, and Broadwell processors, and is ranked 15th in the world at 5.95 petaflops (LINPACK). [13]

As Pleiades has grown, racks that were removed to accommodate the new ones were repurposed into a smaller cluster, Merope, situated in a remote building approximately one mile from the primary NAS facility. [10] Currently, Merope consists of 56 half-populated racks containing 1,792 Westmere compute nodes. Merope is connected to Pleiades through a long-distance InfiniBand network that also allows it to share storage with the other NAS systems. This storage-sharing architecture is important to note, as it provides the basis for a similar scheme used between Pleiades and the MSF. The architecture is described in more detail below.

13.3.2 Interconnect

A Pleiades rack consists of four individual rack units (IRUs), each split into two halves. Each half-IRU has nine compute nodes connected to a single Fourteen Data Rate (FDR) InfiniBand (IB) switch. Because each node has two IB ports—either a dual-port host-channel adapter (HCA) or two single-port HCAs—the second port is connected to a separate IB switch on a second plane. The first IB plane is used for MPI traffic, while the second plane is primarily used for I/O. Both planes are similar hypercubes, so we only describe the construction of the first plane.

Each IB switch is a vertex of a hypercube. The first dimension is built by connecting the two switches in each IRU. Neighboring IRUs are connected on the second dimension, followed by connections between the top IRU pair and the bottom IRU pair in each rack. Neighboring racks are connected on the fourth dimension, and so on. In total, the 160 racks of Pleiades are interconnected in a partial 12-dimension hypercube. Both IB planes are managed using the OpenSM subnet manager from Mellanox OFED. The subnet manager uses the dimension-order routing (DOR) algorithm to program the IB switch forwarding tables. This algorithm uses the Min Hop techniques to pick the shortest route and breaks ties by choosing the lowest-numbered dimension.

13.3.3 Network Connectivity

The NAS high-speed routed data network connects multiple components within the primary NAS facility and the external location containing Merope, but also provides system

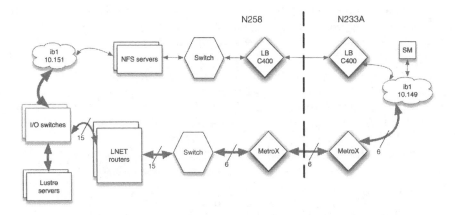

FIGURE 13.1: Components connecting Merope's compute nodes in Building 233A to user filesystems in Building N258, the primary NAS facility.

access to external users. Each month, users move hundreds of terabytes of data over this network that has three major elements: enclave, core, and border. The enclave directly connects the Pleiades compute systems and major subsystems, supporting the overall administrative and IT security requirements. The core provides high-speed Local Area Network (LAN) connectivity for users to access compute resources and services, as well as private networks for system administrators and public-facing networks such as web servers. This LAN has a 10-Gigabit Ethernet (GigE) backbone consisting of many subnets for NAS support functions. The border provides high-speed wide area network (WAN) connections to NASA networks and other partner sites for access by remote users. This advanced peering environment includes 10-GigE connectivity to the NASA Integrated Communications Services (NICS) backbone, and dedicated 10-GigE connectivity to the Jet Propulsion Laboratory and Goddard Space Flight Center.

13.3.4   Storage Resources

NAS provides both Network File System (NFS) storage for home filesystems and software packages, and high-performance Lustre filesystems for reading and writing from HPC jobs. [6] There are six Lustre filesystems, each with between 84 and 312 object storage targets (OSTs), providing a total storage pool of between seven and 19 petabytes (PB) per filesystem. Both the NFS and Lustre servers are connected via InfiniBand (QDR for NFS, FDR for Lustre) to a four-dimensional hypercube of 16 FDR IB switches. This torus has connections throughout Pleiades on the I/O plane, and also to Endeavour and the hyperwall. (Note that the I/O IB plane is a single InfiniBand subnet.) In order to permit DOR to route between three hypercubes—Pleiades, the I/O switch bank, and the hyperwall—NASA engineers worked with SGI (now HPE) to add weights to selective links in the fabric. Each weight (an integer > 1) multiplies the effective distance (number of hops) of the associated link. Since DOR favors shorter paths, this enables the routing to favor paths free of deadlock cycles.

Merope, located in the auxiliary NAS facility in Building 233A, also requires access to the NFS and Lustre filesystems in Building N258, the primary facility. However, since it has its own compute and I/O subnets, a different connection method is required, as shown in Figure 13.1.

In the case of NFS, each server is connected to a QDR IB switch. The latter is then connected to an Obsidian Longbow InfiniBand Range Extender, which connects to a second Longbow next to Merope via approximately 1.2 miles of optical fiber. Finally, this Longbow connects to Merope's I/O plane to allow the sharing of NFS filesystems with Pleiades. For Lustre, several routers (called "LNET routers" in Figure 13.1), which have two IB ports, are used to bridge between Pleiades' I/O plane and Merope's. The Pleiades side of each Lustre router is connected to a Mellanox MetroX long-haul IB switch, which is connected via optical fiber to another MetroX switch that is situated next to Merope. The Lustre connection is completed by several connections between this MetroX switch and Merope's I/O plane.

In addition to the NFS and Lustre filesystems, NAS storage resources include a 525 PB tape system that enables reliable and secure archiving and rapid retrieval. User data is written to two separate tape media in silos located in different buildings. Data migration is managed via SGI's Data Migration Facility (DMF) and OpenVault.

The mass storage system, an SGI parallel DMF cluster with high-availability clustering software, consists of four 32-processor front-end systems with 64 gigabytes (GB) of memory each; 2.9 PB of locally attached SATA RAID Spectra Logic tape storage (525 PB maximum capacity with normal 35-percent compression); six TFinity tape libraries; and 92 LTO-7 tape drives.

13.3.5 Visualization and Hyperwall

The NAS facility's hyperwall, shown in Figure 13.2, is composed of 128 nodes containing NVIDIA GeForce GTX 780 Ti graphics processing units (GPUs) and Intel Xeon Ivy Bridge processor cores, connected to 128 tiled LCD display screens arranged in a wall measuring 23 feet wide by 10 feet high. It has a peak processing power of 57 TF, and directly accesses the NAS facility's online disk storage. [8]

The NAS-developed concurrent visualization framework enables realtime graphical processing and display on the hyperwall while applications are running. This capability is needed to support the visualization of very large datasets that are challenging to store, transfer, and view in their entirety, and provides results that are immediately available for analysis. The framework also enables animations to be rendered and stored showing every time step in the simulation, which allows researchers to see rapid processes in their models—often for the first time—and identify computational problems or optimize parameters on the fly. Production data can be transferred live from the supercomputer to the hyperwall without slowing code performance. A new interactive data analysis tool for the hyperwall, recently developed by the NAS Visualization and Data Analysis team, is described in Section 13.10.

13.3.6 Primary NAS Facility

Constructed in 1985, the primary NAS facility at NASA Ames Research Center is a steel-frame two-story structure with steel-reinforced concrete floor, built to sustain shear loads consistent with the force of a magnitude 8.0+ earthquake. The raised floor includes 15,000 square feet of primary computer floor.

The facility's chiller system has a capacity of 1,800 tons and is capable of achieving a water temperature of 42°F. An intricate plumbing topology and a pumping system able to sustain flow rates in excess of 4000 gallons per minute (gpm) are used to deliver cooling in a precise and efficient manner. The heat load is ultimately ejected to the cooling tower, which uses evaporative and drip technology to lower the water temperature before returning it to the chillers. Electrical consumption by HECC resources at the NAS facility hovers at the current building capacity of 6 megawatts (MW). Electrical service arrives at 13.8 kilo-

FIGURE 13.2: The 128-screen hyperwall, showing part of a visualization of a global ocean circulation simulation (described in Section 13.10).

volts (kV), and is transformed and delivered to electrical switchgear at 480 volts (V) for the HECC systems and 2.4 kV for the chillers. A series of rotary uninterruptible power supplies (RUPS) serve as a backup. All electrical and mechanical infrastructure components, including chillers, pumps, and the cooling tower, are managed by a building management system for electrical efficiency through switchgear, motor control centers, and variable-speed motors.

13.4   Modular Supercomputing Facility

13.4.1   Limitations of the Primary NAS Facility

In its current configuration, Pleiades stresses the primary NAS facility's engineering thresholds in almost every infrastructure category, as the increased processor and memory density of each system augmentation has resulted in more power, cooling, and floor loading requirements. Starting with the integration of new Haswell-based nodes in 2015, the facility could no longer support the power and cooling requirements of new compute nodes without the removal of older-generation nodes that were still cost effective to run. The early retirement of productive nodes effectively drove up the cost of providing additional compute resources.

The HECC project predicts that NASA's requirements for supercomputing capabilities will continue to grow exponentially over time, as the agency leverages HPC to pursue its challenging missions. To meet these requirements, HECC must continue to provide the funding needed to upgrade and replace the supercomputing resources that NAS hosts for the agency. It is critical, therefore, for NAS to realize the full value of adding new compute resources by overcoming the limitations of its current facility space.

13.4.2   Expansion and Integration Strategy

Once it was determined that additional facility space and resources were required for HECC to expand its supercomputing services, NASA commissioned a trade-off study to evaluate its options: (1) restructure the existing NAS facility; (2) construct a new building;

(3) move compute resources offsite to a larger, existing data center; (4) utilize commercial HPC cloud resources; or (5) install a quickly deployable modular data center (MDC). Results indicated that the fastest, most cost-effective approach would be to deploy an MDC. As a lower-risk approach before committing to a large-scale facility, NASA decided to develop a proof-of-concept project, known as the Modular Supercomputing Facility (MSF), with the goals that the system should:

- Represent the most cost-effective way of delivering compute resources that enable science and engineering returns to NASA;

- Be capable of operating in an energy-efficient and environmentally friendly manner; and

- Interoperate with existing InfiniBand-connected Lustre and NFS filesystems in the primary NAS facility.

Potential vendors were asked to propose strategies for a flexible, energy-efficient approach that would meet the project goals. Once the contractors were selected, construction and deployment tasks were divided between two teams. The infrastructure team—a partnership between Cyber Professional Solutions and AECOM—was responsible for concrete slab construction and installation of site utilities, power, water, and drainage. The computer/MDC vendor team—a partnership between SGI, the computer vendor; CommScope, the MDC integrator; and Saiver, the MDC manufacturer—was responsible for module and computer installation, as well as post-installation maintenance.

13.4.3 Site Preparation

The NAS team decided to install the prototype MSF on a 4000-square-foot lot across the street from the primary NAS facility—a distance of about 300 feet. The site is located about a mile from the southern end of San Francisco Bay, so initial groundwork included flood mitigation, including raising the level of the site. Utility duct banks and water lines were installed to connect the site to existing utilities, and a 45x50-foot, 16-inch-thick concrete slab foundation was poured, designed to hold two MDCs weighing up to 135,000 lbs. each. Due to the site's earthquake-prone location, the module was welded to thick steel weld pads embedded in the foundation.

Transformer and switchgear were set onto the slab over conduits for power conductors, which were run under and up through the slab. Power is delivered to the MSF site via 15 kV-rated conductors directly fed from a dedicated breaker in the Ames Research Center substation to a 2,800 kilovolt-amp (kVA) transformer at the site. The transformer steps down from 13.8 kV to 415 V, 3-phase power, which is then distributed through the switchgear; each module has its own dedicated breaker. Ten sets of 750-kcmil conductors run from the transformer secondary to the switchgear main breaker, and four sets of 500-kcmil conductors run from the switchgear into the module's electrical panel.

13.4.4 Module Design

The MDC draws outside air into each end of the module via two fan banks of 12 centrifugal fans each. The air is filtered—and conditioned if required—before it travels into two separate cold aisles and through the racks, and then exhausted into a common hot aisle in the middle of the module for release back to the outdoors.

A programmable logic controller (PLC) controls the operating environment, adjusting dampers for recirculation of hot air, solenoid valves to run water through the evaporative cooler, and fan speeds based on temperature and pressure sensors located inside and outside of the module. Power meters measure total power draw for the module and each of the four Starline busways that feed the compute racks.

The MDC is capable of holding twenty 24-inch wide racks, in two rows of ten each. For our installation, we installed only 18 racks—16 compute racks and two I/O racks—with two blanking panels (to control air circulation) at the end of each cold aisle. The module's four busways each feed power to four compute racks. Each compute rack is powered by two 415 volts-AC (VAC), 3-phase feeds through IEC309 32A, 5-pin connectors. The power distribution units (PDUs) within the rack distribute the 415 V, 3-phase input as 240 VAC single-phase to the 16 power supplies in the rack that output 12 volts-DC (VDC) to the compute and fans. Powering the module at 415 V, 3-phase eliminates the electrical losses associated with the traditional 480–208 V step-down that occur in the the primary facility (Building N258), saving 12 kW.

While the San Francisco Bay Area's weather is mild, there are days when the outside temperature cannot meet the ideal cold aisle settings of 15–27°C (59–81°F). Fortunately, hot days are almost always complemented with low relative humidity, and cooling the supply air can easily be accomplished with an evaporative cooler. When the outside air temperature exceeds 27°C, the air is drawn through an evaporative media—an impregnated glass fiber, honeycomb-like material that has been saturated with water. The heat in the air evaporates the water as it passes through the media, raising the humidity of the air stream and lowering the air temperature. With a maximum cold aisle temperature of 27°C, evaporative cooling will be needed approximately 300 hours per year, requiring an average of about 3.5 gallons per minute of water—for an average yearly water consumption of about 65,000 gallons.

Solenoid valves control the wetting of the evaporative media by pulsing on and off to limit waste. The evaporative cooler has four columns of media, and the PLC controls which columns to wet to provide the proper amount of cooling. The water is run through the evaporative media only once without the use of any water treatment, which allows it to be drained into the center storm drain system. Measurements show that the amount of water lost due to evaporation or drainage in the module is 5% of the amount that would be needed if the compute racks were installed in the conventionally cooled primary NAS facility.

On cold days below 15°C (59°F), the air in the hot aisle can recirculate back to mix with the incoming supply air to increase the air temperature and/or lower the relative humidity (RH) below the 80% maximum setting. In the Bay Area, the recirculating configuration is quite common, as the outside supply is at or above 15°C/80% RH or less for half of the yearly hours.

13.4.5   Power, Cooling, Network

The MDC is controlled by the PLC, which queries sensors throughout the module and makes adjustments to maintain the internal environment within the set operating parameters. Access to the operational control is provided through a user interface (UI) that displays the current module conditions on monitors in three places: inside the module; in the main control room of the primary facility; and in the engineering office. The UI displays detailed measurements for temperature sensors, fan performance, and power/voltage/current draw. The data provided is sampled every 10 seconds and stored in a log file for trending and evaluation. The computer system's power draw is typically about 300 kW, averaging 20–22 kW per rack. (For comparison, LINPACK testing was conducted with an average power consumption of 439 kW). At 22 kW per rack, the fans on the backs of the racks are moving 3,000 cubic feet per minute (CFM) of air per rack. Originally, the racks were not sealed for a tight cold-aisle/hot-aisle configuration, and the module's supply fans had to be overdriven to overpressurize the cold aisle and to keep air from the hot aisle from being drawn back into the cold aisle by the rack fans. When the racks were first powered on to run diagnostic tests, there were several instances where nodes powered off due to overheating because the module's fans were set too low. While overpressurizing the cold aisle was effective in cooling the nodes, it was to the detriment of total power consumption. For the initial setup, depending on how conservative the control parameters were, fan power ranged from 15–45 kW.

Subtle changes were made to the module that improved air management and lowered the fan power. Large metal mesh debris filters in the exhaust airflow of the module were removed to reduce pressure in the hot aisle. Open spaces between the I/O racks and the adjacent compute racks were sealed with large blanking panels. The decorative openings in the top sheet metal enclosure above each rack to contain cables were sealed. The gap between the floor and the rack bottom as well as the gap between the rack sides and module's wall were also sealed. Finally, the open area above the top nodes was blanked off, basically extending the top of the rack. After these changes were made, processor temperature testing was conducted to determine the best operating settings.

The target processor temperature is 70°C, which is a typical high temperature on a 22 kW Broadwell rack in the 20°C (68°F) primary computer room floor. For temperature testing, diagnostic software was run to provide a stable power load on each processor. The total power load was 400 kW (25 kW per rack), about 15% higher than a typical workload. SGI rack management software recorded the processor and air intake temperatures, while the module's PLC recorded airflow. The nodes at the top of the rack are most affected by poor air separation, with hot air spilling over the top of the rack. By setting the module's fans to supply 43,000–45,000 CFM (air flow total to two cold aisles), processor temperatures drop below the 70°C target. When module supply airflow drops below 40,000 CFM, the compute rack fans pull air from the hot aisle to meet their 48,000 CFM requirement (16 racks at 3,000 CFM per rack). Increasing airflow continues to reduce processor temperature, but at the cost of additional fan power. To keep fan power at a minimum, the module is operated at 43,000 CFM, which requires 8 kW of power.

13.4.6   Facility Operations and Maintenance

In this section we present more detailed information about recent operating trends. The data is representative of the facility's performance since it went into production in January 2017.

While the cold aisle temperature increased slightly as summer progressed, we did not need to change our operating parameters from previous months, other than an increase in the running of water. Testing of the evaporative system has shown that passing water over the evaporative media does not require an increase in fan power to improve airflow.

Current operating settings for the cold aisle are a temperature range of 15–27°C (59–81°F) with relative humidity at 20–80%. The lowest airflow setting is 43,000 CFM, which is a setting of 40% fan speed in the PLC, drawing only 350 watts per fan. The airflow will never drop below this setting and will only increase when the hot aisle exceeds 44.5°C (112°F). A 44.5°C hot aisle means that the difference between the cold aisle and hot aisle temperatures, Delta T, is 17.5°C (31°F), at the maximum cold aisle of 27°C.

Electra's Power Effect on Delta T: With the module's fans set to a constant airflow of 43,000 CFM, the hot aisle/cold aisle Delta T is dependent on Electra's power consumption. The Delta T trends at 15–16°C for normal workloads of 350 kW. For the module's control logic, Delta T is not limited until the hot aisle temperature exceeds 44.5°C, at which time the airflow will increase to maintain the hot aisle maximum setting. It should be noted that hot aisle control is just one of five fan strategy programs that can be used to control the module's environment. Each program controls airflow and Delta T in slightly different ways. Because of the significant airflow on the rack fans, hot aisle control has been identified

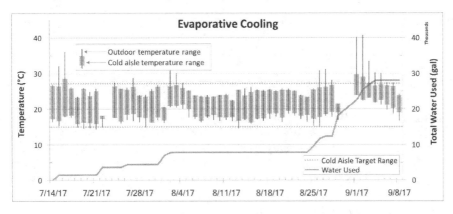

FIGURE 13.3: Evaporative cooling in the MSF over an eight-week period.

as the best fit for our application, but other strategies may be considered as experience is gained from more operating time with the module.

Damper Settings Dependent on Outside Temperature: The module's dampers adjust to maintain a constant cold aisle temperature over a fluctuating outside temperature. When the outside temperature falls, the outside air damper changes from 100% to 20% open while the recirculating air damper acts in a complementary fashion and changes from 95% to 65% closed (35% open). The adjustable dampers allow for a 16°C cold aisle temperature while the outside air varies from 5° to 20°C.

The dampers also adjust to maintain the cold aisle humidity, even if it means raising the cold aisle temperature. In cases where the outside air is within the cold aisle range of 15-27°C, but the outside air relative humidity is over 80%—such as on a rainy day—the recirculating air damper will open to mix hotter air with the incoming air to lower the relative humidity below the set point. In the Bay Area, 27°C dry-bulb temperature days with 80% humidity do not occur, so there is little concern about inability to control the humidity in the module.

Cold Aisle Temperature Compared to Outside Temperature: Figure 13.3 compares the cold aisle temperature ranges on a daily basis with the outside temperature ranges over an eight-week period. For this data set, the cold aisle temperature was set to range between 15–27.2°C (59–81°F). As shown in the chart, the cold aisle ranges generally match the outside ranges; where they do not match, the "Water Used" line shows the effectiveness of the adiabatic system. At the extreme in early September, the outside temperature rose above 40°C on two days. While the adiabatic system was not able to keep the cold aisle temperature in the target range, it did keep it below 30°C. This increases our confidence in the MDC's ability to maintain a cold aisle maximum that is well below the 40+°C set point, at which compute nodes will start to shut themselves off due to heat.

13.4.7 Environmental Impact

As mentioned previously, an important selection criterion for the MSF prototype was that it must be environmentally friendly. The existing NAS supercomputer facility is a traditional data center that uses a chilled water loop for heat transfer from the computer floor. With a constant compute power load of 4.0 MW, Building N258 uses approximately 1.0 MW to power the chillers and cooling tower that cool the computer systems. In addition to its power usage, the cooling system consumes an average of 50,000 gallons of water per day.

Fortunately, the weather in the Bay Area is very temperate and for most hours of the day, the outdoor air temperature is sufficiently cool for computer operation. The MSF prototype design procured by the NAS team is able to exploit the local weather to reduce both water usage and the power needed for cooling.

The Electra system uses an unusual combination of outdoor air and fan technology to remove the heat it generates, and consumes less than 10% of the energy used in traditional supercomputing facilities. As a result, the system has achieved a power usage effectiveness (PUE) rating of 1.03—well below the computing industry standard of 1.7 PUE. The PUE is a measurement that reflects the ratio of energy used by the computing equipment to energy used to power the entire data center, including cooling, lighting, and staff workstations.

The system's power draw varies from a low of 250 kW to a high of 360 kW; the PUE is consistently under 1.03 when Electra is performing a typical workload of 300 kW or higher. Because the module's non-compute power consumption is constant at 8 kW, the PUE only rises above 1.03 when the batch processing system is collecting nodes to run a large job or nodes are taken out of service for system testing. When compared to the resources that would be used if Electra were installed in the conventionally cooled primary NAS facility, this translates to a savings of more than a million kilowatt-hours of energy each year— enough to power five Broadwell racks—and a reduction of more than a million gallons in annual water usage.

13.5 Electra Supercomputer

The computational system installed in the MDC is known as Electra. It consists of 1,152 nodes, installed in 16 racks, and has a theoretical peak performance of 1.24 PF. Each node has two 14-core, 2.4-GHz Intel E5-2680v4 (Broadwell) processor chips and 128 GB of memory. There are 4 IRUs in each rack, with 18 compute nodes per IRU. For every two racks, there is a rack leader controlling them. The nodes are interconnected via two independent FDR InfiniBand fabrics in a hypercube topology. I/O traffic is isolated to the ib1 fabric and MPI/system communication is primarily on the ib0 fabric.

The compute system is mostly self-contained within the module, but from a user perspective, it has been tightly integrated with the Pleiades system in Building N258. Electra users log into Pleiades front ends, and their batch jobs have full access to the NFS and Lustre filesystems, which are located in the primary compute facility and shared by all HECC resources. A single Portable Batch System (PBS) server manages all of the jobs for Pleiades as well as Electra; user jobs are routed to the appropriate system by specifying the hardware model types associated with each system.

13.5.1 Performance

On its very first attempt in October 2016—6 weeks after the start of module assembly— Electra achieved an Rmax of 1.096 PF on the LINPACK benchmark. This was sufficient to place it in the top 100 systems in the November 2016 edition of the TOP500 list. [14] While facility information is not available for some systems in the TOP500 list, we believe Electra to be the top system in the list that is module-based. On the High Performance Conjugate Gradients (HPCG) benchmark, Electra measured 25.2 TF, sufficient to place the system at number 46 in the world on the November 2016 edition of the HPCG list. [7]

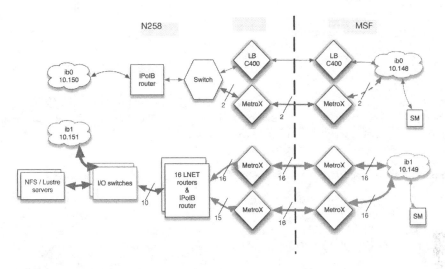

FIGURE 13.4: Components connecting Electra's compute nodes in the MSF to user filesystems in Building N258, the primary NAS facility.

13.5.2   I/O Subsystem Architecture

The cluster management infrastructure used to provision and manage Pleiades and Electra utilizes the same software and hardware components, so the two supercomputers can be managed as a single instance rather than two independent systems. This reduces the amount of required hardware and labor, and maintains consistency between the systems. Although they are highly integrated, the systems are distinct from the user's perspective: jobs are not allowed to span the two systems due to bandwidth limitations.

As shown in Figure 13.4, access to the HECC filesystems is facilitated through Lustre and IP routers connected via Mellanox MetroX long-haul InfiniBand switches and Obsidian Longbow InfiniBand range extenders. As discussed in Section 13.3.2, the Lustre routers were proven in a previous network configured between the primary NAS facility and the Merope supercomputer, located in an auxiliary facility. However, with Electra the IP routers were utilized to minimize the InfiniBand connectivity required on the NFS servers. In the Merope deployment, additional InfiniBand host channel adapters were added to multi-home the NFS servers on all of the required IB fabrics.

With the exception of the I/O subsystem, Electra is very similar to the Broadwell subsystem of Pleiades. Given that fact and that about 900 feet of cabling was needed to reach the user filesystems, we focused on the performance of the I/O infrastructure. In particular, we wanted to determine how many Lustre routers were required to achieve similar I/O performance to Pleiades.

We planned to use up to ten Lustre routers in the I/O infrastructure (these are called "LNET routers" in Figure 13.4). In order to test the sensitivity of I/O performance to the number of routers, we varied the I/O configuration to have two, four, and then ten routers. For each setup, the applications team used a variety of applications from the standard workload on Pleiades to measure I/O performance. Some applications ran stand-alone, filling the system, while others were run with a variety of user jobs sharing the system. We found that application performance suffered significantly when only two or four Lustre routers were available, and consequently the full complement of ten routers was put into production.

13.6   User Environment

13.6.1   System Software

All HECC hosts run Linux. The compute nodes and the Lustre clients run SUSE Linux Enterprise Server (SLES); the Lustre servers run CentOS. All of the InfiniBand software—including the subnet manager, drivers, and libraries—comes from Mellanox OFED.

13.6.2   Resource Allocation and Scheduling

NAS supercomputing resources are shared among hundreds of projects representing NASA's four mission directorates (MDs): Aeronautics Research (ARMD), Human Exploration and Operations (HEOMD), Space Technology (STMD), and Science (SMD). Each MD is allocated a percentage of the total annual node-hours available on the systems (excluding a small fraction reserved for NAS internal use). Allocations are translated into share percentages to help the PBS job scheduler, PBSPro, guarantee that each MD has an appropriate amount of resources at any time. These share percentages are adjusted as needed to ensure high system utilization and best possible job turnaround. The PBSPro software—originally developed at NAS and commercialized through a NASA technology transfer agreement with Altair Engineering—handles job scheduling. Users submit job requests that specify the number and type(s) of node they need, and PBSPro allocates compute resources, taking into account factors such as MD share, job priority within an MD, number of requested nodes, and job wait time.

13.6.3   User Services

The NAS teams listed in this section provide services to assist NASA scientists and engineers through the entire lifecycle of their projects.

24×7 User Support: Ensures that the agency's scientists and engineers can make the most effective, productive use of HECC systems around the clock. The team provides users with immediate responses to their questions, and then coordinates custom support from the other service teams, as well as continuously monitoring all systems.

Application Performance and Productivity: Provides a wide range of consulting services to help users optimize performance of their codes, improve scalability, and port their applications to HECC resources. In addition to helping individual users, code optimization results in improvements to resource availability, thereby benefitting the entire user community.

Data Analysis and Visualization: Develops and implements advanced software tools and data analysis technologies, including a sophisticated concurrent visualization framework that enables users to explore high-resolution results in real time on the hyperwall.

Production Supercomputing and Archive Storage: Evaluates, acquires, installs, and operates new systems; develops custom software tools; and implements advanced IT security methods; also provides customized training and support to help users efficiently manage large amounts of data.

High-Speed Networking: Works closely with remote users to optimize their data flows and select the most efficient transfer methods. Maintains high-capacity connections and resolves network issues so users can transfer massive volumes of data seamlessly between NAS resources and their remote systems.

13.7 Application Benchmarking and Performance

Despite having the capability to run applications at scale, HECC compute resources are not commonly used for applications running on more than 10,000 cores. Rather, the system's primary use is as a capacity resource for projects supporting NASA's future space missions, fundamental aeronautics applications, and Earth and planetary science research. In fact, Pleiades typically runs more than 75,000 jobs each month, and about 50% of the resources are used by jobs requesting 2,400 cores or fewer.

Given this usage pattern, NAS concentrates its benchmarking on modest-sized computations that represent the actual NASA computational workload. In order to be able to compare the capabilities of the different node types comprising HECC systems and also to equitably charge users for their computer usage, NAS embarked on the process of defining a Standard Billing Unit. An SBU reflects the amount of computing power needed to run a representative workload. Each node type can then be tested to determine the amount of resources used to run the workload and establish its SBU charging rate. By using the relative computing power of each node type and its SBU rate, users can run their jobs on the nodes that execute their codes most economically.

Using past accounting data, six application codes that were heavily executed on Pleiades were identified: three codes from SMD and three representing ARMD, HEOMD, and the NASA Engineering and Safety Center (NESC). This suite of codes makes up the application portion of benchmarking requirements in the HECC requests for proposals (RFPs) for supercomputers. In the remainder of this section we describe these applications and give a brief explanation of how they are used to establish charging rates for the different compute resources (see Tables 13.1 and 13.2).

In 2011, a Westmere node was used as a baseline, i.e., the SBU was defined in terms of the application in SBU benchmark suite in such a way that a Westmere node has an SBU rate of 1. In order to choose the number of MPI ranks to use for each application, the benchmarking team first conducted a strong scaling study on the Westmere nodes of Pleiades. They then picked rank counts to reflect typical usage of each application and verified that there was reasonable scaling behavior at that point. Runtime parameters such as iteration counts were then adjusted so that the execution required about 30 minutes on the Westmere nodes.

In 2017, the SBU suite was revamped, using the Broadwell node type as a baseline. The codes were upgraded to use the latest versions, new core counts were chosen and the runtime parameters were adjusted so that the execution required about 30 minutes on the Broadwell nodes.

Following are the six representative codes in the SBU benchmark suite. All of these codes use MPI for interprocess communication.

Enzo v2.5 is an adaptive mesh refinement, grid-based code, developed by a community of academic participants, that is used to simulate cosmological structure formation [3]. Appropriate input files are used to create data in HDF5 format representing initial cosmological conditions in the setup phase. When the benchmark is executed, the cosmos represented by these binary HDF5 files is allowed to evolve. This benchmark case uses 196 MPI ranks.

FUN3D v13.1 is an unstructured computational fluid dynamics (CFD) code from NASA Langley Research Center (LaRC) that is used for aerospace design analysis and optimization [4]. The code uses an adjoint-based error estimation to perform mesh adaptation. The benchmark grid is a wing-body geometry developed as a Common Research Model (CRM) for aerodynamic prediction validation studies of various CFD codes. The

TABLE 13.1: Runtimes (in seconds) for the SBU suite of six applications on different HECC processor types.

Application	Westmere	Sandy Bridge	Ivy Bridge	Haswell	Broadwell
Enzo	2,384	2,524	2,018	1,801	1,616
FUN3D	4,675	4,868	4,144	3,541	3,251
GEOS-5	3,266	3,178	2,373	2,282	2,130
OVERFLOW	4,140	2,728	2,676	2,553	2,555
USM3D	3,299	3,024	2,839	2,290	2,299
nu-WRF	1,076	943	785	751	747

CRM consists of unstructured tetrahedral grids with about 285 million unknowns and 1.7 billion tetrahedral elements. This benchmark uses 2016 MPI ranks.

GEOS v5.16, the Goddard Earth Observing System Model, is the atmospheric general circulation model from NASA Goddard Space Flight Center's suite of models to support climate and weather prediction, data analysis, Earth observing system modeling and design, and basic research [5]. The dataset used is the GMAO global data for year 2000 with a resolution of 360 x 2,160 x 72 for atmosphere and 2,880 x 1,440 x 34 for ocean. The physical problem that it solves is known as the Jablonowski & Williamson Baroclinic Test Case. This benchmark uses 1,344 MPI ranks.

OVERFLOW v2.2l is a CFD code from LaRC for solving complex compressible flow problems. It is widely used to design launch and reentry vehicles, rotorcraft, and commercial aircraft [12]. The dataset used is a three-blade, generic rotor system with a fixed NACA0010 airfoil section and rectangular planform, similar to the UH-60 rotor system. The benchmark geometry consists of about 750 million overset grid points and uses 2,016 MPI ranks.

USM3D v20130926 is an unstructured mesh code from LaRC used to calculate flows over complex geometries such as aerospace vehicles [15]. The dataset used in the benchmark solves the same CRM problem as FUN3D but with slightly different grid size. The wing-body geometry consists of about 105 million unknowns and 623 million tetrahedral elements. This benchmark uses 2,016 MPI ranks.

nu-WRF v8-3.71, the NASA-Unified Weather Research and Forecasting Model, is the latest-generation, mesoscale numerical weather prediction system originated from the National Center for Atmospheric Research. The code has been adapted by NASA for observation-driven regional earth system modeling and assimilation system at satellite-resolvable scale [11]. The Modern-Era Retrospective analysis for Research and Applications, Version 2 (MERRA-2) provides data beginning in 1980, which enables assimilation of modern hyperspectral radiance and microwave observations, along with GPS-Radio Occultation datasets. This benchmark uses a domain size of 600 x 400 x 51 and 1,680 MPI ranks.

To establish the SBU charging rates, each application was run on each node type. The runtimes are shown in Table 13.1. This information is used to calculate the relative number of runs that each application can execute in one hour on 64 nodes (prorated both in time and space, as needed) compared to what could be run in an hour on the baseline 64 Broadwell nodes. Those numbers are shown in Table 13.2. For each node type, the SBU charging rate is a weighted average across all applications of the relative number of runs shown in Table 13.2. This calculation gives the SBU charging rate for each node type, as shown on the last row of the table. Note that the charging factor progressively increases with newer generations of the Intel Xeon architecture.

TABLE 13.2: Relative number of runs for the SBU applications on different HECC processor types.

Application	Weight	Runs relative to Broadwell				
		Westmere	Sandy Bridge	Ivy Bridge	Haswell	Broadwell
Enzo	20%	0.29	0.37	0.57	0.77	1.00
FUN3D	20%	0.30	0.38	0.56	0.79	1.00
GEOS-5	15%	0.28	0.38	0.64	0.80	1.00
OVERFLOW	20%	0.26	0.54	0.68	0.86	1.00
USM3D	10%	0.30	0.43	0.58	0.86	1.00
nu-WRF	15%	0.30	0.45	0.68	0.85	1.00
Weighted Average		0.29	0.43	0.62	0.82	1.00

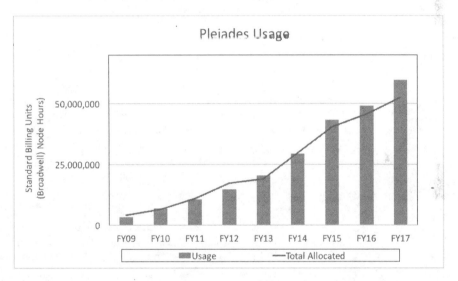

FIGURE 13.5: Compute capacity and utilization growth over the life of Pleiades. The Total Allocated line represents 75% of the maximum theoretically available SBUs.

13.8   Utilization Statistics of HECC Resources

Since their installation, the HECC systems have experienced extremely heavy utilization. In fact, the utilization has closely tracked system expansions over the years. (See Figures 13.5, 13.6, and 13.7 for Pleiades and Electra compute utilization, and HECC storage utilization, respectively.) The NAS operational approach is designed to best meet the needs of NASA's users. For example, the configuration of the different batch queues gives users options for trading off maximum runtime versus likely queue wait time—longer job requests tend to wait longer in the queue. Most of the SBUs delivered on the systems are to jobs that run 24 hours or longer. Job queue limits allow runs of up to five days, and many users take advantage of that. When an application requires even more time, NAS allows jobs up to 16 days if there is a compelling reason and support from the project's MD.

In addition to its continual growth as a capacity resource, Pleiades has also seen an

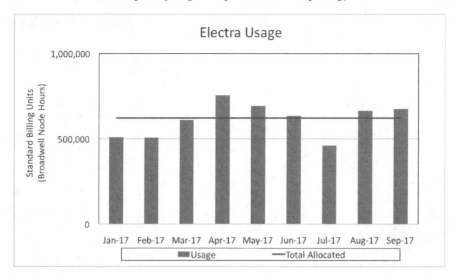

FIGURE 13.6: Compute capacity and utilization growth over the life of Electra. The Total Allocated line represents 75% of the maximum theoretically available SBUs.

increase in its use as a capability resource. In June 2009, jobs requiring between 257 and 512 cores used more SBUs than jobs in any other category, and the widest jobs were under 8,192 cores. However, a year later, jobs between 512 and 1,024 cores represented the largest category of SBU usage, and the widest jobs were between 16,000 and 32,000 cores. In the twelve months from September 1, 2016, to August 31, 2017, 20.9% of the jobs used from 1,025 to 2,048 cores, and 20.6% used from 2,049 to 4,096 cores. Of all the SBUs run on Pleiades during the year, 67.3% were used by jobs requesting 1,025 cores or more. The widest jobs exceeded 70,000 cores.

Because Electra uses the latest Intel processors, Xeon Broadwell, it has been used more as a capability system for larger jobs rather than a capacity resource. Since its installation in January and through August 2017, 32.6% of the SBUs on Electra were used by jobs requesting 8,193 to 16,384 cores—more than double that of any other category. Of all the SBUs used on Electra, 79.4% were used by jobs requesting 1,025 cores or more, while jobs requesting 8,193 to 32,768 cores accounted for 43.8% of the SBUs.

13.9 System Operations and Maintenance

This section provides an overview of the tools and processes used to administer, debug, monitor, and correct problems on HECC systems. Because all the hosts run Linux, there is a variety of open source tools available to our teams for operations and maintenance activities.

13.9.1 Administration Tools

We use SGI's cluster administration package, Tempo, which is based on open source tools such as systemimager, Oscar, C3, and pdsh and customized for the SGI UV and SGI ICE environments. A key element in the administration of these systems is the Rack

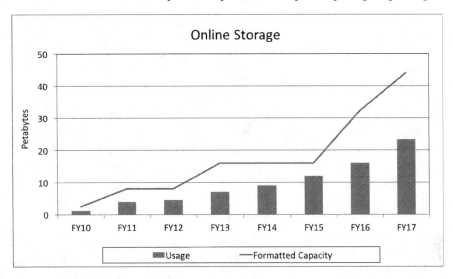

FIGURE 13.7: Storage capacity and utilization growth over the life of the HECC storage system.

Leader Controller (RLC), which communicates with the nodes in the racks it administers over a private 1-Gb Ethernet LAN. The RLC is responsible for all administrative functions within the racks it controls, and is also indirectly responsible for controlling power to the IB switches in each rack.

The RLCs allow the system to scale, as the load on an RLC is nearly independent of the total number of system racks and the racks do not have to compete with each other for LAN bandwidth.

Several "admin nodes" are used for overall administration of HECC resources. The admin nodes communicate with the RLCs rather than the individual compute nodes, providing DHCP, NTP, DNS, and syslog services to the RLCs and to other infrastructure service hosts, such as I/O servers and front-end nodes. All initial install images and updates are built on the admin nodes and then pushed out to the RLCs. Configuration management is handled with CVS and Bcfg2.

13.9.2   Monitoring, Diagnosis, and Repair Tools

Our system administrators use Nagios with several custom plug-ins to monitor infrastructure hosts and filesystems. The Nagios data also provides status information via an at-a-glance display used by 24×7 onsite NAS facility monitors, and via the web for users and program managers.

For the most part, each node runs its own diagnostic and repair tasks. To achieve this, the PBSPro batch scheduling system runs prologue and epilogue scripts at the start and end of every job to perform diagnostic tests on each node used by the job. If a test fails, the node is marked as being offline, and PBSPro selects other nodes for future runs.

All hosts are configured with kdb and crash dumps enabled so administrators can analyze system crashes quickly and develop solutions. It is also fairly common for application codes to exhaust the memory on the nodes; the default Linux behavior is to kill a process in this case, but unfortunately it does not kill the appropriate one. Thus, on HECC systems, Linux is configured to reboot nodes when this occurs so that the error can be handled. A set of scripts using the Simple Event Correlator (SEC) tool monitors system logs and node consoles to detect such out-of-memory (OOM) reboots. SEC then identifies the job and instructs PBSPro to terminate it on the remainder of its nodes.

In addition to these tools, the Application Performance and Productivity team developed a tool called Lumber that is able to collect and scan log messages that result during the running of a job. Despite the fact that such messages can be spread across thousands of files on the system, the tool can locate and gather this information for any job, typically within 30 seconds, automating a process that in the past was laborious to the point of being intractable. Besides facilitating analysis of individual job failures, the tool can be used to find all jobs that experienced a pattern of log messages. Lumber's efficiency has also led to using log files as a mechanism for storing information about a job, such as executable name, I/O statistics, or power usage. It is then straightforward to produce periodic reports about jobs, such as resources used by specific applications.

13.9.3 System Enhancements and Maintenance

NAS teams have developed several processes to minimize the number of full system outages and maximize availability. For example, compute nodes can be booted using one of several images, which facilitates rolling updates—the default operating system of each compute node can be upgraded at the completion of the job executing on that node.

When scheduling a job, PBSPro checks for the availability of necessary resources, including the Lustre scratch filesystem assigned to the user submitting the job. If the filesystem has been taken down for maintenance, the system can still be fully utilized by other jobs. The NFS filesystems are hard mounted, and user applications can reliably withstand reboots (or crashes) of the NFS servers.

HECC systems support live integration, which enables NAS system administrators to augment the systems with new compute nodes while jobs continue to run on the existing hardware, thus increasing overall availability. When the new nodes are ready to be integrated with the existing system, they are powered down, and the subnet manager sweeping is turned off. Then, the new hardware is cabled to the existing hardware, the cabling is verified, and finally the new hardware is powered up and the subnet sweeping is restarted. The subnet manager sweep integrates the new hardware into the overall fabric and the new nodes are added to the PBSPro's list of available resources.

13.10 Featured Application

To study global systems, Earth scientists run ocean, weather, and climate models that require ever-increasing resolution and ever more complex physics representation, driving the need for substantially larger HPC systems than ever before. To help meet these requirements, NAS has been working for over a decade with scientists from the Estimating the Circulation and Climate of the Ocean, Phase II (ECCO2) project, a joint venture led by the Massachusetts Institute of Technology (MIT) and NASA Jet Propulsion Laboratory (JPL) to study ocean currents and their interactions with Earth's atmosphere, sea ice, and marine-terminating glaciers [1]. Their objective is to help monitor and understand the ocean's role in climate variability and changes, as well as to improve the representation of ocean-climate interactions in Earth system models. The ECCO2 project team uses the MIT general circulation model (MITgcm) [9], a numerical model designed to study ocean, atmosphere, and sea ice circulation. MITgcm is combined with observational data from NASA satellites and in-situ ocean probes measuring sea level, temperature, salinity, and momentum, as well as sea ice concentration, motion, and thickness. This model-data combination requires the solution of a huge, nonlinear estimation problem. The result of this estimation is a realistic description of how ocean circulation, temperature, salinity, sea level, and sea ice interact on a global scale.

In 2011, ECCO2 project scientists approached NAS with a request for assistance. They wanted to increase the resolution of their global model from $\frac{1}{24}^\circ$ to an unprecedented $\frac{1}{48}^\circ$ and also increase the number of depth levels in the simulation. In order to accomplish this, NAS estimated that such a simulation would produce data at a sustained rate of 10 GB/s. However, at that time, MITgcm did all of its I/O through rank 0; achieving the project's goals meant that the I/O would need to be parallelized. An evaluation of MPI-IO indicated that its performance would not meet the goals, so the NAS team undertook a custom design and implementation in which auxiliary I/O processes were added to handle data compositing and I/O. For example, suppose there is a large MITgcm run that needs N MPI ranks for computing. The domain decomposition takes place in the horizontal plane (x, y) but not in z—that is, each rank is responsible for the full range of vertical points. The desired output is a collection of M full-range horizontal slices. The new approach is to use M auxiliary ranks for I/O. Each of the N compute ranks will send data to a subset of the M I/O ranks; the I/O ranks will then shuffle data among themselves so that each has the data for the slice it's responsible for. It then outputs the desired plane.

In 2014, the ECCO2 scientists used a new MITgcm code to run a very high-resolution global ocean simulation that covered 14 months of simulated ocean time and used a total of 22 billion grid points (242 million grid points at each of 90 ocean depths). Output was written at each hour of simulated time, totalling 10,311 time steps, each with 20 variables (five 3D fields and 15 2D fields)—a total of 5 PB of stored data. To visualize the data, the NAS Visualization and Data Analysis group created movies that could be both produced and viewed at full resolution on the hyperwall. While ECCO2 project scientists successfully used this method to view their data, it was mutually agreed that a more powerful visualization tool was needed.

The NAS group then began developing an interactive visualization tool that allows browsing, side-by-side comparisons, and dynamic linked scatterplot brushing—enabling researchers to interact with their data in real time. Disk bandwidth requirements are reduced by converting the model's floating-point data to 16-bit fixed point values, and compressing those values with a lossless video encoder, which together allow synchronized playback at 24 time steps per second across all 128 hyperwall displays (see Figure 13.2). The application allows dynamic assignment of any two encoded tiles to any display, and has multiple interfaces for quickly specifying various orderly arrangements of tiles. All subsequent rendering is done on the fly, with runtime control of colormaps, transfer functions, histogram equalization, and labeling. The two data streams on each screen can be rendered independently and combined in various ways, including blending, differencing, horizontal/vertical wipes, and checkerboarding, and can optionally be displayed as a scatterplot in their joint attribute space, as shown in Figure 13.8. All scatterplots and map-view plots from the same (x, y) location and depth are linked so they all show the current brushable selection. ECCO2 project scientists have used the system on several occasions and have found previously unidentified features in the data [2].

During the configuration of Electra, NAS teams used output-intensive runs of MITgcm to size the I/O system. In particular, runs were made with varying numbers of Lustre routers to find out how many were needed. In the end, the NAS Systems team decided on 10 routers; this enabled MITgcm to achieve 40 GB/s of output bandwidth.

During Electra's system testing period, NAS wanted to use short-term runs of MITgcm to fill in the gaps between tests. Unfortunately, initializing each run took about an hour as a

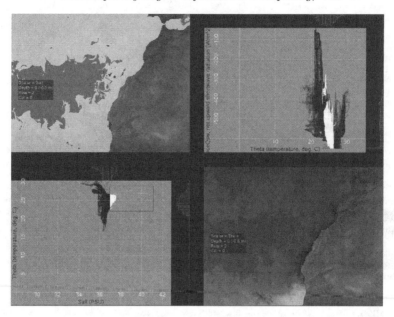

FIGURE 13.8: A portion of the ECCO2 MITgcm visualization on the hyperwall, showing scatterplots and map-view displays for the same geographical location.

single rank read in the startup files; after parallelizing the input routines, the initialization time dropped to a few minutes. This shortened the restart overhead, allowing productive use of the code to fill in the gaps.

13.11   Conclusions

In this chapter, we have focused on the Electra system housed in the Modular Supercomputing Facility (MSF) at NASA Ames Research Center in Silicon Valley, Calif.—an approach that has provided NASA with extended high-performance computing resources while reducing energy costs and minimizing the environmental impact of the facility. Facing a situation where its primary supercomputer facility could not economically support the addition of new equipment, the NAS Division elected to conduct an experiment to study whether HPC equipment was compatible with Modular Data Center (MDC) technology. Specifically, we undertook the design, installation, and deployment of the MSF prototype, which resulted in the Electra supercomputer being housed in a 1,000-square foot module about 100 meters from the primary facility while being integrated into the current HPC environment. Overall, the prototype has been a huge success. The MSF site was transformed from an unimproved lot to a production supercomputer in less than six months. The additional compute resources increased the capacity available for NASA's large-scale simulations by 16%. In addition, in the nine months since it went into operation, the facility has returned an average PUE of under 1.03. Also during this time period, it has utilized approximately 65,000 gallons of water for cooling the systems—a 95% reduction relative to the same system being housed in a traditional data center facility.

Building on the success of the prototype, NAS plans to use MDC technology for two future expansions. One, which is already underway, has added a second module on the current pad next to the first. Rather than using outside air for directly cooling the compute nodes, NAS aims to gain experience with warm-water cooling in the new module. While the Electra system uses a traditional hot/cold aisle setup, the next iteration is utilizing the HPE water-cooled E-Cell technology, which allows for a higher density configuration. Although the PUE is expected to rise, we expect that the Total-power Usage Effectiveness (TUE) measurement will improve; this is due to the integrated fans in the existing Electra racks being counted as compute load for its PUE calculation and as cooling load in its TUE calculation. In the longer term, NAS plans to significantly expand its available facility space. A Request for Proposals is underway for computer systems and facility space that would support a growth path to 30 MW of equipment over the next five years.

The modular facility approach described here pushes HPC technology to meet NASA's evolving computing requirements, and makes it possible for the agency to be flexible and add computing resources as needed. NASA will save about half the cost of building another big brick-and-mortar facility, and the MSF can serve as a model for expanding supercomputing facilities in the future.

Acknowledgments

The authors would like to thank Christopher Buchanan, Johnny Chang, Michael Hartman, Henry Jin, Catherine Schulbach, and Dale Talcott for their contributions to this chapter. We are also indebted to our colleagues in the entire NAS Division for their hard work in acquiring, running, and maintaining HECC systems and providing outstanding services to users.

Bibliography

[1] Estimating the Circulation and Climate of the Ocean Consortium, Phase II (ECCO2). Website. http://ecco.jpl.nasa.gov/.

[2] D. Ellsworth, C. Henze, and B. Nelson. Interactive Visualization of High-Dimensional Petascale Ocean Data. *2017 IEEE 7th Symposium on Large Data Analysis and Visualization (LDAV)*. Phoenix, AZ, 2017.

[3] The Enzo Project. Website. http://enzo-project.org/.

[4] FUN3D: Fully Unstructured Navier-Stokes. Website. http://fun3d.larc.nasa.gov/.

[5] The GEOS-5 System. Website. http://gmao.gsfc.nasa.gov/systems/geos5/.

[6] HECC Storage Resources. Website. https://www.nas.nasa.gov/hecc/resources/storage_systems.html.

[7] High Performance Conjugate Gradients, November 2016. Website. http://www.hpcg-benchmark.org/custom/index.html?lid=155&slid=289.

[8] hyperwall Visualization System. Website. https://www.nas.nasa.gov/hecc/resources/viz_systems.html.

[9] Massachusetts Institute of Technology General Circulation Model (mitgcm). Website. http://mitgcm.org/.

[10] Merope Supercomputer. Website. https://www.nas.nasa.gov/hecc/resources/merope.html.

[11] nu-WRF: NASA-Unified Weather Research and Forecasting (nu-WRF). Website. https://modelingguru.nasa.gov/community/atmospheric/nuwrf.

[12] OVERFLOW Computational Fluid Dynamics (CFD) flow solver. Website. https://overflow.larc.nasa.gov/.

[13] Pleiades Supercomputer. Website. https://www.nas.nasa.gov/hecc/resources/pleiades.html.

[14] TOP500 – November 2016. Website. https://www.top500.org/lists/2016/11/.

[15] USM3D NASA Common Research Model (USM3D). Website. https://commonresearchmodel.larc.nasa.gov/computational-approach/flow-solvers-used/usm3d/.

Chapter 14

Bridges: Converging HPC, AI, and Big Data for Enabling Discovery

Nicholas A. Nystrom

PSC, Carnegie Mellon University

Paola A. Buitrago

PSC, Carnegie Mellon University

Philip D. Blood

PSC, Carnegie Mellon University

14.1 Overview

Physical science and engineering communities have used and driven high-performance computing (HPC) for many decades. Examples include cosmology, quantum chromodynamics, quantum chemistry, molecular dynamics, weather and climate modeling, and computational fluid dynamics and structural mechanics. Such communities have scalable applications, a culture of computational science, proficiency with Linux and HPC systems, and access to extremely large computational resources. Their applications are parallelized through a combination of message passing and threading (most often, MPI and OpenMP) with source code in C++, C, or Fortran. Priority is often placed on running an application on as many compute cores as possible, potentially using a whole supercomputer for one application at a time. Collectively, this has come to be called "traditional HPC".

Conversely, many other research communities, such as genomics, neuroscience, medicine, computer science, ecology, economics, public policy, business, and the humanities historically tended to avoid supercomputers. At the time, the applications and algorithms of these "nontraditional HPC" communities did not yet require massive scalability. Those applications are generally expressed in high-productivity languages such as Python, R, Java, and MATLAB, and they often access persistent databases. Nontraditional HPC research communities have been fairly well served – to a point – by laptop and desktop windowed and GUI environments, compared to which traditional HPC batch queuing systems and command lines are unwelcome hindrances. These communities are largely focused on data, developing, integrating, and using a different set of applications built on foundations such as statistics, natural language processing, image and video processing, machine learning, and artificial intelligence. As their data expanded, its analysis required a computer more powerful than their local resources but still supporting familiar applications and tools. Their analyses have vital societal importance, addressing topics such as the microbiome and its relation to disease, national economic policy, biodiversity and sustaining the environment, and root causes of cancers.

PSC, whose scope spans a broad portfolio of research and services in scalable analytics, simulation, and modeling, integrating HPC, AI, and data to enable discovery, designed Bridges [31] to meet the requirements of nontraditional HPC communities. Bridges, funded by National Science Foundation award 1445606, converges high-performance computing (HPC), artificial intelligence (AI), and Big Data, and it offers a familiar, exceptionally flexible user environment to help researchers work more intuitively. Its highly heterogeneous architecture features large memory – 4 compute nodes with 12 TB of RAM, 42 with 3 TB, and 800 with 128 GB – and powerful new Intel® Xeon CPUs and NVIDIA Tesla GPUs for exceptional performance. Bridges also includes database and web servers to support web-based science (gateways), collaboration, and data management, and it includes 10 PB usable of shared, parallel storage, plus local storage on each of its compute nodes. Hewlett Packard Enterprise (HPE) delivered Bridges. PSC chose HPE for Bridges because of HPE's broad range of servers, particularly with large memory, high reliability, and outstanding engineering. At the time of its installation, Bridges was the first production deployment of the Intel® Omni-Path Architecture (OPA) Fabric. OPA's high-radix (48-port) switches enable interconnecting all of Bridges' compute, storage, and utility nodes in a PSC-designed topology designed for converged HPC, AI, and data. Bridges prioritizes usability and flexibility by supporting a high degree of interactivity, gateways and tools for gateway-building, and a very flexible user environment. Widely-used languages and frameworks such as Python, R, MATLAB®, Spark, Hadoop, and Java benefit transparently from Bridges' large memory and its high-performance OPA fabric, for example, running an R script unchanged and accessing 12 TB of RAM. Virtualization and containers enable hosting web services, NoSQL databases, and application-specific environments, enhance reproducibility, and support interoperation with clouds. Access to Bridges is available at no charge for open research and education, and by arrangement to industry through PSC's corporate program. Access to Bridges can include collaboration with an expert to help with development, also at no charge (see section 14.2.5, Allocations).

Bridges is allocated through XSEDE, the Extreme Science and Engineering Discovery Environment [42], the cyberinfrastructure umbrella organization funded by the National Science Foundation (NSF) to enable the sharing of computing resources, data, and expertise, of which PSC is a founding member and Level 1 Service Provider. Bridges is in high demand for an extremely wide range of research. As of May 2018, Bridges is serving 1,421 projects and 7,340 users at 349 institutions and representing 110 principal fields of study. Additional users access Bridges through gateways (see section 14.2.4, Gateways). For example, Galaxy Main [4] reports over 100,000 users [5], any of whom may use Bridges through the Galaxy Main gateway.

PSC is a joint effort of Carnegie Mellon University (CMU) and the University of Pittsburgh (Pitt). PSC began operations in 1986 and has installed and operated 19 supercomputers, many the first of their kind and some unique. For example, PSC developed applications using an FPGA simulator for the interconnect of the Cray T3D, then pioneered development of massively parallel applications on its very early T3D. PSC designed and operated LeMieux, which extended the limits of clustered systems using AlphaServer SC servers and a dual-rail Quadrics interconnect to become the #2 system on the Top500. PSC then hosted the first Cray XT3 and, working with Cray, improved its interconnect performance by 70%. PSC then hosted Blacklight [32], which was the world's largest shared-memory computer. Bridges, shown in Figure 14.1, is the eighteenth in that sequence.

14.1.1 Sponsor/Program Background

The National Science Foundation (NSF) is an independent United States federal agency that advances the progress of science through grants for discovery, learning, research infrastructure and stewardship. In 2014, NSF issued solicitation 14-536, "High Performance Computing System Acquisition: Continuing the Building of a More Inclusive Computing Environment for Science and Engineering." The solicitation sought proposals addressing less traditional computational science communities, complex and dynamic workflows, new, flexible, and highly usable capabilities, connections to other parts of the national cyberinfrastructure and campus cyberinfrastructure, expanding the range of computationally challenging science and engineering applications that can be tackled, and providing a flexible and user-friendly environment.

FIGURE 14.1: Bridges, in PSC's datacenter.

14.1.2   Timeline

NSF issued solicitation 14-536 in February 2014, with responses due May 14, 2014. The design of Bridges began earlier, based on PSC's deep connection to the research community and experience with making advanced computing more usable, and completed in May 2014, with the submission of PSC's proposal. Following review, the Bridges project was awarded with a start date of December 1, 2014. Pursuant to the solicitation, acquisition of the initial system was planned to intercept emerging hardware for January 2016.

Bridges was implemented in two phases to ensure rapid, high scientific impact and also include important new technologies. Phase 1 included representative nodes of all types that would be in the completed system, including all dual-socket CPU nodes, initial GPU and large-memory nodes, and the world's first deployment of the Intel Omni-Path Architecture (OPA) fabric. Initial Phase 1 Bridges hardware was delivered to PSC's datacenter in late 2015. Additional Phase 1 hardware was delivered in January 2016, at which time assembly began. An HPE team led the integration, and an Intel team led installation and testing of this flagship deployment of Omni-Path. All Phase 1 performance targets were achieved. External users began using Bridges in February 2016 for the MIDAS MISSION Public Health Hackathon [6], during which twelve teams from across the United States and India developed applications to better visualize complex, multidimensional public health data. The Phase 1 early-user period demonstrated substantial scientific impact, high degrees of stability and usability, and the ability to successfully onboard nontraditional communities. February began the Phase 1 "early user period". A successful NSF review of the Phase 1 acquisition then led to Bridges running production jobs starting in June 2016. In June, accounting for allocations was updated to reflect utilization during the early user period.

Phase 2 then added compute nodes featuring new technologies and completed the parallel storage system, including additional OPA hardware to integrate those new components. Installation of Phase 2 was completed in early October 2016. Phase 2 hardware also met all performance targets. An early-user period from October 2016 to February 2017 for the fully-integrated system, including the new Phase 2 components, again demonstrated substantial scientific impact, high degrees of stability and usability, and successful onboarding of nontraditional communities. Following a successful review of the complete Bridges acquisition, the full Bridges system entered production in February 2017. As before, accounting for allocations was updated to reflect utilization during the Phase 2 early user period.

Figure 14.2 illustrates Bridges' two phases and lists the hardware components introduced in each of them. Section 14.4 details the hardware architecture.

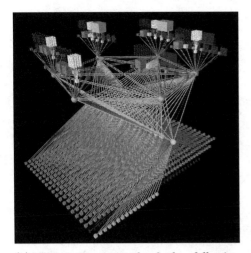

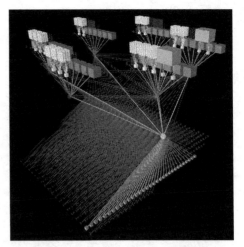

(a) Phase 1 consisted of the following components: 752 Regular Shared Memory (RSM) nodes with 2 Intel Xeon 2695v3 ("Haswell EP" CPUs) each (HPE Apollo 2000); 16 RSM nodes with 2 NVIDIA Tesla K80 GPUs each (HPE Apollo 2000); 8 Large Shared Memory (LSM) nodes (HPE ProLiant DL580); 2 Extreme Shared Memory (ESM) nodes (HPE Integrity Superdome X); 5 Storage Building Blocks (SBBs); Intel Omni-Path Architecture (OPA) fabric; and Database, Web, Front-end, and Management nodes.

(b) Phase 2 added 32 RSM nodes with 2 Tesla P100 GPUs each (HPE Apollo 2000); 34 LSM nodes with Intel Xeon v4 ("Broadwell EX") CPUs (HPE ProLiant DL580); 2 ESM nodes also with Intel Xeon v4 CPUs (HPE Integrity Superdome X), 15 Storage Building Blocks, all connected through the Intel OPA fabric to the Phase 1 components.

FIGURE 14.2: Components in Phase 1 and Phase 2 of Bridges.

14.2   Applications and Workloads

Bridges' primary goal is to enable non-traditional applications and communities. As one measure of success, PSC categorizes Bridges projects as traditional or nontraditional based on the research being done, the field of the principal investigator (PI) leading it, and how it is implemented. The Bridges PI reads all proposals and makes the primary determination, which is recorded and open to revision. Examples of projects that would be classified as "nontraditional" are as follows:

- Projects in nontraditional HPC fields such as economics, machine learning, graph analytics, and genome sequence assembly.

- Nontraditional approaches to traditional fields, for example, applying machine learning to develop better force fields for materials science, combining deep learning with molecular dynamics simulation to make longer time scales accessible, or applying machine learning to spot features of interest in simulation data and focusing resolution.

- Projects implemented in high-productivity programming languages, for example, R and MATLAB leveraging large memory (3–12 TB, allowing researchers to scale beyond their desktop systems).

- Projects implemented as workflows involving integration of high-productivity components, interactivity, visualization, databases, etc.

- Projects implemented wholly or partially using Spark, Hadoop, and other emerging frameworks.

- Science gateways [24], which make HPC Software as a Service (HPCSaaS) available through easy-to-use, domain-oriented web portals.

The Bridges team has found that, by far, the most effective way to onboard new nontraditional projects is through in-person engagements. Expanding awareness through outreach, publication of success stories, and community engagement is an ongoing focus for the Bridges team.

Bridges serves hundreds of applications, none of which is clearly dominant. Grouping projects by field of study as reported by their principal investigators, the largest single category is Training, with 11.3% of Bridges projects. This includes university and even high school courses using Bridges, domain-specific workshops, XSEDE workshops, PSC's summer boot camp, and the International Summer School on HPC Challenges in Computational Sciences. The fields of study with the next-largest numbers of projects, in decreasing order, are Biophysics (7.8%), Advanced Scientific Computing (7.0%), Materials Research (6.4%), and Biological Sciences (6.1%). These fields of study with at least 5% each of all projects make up only 38.6% of the total. The remaining 61.4% of projects are comprised of 105 other fields of study. This includes, for example, Genetics and Nucleic Acids (2.7%), Economics (1.3%), Visualization, Graphics, and Image Processing (1.0%), Neuroscience Biology (0.8%), Robotics and Machine Intelligence (0.6%), and Ecological Studies (0.5%). The actual applications are a mix of community applications, some commercial applications, and users' own applications.

Figure 14.3 illustrates the distribution of applications on the system. The 110 fields of study represented by projects being done on Bridges are folded into top-level directorates MPS (Math and Physical Sciences), CISE (Computer and Information Science and Engineering), BIO (Biological Sciences), SBE (Social, Behavioral, and Economic Sciences), GEO (Geological Sciences), ENG (Engineering), and Other. The top bar shows the relative numbers of projects in each of the five directorates, and the second through fifth bars show distributions of RM allocations (regular-memory, in core-hours), LM allocations (large-memory, in TB-hours), GPU allocations (in GPU-hours), and Pylon allocations (storage, in TBs).

Supporting nontraditional communities requires a high level of effort. Effort is highest for users who wish to develop collaborative environments or migrate specific software environments. Some examples are building gateways to enable geographically distributed scholarship, supporting data-intensive workflows composed of specific software stacks, and making valuable data available by transitioning from a desktop database to a flexible, scalable implementation on a publicly-accessible resource. Achieving such goals requires collaboration between the user, user support staff, and systems staff. The Bridges project provides some user support, which PSC augments by leveraging XSEDE's Extended Collaborative Support Service (ECSS).

14.2.1 Highlights of Main Applications and Data

As noted, Bridges runs an extremely broad set of workloads. Two specific application areas where Bridges is making very strong contributions are artificial intelligence and genomics. For AI, Bridges introduced powerful, large-memory GPUs ideal for deep learning

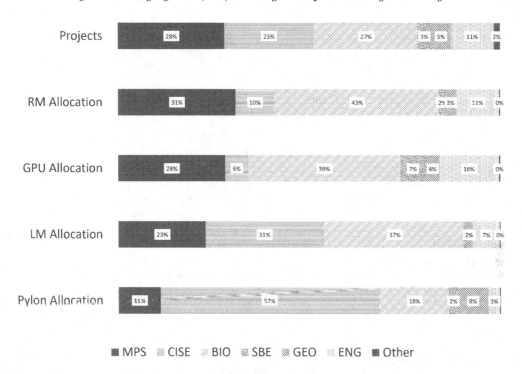

FIGURE 14.3: Distribution of Bridges projects by resource type and NSF directorate. Resource types are regular memory (RM), graphics processing unit (GPU), large memory (LM), and storage (Pylon).

training and OPA-connected Xeon CPUs for scalable AI and additional capacity. For genomics, Bridges' large-memory nodes with 3 TB and 12 TB are the platform of choice for genome and metagenome sequence assembly. AI and genomics have in common the need to access extremely large data.

Sections 14.2.2, 14.2.3, and 14.2.4 survey AI, genomics, and gateways on Bridges, and sections 14.11.1 and 14.11.2 highlight breakthroughs in AI and genomics.

14.2.2 Artificial Intelligence

In recent years, the convergence of vast computing power and very large data has led to the development of representation learning techniques based on very deep neural networks, commonly referred to as "deep learning." With deep learning, researchers in computer vision, machine translation, and medicine have broken through prior performance plateaus. For example, in 2012, Krizhevsky's AlexNet achieved a performance improvement in object detection that, at the time, was expected to take many years [22]. It sparked intense activity that now touches on many aspects of science, business, and daily life.

Deep learning has shown excellent results for diverse topics including computer vision, speech recognition, natural language processing, recommender systems and knowledge representation (reasoning and question answering) in the past 5 years. In 2017, AI enabled achievement of significant milestones including AlphaGo [40], Libratus [12, 11] for decision making with incomplete information and adversaries having their own unknown and changing strategies, a dermatologist-level model for skin cancer classification [16], and cardiologist-level arrhythmia detection model based on convolutional neural networks [36].

The field is exploding, and many challenges are on the horizon. The field is expected to deliver models or solutions with improved performance at the tasks already being considered and models that offer satisfactory results in new and more complex endeavors. The trend has been to use more complex models with proportionally higher computational complexity. Alternatively, simple, well-tuned models (using expensive hyperparameter searches) have in cases beaten more sophisticated approaches that claimed to be superior [26, 15]. In both cases, the computational demand will increase as researchers explore new frontiers. The leveraging of well-integrated scalability and performance is mandatory for materializing the next breakthroughs. Bridges makes these advances possible.

Examples of AI projects on Bridges, most of which involve deep learning, are addressing the genomics of tumors such as glioblastoma multiforme [46], medical image enhancement [43], detecting severe storm-causing clouds using big satellite, radar, and weather report data [45, 48], AI for strategic reasoning [12, 11], machine translation, conversational speech, and grounded linguistic units [3], predicting the severity of lung disease, development of methods for digital pathology, image and video analysis, economics, drug-protein interactions, and neuroscience.

Deep learning requires very fast arithmetic and hardware platforms for which specialized frameworks are well-optimized. Deep learning training calls for fast execution of vast numbers of matrix multiplications and large enough memory to support deep network models and manage sufficient data precision.

Bridges' NVIDIA Tesla P100 GPUs and deep learning frameworks (e.g., TensorFlow, Keras, Theano, Caffe, PyTorch, Chainer) provide excellent performance for deep learning training and are being very heavily used for a wide range of deep learning applications and graduate and undergraduate courses. Multiple versions (e.g., TensorFlow 1.3 to 1.8, including GPU and CPU builds) are available on Bridges for most deep learning frameworks to accommodate users who have networks built for specific framework versions.

It is important for users to be able to customize their environments, for which Bridges supports Anaconda 4 and 5 with builds for Python 2.7 and 3.x. Bridges also supports Jupyter, which has become very popular for implementing, sharing, and communicating deep learning research and results. Jupyter is available directly on Bridges and also through Bridges' Open OnDemand [20] interface, which provides an easy-to-use web interface to start Jupyter (and other) jobs.

14.2.3 Genomics

Rapid advancements in second-generation (next-generation) nucleic acid sequencing technologies over the last decade, together with innovations in algorithms for analyzing these data, have dramatically increased the number and type of genomes that can be assembled (i.e., short sequence reads placed in the correct order to form a complete genome) and analyzed by biologists and bioinformaticians [37]. Assembly of short-read data is generally done with de Bruijn graph algorithms [34, 47], whose memory requirements scale with the number of unique sequences of a given length k (k-mers). The large memory requirements of de Bruijn graph genome assembly has presented a significant computational challenge. Recently, third-generation sequencing technologies have made it possible to greatly improve the quality of genome assemblies and analyses thanks to longer read lengths and other innovative technologies that span regions of repeating sequences that are impossible to resolve with short reads alone. Due to the longer read lengths, genome assemblers for third-generation sequencing technologies can use overlap-layout-consensus algorithms [10] that are more parallelizable and require less shared memory. Nevertheless, second-generation short-read technologies are still extensively used due to their low cost and low error rates.

Metagenomics [19], the analysis of the genomes of all microorganisms living in a particular environment, represents a significant opportunity and challenge. The uncovering and classification of new organisms, genes, and gene pathways has great potential to lead to breakthroughs in treating disease, establishing alternative energy sources, improving food production, and many more applications. To tap this potential, scientists are sequencing diverse environments at an increasing rate, but often do not have the computational resources necessary to assemble and fully analyze these data. Each genome of distinct but similar organisms in a sample is essentially a genome-length repeat sequence. Thus, to correctly resolve individual genomes from a diverse environment with many related species is extremely challenging and requires a high depth of sequence coverage for even partial success. Unfortunately, due to the high coverage required, the more expensive third-generation sequencing technologies are often not yet feasible for metagenomics studies, so most current studies are done with short read data. Together, the high coverage and high k-mer diversity of metagenome assemblies makes them one of the most memory-hungry data science applications.

Bridges is an ideal fit for the diversity of computational requirements presented by genomics applications. *De novo* assembly of short-read data to build genomes, transcriptomes, metagenomes, and metatranscriptomes is greatly facilitated by Bridges' forty-two 3 TB nodes and four 12 TB nodes. Assembly of long-read sequence data is also facilitated by these large shared memory nodes, along with the large number of regular memory nodes available. In both cases, I/O-intensive sections of genomics pipelines are benefitted by fast node-local storage on all Bridges nodes and in some cases by the use of RAM disk for I/O. Downstream analyses required to classify genes (and organisms in the case of metagenomes), e.g. BLAST, are often trivially parallelizable and I/O intensive and hence benefit from the large number of nodes with node-local storage. Bridges' flexibility is key to lowering computational barriers in genomics, since these diverse computational requirements may all be present in a single genomics analysis pipeline.

Bridges' integration with gateways provides another pillar of support to the genomics community, since many biologists who wish to use genomics tools are not familiar with command-line environments. Through a collaboration with the Galaxy team, XSEDE, and PSC, the popular Galaxy Main [4] gateway was able to offer genome and transcriptome assembly tools for the first time. These Galaxy Main assembly tools currently run exclusively on Bridges large memory nodes. PSC also maintains our own Galaxy gateway where we can capture important workflows and offer these to users for training or research.

A few of the many genomics projects using Bridges include the NASA Twins study of the effects of space travel on the human genome [18]; efforts to improve metagenomics methods, e.g., via the Critical Assessment of Metagenome Interpretation (CAMI) [39]; assembly and analysis of terabase-scale metagenomics data sets in the Sequence Read Archive (SRA) to identify novel genes and organisms; creation and/or support of genomic data resources such as The Cancer Genome Atlas [14] and the Non-Human Primate Reference Transcriptome Resource [35, 33]; improvement of model organism reference genomes [13]; and *de novo* genome and transcriptome assembly of non-model organisms [27].

14.2.4   Gateways

The Causal Web is a science gateway that highlights many of Bridges' innovative features. Developed through the Center for Causal Discovery (CCD), an NIH Big Data to Knowledge (BD2K) Center of Excellence, The Causal Web provides an easy-to-use, web-based interface to sophisticated algorithms for identifying potential cause-and-effect relationships in big data. Figure 14.4 shows the high-level architecture. A browser-based client written in standard HTML5, JavaScript, and CSS provides an intuitive interface to preparing and uploading data, running causal discovery algorithms, and visualizing results. A file transfer client runs over commodity Internet (red links) to a web server continuously running in a virtual machine on one of Bridges' web server nodes. Applications embedded in the web server communicate with databases that are also continuously running on Bridges' database nodes to authenticate the user, manage the user's data, and maintain provenance information. Users establish accounts directly with the Causal Web portal, leveraging a community allocation obtained by the CCD team. This greatly lowers the barrier to entry for new users who would not be prepared to write a detailed proposal to request their own allocation on XSEDE. Once the user's data is uploaded, or if the user specifies a run to be made against data that is already resident on Bridges' Pylon file system (such as The Cancer Genome Atlas), the Causal Web portal launches the algorithm on an appropriate node of Bridges. Deep searches on large datasets can require multiple terabytes of RAM and execute on Bridges' 12 TB or 3 TB nodes. The novel features of Bridges that are required by the Causal Web portal are persistent web server and database nodes, a range of compute nodes including large memory, and resident large datasets (Big Data as a Service) on a parallel file system, all interconnected by a high-performance fabric.

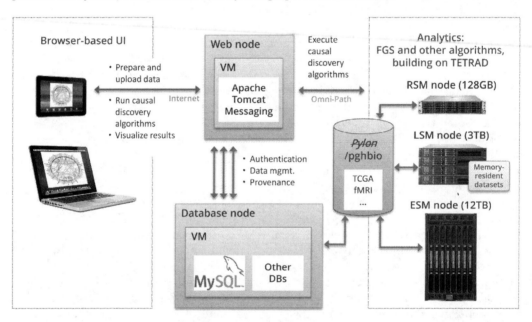

FIGURE 14.4: The Causal Web.

14.2.5   Allocations

Allocations on Bridges are available at no charge for open research led by researchers and educators at U.S.-based institutions. Proprietary research to foster discovery and innovation and broaden participation in data-intensive computing can be accommodated through PSC's Corporate Affiliates program. 90% of Bridges' capacity is allocated through XSEDE, and up to 10% is made available on a discretionary basis.

For open research, the primary way to obtain an allocation is through XSEDE. There are three main types of XSEDE allocations:

- **Start-up allocations**, reviewed quickly by PSC staff, provide modest resources for development, support benchmarking to justify potentially much larger requests, and are adequate by themselves for some projects.

- **Research allocations**, reviewed quarterly by the XSEDE Resource Allocations Committee, can be much larger, technically bounded only by the available capacity.

- **Educational allocations** provide access to supplement university, college, and even high school courses and programs, workshops, summer institutes, and other educational activities.

From the discretionary pool, faculty at Carnegie Mellon University and the University of Pittsburgh can apply for access to Bridges through the Pittsburgh Research Computing Initiative, with resource limits similar to those for XSEDE start-up allocations but a simpler application process.

14.3   System Overview

Bridges is an extremely heterogeneous system, integrating node types having three tiers of coherent shared memory (12 TB, 3 TB, and 128 GB), GPUs, persistent services, and high-performance parallel and local storage. Over several generations of large-memory supercomputers recently including Blacklight [32], PSC found that large memory is extremely valuable for enabling new users to scale up and to maximize human productivity. Bridges amplifies that capability and combines it with standard compute nodes for MPI+X applications and GPUs for deep learning and accelerated applications. It is a unique hardware and software architecture that converges HPC, artificial intelligence, and Big Data to provide unprecedented capability for data-driven discovery and ease of use. The architecture is readily extensible in scale and can be tuned to different workloads.

Figure 14.5 is a visual representation of Bridges' topology, compute and utility nodes, and storage. The image is a rendering from the Bridges Virtual Tour [30], an interactive tool that explains Bridges, its components, and how they interoperate and contribute to use cases such as HPC, AI, Spark, and gateways. Table 14.1 summarizes Bridges' floating-point speed, memory, and storage. Table 14.2 details the CPUs, GPUs, memory, and server types for Bridges' 908 nodes.

Interconnect The central network of orange and yellow spheres interconnected by blue, green, orange, and violet lines is the Intel Omni-Path Architecture fabric, configured in a custom topology developed by PSC for cost-effective, data-intensive computing. The orange and yellow spheres are 48-port Omni-Path edge switches. The lines connecting edge switches are Omni-Path cables, some copper and some optical, depending on length. The cables are colored differently only to show the topology more clearly. See Section 14.4.4.

Compute Nodes At the bottom of the figure are 800 red and green cubes, representing HPE Apollo 2000 compute nodes, each having two Intel Xeon CPUs and 128GB of RAM. The 752 red nodes are "regular shared memory" (RSM) nodes, the 16 light green nodes are Phase 1 GPU nodes each with two NVIDIA Tesla K80 GPUs, and the 32 dark green nodes are Phase 2 GPU nodes each with two NVIDIA Tesla P100 GPUs. At the top of the figure are 42 larger violet cubes, representing HPE ProLiant DL580 servers. These are "large shared memory" (LSM) nodes, each having 4 Intel

Xeon CPUs and 3 TB of RAM. Also at the top are four even larger orange cubes, representing HPE Integrity Superdome X servers. These are "extreme shared memory" (ESM) nodes, each having 16 Intel Xeon CPUs and 12 TB of RAM. See Sections 14.4.1, 14.4.2, and 14.4.3 and Table 14.2.

Other Nodes Dark red, dark blue, dark green, pink, and light blue cubes represent database, web server, login, management, boot, and nodes, respectively. These are all dual-CPU, 128GB servers, implemented as either HPE ProLiant DL360 and DL380 servers, depending on function. See Sections 14.4.1, 14.4.2, and 14.4.3 and Table 14.2.

Storage The 20 white cubes represent storage servers. Each is backed by 4 JBODs, totaling 176 hard disks and providing 0.5 PB of usable storage (after RAID). Together, those 20 "storage building blocks" (SBBs) provide 10 PB aggregate shared, parallel storage. See Sections 14.4.5 and Table 14.2.

TABLE 14.1: Capacities of Bridges' compute nodes, by phase and aggregate.

	Phase 1					Phase 2					Total
	RSM	GPU	LSM	ESM	Total	GPU	LSM	ESM	Total		
Peak fp64 (Tf/s)	774.9	80.5	18.0	21.2	895	335.2	91.4	24.8	451		1,346
RAM (TB)	94	2	24	24	144	4	102	24	130		274
HDD (TB)	6,016	128	128	128	6,400	256	544	128	928		7,328

14.4 Hardware Architecture

Physically, Bridges consists of 37 racks, arranged in two rows of 13 and one row of 11. Interconnect cabling runs over the racks, and power comes up through the raised floor in PSC's datacenter. Bridges is air-cooled front-to-back, with "cold aisles" at the front (shown) and between rows 2 and 3 and the "hot aisle" between rows 1 and 2. Figure 14.1 portrays most of the Bridges' front row.

14.4.1 Processors and Accelerators

Bridges' compute nodes feature Intel Xeon v3 ("Haswell") and v4 ("Broadwell") CPUs and NVIDIA Tesla K80 and P100 GPUs.

Each Extreme Shared Memory (ESM) node contains 16 Intel Xeon E7-8880 v3 (Phase 1) or E7-8880 v4 (Phase 2) CPUs. The Phase 1 E7-8880 v3 CPUs have 18 cores, 2.3 GHz base frequency, 3 GHz maximum turbo frequency, 45 MB last-level cache, and 3 QPI links at 9.6 GT/s. The Phase 2 E7-8880 v4 CPUs have 22 cores, 2.2 GHz base frequency, 3.3 GHz maximum turbo frequency, 55 MB last-level cache, and 3 QPI links at 9.6 GT/s.

Each Large Shared Memory (LSM) node contains 4 Intel Xeon E7-8860 v3 (Phase 1) or E7-8870 v4 (Phase 2) CPUs. The Phase 1 E7-8860 v3 CPUs have 16 cores, 2.2 GHz base frequency, 3.2 GHz maximum turbo frequency, 40 MB last-level cache, and 3 QPI links at

FIGURE 14.5: Bridges topology.

9.6 GT/s. The Phase 2 E7-8870 v4 CPUs have 20 cores, 2.1 GHz base frequency, 3.0 GHz maximum turbo frequency, 50 MB last-level cache, and 3 QPI links at 9.6 GT/s.

Each Regular Shared Memory (RSM) node contains 2 Intel Xeon E5-2695 v3 (Phase 1 and Phase 1 GPU) or E5-2683 v4 (Phase 2 GPU) CPUs. The Phase 1 E5-2695 v3 CPUs have 14 cores, 2.3 GHz base frequency, 3.3 GHz maximum turbo frequency, 35 MB last-level cache, and 2 QPI links at 9.6 GT/s. The Phase 2 E5-2683 v4 CPUs have 16 cores, 2.1 GHz base frequency, 3.0 GHz maximum turbo frequency, 40 MB last-level cache, and 2 QPI links at 9.6 GT/s.

The 32 NVIDIA Tesla K80 GPUs in Bridges' Phase 1 GPU nodes implement the Kepler architecture. Each has 2496 CUDA cores (128 per streaming multiprocessor (SM)), 2×24 GB of GDDR5 memory delivering 2×240.6 GB/s of memory bandwidth, with base and boost clocks of 562 MHz and 876 MHz, respectively. The theoretical peak of each K80 is 2.91 Tf/s (64b) and 8.73 Tf/s (32b).

The 64 NVIDIA Tesla P100 GPUs in Bridges' Phase 2 GPU nodes implement the Pascal architecture. Each has 3584 CUDA cores (64 per SM), 16 GB HBM2 memory at 720 GB/s with ECC, and base and boost clocks of 1126 MHz and 1303 MHz, respectively. The theoretical peak of each P100 is 4.7 Tf/s (64b), 9.3 Tf/s (32b), and 18.7 Tf/s (16b). The new 16b precision provides acceleration that is particularly valuable for deep learning training.

14.4.2   Node Design

Bridges contains 908 nodes, including 4 Extreme Shared Memory (ESM) nodes that are HPE Superdome Integrity X servers; 42 Large Shared Memory (LSM) nodes that are HPE ProLiant DL580 servers; 752 Regular Shared Memory (RSM) nodes, 48 GPU nodes, 12 database nodes, 6 web nodes, 16 utility nodes, 8 gateway nodes (connecting ESM nodes to OPA), all of which are HPE Apollo 2000 servers; and 20 storage nodes.

TABLE 14.2: Bridges node types.

Node type	RAM	Phase	Count	Processor	Server
ESM	12TB	1	2	16 × Intel Xeon E7-8880 v3 (18c, 2.3/3.1 GHz, 45MB LLC)	HPE Integrity Superdome X
	12TB	2	2	16 × Intel Xeon E7-8880 v4 (22c, 2.2/3.3 GHz, 55MB LLC)	
LSM	3TB	1	8	4 × Intel Xeon E7-8860 v3 (16c, 2.2/3.2 GHz, 40 MB LLC)	HPE ProLiant DL580
	3TB	2	34	4 × Intel Xeon E7-8870 v4 (20c, 2.1/3.0 GHz, 50 MB LLC)	
RSM	128GB	1	752	2 × Intel Xeon E5-2695 v3 (14c, 2.3/3.3 GHz, 35MB LLC)	HPE Apollo 2000
GPU	128GB	1	16	2 × Intel Xeon E5-2695 v3 + 2 × NVIDIA Tesla K80	
GPU	128GB	2	32	2 × Intel Xeon E5-2683 v4 (16c, 2.1/3.0 GHz, 40MB LLC) + 2 × NVIDIA Tesla P100	
DB-s	128GB	1	6	2 × Intel Xeon E5-2695 v3 + SSD	HPE ProLiant DL360
DB-h	128GB	1	6	2 × Intel Xeon E5-2695 v3 + HDDs	HPE ProLiant DL380
Web	128GB	1	6	2 × Intel Xeon E5-2695 v3	HPE ProLiant DL360
Other	128GB	1	16	2 × Intel Xeon E5-2695 v3	HPE ProLiant DL360, 380
Gateway	64GB	1	4	2 × Intel Xeon E5-2683 v3 (14c, 2.0/3.0 GHz, 35MB LLC)	HPE ProLiant DL380
	64GB	2	4	2 × Intel Xeon E5-2683 v3	
Storage	128GB	1	5	2 × Intel Xeon E5-2680 v3 (12c, 2.5/3.3 GHz, 30 MB LLC)	Supermicro X10DRi
	256GB	2	15	2 × Intel Xeon E5-2680 v4 (14c, 2.4/3.3 GHz, 35 MB LLC)	

14.4.3 Memory

Bridges' Phase 1 and Phase 2 nodes feature DDR4-2133 memory and DDR4-2400 memory, respectively.

Compute nodes contain an aggregate of 274 TB of RAM and 1.75 TB of GDDR5 and HBM2 memory on GPUs. Including database, web, and utility nodes, aggregate system RAM is 283.5 TB.

14.4.4 Interconnect

Bridges' Phase 1 installation was the first deployment of the Intel Omni-Path Architecture (OPA) fabric. Omni-Path unifies all of Bridges' compute nodes, database, web server, and other utility nodes, and parallel file systems, achieving convergence of HPC, AI, and Big Data capabilities.

OPA features salient to Bridges are as follows. Signaling is at 100 Gbps, yielding very high link bandwidth of 12.5 GB/s/direction. PSC measured 12.36 GB/s/direction for MPI, 98.9% of the theoretical maximum. The message injection rate is 160 million messages per second per port. The 48-port edge switches of first-generation OPA interconnect increase performance and reduce cost. Specifically, fewer switches translates to fewer hops, which reduces latency. OPA incorporates optimizations for HPC performance, reliability, and quality of service (QoS). Open Fabrics Alliance (OFA) compliant applications run without modification.

Bridges deploys OPA in a two-tier island topology developed by PSC and validated by Intel for cost-effective, data-intensive HPC. The top tier (see Figure 14.5) is a dual-rail mesh of six "core" switches, which are fully interconnected (single-rail) to twenty "leaf" switches. The core switches connect directly to all of Bridges' parallel storage, large and extreme memory nodes, and utility nodes. The leaf switches connect directly to all of Bridges' regular shared memory and GPU nodes, with up to 42 RSM nodes per "island". The bisection bandwidth within each of the 42-node islands is 525/, GB/s, full duplex, i.e., full bisection. Within an island, nodes are separated by two hops. Nodes are separate from storage by 2–6 hops.

This topology has several advantages. First, the core mesh provides multiple paths between each compute node and each piece of data, reducing congestion. Second, building the topology exclusively from leaf switches reduced the cost of the interconnection fabric, allowing more budget to be put in compute nodes, while maintaining full bisection bandwidth for jobs of up to 1,176 cores (many of which can be run concurrently) and also allowing full-machine runs for applications that are not primarily constrained by bisection bandwidth. The 48-port switches allowed the topology to be built with fewer switches, reducing the number of hops to reduce latency and reducing cost. Third, the fabric has open ports to which additional nodes or storage can be connected, and it can easily be expanded if needed.

PSC initiated the Omni-Path User Group (OPUG) to facilitate community discussion, sharing of experiences, and potentially advanced development. OPUG meets in person at major conferences and by teleconference, and an email distribution list facilitates timely sharing of information.

14.4.5 Storage System

Bridges implements three types of storage: shared parallel file systems, node-local storage, and RAM disk. PSC designed and built Pylon, Bridges' storage system for shared parallel file systems, on which Lustre and SLASH2 [29, 44] file systems are mounted (see Section 14.5.2).

Both Lustre and SLASH2 file systems federate separate file systems storage building blocks (SBBs). Each SBB consists of a storage server and four JBODs with forty-four 4 TB hard disk drives each (176 hard disk drives per SBB). A ZFS file system runs on each SBB, with 8+3 RAID providing extremely high reliability. Those ZFS file systems are then federated into parallel Lustre and SLASH2 file systems, which are exposed as standard mount points to users.

Bridges' aggregate shared parallel file system usable capacity is 10 PB. Node-local storage adds 7.3 PB raw storage.

14.5 System Software

PSC configured all system software for Bridges, including the operating system, file systems, management and monitoring tools, and user environment. Table 14.3 lists basic system software elements, and the following sections briefly describe Bridges' system software environment. The Bridges User Guide, available on PSC's website, provides much greater detail on applications, libraries, and the user environment.

TABLE 14.3: Software configuration.

Feature	Software
Login Node OS	CentOS
Compute Node OS	CentOS
Parallel Filesystems	Lustre, SLASH2
Container Technologies	Singularity, Docker
Compilers	Intel, PGI, GNU, NVIDIA
MPI	Intel MPI, OpenMPI, MVAPICH
Notable Frameworks	Anaconda, Jupyter, RStudio, MATLAB TensorFlow, Keras, PyTorch, Caffe, Caffe2, Theano Spark, Hadoop
Notable Libraries	HDF5, NetCDF Intel MKL, CUDA Trilinos, Boost, Magma, FFTW OpenCV, parseltongue
Job Scheduler	Slurm
Resource Manager	OpenStack
Debugging Tools	Allinea DDT, NVIDIA cuda-gdb
Performance Tools	TAU, VTune, PAPI, NVIDIA Visual Profiler

14.5.1 Operating System

Bridges runs the CentOS operating system (OS). PSC keeps the OS up-to-date subject to constraints imposed by device drivers such as for network interfaces. Between releases, patches are installed as necessary to maintain security and provide important new features.

Other operating systems such as Ubuntu Linux and Microsoft Windows are supported through containers and virtual machines.

14.5.2   File Systems

Shared parallel file systems are used for persistent storage and scratch space. Bridges implements two shared parallel file systems: Lustre and SLASH2. Lustre provides high performance over Omni-Path and benefits from broad community support. SLASH2 [29, 44], developed by PSC, provides additional wide-area capabilities for cross-site collaboration.

On Bridges, both Lustre and SLASH2 file systems federate separate file systems storage building blocks (SBBs). Each SBB consists of a storage server and four JBODs with forty-four 4 TB hard disk drives each (176 hard disk drives per SBB). A ZFS file system runs on each SBB, with 8+3 RAID providing extremely high reliability. Those ZFS file systems are then federated into parallel Lustre and SLASH2 file systems, which are exposed as standard mount points to users.

Bridges' aggregate file system capacity is 10 PB. The amount allocated to Lustre versus SLASH2 is not fixed and can vary over time pursuant to users' needs.

Each Bridges compute node contains local storage, mounted as $LOCAL. RSM, LSM, and ESM nodes have two, four, and 16 hard disk drives each, where each of those drives is 4 TB. Bridges' node-local storage serves three roles. First, it improves portability for Hadoop, sharded databases, and other applications written for distributed storage. Second, it increases aggregate system bandwidth and adds 7.3 PB of aggregate capacity for short-term use. Third, by localizing I/O within nodes, the node-local storage improves performance and performance consistency for other applications using Bridges' shared parallel file systems.

RAM on Bridges' large-memory nodes can also be used very productively for memory-resident file systems. This has proven especially valuable for genome sequence assembly applications, which benefit transparently from RAM disk performance without requiring any changes to their source code.

14.5.3   System Administration

Bridges' nodes are provisioned using OpenStack[17]. For Bridges, PSC pioneered use of OpenStack Ironic [7] for bare-metal provisioning at scale. OpenStack is also used to provision virtual machines (VMs), including provisioning of additional VM block and object storage.

Central to Bridges' architecture is the notion that nodes can be repurposed for different uses. For example, a Regular Shared Memory node may be configured for HPC or Hadoop, and if additional nodes for persistent services are eventually required, RSM nodes can also be repurposed for that. PSC uses Puppet for rolling out specific node configurations in a consistent, manageable way. PSC has developed several hundred custom Puppet scripts to support Bridges. Puppet infrastructure is integrated into PSC-managed VMs.

PSC employs a wide range of tools for system management, monitoring, and reporting. Naemon is used for monitoring and alerting, where Puppet dynamically sends new nodes and services to be monitored to Naemon as they are configured.

Bridges is integrated with the XDMoD SUPReMM system [25] for instrumentation, which included development of a collection workflow and uploading of aggregate data. Fine-grained monitoring, for example, measurement of power and cooling, is stored in an InfluxDB database and visualized with Grafana. Queue utilization and wait statistics are collected and used for ongoing system tuning.

14.5.4   Scheduler

Bridges uses Slurm [21] for its reasonably robust feature set and to provide uniformity across XSEDE resources. All resources on Bridges are scheduled through Slurm, including reserving nodes to host persistent services and to run Hadoop.

Separate partitions allow selection of regular memory, large memory, or GPU nodes, as required for specific job types. Job submissions are constrained by users' allocations. Users who require a particular type of GPU or CPU can identify the specific resource(s) they require. For example, Bridges' P100 GPUs are optimal for deep learning training, whereas its K80 GPUs are a good choice for scale-out acceleration of molecular dynamics applications.

Regular shared memory nodes are requested by number of nodes or by number of cores, where individual jobs can use anywhere from one core to all compute nodes. Large shared memory nodes are requested by the amount of memory, with the number of cores automatically allocated based on the amount of memory per core on each of the four large memory node types (LSM and ESM, Phase 1 and 2). GPU nodes are requested by the number of GPUs, where each K80 presents two allocatable GPUs and each P100 presents one allocatable GPU.

14.6   Interactivity

New and nontraditional users expect interactivity. Even for seasoned users, interactivity greatly increases productivity for data analytics, development, and debugging. Individuals who do not have background in HPC systems and batch schedulers are accustomed to web and mobile devices that transparently interoperate with cloud services. Submitting even simple tasks to a batch scheduler and potentially waiting hours to days to see results can be perceived as an unexpected and unwelcome barrier. Interactivity is also critical for analytics that are inherently iterative, alternating between testing ideas and tuning the approach.

Bridges provides interactivity via a simple *interact* command, implemented for convenience as a wrapper for Slurm's *srun* command. Using *interact*, users can usually obtain immediate access to regular shared memory, GPU, and large shared memory nodes. As with batch access, users can specify their requirements, ranging from one core to multiple nodes. PSC sizes the pool of resources that is reserved for interactive access according to demand, revisiting utilization weekly.

14.6.1   Virtualization and Containers

Virtualization serves two main roles on Bridges. Primarily, virtual machines (VMs) are deployed on a persistent, project-specific basis to provide encapsulation, specific software environments, and security. To a lesser extent, a few projects have requested VMs to develop scalable software that requires a certain operating system or other specific components in their software environment. In most cases, VMs are not needed on Bridges because PSC already supports a very rich software stack on bare metal. Also, PSC has observed a shift in users' requests from VMs to containers.

For containers, PSC recommends the use of Singularity [23]. Singularity is designed to support scientific application workloads securely on HPC resources. In particular, Singularity does not require a privileged daemon and runs in user space. Users can therefore run Singularity images directly, without needing any special steps or interaction with system administrators. Importantly, Singularity can bootstrap Docker [28] containers and download layers from the Docker Registry. Its interoperating with Docker is extremely valuable to support the large number of Docker images in use, particularly for computational biology.

14.7 User Environment

A significant difference between traditional and nontraditional HPC communities is their difference in preferred programming models and languages.

For traditional HPC applications written to solve well-defined differential equations, writing in C++, C, or Fortran and using message-passing and threading libraries or directives is relatively well-understood. Such programming can be detailed and tedious, but the effort is amortized over large amounts of simulation time. There exist abundant libraries for solvers, linear algebra, fast Fourier transforms (FFTs), meshing, and other common operations. Floating-point speed and efficiency are paramount. Data for these applications tends to be structured and regular, and there are widely-used, mature libraries for the resulting I/O patterns.

For nontraditional applications, the situation is quite different. Various nontraditional HPC communities draw heavily on unstructured, irregular, and disparate data such as natural language, medical records, images, audio, video, and data from diverse sensors and instruments. Their applications tend to focus on data analytics involving statistics, machine learning, visualization, and collaboration, and they are written using high-productivity programming models to accommodate rapidly-changing questions and iterative model building and refinement.

The user environment for Bridges is designed to accommodate both traditional and nontraditional applications. Bridges' rich user environment reflects its highly heterogeneous hardware architecture. Its user environment is based on recognition that large-memory nodes, cross-cutting filesystems, and the ability to couple HPC with AI and Big Data would provide nontraditional communities with orders of magnitude more capability without requiring them to change their way of working.

14.7.1 User Environment Customization

PSC's diverse user requirements require providing powerful tools for letting users customize their environments. Examples include selecting a particular compiler (vendor, version) and MPI implementation (compiler-specific build, version), application (e.g., GATK 3.7), or library (e.g., HDF 1.8.16, for use with Intel compiler builds). Bridges uses the *modules* utility to manage those selections and their dependencies. For example, by default each user's environment is pre-loaded with the Intel (and GNU) compiler and with Intel MPI. To use OpenMPI, the following command *module load mpi/intel_openmpi* replaces Intel MPI with the default version of OpenMPI in the user's environment. For each package being installed, the corresponding Puppet specification for package management also includes generation of the appropriate *module* file.

Python also requires frequent customization. Bridges supports Python 2.7, 3.*x*, and some other versions that are needed for specific projects. Users can add packages to their own file spaces with *pip* and *pip3* for Python 2.7 and 3.*x*, respectively. Bridges also supports Anaconda to allow users to better manage complex collections of Python and R software.

14.7.2   Programming Models

Bridges supports MPI+X for scalable computing, CUDA, MPI+CUDA and MPI+OpenACC for GPU programming, and a wide variety of options for threading from various programming languages including C++, C, Fortran, Java, Python, and R.

14.7.3   Languages and Compilers

Bridges supports Python (2.7 and 3.x), R, Java, MATLAB, Scala, Julia, and Lua, in addition to C++, C, Fortran, MPI, OpenMP, and OpenACC. Bridges supports Intel, PGI, and GNU compilers for C++, C, and Fortran. Where available, implementations of high-productivity programming languages optimized for specific hardware are provided; for example, the Intel Python Distribution.

Accelerators are important to Bridges for deep learning, simulation, and analytics. For those wishing to program GPUs, Bridges supports OpenACC through PGI's compiler and CUDA.

OpenACC provides an easy-to-use directive-based approach with strong potential for performance portability across new generations and different types of processors and accelerators. PSC has led OpenACC training for the NSF research community from OpenACC's inception.

14.7.4   Programming Tools

Bridges' familiar, flexible user environment builds heavily on its broad range of programming tools and frameworks.

Python is now of great importance for data analytics, computation, coupling applications, and coursework. Users can customize their environments on Bridges using Anaconda and virtualenv. Jupyter has also become popular. On Bridges, users can launch Jupyter notebooks with Python 2.7 or 3.x environments, including from an Open OnDemand web interface.

For more traditional software development, Bridges supports Allinea's DDT parallel debugger, provisioned for routine use and allowing occasional bursting to much larger core counts for problems that manifest only at scale, and PGI's Graphical OpenMP/MPI parallel debugger. For performance optimization, Bridges features an effective suite of tools including TAU, PAPI, Intel VTune, and the NVIDIA Visual Profiler.

14.7.5   Spark and Hadoop

Spark is available through the *modules* utility and can be run with or without the Hadoop filesystem (HDFS) and resource management daemons (YARN), depending on need. Spark applications can benefit greatly from Bridges' large-memory nodes to increase the performance of databases, graph analytics (e.g., GraphX), and other memory-intensive tasks. Spark runs in user space, making it very easy for users to initiate. Spark can leverage Bridges' large memory, node-local storage, and/or parallel file systems. PSC has run Big Data workshops successfully with hundreds of concurrent Spark users.

Bridges also supports Hadoop to allow users to leverage popular tools such as Cassandra, Hive, HBase, Hive, and other community software. Hadoop-on-Demand is the default, with reservations taken for larger or special configurations. The filesystem can be tailored to the application, using local disk for performance or Pylon for convenience and persistence.

14.7.6 Databases

Prior to Bridges, PSC began receiving many requests for persistent databases on Blacklight [32], PSC's previous large-memory system.

An innovative and vital feature of Bridges is its support for persistent databases that support gateways, workflow management systems, metadata for community datasets, and other advanced data management.

Examples of databases that researchers working in data fusion, genomics, radio astronomy, and machine learning are already requesting include relational (MySQL, PostgreSQL), document (MongoDB, CouchDB), column (Cassandra), graph (Neo4j), and XML (eXistdb). Bridges database nodes will be configured with either solid-state drives (SSDs) for high IOPs or hard disk drives (HDDs) for high capacity and will be strong enough to host multiple projects database needs, isolated by virtualization where security or implementation concerns so require, although a particularly demanding project may require its own node.

14.7.7 Domain-Specific Frameworks and Libraries

Bridges supports a broad range of domain-specific frameworks and libraries with specific concentrations in computational biology and deep learning. Also supported are a wide range of traditional applications for domains such as engineering, chemistry, and physics.

14.7.8 Gateways, Workflows, and Distributed Applications

Science gateways (or, more simply, "gateways") are domain-specific, Internet-based interfaces to applications, data, workflows, collaborative functionality, and resources that allow end users to focus on their research rather than on programming, interacting with different computers, and queuing jobs. They can orchestrate complex workflows, manage security constraints, track provenance, and provide capabilities for reproducibility and linking digital assets from the scholarly record.

Gateways are the most effective way to enable new users to exploit HPC resources and extensive data collections. Significantly, the number of XSEDE gateway users surpassed the number of non-gateway users in 2015 [41]. Coming in through a gateway, users do not have to become programmers, understand how to work with the Linux command line or schedulers, or deal with the idiosyncrasies of different supercomputers. Well-designed gateways present interfaces using the language, context, and tools with which their communities are already familiar. In some cases, end users do not even have to obtain their own allocations on XSEDE. Instead, gateway providers obtain "community accounts" that users can leverage, thereby removing a significant barrier to entry for new and occasional users.

Users interact with gateways through interfaces typically implemented in web browsers, allowing abstraction of the complexities of Bridges to realize HPC, Big Data, and AI as a Service. This is extremely powerful, and it lets users easily scale their problems up and access data collections that they could not host on their local systems.

There are 37 science gateways currently registered with XSEDE[8], including some that run on Bridges and others that use Bridges as a computational resource. For example, Galaxy Main, hosted at the Texas Advanced Computing Center (TACC), transparently sends genome assembly jobs requiring large memory to Bridges. Bridges also runs other gateways that are not (yet) registered with XSEDE, for example, the Causal Web[1, 2] and additional instances of Galaxy.

Provenance: A vital role for gateways is implementation of workflows. Well-designed workflows enable reproducibility of results and extending research by supporting provenance, i.e., maintaining all the artifacts and configuration that produced the results. Bridges' database nodes and support for virtual machines and containers provide the basic infrastructure on which workflow frameworks, data management, and provenance are built.

14.8   Storage, Visualization, and Analytics

Data is foundational to Bridges for its role in driving analytics. All data is online, not in an archival system, to enable low-latency, high-bandwidth access. Researchers on Bridges make extensive use of Python, Jupyter, R, and MATLAB for their data analytic and visualization capabilities. Also supported are parallel visualization packages such as VisIt and ParaView.

14.8.1   Community Datasets and Big Data as a Service

Science is driven by data, and AI is most effective when presented with substantial datasets on which to train. Having data readily available, and hosting multiple datasets on the same computational resource to allow cross-correlation, offers valuable support for research and fosters multidisciplinary collaboration. Hosting a single copy of data used by multiple projects also uses storage space more efficiently.

To address these important factors, PSC's AI & Big Data group, working with other domain specialists at PSC, curates and makes available community datasets. Examples include benchmark data for natural language processing, ImageNet [38], GDELT [9], and various genomic data.

Big Data as a Service, or BDaaS, builds on community datasets by coupling tools for access and analysis to datasets. Like gateways, BDaaS can be democratizing by enabling access to large data and tools for domain experts to perform high-impact, compute-intensive analyses without specialized HPC skills.

In Bridges, the active effort to bring HPC capabilities to Big Data is being realized through BDaaS. This is of particular value where data cannot be processed completely independently, in which case the coupling and scalability of HPC allows researchers to address a different and important class of problems. The challenging convergence of the HPC and Big Data paradigms presents exciting opportunities driven by exploiting complex data.

14.9   Datacenter

Bridges is housed in PSC's datacenter, located in Monroeville, Pennsylvania. This controlled-access facility is 21 km from PSC's headquarters, which are located at the junction of the Carnegie Mellon and Pittsburgh campuses in the Oakland area of Pittsburgh. Also housed in PSC's datacenter are an Anton 2 special-purpose supercomputer for biomolecular simulation designed and constructed by D. E. Shaw Research (DESRES), high-performance networking equipment, and various other high-performance, cluster, and storage resources.

The datacenter features dual feeds from the electric utility, coupled with high-speed switching between feeds, to minimize the effect of short power interruptions. Diesel generators support the site during longer power outages. Cooling is from a central chilled water plant with an ample water reserve for emergency backup.

14.10   System Statistics

As of May 2018, Bridges is serving 1,421 projects and 7,340 users at 349 institutions and representing 110 principal fields of study. Institutions include universities, colleges, high schools, national labs, federal reserve banks, and private-sector companies. Requests for Bridges regular-memory nodes exceed capacity by approximately a factor of three, and requests for its GPU nodes exceed capacity by approximately a factor of five. Bridges has been executing approximately one million jobs per year.

14.10.1   Reliability and Uptime

Bridges' uptime has been 97%. Over the past year, this included scheduled outages to upgrade to Omni-Path 10.4 and CentOS 7.3. Because of Bridges' distributed architecture, an interruption on a compute node is isolated to that node, leading to high overall reliability.

To minimize disruptions to users, updates are bundled to the maximum extent possible into fewer outages. This is especially important on Bridges because many large-memory genome sequence assembly jobs run for weeks, precluding frequent outages.

Utilization shows a preponderance of small jobs, including jobs that run on only one node. This is to be expected for a machine focused on nontraditional applications, many of which involve large ensembles of individually small runs.

The primary challenge is balancing interactive access, which is essential for data analytics and new communities, against maintaining reasonably high system utilization. Pools of nodes are set aside in queues with short time limits (typically 8 hours) to provide availability for interactive jobs. The number of nodes in those pools is adjusted based on anticipated demand, and related queue policies, such as number of jobs per user and number of GPUs per user, are also adjusted. This has provided users with sufficient resources, including during peak periods such as when hundreds of students are using Bridges to complete AI coursework or when reservations are required to meet specific goals. The Bridges team is continuing to refine this process.

14.11   Science Highlights: Bridges-Enabled Breakthroughs

We conclude this overview of Bridges with two breakthroughs: one in AI and the other in genomics.

14.11.1   Artificial Intelligence and Big Data

In January 2017, Prof. Tuomas Sandholm and Noam Brown of Carnegie Mellon University made history when their AI, Libratus, defeated four of the world's top professional heads-up no-limit Texas hold'em poker players [12, 11]. This is a remarkable achievement since poker is a surrogate for real-world situations that require making decisions with imperfect information and where adversaries change their strategies, act to deceive, and also learn. More than just a game, poker is a benchmark through which algorithms can compete with clear results. Real-world applications to which closely related algorithms are likely to apply include negotiation, strategic pricing, medical treatment planning, and auctions.

Heads-up no-limit Texas holdem poker is exceedingly complex, with 10^{161} situations. A total of 120,000 hands were played over 20 days. Libratus won decisively, achieving 99.98% statistical significance. Libratus went beyond previous best algorithms by incorporating real-time improvements in its strategy.

Bridges made this groundbreaking result in scalable AI possible by supplying Libratus with real-time access to high-performance computing and storage for the 20-day experiment. PSC contributed to Libratus and its predecessors by helping with parallelization and optimization of the code.

Libratus ran on 600 nodes of Bridges: 50 nodes per hand for each of the 8 hands being played concurrently, and 200 nodes for additional ongoing training. Overall, Libratus required 19M core-hours and generated a knowledge base of 2.6 PB. The intense rate of play of the competition demanded highly reliable performance across all nodes, requiring the HPC capability of Bridges.

This work was published at the Neural Information Processing Systems (NIPS) 2017 conference [11], the most highly respected publication venue for advances in AI, where it was awarded Best Paper, along with a companion paper in Science [12].

14.11.2   Genomics

In 2016, a team from Marshall University, led by Herman Mays, an evolutionary biologist, and Jim Denvir, co-director of Marshall's genomics facility, used Bridges to assemble the first genome of the Sumatran rhinoceros, one of the world's most endangered mammals. The assembly and subsequent analysis of the Sumatran rhino genome [27], published in Current Biology, provides a reference genome from which other researchers may conduct larger population studies to help develop strategies for saving this endangered species. In addition, the study provides evolutionary and ecological context for the current status of the Sumatran rhino population. Analysis of the genome together with other modeling techniques provide insight into how the population of Sumatran rhinos changed throughout their evolutionary history and the likely role of climate change in their decline. These analyses indicate that the loss of genetic diversity since the Pleistocene made the species more susceptible to later pressure by humans and habitat loss.

Bridges was critical to the successful assembly of the first Sumatran rhino genome. Researchers used 116 billion bases of raw sequence data, consisting of 250-base short-read sequence fragments, to determine the sequence of the 2.5 billion base rhino genome. Although the researchers had local access to large memory systems with 500 GB of RAM, initial attempts to assemble the genome on these resources with a state-of-the-art genome assembler failed. Searching for resources that might be suitable for this task, the team identified the 3 TB nodes on Bridges and worked closely with PSC to assemble the genome. The final assembly required 2 TB of RAM on a Bridges 3 TB node and completed 4x faster than the team had anticipated based on assemblies of fractions of their data sets on local systems.

These results, and the approach presented in this study, may help scientists devise conservation strategies, not only for the Sumatran rhino, but also for other critically endangered species.

14.12 Acknowledgments

Bridges is supported by National Science Foundation award 1445606. Bridges is a resource in the Extreme Science and Engineering Discovery Environment (XSEDE), which is supported by National Science Foundation grant number 1548562. Thanks to Michael J. Levine, Ralph Z. Roskies, J. Ray Scott, Jason Sommerfield, John Urbanic, Ken Goodwin, Robin Scibek, Sergiu Sanielevici, David Moses, Jim Marsteller, and the PSC technical facilities, networking, security, and user services groups for contributions to Bridges' design, deployment, and operation.

Bibliography

[1] Causal web. https://ccd2.vm.bridges.psc.edu/ccd/login.

[2] Causal web application quick start and user guide. http://www.ccd.pitt.edu/wiki/index.php?title=Causal_Web_Application_Quick_Start_and_User_Guide.

[3] Frederick Jelinek Memorial Summer Workshop. https://www.lti.cs.cmu.edu/frederick-jelinek-memorial-summer-workshop-closing-day-schedule.

[4] Galaxy Main. https://usegalaxy.org.

[5] Galaxy Project Stats. https://galaxyproject.org/galaxy-project/statistics/#usegalaxyorg-usage.

[6] MIDAS MISSION Public Health Hackathon - Visualizing the future of public health. https://midas-publichealth-hack-3336.devpost.com.

[7] Openstack bare metal provisioning program. https://wiki.openstack.org/wiki/Ironic.

[8] Science gateways listing. https://www.xsede.org/gateways-listing.

[9] The GDELT Project. https://www.gdeltproject.org.

[10] Serafim Batzoglou. Algorithmic challenges in mammalian whole-genome assembly. In *Encyclopedia of Genetics, Genomics, Proteomics and Bioinformatics*. American Cancer Society, 2005.

[11] Noam Brown and Tuomas Sandholm. Safe and Nested Subgame Solving for Imperfect-Information Games. In I Guyon, U V Luxburg, S Bengio, H Wallach, R Fergus, S Vishwanathan, and R Garnett, editors, *ArXiv e-prints*, volume Advances i, pages 689–699, Long Beach, California, 2017. Curran Associates, Inc.

[12] Noam Brown and Tuomas Sandholm. Superhuman AI for heads-up no-limit poker: Libratus beats top professionals. *Science*, 2017.

[13] Gregory A. Cary, R. Andrew Cameron, and Veronica F. Hinman. EchinoBase: Tools for Echinoderm Genome Analyses. In *Eukaryotic Genomic Databases*, Methods in Molecular Biology, pages 349–369. Humana Press, New York, NY, 2018.

[14] Uma R. Chandran, Olga P. Medvedeva, M. Michael Barmada, Philip D. Blood, Anish Chakka, Soumya Luthra, Antonio Ferreira, Kim F. Wong, Adrian V. Lee, Zhihui Zhang, Robert Budden, J. Ray Scott, Annerose Berndt, Jeremy M. Berg, and Rebecca S. Jacobson. TCGA Expedition: A Data Acquisition and Management System for TCGA Data. *PLOS ONE*, 11(10):e0165395, October 2016.

[15] Chris Dyer and Phil Blunsom. On the State of the Art of Evaluation in Neural Language Models. pages 1–10, 2018.

[16] Andre Esteva, Brett Kuprel, Roberto A Novoa, Justin Ko, Susan M Swetter, Helen M Blau, and Sebastian Thrun. Dermatologist-level classification of skin cancer with deep neural networks. *Nature Publishing Group*, 2017.

[17] O.S. Foundation. *The Crossroads of Cloud and HPC: OpenStack for Scientific Research: Exploring OpenStack Cloud Computing for Scientific Workloads.* CreateSpace Independent Publishing Platform, 2016.

[18] Timothy Gushanas. NASA Twins Study Investigators to Release Integrated Paper in 2018. 2018.

[19] Jo Handelsman. Metagenomics: Application of Genomics to Uncultured Microorganisms. *Microbiology and Molecular Biology Reviews*, 68(4):669–685, December 2004.

[20] David E Hudak, Douglas Johnson, Jeremy Nicklas, Eric Franz, Brian McMichael, and Basil Gohar. Open OnDemand: Transforming Computational Science Through Omnidisciplinary Software Cyberinfrastructure. In *Proceedings of the XSEDE16 Conference on Diversity, Big Data, and Science at Scale*, pages 1–7, Miami, USA, 2016. ACM.

[21] Morris A. Jette, Andy B. Yoo, and Mark Grondona. Slurm: Simple linux utility for resource management. In *In Lecture Notes in Computer Science: Proceedings of Job Scheduling Strategies for Parallel Processing (JSSPP) 2003*, pages 44–60. Springer-Verlag, 2002.

[22] Alex Krizhevsky, Ilya Sutskever, and Geoffrey E. Hinton. *ImageNet Classification with Deep Convolutional Neural Networks*, pages 1097–1105. Curran Associates, Inc., 2012.

[23] Gregory M. Kurtzer, Vanessa Sochat, and Michael W. Bauer. Singularity: Scientific containers for mobility of compute. *PLOS ONE*, 12(5):1–20, 05 2017.

[24] Katherine A Lawrence, Michael Zentner, Nancy Wilkins-Diehr, Julie A Wernert, Marlon Pierce, Suresh Marru, and Scott Michael. Science gateways today and tomorrow: positive perspectives of nearly 5000 members of the research community. *Concurrency and Computation: Practice and Experience*, 27(16):4252–4268, 2015.

[25] Charng-Da Lu, James Browne, Robert L. DeLeon, John Hammond, William Barth, Thomas R. Furlani, Steven M. Gallo, Matthew D. Jones, and Abani K. Patra. Comprehensive job level resource usage measurement and analysis for XSEDE HPC systems. *Proceedings of the Conference on Extreme Science and Engineering Discovery Environment Gateway to Discovery - XSEDE '13*, page 1, 2013.

[26] Mario Lucic, Karol Kurach, Marcin Michalski, Sylvain Gelly, and Olivier Bousquet. Are GANs Created Equal? A Large-Scale Study. *arXiv:1711.10337 [cs, stat]*, November 2017. arXiv: 1711.10337.

[27] Herman L. Mays, Chih-Ming Hung, Pei-Jen Shaner, James Denvir, Megan Justice, Shang-Fang Yang, Terri L. Roth, David A. Oehler, Jun Fan, Swanthana Rekulapally, and Donald A. Primerano. Genomic Analysis of Demographic History and Ecological Niche Modeling in the Endangered Sumatran Rhinoceros Dicerorhinus sumatrensis. *Current Biology*, 28(1):70–76.e4, January 2018.

[28] Dirk Merkel. Docker: lightweight Linux containers for consistent development and deployment. *Linux Journal*, 2014(239), 2014.

[29] Paul Nowoczynski, Jason Sommerfield, Jared Yanovich, J. Ray Scott, Zhihui Zhang, and Michael Levine. The data supercell. In *Proceedings of the 1st Conference of the Extreme Science and Engineering Discovery Environment: Bridging from the eXtreme to the Campus and Beyond*, XSEDE '12, pages 13:1–13:11, New York, NY, USA, 2012. ACM.

[30] Nicholas A. Nystrom. Bridges virtual tour. https://psc.edu/bvt.

[31] Nicholas A. Nystrom, Michael J. Levine, Ralph Z. Roskies, and J. Ray Scott. Bridges: A uniquely flexible hpc resource for new communities and data analytics. In *Proceedings of the 2015 XSEDE Conference: Scientific Advancements Enabled by Enhanced Cyberinfrastructure*, XSEDE '15, pages 30:1–30:8, New York, NY, USA, 2015. ACM.

[32] Nick Nystrom, Joel Welling, Phil Blood, and Eng Lim Goh. Blacklight: Coherent Shared Memory for Enabling Science. In *Contemporary High Performance Computing*, Chapman & Hall/CRC Computational Science, pages 421–440. Chapman and Hall/CRC, July 2013.

[33] David Palesch, Steven E. Bosinger, Gregory K. Tharp, Thomas H. Vanderford, Mirko Paiardini, Ann Chahroudi, Zachary P. Johnson, Frank Kirchhoff, Beatrice H. Hahn, Robert B. Norgren, Nirav B. Patel, Donald L. Sodora, Reem A. Dawoud, Caro-Beth Stewart, Sara M. Seepo, R. Alan Harris, Yue Liu, Muthuswamy Raveendran, Yi Han, Adam English, Gregg W. C. Thomas, Matthew W. Hahn, Lenore Pipes, Christopher E. Mason, Donna M. Muzny, Richard A. Gibbs, Daniel Sauter, Kim Worley, Jeffrey Rogers, and Guido Silvestri. Sooty mangabey genome sequence provides insight into AIDS resistance in a natural SIV host. *Nature*, 553(7686):77–81, January 2018.

[34] Pavel A. Pevzner, Haixu Tang, and Michael S. Waterman. An Eulerian path approach to DNA fragment assembly. *Proceedings of the National Academy of Sciences*, 98(17):9748–9753, August 2001.

[35] Lenore Pipes, Sheng Li, Marjan Bozinoski, Robert Palermo, Xinxia Peng, Phillip Blood, Sara Kelly, Jeffrey M. Weiss, Jean Thierry-Mieg, Danielle Thierry-Mieg, Paul Zumbo, Ronghua Chen, Gary P. Schroth, Christopher E. Mason, and Michael G. Katze. The non-human primate reference transcriptome resource (NHPRTR) for comparative functional genomics. *Nucleic Acids Research*, 41(D1):D906–D914, January 2013.

[36] Pranav Rajpurkar, Awni Y. Hannun, Masoumeh Haghpanahi, Codie Bourn, and Andrew Y. Ng. Cardiologist-Level Arrhythmia Detection with Convolutional Neural Networks. *arXiv:1707.01836 [cs]*, July 2017. arXiv: 1707.01836.

[37] Jason A. Reuter, Damek V. Spacek, and Michael P. Snyder. High-throughput sequencing technologies. *Molecular Cell*, 58(4):586–597, May 2015.

[38] Olga Russakovsky, Jia Deng, Hao Su, Jonathan Krause, Sanjeev Satheesh, Sean Ma, Zhiheng Huang, Andrej Karpathy, Aditya Khosla, Michael Bernstein, Alexander C Berg, and Li Fei-Fei. ImageNet Large Scale Visual Recognition Challenge. *International Journal of Computer Vision*, 115(3):211–252, 2015.

[39] Alexander Sczyrba, Peter Hofmann, Peter Belmann, David Koslicki, Stefan Janssen, Johannes Dröge, Ivan Gregor, Stephan Majda, Jessika Fiedler, Eik Dahms, Andreas Bremges, Adrian Fritz, Ruben Garrido-Oter, Tue Sparholt Jørgensen, Nicole Shapiro, Philip D Blood, Alexey Gurevich, Yang Bai, Dmitrij Turaev, Matthew Z DeMaere, Rayan Chikhi, Niranjan Nagarajan, Christopher Quince, Fernando Meyer, Monika Balvočit, Lars Hestbjerg Hansen, Søren J Sørensen, Burton K H Chia, Bertrand Denis, Jeff L Froula, Zhong Wang, Robert Egan, Dongwan Don Kang, Jeffrey J Cook, Charles Deltel, Michael Beckstette, Claire Lemaitre, Pierre Peterlongo, Guillaume Rizk, Dominique Lavenier, Yu-Wei Wu, Steven W Singer, Chirag Jain, Marc Strous, Heiner Klingenberg, Peter Meinicke, Michael D Barton, Thomas Lingner, Hsin-Hung Lin, Yu-Chieh Liao, Genivaldo Gueiros Z Silva, Daniel A Cuevas, Robert A Edwards, Surya Saha, Vitor C Piro, Bernhard Y Renard, Mihai Pop, Hans-Peter Klenk, Markus Göker, Nikos C Kyrpides, Tanja Woyke, Julia A Vorholt, Paul Schulze-Lefert, Edward M Rubin, Aaron E Darling, Thomas Rattei, and Alice C McHardy. Critical Assessment of Metagenome Interpretation—a benchmark of metagenomics software. *Nature Methods*, 14:1063, Oct 2017.

[40] David Silver, Aja Huang, Chris J Maddison, Arthur Guez, Laurent Sifre, George van den Driessche, Julian Schrittwieser, Ioannis Antonoglou, Veda Panneershelvam, Marc Lanctot, Sander Dieleman, Dominik Grewe, John Nham, Nal Kalchbrenner, Ilya Sutskever, Timothy Lillicrap, Madeleine Leach, Koray Kavukcuoglu, Thore Graepel, and Demis Hassabis. Mastering the game of Go with deep neural networks and tree search. *Nature*, 529(7587):484–489, 2016.

[41] Nikolay A. Simakov, Joseph P. White, Robert L. DeLeon, Steven M. Gallo, Matthew D. Jones, Jeffrey T. Palmer, Benjamin Plessinger, and Thomas R. Furlani. A Workload Analysis of NSF's Innovative HPC Resources Using XDMoD. *arXiv:1801.04306 [cs]*, January 2018. arXiv: 1801.04306.

[42] John Towns, Timothy Cockerill, Maytal Dahan, Ian Foster, Kelly Gaither, Andrew Grimshaw, Victor Hazlewood, Scott Lathrop, Dave Lifka, Gregory D Peterson, Ralph Roskies, J Ray Scott, and Nancy Wilkens-Diehr. XSEDE: Accelerating Scientific Discovery. *Computing in Science & Engineering*, 16(5):62–74, 9 2014.

[43] B Yang, L Ying, and J Tang. Artificial Neural Network Enhanced Bayesian PET Image Reconstruction. *IEEE Transactions on Medical Imaging*, PP(99):1, 2018.

[44] Jared Yanovich. Slash2 file system. https://github.com/pscedu/slash2.

[45] J Ye, P Wu, J Z Wang, and J Li. Fast Discrete Distribution Clustering Using Wasserstein Barycenter With Sparse Support. *IEEE Transactions on Signal Processing*, 65(9):2317–2332, 2017.

[46] Jonathan D. Young, Chunhui Cai, and Xinghua Lu. Unsupervised deep learning reveals prognostically relevant subtypes of glioblastoma. *BMC Bioinformatics*, 18(Suppl 11):381, October 2017.

[47] Daniel R. Zerbino and Ewan Birney. Velvet: Algorithms for de novo short read assembly using de Bruijn graphs. *Genome Research*, 18(5):821–829, May 2008.

[48] Xinye Zheng, Jianbo Ye, Yukun Chen, Stephen Wistar, Jia Li, Jose A. Piedra-Fernndez, Michael A. Steinberg, and James Z. Wang. Detecting Comma-shaped Clouds for Severe Weather Forecasting using Shape and Motion. *arXiv:1802.08937 [cs]*, February 2018. arXiv: 1802.08937.

Chapter 15

The Evolution of the Stampede Project at TACC and the Design of Stampede 2

Dan Stanzione and John West

Texas Advanced Computing Center, The University of Texas at Austin

15.1 Overview

The US National Science Foundation (NSF) vision for cyberinfrastructure (CI) [10] recognizes the need for high capability and capacity HPC systems as part of a comprehensive national operational CI that enables open science research and education. The "Stampede" and follow-on "Stampede 2" HPC systems [25], both at the Texas Advanced Computing Center (TACC) at The University of Texas at Austin (UT), were deployed to address this need.

Stampede should be understood not simply as the individual systems bearing the name, but rather as a computational ecosystem that enables petascale computing and complements other major national investments in open science CI. The design for the Stampede project enhances petascale productivity with a highly usable and balanced system that includes integrated data analysis capabilities and extensive support and outreach. By using commodity technologies and offering a familiar programming model, and through campus bridging efforts and industrial partnerships, Stampede is extending the adoption of petascale computing while providing a compelling new path towards exascale computing. The Stampede project is a key part of the national CI coordinated by the eXtreme Science & Engineering Discovery Environment (XSEDE) partnership [27], of which TACC is a co-lead partner. The first Stampede system was very successful, delivering up to 80% of all HPC cycles provided within XSEDE to the open science community; the success of this design and the lessons we learned from it drove the design of Stampede 2 and positioned users for success on day one of system operation.

15.1.1 Program Background

The goals of the strategic plan for the NSF's advanced cyberinfrastructure are to provide advanced computing technologies to the entire spectrum of NSF-funded research while providing the training and expertise needed for effective multidisciplinary computational and data-enabled science and engineering [10]. The Stampede project supports many facets of this vision, but it most directly relates to:

> Building, testing, and deploying both sustainable and innovative resources into a collaborative ecosystem that encompasses integration/coordination with campus and regional systems, networks, cloud services, and/or data centers in partnerships with scientific domains.

As elaborated in the strategic plan, it is not sufficient to simply *provide* computing resources, even advanced leadership-scale systems; scientists and engineers need access to the resources and expertise required to use the computing systems effectively. These resources include user assistance, archival data storage, integration of data- and compute-intensive science, and transfer of the knowledge and skills needed for new communities of users to adopt advanced computing as part of their routine workflow. The importance of the last point — transfer of knowledge and skills — is highlighted by the inclusion of workforce development as a key attribute of the National Scalable Computing Initiative (NSCI) established by executive order of the President of the United States[3]. The NSF is designated the lead on this part of NSCI.

15.1.2 Lessons Learned on the Path to Stampede 2

TACC was awarded the grant to build the first Stampede system in 2012 through the NSF's "Equipment Acquisitions, Petascale — Track 1" program, and the system became available to users in January 2013. At the time of its deployment, Stampede was the largest open science system in the world and debuted as the seventh fastest system among all systems. The system concluded operations in late 2017.

At the peak of its deployment, Stampede was an 11 petaFLOPS (PF) system designed for a very diverse population of applications. Intel's Xeon E5 (Sandy Bridge) processors powered the base system, augmented by the first large-scale deployment of Intel's first-generation Xeon Phi processors (Knights Corner, or KNC). The Xeon E5 nodes provided 2.2 PF of the system's total capability, and the Xeon Phi co-processors provided the remaining 7.3 PF. Next-generation Xeon Phi processors (Knights Landing) were added to Stampede in 2016, resulting in an additional 508 nodes and 1.5 PF of capacity. With 272 TB of memory and 14 PB of local disk, Stampede also had excellent memory and I/O bandwidth, enabling both large simulations and data-driven applications. Stampede's InfiniBand interconnect provided a low latency, high bandwidth path between nodes and to parallel file systems, with a total of 35 TB/s of backplane bandwidth.

The wide applicability of Stampede's architecture is reflected in usage statistics. Over the system's operational life more than 12,000 users participating in 3,600 projects logged in directly to use the machine, and tens of thousands more used Stampede indirectly through web portals created as part of the NSF's CyVerse [20] and DesignSafe [23] initiatives (among others). Throughout its operation Stampede performed more than 8.2 million simulations and data analysis runs, totaling more than 3.3 billion processor core hours.

Stampede enabled groundbreaking science, contributing to the LIGO measurement of gravitational waves [4], helping to determine how the first stars formed [15], providing insights into the fundamental driving mechanisms of plate tectonics, and thousands of other innovations. Calculations performed on Stampede were featured on the covers of many journals, including *Science*, and contributed to Gordon Bell prize-winning simulations [22, 24].

The success (and challenges) of Stampede in serving the needs of a very broad range of science and engineering applications provided an informative perspective through which to evaluate possible designs for Stampede 2. User success in transitioning work to Intel's Xeon Phi processors, although far from universal, was substantial enough to convince the design team that Phi continued to be a viable alternative to GPUs. A key design point for Stampede 2 was that it should prepare the science community for future exascale machines. All likely exascale technology paths at the time of design indicated a future dominated by "manycore" processors. While both GPUs and Phi processors offer a manycore platform, the convergence of the Xeon and Xeon Phi platforms has practical advantages over GPUs, as software investments made to improve performance on Xeon will improve Phi performance as well (and vice versa).

We recognized that programming complexity is increasing, presenting a challenge for all of scientific computing. However, the complexities inherent in the manycore future appear to be inevitable, at least through the initial round of exascale deployments. When first deployed as part of the Stampede project, the Intel Knights Corner co-processors represented a significant technology risk, as they had never been deployed at scale. KNC also represented a significant performance risk for the user community, as applications needed to be adapted to use the new chips successfully. TACC's approach to minimizing both of these risks was to deploy early access nodes featuring KNC processors. These nodes provided TACC and its users with a test platform to validate that the processors delivered the expected performance and could be an effective component of a stable, large-scale production HPC system.

This approach to risk mitigation and user productivity continued into the design and deployment of Stampede 2. When TACC deployed the first 508 production nodes of Intel's next-generation Phi processor as part of the first Stampede system, it again provided both users and center staff with the opportunity to assess technological and performance risks before fully committing to the technology in Stampede 2. Those risk gates were passed successfully, and a phased deployment is underway at the time of writing. Phase 1, currently in operation, consists of 4,204 Xeon Phi (Knights Landing) nodes, a 25PB Lustre parallel filesystem, and an Omni-Path interconnect. Phase 2, scheduled for operation in October 2017, will add 1,736 Intel Xeon (Sky Lake) nodes. A final phase in 2018 will add 2TB of NVDIMM capacity to 50 nodes as part of an advanced technology evaluation. The resulting system will provide roughly double the peak performance of the original Stampede system, and is expected to remain operational through 2021.

15.2   Workload and the Design of Stampede 2

As mentioned above, Stampede 2 is the second system in the Stampede project. As both systems are designed to serve the same computational communities, it was instructive to study Stampede's performance and workload data in designing Stampede 2.

The system design team analyzed utilization and application performance for the most recent sixteen month period preceding the start of design. During this single period over 1.5 billion node hours were consumed, about 1 billion of which were consumed by jobs executed using TACC-developed tools that permit detailed analysis [5, 9]; this is the population on which our design analysis focuses. The data for this period includes information on over one million individual jobs and more than 5,000 unique application names.

The challenge was to reduce the sheer volume of data to a smaller number of characteristic dimensions that would inform system design. Utilization over the period was dominated by a relatively small number of major applications, with the bulk of the individual applications in the long tail. In order to limit the data to a meaningful subset that could drive design, we looked at applications that used 2 million or more node hours over all jobs during the period. This group included 60 applications, the top 34 of which consume 50% of all node hours consumed during the sample period.

Of the 500 million node hours consumed by these applications, 47% of usage was from applications that solve partial differential equations (PDEs) in a very wide range of disciplines, 45% of usage was from molecular dynamics (MD) applications, 6% of total usage was consumed by lattice QCD, and the remaining 2% was consumed by applications performing n-body calculations. The largest single application on Stampede during this period was NAMD, a popular molecular dynamics application [21]. This code alone accounts for 13.5% of all node hours consumed, nearly twice the number of hours consumed by the next largest application.

Despite this clustering of utilization in a small number of applications, the tail of the utilization curve is very long: although only 60 codes consume 50% of the node hours used during the sample period, the remaining 50% is divided among more than 5,000 individual applications. Interactions with Stampede's many users lead us to believe that the bulk of this long tail is PDE-based applications, but the population size is too large and too fractured to reward detailed study.

Examination of the performance characteristics of the four dominant application categories provided motivation for specific decisions about the Stampede 2 architecture. In general, mature parallel PDE applications used by a wide community of users employ explicit solution methods that scale well on distributed memory systems. Implicitly-solved PDEs are less common among the largest projects but are an important class for which a global solve is required, and for which effective memory use is a significant challenge. Nonetheless, our experience is that PDE applications can scale effectively to tens of thousands and, less frequently, many hundreds of thousands of cores.

The other large applications that dominate the portfolio — MD, lattice gauge QCD, and n-body problems — also have potential to make effective use of distributed memory systems with accelerators. Lattice gauge QCD methods resemble PDEs in their execution of sparse, local matrix-vector products, but with a 4D grid, and good performance is now being achieved for some problems in this class on accelerator-based systems [6]. MD, n-body, and many-body problems feature potentials that incorporate non-local interactions. In many cases these non-local interactions can be transformed in a way that localizes them, for example by neglecting their effects beyond some cut-off radius; effective parallel solvers are available for these cases. Dense local interactions mean that, with sufficient effort, good performance is also possible for these problems on accelerators, as demonstrated by the inclusion of a Xeon Phi-accelerated application in the finalists for the 2014 Gordon Bell prize [14]. As with PDEs, a low-latency/high-bandwidth network is the key to scalability for many of these applications.

In addition to large HPC projects that dominate the current workload for the Stampede project, it was important during the design to consider emerging application domains that may not use large-scale computers in the same way as established disciplines. Data-driven and data-intensive applications featured prominently in this group. Generally, these simulations use observed or collected digital data for either data assimilation (inverse problems), in which observational data is used to infer uncertain states or uncertain parameters, or statistics, informatics, and analytics methods in which the data, not the physics, is the primary driver of discovery. These data applications often require software that is quite different from classic HPC applications (e.g. parallel R and Matlab), and I/O read performance can be even more important than write performance.

15.2.1   Science Highlights

It is instructive to more closely examine a few of the individual projects that are aggregated in the system-level description of the Stampede design workload as just described. The following projects illustrate the benefits realized by some very diverse projects, through the improved capabilities and capacities provided by Stampede, as well as through collaboration with TACC staff to improve codes and workflows that enable more productive research.

Of the over 3,000 projects that relied on resources of the Stampede project, the discovery of gravitational waves by the NSF-funded Laser Interferometer Gravitational-Wave Observatory (LIGO) in 2015 is one of the most important [4]. Gravitational waves are ripples in the fabric of space-time created by black hole collisions. The waves are spaced apart by only 1/1000th the diameter of a proton, so tiny that until recently they've eluded efforts to extract their signal from background noise. Researchers used roughly seven million core hours on Stampede to analyze the dataset containing the first gravitational waves ever detected, and worked with TACC researchers to improve their workflow for more productive discovery work.

Forecasting the correct track and intensity for an expected hurricane enables emergency management officials to more effectively protect life and property for communities near the coast. The methods that Penn State University researcher Fuqing Zhang developed in a 2015 Stampede-enabled study of 100 tropical storms between 2008-2012 reduced errors by 25 to 28 percent in forecast intensity, compared to the corresponding forecasts issued by the National Hurricane Center [29]. Earlier and more accurate predictions can provide residents and local officials the time they need to plan evacuation and emergency response when a hurricane threatens.

DNA, the fundamental building block of life, uses electrostatic attraction or repulsion to fold together or come apart. This property enables cells to store genetic information, to replicate and repair that information, and to regulate how that information is expressed. Computational physicist Aleksei Aksimentiev of the University of Illinois at Urbana-Champaign used large-scale simulations on Stampede to explore the nature of DNA-DNA interactions [18]. The large scale of Stampede reduced the time for a computational study from more than a month to less than a week, enabling a simulation research and development cycle that matched that of experimental biophysics, and allowed for an iterative approach to the solving of the same scientific problem. Aksimentiev's research helps explain why DNA — a highly charged polymer — can fold into compact structures at the cell's nucleus in spite of the fact that like charges should force the molecule into a much larger structure. The

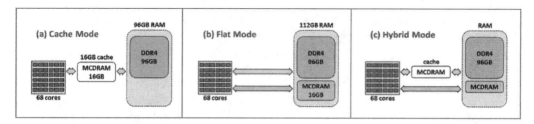

FIGURE 15.1: KNL Memory Modes on Stampede 2.

new techniques that led to key insights on this problem are now being used to design DNA nanostructures that deliver drugs into cancerous cells.

15.3   System Configuration

The final design for Stampede 2 includes 5,928 total compute nodes, a 28 petaByte storage subsystem, and 24 additional login and management servers. The nodes are interconnected by an Intel Omni-Path network. The compute nodes are based on two processors: 1,728 nodes provisioned with dual-socket Intel Xeon "Skylake" (SKX) processors, and 4,200 nodes provisioned with an Intel Xeon Phi "Knights Landing" (KNL) bootable processor.

The compute nodes are deployed in 107 total racks, 75 of which contain 56 KNL compute nodes each. The remaining 32 racks contain the 54 Skylake compute nodes each. The compute racks include two Omni-Path 48-port leaf switches each, along with two 48-port gigabit Ethernet switches with a 10-gigabit uplink to aggregation switches. Eight additional racks hold login, data transfer, management, and storage servers, while six wider racks house the core Omni-Path Director Class Switches and cabling. Total peak system power for the complete system is approximately 4MW.

15.3.1   Processors and Memory

Unlike the earlier generation Knights Core processors, each 68-core "Knights Landing" (KNL) processor in Stampede 2 is a stand-alone, self-booting processor that is the sole processor in its node. KNL has four hardware threads per core, and two 512-byte vector units per core. The vector units use the same AVX512 instruction set that is used for the Xeon processors, meaning that applications compiled for KNL will run on SKX without recompilation.

KNL has two kinds of memory: high bandwidth MCDRAM on package, and six channels of off-package RAM. Each of the six channels on Stampede 2 is provisioned with a single 16GB DDR-4 DIMM to improve performance, providing a total of 96GB of DDR-4 RAM. As shown in Figure 15.1, these two memories can be configured in three modes. Most Stampede 2 queues are configured to automatically run in cache mode; hybrid mode is not available to users on Stampede 2.

The "Skylake" (SKX) processors in Stampede 2 are the successors to the Intel Sandy Bridge processor. The instruction set for SKX is compatible with the KNL processor (except for a few specialized uncommon instructions). Each SKX node in Stampede 2 has two SKX sockets with 48 cores each; each core supports two hardware threads. A total of 192GB of RAM is provisioned on each node and shared by the two sockets.

15.3.2   Interconnect

The tightly-coupled scientific applications that dominate Stampede's workload (see Section 15.2) require a high-bandwidth, low-latency network. Stampede 2 uses the 100 Gb/s Intel Omni-Path network to support all inter-node application communications (e.g. MPI messages and shared file system transfers). The interconnect is a fat tree using six 768-port Director Class core switches, with two 48-port Omni-Path leaf switches installed into each compute rack. Up to 28 ports in each leaf switch are connected to compute nodes, with the remaining 20 ports uplinked to the core switches. This design yields a marginal oversubscription of 7:5.

The I/O servers have full non-blocking connectivity to ensure maximum network bandwidth is available to the storage subsystem. The remaining login and support nodes also have non-blocking connectivity to the core switches; however, no MPI communication traffic will run across these uplinks. This design leaves 40 ports free on each of the 768-port core switches, building in an upgrade path for the system.

15.3.3   Disk I/O Subsystem

The Stampede 2 storage system is based on Seagate's ClusterStor product, originally developed by Xyratex. ClusterStor was selected for improved performance to a single Lustre target, shorter rebuild times after drive failure, and automatic active/active failover of the servers. The storage subsystem consists of six metadata servers with 18TB of SAS disk and 35 ClusterStor Scalable Storage Units (SSUs). An SSU is essentially a storage "building block" that includes two servers, 82 10TB drives and two SSDs for external journals; the total capacity is 28PB.

The storage subsystem is divided into two filesystems, *home* and *scratch*. The *home* filesystem is not intended for high-intensity file operations and is backed up regularly. It consists of two metadata servers (MDSs) and two SSUs, with a usable capacity of almost 1.2PB and 20GB/s of aggregate bandwidth. *scratch*, designed to support high-volume, fast file I/O for parallel jobs, uses four MDSs and 33 SSUs to provide a usable capacity of 20PB and overall aggregated bandwidth of 330GB/s. *scratch* includes enough metadata capacity to support four billion files. All of the storage servers are connected into the Omni-Path fabric with non-blocking connectivity to provide maximum bandwidth to the rest of the system.

TABLE 15.1: Stampede 2 Hardware Configuration.

Feature	Phase 1 (Jul 2017)	Phase 2 (Nov 2017)	Total
CPU	Intel Xeon Phi 7250	Intel Xeon 8160	
CPU microarchitecture	Knights Landing	Skylake	
CPU Frequency (GHz)	1.4	2.1	
Sockets per Node	1	2	
Cores per Socket	68	24	
Node Memory Capacity	96GB DDR4 16GB MCDRAM	192GB	
Interconnection Network	Intel Omni-Path		
Compute Racks	75	32	107
Compute Nodes	4,200	1,728	5,928
Login and Mgmt. Nodes	24	24	24
Peak FLOP Rate (TF)	14,280	3,802	18,082

15.3.4   Non-volatile Memory

Many of TACC's leading supercomputing systems have included an effort to evaluate new and potentially transformative technologies. The innovative component in Stampede, the first-generation Xeon Phi, became the basis for the majority of the Stampede 2 compute nodes. In Stampede 2 we continue to explore new technology with the installation of Intel's "Apache Pass" (AP) non-volatile memory DIMMs. These devices preserve stored data across power losses and reboots — the way disks do, for example — and have performance much closer to that of DRAM.

At the mid-point of the operational life of the system, we will add four 512GB AP DIMMs on fifty of the Skylake compute nodes, boosting node memory to 2TB per node. The AP devices can be used in multiple modes. Some modes offer programming and performance characteristics similar to normal memory, either using the conventional DDR DRAM as a cache or managed by the application in much the same way as the MCDRAM on the KNL interacts with DDR DRAM. In other modes, the AP devices can be configured as a block device and treated as permanent storage. Once installed, TACC staff and interested users will evaluate the effectiveness of this new type of memory in several use cases: using these nodes as very large memory nodes, as nodes with hyper-speed local storage, or for experiments in memory resilience or burst buffer capability.

15.4   System Software

TACC-deployed systems, including all of the supercomputing platforms, are provisioned from "bare metal" using TACC developed and enhanced cluster tools, rather than vendor-provided operating system distributions. This allows the center to support a common look and feel for all TACC users, and to incorporate monitoring tools that provided significant additional insight for center operations and user support. Figure 15.2 gives a graphical overview of the components of TACC's system, performance, and application development tools and how they relate to one another.

15.4.1   System Performance Monitoring and Administration

TACC systems are built on Red Hat Enterprise Linux (RHEL). Overall cluster management and provisioning are managed by TACC's Linux operating System Framework (LoSF), which combines bare-metal provisioning via Cobbler with an integrated software/configuration toolkit that is used on all TACC HPC resources [19]. LoSF integrates RPM software builds that configure, modify, and regression test all system software before provisioning to maintain a consistent, traceable software environment.

TACC has also developed and integrated tools to support lights-out management, enabling remote power up/down operations, hardware sensor information, and remote console access to all servers in the system. TACC operates multiple Nagios instances for automatic notification of problems on the production systems.

The operating system on Stampede 2 is configured to allow access to hardware performance counters including cache and TLB misses, FLOPS rates, and branch mispredictions, among others. TACC's performance monitoring suite includes lltop [12] and xltop [13], which provide real-time Lustre load monitoring, as well as TACC Stats [9] and XALT [5]. TACC Stats is an infrastructure for the low-overhead collection of system-wide performance data that integrates information from a variety of sources and performance counters. XALT,

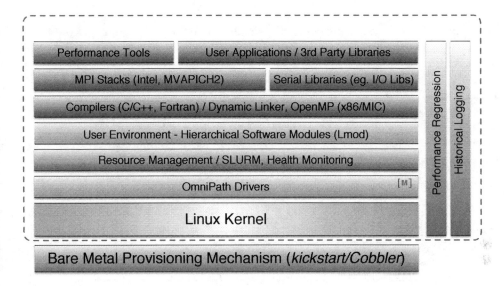

FIGURE 15.2: Overview of the software stack deployed on Stampede 2.

jointly developed by XSEDE partners including TACC, is a tool that allows supercomputer support staff to collect and understand job-level information about the libraries and executables that end-users access during their jobs.

Having granular performance information like this available for every job is invaluable to HPC application developers interested in maximizing overall performance. TACC's user support and administration staff also use this data to identify applications with ineffective resource utilization patterns for performance consulting as well as diagnosing the root cause of systems problems that are sometimes triggered by specific applications. The performance monitoring systems automatically create a set of standard reports indicating potentially poor-performing applications over the past day, week, and month; these reports are used for proactive engagement with users to improve either their application performance or their job-staging parameters, as appropriate. The system is also front-ended by a web interface that users or consultants can use to explore specific users, applications, or jobs when questions arise.

15.4.2   Job Submission and System Health

TACC uses SLURM for resource management and batch queuing of user jobs on Stampede 2 and all of its recent Linux-based systems [16]. TACC has made modifications to SLURM to integrate lightweight monitoring of filesystem availability, InfiniBand connectivity, and correct functionality of important OS components. This integration enhances reliability and reduces the number of job faults on the system due to undetected problems in compute node operation. When a failure of any of these resources is detected, SLURM disables scheduling to the node and notifies the system administrator of the problem.

15.4.3   Application Development Tools

C, C++, and Fortran compilers — and high-performance MPI stacks for these languages — represent the dominant toolchain for application scientists using the Stampede project. Stampede 2 is provisioned with the latest Intel Compiler packages to provide a unified, x86-

based compiler toolchain for Skylake and KNL processors. To maximize performance and functionality for a diverse set of user applications, TACC supports multiple MPI families on Stampede 2, including both MVAPICH2 [17] and Intel MPI, as well as on-node parallelism through threading APIs.

Beyond languages and process communication, TACC has considerable experience building, testing, packaging, and deploying a large matrix of scientific, mathematical, and profiling/optimization libraries for its user community. There are too many of these for an exhaustive list, but examples include NetCDF, HDF, PETSc, Trilinos, METIS, ParMETIS, FFTW, GSL, Boost, ScaLAPACK, SLEPc, PLAPACK, ARPACK, and the Intel Math Kernel Library. For debugging, optimization, and analysis purposes, TACC provides the Intel Debugger, Allinea's DDT parallel graphical debugger, MPIp, and TACC's PerfExpert [8], among others.

TABLE 15.2: Stampede 2 software stack.

Login Node OS	Red Hat Enterprise Linux 7
Compute Node OS	Red Hat Enterprise Linux 7
Parallel Filesystem	Seagate Lustre release 2.7.19
Compilers	Intel 17 GNU 7.1
MPI	Intel MPI MVAPICH 2.1
Notable Libraries	HDF5 NetCDF/pNetCDF Intel Math Kernel Library PetSC Boost FFTW
Job Scheduler	SLURM
Debugging Tools Performance Tools	Intel Debugger Allinea DDT TAU PerfExpert PAPI

15.5   Visualization and Analytics

The modeling and simulation capability of Stampede 2 is complemented by support on the system for data analysis and visualization, either in interactive sessions or using the batch queue for offline rendering.

15.5.1   Visualization on Stampede 2

Interactive visualization has traditionally been difficult to incorporate into a homogenous system due to dependence on graphics processing units (GPUs) for rendering that is fast enough to be useful to users. Recent developments in software-based visualization have made this possible on general computing platforms. The Stampede 2 capability relies on two open source Intel-developed tools that are targeted for graphics and visualization tasks: OpenSWR, a performant threaded software-based rasterization library [2], and OS-PRay [28], an efficient parallel ray tracer. TACC has built additional capability on top of these tools to improve the productivity of users analyzing their data. First, TACC has implemented a VTK interface for OSPRay to simplify its use in VTK-based visualization applications (like ParaView and VisIt). Second, TACC has integrated OpenSWR and OS-PRay with TACC's GLuRay OpenGL-based ray tracing interface [7], allowing users to combine rasterization and ray tracing via OpenGL without code modification. In addition, TACC's NSF-funded GravIT project [1] creates a general interface for ray tracing for use by applications, independent of the underlying hardware platform.

With these tools, Stampede 2 provides a fully scalable visualization environment without the need for GPUs that enables analysis applications to run on any of the system's hardware. Importantly, the performance and visual fidelity are at least as good as current GPU-based methods for both *in-situ* and interactive visualizations. Implementing efficient visualization on the primary compute platform facilitates development of the *in-situ* "zero-copy" analysis capabilities required for efficient analysis at exascale and beyond.

15.5.2 Data Analysis

The National Science Foundation today provides a range of resources specifically targeted at data-oriented workflows: Wrangler, (TACC resource) is designed to provide high I/O throughput and transaction processing rates for big data applications [11], Jetstream (a joint project of Indiana University and TACC) enables cloud computing-based workflows [26], and Bridges (hosted at the Pittsburgh Supercomputing Center) supports applications that require large shared memory. However, many data workflows are still best supported by Stampede 2, as it provides several key capabilities needed for many computationally-intensive data problems. Projects with large datasets benefit from the sheer scale of processing and I/O available on the system. And users of languages such as R and Python can take advantage of installations that are optimized to run on Stampede 2, enabling large data sets to be analyzed without the costs of transferring the data to special-purpose visualization and analytics resources.

In the future, phase change memory will provide users with new technology that may change the costs of doing computations that are currently not practical, such as out of core computations and large-scale data comparisons. We will explore these methods for advancing data compute and promote these methods for code bases that will benefit from this new technology.

15.6 Datacenter, Layout, and Cybersecurity

Stampede 2 is housed in the TACC data center at The University of Texas at Austin. The datacenter has more than 15,000 square feet of air-conditioned, raised-floor space, supporting up to 10 MW of computing load. The center is served by a dedicated chilling plant capable of producing 3,750 tons of water cooling. Cooling for all large-scale systems, including Stampede 2, is provided with in-row chillers in an enclosed hot aisle configuration that brings chilled water next to each compute rack. Chilled water for the data center is delivered from a one million gallon thermal storage tank that allows TACC to shift demand for chilled water production to off-peak times, reducing overall peak load on the power grid and creating a more efficient allocation of energy resources. A 400 KVA UPS covers critical storage systems with backup power, and the data center is monitored 24x7 by TACC operations staff and UT facilities personnel.

15.6.1 System Layout and Phased Deployment

Stampede 2 includes a total of 121 racks and has a peak power requirement of 4 MW. The existing hot-aisle containment structure of the first Stampede system was redeployed for Stampede 2, resulting in improved efficiency of the cooling system.

Stampede 2 was deployed in phases in the existing footprint of Stampede 1, which was decommissioned in corresponding phases. Stampede racks were incrementally removed as new racks arrived, leaving substantial portions of the original system up and available to run jobs. The first phase of deployment included 75 KNL racks and began in the last three months of the original system's operational life. This left more than half of the existing compute capability in operation during the final three months. The second stage of installation included the new filesystem and required a one-day downtime on the existing system to move the existing storage off of UPS backup power and install the new storage on the UPS. The final phase of deployment included all of the SKX nodes and the remaining Omni-Path switches.

15.6.2 Cybersecurity and Identity Management

TACC's cybersecurity program is designed to control the risk and magnitude of harm that could result from the loss, misuse, disclosure, or modification of TACC computers, or data stored on those computers. The program is generally designed around Federal Information Processing Standards (FIPS) security documents as best practice, with changes as needed to reflect the (often more stringent) requirements of UT-Austin and its established Information Technology (IT) security practices. The policy and procedures specifically focus on the people, equipment, network, and software components of the information system within the TACC network boundary. TACC's IT Security Policy and Procedures are audited on a regular basis by an external security consulting firm.

Identity management for all TACC users (including administrators and local staff) conforms to the NIST 800-53 standard for account verification, activation, authentication, and deactivation. TACC uses Lightweight Directory Access Protocol (LDAP) for user authentication and a two-factor authentication mechanism for user access with an additional layer of RSA tokens for system administrators to gain root access.

15.7 Conclusion

The Stampede project has now led to multiple successful large-scale supercomputers. The first Stampede system was remarkably productive, completing over eight million lives in its production life. Lessons from the first system helped inform the design of the second system, and Stampede2 has now been launched as a productive system for both large-scale MPI jobs and for high throughput computing.

Bibliography

[1] The gravIT github repository.

[2] OpenSWR.

[3] *Presidential Executive Order No. 13702*. 2015.

[4] B. P. Abbott et al. Observation of gravitational waves from a binary black hole merger. *Phys. Rev. Lett.*, 116:061102, February 2016.

[5] Kapil Agrawal, Mark R. Fahey, Robert McLay, and Doug James. User environment tracking and problem detection with XALT. In *Proceedings of the First International Workshop on HPC User Support Tools*, HUST '14, pages 32–40, Piscataway, NJ, USA, 2014. IEEE Press.

[6] Ronald Babich, Michael A. Clark, and Bálint Joó. Parallelizing the QUDA library for multi-GPU calculations in lattice quantum chromodynamics. In *Proceedings of the 2010 ACM/IEEE International Conference for High Performance Computing, Networking, Storage and Analysis*, SC '10, pages 1–11, Washington, DC, USA, 2010. IEEE Computer Society.

[7] Carson Brownlee, Thiago Ize, and Charles D. Hansen. Image-parallel ray tracing using openGL interception. In *Proceedings of the 13th Eurographics Symposium on Parallel Graphics and Visualization*, EGPGV '13, pages 65–72, Aire-la-Ville, Switzerland, 2013. Eurographics Association.

[8] Martin Burtscher, Byoung-Do Kim, Jeff Diamond, John McCalpin, Lars Koesterke, and James Browne. Perfexpert: An easy-to-use performance diagnosis tool for HPC applications. In *Proceedings of the 2010 ACM/IEEE International Conference for High Performance Computing, Networking, Storage and Analysis*, SC '10, pages 1–11, Washington, DC, USA, 2010. IEEE Computer Society.

[9] Todd Evans, William L. Barth, James C. Browne, Robert L. DeLeon, Thomas R. Furlani, Steven M. Gallo, Matthew D. Jones, and Abani K. Patra. Comprehensive resource use monitoring for HPC systems with TACC stats. In *Proceedings of the First International Workshop on HPC User Support Tools*, HUST '14, pages 13–21, Piscataway, NJ, USA, 2014. IEEE Press.

[10] National Science Foundation. Advanced computing infrastructure strategic plan. Technical Report NSF-12-051, 2012.

[11] Niall Gaffney, Christopher Jordan, Tommy Minyard, and Dan Stanzione. Building wrangler: A transformational data intensive resource for the open science community. *2014 IEEE International Conference on Big Data (Big Data)*, pages 20–22, 2014.

[12] J. Hammond. The lltop github repository.

[13] J. Hammond. The xltop github repository.

[14] Alexander Heinecke, Alexander Breuer, Sebastian Rettenberger, Michael Bader, Alice-Agnes Gabriel, Christian Pelties, Arndt Bode, William Barth, Xiang-Ke Liao, Karthikeyan Vaidyanathan, Mikhail Smelyanskiy, and Pradeep Dubey. Petascale high order dynamic rupture earthquake simulations on heterogeneous supercomputers. In

Proceedings of the International Conference for High Performance Computing, Networking, Storage and Analysis, SC '14, pages 3–14, Piscataway, NJ, USA, 2014. IEEE Press.

[15] Jacob A. Hummel, Athena Stacy, and Volker Bromm. The First Stars: formation under cosmic ray feedback. *Mon. Not. Roy. Astron. Soc.*, 460(3):2432–2444, 2016.

[16] Morris A. Jette, Andy B. Yoo, and Mark Grondona. SLURM: Simple linux utility for resource management. In *In Lecture Notes in Computer Science: Proceedings of Job Scheduling Strategies for Parallel Processing (JSSPP) 2003*, pages 44–60. Springer-Verlag, 2002.

[17] Jiuxing Liu, Jiesheng Wu, and Dhabaleswar K. Panda. High performance RDMA-based MPI implementation over infiniband. *Int. J. Parallel Program.*, 32(3):167–198, June 2004.

[18] Christopher Maffeo, Binquan Luan, and Aleksei Aksimentiev. End-to-end attraction of duplex DNA. *Nucleic Acids Research*, 40(9):3812–3821, 2012.

[19] Robert McLay, Karl W. Schulz, William L. Barth, and Tommy Minyard. Best practices for the deployment and management of production HPC clusters. In *State of the Practice Reports*, SC '11, pages 1–11, New York, NY, USA, 2011. ACM.

[20] Nirav Merchant, Eric Lyons, Stephen Goff, Matthew Vaughn, Doreen Ware, David Micklos, and Parker Antin. The iplant collaborative: Cyberinfrastructure for enabling data to discovery for the life sciences. *PLOS Biology*, 14(1):1–9, January 2016.

[21] James C. Phillips, Rosemary Braun, Wei Wang, James Gumbart, Emad Tajkhorshid, Elizabeth Villa, Christophe Chipot, Robert D. Skeel, Laxmikant Kal, and Klaus Schulten. Scalable molecular dynamics with NAMD. *Journal of Computational Chemistry*, 26(16):1781–1802, 2005.

[22] Abtin Rahimian, Ilya Lashuk, Shravan Veerapaneni, Aparna Chandramowlishwaran, Dhairya Malhotra, Logan Moon, Rahul Sampath, Aashay Shringarpure, Jeffrey Vetter, Richard Vuduc, Denis Zorin, and George Biros. Petascale direct numerical simulation of blood flow on 200K cores and heterogeneous architectures. In *Proceedings of the 2010 ACM/IEEE International Conference for High Performance Computing, Networking, Storage and Analysis*, SC '10, pages 1–11, Washington, DC, USA, 2010. IEEE Computer Society.

[23] Ellen M. Rathje, Clint Dawson, Jamie E. Padgett, Jean-Paul Pinelli, Dan Stanzione, Ashley Adair, Pedro Arduino, Scott J. Brandenberg, Tim Cockerill, Charlie Dey, Maria Esteva, Fred L. Haan, Matthew Hanlon, Ahsan Kareem, Laura Lowes, Stephen Mock, and Gilberto Mosqueda. Designsafe: New cyberinfrastructure for natural hazards engineering. *Natural Hazards Review*, 18(3):06017001, 2017.

[24] Johann Rudi, A. Cristiano, I. Malossi, Tobin Isaac, Georg Stadler, Michael Gurnis, Peter W. J. Staar, Yves Ineichen, Costas Bekas, Alessandro Curioni, and Omar Ghattas. An extreme-scale implicit solver for complex PDEs: Highly heterogeneous flow in earth's mantle. In *Proceedings of the International Conference for High Performance Computing, Networking, Storage and Analysis*, SC '15, pages 1–12, New York, NY, USA, 2015. ACM.

[25] Dan Stanzione, Bill Barth, Niall Gaffney, Kelly Gaither, Chris Hempel, Tommy Minyard, S. Mehringer, Eric Wernert, H. Tufo, D. Panda, and P. Teller. Stampede 2: The evolution of an XSEDE supercomputer. In *Proceedings of the Practice and Experience in Advanced Research Computing 2017 on Sustainability, Success and Impact*, PEARC17, pages 1–8, New York, NY, USA, 2017. ACM.

[26] Craig A. Stewart, Timothy M. Cockerill, Ian Foster, David Hancock, Nirav Merchant, Edwin Skidmore, Daniel Stanzione, James Taylor, Steven Tuecke, George Turner, Matthew Vaughn, and Niall I. Gaffney. Jetstream: A self-provisioned, scalable science and engineering cloud environment. In *Proceedings of the 2015 XSEDE Conference: Scientific Advancements Enabled by Enhanced Cyberinfrastructure*, XSEDE '15, pages 1–8, New York, NY, USA, 2015. ACM.

[27] John Towns, Timothy Cockerill, Maytal Dahan, Ian Foster, Kelly Gaither, Andrew Grimshaw, Victor Hazlewood, Scott Lathrop, Dave Lifka, Gregory D. Peterson, Ralph Roskies, J. Ray Scott, and Nancy Wilkins-Diehr. XSEDE: Accelerating scientific discovery. *Computing in Science & Engineering*, 16(5):62–74, 2014.

[28] I. Wald, G. P. Johnson, J. Amstutz, et al. OSPRay - A CPU ray tracing framework for scientific visualization. *IEEE Transactions on Visualization & Computer Graphics*, 23(1):931–940, 2017.

[29] Fuqing Zhang and Yonghui Weng. Predicting hurricane intensity and associated hazards: A five-year real-time forecast experiment with assimilation of airborne Doppler radar observations. *Bulletin of the American Meteorological Society*, 96(1):25–33, 2015.

Chapter 16

Oakforest-PACS: Advanced KNL Cluster System

Taisuke Boku, Osamu Tatebe, Daisuke Takahashi, Kazuhiro Yabana, Yuta Hirokawa, and Masayuki Umemura

Center for Computational Sciences, University of Tsukuba

Toshihiro Hanawa, Kengo Nakajima, and Hiroshi Nakamura

Information Technology Center, the University of Tokyo

Tsuyoshi Ichimura and Kohei Fujita

Earthquake Research Institute, the University of Tokyo

Yutaka Ishikawa, Mitsuhisa Sato, Balazs Gerofi, and Masamichi Takagi

Center for Computational Science, RIKEN

16.1 Overview

Oakforest-PACS (OFP for short) is a large scale cluster system installed on December 2016 which was recorded as a new Japan's fastest supercomputer on TOP500 List on Novemeber 2016 overcoming the previous record set by the K Computer. OFP is designed, procured and operated under a joint organization named JCAHPC (Joint Center for Advanced High Performance Computing) under the cooperation between the University of Tokyo and University of Tsukuba, Japan.

On April 2013, two universities organizing JCAHPC agreed to collaborate for introduction of new supercomputer with state-of-the-art technology on both computation node and interconnection as a shared resource. The actual contributing members for JCAHPC belong to Information Technology Center (ITC) at the University of Tokyo and Center for Computational Sciences (CCS) at University of Tsukuba. These two centers have a long term history and background to operate a number of supercomputers to represent Japan's HPC technology, and these resources have been shared by nationwide computational science/engineering researchers so far.

In the agreement of JCAHPC, both universities contribute to procure and operate the latest supercomputer in Japan, later named Oakforest-PACS, as the top class system in the world. The target performance is more than K Computer which was previously Japan's top machine for five years since 2011. There is a new project to build the next generation of national flagship machine in Japan, so called Post-K Computer and Flagship2020 Project, however, we need a strong system to bridge K Computer and Post-K Computer to support computation requirement by nation wide researchers. JCAHPC was established under such a background.

Since the new machine is expected to support a wide variety of application fields with easy programming to port various applications, we decided to introduce a general purpose architecture for node processor, not introducing accelerators such as GPUs. The reasonable solution is introducing Intel's IA32 (x86-64) architecture with very high potential performance. We focused on the many-core processor rather than multi-core one since our main target applications are scientific codes with a large amount of parallelism even within a node processor. The interconnection network should also be a generic one to support high bandwidth and low latency as well as high aggregated bandwidth in a large scale cluster system.

Based on the above architectural specification, we finally introduced an advanced cluster system with the 2nd generation of Intel Xeon Phi (code name: Knights Landing) as the CPU. We also introduced the latest Intel Omni Path Architecture (OPA) for interconnection among all nodes to configure a full-bisection bandwidth Fat Tree network. As on October 2017, OFP is the world-largest cluster system based on Intel Xeon Phi, Knights Landing processor, as well as the largest OPA configuration with 8208 nodes.

16.2 Timeline

April 2013 The collaboration agreement of JCAHPC by the University of Tokyo and University of Tsukuba was established. After the agreement, two centers of these universities started the procurement process of the system.

FIGURE 16.1: Panoramatic view of Oakforest-PACS

June 2015 The specification of OFP was announced with the Request for Proposal to supercomputer venders.

April 2016 Fujitsu was awarded as the primary vendor to install Oakforest-PACS. The proposal includes a system with Intel Xeon Phi (Knights Landing) as the CPU, Intel Omni Path Architecture as the interconnect and DDN Lustre and IME for shared file system.

October 2016 A small system for performance tuning and system test was installed as the first part of Oakforest-PACS.

December 2016 The full system of Oakforest-PACS was finished to install and started the operation for test users.

April 2017 The official full system operation was started to share the entire system for various operation programs managed by two universities and JCAHPC.

Mar 2022 The system will be shutdown after 66 months of operation.

16.3 Applications and Workloads

16.3.1 GAMERA/GHYDRA

Enhancement of earthquake simulation for disaster reduction requires fast analysis of very large scale low-order finite-element analyses. Low-order finite-element analysis is difficult to attain performance on recent compute architecture since its cost is dominated by computation with random data access. Group led by Earthquake Research Institute, the University of Tokyo has been developing high-performance low-order finite-element solvers by designing algorithms suitable for current computer architecture. The developed code was named GAMERA (multi-Grid method, Adaptive conjugate gradient method, Multi-precision arithmetic, Element-by-element method, pRedictor with Adams-bashworth method). Achievements by GAMERA on the *K computer* have been recognized as SC14 Gordon Bell Prize finalist [14], SC15 Gordon Bell Prize finalist [13], and SC16 Best Poster Award [8].

GAMERA enabled 1.08 trillion degrees-of-freedom analysis using the full system of the K computer (Figure 16.2). The solver attained high performance by developing suitable algorithm and implementation for the K computer:

- Size-up scalability: 96.6% (from 9,216 cores to 663,552 cores of the K computer (*full system*))

- Speed-up scalability: 76% (from 9,216 cores to 294,912 cores of the K computer)

- 18.6% of peak (=1.97 PFLOPS) on the full system of the K computer

Research is continuing to attain high-performance on Oakforest-PACS by developing time-parallel algorithms. The new code is called *GHYDRA* (Great-HYDRA, HYbird tempo-spatial-arithmetic multi-griD solveR with concentrated computAtion). Developed solvers are planned to be used for three-dimensional ground motion analysis for earthquake disaster estimation, as well as crust-deformation analysis for estimating earthquake generation cycles.

FIGURE 16.2: Example of Simlation by *GAMERA*: Earthquake simulation of 10.25 km x 9.25 km area of central Tokyo using the full system of the K computer. Response of 328 thousand buildings are evaluated using three-dimensional ground data and building data. Analyzed using a 133 billion degrees-of-freedom nonlinear finite-element model.

16.3.2 ARTED

Ab-initio Real-time Electron Dynamics simulator (ARTED) is a multi-scale electron dynamics simulator based on Real-Time Real-Space Density Functional Theory (RTRSDFT), developed in the Center for Computational Sciences (CCS), University of Tsukuba [17]. The

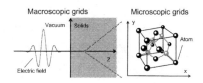

FIGURE 16.3: Two level grids on ARTED solver

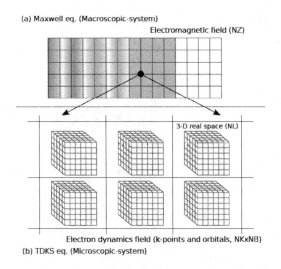

FIGURE 16.4: ARTED computation fields (Maxwell + TDKS equations)

application simulates the interaction between pulse light and matter to solve RTRSDFT by coupled electron dynamics (Time-Dependent Kohn-Sham equation, TDKS) and electromagnetic fields (Maxwell equation) in multi-level grids (Figure 16.3). The purpose of the application is to contribute for optoelectronics which is one of the frontiers in computational sciences. The performance of ARTED was evaluated on the K Computer with up to 11,520 nodes (92,160 cores). We have been porting this code to fit the characteristics of Intel Xeon Phi, both for Knights Corner (KNC) and Knights Landing (KNL) architectures. The code of all versions are available in [1].

Here a time-development loop computes the wave function with a time-dependent Kohn-Sham equation. The time-development loop is a sort of 3D stencil computation where the physical domain is decomposed and computed, reflecting the variables in the surrounding external area. This 3D stencil computation is applied for every wave band, and we get a considerable degree of parallelism in total. Actually, we do not apply domain decomposition for 3-D stencil computation to avoid a communication overhead on the halo region as shown in Figure 16.4. While the real space domain size of 3-D stencil computation is not quite large, a large degree of wave space computation result should be aggregated. Therefore, we need to perform an allreduce operation over the wave space processes after real space computation within each process. Finally, the time-step development for entire Hamiltonian solver is iterated in a range of 10,000–100,000 steps.

For the development of code to fit Oakforest-PACS, we have developed a version based on the KNC accelerated cluster named COMA[4] at CCS where each node is equipped with two sockets of IvyBridge Intel Xeon CPUs and two cards of KNC coprocessor (Intel 7110P). The

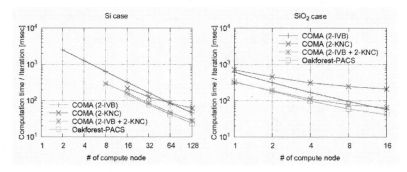

FIGURE 16.5: ARTED computation fields (Maxwell + TDKS equations)

basic techniques for KNC optimization includes the array allocation to fit SIMD load/store instructions, software prefetching, indirect vector addressing to avoid integer divide (which is very slow on Xeon Phi), and introduction of non-temporal store for cache cleanness, etc. The detailed optimization is shown in [12].

Figure 16.5 shows the strong scaling results for Si and SiO2 materials on COMA and Oakforest-PACS. Since the Si case implies a larger degree of parallelism, we can apply much larger scale computation. With up to 128 nodes of COMA and Oakforest-PACS runs, we observed that a single socket of KNL achieves more than double the performance of a KNC card. Since the MPI communication cost on ARTED code is negligible with just a small vector length of MPI_Allreguce, we have very good scalability on Si case. The stencil computation part dominates the computation, and we observed approximately 25% of sutained performance against to the theoretical peak performance on the KNL socket of Oakforest-PACS.

16.3.3   Benchmark Results

16.3.3.1   HPL

High-Performance Linpack Benchmark (HPL) [7, 16] is an implementation of the Linpack benchmark for distributed-memory parallel computers. The HPL benchmark solves a dense linear system of equations in double-precision arithmetic. In the HPL benchmark, it is possible to change various parameters at the time of execution such as problem size N, block size NB, and communication pattern. The MPI processes in the HPL benchmark are mapped into a $P \times Q$ two-dimensional process grid. The coefficient matrix is distributed and allocated to each node according to a two-dimensional block-cyclic distribution on the $P \times Q$ process grid, and the right-looking LU factorization algorithm is applied. When the HPL problem size is set to N, the computational amount is $O(N^3)$ and the communication amount is $O(N^2)$, so as N increases, the performance improves.

Table 16.1 shows a summary of the HPL benchmark run on Oakforest-PACS. The HPL benchmark run on Oakforest-PACS achieved 13.55 PFlops out of a theoretical peak performance of 25 PFlops, which is an efficiency of 54.41% of the theoretical peak performance. The performance of the HPL benchmark on Oakforest-PACS is reasonable as a result of a cluster of Knights Landing processors. Oakforest-PACS was ranked 6th in the TOP500 list of November 2016 [5].

The Green500 list [2] is a ranking for evaluating power efficiency based on a value obtained by dividing the performance of the HPL benchmark on each supercomputer of the TOP500 list by its power consumption. The value obtained by dividing the performance of

TABLE 16.1: Summary of HPL benchmark run on Oakforest-PACS.

Memory mode	Flat mode
Cluster mode	Quadrant
Number of MPI processes	8178 (= 1 MPI process / node × 8178 nodes)
Hyper-Threading	Disabled
Problem size (N)	9,938,880
Block size (NB)	336
Process grid ($P \times Q$)	47 × 174
Performance (PFlops)	13.5546
Power consumption (kW)	2718.7

TABLE 16.2: Summary of HPCG benchmark run on Oakforest-PACS.

Memory mode	Flat mode
Cluster mode	Quadrant
Number of MPI processes	32768 (= 4 MPI processes / node × 8192 nodes)
Hyper-Threading	Disabled
nx	104
ny	104
nz	384
Performance (PFlops)	0.3855

the HPL benchmark by the power consumption shown in Table 16.1 is 4985.7 MFlops/W. Oakforest-PACS was ranked 6th in the Green500 list of November 2016 [2].

16.3.3.2 HPCG

The High Performance Conjugate Gradients (HPCG) benchmark [6, 3] is a benchmark program for supercomputers. In order to achieve high performance in the HPL benchmark, it is necessary to increase the size N of the matrix as much as possible. However, since the computation amount of the HPL benchmark is $O(N^3)$, computation time becomes longer as N is increased, and a computation time of more than one day is required for a PFlops-class system. The computations performed in the HPL benchmark differ greatly from those of applications running on supercomputers, and so the establishment of a benchmark closer to real applications has been discussed. The HPCG benchmark is a supercomputing benchmark developed with this fact in mind. In the HPCG benchmark, a regular sparse linear system obtained using the finite element method is solved. Compared with the HPL benchmark, which is a dense matrix solver, the HPCG benchmark is a sparse matrix solver, and data access is irregular, so it is difficult to achieve high performance.

Table 16.2 shows a summary of the HPCG benchmark run on Oakforest-PACS. The HPCG benchmark run on Oakforest-PACS achieved 0.3855 PFlops out of a theoretical peak performance of 25 PFlops, which is an efficiency of 1.54% of the theoretical peak performance. Oakforest-PACS was ranked 3rd in the HPCG performance list of November 2016 [3].

16.4 System Overview

Oakforest-PACS is a large scale PC cluster with the latest technology for CPU and interconnection as in 2016, where Intel Xeon Phi (Knights Landing) and Intel Omni Path

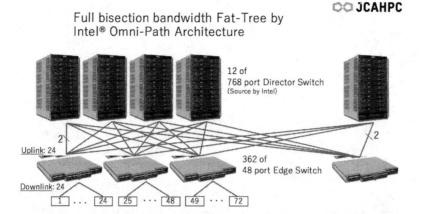

FIGURE 16.6: Block Diagram of Interconnection Network of Oakforest-PACS

Architecture (OPA) were introduced for the world largest cluster based on these technologies. As on October 2017, it is still the largest configuration of Intel OPA in the world.

To configure the largest scale of KNL based cluster system, we introduced several key technologies such as hybrid cooling for computation nodes and rear-door water cooling in the encloure rack. In a computation node, the KNL CPU is cooled by the direct mounted water pipe on the chip and the node is equipped with in/out water pipes while all other parts are cooled by air with ordinary fans. By this configuration, a computation node is implemented as a compact board and eight of the nodes are included in a chassis.

The total number of computation nodes is 8208, and there are 20 of login nodes and 8 of system management nodes. In addition, DDN IME servers and DDN Lustre servers use 300 ports and 64 ports, respectively. To connect all these nodes and servers with full bisection bandwidth of Fat-Tree network, the interconnection network consists of 362 of 48-port edge switches and 12 of 768-port director switch as shown in Figure 16.6. Here, the copper cables are used between computation nodes and edge switches while the edge switches and director switches are connected by optical cables. Each edge switch is installed in the same rack of connected nodes to minimize the cable length for low cost copper cable connections.

All the computation nodes are not directly visible by users, and they can only access 20 of login nodes to be opened to internet access. The users submit their jobs through the job scheduler and access files on the Lustre shared file system over Intel OPA network.

16.5   Hardware Architecture

1. Processor: Intel Xeon Phi 7250 (Knights Landing, 68 core, 1.4 GHz)

2. Node design: 8 nodes for 2U chassis (Front-side: 4 node, Back-side: 4 node)

3. Memory:

   - MCDRAM 16 GB, 490 GB/sec (effective rate)
   - DDR4-2400 96 GB, 115.2 GB/sec peak

4. Interconnect: Intel Omni-Path Architecture 100 Series, fat-tree network with full-bisection bandwidth. Aggregated system bandwidth: 102.6 TB/sec

5. Storage system: 26 PB Lustre file system and 960 TB file cache system (burst buffer) via Omni-Path Architecture, directly accesible from all compute nodes, with DataDirect Networks SFA14KE and IME14K, respectively. (See Section 16.8.)

TABLE 16.3: Oakforest-PACS Hardware Configuration.

Feature	Component
Node Architecture	Fujitsu PRIMERGY CX1640 M1
	Fujitsu PRIMERGY CX600 M1 (2U chassis which contains 8 nodes)
CPU	Intel Xeon Phi 7250
CPU microarchitecture	Knights Landing
CPU Frequency (GHz)	1.4
CPU Count per Node	68 (HyperThreading: 272)
Node Memory Capacity (GB)	Flat mode: 16 GB (MCDRAM) + 96 GB (DDR4)
	Cache mode: 96 GB
Node PCIe	Gen 3
Interconnection Network	Omni-Path Architecture
Network Ports per Node	1 OPA HFI
Compute Racks	69
Total number of nodes	8,208
Peak FLOP Rate (TF)	25,004

16.6 System Software

16.6.1 Basic System Software

1. Operating system: RedHat Enterprise Linux 7.4 for login nodes and other frontend servers, CentOS 7.4 with XPPSL (Intel Xeon Phi processor software) for compute nodes
   McKernel, a lightweight kernel for manycore systems developed by Riken AICS, is also available on compute nodes (See Section 16.6.2.)

2. Filesystem: Lustre file system with file cache system (burst buffer) (See Section 16.8.)

3. System administration: Fujitsu Technical Computing Suite (TCS)

4. Schedulers: Fujitsu Technical Computing Suite (TCS)

5. Virtualization: No

16.6.2 IHK/McKernel

IHK/McKernel is a lightweight multi-kernel operating system that runs Linux and a lightweight kernel simultaneously on many-core CPUs. An overview of IHK/McKernel is

TABLE 16.4: Oakforest-PACS Software Configuration.

Feature	Software
Login Node OS Compute Node OS Parallel Filesystem	RedHat 7.4 CentOS 7.4 with XPPSL, McKernel (Sec. 16.6.2) (dynamically selectable) Lustre 2.7 (Sec. 16.8)
Compilers	Intel 16, 17, 18 GNU 4.8 XcalableMP (Sec. 16.7.2)
MPI	Intel MPI (default) MVAPICH2 (for IME ROMIO)
Notable Libraries	Intel Math Kernel Library HDF5 netcdf/pNetCDF FFTW SuperLU LAPACK, ScaLAPACK PETSc METIS ppOpen-HPC [15]
Notable Applications	OpenFOAM ABINIT-MP, PHASE system, FrontFlow/blue, FrontISTR, and REVOCAP, developed by Center for Research on Innovative Simulation Software (CISS), the Univ. of Tokyo
Job Scheduler Resource Manager	Fujitsu Technical Computing Suite (TCS) Fujitsu Technical Computing Suite (TCS)
Debugging Tools Performance Tools	Allinea DDT Intel VTune

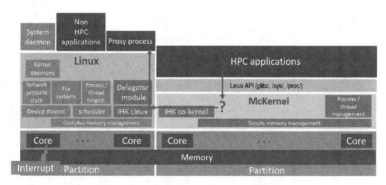

FIGURE 16.7: An Overview of IHK/McKernel

illustrated in Figure 16.7. Interface for Heterogeneous Kernels (IHK) [19] is a general framework that provides resources partitioning in a many-core environment (e.g., CPU cores and physical memory) as well as co-processor based environments (e.g., Intel Knights Corner). It is implemented as a set of Linux kernel modules without any modifications to the Linux kernel. IHK manages node resources and lightweight kernel instances and it enables inter-kernel communication (IKC) between Linux and the LWKs. Upon IKC a mechanism of system call delegation to Linux is also implemented.

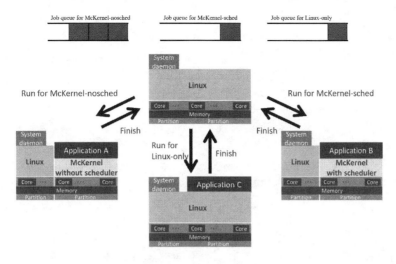

FIGURE 16.8: An Example of McKernel with Batch Job System

McKernel [9, 10, 11], whose pronunciation is émsí:k'ə:nl, is a lightweight kernel designed for HPC and is written from scratch. McKernel retains a binary compatible ABI with Linux, but it implements only a small set of performance sensitive system calls and the rest are delegated to Linux. Specifically, McKernel implements its own memory management, and it supports multi-process and multi-thread management with a simple round-robin cooperative (tick-less) scheduler and optional time-sharing. McKernel also allows inter-process memory mappings and it provides interfaces to hardware performance counters.

IHK's dynamic deployment feature enables custom configurations for McKernel. A system administrator may provide multiple batch job queues, e.g., one for Linux only and others for different McKernel configurations, as shown in Figure 16.8. In this figure, the *Linux* batch job queue is for applications that run exclusively on Linux. Many HPC applications run the same number of processes as the number of physical cores in compute nodes. The *McKernel-without-schedule* job queue is provided for such cases. Users may benefit from McKernel without the time-sharing feature because OS jitter of the OS kernel is almost completely eliminated. In case of applications requiring time-sharing feature, the *McKernel-with-schedule* job queue is used.

IHK/McKernel has primarily the following three advantages: Since IHK/McKernel does not require Linux kernel modifications, it is easily deployable to production environments in supercomputer centers. Users do not need to recompile their application code because McKernel is compatible with Linux. Because IHK/McKernel's source code is small and simple, it works as a research vehicle in the sense that developers can easily modify it or experiment with new OS capabilities. At the same time, because IHK is designed independently of McKernel, a developer may create new, specialized OS kernels easier than developing everything from scratch.

One of the significant results, the noise-less environment, is shown in Figure 16.9. The Fixed Work Quanta benchmark, provided by Sandia National Laboratory, reports how much the execution times of fixed work quantas deviate. The result shows that execution time in McKernel is constant, while much larger deviation can be observed in Linux.

Figure 16.10 shows results of two applications running on Oakforest-PACS: GeoFEM, ICCG with additive Schwartz domain decomposition, developed at the University of Tokyo, and CCS-QCD, lattice quantum chromodynamics code developed at the Univer-

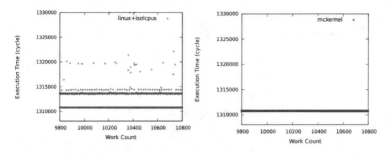

FIGURE 16.9: Results of Fixed Work Quanta (FWQ)

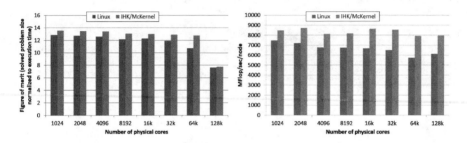

FIGURE 16.10: Results of GeoFEM and CCS-QCD

sity Tsukuba. Both applications are weak scaled running in KNL's SNC-4 flat memory mode. GeoFEM and CCS-QCD achieve up to 18% and 38% improvement, respectively.

IHK/McKernel was originally designed at the Japanese national project, "feasibility study on advanced and efficient latency core-based architecture for future HPCI", lasting from 2012 through 2013. It was derived from a research work done by Taku Shimosawa as a part of his Ph.D thesis [18] and a part of the "Parallel System Software for Multi-core and Many-core" research under a JST CREST program.

RIKEN has taken over the IHK/McKernel development for x86_64 architectures. IHK/McKernel for ARM architecture is cooperatively being developed with Fujitsu. The PC Cluster Consortium in Japan provides a git repository and mailing lists, and holds tutorials. IHK/McKernel is being distributed under the GNU license.

16.7   Programming System

16.7.1   Basic Programming Environment

1. Programming models: MPI + OpenMP

2. Languages and Compilers: C/C++, Fortran90

3. A special language in PGAS model: XcalableMP

4. Tools - correctness, debugging, performance: Intel Parallel Studio

16.7.2 XcalableMP: A PGAS Parallel Programming Language for Parallel Many-core Processor System

XcalableMP (XMP) is a Partitioned Global Address Space (PGAS) style of language for describing large-scale scientific code for parallel systems with distributed memory architecture. With simplification for easy understanding, XMP is a directive-based parallelizing language with grammar similar to the grammar of OpenMP.

XMP has been designed by the XMP Specification Working Group and its reference implementation, the Omni XcalableMP (XMP) compiler, is being developed by RIKEN and University of Tsukuba. The Omni XMP compiler is a source-to-source compiler and it translates C or Fortran codes with XMP directives to XMP runtime calls. XMP is an extension of existing languages such as C and Fortran by directives for distributed-memory programming.

Currently, we are working on the next version of XcalableMP specification, called XcalableMP 2.0. The important topics for XcalableMP 2.0 might include the support for many-core clusters, that is multitasking with integrations of PGAS model and synchronization models for dataflow/multitasking executions. For this issue, we propose an extension by a new directive called tasklet to describe a multithreaded programming model. We expect this model will enable less overhead of synchronization eliminating expensive global synchronization, overlap between computation and communication in manycore, and light-weight communication by RDMA in the PGAS model.

16.7.2.1 Overview of XcalableMP

XMP is an extension of existing languages such as C and Fortran by directives for distributed-memory programming and supports two programming models: global-view and local-view models.

The global-view programming model supports data distribution on computational *nodes* set, and parallel operations on the distributed data. The model makes it easy for users to program typical data parallel processing based on a data distribution with directives. The data distribution uses a virtual array called *template*. Figure 16.11 shows an example of the global-view programming model using the data distribution. First, the number of execution nodes (processes) and the template size are determined by the node and template directives. Second, the distribute directive specifies a distribution of the target template. Third, an array is aligned with a template using the align directive. As a result, each element of the array is distributed among nodes via the distributed template. In this example, the loop directive is then executed in parallel by the executing nodes and collective communication is enabled by the reduction clause on the loop directive, as shown in Figure 16.11.

The global-view programming model provides some directives for typical data communication. Figure 16.12 shows an example of shadow and reflect directives for data exchange among neighboring nodes. The shadow directive defines halo regions around the specified distributed data. The halo region is used for saving neighbor's top or bottom elements in case of distributed one-dimensional array. The reflect directive updates halo regions of the array by exchanging elements among neighboring nodes. These directives are usually used in stencil computations. Figure 16.13 shows an example of gmove directive. This directive copies the value of the right-hand side into the left-hand side of the associated assignment statement for variable and distributed data. Array *A[]* is distributed to 4 nodes as equal-sized contiguous blocks in Figure 16.11. For example, node 1 deals with indices 0 to 3 in array *A[]*. In this example, elements from indices 0 to 3 on node1 are copied to indices 12 to 15 on node 4 as point-to-point communication by the gmove directive. The reflect and gmove directives execute the communication collectively and cause an implicit synchronization among the executing nodes.

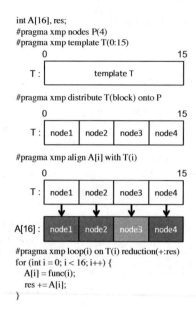

```
int A[16], res;
#pragma xmp nodes P(4)
#pragma xmp template T(0:15)
```

```
#pragma xmp distribute T(block) onto P
```

```
#pragma xmp align A[i] with T(i)
```

```
#pragma xmp loop(i) on T(i) reduction(+:res)
for (int i = 0; i < 16; i++) {
    A[i] = func(i);
    res += A[i];
}
```

FIGURE 16.11: Example of the XMP global-view model programming.

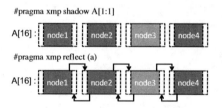

```
#pragma xmp shadow A[1:1]
```

```
#pragma xmp reflect (a)
```

FIGURE 16.12: Example of the shadow and reflect directives.

The local-view programming model supports a function that performs the one-sided communication for the local data on each node. XMP employs coarray notation as an extension of Coarray Fortran and the function is described in the form of an array assignment statement.

16.7.2.2 OpenMP and XMP Tasklet Directive

Although OpenMP originally focuses on work sharing for loops as the `parallel for` directive, OpenMP 3.0 introduces task parallelism using the `task` directive. It facilitates the parallelization where work is generated dynamically and irregularly as in recursive structures or unbounded loops. The `depend` clause on the `task` directive is supported from OpenMP 4.0 and specifies data dependencies with dependence-type `in`, `out`, and `inout`. Task dependency can reduce the global synchronization of a thread team because it can execute fine-grained synchronization between tasks through user-specified data dependencies.

To support task parallelism in XMP as in OpenMP, the `tasklet` directive is proposed. Figure 16.14 describes the syntax of the `tasklet`, `tasklets`, and `taskletwait` directives for the multi-tasking execution in XMP. The `tasklet` directive generates a task for the associated structured block on the node specified by the `on` clause, and the task is sched-

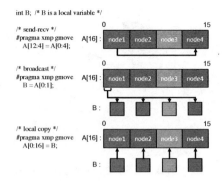

int B; /* B is a local variable */

/* send-recv */
#pragma xmp gmove
    A[12:4] = A[0:4];

/* broadcast */
#pragma xmp gmove
    B = A[0:1];

/* local copy */
#pragma xmp gmove
    A[0:16] = B;

FIGURE 16.13: Example of the gmove directive.

```
#pragma xmp tasklet [clause[, clause] ... ] [on { node-ref | template-ref } ]
    (structured-block)

#pragma xmp taskletwait [on { node-ref | template-ref } ]

#pragma xmp tasklets
    (structured-block)

where clause is :
    {in | out | inout} (variable[, variable] ... ])
```

FIGURE 16.14: Syntax of the `tasklet`, `taskletwait`, and `tasklets` directives in XMP.

uled and immediately executed by an arbitrary thread in the specified node if there is no task dependency. If it has any task dependencies, the task execution is postponed until all dependencies are resolved. These behaviors occur when these tasks are surrounded by `tasklets` directive. The `taskletwait` directive waits on the completion of the generated tasks on each node.

16.7.2.3 Multi-tasking Execution Model in XcalableMP between Nodes

In OpenMP, the task dependency in a node depends on the order of reading and writing to data based on the sequential execution. Therefore, the OpenMP multi-tasking model cannot be applied to describe the dependency between tasks running in different nodes since threads of each node are running in parallel. In OmpSs, interactions between nodes are described through the MPI task that is executing MPI communications. Task dependency between nodes is guaranteed by the completion of MPI point-to-point communication in tasks. While this approach can satisfy dependencies between nodes, it may cause further productivity degradation because it forces users to use a combination of two programming models that are based on different description formats. Therefore, we propose new directives for communication with tasks in XMP, and they enable users to easily write the multi-tasking execution for clusters by only using language constructs.

We propose two new directives, `tasklet gmove` and `tasklet reflect` directives to describe interactions between nodes in tasks by point-to-point communication for the inter-node data dependency, and these communications are synchronized only between sender and receiver of communication in each task.

The `tasklet gmove` directive copies the variable of the right-hand side (rhs) into the left-hand side (lhs) of the associated assignment statement for local or distributed data in tasks. If the variable of the rhs or the lhs is the distributed data, this directive may execute communication. The communication is detected and performed automatically by the XMP

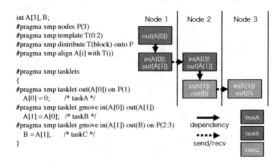

FIGURE 16.15: Example of the `tasklet` and `tasklet gmove` directives.

runtime system. This directive must be executed by all nodes in the current executing node set specified by the **on** clause. When **in**, **out**, or **inout** clause presents on the `tasklet gmove` directive, the generated task have each data dependency in a node similar to the `tasklet` directive.

Figure 16.15 shows an example of the `tasklet` and `tasklet gmove` directives. In this example, array *A[]* of length 4 is distributed to 2 nodes as equal-size contiguous blocks; therefore, node 1 and 2 can deal with indices 0 to 1 and 2 to 3, respectively. This code has three tasks, taskA and taskB are executed on node 1, and taskB and taskC are executed on node 2, that these execution nodes are specified by the **on** clause. There is flow dependency between taskA and taskB by *A[0]*, and taskB and taskC by *B*. After the execution of taskA, taskB on node 1 sends *A[0]* to node 2 which is determined by the execution nodes set by the **on** clause. In node 2, taskB receives *A[0]* from node 1 in *B*. When finishing the receive operation in taskB, taskC is immediately started on node 2 because the flow dependency by *B* is satisfied.

The `tasklet reflect` directive is a task-version of reflect operation. It updates halo regions of the array specified to `array-name` in tasks. In this directive, data dependency is automatically added to these tasks based on the communication data because the boundary index of the distributed data is dynamically determined by XMP runtime system.

16.7.2.4   Preliminary Performance Evaluation on Oakforest-PACS

We have designed a simple code translation algorithm from the proposed directives to XMP runtime calls with MPI and OpenMP.

We have evaluated the performance on our Oakforest-PACS. We select the Flat and Quadrant mode for KNL. While the Intel Xeon Phi 7250 has 68 cores, 64 cores usage per a node is recommended in this system. As our benchmark program, we used the Blocked Cholesky factorization program which calculates a decomposition of a Hermitian, positive-definite blocked matrix as the product of a lower triangular matrix and its conjugate transpose. We implemented tow versions in different parallelization approaches: "Parallel Loop" and "Task", in MPI and OpenMP. The "Parallel Loop" version is the conventional barrier-based implementation described by work sharing for loops by the `parallel for` directive and independent tasks using the `task` directive without the `depend` clause. Although this version of the blocked Cholesky factorization is applied the overlap of the communication and computation at the process level, it performs the global synchronization in work sharing. The "Parallel Loop" version of Laplace equation solver does not include the overlap of the communication and computation. The "Task" version is implemented using our proposed model by task dependency using the `depend` clause instead of global synchronization.

We measured the performance using from one to 32 nodes, 1 process per node, 64 cores per process, and 1 thread per core. As problem size of these benchmarks, the matrix size is 32768 × 32768 and the block size is 512 × 512 in double precision arithmetic. The matrix is distributed by two-dimensional block-cyclic data distribution in blocked Cholesky factorization and two-dimensional block data distribution in Laplace equation solver.

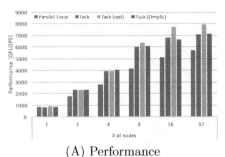

(A) Performance

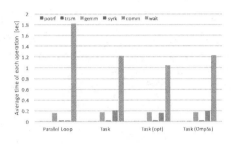

(B) Breakdown at 32 nodes execution

FIGURE 16.16: Performance and breakdown of the blocked Cholesky factorization on Oakforest-PACS system.

Figure 16.16 show the performance and breakdown of the blocked Cholesky factorization on the Oakforest-PACS. The breakdown indicates the average time of each operations performed on all threads because tasks executed on threads differ each time the program is executed. The "wait" in breakdown represents the waiting time of the thread including the global synchronization. In Figure 16.16 (A), the "Task" version shows better performance than the barrier-based implementations, "Parallel Loop" version. The reason why "Task" version outperforms "Parallel Loop" version is that the global synchronization spends more cost in work sharing of loops and among tasks as the "wait" shown in Figure 16.16 (B). The relative performances of "Task" version against the barrier-based implementation, "Parallel Loop" version, is 123%.

16.7.2.5 Communication Optimization for Many-Core Clusters

In the version reported in the previous subsection, the communications are executed in MPI_THREAD_MULTIPLE as MPI thread-safety level since tasks executed on threads may communicate simultaneously. Our basic performance analysis of point-to-point communication using OSU Micro-Benchmarks indicates that the performance of multi-threaded communication with MPI_THREAD_MULTIPLE degrades when increasing the number of threads, compared to a single-threaded communication.

According to the observation above, we optimize the communication by delegating all communications to the communication thread. To delegate the communication to a single thread, we make a global queue accessible by all threads so that the tasks enqueues the communication requests into its queue and wait for the communication completion. Meanwhile, the communication thread dequeues the requests for communication to perform the requested communications, and check the communication completion, respectively. The communication thread executes only the communication, and the other threads perform computation tasks.

In Figure 16.16 (A), "Task (opt)" version are higher than that of the multi-tasking execution with MPI_THREAD_MULTIPLE. The reason is that the communication time is reduced compared with the "Task" version as shown in Figure 16.16 (B). The relative performance against the barrier-based implementation, "Parallel Loop" in Figure 16.16, are improved to 138% and 141%, respectively. For comparison, Figure 16.16 (A) includes the the performance of OmpSS version.

TABLE 16.5: Overall storage specification

	Capacity (TB)	Bandwidth (GB/s)
File System Cache	864	1,560
Parallel File System	26,000	500

In near future, we expect the performance of MPI_THREAD_MULTIPLE will also be improved as the design and implementation is getting mature for parallel manycore system. Currently, we are investigating a lower-level communication API for efficient one-sided communication of PGAS operations in a multithreaded execution environment.

16.8   Storage System

Performance of storage system needs to be balanced with CPU performance. A rule of thumb indicates we need over 25 PB capacity since the peak CPU performance is about 25 PFlops. On the other hand, the total memory capacity of Oakforest-PACS is about 900 TB. To store all memory data to storage system in 10 minutes, the required storage bandwidth is 1.5 TB/s. The number of compute nodes is around 8,000. File creation performance in a single directory requires more than 8,000 in a second, which means it takes one second to create a file using 8,000 processes. This is not ideal but a minimum requirement. These are a baseline of the storage performance requirement.

1.5 TB/s of storage bandwidth is quite challenging. Regarding an N-N access pattern, where each process accesses its own file, when assuming a hard disk drive (HDD) achieves 200 MB/s of bandwidth for sequential access, it requires 7,500 HDDs to achieve 1.5 TB/s. When each HDD has 6 TB capacity, the total capacity will be 45 PB, which is much more than required. A more difficult issue is an N-1 access pattern, where each process accesses a shared file but a different part of it. There are several research efforts to transfer N-1 access to N-N access, which introduce an intermediate layer between applications and a parallel file system. To achieve 1.5 TB/s of storage bandwidth in an N-1 access pattern, we introduce a file system cache layer between applications and a parallel file system.

Overall storage specification of Oakforest-PACS is shown in Table 16.5. To fill the bandwidth requirement, a file system cache is introduced. The capacity of the file system cache is almost the same as the total memory capacity, which is not considered to be enough, but minimum capacity. The capacity of the file system is almost the same as required. The bandwidth is a peak bandwidth for an N-N sequential access pattern, assuming a file system cache layer arranges all access patterns to an N-N sequential access pattern. In this case, still 1.5 TB/s of bandwidth is desired for a parallel file system, but it requires more storage capacity. 500 GB/s of bandwidth is considered to be balanced bandwidth with 26 PB of capacity.

The file system cache consists of 25 sets of DDN IME 14K, each has two servers in active-active redundant configuration. Each IME 14K has 48 800GB NVMe SSDs, and it is connected with 8 links of 100Gbps Omni-Path network. Assuming each NVMe SSD achieves 1,300 MB/s of bandwidth, 25 sets of DDN IME 14K provides 1,560 GB/s of bandwidth. Total physical SSD capacity is 960 TB, but the available capacity is 864 TB due to 10D+1P erasure coding.

The parallel file system consists of 3 sets of metadata servers (MDSs) and 40 object storage servers (OSSs). Each MDS consists of 4 servers and 26 480GB SAS SSDs that is

FIGURE 16.17: Compute node (a), chassis for compute nodes (b), racks for compute node (c), and rear-door of compute node rack (d)

configured with 4 groups of 4D+2P RAID6 plus 2 hot spare disks. Total metadata capacity is 23 TB. Assuming each inode consumes 2KB, 11.5 billion files can be stored. The object storage target consists of 4,200 8TB NL-SAS HDDs that is configured with 410 groups of 8D+2P RAID6 plus 100 hot spare disks. Total available capacity is 26.24 PB. Each OSS is connected with 1 link of 100Gbps Omni-Path. Physical bandwidth to OSSs is 500 GB/s.

Software for the file system cache is DDN infinite memory engine (IME), which is an intermediate layer based on a parallel log structured file system. From compute nodes, applications can access IME using POSIX and MPI-IO. File staging between the parallel file sytem and the file system cache is integrated with a batch job queuing system. There are several commands to check staging status, manually stage-in, stage-out, and release operations.

Software for the parallel file system is Lustre file system. Metadata operations are balanced using Lustre DNE (Distributed Namespace) with 3 sets of MDSs.

16.9 Data Center/Facility

1. System installation site: Kashiwa Campus, Information Technology Center, The University of Tokyo, Japan

2.
   - Floorspace: 962 m^2
   - Power consumption: 3.37 MW (rating), 2.72 MW (HPL for Top500)

- Cooling: Warm-water cooling (Cooling tower + Chiller (for summer-time)) + Air cooling.

  Each CPU is directly cooled by autonomous water pump. Other components on the compute nodes, such as DDR4 memory and HFI, are cooled by air flow; however, each rack is equipped with rear-door cooling by water.

  Power consumption of cooling facility is 870 kW.

3. Facility challenge: Oakforest-PACS is high-density cluster using water cooling. Power consumption and cooling capacility are limited due to the facility and equipments.

4. Figure 16.1 shows the full system view, and Figure 16.17 shows compute node, chassis for compute node, racks for compute node, and rear-door of compute node rack.

Bibliography

[1] Github: ARTED. https://github.com/ARTED/ARTED.

[2] Green500 | TOP500 Supercomputer Sites.

[3] HPCG.

[4] KNC cluster COMA. https://www.ccs.tsukuba.ac.jp/eng/supercomputers/.

[5] TOP500 Supercomputer Sites.

[6] Jack Dongarra, Michael A. Heroux, and Piotr Luszczek. High-performance conjugate-gradient benchmark: A new metric for ranking high-performance computing systems. *The International Journal of High Performance Computing Applications*, 30(1):3–10, 2016.

[7] Jack J. Dongarra, Piotr Luszczek, and Antoine Petitet. The LINPACK benchmark: past, present and future. *Concurrency and Computation: Practice and Experience*, 15(9):803–820, 2003.

[8] K. Fujita, T. Ichimura, K. Koyama, M. Horikoshi, H. Inoue, L. Meadows, S. Tanaka, M. Hori, M. Lalith, and T. Hori. A fast implicit solver with low memory footprint and high scalability for comprehensive earthquake simulation system. In *Research Poster for SC16, International Conference for High Performance Computing, Networking, Storage and Analysis*, November 2016.

[9] Balazs Gerofi, Akio Shimada, Atsushi Hori, and Yutaka Ishikawa. Partially Separated Page Tables for Efficient Operating System Assisted Hierarchical Memory Management on Heterogeneous Architectures. In *2013 13th IEEE/ACM International Symposium on Cluster, Cloud and Grid Computing (CCGrid)*, May 2013.

[10] Balazs Gerofi, Akio Shimada, Atsushi Hori, Takagi Masamichi, and Yutaka Ishikawa. CMCP: A Novel Page Replacement Policy for System Level Hierarchical Memory Management on Many-cores. In *Proceedings of the 23rd International Symposium on High-performance Parallel and Distributed Computing*, HPDC '14, pages 73–84, New York, NY, USA, 2014. ACM.

[11] Balazs Gerofi, Masamichi Takagi, Yutaka Ishikawa, Rolf Riesen, Evan Powers, and Robert W. Wisniewski. Exploring the Design Space of Combining Linux with Lightweight Kernels for Extreme Scale Computing. In *Proceedings of ROSS'15*, pages 1–8. ACM, 2015.

[12] Y. Hirokawa, T. Boku, S. A. Sato, and K. Yabana. Performance evaluation of large scale electron dynamics simulation under many-core cluster based on Knights Landing. In *HPC Asia 2018*, January 2018.

[13] T. Ichimura, K. Fujita, P. E. B. Quinay, L. Maddegedara, M. Hori, S. Tanaka, Y. Shizawa, H. Kobayashi, and K. Minami. Implicit nonlinear wave simulation with 1.08T DOF and 0.270T unstructured finite elements to enhance comprehensive earthquake simulation. In *ACM Proceedings of the International Conference on High Performance Computing, Networking, Storage and Analysis (SC'15)*, November 2015.

[14] T. Ichimura, K. Fujita, S. Tanaka, M. Hori, M. Lalith, Y. Shizawa, and H. Kobayashi. Physics-based urban earthquake simulation enhanced by 10.7 BlnDOF x 30K timestep unstructured FE non-linear seismic wave simulation. In *IEEE Proceedings of the International Conference on High Performance Computing, Networking, Storage and Analysis (SC'14)*, November 2014.

[15] K. Nakajima, M. Satoh, T. Furumura, H. Okuda, T. Iwashita, H. Sakaguchi, T. Katagiri, M. Matsumoto, S. Ohshima, H. Jitsumoto, T. Arakawa, F. Mori, T. Kitayama, A. Ida, and M. Y. Matsuo. ppOpen-HPC: Open source infrastructure for development and execution of large-scale scientific applications on post-peta-scale supercomputers with automatic tuning (AT). In *Optimization in the Real World — Towards Solving Real-Worlds Optimization Problems*, volume 13 of *Mathematics for Industry*, pages 15–35, 2015.

[16] A. Petitet, R. C. Whaley, J. Dongarra, and A. Cleary. HPL - A Portable Implementation of the High-Performance Linpack Benchmark for Distributed-Memory Computers.

[17] S. A. Sato and K. Yabana. Maxwell + TDDFT multi-scale simulation for laser-matter interactions. *J. Adv. Simulat. Sci. Eng.*, 1(1), 2014.

[18] Taku Shimosawa. *Operating System Organization for Manycore Systems.* dissertation, The University of Tokyo, 2012.

[19] Taku Shimosawa, Balazs Gerofi, Masamichi Takagi, Gou Nakamura, Tomoki Shirasawa, Yuji Saeki, Masaaki Shimizu, Atsushi Hori, and Yutaka Ishikawa. Interface for Heterogeneous Kernels: A Framework to Enable Hybrid OS Designs targeting High Performance Computing on Manycore Architectures. In *2014 21th International Conference on High Performance Computing (HiPC)*, December 2014.

Chapter 17

Center for High Performance Computing in South Africa

Happy M Sithole, Werner Janse Van Rensburg, Dorah Thobye, Krishna Govender, Charles Crosby, Kevin Colville, and Anita Loots

Center for High Performance Computing

17.1 Overview

17.1.1 Sponsor/Program Background

The Center for High Performance Computing provides the high-end computational resources for researchers in South African academia, science councils and industry. The Center is fully funded by the Department of Science and Technology to provide this service. The Center is hosted under the National Integrated Cyber-Infrastructure (NICIS) within the Council for Scientific and Industrial Research (CSIR). The CISR is one of the oldest science councils in South Africa, and focuses on developing technologies in various fields, ranging from defense, materials, built-environment and biosciences. Apart from providing the computing resources, the center has in-house scientists and engineers, who advise users on various fields of science and engineering, on applications performance in high performance computing environment. Training of Users is a corner stone of efficient utilization of the

HPC systems. The training programs are domain specific and also general HPC skills, such as introductory parallel programming and Linux courses.

17.1.2 Business Case of the Installation of Lengau

The Center for High Performance Computing started operations in June 2007 with an initial system of 640 processors, with compute capacity of 2.5 TFLOPS. The current system to be replaced by Lengau, TSESSEBE, was installed in 2009 with initial performance of 24.5 TFLOPS, and with interim upgrades over the years, it had an overall performance of 61.44 TFLOPS. With this installation, CHPC has:

- Provided a stable and reliable service to the community, with availability of the HPC system averaging over 90% annually and the utilization of the resources by users above 86%.

- Managed to provide researchers with relevant technologies to enable cutting-edge research evidenced by the increased number of publications[1] in HPC related fields (267 publications between 2009 and 2014) and over 55 post-graduate students in science and engineering disciplines with focus on HPC during the 2013/14 financial year.

- Developed the HPC integration skills, allowing the Center to procure HPC systems with less dependence on the vendor, as is evident with the current 61.4 TFLOP system which has various components from SUN Microsystems to DELL and XYRATEX that have been fully integrated into a single HPC service by CHPC personnel.

- Performed the benchmarks on the HPC system for acceptance in the TOP500 supercomputers in the world, the status that has attracted recognition of South African's ability to provide computational facilities for international projects. Currently, 1,600 jobs are processed per day for CERN[2] experiments.

- Formed part of the international consortium that is tasked with developing prototypes for the Science Data Processing (SDP) facilities around the world, which will provide second level processing for the Square Kilometer Array (SKA). Presently, the center, with its limited resources, provides the test-facility for SKA and also processing capacity for KAT-7 data.

- Provided inspiration to undergraduate students to acquire critical skills of HPC at an early stage, which has resulted in South African Student Cluster team attaining international championship at International Supercomputing Meeting, 5 years in a row, where the students became champions three times, and won second prize twice.

However, the growth in the HPC facility has also resulted in growing demand of resources, which presents the following challenges:

- The growing demand of researchers from various science and engineering disciplines for the resources, has escalated to the level where waiting in the queue for processing approaches 30 days, a waiting period unacceptable within any standards of service for HPC centers.

- The maintenance of the system is becoming increasingly costly (e.g., human resource time to replace the spares) and the acquisition of spares. As some of the components

---

[1] http://www.chpc.ac.za/index.php/research-and-collaboration/publication
[2] http://home.web.cern.ch/topics/large-hadron-collider

are going out of their life-cycle, from the initial 7500 processors, the system is operating with close to 6000 processors.

- Due to some of the pressures for delivering on international projects such as the H3Africa and the International Protocol on Climate Change (IPCC), 240 nodes = 2880 processors resources are reserved for these projects, further depleting the already limited resources.

In responding to these challenges, CHPC held a User Requirement meeting with the researchers around the country mainly to:

- Provide them with the current challenges on the high demand of the system.

- Present users with different technology scans, on what is available and time lines from different vendors.

- Understand from the researchers the time lines of their research programs and projections on resources they will require.

This information was used to determine the type of technology required, and also the architecture of the system most suitable for the Users Community.

17.1.3 Timeline

Following the trends of the technology roadmap from the processor technologies [Insert Intel Reference] , and guided by Moore's Law [Reference], CHPC has developed a roadmap to deploy HPC systems. This can be summarized in Figure 17.1. In the same figure, a projection on the deployment of future systems is made. This projection is guided by the TOP500 list, as can also be seen by the requirement of a Petascale machine in 2018. Hence the deployment of Lengau falls within this projected timelines.

In summary, the deployment of HPC systems for South Africa are defined as follows:

- After two years of commissioning a system, upgrade to the new chipset technology is planned;

- The introduction of the new chipset is in a phased-in approach, where 50% of the system is upgraded to provide users with an opportunity to port their applications;

- A revamp of the system should then be deployed after four years, guided by the technology implemented in a past upgrade;

- There should be an overlap of two years for the two generations of technologies, to afford users an opportunity to effectively migrate their applications to the new platform;

- Two years after the successful production life of the system, an HPC system will either require a complete refurbishment or be used only for test purposes as it will be costly to keep it maintained for a full production purpose;

It is highly desirable to understand the technology partners roadmap so that the phased-in upgrades can be performed without a major revamp of the architecture.

The actual implementation of Lengau followed the following time-lines:

- Stage 1: Exploration of technology options to be considered: 2010

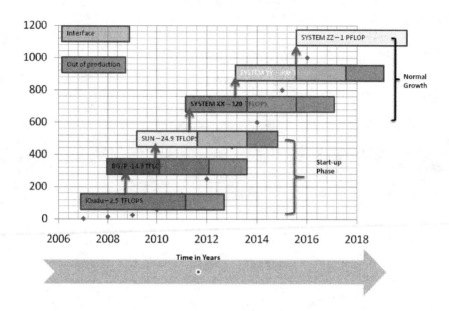

FIGURE 17.1: Roadmap for deployment of HPC systems for CHPC.

- Stage 2: Deployment of 6 node GPU and Xeon-phi test-bed: 2012

- Stage 3: User engagements for user specific requirements: 2014

- Stage 4: Design and architect of the system: 2014

- Stage 5: Procurement of the system: 2015

- Stage 6: Installation of the system in two phases: (2015 -2017)

17.2 Applications and Workloads

17.2.1 Highlights of Main Applications

The status of the CHPC as a national HPC facility for South Africa is reflected well in the diverse research application areas being studied on the Lengau cluster. The domains with highest CPU usage include Materials Science, Chemistry, Earth Sciences, Health and Bioinformatics. A significant fraction of CPU usage for domains such as Computational Mechanics, Astrophysics, Physics and Computer Science is also observed.

The largest independent programs making use of the CHPC in terms of total CPU hours used are in the Materials Science, Earth Science and Drug Discovery domains. In particular, the Materials Science program entitled 'Energy Materials: Numerical Explorations' from the School of Physics, University of the Witwatersrand, Johannesburg is the single largest program at the CHPC. The main focus of this research is on the application of Density Functional Theory (DFT) towards property (optical, thermoelectric, photo-catalytic, etc.) determinations for energy materials.

Another large research programme making use of the CHPC is in the Earth Science domain and is focused on the development of the first African-based earth systems model with variable resolution and its projection of future climate change over Africa. The climate modeling research is being conducted by the Council for Scientific and Industrial Research (CSIR) based in Pretoria, as part of the International Protocol on Climate Change (IPCC)[3]. The simulations for this project represent the single largest runs being executed on Lengau on a routine basis.

A number of prominent Drug Discovery research programs, e.g. computer-aided HIV/TB drug design, mainly involving researchers from the University of KwaZulu Natal in Durban, make use of the CHPC, while Bioinformatics applications have grown in prominence. An example of the latter of contributions made internationally is for the H3Africa program conducted by the University of Cape Town.

A number of other noteworthy programs making use of compute resources include studies towards gravitational waves from binary black hole mergers (Astrophysics, Rhodes University, Grahamstown), modeling of analytical methods for South African water systems (Chemistry, University of Johannesburg, Johannesburg), modeling of battery materials and minerals processing (Materials Science, University of Limpopo, Polokwane), investigations towards nature inspired computing optimization (Computer Science, University of KwaZulu Natal, Pietermaritzburg) and computational fluid dynamics modeling of concentrated solar power applications (Computational Mechanics, University of Pretoria, Pretoria).

17.2.2 Benchmark Results

HPL was run twice in order to submit for the TOP500 list. These runs are described as phase 1 and phase 2. Phase 1 run occurred on the 26th April 2016. Phase 2 was run on the 1st March 2017.

TABLE 17.1: HPL run for Lengau.

	Phase 1	Phase 2
Number of Nodes	1008	1369
MPI Ranks	1008	1369
Total Threads	24192	32856
Problem Size (N)	3836736	3105408
P & Q Grid Size	28 X 36	37 X 37
Result	782.9TF	1029.3TF

These results were achieved using Intel MKL, and Intel MPI binaries, with one MPI rank per node and 24 threads per rank. This matched the physical hardware: Dual 12-core Xeons per compute node. Memory configuration played a huge part in terms of the problem size (N) across the two runs. The phase 1 nodes (1008) were configured with 128GB of memory whilst the additional nodes added during phase 2 (360) had a memory configuration of 64GB per node. Thus the N value was calculated based on 64GB memory across all 1369 nodes for the phase 2 run were as during the phase 1 the full 128GB per node was used to

---

[3]http://www.eolss.net/sample-chapters/c07/e2-25-02-05.pdf

calculate the value. System efficiency was calculated at 78% during phase 1 and 75% during phase 2.

TABLE 17.2: HPC run for Lengau.

Compute size	1 000 nodes
MPI ranks	2 000 processors
Total threads	24 000 cores
Result	15 650.8 Gflop/s

On 21 July 2017, shortly after the production cluster had passed its burn-in tests and proven itself, we ran the HPCG on 1000 (of the 1008 available) nodes. This took place before the expansion to 1360 nodes was implemented.

Using a processor grid of 101020 with the standard local grid size $n = 192$, the HPCG result was 15650.8 Gflop/s. This was executed using Intel's AVX2 optimised binary, with two MPI ranks per node and 12 OpenMP threads per rank. This matched the physical hardware: dual 12-core Xeons per compute node.

The HPCG benchmark is limited by two hardware characteristics: effective memory bandwidth and interconnect latency. Extrapolating, we expect the full upgraded result for 1360 nodes (2720 processors) to be approximately 21 Tflop/s, or 2% of the HPL result. We believe there is room for improvement as other clusters using a similar hardware configuration that has achieved 3% of HPL. However, the main weakness of the CHPC cluster is the restrictive 2:1 tree topology of the IB interconnect. This can increase latency as contention will occur at the core switch.

17.2.2.1 Computational Mechanics

The three most widely used computational mechanics codes at the CHPC are the commercial fluid dynamics solvers Ansys Fluent and Siemens STAR-CCM+ and the open-source OpenFOAM library. These are all very mature codes, with highly developed parallelisation. Because the Lengau cluster is a very conventional CPU-based system, these benchmarks mainly serve to verify that the codes and system work together as expected. Both Ansys and Siemens provide a range of standard benchmark cases to facilitate comparison. In general, the CHPC has focused attention on benchmarks that are similar in size to the models typically built by the system's users.

Ansys Fluent The parallel scaling for the smaller case (Figure 17.2) compares very favourably to the results published by Ansys for a cluster of similar architecture. Large test cases generally scale very well – it is the smaller ones that highlight the performance bottlenecks. In this case it can be seen that the performance per core is substantially improved by not using all the cores on each node.

Figure 17.3 shows that linear scaling up to software license limits is achieved with a much larger model. Lengau single precision results once again compare well with double precision results published by Ansys, with the expected ratio of single precision to double precision performance.

Siemens STAR-CCM+ The results for a 105 million cell racing car model shown in Figure 17.3 display linear scaling up to the limit imposed by the Platform MPI license for Siemens STAR-CCM+. The user has a choice of MPI implementations, and although there

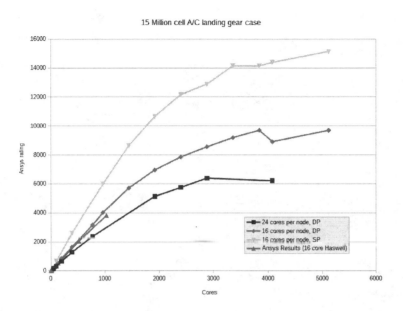

FIGURE 17.2: Ansys standard benchmark case - aircraft landing gear, 15 million finite volume cells. Lengau results compare favorably with published Ansys results on similar Haswell architecture.

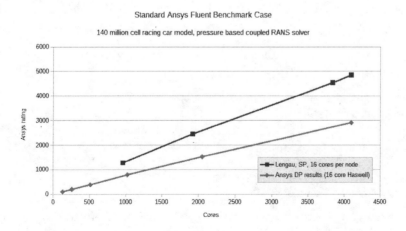

FIGURE 17.3: Standard Ansys benchmark case - 140 million cell racing car model. The Lengau single precision results show linear scaling up to the limit imposed by the available software license.

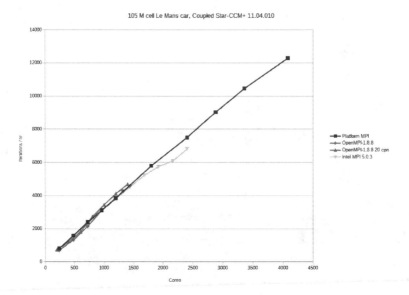

FIGURE 17.4: STAR-CCM+ scaling results for a 105 million cell racing car model, comparing various MPI implementations.

is little to choose between the different MPI's for lower core counts, Platform MPI performs substantially better when using more cores.

OpenFOAM   The parallel performance of a standard OpenFOAM solver on the Lengau cluster is shown in Figure 17.5. The comparison to the performance of a desktop workstation is particularly dramatic, and serves as a useful method of persuading modeling and simulation practitioners of the value of high performance computing.

By contrast, Figure 17.6 has useful information for an existing HPC user, who may need advice on the number of cores to be used for a particular size of model. In this case, excellent parallel scaling is evident down to as few as 12000 cells per core, and it may even be justifiable to drop as low as 6000 cells per core.

17.2.2.2   Earth Sciences

Various variants of the open-source weather modelling code WRF is used on Lengau, where it is implemented with Intel's compiler and MPI, as well as parallel NetCDF. The satisfactory parallel scaling for a typical model is shown in Figure 17.7. When using high core counts, I/O becomes a serious bottleneck, which can be alleviated with the parallel version of NetCDF.

17.2.2.3   Computational Chemistry

When it comes to drug design and molecular dynamics simulations of various biological based systems, the NAMD and AMBER software packages are widely used at the CHPC. The tests run for these applications were obtained from the software vendors and are usually used in order to evaluate the package's scalability. The results given below show the scaling performance of these codes on the Lengau cluster.

The results provided in Figure 17.8 show good scaling for both versions of NAMD that are currently on Lengau. There is a considerable improvement observed for NAMD 2.12

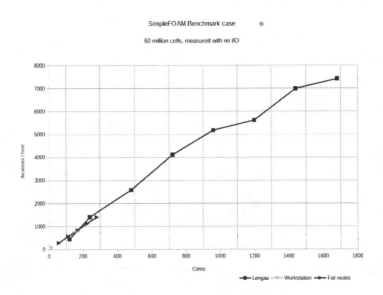

FIGURE 17.5: OpenFOAM scaling for an intermediate size problem of 60 million cells.

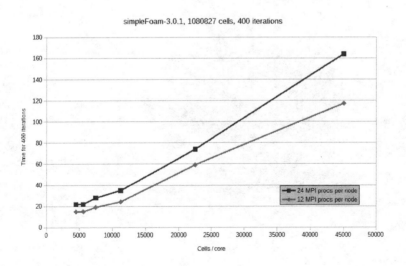

FIGURE 17.6: The minimum number of cells that should be used is a good practical guide-line to a user of an HPC system.

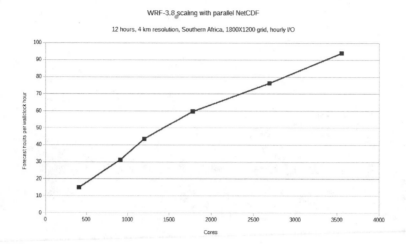

FIGURE 17.7: Parallel scaling of the weather modelling code WRF on Lengau. Parallel I/O is essential to maintain scaling when writing outputs at frequent intervals.

FIGURE 17.8: Visualization of molecular dynamics simulation of Apolipoprotein A1 (ApoA1) using the NAMD code on Lengau.

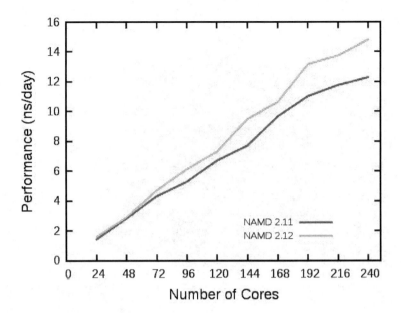

FIGURE 17.9: Parallel scaling of molecular dynamics simulation of Apolipoprotein A1 (ApoA1) using the NAMD code on Lengau.

when compared to the earlier version of NAMD. The results show an 8.5x speedup when using 240 cores as opposed to 24 cores for NAMD 2.11, whereas NAMD 2.12 produces a 9.2x speedup.

Figure 17.8 and Figure 17.9 show that AMBER14 has a slightly better performance than AMBER12. From Figure 17.8 it can be seen that there is no linear scaling. This is due to the system size as the system is not large enough to take advantage of all the cores that have been assigned to the job. This is a good example for the users of the cluster to illustrate that if you have a smaller system, you should not submit such a job on all 240 cores, but instead run the job on 192 or 120 cores as you do not gain a substantial amount of simulation time by running the job on the additional cores.

From Figure 17.9 we see that AMBER14 has a good linear scaling. It should also be noted that the system is this case is substantially larger than that used in Figure 17.8. This provides users of Lengau with an idea of the sizes of systems they should be considering when they wish to make effective use of 240 cores.

17.2.2.4 Astronomy

The most well-known, and perhaps most used, astronomy application at the CHPC has been the GADGET code. In particular, version 2, which is publicly available, has served as the de facto standard for the most part. Nowadays, as theoretical modeling has improved, most users are making use of privately available versions (e.g. GADGET -3) that capture a plethora of physics recipes of interest to various research groups. Nevertheless, reasonable insight into the scaling nature of a typical Gadget simulation can be captured by focusing on a simple setup within GADGET -2 – specifically, we consider dark matter (DM) only runs.

We characterize our different simulations by the number of particles along one dimension of the cubic volume by N, and the length (in megaparsecs) of one size of the cube by L.

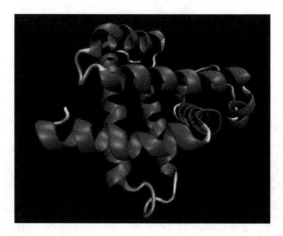

FIGURE 17.10: Visualization of molecular dynamics simulation of Myoglobin using the AMBER code on Lengau.

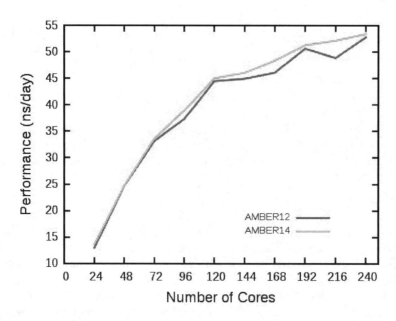

FIGURE 17.11: Parallel scaling of molecular dynamics simulation of Myoglobin using the AMBER code on Lengau.

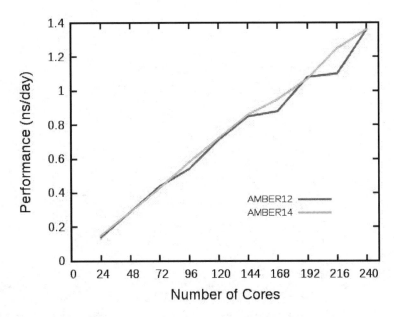

FIGURE 17.12: Parallel scaling of molecular dynamics simulation of Nucleosome using the AMBER Code on Lengau.

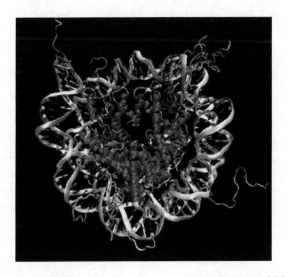

FIGURE 17.13: Visualization of molecular dynamics simulation of Nucleosome using the AMBER Code on Lengau.

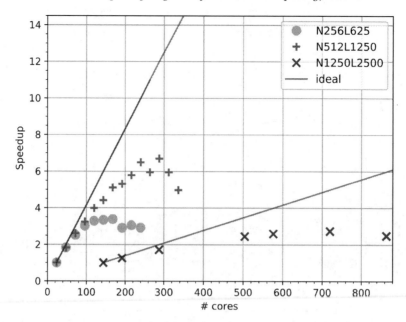

FIGURE 17.14: GADGET-2 benchmark case: varying the problem size while keeping the resolution fixed. This suggests that there may be some sweet-spot in terms of which problem-size can achieve the best level of speedup. Nevertheless, the larger the problem size, the more memory is required (which is why the N1250L2500 cannot run on less than a few nodes) and the higher the core count possible before speedup diminishes due to MPI communication overhead.

In Figure 17.11, we vary the problem size (doubling N means a problem size eight times larger), but fix the simulation resolution (i.e. L/N).

In Figure 17.11 , we vary the resolution, but fix the problem size.

Finally, in Figure 17.12, we vary the number of cores per node for N512L1250 case.

17.3   System Overview

The CHPC HPC cluster is named Lengau owing to its speed of 1029 teraflops, its small framework as opposed to its predecessor and the conventional naming of system at CHPC, where we use our fastest animals. The advancement in technology enabled us to build a much bigger system with a small footprint. The Dell HPC system comprised of 1638 C6320 Dell PowerEdge servers, based on Intel Xeon processors totaling 19 racks of administration, compute and storage nodes. It has a total storage capacity of five petabytes, and uses Dell Networking Ethernet switches and Mellanox FDR InfiniBand with a maximum interconnect speed of 56 Gb/s.

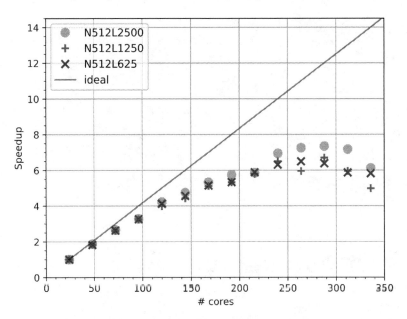

FIGURE 17.15: GADGET-2 benchmark case: varying the resolution size while keeping the problem size fixed. Similar performance is observed for the most part up to about 200 cores, after which the higher resolution versions (L1250 and L625) begin to slow down compared to the lower resolution version (L2500), mainly due to more time spent in the hierarchical tree search algorithm that operates on the close-range gravitational forces.

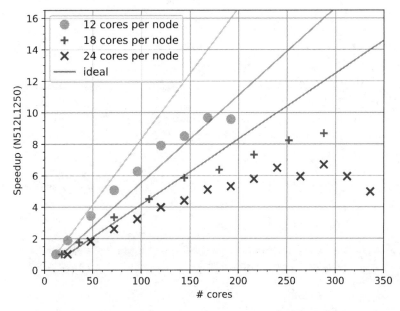

FIGURE 17.16: GADGET-2 benchmark case: varying the number of cores per node for the N512L1250 case. This suggests that there may be some sweet-spot in terms of the number of cores per node that can achieve the best level of speedup. [Indeed, most users are more interested in completing the job quicker, so they will prefer utilising all the available cores per node (e.g. 24 cores per node runs on average about 1.6 times faster than 12 cores per node up to about 10 nodes).]

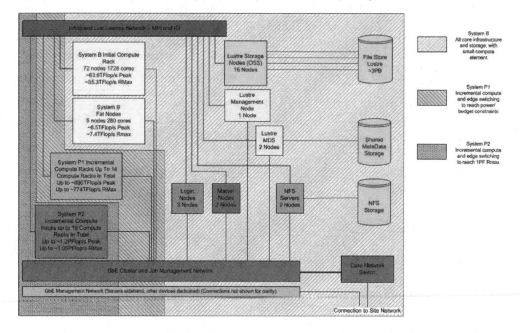

CHPC System Outline

FIGURE 17.17: CHPC Lengau system outline.

17.4   Storage, Visualisation and Analytics

The Lengau cluster is equipped with two visualization servers, each with 64 GB of RAM, 12 cores and one NVidia K20M card. The open-source remote visualization software stack consisting of VirtualGL and TurboVNC is used. On the visualization software side, Paraview and VisIt are supported. By means of the Mesa library, standard and fat compute nodes can be used when parallel visualization is required.

17.5   Data Center/Facility

The Center for High Performance Computing (CHPC) is situated in Rosebank Southern Suburb of Cape Town in Western Cape of South Africa, alongside the banks of Liesbeek River and is physically located at 15 Lower Hope Road, Rosebank, Cape Town, 7700. The Data Center is approximately 145 sqm of floor space capable of accommodating maximum 20 42U Standard Rack Enclosure, see Figure 17.15. The facility is powered by the utility power of 2 MVA supported by 1 resilient diesel backup generators capable to provide a minimum of 8 hours of power boosted by guaranteed diesel delivery should the municipal supply fail. The power is cascaded to multiple resilient distribution boards that enable the servicing of multiple zones of the data center. The Data Center has 2 fully online 500 kVA UPS systems to ensure frequency, voltage and surge stability.

TABLE 17.3: System architecture and details.

FEATURE	PHASE 1 Date: 2017/06/15	PHASE 2
Node Architecture	Dell PowerEdge	Dell PowerEdge
	C6320 Quad Node	C6320 Quad Node
CPU	Intel Xeon E5-2690	Intel Xeon E5-2690
CPU Microarchitecture	Haswell	Haswell
CPU Frequency (GHz)	2.60GHz	2.60GHz
CPU Count per Node	2	2
Node Memory Capacity (GB)	128 GB	64 GB
Node PCIe	PCIe Gen 3	PCIe Gen 3
Interconnection Network	Mellanox IB FDR	Mellanox IB FDR
	Mellanox ConnectX-3 FDR	Mellanox ConnectX-3 FDR
Network Ports per Node	1	1
Compute Racks	14	19
Total Number of Nodes	1008	1368
Peak FLOP Rate (TF)	1,006	1,365
HPL FLOP Rate (TF)	782.9	1,029.3
Storage System	NFS : 90 TB	
Lustre : 5 PB		

Multiple independent CRAC units are maintained to control temperature and cooling in the server rooms through floor grilles with 2 chilled water loops existing below raised floor of the data center to provide thermal cooling up to a combined maximum of 450 kW. The cooling system for the data center is supported by 3 TRANE Chillers working on the weekly rotational basis to provide circulating water to high temperature loops at maximum flow rate of 24 kg/s and 18 degree Celsius to the rear door of the server racks and to low temperature loops at 10 degree Celsius to the CRAC units. See Figure 17.16 for details of the chillers.

The facility has a comprehensive perimeter and building security. Pre-authorization is required for data center access according to the CHPC's Access Policy. There is continuous video surveillance of all zones in the server room, and entry access is enforced through additional card and pin control systems.

17.6   System Statistics

1. Number of users and projects

   Since the launch of Lengau at the CHPC in April 2016 a significant growth in the number of users of the facility has been observed. By 31 August 2017 the total number of registered Research Programmes have grown to 266, which is associated with a total number of 1050 users. Of these registered programmes, 197 are classified as active when actual CPU hour usage on Lengau is considered.

TABLE 17.4: Software configuration.

Feature	Phase 1	Phase 2 System
Login Node OS	Centos 7.1	Centos 7.3
Compute Node OS	Centos 7.1	Centos 7.3
Parallel Filesystem	Intel Lustre 2.4	Intel Lustre 2.5
Compilers	<ul><li>gcc 4.8.5</li><li>gcc 5.1.0</li><li>Intel Parallel Studio XE Cluster Edition 16.0.1</li><li>Intel Parallel Studio XE Cluster Edition 17.0.4</li></ul>	
MPI	<ul><li>OpenMPI</li><li>MVAPICH</li><li>Intel MPI</li></ul>	
Notable Libraries	<ul><li>NetCDF</li><li>Intel MKL</li><li>Intel Integrated Performance Primitive</li><li>Intel Data Analytics Acceleration Library</li></ul>	
Job Scheduler Resource Manager	PBSPro 13.0	
System Administration and Monitoring.	Bright Manager 7.1 <ul><li>Intel Manager For Lustre (IML 2.4)</li><li>Unified Manager For Fabric (UFM 5.5)</li></ul>	Bright Provisioning Manager 7.3
Debugging Tools	<ul><li>TAU</li><li>Intel Trace Analyzer and Collector</li><li>Intel Inspector</li><li>Intel Cluster Checker</li></ul>	
Performance Tools	<ul><li>Intel VTune Amplifier</li><li>Intel Threading Building Blocks</li></ul>	

TABLE 17.5: Table of research application domain distribution of Research Programmes at the CHPC on 31 August 2017.

Research Domain Application	Number of Research Programmes
Materials Science	33
Chemistry	39
Earth Science	17
Health	13
Bioinformatics	33
Computational Mechanics	33
Astrophysics	12
Physics	7
Computer Science	9
Economics and Finance	1
TOTAL	**197**

The research domain application distribution of the total number of active programmes as recorded by 31 August 2017 at the CHPC is summarized in Table 17.5.

The research programme distribution summarized in Table 17.5 is also displayed in Figure 17.17.

The user base of the CHPC may be classified into one of four classifications, viz. South African academic institutions, South African public sector institutions, South African industry and other African partner academic institutions (i.e. SKA partner countries which includes Namibia, Botswana, Mozambique, Madagascar, Mauritius, Zambia, Kenya and Ghana). The distribution of the 197 active research programs at the CHPC according to these four classifications on 31 August 2017 is illustrated in Figure 17.18. It is evident that almost three quarters of the active research programmes are associated with South African academic institutions, while ca. a quarter of the programmes are from the other three sectors.

1. System usage patterns

    Figure 17.19 illustrates the CPU hour distribution recorded for different domain applications since the commissioning of the Lengau cluster in April 2016 until 31 August 2017. During this period a total number of 162.5 million CPU hours have been used, more than half of which were consumed for Materials Science and Chemistry applications. Slightly more than a third of the usage was distributed amongst Earth Science (mostly climate modeling), Health (Drug Design) and Bioinformatics applications, whereas the remaining 12% of the usage shared amongst Computational Mechanics, Astrophysics, Physics and Computer Science.

It is interesting to compare the CPU hour usage distribution according to the user classification that was introduced in Figure 17.18. This is illustrated by the graph in Figure 17.20

From the information in Figure 17.20 it is evident that the CPU hour usage on Lengau is dominated by the South African academic and public sector users, effectively accounting for 97% of all CPU hours used in the period 1 April 2016 – 31 August 2017. The uptake of HPC resources, in terms of CPU hours used, is still relatively small at 1% and represents an area where growth is desired. The 2% CPU hour usage by African partner country researchers is expected to increase with increased awareness of HPC opportunities and training programs in these countries.

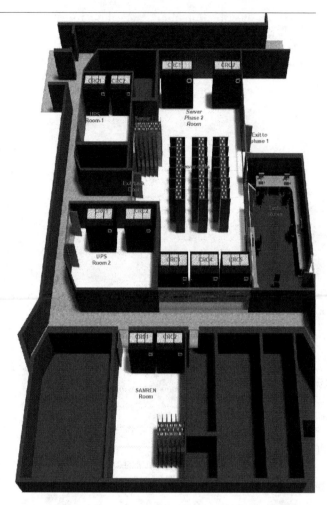

FIGURE 17.18: CHPC Data Center Layout

- Reliability: The system has been extremely reliable ever since it has been commissioned. We had a negligible amount of hardware failures given the size of the cluster. Recently, due to the high usage of the Lustre storage FS, we have noticed some instability of the FS, which is expected. However, the recovery of the MDS after failing is taking longer than expected. There is only one single point of failure that can result in the cluster being unavailable and that is the Storage (Lustre and/or NFS)

- Utilization: The CHPC has achieved an average system utilization of 80% since the system was opened to the users on the 3rd of May 2016, and sometimes it has reached 100% capacity. See details in Figure 17.21.

- Uptime: The centre has achieved the total average uptime from of 88.6% since the system was handed over to the user on May 2016. The bulk of the shutdown was due to the implementation of phase 2.

Implementation Challenges:

- Integration between Bright Cluster Manager and Intel Enterprise Lustre.

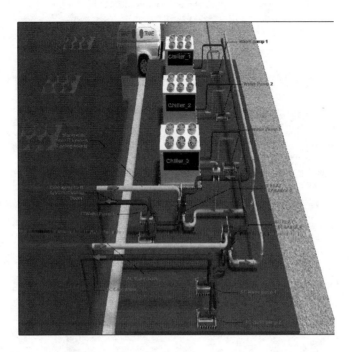

FIGURE 17.19: The Data Center Chillers

The removal and overwriting of Intel Lustre files by Bright via the software image. Exclude lists were implemented on Bright in order to preserve these files.

- Cabling of InfiniBand uplinks due to the height constraints of the DC.

  Additional overhead fibre trays were installed.

- Rear Water Cooled Door plumbing installation.

  Additional high pressure hydraulic hoses were installed with special couplings to allow for water flow from under the floor to inlet and outlet tails situated at the top of the door.

- NFS configuration.

  The issues we were experiencing were slow NFS reads and writes. NFS was being exported over the 1Gb Ethernet network. In order to resolve this we moved the exports over to the IB hardware and configured IPoIB. We also changed some mount options like hard/soft mounts and sync options which increased the performance.

  During Operation:

- Users running jobs on the login node.

- Users writing output of jobs to the NFS rather than Lustre.

During Benchmarking:

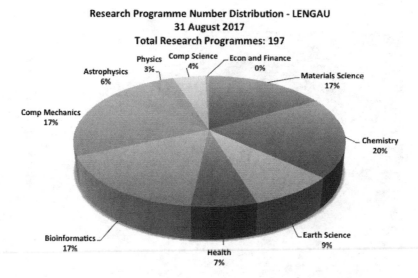

FIGURE 17.20: Research programme number distribution according to research application domains at the CHPC on 31 August 2017.

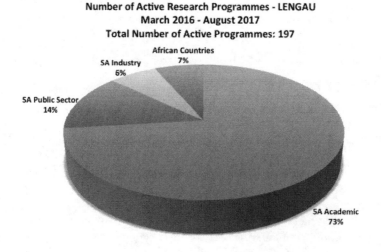

FIGURE 17.21: Distribution of number of research programs at the CHPC according to the four user classifications on 31 August 2017.

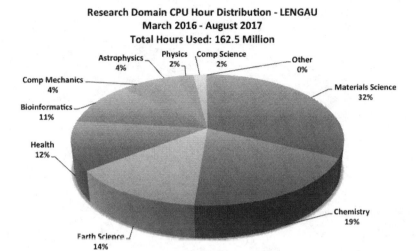

FIGURE 17.22: CPU hour usage distribution according to research application domains at the CHPC for the period 1 April 2016 – 31 August 2017.

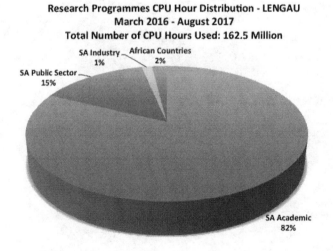

FIGURE 17.23: CPU hour usages distribution according to user classification at the CHPC for the period 1 April 2016 – 31 August 2017.

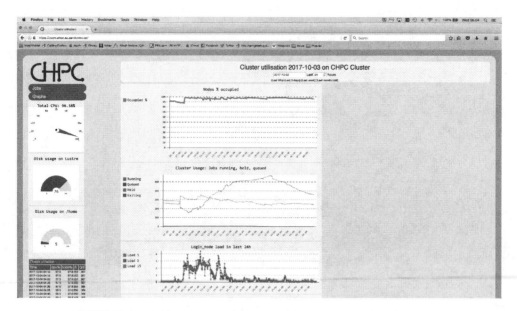

FIGURE 17.24: Resource utilization of Lengau on 3 October 2017.

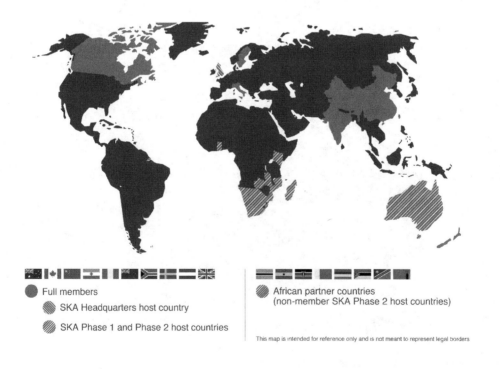

FIGURE 17.25: Countries participating in the SKA

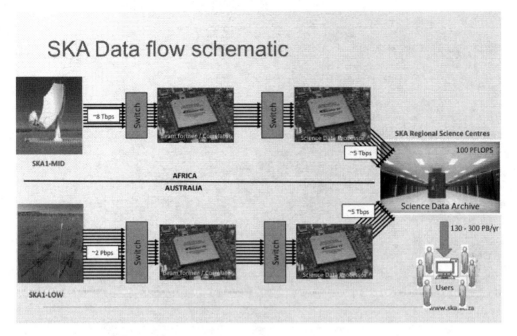

FIGURE 17.26: Schematic diagram of data flow for SKA

- Nodes would randomly power off during HPL runs.

  Dell supplied a custom firmware that would rectify this issue.

- PDU's would trip during HPL runs due to overload.

  Redistribution of power cabling on the PDU to cater for increase requirements of power during heavy load.

- Memory failures on nodes implemented during phase 1 were higher than normal during the phase 2 benchmarking.

- Positive Surprises: The nodes failure rate is extremely low, which is rare for a system of this magnitude.

17.7 Square Kilometer Array

The Center for High Performance Computing, as the National Facility, supports large-scale science projects around the globe. The Square Kilometer Array is an interesting project that South Africa is hosting, which will be the largest Radio telescope in the world [Reference for SKA]. The SKA is a global project with many countries already forming the consortium and other countries still planning to join. Figure 17.22 shows the countries, with color-coding on various categories.

It is widely coined, "a large ICT project, with an astronomy question", owing to the large amount of data to be produced by the telescope and requiring processing. The projections of the project, which will start construction in 2018, will produce Exabytes of data and

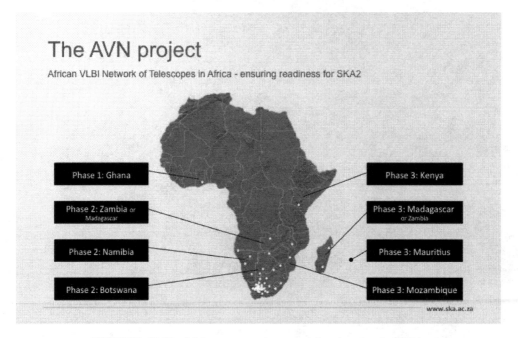

FIGURE 17.27: African countries participating in the SKA

require ExaFLOPS of compute capacity. This computing capacity will be required for the SKA low frequency experiment in Australia and the SKA medium frequency experiment in South Africa [Reference on the classification]. However the computing will be combined to give the end-user the overall observation data, as is depicted on Figure 17.23.

As part of this project, Lengau will be used to provide a test-bed environment, alongside other HPC centers around SKA countries, for the SKA data flow, which will later determine the final configuration of the computing requirements of SKA.

It should also be emphasized that South Africa included other eight partner countries in the SKA delivery; these countries are shown in Figure 17.24. Hence Lengau also play an important role by providing, to the African researchers from these countries, access to computing capacity and training in HPC skills. The training program is named the SKA Readiness project, and also includes the strategy of re-purposing the HPC systems when they are decommissioned, and provided as single racks of computing to various countries. This will be the destiny of Lengau at its retirement age, following successful retirement of HPC systems such as NSF TACC Ranger, NSF TACC Stampede and Cambridge systems. Already all the countries except Mozambique and Kenya have received computing infrastructure through this program.

Bibliography

[1] Github: ARTED. https://github.com/ARTED/ARTED.

[2] Green500 | TOP500 Supercomputer Sites.

[3] HPCG.

[4] KNC cluster COMA. https://www.ccs.tsukuba.ac.jp/eng/supercomputers/.

[5] TOP500 Supercomputer Sites.

[6] Jack Dongarra, Michael A. Heroux, and Piotr Luszczek. High-performance conjugate-gradient benchmark: A new metric for ranking high-performance computing systems. *The International Journal of High Performance Computing Applications*, 30(1):3–10, 2016.

[7] Jack J. Dongarra, Piotr Luszczek, and Antoine Petitet. The LINPACK benchmark: past, present and future. *Concurrency and Computation: Practice and Experience*, 15(9):803–820, 2003.

[8] K. Fujita, T. Ichimura, K. Koyama, M. Horikoshi, H. Inoue, L. Meadows, S. Tanaka, M. Hori, M. Lalith, and T. Hori. A fast implicit solver with low memory footprint and high scalability for comprehensive earthquake simulation system. In *Research Poster for SC16, International Conference for High Performance Computing, Networking, Storage and Analysis*, November 2016.

[9] Balazs Gerofi, Akio Shimada, Atsushi Hori, and Yutaka Ishikawa. Partially Separated Page Tables for Efficient Operating System Assisted Hierarchical Memory Management on Heterogeneous Architectures. In *Cluster, Cloud and Grid Computing (CCGrid), 2013 13th IEEE/ACM International Symposium on*, May 2013.

[10] Balazs Gerofi, Akio Shimada, Atsushi Hori, Takagi Masamichi, and Yutaka Ishikawa. CMCP: A Novel Page Replacement Policy for System Level Hierarchical Memory Management on Many-cores. In *Proceedings of the 23rd International Symposium on High-performance Parallel and Distributed Computing*, HPDC '14, pages 73–84, New York, NY, USA, 2014. ACM.

[11] Balazs Gerofi, Masamichi Takagi, Yutaka Ishikawa, Rolf Riesen, Evan Powers, and Robert W. Wisniewski. Exploring the Design Space of Combining Linux with Lightweight Kernels for Extreme Scale Computing. In *Proceedings of ROSS'15*, pages 1–8. ACM, 2015.

[12] Y. Hirokawa, T. Boku, S. A. Sato, and K. Yabana. Performance evaluation of large scale electron dynamics simulation under many-core cluster based on Knights Landing. In *HPC Asia 2018*, January 2018.

[13] T. Ichimura, K. Fujita, P. E. B. Quinay, L. Maddegedara, M. Hori, S. Tanaka, Y. Shizawa, H. Kobayashi, and K. Minami. Implicit nonlinear wave simulation with 1.08T DOF and 0.270T unstructured finite elements to enhance comprehensive earthquake simulation. In *ACM Proceedings of the International Conference on High Performance Computing, Networking, Storage and Analysis (SC'15)*, November 2015.

[14] T. Ichimura, K. Fujita, S. Tanaka, M. Hori, M. Lalith, Y. Shizawa, and H. Kobayashi. Physics-based urban earthquake simulation enhanced by 10.7 BlnDOF x 30K time-step unstructured FE non-linear seismic wave simulation. In *IEEE Proceedings of the International Conference on High Performance Computing, Networking, Storage and Analysis (SC'14)*, November 2014.

[15] K. Nakajima, M. Satoh, T. Furumura, H. Okuda, T. Iwashita, H. Sakaguchi, T. Katagiri, M. Matsumoto, S. Ohshima, H. Jitsumoto, T. Arakawa, F. Mori, T. Kitayama, A. Ida, and M. Y. Matsuo. ppOpen-HPC: Open source infrastructure for development and execution of large-scale scientific applications on post-peta-scale supercomputers

with automatic tuning (AT). In *Optimization in the Real World — Towards Solving Real-Worlds Optimization Problems*, volume 13 of *Mathematics for Industry*, pages 15–35, 2015.

[16] A. Petitet, R. C. Whaley, J. Dongarra, and A. Cleary. HPL - A Portable Implementation of the High-Performance Linpack Benchmark for Distributed-Memory Computers.

[17] S. A. Sato and K. Yabana. Maxwell + TDDFT multi-scale simulation for laser-matter interactions. *J. Adv. Simulat. Sci. Eng.*, 1(1), 2014.

[18] Taku Shimosawa. *Operating System Organization for Manycore Systems.* dissertation, The University of Tokyo, 2012.

[19] Taku Shimosawa, Balazs Gerofi, Masamichi Takagi, Gou Nakamura, Tomoki Shirasawa, Yuji Saeki, Masaaki Shimizu, Atsushi Hori, and Yutaka Ishikawa. Interface for Heterogeneous Kernels: A Framework to Enable Hybrid OS Designs targeting High Performance Computing on Manycore Architectures. In *High Performance Computing (HiPC), 2014 21th International Conference on*, HiPC '14, December 2014.

Index